Contents

*The Michelin maps
you will need
with this guide
are:*

*For more detailed
maps of Paris and
its outskirts use
the Michelin plans
18, 20, 22 and 24
scale 1:15 000
12 or 14
scale 1:10 000*

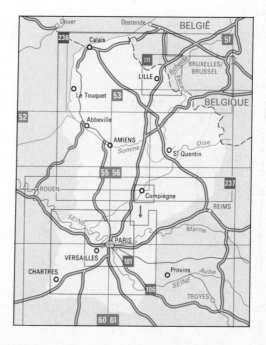

Fla. Ang. 1

3

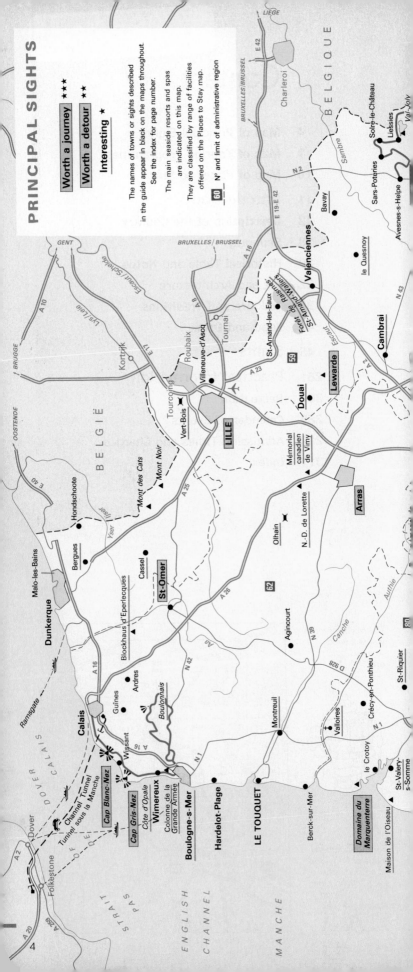

PRINCIPAL SIGHTS

Worth a journey ★★★

Worth a detour ★★

Interesting ★

The names of towns or sights described in the guide appear in black on the maps throughout. See the index for page number.

The main seaside resorts and spas are indicated on this map.

They are classified by range of facilities offered on the Places to Stay map.

60 N° and limit of administrative region

PLACES TO STAY

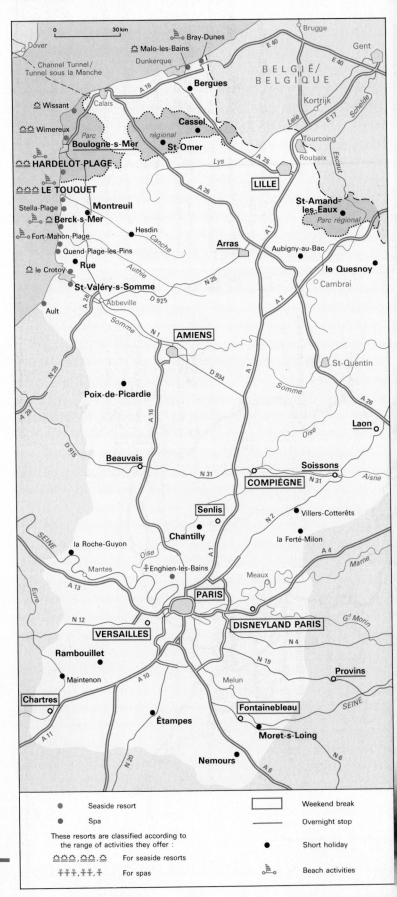

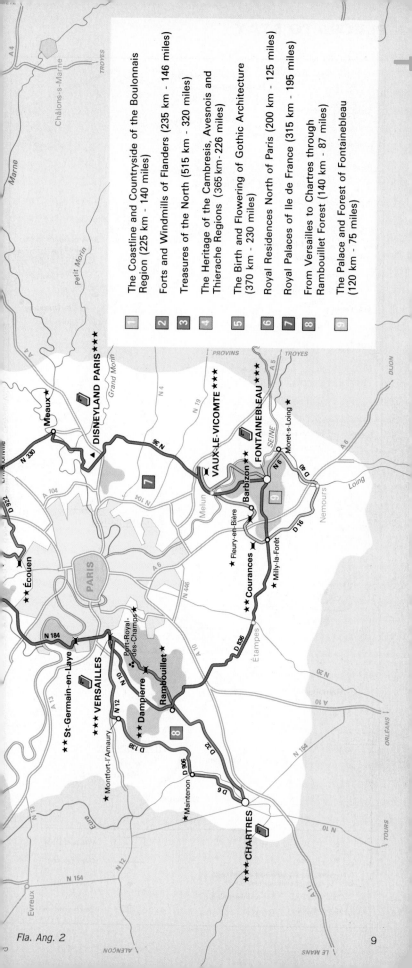

The Coastline and Countryside of the Boulonnais Region (225 km - 140 miles)

Forts and Windmills of Flanders (235 km - 146 miles)

Treasures of the North (515 km - 320 miles)

The Heritage of the Cambresis, Avesnois and Thierache Regions (365 km - 226 miles)

The Birth and Flowering of Gothic Architecture (370 km - 230 miles)

Royal Residences North of Paris (200 km - 125 miles)

Royal Palaces of Ile de France (315 km - 195 miles)

From Versailles to Chartres through Rambouillet Forest (140 km - 87 miles)

The Palace and Forest of Fontainebleau (120 km - 75 miles)

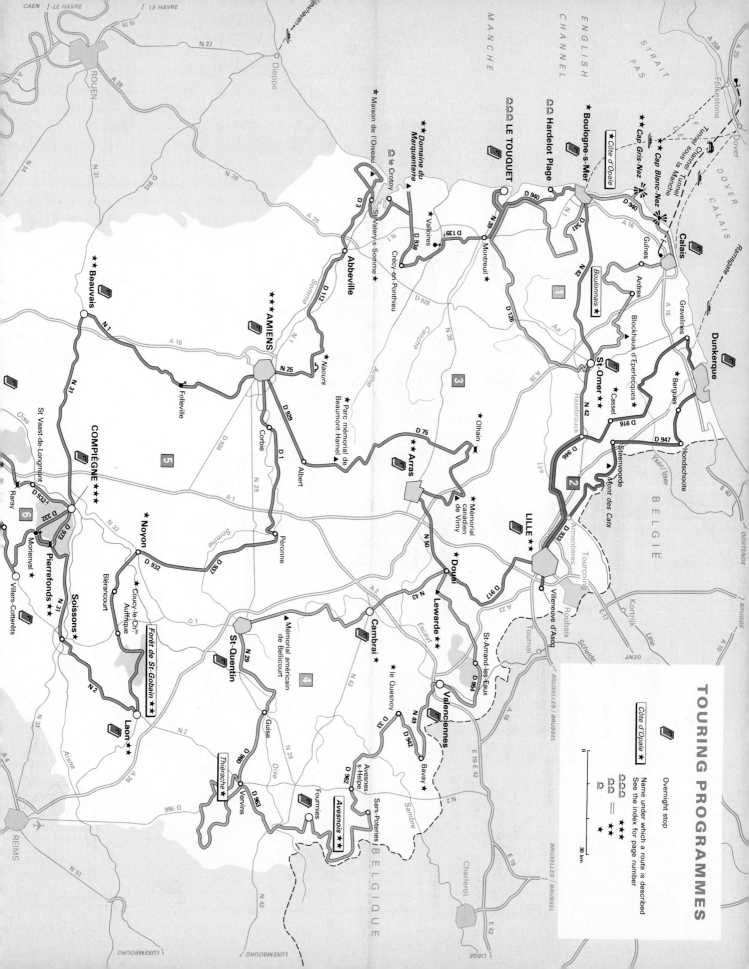

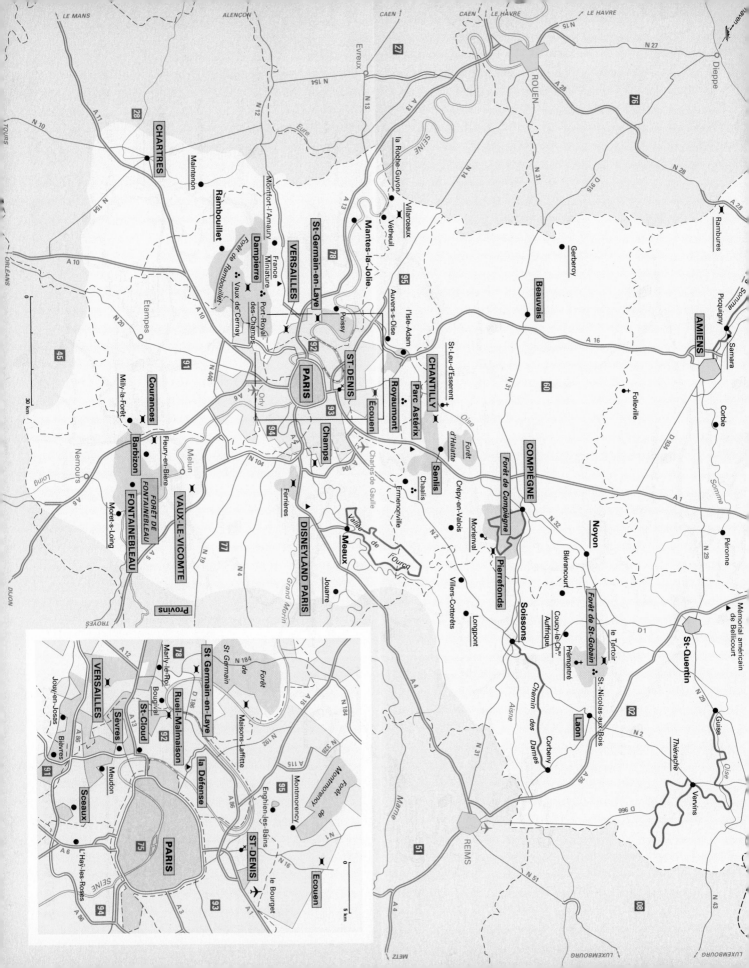

Introduction

J. Bernard/DIAPHOR LA PHOTOTHEQUE, Lille

Description of the country

Picardy, Artois, Ile-de-France (the province around Paris) and Paris itself all lie within the vast geological region known as the Paris Basin which borders on Flanders and the great plain of Northern Europe beyond. The Paris Basin is linked by the Burgundy sill to the Rhône Basin (southeast) and by the Poitou sill to the Aquitaine Basin (west). The landscape of the Paris Basin comprises forests, lush alluvial valleys with slow-flowing rivers and limestone plateaux providing arable land, dotted with sandy patches. The climate tends towards stormy summers and cool winters interspersed with rainy spells. Under Clovis, Ile-de-France was part of the Frankish kingdom, the first French territory with its two capitals Soissons and Compiègne. Clovis' descendants were deposed in 751 by Pépin the Short, whose son Charlemagne was consecrated King of the Franks by the Pope in Rome in 774. In 843 Charlemagne's kingdom was carved up and France was designated the land lying west of the provinces bordering the Meuse, Saône and Rhône rivers. The former territory of the Franks was reduced to the Duchy of France and the two counties of Orléans and Étampes. It was only four centuries later that this duchy was called Ile-de-France (the 'island of France' because of its position between the rivers Seine, Aisne, Oise and Marne). During the Norman invasion, the Duc de France valiantly defended Paris and one of the members of this House – Hugh Capet – was elected King of France at Senlis in 987. Hugh Capet's descendants governed France until 1848, except during the Revolution and the First Empire (1793 to 1814).

Picardy – This area northwest of Paris and Ile-de-France is a land of plateaux and valleys but it also has a long coastline.

Plateaux – The wide and virtually flat plateaux of the province are covered with a thick layer of silt which makes them very fertile and well suited to the cultivation of sugar-beet and cereals, fields of which stretch without interruption as far as the eye can see.

To the east, the **Santerre** (*Sana terra* : healthy earth) and **Vermandois** regions are characterised by large farming areas, often complemented by a sugar refinery or a distillery. St-Quentin, the administrative and industrial centre of the Aisne *département*, is the principal town.

To the east and south, the **Laonnois, Noyonnais** and **Soissonnais** regions make the transition to Ile-de-France, in particular to the prestigious Valois region with its mantle of forests. Western Picardy is sliced by wide valleys. Where the silt on the plateau was swept away the soil is poorer, as in the **Ponthieu** region where the villages have long, daubed blind walls. In the **Vimeu** region, where the chalk has decomposed into flinty clay, the cold, damp ground has created a mixed landscape of farmland crisscrossed by hedges and trees, cider-apple orchards and small, scattered villages. Near Beauvais the chalky, silt-covered plateau suddenly reveals a verdant hollow: the clayey **Pays de Bray**, a wooded area interspersed with meadows, which lives by stock-farming.

Valleys – The verdant and wide-mouthed valleys are bisected by the Somme, Authie and Canche rivers. These waters flow so slowly they have difficulty in making their way, losing themselves in ponds and marshes full of fish and waterfowl. The floors of the valleys are a mix of old peat bogs, rows of poplars, stock-farming fields and, on the outskirts of towns (Abbeville, Amiens, Péronne, Montdidier), marsh gardens *(hortillon-nages)* surrounded by canals.

Towns have developed along these valleys: Montreuil on the Canche, Doullens on the Authie, Péronne, Amiens, Abbeville on the Somme.

The capital of this region is Amiens, a great industrial centre with factories producing tyres, electronics, car parts and chemical products.

Coast – To the south near Ault the Picardy plateau meets the sea, ending in a sharp cliff of white chalk banded with flint. North of the Somme Bay a maritime plain called the Marquenterre area has been created by debris torn from the Normandy coast and carried northward by the currents, gradually forming an offshore bar. Only the Somme, Authie and Canche rivers have carved a passage to the sea ; there are therefore few large ports but several seaside resorts, the largest of them Le Touquet, beside the dunes.

The coastal plain lies between the dunes and the old coastal bar, which is marked by a noticeable cliff. The drained and dried plain is now used for fields of wheat and oats, and for raising salt-pasture lambs on the grassy shores known as *mollières*.

In the past St-Valery-sur-Somme, Le Crotoy and Étaples were important ports; today they harbour only fishing and pleasure boats.

Artois – The province of Artois, which lies on an extension of the Picardy plateaux, is a rise of land running northwest to southeast. It ends in an escarpment of about a hundred metres (Vimy Ridge, Notre-Dame de Lorette Hill) which divides the Paris Basin from the Anglo-Belgian Basin. The great plain of Flanders begins at the foot of this escarpment. The Artois hills overlook the Boulonnais region to the northwest and the Lens plain and Arras' agricultural plain, fed by the Scarpe River, to the southwest.

The well-watered hills of Artois are however bare to the southeast, in the **Ternois** region where there are outcrops of chalk; to the northwest, the chalky top layer of soil has decomposed into flinty clay resulting in lush, damp countryside which includes Hesdin forest and mixed agricultural and meadow land.

The **Boulonnais** region forms an enclave in the chalk layer, revealing outcrops of harder, older rocks; this "buttonhole" ends below the Channel.

The landscape of the Boulonnais is very different from neighbouring areas. In the north, where Artois rises again, the Upper Boulonnais forms a chalky plateau which in places reaches over 200m-650ft in altitude.

In the area where the land forms a hollow, the Lower Boulonnais, the wooded countryside is dotted with white, limewashed farms. The clay creates meadows used for rearing the dappled-grey "Boulonnais draughthorses" and for other stock-breeding; the soil also supports Desvres and Boulogne forests, while Hardelot Forest grows in sandier soil.

Boulogne itself, France's foremost fishing port, stands at the mouth of the River Liane. To the north, the edge of the calcareous plateau forms the cliffs of the Opal Coast.

Hainault and Cambrésis – Hainault (capital: Valenciennes) and Cambrésis (capital: Cambrai) are extensions of the chalky plateaux of Artois and Picardy, but are in addition covered with a thick layer of silt which is ideal for growing sugar beet and wheat; the per-acre harvests are excellent. The plateaux are divided by wide river valleys such as those of the Scarpe, Sambre, Selle and Escaut (Scheldt); meadows of fodder crops and pasture give them the look of farming country. The forests of St Amand and Mormal appear where there is flinty clay, the result of decomposition of the chalk.

Thiérache and Avesnois – These two relatively hilly regions form the tail of the Ardennes mountain mass, which is covered at its western end by marl and chalk mixed with marl. The **Thiérache** is a damp region, part forest and part farmland. When carefully drained the cold, non-porous ground provides pasture for cows. The dairies produce butter, cheese and condensed milk. The **Avesnois** is crossed by the Helpe Majeure and the Helpe Mineure rivers, tributaries of the Sambre River. This region resembles the Thiérache but is marked by summits which rise to over 250m-820ft in places. It is also a region of pastures and is known for its dairy cows and its cheeses, especially Maroilles.

Flanders – The Flemish plain, which continues into Belgium, is bounded to the south by the hills of Artois and to the east by the plateaux of Hainault and Cambrésis.

Coastal Flanders – The wet and windy *Blooteland* (bare land) has been gradually clawed back from the sea since the Middle Ages. The engineers, including the famous **Coebergher** *(qv)*, came mostly from the Low Countries: protected by dunes separating the area from the sea, they were able to drain the land gradually using great dams, canals and pumps, thus creating the marshes *(Moëres – qv)*. It is today a low-lying region where the grey clay yields crops of sugar-beet, cereals, flax and chicory and the nearby pastures are grazed by sheep, pigs, horses and cattle. The flat countryside, scattered with great isolated farms built around square courtyards, is dominated by belltowers, windmills and, on the coast, the factory chimneys and harbour cranes of Dunkirk and Calais.

Inland Flanders – Known as *Houtland* (wooded land), in contrast with the bare maritime Flanders, the "Flemish lowlands" consist of lush countryside divided by rows of poplars, willows or elms. The *censes*, white-walled Flemish farms with red roofs, stand out against this green background.

A series of summits extends into Belgium; each standing independently from the others, they make up the chain of the **Flemish hill-range**. As well as providing beautiful meadows where cows, horses and pigs thrive, the rich soil is also used to grow various crops: cereals, fruit and vegetables in marsh gardens among the St-Omer canals, plants for industrial processing (hops near Bailleul, flax in the Lys Valley, chicory, sugar beet).

Two small areas between Lille and Douai are different, however: they are the bare plateaux of the **Mélantois** and the **Pévèle** regions. The coal fields *(see Economy)* stretch from Béthune to Valenciennes and have given rise to a "black country" marked by coal slag-heaps, brick mining towns and mine-shaft frames.

Between the Lys Valley and the Escaut (Scheldt) River, there lies the industrial area of Lille – Roubaix – Tourcoing – Armentières, traditionally largely devoted to textiles *(see Lille)*.

THE REGIONS WITHIN ILE-DE-FRANCE

Pays de France – This arable plateau extending between St-Denis, Luzarches and the Dammartin-en-Goële ridge lay at the heart of royal territory. The layer of marl covering the subsoil has made the area extremely fertile and the huge fields are planted with wheat and beetroot.

Parisis – Parisis lies between the Oise and the Seine rivers and the Pays de France. This area was once occupied by the Gauls, who gave it its name and who christened the French capital. Parisis is an alluvial plain with few rivers which slopes towards the Seine; it is dominated by limestone buttes covered in sand or grit.

Beyond the industrial suburbs of Paris, market gardens and orchards spread along the limestone slopes of the plain, while the sandy stretches bear forests.

Senlisis – This region has often been bracketed with Valois by geographers and historians but in fact it was part of the king's dominion, the central core of Ile-de-France. Senlisis, which is bordered by the Oise, the Dammartin-en-Goële ridge and the Valois itself, is one of the most picturesque regions near the capital. Arable land is found on the silty soils while the sandy areas have favoured the development of forestry.

Valois – Valois is surrounded by Senlisis and the rivers Oise, Automne and Ourcq; it acquired strategic importance as early as Roman times and has remained one of the most important regions in French history. First a county, then a duchy, Valois was twice given to one of the king's brothers. Twice the descendants of this royal line, known as the Princes de Valois, acceded to the throne.

Multien – Multien is an area of rolling landscapes and ploughed fields, bounded by the River Marne, the Valois and the Croële ridge. It was the scene of the fighting in September 1914.

French Vexin – Three rivers border this limestone platform: the Oise, the Epte and the Seine. West of the River Epte is the Normandy Vexin. The loess covering is an extremely fertile topsoil which favours cereal cultivation, especially wheat. Cattle rearing is concentrated in the sylvan valleys planted with poplar trees. The Rosne Buttes, a series of outliers stretching from Monneville to Vallangoujard, are covered in woods. They include the strip of land running north of the Seine.

Mantois – Mantois is an enormous plateau situated between the rivers Eure and Oise; it consists of forests to the east and arable land to the west. The many brooks and streams which cut across it provide a pleasantly fresh, undulating appearance.

Hurepoix – It is bounded by Mantois, Beauce, Fontainebleau Forest and the Seine. Like other areas in Ile-de-France, Hurepoix features a number of buttes capped with limestone which rise between the valleys. In some places, rain and wind have eroded the limestone to reveal the sandstone and its underlying stratum of sand. Such geological diversity – sand, sandstone and limestone in the hills, marl in the vales – has produced a varied landscape and vegetation, which is one of the main attractions of the Hurepoix: market gardens spread along the valleys of the rivers Bièvre, Yvette and Essonne, the hillsides are covered in woodland and the plains below offer lush green pastures.

Gâtinais – The Gâtinais is defined by the River Seine, Hurepoix, Beauce and Champagne. The French Gâtinais, a clay plateau, lies east of the river Loing while the Orléanais Gâtinais (to the west) is an area of sand and sandstone. This second area is covered by Fontainebleau Forest, popular because of its splendid groves and sandstone boulders. The lush valley of the Loing is dotted with charming small towns.

French Brie – French Brie is located between the Seine and the Grand Morin rivers and has Champagne Brie as its northern border. These two regions differ for historical reasons: the former belonged to the King of France while the latter was the property of the Comte de Champagne. This area is watered by four meandering rivers: the Seine, Marne, Petit Morin and Grand Morin. A layer of non-porous marl which retains moisture is topped by a covering of millstone and siliceous limestone. This is the famous Brie limestone, which is itself covered with a fine blanket of fertile loess. The area has many large farms specialising in large-scale wheat and sugar-beet cultivation. The vast expanse of arable land is dotted with small groves and spinneys. The less fertile pockets of land, around Sénart and Ferrières for instance, have been planted with forest.

FORESTS

France has some magnificent forests, among them those of Rambouillet, Compiègne and Fontainebleau which feature among the finest sights in the country.

Woods and forests have a timeless appeal due to their peaceful and soothing atmosphere combined with an endlessly fascinating and constantly-changing character: lush greenery in springtime, shaded groves in summer, the deep russet tones of autumn or the crisp frosts of winter. Forests also provide a multitude of fauna and flora to study or just ramble through and flowers, fruit, nuts and mushrooms to harvest in season. Many also have charming picnic areas.

State forests and private forests – Three types of forest exist in France: state, private and local authority forests. The most interesting for ramblers are state forests, run by the French Forestry Commission (ONF) since 1966: they have an extensive network of roads, paths and lanes, and their magnificent groves form a picturesque setting. The aim of the arborists in charge is to preserve the natural habitat. The most beautiful French forests used to feature protected forest zones known as "artistic reserves" in which unusually striking trees were left untouched by the axe, even when they died. This practice was given up in favour of "biological reserves". Forests on private estates are not open to the public, apart from the footpaths which occasionally cross them.

Trees – Like all living things, trees breathe, reproduce and need nourishment. Mineral nutrients are drawn from the earth by the roots and distributed to all parts of the tree via the sap running through the trunk and leaves.

Every type of terrain does not necessarily suit every species of tree. Chestnut trees, for instance, cannot survive on limestone sites, whereas oaks will flourish on a variety of soils and firs can live in very poor ground.

Trees, like other plants, breathe through their leaves and reproduce through their flowers. Flowers will bear fruit providing they are fertilised by pollen of their own species. Very few trees have hermaphrodite flowers – presenting both male and female characteristics – like roses, acacias etc, and consequently the pollen is usually carried from the male flower to the female flower by insects, or sometimes by the wind. Trees may also reproduce by their shoots: if a youngish tree trunk is razed to the ground, a number of stool shoots will emerge from the stump. Conifers do not produce offshoots.

The trees of Ile-de-France fall into two categories: deciduous and coniferous.

Deciduous – These trees shed their leaves every autumn and grow them again in the spring. Beeches, oaks, hornbeams, birches and chestnut trees belong to this category.

Coniferous – Coniferous species do not have leaves but needles instead, which they shed regularly throughout the year. The needles are renewed every four to five years. Their sap contains resin – they are also known as resinous trees – and the fruit is generally cone-shaped. Pines, cypresses, cedars and fir trees are all conifers, as is the larch, which loses its needles every year.

The trees of the Ile-de-France forests – Most species of deciduous trees can be found around Paris; the most common are listed below.

Oak – One of the most esteemed forest trees, its hard but beautiful wood is used for both carpentry and ornamental woodwork. In former times oak bark was much sought-after by local tanners. Some of the oaks tower 40m-132ft high with trunks over 1m-3ft in diameter. The species may be exploited up to the age of 250.

Oak   Beech

Beech – Although it resembles the oak in its habit, beech is slightly more elegant. The wood is mainly used for modern furniture and railway sleepers but it is also popular as fuel. The trunk is cylindrical, the bark smooth and shiny; young shoots have a crooked, gnarled appearance. Beeches grow as tall as oaks but are no longer commercially viable beyond 120 years.

Hornbeam – A remarkably tough species, the hornbeam resembles beech; it also lives to the same age, but is shorter and its bark features numerous fissures.

Chestnut – This tree can grow to great heights and can live for several hundred years but is generally felled much younger as very old chestnut trees become hollow and prone to disease. Its wood was traditionally used by the cooperage industry for making staves, posts and stakes; nowadays it is used in the production of chip-board. Chestnut trees will grow only on siliceous soil.

Birch – Even when it reaches 25m - 82ft in height the birch retains a graceful, slim trunk of white bark – which peels off in fine layers – and shimmering leaves. Damp, sandy soil is an excellent terrain for all varieties of birch. It makes excellent firewood but it is principally used for making wood pulp, paper fibre and other industrial products.

Scots Pine – This species, the most commonly-found conifer in Ile-de-France, is ideal for reafforestation, particularly in sandy terrain; since the mid-19C it has been planted in plots of land where there is meagre or non-existent vegetation. Scots pines have short needles (4 to 6cm - 1 1/2 to 2 1/2in) which grow in pairs, smallish cones (3 to 5cm - 1 to 2in) and reddish-ochre bark.

Foresters often plant Scots pines alongside exotic or Mediterranean (maritime pine) resinous species. A great favourite is the Corsican pine, a tall, handsome tree with a perfectly straight trunk; it can grow to 50m - 165ft but old trees develop large grey patches on their bark.

The science of forestry – If a forest is not tended it will invariably deteriorate. In order to develop fully and reach their proper size, trees must be given breathing space and be placed in an environment which meets their specific requirements. The first step in a reafforestation campaign is to plant fir trees, which have few needs and which produce wood in a very short time. Their roots retain the earth, which the surface water otherwise washes away, and the needles build up thick layers on the ground. Next, hornbeams, birches and beeches are planted to increase the fertility of the soil, and finally oaks. Many of the beech groves are left as this species is considered to be commercially profitable.

Rotations – The prime concern of foresters is always to have trees ready for felling; consequently, when trees are felled foresters ensure they are immediately replaced with seedlings. For example, a forest may be divided into ten units and every five years the unit with the oldest trees is cleared and then replanted; this means that within 50 years the forest is entirely renewed while remaining commercially viable. This technique is known as rotation. Forest managers try to avoid exposing a large sector of the forest as leafy plants such as hazel and mulberry trees can set in, which might choke the young shoots. Within each sector 2, 3 or 4 groups are formed according to the trees' approximate age and a programme of successive felling is planned. This ensures that only limited areas are deforested at any one time.

Whatever the rotation for a given forest, its appearance is bound to change depending on the thickness of the vegetation and the forestry techniques which have been applied. There are three types of plantation in Ile-de-France:

Groves – After the land has been sown, natural selection sees that the weaker shoots are choked by the stronger ones. The trees – planted fairly close to one another – grow vertically in an upward direction. After some time the land is cleared around the finer species, to encourage them to develop, and eventually these are the only ones which remain. This grove, where the widely-spaced trees are all the same age, is called a *futaie pleine*; the rotation is rather long, 50 years or even 80 for very tall trees. *Futaie jardinée* is another type of grove, in which the trees are planted and cut at different times, so that the sector features a variety of "age groups"; older trees are always felled first.

Copses – The trees are younger. Rotation ranges from 5 to 30 years, depending on whether pit props, logs for heating or firewood is wanted. A copse is a sector of forest where a group of mature trees are razed to the ground once they have been cut. The shoots growing around the stump develop into a multitude of young bushy, leafy trees.

Copses with Standards – If, when cutting a copse, the finest trees are left standing, these will dominate the new shoots. If they survive a series of fellings, they will grow to be extremely strong. The utilisation of copses with standards produces both fuel wood (from the copses) and timber for industrial purposes (from the older species).

Fauna and flora – Forests contain not only trees but also countless varieties of plants and animals; stag hunts are still organised in certain forests.

Nature lovers always find forests fascinating as the rich, damp soil is remarkably fertile and can sustain moss, lichen, mushrooms, flowers, shrubs and ferns.

Flowers – April is the season of laburnum, hyacinths and daffodils. May brings hawthorn, lily-of-the-valley, columbine and the delightful catkins of the hazel tree. In June there is broom, heather, campanula, scabious and wild pinks. During the autumn season the tall, slender ferns and the russet and gold leaves are as attractive as the forest flowers.

Fruit – Wild strawberries and succulent raspberries ripen during July and August, while blackberries can be harvested in September together with the new crop of hazel nuts. October is the time for sloes and sweet chestnuts.

Mushrooms – Some varieties of mushrooms – the *Russula virescens, chanterelle comestible* and *mousseron* – are always edible. Other species are difficult to identify and may be dangerous. If in doubt, mushroom pickers should consult a professional mycologist or the local chemist (*pharmacien*).

GARDENS IN ILE-DE-FRANCE

Three successive trends defined the official canons of ornamental gardening in Ile-de-France, the home of many royal residences.

16C – During the 16C gardens were not considered an essential part of an estate, merely of the same category as outbuildings. They were generally of geometric shape and resembled a chessboard where each of the squares contained carefully-trimmed spindle and box forming arabesques and other elaborate patterns; these motifs were called *broderies*. Gardens were enclosed within a sort of cloister, made from stonework or greenery, from which visitors could enjoy a good view of the garden. The grounds themselves were cut across by paths featuring fragments of marble, pottery and brick. Though water did not play any significant part in the general appearance of the gardens, there were basins and fountains encircled by balustrades or tall plants; they were there to be observed in their own right and for people to admire their ornamental statues and water displays.

17C - early 18C: The Formal Garden – André le Nôtre (1613-1700) was the creator of the formal French garden. Its purpose was two fold: to enhance the beauty of the château it surrounded and to provide a superb view from within. The garden's main features were fountains, trees, statues, terraces and a sweeping perspective.

The château was fronted by a "Turkish carpet" of parterres with flowers and evergreen shrubs forming arabesques and intricate patterns. These were symmetrically flanked by basins with fountains, usually adorned with statues. Fountains were also placed on the terrace bearing the château and the upper lawns, which was the starting-point of the central perspective along a canal or a green carpet of lawn (*tapis vert*) lined with elegant groves of tall trees.

The groups of trees planted along the perspective were designed to be perfectly symmetrical. They were crossed by a network of paths: the clearings at the inter-sections offered splendid vistas extending into the far distance. Hedges lined the paths, concealing the massive tree trunks and providing a backdrop for marble statues; as hedges were fragile and expensive to maintain, however, most were later removed or greatly reduced in height from their original 6-8m - *c*20-26ft. Each grove of trees featured a "curiosity": a fountain with elaborate waterworks, perhaps, or a colonnade or a group of sculpted figures.

Aerial view of Vaux-le-Vicomte Château and Gardens

The enormous variety in designs and styles of the parterres and surrounding trees, bushes and hedges ensured that these formal gardens were never monotonous. They were conceived as an intellectual pursuit, giving pleasure through their stately proportions and perspectives, the skilful design and the sheer beauty of each detail.

Late 18C - 19C: The Landscape Garden – In the 18C manipulating the landscape into rigid geometric patterns was deemed to be no longer fashionable: instead the tendency was to imitate nature. The landscape garden – also called the Anglo-Chinese garden – consisted of lush, rolling grounds dotted with great trees and rocks, pleasantly refreshed by swirling streams and tiny cascades. A rustic bridge might cross a river flowing into a pond or lake covered with water-lilies and surrounded by willow trees, and a mill or dairy might add the final touch to this Arcadian scene.

The 18C fascination for philosophy which characterised the Age of Enlightenment was also reflected in contemporary gardening which saw the introduction of symbolic or exotic monuments or "**fabriques**" (a technical term which originally referred to architectural works depicted in paintings). These follies were dotted throughout the grounds to enhance the landscape.

Antique temples and medieval ruins were particular favourites, and tombs and mausoleums became popular just before the Revolution; Chinese and Turkish sculptures were also fashionable. An unfinished temple, for instance, would remind visitors of the limits of science, while an oriental pagoda standing beside a crumbling tower symbolised the fragility of human achievements.

Sentimentality, romance and melodrama were popular features of many art forms in the 18C and the trend also affected landscape gardens: a number of new sights made their appearance including the secret lovers' grotto, the bench of the grieving mother, the grave of the rejected suitor etc.

Most of these estates were ravaged during the Revolution and few of their fragile monuments survived. The most outstanding example of an 18C folly in the region is the Cassan Pagoda at L'Isle-Adam (qv).

Particularly fine gardens may still be found at Versailles, Vaux-le-Vicomte, Chantilly, Courances, St. Cloud, Sceaux, Champs, Fontainebleau, Rambouillet and Ferrières.

Economy

NORD – PAS-DE-CALAIS

The Nord – Pas-de-Calais region has for a long time played a major role in the French economy. This success is due to its privileged geographical position linking with productive regions of the Common Market, to its high population – more than three times above the French average – and to the natural agricultural and mining resources. In the late 1950s regional industry was restructured, largely because of international competition, the exhaustion of the coal fields and the loss of advantageous colonial markets: the coal-mines, which were closed in 1990, have undergone important transformations; the scattered textile industries have merged into large groups; metallurgy has branched into new directions, among them iron and steel production on the coast. Consumer product industries, such as car manufacturing, were also established in this area.

At the close of the 20C, the Nord – Pas-de-Calais region is now one of the major players in the fields of electricity production (Gravelines nuclear power station), electronics and information technology. Its position on one of the major transportation networks (TGV, Channel Tunnel, motorways) has attracted foreign investment, and the region is the third largest exporter in France.

Metallurgy – Local metallurgy accounts for a quarter of France's steel production, 15% of its iron production, half of its railway rolling stock and 10% of its cars. The iron and steel industry has suffered many upheavals in the last few decades: metallurgical industries in the north of France traditionally used ore from Lorraine and coal as their energy source, hence their establishment by the coal fields (between Douai and Valenciennes) and in the Sambre valley (Maubeuge); coal shortages, problems in Lorraine's industry, and outdated plants, however, caused many iron and steel works to close.

During the 1960s steel-making by the coast developed, using cheaper and richer imported ore. The new metalworks were established in Dunkirk which has become one of the most modern and efficient complexes in Europe. The Sollac company's Dunkirk plant, with its four tall blast furnaces, produces almost half of France's rolled steel and the Société Ascométal factory at Dunes is one of the foremost production sites of forged train-wheels in the world. Manganese used in the production of special steels is treated at Boulogne.

Supplies for the French railways are made largely in the Valenciennes and Douai areas, and car manufacturing is based at Douai (Renault), Maubeuge (Chausson) and Bouchain (Peugeot).

Textiles – The textile industry, which has been a traditional activity in the region since the Middle Ages, is today one of the areas worst hit by the crisis. Numerous efforts have been made to modernise equipment, to adapt to synthetic fibres and for family businesses to link up with large, powerful companies but the French textile industry continues to suffer from the competition of imported goods from Third World countries.

In spite of these problems, the Nord – Pas-de-Calais region manufactures 95% of the country's linen (Lys Valley), 85% of its worsteds (Roubaix-Tourcoing), 83% of its thread, 42% of its cotton and 40% of its weaving wools. Lacemaking in France is largely based in Calais and at Caudry nearby.

Chemicals – The chemical industry of the North developed with organic chemistry using tar and other coal by-products. The region specialises in soap and detergent manufacturing and in paints (Ripolin in Ruitz) and varnishes.

Two important oil refineries operate in Dunkirk and Valenciennes.

The Copenor company, in collaboration with the State of Qatar, has established in Dunkirk a steam cracker which produces ethylene and propylene.

The region also produces sheet glass and window glass, partly at the BSN factory in Boussois and at Sicover in Aniche.

The famous crystal factory at Arques has expanded enormously and now exports to 140 countries.

Farm Produce Industries – These are numerous in this region where agriculture is geared to industrial production: wheat for the flour mills and biscuit factories around Lille, potatoes for two large starch manufacturers, barley and hops for the breweries *(see Food and Drink, qv)*. The local chicory refineries have a worldwide reputation. An active industry has developed around sugar-beet resulting in crushing mills, sugar-works, refineries and distilleries which give a particular look to the plains here, in the Cambrésis and at Thumeries. The preserving industry is also important: 30% of the country's canned vegetables and pre-cooked foods are produced here and 50% of the country's preserved fish (processed largely in Boulogne, France's foremost fishing port).

New businesses: mail order and direct selling – Mail order selling in the Nord – Pas-de-Calais region makes up 75% of the turnover from all such sales in France. 17 000 people in the region are employed in direct selling, which has become a prosperous activity offering numerous markets for local businesses. Among the ten largest mail order companies in France, five are located in the region; La Redoute and Les Trois Suisses occupy the top two positions.

Coal Fields – Coal extraction in the coal fields of the Nord – Pas-de-Calais dates from the 18C. This deposit in this region lies at the western end of a large coal depression which extends into Belgium (Borinage at Mons, Charleroi coal fields) and Germany (Ruhr coal fields).

After 270 years of extraction, all activity has now ceased.

The deposit – The coal fields extend eastwards from the hills of the Artois region for about 120km - 75 miles to the Belgian border; the deposit is from 4 to 12km - 2 1/2 to 7 1/2 miles wide and was mined to a depth of 1 200m - 3 937ft. The irregularity of the seams, however, their small openings (sometimes less than 0.80m - 3ft) and the presence of numerous geological flaws made extraction progressively harder and led to an increasing deficit.

Closure of the mines – A decline in the yield from these mines first appeared in the late 1950s. In 1959, when productivity still reached 29 million tonnes, a plan of progressive shutting down was implemented which led to the closure of the last pit on 21 December 1990.

Industrial Recycling – Following the closure of the mines, which had employed up to 220 000 people in 1947, other businesses developed around the working of the mines: production of oval coal briquettes, foundry and special coke; the manufacture of decorative bricks; sales of mine gas; the production of electricity in power stations which run largely on combustible products gathered from the slag heaps; the use of shale, also from slag heaps, for road foundations and as ballast for railway lines. Over 350 either flat or conical slag heaps remain today, of which about 70 are still commercially exploitable.

With the prospect of imminent closure, the mining companies formed subsidiaries to take over from them; these make up the regional industrial group Filianor.

PICARDY

Despite being a rural area, Picardy nonetheless sustains lively industrial activity. Traditionally the region's industry was textiles but this has largely been replaced by metal-based industries (agricultural and car equipment, mopeds etc). Chemical products include glass (St Gobain) and rubber (tyres in Amiens) in particular.

Linked to agriculture, the sugar-works, food manufacturing plants and especially the canning factories – based in the Santerre area at Estrée, Rosières and Péronne – all play an important part in the region.

ILE-DE-FRANCE

A high population density – Although Ile-de-France covers only 2.2% of the surface area of France, over 18% of the French population resides in the province. This huge concentration of over 10 million inhabitants has gradually focused around the natural junctions of the Seine, Marne and Oise river basins. These large, slow rivers separate vast plateaux bearing rich countryside including the Brie and Beauce regions, and the large forests of Fontainebleau, Halatte, Rambouillet, Marly and St Germain.

Today the development of the Paris region tends to respect these natural tracts and instead focuses urban and economic growth around the new towns: Cergy-Pontoise, Évry, St Quentin-en-Yvelines, Marne-la-Vallée and Melun-Sénart.

The foremost industrial region in France – The Paris region employs over 15% of the national labour force. Alongside the various industries (metallurgy, mechanical construction, electrical and electronics manufacturing, chemicals, clothing and fashion), highly specialised and ultra-modern businesses have also developed.

The Paris and Ile-de-France region is the foremost business market in France.

Historical table and notes

Celts and Romans

BC	
Circa 300	The north of Gaul taken by a Celto-Germanic tribe, the Belgae.
57	Belgian Gaul brought into subjection by Caesar. Bavay, Boulogne and Amiens became important Roman centres.
AD 1C-3C	Roman peace. Northern France became part of the province of Second Belgium (capital Rheims).
406	Frankish invasion.

Merovingians and Carolingians

486	Territory from the Somme to the Loire rivers occupied by Clovis following the defeat of the Roman army at Soissons: his kingdom was called Francia in Latin.
561	The kingdom of France divided into three parts: northern France incorporated into Neustria.
6C and 7C	Creation of bishoprics and founding of many abbeys.
768	Charlemagne crowned King of Neustria in Noyon.
800	Charlemagne proclaimed Emperor of the western world.
9C and 10C	Norman, Hungarian and Vandal invasions. Withdrawal of the abbeys into the towns.
911	The Duchy of Normandy created after the Treaty of St Clair-sur-Epte, ending Normans' ambitions in Ile-de-France.
987	Hugh Capet, duke and suzerain of the land extending from the Somme to the Loire rivers, elected King of France in Senlis.

The Middle Ages

11C and 12C	Period of prosperity. Development of the clothmaking industry in Flanders, Artois and Picardy. Towns obtained charters and built belfries.
1180-1223	The Valois, Clermont, Meulan, Artois and Vermandois regions and the region around Amiens and Lille annexed to the royal kingdom by Philippe Auguste.
1214	Battle of Bouvines: victory for Philippe Auguste over the Count of Flanders and his allies King John of England, the Holy Roman Emperor Otto IV and the counts of Boulogne and Hainault.
1272	Ponthieu under the authority of the kings of England.
1314	Flanders annexed by Philip the Fair.
1337	Beginning of the Hundred Years War. The death of Philip the Fair and his three sons ('the cursed kings') resulted in a problem of succession: Philip the Fair's nephew, Philip de Valois, preferred by the French barons over his grandson, Edward II, King of England. The following century marked by battles between the English and the French who laid claim to the French Crown, as well as between the Armagnacs, supporters of the family of Orléans, and the Burgundians, supporters of the dukes of Burgundy.
1346	Battle of Crécy: victory for Edward III of England.
1347	Calais surrendered to the English with the famous episode of the Burghers of Calais.
1369	Marriage of Philip the Bold, Duke of Burgundy, with Marguerite, daughter of the Count of Flanders: Flanders under Burgundian authority.
1415	Battle of Agincourt: victory for Henry V of England.
1420	The Treaty of Troyes signed by Isabeau of Bavaria, wife of the mad king Charles VI, depriving the Dauphin of his rights of succession and designating her son-in-law, Henry V of England, heir to the French throne.
1422	Death of Charles VI. France divided between the English, the Burgundians and the Armagnacs.
1430	Joan of Arc taken prisoner at Compiègne.
1435	Picardy and the Boulonnais region yielded to the Duchy of Burgundy in the Treaty of Arras.
1441	English supremacy over Ile-de-France ended with the liberation of Pontoise.
1477	Invasion of Picardy, Artois, Boulonnais and Hainault by Louis XI following the death of Charles the Bold; only Picardy subsequently held. Marriage of Marie of Burgundy, daughter of Charles the Bold, to Maximilian of Austria: Flanders brought under Hapsburg control.

From the Bourbons to the Revolution

16C	Through the House of Hapsburg, Flanders included in the empire of Charles V of Spain.
1520	Meeting between Henry VIII of England and François I at the Field of the Cloth of Gold, Guînes.
1529	Peace of Dames signed at Cambrai: claims to Artois and Flanders renounced by François I.

1557	St-Quentin taken by the Spanish.
1558	Calais taken from the English by the Duke of Guise.
1562	Beginning of the Wars of Religion.
1585	Philip II of Spain allied with the Catholic League under the Treaty of Joinville.
1593	Henry of Navarre converted to Catholicism after convincing most of his subjects; crowned King Henri IV of France.
1598	Edict of Nantes.
1659	Following the Treaty of the Pyrenees, marriage agreed between Louis XIV and Maria-Theresa of Spain; Artois brought under French sovereignty.
1661	The construction of a huge palace at Versailles commissioned by Louis XIV.
1663	Marriage of Louis XIV with Maria-Theresa, who according to local custom was to inherit all of the Brabant region from her mother. When the inheritance passed to another heir, Louis XIV declared the war of "Devolution" on the Spanish Low Countries.
1668	Walloon Flanders given to Louis XIV under the Treaty of Aix-la-Chapelle.
1678	Louis XIV allowed to annexe the other northern towns under the Treaty of Nimegen.
1713	The frontiers of northern France definitively fixed under the Treaty of Utrecht.
1789	French Revolution.

From the First to the Second Empire

1803	Napoleon's army mustered at the Boulogne Camp for a possible invasion of England.
1804	Napoleon crowned Emperor of the French.
1812	Russia invaded by Napoleon's troops.
1814	France invaded. Forced abdication by Napoleon at Fontainebleau as all Europe lined up against him. Louis XVIII returned from exile in England and enthroned in 1815.
1840	Attempted uprising against King Louis-Philippe organised by Louis-Napoleon.
1848	Louis-Napoleon elected President of the Republic; crowned Emperor (Napoleon III) in 1852.
1870-71	Franco-German War. End of the Second Empire signalled by the defeat at Sedan: the Third Republic proclaimed. Paris besieged by Prussians: Alsace and part of Lorraine given up under the Treaty of Frankfurt.

World War I (1914-1918)

1914	Outbreak of the First World War: France attacked by German armies through neutral Belgium; four years of bloody trench warfare followed.
1915 to 1918	Battles throughout northern France and Flanders: in Artois (Neuville-St-Vaast, Vimy), in Picardy (Somme Valley, Chemin des Dames in the Aisne Valley, St Quentin) and in Ile-de-France (Ourcq Valley, Battle of the Marne). 11 November: armistice signed in Compiègne forest.
1919	End of the War with the Treaty of Versailles.

World War II (1939-1945)

1939	Outbreak of the Second World War. In June 1940 France overrun by the German army: occupation of much of the country. The "French State", established at Vichy, collaborated closely with the Germans. The north of France cut off from the rest of the country by a boundary. France's honour saved by General de Gaulle's Free French forces and by the courage of the men and women of the Resistance. By 1942 all France occupied; the French fleet scuttled at Toulon. Allied landing in Normandy in June 1944, and in the south of France in August: Paris liberated. The "Dunkirk pocket" retaken by the Allies. The German surrender signed at Rheims on 7 May 1945.
1976	Creation of the "Ile de France" region.
1987	Start of building works for the latest tunnel under the Channel linking France and England.
1994	6 May: official opening of the Channel Tunnel.

Art

ABC OF ARCHITECTURE

To assist readers unfamiliar with the terminology employed in architecture, we describe below the most commonly used terms, which we hope will make their visits to ecclesiastical, military and civil buildings more interesting.

Ecclesiastical architecture

illustration I ▶

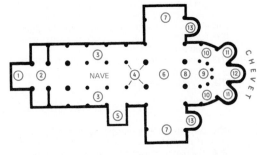

Ground plan: The more usual Catholic form is based on the outline of a cross with the two arms of the cross forming the transept: ① Porch – ② Narthex – ③ Side aisles (sometimes double) – ④ Bay (transverse section of the nave between 2 pillars) – ⑤ Side chapel (often predates the church) – ⑥ Transept crossing – ⑦ Arms of the transept, sometimes with a side doorway – ⑧ Chancel, nearly always facing east towards Jerusalem; the chancel, often vast in size, was reserved for the monks in abbatial churches – ⑨ High altar – ⑩ Ambulatory: in pilgrimage churches the aisles were extended round the chancel, forming the ambulatory, to allow the faithful to file past the relics – ⑪ Radiating or apsidal chapel – ⑫ Axial chapel. In churches which are not dedicated to Our Lady this chapel, in the main axis of the building, is often consecrated to her (Lady Chapel) – ⑬ Transept chapel

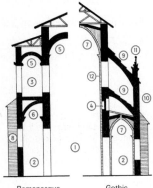

Romanesque   Gothic

◀ illustration II

Cross-section: ① Nave – ② Aisle – ③ Tribune or Gallery – ④ Triforium – ⑤ Barrel vault – ⑥ Half-barrel vault – ⑦ Pointed vault – ⑧ Buttress – ⑨ Flying buttress – ⑩ Pier of a flying buttress – ⑪ Pinnacle – ⑫ Clerestory window

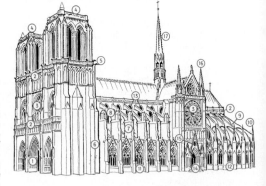

illustration III ▶

Gothic cathedral: ① Porch – ② Gallery – ③ Rose window – ④ Belfry (sometimes with a spire) – ⑤ Gargoyle acting as a waterspout for the roof gutter – ⑥ Buttress – ⑦ Pier of a flying buttress (abutment) – ⑧ Flight or span of flying buttress – ⑨ Double-course flying buttress – ⑩ Pinnacle – ⑪ Side chapel – ⑫ Radiating or apsidal chapel – ⑬ Clerestory windows – ⑭ Side doorway – ⑮ Gable – ⑯ Pinnacle – ⑰ Spire over the transept crossing

◀ illustration IV

Groined vaulting:
① Main arch –
② Groin –
③ Transverse arch

illustration V ▶

Oven vault:
termination of a
barrel vaulted nave

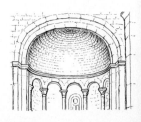

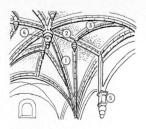

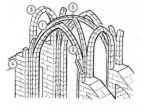

illustration VI
Lierne and tierceron vaulting:
① Diagonal – ② Lierne –
③ Tierceron – ④ Pendant –
⑤ Corbel

illustration VII
Quadripartite vaulting:
① Diagonal – ② Transverse –
③ Stringer – ④ Flying buttress –
⑤ Keystone

▼ **illustration VIII**

Doorway: ① Archivolt. Depending on the architectural style of the building this can be rounded, pointed, basket-handled, ogee or even adorned with a gable – ② Arching, covings (with string courses, mouldings, carvings or adorned with statues). Recessed arches or orders form the archivolt – ③ Tympanum – ④ Lintel – ⑤ Arch shafts – ⑥ Embrasures. Arch shafts, splaying, sometimes adorned with statues or columns – ⑦ Pier (often adorned with a statue) – ⑧ Hinges and other ironwork

illustration IX ▶
Arches and pillars: ① Ribs or ribbed vaulting – ② Abacus – ③ Capital – ④ Shaft – ⑤ Base – ⑥ Engaged column – ⑦ Pier of arch wall – ⑧ Lintel – ⑨ Discharging or relieving arch – ⑩ Frieze

Military architecture

illustration X
Fortified enclosure: ① Hoarding (projecting timber gallery) – ② Machicolations (corbelled crenellations) – ③ Barbican – ④ Keep or donjon – ⑤ Covered watchpath – ⑥ Curtain wall – ⑦ Outer curtain wall – ⑧ Postern

illustration XI
Towers and curtain walls:
① Hoarding – ② Crenellations – ③ Merlon – ④ Loophole or arrow slit – ⑤ Curtain wall – ⑥ Bridge or drawbridge

◀ **illustration XII**
Fortified gatehouse:
① Machicolations –
② Watch turret or bartizan – ③ Slots for the arms of the drawbridge – ④ Postern

illustration XIII ▶
Star fortress: ① Entrance – ② Drawbridge – ③ Glacis – ④ Ravelin or half-moon – ⑤ Moat – ⑥ Bastion – ⑦ Watch turret – ⑧ Town – ⑨ Assembly area

ART AND ARCHITECTURAL TERMS USED IN THE GUIDE

Abacus: illustration IX.

Aisle: illustration I.

Altarpiece or **retable:** illustration XVIII.

Ambo: an elevated lectern or pulpit situated in the chancel; usually occur in pairs.

Ambulatory: illustration I.

Apsidal or **radiating chapel:** illustration I.

Arcade: succession of small arches; when attached to a wall they are known as blind arcades.

Arching: illustration VIII.

Archivolt: illustration VIII.

Arch shaft: illustration VIII.

Arms of the transept: illustration I.

Asymmetrical merlon: oblong-shaped merlon in which length exceeds width.

Atlante: male figure used as a support.

Attic: a low storey over main cornice.

Axial or **Lady Chapel:** illustration I.

Baluster or **banister:** uprights (posts or pillars) supporting the handrail of a staircase.

Barrel vaulting: illustration II.

Bay: illustration I.

Buttress: illustration III.

Campanile: a belltower, usually separate from the main building.

Capital: illustration IX.

Caryatid: female figure used as a support.

Chevet: French term for the east end of a church; illustration I.

Coffered ceiling: vault or ceiling decorated with sunken panels.

Coping: protective covering of stone or brick around the edge of a well.

Corbel: illustration VI.

Corinthian order: Greek architectural order characterised by scroll capitals almost entirely covered in curled acanthus leaves.

illustration XIV

Organ
① Great organ case –
② Little organ case –
③ Caryatids – ④ Loft

◄ illustration XV

Dome on squinches:
① Octagonal dome – ② Squinch –
③ Arches of transept crossing

illustration XVI ►

Dome on pendentives:
① Circular dome – ② Pendentive –
③ Arches of transept crossing

Crypt: underground chamber or chapel.

Curtain wall: illustration X.

Diagonal arch: illustrations VI and VII.

Dome: illustrations XV and XVI.

Doric order: Greek architectural order with plain capitals.

Embrasures: illustration VIII.

Equilateral arch: pointed arch with its radii equal to the span.

Ex-voto: offering or inscription made in pursuance of a vow.

Flamboyant: latest phase (15C) of French Gothic architecture; name taken from the undulating (flame-like) lines of the window tracery.

Fluted: vertical grooves in column shafts.

Flying buttress: illustration II.

Fresco: mural painting executed on wet plaster.

Gable: triangular part of an end wall carrying a sloping roof; also applied to the steeply pitched ornamental pediments of Gothic architecture; illustration III and above.

Gallery: illustration III and above.

Gargoyle: illustration III.

Groined vaulting: illustration IV.

Haut-relief: sculpture or carved work projecting more than one half of its true proportions from the background.

High altar: main altar usually placed in the chancel.

High relief: haut-relief.

Historiated: decorated with figures of people or animals.

Ionic order: Greek architectural order with double scroll capitals.

Keep or **donjon:** illustration X.

Keystone: illustration VII.

Lancet arch: narrow arch with a sharply pointed head.

Leaf: one of two or more parts of a door or shutter.

Lintel: illustrations VIII and IX.

Loophole or **arrow slit:** illustration XI.

Low relief: sculpture or carved work projecting very slightly from the background.
Machicolations: illustrations X and XII.
Merlon: raised part of an embattled parapet between two embrasures; illustration XI.
Moat: ditch surrounding a fortress, generally filled with water.
Mullion: a vertical post dividing a window.
Narthex: illustration I.
Nave: illustration I.
Oculus: small round window.
Organ case: illustration XIV.
Oven vaulting: illustration V.
Parclose screen: screen separating a chapel or the chancel from the rest of the church.
Pendant: illustration VI.
Pepperpot roof: conical roof.
Peristyle: row of columns surrounding or adorning the façade of a building.
Pilaster: engaged rectangular column.
Pinnacle: illustrations II and III.
Piscina: basin for washing the sacred vessels.
Pointed arch: diagonal arch supporting a vault; illustrations VI and VII.
Porch: covered entrance to a building.
Portico: a space enclosed by colonnades fronting a building or located in an inner court.
Projection: any part of a structure that is cantilevered, jetties out or projects.
Quadripartite vaulting: illustration VII.
Reliquary: casket containing the relics of a saint.
Retable or **altarpiece:** illustration XVIII.
Rose or **wheel window:** illustration III.
Semicircular arch: roundheaded arch.
Shaft or **column:** illustration VIII.
Shingles: wooden slips used as roofing tiles.
Side aisle: illustration I.
Side chapel: illustrations I and III.
Spire: illustration III.
Stalls: illustration XIX.
Tracery: intersecting stone ribwork in the upper part of a window.
Transept: illustration I.
Tribune: illustration II.
Triforium: small arcaded gallery above the aisles; illustration II.
Twinned or **paired:** applied to columns or pilasters grouped in twos.
Tympanum: illustration VIII.
Wainscot or **panelling:** timber lining to walls.
Watch turret or **bartizan:** illustration XII.

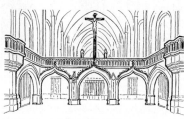

illustration XVII

Roodscreen: this replaces the rood-beam in larger churches, and may be used for preaching and reading of the Epistles and Gospel. Many disappeared from the 17C onwards as they tended to hide the altar.

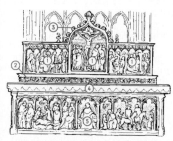

illustration XVIII

Altar with retable or altarpiece
① Retable or altarpiece – ② Predella –
③ Crowning piece – ④ Altar table –
⑤ Altar front

illustration XIX

Stalls
① High back – ② Elbow
rest – ③ Cheek-piece –
④ Misericord

RELIGIOUS ARCHITECTURE

Ile-de-France and the regions north of Paris offer a rich variety of architectural styles: Gallo-Roman at Bavay and Romanesque at Morienval, Rhuis and Chartres; Gothic architecture throughout Ile-de-France where it was born and the later Flamboyant Gothic in Picardy especially; Renaissance influence may be found at Amiens and Cassel; Classical architecture flourished in and around Paris and the Baroque was embraced in Flanders. Many of the earliest buildings of note were constructed for religious purposes and it is through these buildings that the development of architectural styles can best be followed. A church was basically a chancel reserved for members of the clergy, where the high altar and the reliquary were located, and a nave which accommodated the congregation. This simple layout characterised the early churches which were built on a basilical plan. During the Romanesque period the plan of the church developed into a cross; the narthex at the entrance received those who had not been baptised; the nave was enlarged by aisles. In places of pilgrimage, an ambulatory and side aisles were added to the chancel to facilitate processions. Architects followed this layout as it was convenient for celebrating Mass and easy to build.

Romanesque (11C-12C)

Architects in Romanesque times knew how to build huge, lofty churches but, as the heavy stone vaulting often caused the walls to settle or cave in, they made the windows as small as possible and added aisles surmounted by galleries to support the sombre nave.

Romanesque statue-columns
The Royal Doorway of Chartres Cathedral

Romanesque Spire
Chartres Cathedral

One of the main types of roofing in Romanesque churches is groined vaulting *(qv)*, in which two identical barrels meet at night angles. The barrel in the axis of the nave rests upon the transverse arch, while that set at a right angle is supported by the main arch or by a recess in the wall. Rhuis and Morienval churches and the Royal Doorway of Chartres Cathedral are splendid examples of Romanesque art.

Gothic (12C-15C)

The transition from Romanesque to Gothic architecture – which originated in Ile-de-France – was a slow, natural process that developed in response to the demand for wider, higher and lighter churches. Typified by quadripartite vaulting and the use of pointed arches, Gothic art evolved from the sombre 12C Romanesque sanctuaries to the light 13C churches and the extravagantly ornate buildings of the 15C. It is rare, however, to find a church with entirely unified features reflecting a given period in history: building a church was a costly and lengthy operation subject to changes in public taste and building methods as the work progressed. Towards the late 13C famous personalities and guilds were granted the privilege of having a chapel built in their honour in one of the side aisles. In exchange they were expected to make a generous contribution towards the building or its maintenance.

Architects – The names of the architects of the great religious edifices are known to us only from the Gothic period onwards, through texts or through inscriptions carved around the "labyrinths" outlined on the floor of cathedrals; that is how Robert de Luzarches was revealed as responsible for the plans of Amiens Cathedral.

The most outstanding master builder in the north of France, however, was undoubtedly **Villard de Honnécourt**, born near Cambrai. The towers of Laon Cathedral, Vaucelles Abbey *(south of Cambrai)*, the chancels at St Quentin and Cambrai *(no longer extant)* have all been attributed to him.

West Fronts – Most main façades were set facing west. Nave and aisles had their own doorway flanked by buttresses which were bare in the 12C and 13C, ornate in the 15C. The tympanum featured ornamentation and in the 14C its gable was elaborately carved, with crockets adorning the sides. 13C rose windows were fairly small; in the 14C they were enlarged across the west front to provide light for the nave. As windows grew larger, façades became more delicate. A gallery was built at the base of the towers to break the rigid vertical perspective created by the buttresses and belltowers; in the 15C this was reduced to a balustrade and the gables further embellished. Ideally west fronts were to be richly decorated with stone carvings but in many cases they were the last part to be completed and architects were often obliged to forego ornamentation, and even towers, owing to insufficient funds; in others, however, even the transepts were given remarkable façades (see Chartres).

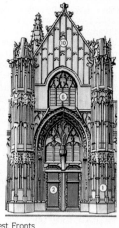

Gothic West Fronts

12C and 13C
Collegiate Church, Mantes

15C
St Peter's Church, Senlis

1) Buttresses - 2) Doorways - 3) Tympanum - 4) Gable -
5) Sloping features - 6) Windows - 7) Rose window - 8) Gallery -
9) Tower with platform - 10) Gable

Spires – After lightening the façades of Gothic churches architects turned to the spires; by the Flamboyant period the open-work masonry was markedly ornate. In the 19C numerous belltowers in the region were given a spire by disciples of Viollet-le-Duc.

Flying buttresses – In early Gothic churches the pillars in the nave were supported by masonry concealed in the galleries. During the 12C these walls were reduced to arches (see below) supported by sturdy piers. Soon afterwards the galleries themselves were replaced with a row of flying buttresses outside. A number of high openings could therefore be incorporated into the church interior, producing a far more luminous nave. Tall churches from then on can be schematically described as stone frames consisting of columns supporting diagonal arches and resting on two or three levels of flying buttresses. The buttresses were in turn supported by a series of tall pillars bearing pinnacles.

Diagonal arches – Towards the end of the 11C groined vaulting was extremely common but, as it was difficult to build and liable to crack, a group of architects from England, Milan and Ile-de-France decided to reinforce the groins.
They found that by building the diagonal arches first and by consolidating them with a small amount of rubble, vaulting that was both sturdy and light was achieved.
By supporting this vaulting on a series of arches, so that the weight of the masonry would have to be borne at the springing, the architects could dispense with the walls in between the arches and replace them with stained-glass windows; this in turn greatly enhanced the luminosity of the interiors.
This significant development heralded the age of quadripartite vaulting.

Vaulting – Illustrations see above. Quadripartite vaulting, in which the thrust is supported by four main arches, is easy to install in a square-shaped bay. In the 12C bays were enlarged and it was no longer possible to build them square: the pillars propping up the walls would have been too far apart. The problem was initially resolved by covering the bays two by two thus forming a square again: an extra transverse arch was then added and made to rest on slim pillars alternating with stout piers.
This type of vaulting – upheld by three diagonal arches – is known as sexpartite vaulting because of the number of its divisions.

Gothic Spires

13C
Former Cathedral,
Senlis

16C
New Bell Tower,
Chartres

When more sophisticated diagonal arches were able to support the vaulting above rectangular bays, the intermediary resting points were eventually discarded.

After the 15C Flamboyant architects put in additional, decorative ribbing of complex design: it formed liernes and tiercerons, and subsequently stars and intricate networks. The main supporting arches were flanked by ornamental arches of no practical use. The keystones – usually pendant – grew thinner and longer.

Elevations – *(illustrations below)* Gothic elevations reflect the continual search for higher and lighter buildings.

Transitional Gothic (A) – The term Transitional Gothic covers the birth and early stages of Gothic architecture, from about 1125 to 1190. The first use of diagonal vaulting in France appeared over the ambulatory in the Romanesque abbey church at Morienval. Though some Romanesque details, such as semicircular arches, can still be observed in early Gothic buildings, there were several significant

Notre-Dame Cathedral, Senlis

changes. The new interiors presented four-storey elevations consisting of high clerestory windows at the top which lit the nave directly, a triforium (a narrow, arcaded passageway below the clerestory) and a gallery, which were instrumental in supporting the walls as high up as possible, and arcading at ground level. There were often openings behind the gallery but never behind the triforium.

The pillars of the main arches initially consisted of a thick column; this was later replaced by twinned columns supporting the arches and the colonnettes above. Laon Cathedral is a good example of early Gothic architecture. Semicircular transept endings like the famous south arm at Soissons Cathedral were also a feature.

Lancet Gothic (B) – This great period (*c*1180 to 1250) when Gothic architecture was in its ascendancy produced some of France's finest masterpieces, among them Chartres Cathedral.

Characteristics include arches and windows pointed and shaped like a lancet; clerestory windows surmounted by a round opening; the gallery replaced by external flying buttresses. The numerous colonnettes originating from the vaulting rested on the shaft which bore the weight of all the main arches. This pier was generally a large round column flanked by four colonnettes.

Radiant Gothic (C) – This was the golden age of the great cathedrals in France, lasting from about 1250 and the reign of St Louis to around 1375 when the Hundred Years War blocked the progress made by medieval architects.

Transitional
(12C)

Lancet
(early 13C)

Radiant
(late 13C - early 14C)

Flamboyant
(15C and 16C)

The Gothic style was at its summit: the three-storey elevation (large arcades, triforium – the wall at the back now pierced with stained-glass – and tall clerestory windows) lightened the nave and formed one huge single stained-glass window in the chancels of churches with no ambulatory; the wall area was reduced to a minimum and the stringers supporting the vaulting were doubled by another series of arches. In many cases the colonnettes started from the ground, at the point where they surround the pillar of the main arches. Two slight mouldings – level with the main arches and the springers – were the only features to break the vertiginous ascent. Beauvais Cathedral is the most remarkable example of Radiant Gothic.

Flamboyant Gothic (D) – This last stage in Gothic architecture, which could develop no further, succumbed to ornamental excess, aided by the fine, easily worked Picardy stone. The style owes its name to the flame shapes in the tracery of the openings and rose windows, and to the exuberant carved and sculpted decoration which tended to obscure the structural lines of the buildings: doorways were crowned with open-work gables, balustrades were surmounted by pinnacles, vaulting featured complex designs with purely decorative arches (called liernes and tiercerons) converging on ornately-worked keystones. The triforium disappeared, replaced by larger clerestory windows. Arches came to rest on columns or were continued by ribbing level with the pillars. The latter were no longer flanked by colonnettes. In some churches, the ribs formed a spiral around the column.

Flemish civil architecture – From the late 13C the particular nature of Flemish Gothic architecture manifested itself in the civic buildings, belfries and town halls erected by the cities which had obtained charters.

Belfries – Symbol of the town's power, the belfry rose either as an isolated building (Bergues, Béthune) or as part of the town hall (Douai, Arras, Calais). It was built like a keep with watchtowers and machicolations. The rooms above the foundations – which housed the prison – had diverse functions, such as Guard Room. At the top, the Bell Room enclosed the **chimes**. Originally these consisted of only four bells; today they often number at least 47 bells which play every hour and on the quarters. The Bell Room is surrounded by watchtowers from which the sentry looked out for enemies and fires. The whole is crowned by a weather vane symbolising the city: thus the lion of Flanders stands at Arras, Bergues and Douai.

Town halls – The town halls are often imposing with striking, richly embellished façades: niches, statues, gables and pinnacles might adorn the exterior. Inside, the large council chamber or function room had walls decorated with frescoes illustrating the history of the town.

The most beautiful town halls (Douai, Arras, St-Quentin, Hondschoote, Compiègne) were built in the 15C and 16C. Many suffered damage and modification over the centuries and some were completely rebuilt in their original style, as at Arras.

Renaissance (16C)

Renaissance architecture, under the influence of Italian culture, favoured a return to antique themes: columns with capitals imitating the Ionic and Corinthian orders; façades decorated with niches, statues and roundels; pilasters flanking the windows. Quadripartite vaulting was replaced by coffered ceilings and barrel vaulting. Architects introduced basket-handled arches and semicircular or rectangular openings. Inverted brackets replaced flying buttresses. West fronts, and sometimes the north and south façades too, kept their heavy ornamentation. Spires were replaced by small domes and open-work pinnacles.

Isolated examples of Renaissance art – not widely adopted in the north of France – are in the Sagittarius House, Amiens and the Hôtel de la Noble Cour, Cassel.

Baroque and Classical (17C-18C)

Architecture – Through the 17C and 18C architecture presented two different faces, one Baroque – dominated by irregular contours, an abundance of exuberant shapes, generous carving and much ornamentation; the other Classical – a model of stateliness and restraint, adhering strictly to the rules of the Antique: rows of Greek columns (Doric, Ionic and Corinthian), pedimented doorways, imposing domes and scrolled architraves. The Baroque style flourished in Flanders, Hainault and Artois which fell under Spanish influence, while the Classical style found favour in Picardy and Ile-de-France.

The Baroque Seminary Chapel in Cambrai is one of many religious buildings erected in the 17C following the influence of the Counter-Reformation and its main engineers, the Jesuits. Civil buildings include the House of Gilles de la Boé in Lille and the Mont-de-Piété, Bergues; the Mint in Lille, with its bosses and richly carved ornamentation, exemplifies **Flemish Baroque**.

The Seminary Chapel, Cambrai

The Petit Trianon at Versailles is a famous example of Classical architecture.
In Arras Baroque and Classical elements were combined for the town's splendid main squares framed by houses with arcades and volutes. Combined elements can also be seen at Valloires and Prémontré abbeys and at Long and Bagatelle châteaux.

Sculpture – The finely grained and easily worked chalky stone found in Picardy was used for much decorative work and by the 13C the "picture carvers" in Amiens and Arras were already displaying the specific Picardy traits discernible throughout later centuries: lively, finely detailed figures going about their everyday life. The calendar at Amiens is a good example of this engaging art.
In the late 15C and early 16C the Picardy wood carvers *("huchiers")* became renowned through their work on the stalls in Amiens Cathedral; the door panels in St Wulfram's, Abbeville; the finely-worked frames of the "Puy-Notre-Dame" *(qv)* paintings.
Baroque art favoured abundant decorative sculpture: buildings were covered with a profusion of ornamental fruit, flowers, cornucopias, *putti*, niches, statues, vases...

THE MONASTERIES OF ILE-DE-FRANCE

A considerable number of priory, convent and abbey ruins are to be found in Ile-de-France, and numerous districts and street names recall the many religious communities which have not survived.

Abbeys in the history of Ile-de-France – Abbeys would not exist if people did not feel a strong calling to take up ecclesiastical duties; but equally abbeys would not exist if the clergy were not given land. After the 5C, when the victorious Franks carved up the Gallo-Roman territory, it would have been impossible for any religious community to survive without the help of donations. There were a great many aspiring monks in France up to the 19C and the different communities were almost entirely dependent on the generosity of benefactors. As the suzerain of Ile-de-France was none other than the supreme ruler of France, the king, this region was graced with an abundance of local monasteries.
In the early days of Christianity, towards the late 4C, Ile-de-France was covered with forests and therefore quite fertile; the area attracted monks who wanted to live in peace and escape the terrible famine ravaging the country. Soon afterwards the Merovingian monarchs, who had been strongly backed by the clergy, encouraged the creation of religious foundations, to which they contributed quite considerably. The wealthy Carolingians continued to enrich these abbeys and the practice was kept up by the Capetians and their vassals for over 800 years (Chaâlis and Royaumont).
French kings favoured monasteries because the monks used to reclaim uncultivated land and because the monasteries were constantly praying for their patrons. Religious faith was strong from the 10C to the 17C, so a king might donate an abbey for a variety of reasons: to thank God for a victory, to seek expiation for an offence committed against the Church, to express his own personal belief or to offer a dowry to dowager queens or royal princesses about to take the veil.

Religious Orders – The term abbey does not apply to just any Christian community whose members lead a frugal, secluded life; it in fact designates a group of men or women placed under the authority of an abbot or an abbess, who live according to a rule approved by the Pope. The monks' day is usually divided into chores related to community life, and spiritual and liturgical duties, which are the main purpose of the association.
All abbeys have an abbot or abbess, who generally enjoys the same rank as a bishop. He or she is elected by fellow companions and incarnates the spiritual and temporal leader of the abbey. After the 16C, the Pope gave the king of France the right to appoint abbots and abbesses: these prelates were called commendatory abbots and usually lived in the king's entourage.

Royaumont Abbey Cloisters

Sometimes, to administer new domains or to fulfil the wish of a patron who wanted to receive monks on his land, the abbots would build a priory. This small community was supervised by a prior who was answerable to the abbey. The Cistercians set up numerous *granges*, farming colonies run by lay brothers.

Monastic Rules – The Benedictine Order – created by St Benedict in the 6C – was undoubtedly the order which flourished the most in France: its members founded over one thousand abbeys throughout the country. The Benedictine rule was subsequently reformed and this led to the creation of separate orders.

The first originated in the 10C from Cluny in Burgundy but unfortunately all the Cluniac houses died out during the Revolution. The second – the Cistercian Order – was, and still is, extremely powerful. It was St Bernard of Cîteaux, also a native of Burgundy, who founded the order in the 11C. He was a firm believer in asceticism and introduced a number of new rules: he condemned elaborate ceremonial and the decoration of churches; monks could no longer be paid tithes, neither could they receive or acquire land; strict rules were laid down on diet, rest was limited to seven hours and the friars had to sleep in their clothes in a common dormitory.

The monks shared their time between liturgical worship – 6 to 7 hours a day – manual labour, study and contemplation. In the 17C, Abbot Rancé added further austerities to the Cistercian rule (silence, diet). This new rule was named after La Trappe, the monastery near Perseigne where it originated. It is presently enforced in abbeys of strict observance.

The two other main orders which founded abbeys in France were the Augustinian friars and the Premonstratensian canons, both dating from the 12C.

Other communities include the Carmelite Order, the Order of St Francis (Franciscans and Capuchins), the Order of Preachers and the Society of Jesus (Jesuits). These however do not follow monastic rules and they do not found abbeys. Their activities (missionary work, caring for the sick) bring them into contact with the lay world. They live in convents under the authority of the prior, the Mother Superior etc.

A collegiate church is occupied by a community of canons accountable to their bishop.

Monastic buildings – The cloister is the centre of an abbey; its four galleries allow the nuns and monks to take their walks undercover. One of the cloister walls adjoins the abbey church, while another gives onto the chapter-house where monks meet to discuss community problems under the presidency of the abbot. The third gallery opens onto the refectory and the fourth onto the calefactory, the only room with heating where the monks study or do manual labour.

The dormitory is generally placed above the chapter-house. It communicates with the church by means of a direct staircase so that the monks may readily attend early morning and night mass. Lay brothers – believers who cannot or will not take holy orders – are granted a separate status. They spend most of their time in the fields and the workshops, and have their own dormitory and refectory. They may not enter the chapter-house or visit the chancel of the church. Since the Vatican II Council (1962-65) lay brothers have become more and more involved in the life of the community.

Visitors are not allowed to enter the monastic buildings and are lodged in the guest house. The poor are housed in the almshouse.

Monasteries also include an infirmary, a novitiate, sometimes a school, and the buildings needed to run the abbey: barns, cellars, wine press, stables and cowsheds.

CIVIL ARCHITECTURE

Three great periods in architecture – widely admired and imitated throughout Europe – originated from Ile-de-France: the Louis XIV, Louis XV and Louis XVI styles.

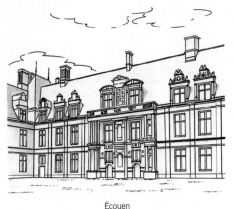

Écouen

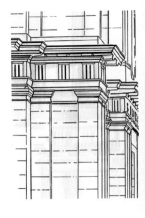

François I's House at Moret-sur-Loing

Renaissance style (16C). – After the 15C, medieval castles were converted into residential châteaux. Windows were enlarged, doors and openings were richly adorned. The towers were only there for decorative purposes and by the second half of the 16C they were considered superfluous. Façades were embellished with statues and rows of superimposed columns. Roofs were high and presented a single slope.

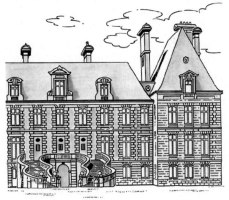

Courances

Louis XIII style (1580-1640). – Principal characteristics were the exact symmetry of the main building and the use of brick panels set into white stonework. Carved ornamentation was either limited in the extreme or non-existent. The proportions of these châteaux were of the utmost simplicity. They usually consisted of a central block flanked by two end pavilions.

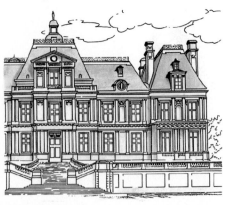

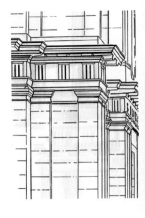

Maisons-Laffitte

Louis XIV style, first period (1640-1660). – Under the skilful hand of François Mansart, civil architecture gave up the amiable character it still showed during the Louis XIII period and acquired a far more noble appearance. Columns and pilasters never ran higher than a single floor of the château. Triangular and arched pediments were becoming popular. Roofs were still fairly high and featured numerous chimneys.

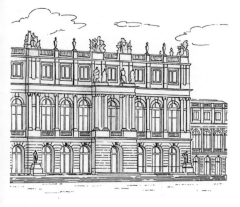

Versailles

Louis XIV style, second period (1662-1710). – The ground floor was taller, the first floor fairly high, while the second floor remained low. The flat roof was concealed by a balustrade. The horizontal lines of the building were broken by the rows of sturdy columns and tall windows. Ornamental sculpture was limited to the rooftop and the summit of the front pavilions. The statues were inspired by antique models.

The Great Stables at Chantilly

Louis XV style (1700-1750). – After 1700, the Louis XIV style and its harsh angles were mellowed by soft, rounded contours. Under Louis XV, curves were favoured. Windows and pediments featured intricate ornamentation, while the decoration of the façades remained somewhat austere. Generally speaking, the châteaux resumed modest proportions. Columns disappeared and roofs consisted of two sloping planes.

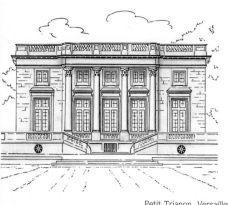

Petit Trianon, Versailles

Louis XVI style (1750-1793). – The Louis XV elegance was still felt but the excessive use of curves brought back right angles. Columns made a marked comeback. The ornamentation of the façades was severe in the extreme. Many of the motifs were taken from Antiquity, a trend that introduced the Pompeian (1790-1804) and the Empire style, characterised by simple design and tall, imposing columns.

Fla. Ang. 3

33

RURAL HOUSING IN THE NORTH

Homes of the Coast, Inland Flanders and Artois – Whether in Picardy, Artois or Flanders, the same types of houses can be found along the coast: long and low to form a defence against the west winds which often bring rain. The houses are capped by high-pitched roofs covered with Flemish S-shaped tiles called *pannes*. The whitewashed

Rue du Clape-en-Bas, Montreuil

walls are cheered by brightly-coloured doors and shutters; the bases of the buildings are tarred against the damp.

Behind this apparent uniformity lie very different construction techniques.

In Picardy the walls consist of daubing on wood laths; in certain areas the surface is left plain, as in Ponthieu, but it is more usually whitewashed, giving a spruce look in summer to the flower-bedecked villages along the Canche and Authie rivers.

In Flanders the usual building material is more generally brick, sandy-coloured in the maritime region and ranging from red to purplish or brown further inland. The great Lille and Artois regional farms, known as « censes », are built around a courtyard with access through a carriage gateway often surmounted by a dovecote.

Some large, partly stone-built farms in the Boulonnais hills are actually old seignorial homes and include a turret or fortifications, giving the impression of a manor house.

Homes in Hainault, Avesnois, Thiérache and Soissonnais – In the Hainault and Avesnois regions houses are massively built: they usually consist of brick buildings with facings and foundations in regional blue stone.

Château de la Motte, Liessies

Their slate roofs are reminiscent of the nearby Ardennes region.

Construction in the Thiérache region, the land of clay and wood, consists of daubing and brick with slate roofs. There are many old dovecotes in the region, either over carriage gates or free-standing in courtyards. The fairly thickly-scattered villages huddle around their fortified churches *(see the Thiérache)*.

The houses in the Soissonnais region are similar to those of Ile-de-France. Beautiful white limestone ashlars are used for walls and crow-stepped gables, contrasting with flat red roof tiles which take on a patina with the years.

Windmills – Up to the last century there were windmills throughout the windswept northern regions of France. In the early 19C there were 800 in the Somme district alone and over 250 in the countryside south of Lille. Today no more than a few dozen still exist, registered, protected and restored by the Association Régionale des Amis des Moulins du Nord – Pas-de-Calais (ARAM).

Post mills, which are built of wood, are the most common in Flanders. The main body of the structure and the sails turn around a vertical post. On the exterior, on the side opposite the sails, a beam known as the « tail » is linked to a wheel which is turned to position the entire mill according to the wind direction *(illustration see Hondschoote)*. Some dozen of this type remain in northern France, including those at Boeschepe, Cassel, Hondschoote, Steenvoorde, Villeneuve d'Ascq and St-Maxent.

On a **tower mill** (or smock mill when made of wood) only the roof, to which the sails are attached, turns. This type of mill is more massive and is usually built of brick or stone; Terdeghem windmill near Steenvoorde is the most famous of these.

Terdeghem windmill

Consult the index to find an individual town or sight.

MILITARY ARCHITECTURE

Of the defensive systems in the north of France, relatively few date from the Middle Ages: the town walls of Boulogne and Laon, and the castles at Coucy *(qv)*, Rambures *(qv)*, Picquigny, Lucheux, Septmonts and Pierrefonds *(qv)*.

In contrast, numerous classic, 17C star fortifications along the northeastern border have been preserved, some in their entirety, as at Bergues *(qv)* and Le Quesnoy *(qv)*, others only partially: Avesnes *(qv)*, Maubeuge, Cambrai *(qv)*, Douai *(qv)*, St-Omer *(qv)*, Péronne *(qv)*.

Before Vauban – It was under the last of the Valois kings that the military engineers, who had studied Italian examples, adopted a system of curtain walls defended at the corners by bastions. Bastions with orillions – bastions in the shape of an ace of spades with projections to protect the men defending the curtain wall from their assailants' fire – were introduced: this feature can be seen at Le Quesnoy. Bastions and curtain walls, usually made of stone, were crowned with platforms bearing cannons; raised towers allowed the moats or ditches and surrounding area to be watched.

At the beginning of the 17C, Henri IV employed an engineer specialising in « castrametation » (fortification-building) as it was called: **Jean Errard** (1554-1610) from Bar-le-Duc, nicknamed The Father of French Fortification. In the north Errard fortified Ham and Montreuil *(qv)* and built the citadels at Calais *(qv)*, Laon *(qv)*, Doullens and Amiens *(qv)* which still stand today; in 1600 he published an authoritative *Treatise on Fortification* which served until Vauban's time.

The Age of Vauban – Inspired by his predecessors, **Sébastien le Prestre de Vauban** (1633-1707) established a system of his own *(illustration p 23)* characterised by bastions with half-moons surrounded by deep moats. Making the most of the natural obstacles and using local materials (brick in the north), he also tried to give an aesthetic quality to his works by giving them monumental stone gateways which were often carved.

On the coast and along the border of Flanders and Hainault, Vauban established a long line of double defences, known as the **« Pré carré »**. These two close lines of fortresses and citadels were to prevent the enemy's passage and to provide a haven in case of attack. The first line consists of 15 sites from Dunkirk and Bergues to Maubeuge, Philippeville and Dinant; the second runs a little way behind and includes 13 towns extending from Gravelines and St-Omer to Avesnes, Marienbourg, Rocroi and Mézières. Some of these strongpoints were Vauban's own creations such as the citadel at Lille, which he himself called the queen of citadels; others existed already and were remodelled.

For over a century this group of fortifications succeeded in defending the north of France, until the invasions of 1814 and 1815.

During the French campaign in 1940 Le Quesnoy, Lille, Bergues, Dunkirk, Gravelines and Calais all formed solid strongholds protecting the retreat of the Franco-British armies.

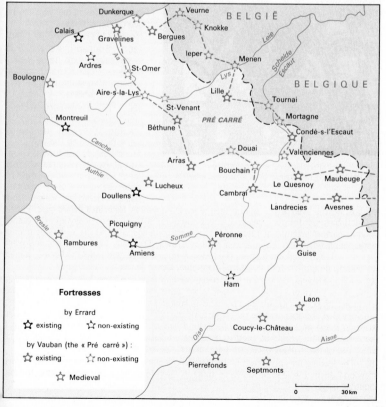

Atlantic Wall – The blockhouses of the Atlantic Wall which stretch along the coastline are examples of a more recent type of military architecture. They were erected by the **Todt Organisation** which from 1940 used prisoners of war for the labour. In 1944 about 10 000 constructions were counted on the French coast: the Nord – Pas-de-Calais region was considered a war zone against England. In the deep forests of Eperlecques and Clairmarais enormous concrete installations were built for launching the V1 and V2 rockets on London. The Eperlecques Blockhouse *(qv)*, today designated a Historic Monument, is one of the most impressive examples of this type of monumental concrete architecture.

STAINED GLASS

Since the early Middle Ages church windows have been adorned with coloured glass; unfortunately, few of these early works have survived.
During the Gothic period, master glass-makers played an important role in the completion and the ornamentation of churches: thanks to them, both the clergy and the congregation could appreciate the shimmering light that came streaming through the roundels. Stained glass is not purely decorative, however: to the Church it is an invaluable teaching aid, permanently communicating catechism, sacred history and the lives of the saints.

The art of making stained glass – Stained-glass windows consist of juxtaposed pieces of coloured glass held together by strips of lead. The window is divided into panels to ensure perfect solidity. When the various coloured pieces have been selected and cut to shape, the glass-maker completes the shading and details of the figures with touches of *grisaille*: this is a brownish pigment containing silica which is painted on and which blends with the glass in the melt. The glass panels are then reassembled and fixed in place in the window. Patches of lichen may develop on stained-glass windows; it starts to attack the lead after 100 years and has been known to break through the glass after 300 to 400 years. It is man, however, rather than erosion which is to blame for the disappearance of numerous early stained-glass windows: in the 18C many were dismantled and replaced by plain glass, which afforded a better view of the nave.

Notre-Dame de la Belle-Verrière
Detail of 12C-13C stained glass, Chartres Cathedral

The development of stained glass – Technical developments in glass-making were prompted by artistic trends but also by the search for greater economy and the wish to produce lighter tones.

12C – Stained-glass windows were small, with fairly heavy borders. The ornamentation around the main figures was extremely limited.

13C – To ensure perfect cohesion between the panels and the leading, the iron armatures were fastened to the walls. The clerestory windows presented tall, isolated figures whereas lower windows, which could be observed more closely, had medallions depicting scenes from legends, eg the lives of the saints: this genre is known as **historiated stained glass**. Panels included architectural features and embellishments. Borders were heavy and the scenes show a marked attempt at realism. Historiated roundels were set in a *grisaille* framework enhanced by brightly-painted rose windows. The daily lives of craftsmen were evoked in lively anecdotal scenes. The lower windows were generally divided into panels composing geometric motifs (stars, diamonds, clover leaves).

14C – A combination of architectural advances and loss of wealth led to a considerable increase in window space. For reasons of economy, more and more *grisaille* was produced, its starkness softened by delicate shading and graceful foliage motifs. Angels and rosy cherubs adorned the barer parts of the windows. Borders became smaller and lettering made an appearance. In the second half of the 14C glass-makers discovered that silver staining could be used to accentuate a variety of bright colours: yellow on a white background, light green on blue, amber on red etc.

15C – The leading was no longer produced using a plane, but instead stretched on a wire drawing bench: the lead strips were thinner, therefore more supple and able to hold together larger and flatter panes of glass than previously. Glass-makers worked with a lighter type of glass and the colours used in the decoration were less vivid. In some churches, two thirds of the window was taken up by *grisaille*: these panels featured Gothic canopies with high gables and open-work pinnacles. The craftsmanship was of a remarkable quality: master glass-makers began to sign their own work and to introduce original themes.

16C – Stained glass drew inspiration from the works of the great painters and from contemporary engravings. Glass-makers had become masters at cutting the glass from large sheets – using a diamond and no longer a red-hot iron – and they also excelled at painting with enamels. Stained-glass windows developed into large, transparent paintings in which minute attention was given to detail, perspective and design. In some buildings religious themes were replaced by classical scenes taken from Antiquity.

17C and 18C – The use of coloured glass decreased. Stained glass was painted and decorated with enamels.

LANDSCAPE PAINTING

Although many painters were employed in the internal decoration of châteaux and abbeys around Paris, it was not until the 19C that painters began to show an interest in the surrounding landscapes.

Until the 18C, French masters had used landscapes merely as a background to their work, either as a decorative element or to enhance the atmosphere through composition and colour. It was so poorly regarded that often a major artist painting a portrait or other subject would leave the background landscape to be painted by a studio assistant. The two most celebrated French landscape painters were the 17C classicists Nicolas Poussin and Claude Lorrain: Poussin gave his views the heroic qualities of his subject and Lorrain painted scenes of a lost, idyllic Antiquity.

Camille Corot (1796-1875) – Corot was the pioneer of contemporary landscape painting in France. He lived in Barbizon from 1830-35 and worked outdoors in Fontainebleau Forest and all over Ile-de-France, studying the contrasts and soft hues of light in the undergrowth, along shaded paths and on the edge of the plain. He later took up painting lakes in a search for more delicate variations; the ponds at Ville-d'Avray (south of St-Cloud), with their subtle reflections, were his favourites.

Mantes Bridge by Camille Corot

Painters of the Oise – The group was founded in 1845 by two of Corot's disciples, Charles-François Daubigny and Jules Dupré. Daubigny (1817-78) liked to paint the rippling waters of the River Oise and the greenery and blossoms of the orchards and groves. He led a peaceful life: his work paid well and received universal acclaim. He could often be found working on the Ile de Vaux near Auvers, or in a small rowing boat he had converted into a studio. Jules Dupré (1811-89), a close friend of Théodore Rousseau, used darker colours and belonged to the Barbizon School. He seldom left his house in L'Isle-Adam.

In 1865 the lithographer and satirical cartoonist Honoré Daumier (1808-79) moved from the capital to Ile-de-France, to Valmondois, when he met with serious financial difficulties.

In 1866 **Camille Pissarro** (1830-1903) settled in Pontoise for a first two-year stay. Uninterested in the nearby streams and rivers, he concentrated on meadows, grassy slopes, country villages and street scenes featuring peasant women, which he portrayed in a deliberately poetic manner. His gift for expressing light, his qualities as a teacher and his kindliness made him the father figure of the Impressionist movement.

The Barbizon School – Its representatives drew inspiration from the landscapes of Fontainebleau forest and the nearby Bière plain. The founder of the movement was **Théodore Rousseau** (1812-67) who settled in a modest country cottage in 1847 and stayed there until his death. Diaz and Charles Jacque were among his close friends. They remained cheerful and humorous despite their paintings not fetching high prices and their consequent penury; it was only towards the end of the Second Empire that their talent was acknowledged. Troyon (1810-65) specialised in rural scenes representing cattle. Barye, the highly-respected sculptor of animals, also took up landscape painting because of his love of nature. The charms and hardships of country life were particularly evoked in the work of **Jean-François Millet** (1814-75), who lived in Barbizon from 1849 until his death.

The artists of this school generally favoured the dark colours of tree bark and undergrowth and their preferred subjects included dusk, filtered sunlight and stormy skies; these sombre tones were criticised by their detractors who claimed they painted with "prune juice".

Around 1865 a new group of artists fell under the spell of these magical woodlands: Pierre-Auguste Renoir, Alfred Sisley, Claude Monet and Frédéric Bazille settled in Chailly. Though they did not associate themselves with the Barbizon community, they did however accept advice from their elders: Diaz encouraged the young Renoir to work with lighter tones. Here too the seeds of Impressionism were being sown.

Impressionism – The second-generation artists wanted their work to capture the essence of light itself and to reflect the resonance of colour; the term "Impressionist" was actually coined by a sarcastic journalist in 1874, but was adopted by the group as they felt it conveyed the double revolution they had brought about in the field of painting.

The Impressionist Revolution – The Impressionist movement revolutionised artistic conventions on two counts: it paid little attention to form and it invented a new technique. Until then, the representation of reality was fundamentally important and no artist would have dared to neglect the lines and shapes of his subject, whether a portrait, still-life or landscape. Painters showed little concern for light and its effects, considered a minor component: priority was given to subject matter. For the Impressionists, light and the analysis of its effects became the principal subject; all the rest – contours, scenes, people – was simply an excuse to paint light.

Religious and historical works as well as family portraits and everyday scenes were no longer interesting in themselves. The Impressionists' favourite subjects were those which played with light: water, snow, material, flesh, flowers, leaves, fruit, mist and smoke. They wished to capture the infinite depths of the skies, the shimmering of light on water, a dress or a human face. When depicting the undergrowth, they wanted to show how the russet tones glitter in sunlight, how bright colours sparkle when the light changes and how colours are perceived in misty and smoky atmospheres.

Such fleeting and indefinite concepts were no longer attainable using traditional techniques. As priority was given to the vibration of light around the edges of objects, the process that applied paint along contours was banished. Traditionally, the layers of paint were applied slowly and acquired their definite colour after the oil had solidified; they were then coated with varnish to produce a transparent effect and to give depth to the colours. Naturally this technique was far too lengthy to capture the ephemeral quality of light and as a consequence the Impressionists developed a technique more suited to their purpose, one which involved very little oil and which dispensed with varnish: their art consisted of applying quick, small dabs of colour. The exact shade was conveyed by the juxtaposition of touches of pure colour, the final effect being assessed by the eye of the viewer.

The Impressionists were harshly criticised, even insulted at times, and it was only after a twenty-year struggle that their work was fully acknowledged.

The Painters – The Impressionist School was founded in Honfleur where Claude Monet (1840-1926), a painter from Le Havre, was encouraged by the seascape specialist Eugène Boudin to paint landscapes. Boudin (1824-98), a friend of Corot's, was also a precursor of Impressionism: his paintings are full of air and light. Following his example, Monet and later the Dutch artist Jongkind worked on the luminosity of the landscapes around the Seine estuary. They were joined by Bazille and **Sisley**, whom they had befriended in Gleyre's studio, and began to paint around Fontainebleau forest too, though they remained separate from the Barbizon School. Pissarro, Cézanne and Guillaumin, who met at the Swiss Academy, were called "The Famous Three" *(Le Groupe des Trois)*.

The painters were strongly supported by Édouard Manet (1832-83), one of their elders who was upsetting artistic conventions and scandalising the public with his bold colours and compositions. It was Manet who encouraged the Impressionists to pursue their efforts at painting light. In 1863, following clashes between the artists and the official salons which refused to show these new works, a now-famous independent exhibition of the rejected works (Salon des Refusés) was set up which gave birth to and led to the naming of the Impressionist movement.

In 1871 small groups of amateur painters, pupils and friends, including Paul Cézanne, gathered with Pissarro at Pontoise and with Docteur Gachet in Auvers. Another group based in Argenteuil and Louveciennes included Renoir, Monet, Sisley and Edgar Degas, who had originally studied under Ingres. Monet's innovative technique put him at the head of the movement and inspired both Manet and later Berthe Morisot. After 1880 the group broke up but its members remained faithful to painting light.

Sisley moved to Moret, seduced by the River Loing, while Monet settled in Giverny on the banks of the Epte *(see Michelin Green Guide Normandy)*. For practical reasons, Pissarro left the Oise valley to live in Eragny, near Gisors.

Georges Seurat (1859-91) remained in Paris but concentrated on the landscapes around the capital and along the coasts of the Channel. His technique consisted of breaking down the subject matter into small dabs of colour, each consisting of a series of dots *(points)*. Maximilien Luce (1858-1941) also experimented with this method – known as Pointillism or Divisionism – in the vicinity of Mantes.

Cézanne later returned to Aix-en-Provence where through the use of colour, tone and accentuated outlines he developed stylised masses which laid the foundations for the Cubist movement.

Renoir travelled to Algeria and Venice which inspired him to paint some of his finest works. Degas and Toulouse-Lautrec (1846-1901) lived in Paris; they were fascinated by circuses and theatres where the swirling dancers and performers were showered with complex illuminations created by artificial lighting.

The Dawn of the Twentieth Century – The **Nabis** and **Fauve** movements, which preceded Cubism and the new art forms which emerged in the wake of the First World War, also set up their easel or sometimes even their studio in the picturesque outskirts of Paris. On his return from a stay in Pont-Aven where Paul Gauguin had shown him the magic of composing in flat, bold colours, Paul Sérusier converted his friends from the Académie Julian to the same style and formed the Nabi movement (a Hebrew word meaning prophet). **Maurice Denis** (1870-1943) became the leader of the group, which included Bonnard, Roussel, Vuillard, Maillol, Vallotton and others.

The early Fauves (meaning "wild beasts") included extremely diverse artists – Matisse, Dufy, Braque, Derain, Vlamick, Rouault, Marquet. Their paintings of flat pattern and bright, even violent colour created an uproar when they were first shown. The painters, never a coherent group, were influenced by the paintings of **Van Gogh** who had died in 1890 leaving a collection of brilliant canvases composed of strong, vigorous touches of pure colour *(p 59)*.

The coasts and countryside of the north of France and the region around Paris still attract many artists to this day.

Folklore and Traditions of the North

For dates of festivals and other events see the Calendar of Events at the end of the guide.

The people of Picardy and the north of France belong to the "Picardy nation" which spreads from Beauvais to Lille and from Calais to Laon, extending as far as Tournai and Mons. The common language of this "nation" formed a bond between its inhabitants, who are known for being hard workers with a taste for good and lively merry-making. Even now, the slightest excuse can be found to organise a feast or a get-together in an *estaminet* (the Walloon word for a café) for a beer or two. Natives of Flanders, Artois, Lille and Picardy all have this same fondness for gatherings which is reflected in their many group activities: carnivals, holidays, patron saint days, village fairs and associations (each village has its own band).

The Ducasse or Kermesse – The words *ducasse* (from *dédicace*, meaning a Catholic holiday) and *kermesse* ("church fair" in Flemish) now both designate a town or village patron saint's day. This holiday has preserved aspects of its religious origins (Mass and procession) but today also includes stalls, competitions, traditional games, jumble sales...

Carnivals – Carnival-time is an occasion to dress up in costume and watch parades of floats and giant figures; it traditionally takes place on Shrove Tuesday *(Mardi Gras)* – as in Dunkirk, where it lasts for three days – but in reality, however, carnival parades take place throughout the year in the North.

Famous Giants – The giants originate from various myths, legends and stories and include:
– legendary founders, such as Lydéric and Phinaert in Lille.
– famous warriors like the Reuzes from Dunkirk and Cassel, who were originally from Scandinavia.
– historic figures, such as Jeanne Maillotte in Lille, the inn-keeper who fought off the "Howlers"; the beautiful Roze in Ardres, who saved the town from dragonnades; the Elector of Bergues, which portrays Lamartine; Roland in Hazebrouck, one of Baudouin of Flanders' Crusaders, who distinguished himself at the taking of Constantinople.
– famous couples, like Martin and Martine, the two jack o' the clocks of Cambrai; Colas and Jacqueline, the gardeners of Arras; Arlequin and Colombine in Bruay-en-Artois; Manon and Des Grieux in Hesdin.
– popular figures, like Gédéon, the bellringer of Bourbourg

Procession of the Reuze giants, Cassel

Boudin/EXPLORER

who saved the belfry chimes from being stolen; the pedlar Tisje Tasje of Hazebrouck, symbol of the Flemish spirit, with his wife Toria and his daughter Babe Tisje; Pierrot Bimberlot in Le Quesnoy; and Ko Pierre, a drum major, in Aniche.
– legendary heroes: Gargantua in Bailleul; Gambrinus, the king of beer, in Armentières; Yan den Houtkapper, the woodcutter who made a pair of wooden boots for Charlemagne, in Steenvoorde; Gayant of Douai, who delivered the town from brigands.
– representatives of trades, like the marsh gardener Baptistin in St Omer; the miner Cafougnette in Denain; and the fisherman Batisse in Boulogne.
– or simply a child, like the famous Binbin in Valenciennes.
The giants are often accompanied by their families – as they do marry and are given large families – and are surrounded by skirted horses, devils, bodyguards and wheels of fortune. Sometimes they have their own hymn, such as the Reuzelieds in Dunkirk and Cassel.

Materials – Traditionally the giants' bodies are made from a willow frame on which a painted *papier-mâché* head is placed. Once dressed in their costumes, the giants are then carried by one or more people who make them dance in the procession.
The tallest is Gayant in Douai, who is 7.50m - 25ft tall.
As giants are often now made of heavier materials (steel tubing, caning, plastic), they are frequently pulled along in carts or on wheels rather than carried.

Town Chimes – The chimes in the town belfry which regularly sound out their melodic tunes lend a rhythm to life in northern French towns. Since the Middle Ages, when four bells were tapped by hand with a hammer, there have been many additions: a mechanism, a manual keyboard, pedals, all of which have made it possible to increase the number of bells (62 in Douai) and to enrich the variety of their sounds.
Carillon concerts are held in Douai, St-Amand-les-Eaux and Maubeuge (east of Valenciennes).

Traditional Games and Sports – Traditional entertainments remain popular: marionettes, ball games, real tennis, ninepins, darts, lacrosse (an ancestor of golf), archery (which is also a traditional sport of the Valois area), cock-fighting, pigeon-breeding etc.

Archery – In the Middle Ages archers were already the pride of the Counts of Flanders, who would have the archers accompany them on all their expeditions. As soon as individual towns were founded the archers formed associations or guilds. They appeared at all public ceremonies, dressed in brightly-coloured costumes, brandishing the great standard of their association.
Today archery is practised in several ways. A method particular to the North is vertical or "perch" shooting, which consists of firing arrows upward to hit dummy birds attached to gratings suspended from a pole. At the top of this pole, about 30m - 98ft off the ground, is the hardest target of all, the **"papegaï"**. Archers must hit this bird with a long, ball-tipped arrow and the winner is proclaimed "King of the perch". In winter the sport is practised indoors: arrows are shot horizontally at a slightly tilted grating. Still grouped in brotherhoods, the archers gather every year to honour their patron, St Sebastian.

Crossbow – The art of the crossbow, which also dates from the Middle Ages, has its own circle of enthusiasts organised into brotherhoods. Their gatherings, colourful events featuring these curious weapons from another time, are often given evocative names such as The King's Crossbow Shoot.

Javelin – This feathered arrow measuring 50-60cm - 20-24in is thrown into a tightly-tied bundle of straw which serves as a target. It is the same principle as for the game of darts, which is played in many cafés.

The Game of "Billons" – A *billon* is a tapering wooden club about 1m - 3ft long, weighing about 2-3kg - 4-7lbs. Two teams throw their *billons* in turn towards a post 9m-30ft away; the aim is to land the narrower end of the club nearest to the post and this may be achieved by dislodging the *billons* of the opposing team.

Bouchon – Teams face each other in cafés, and knock down the cork and wood "targets" with their metal paddles. The best players participate in competitions at local festivals.

Cock-Fighting – Cock-breeders and anxious gamblers watch bloody and vicious fights to the death between roosters.

Pigeon-Breeding – Pigeon fanciers *(coulonneux)* raise their birds to fly back to the nest as quickly as possible: for pigeon-racing competitions, which are very popular, the birds are carried in special baskets to a distance of up to 500km - 310 miles and must then return to their dovecote at record speed. A pigeon can fly over 100km - 60 miles per hour on average.

Singing Finch Competitions – Finches have also become part of the folklore in the north of France, where they participate in trilling contests. Some can trill as many as 800 times an hour.

Ratting Dogs – Cruel ratting competitions have always had a certain popularity in this region. Three rats are put in a cage, then a dog; spectators time how long it takes the dog to kill its adversaries; the fastest dog is the victor.

Food and Drink

The people of the north of France are *bon vivants* who like to live well and enjoy their food; this is reflected in the cuisine of Flanders and Picardy which offers rich, savoury dishes.

The Cuisine of Picardy – Soups are the great local specialities, in particular those made from tripe *(tripe)*, pumpkin *(potiron)* or frogs *(grenouille)*, as well as the famous vegetable Gardener's Soup *(soupe des hortillons)*. The people of Picardy and Artois love their vegetables: St Omer cauliflowers, beans from Soissons, Laon artichokes, St Valery carrots, peas from the Vermandois and leeks which are used in a delicious pie, the *tarte aux porions*.

Main dishes include duck pâté in a pastry case *(pâté de canard en croûte)* (prepared in Amiens since the 17C), snipe pâté *(pâté de bécassines)* from Abbeville and Montreuil, eel pâté *(pâté d'anguilles)* from Péronne and chitterling sausages *(andouillettes)* from Arras and Cambrai. The *ficelle picarde* is a ham pancake in a creamy mushroom sauce. Duck, snipe and plover, trout from the Canche and the Course rivers, and eel, carp and pike from the River Somme are often on the menu. Seafood (shrimps known as *sauterelles*, cockles called *hemons*) is common, as well as sole, turbot, fresh herring and cod, often cooked with cream.

Flemish Cuisine – Flemish cooking, washed down with beer and often followed by a glass of gin or a *bistouille* (coffee with a dash of alcohol), contains several typical dishes:
– rabbit with prunes or raisins and pigeon with cherries.
– home-made potted meat made from veal, lard and rabbit *(potjevleesch)*.
– mixed stew of veal, mutton, pork, lard and vegetables *(hochepot)*.
– braised beef in a beer sauce flavoured with onions and spices *(carbonade)*.
– eel sautéed in butter and stewed in a wine sauce with herbs *(anguille au vert)*.
– small smoked herrings, a speciality of Dunkirk *(craquelots)*.

Cheeses of the North – Local cheeses, except for that from **Mont des Cats**, are strong; most come from the Thiérache and Avesnois regions, areas rich in pasture. The best in **Maroilles**, created in the 10C by monks from Maroilles abbey: it has a soft centre with a crust washed in beer, similar to cheese from Munster. The other cheeses in the region are derived from it: **Vieux Lille**, also called Maroilles gris (grey Maroilles); **Dauphin** (Maroilles with herbs and spices); **Cœur d'Avesnes** or Rollot; and the delicious **Boulette d'Avesnes** (Maroilles with spices, rolled in paprika). **Flamiche au Maroilles**, a creamy, highly-flavoured quiche, is one of the most famous dishes from the northern region of France. The most famous cheese from the Paris region is Brie.

Local cheeses

Cakes – The local pancakes *(crêpes)*, waffles and sweet breads *(tartines* and *brioches)* can make entire meals in themselves; the *brioches* with bulging middles are called *coquilles*.

Tarts, such as the delicious *tartes au sucre* sprinkled with brown sugar, are often served for dessert. Sweets are accompanied by the light, chicory coffee which people from the region drink at any time of the day.

The Flemish "Vivat" – Games and fêtes invariably conclude with banquets during which cheering participants intone the Flemish toast *(vivat)*; the person to be honoured has their health sung to while beer or champagne is poured into a napkin held above their head.

BEER

Gambrinus, the king of beer, is greatly revered in the north of France as is St Arnould, the patron saint of brewers. Beer *(la bière)* was already known in Antiquity; in Gaul, later, it was called *cervoise*. During the Middle Ages brewing beer was a privilege of the monasteries; it spread enormously in Flanders under John the Fearless, Duke of Burgundy and Count of Flanders, who developed the use of hops.

The Brewing Process – Beer is obtained by the mashing and fermentation of a mixture of water and malt, flavoured with hops. Barley grains are soaked in water (malting) until they germinate. The sprouting seeds are then dried and roasted in a kiln: **malt**. This is powdered and then mixed with pure water and hops and cooked, according to each manufacturer's secret procedure. This operation, called brewing, transforms the starch in the malt into sugar and makes it possible to obtain the **wort**. With the addition of a raising agent, the wort begins to ferment. Beer brewing was formerly undertaken simply by a brewer, with his boy handling a sort of pointed shovel *(fourquet)*, but is now a large and sophisticated industry. Much of French beer and lager (paler, 'aged' beer containing more bubbles and often less alcohol) is produced in the Pas-de-Calais region, which is rich in water, barley and hops; the hops grown in Flanders have a particularly strong flavour. The biggest breweries are in the areas around Lille-Roubaix and Armentières, and the Scarpe and Escaut (Scheldt) river valleys.

Different beers have their own characteristics: the traditional, slightly-bitter lager *(bière blonde)* of the north; the relatively sweet and fruity regional dark beer *(bière brune)* or the richly-flavoured, amber-red beer *(bière rousse)*.

Consumption has decreased over the past dozen years or so and is now at the level of 40 litres – 35 pints per person a year.

Traditional Brasseries – In the Nord – Pas-de-Calais region there are still a number of companies making lager in the traditional way, even if modern equipment is used. Some of these may be visited:

Brasserie Castelain, 13 rue Pasteur, 62410 Benifontaine. Tel: 21 40 38 38.

Brasserie Bailleux, café-restaurant Au Baron, Place du fond des rocs, 59570 Gussignies. Tel: 27 66 88 61.

Les Brasseurs, micro-brasserie, 22 place de la Gare, 59800 Lille. Tel: 20 06 46 25.

Brasserie d'Annœullin, 4 Grand Place, 59112 Annœullin. Tel: 20 85 78 57.

Brasserie Steinbeer, 20 rue Basly, 62141 Evin-Malmaison. Tel: 21 77 92 12.

F. Jalain/EXPLORER

Brewers in Lille

The area covered by this guide is one of contrasts. The coastal resorts, captured on canvas by Boudin, Monet and Sisley, traditionally attracted the inhabitants of industrial towns of the north seeking fresh air and sun. Veterans of two world wars return to the battlefields of their youth. The flat agricultural land of the Beauce, a golden sea of ripening corn in the autumn, is dominated by the majestic Gothic cathedral of Chartres, which together with Amiens, Beauvais and Laon, continues to draw pilgrims.

The châteaux of the French kings and emperors in the Ile-de-France are set in formal gardens with sculptured fountains, surrounded by the parks and forests where the court rode to hounds. All roads lead to Paris, where the traditional beer of Flanders and Picardy and the wine of the other provinces are enjoyed in the pavement-cafés. Astérix and his new rival, Mickey Mouse at Disneyland, provide entertainment for the whole family.

The Apollo Basin, Versailles

Sights

ABBEVILLE

Population 23 787
Michelin map 52 folds 6, 7 or 236 fold 22
Town plan in the current Michelin Red Guide France

Abbeville (pronounced Abb'ville) is the capital of the Ponthieu region and stands on the edge of the River Somme, about 20km - 12 miles from the sea. In the 19C artists flocked to its medieval streets overlooked by the towers of St Wulfram's church; since the Second World War it has taken on a more modern aspect.

HISTORICAL NOTES

The town derives its name from the Latin *Abbatis Villa* meaning abbot's villa, and originally grew up around the country house of the abbot of St-Riquier *(qv)*. From the 13C to the 15C Abbeville became the property of the English, the Burgundians and the French, depending on the outcome of the struggles for possession of the Somme Valley. Abbeville finally became French under Louis XI in the 18C.

In 1542 the young and attractive Mary of England (Henry VIII's sister) was married to King Louis XII – then aged 52 – here; he died of consumption the following year.

Enlightened Capitalists: the Van Robais – This Dutch family settled in Abbeville as a result of Colbert's wish to free the national economy from its dependence on foreign imports by manufacturing products in France.

Josse Van Robais arrived in Abbeville in 1665 to establish a factory making fine cloth, aided by various privileges, not least of which was a guaranteed monopoly.

Van Robais brought with him his family, his Protestant chaplain, about 50 workers and his weaving looms, which he installed in Faubourg Hocquet.

Thus the Royal Tenter Works (Manufacture Royale des Rames) was founded, one of the first 'integrated' businesses, dealing not only with all aspects of spinning and weaving but also with the finishing (dressing, fulling, dyeing...).

The firm's success was consolidated by Josse's grandson, Abraham Van Robais (1698-1779): during the 18C about 2 500 people were employed, 250 of whom were weavers.

The Father of Prehistory: Boucher de Perthes (1788-1868) – Jacques Boucher de Perthes was a handsome and intelligent man, the multi-talented author of a minor masterpiece and painter of portraits in the style of La Bruyère. In 1825 after a wild and worldly youth he succeeded his father as Head of Customs in Abbeville, which at the time was a busy seaport.

He became passionately interested in prehistory, scanning the alluvial layers of the Somme – exposed by dredgers widening the canal – in search of the sharpened flints which, he believed, should accompany the bones of antediluvian man. From 1830 he was assisted by the doctor, **Casimir Picard.** Following Picard's death in 1841, Boucher de Perthes struggled on, continuing to explore the woodland peat of La Portelette – close to what is now Abbeville station – and the quarries of St-Acheul, near Amiens. From the study of his finds he gathered material for a work on "Celtic and Antediluvian Antiquities" in which he asserted his belief in the existence of paleolithic man, contemporary to the large extinct pachyderms.

His discoveries were met with scepticism. Boucher de Perthes would pay 10 centimes for an oddly-shaped rock or stone, and one of his cousins recalled how, on meeting a peasant breaking rocks, she asked what he was doing: "Making prehistoric axes for M Boucher de Perthes" was the reply.

The tragic days of May-June 1940 – After the German breakthrough at Sedan and the Panzer drive to the sea, Abbeville became a nerve centre for the French Resistance.

From 20 May intense bombing by Stukas struck the urban centre, almost all of which burned, destroying 2 000 houses and leaving hundreds of people dead or wounded. At night, the Germans entered the town and constructed a large bridgehead on the south bank of the Somme, extending as far as Huppy and Bray-lès-Mareuil, with the well-fortified Caubert Heights (Monts de Caubert) as a strong point.

A fierce counter-attack by the French under **Colonel de Gaulle** at the end of May for 3 days, and by the Scots for another 2 days in early June, reduced the German pocket but did not succeed in breaching the Caubert Heights' defences.

SIGHTS *2 hours*

Collégiale St-Vulfran (St Wulfram's Collegiate Church) ⊙ – This church, which resembles a cathedral, was begun in 1488; the west front was built first, but construction of the nave was interrupted in 1539 owing to lack of money, and it was not until the 17C that the chancel was finished in neo-Gothic style. During the bombing of 1940 the nave and chancel vaults collapsed. The west front is best viewed from the west side of the square. The interior is undergoing restoration.

It was in this square that a young man of 19, Chevalier de la Barre, was condemned to be beheaded and burnt at the stake after being accused of damaging one of the crucifixes on the bridges in Abbeville. Voltaire tried in vain to obtain a pardon for him.

★West Front – The Flamboyant west front shows how late-15C architecture had become merely a vehicle for sculpture. Flanked by small watch-turrets, the towers rise to 55m - 180ft; between them the open gable supports a statue of the Virgin accompanied by St Wulfram and St Nicholas. In the pointed angle of the gable above the centre doorway stands a group representing the Trinity.

Central Doorway – The piers are decorated with statues of bishops: St Nicholas *(left)* and St Firmin of Amiens *(right)* standing on a sculpted base, showing his martyrdom, and the emblem of the coopers of whom he was patron.

The door has preserved its Renaissance panels, masterpieces by the Picardy woodcarvers *("huchiers")*. In the centre the figures of the Evangelists are framed by St Peter *(left)* and St Paul *(right)*. Above are scenes from the life of the Virgin.

The panels were given by Jehan Mourette, the head of a brotherhood of poets (Confrérie du Puy Notre-Dame d'Abbeville), who is commemorated in an inscription dated 1550.

Left Doorway – This doorway tells the legend of St Eustace: on the tympanum, his foot on the shield of the draper-hosiers, St Eustace sees his children being eaten, one by a lion, the other by a wolf; to the left, a relief shows him being thrown into the sea by a sailor, in front of his wife, from a ship on which he had tried to stow away.

Right Doorway – This doorway was the gift of the guild of haberdashers; their shield of a purse and scales can be seen under the three famous statues carved by Pierre Lheureux in 1501-02.

These statues represent: the Assumption of the Virgin *(on the tympanum)* and the Virgin's sisters *(on the piers)*: bare-breasted Mary Cleopas with her four children on the left; on the right, Mary Salome and her two children, John and James the Great.

Buttresses – The second buttress on the left features figures of St Peter and St Andrew, the latter carrying the cross of his martyrdom, with the bull's head emblem of the butchers at his feet.

Interior – From the nave, notice the abstract stained-glass windows of the chancel which were designed by William Epstein.

★**Musée Boucher de Perthes (Boucher de Perthes Museum)** ☉ – Facing the square, which is graced by the statue of the local sailor Courbet (1827-1885), stand the museum buildings: a 13C belfry, a small 15C edifice (formerly the Mint) and a new building to the rear.

The main room on the ground floor displays paintings: 16C works from the Confrérie du Puy Notre-Dame (portrait of Jehan Mourette and his wife), a 17C *Descent from the Cross* by the Flemish artist Van Mol, and from the 18C four mythological canvases by François le Moine, portraits by Largillière, a self-portrait by Lépicié and genre scenes by the local artist Choquet.

The Mint and the grand staircase exhibit medieval sculpture (corbels and friezes from local houses, 15C altarpiece from the Charterhouse at Thuison), local ceramics (faience from Vron, glazed earthenware from Sorrus) and tapestries (fragment from the Artemis series).

The vaulted rooms of the old belfry provide an ideal setting for the medieval statues and ivories, in particular the superb silver Virgin and Child (1568).

The second floor houses the Boucher de Perthes prehistoric collections and the archeological discoveries made around the Somme and in St-Acheul.

The Natural History section has a good display of birds.

Église du St-Sépulcre (St Sepulchre Church) – Only the belltower, the piers and archivolts of the nave, the two side chapels and the St-Sepulchre Chapel remain from the original 15C building, which was altered substantially in the late 19C into Flamboyant Gothic style. The vaulting and paving were renovated following severe damage during the Second World War. The contemporary **stained-glass windows★** by Alfred Manessier represent The Passion and the Resurrection of Christ.

Old House – *29 Rue des Capucins, on the corner of Rue des Teinturiers.* This corbelled house is an example of 15C-16C urban housing.

★**Château de Bagatelle (Bagatelle Château)** ☉ – *Southeast of the town, at 133 Route de Paris.*

Abraham Van Robais had Bagatelle built from 1752-54 as his villa in the country, where he could relax and receive his business clients. It originally consisted of only the ground floor to which was added, 15 years later, an attic storey with bull's-eye windows to provide living accommodation; the mansard roof dates from about 1790. In spite of subsequent additions this is a charming residence, characterised by a harmony and unity of style.

On the ground floor, the Rococo decoration of the rooms – furnished with period pieces – has a light and elegant touch. The hall leads into the summer salon, a room with no fireplace. The picture panels above the door cases are painted with love scenes showing Morning, Noon and Night; the panelling is carved with arabesques in the Pompeiian style.

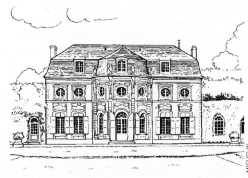

Bagatelle Château, Abbeville

In the winter salon the decoration of the sculpted panels and chimneypiece is highlighted in blue. The fine chandelier with porcelain flowers from the Royal Vincennes factory, the applied ornament, the panelling and the consoles in the dining room all belonged to the Van Robais; the rest of the furniture is also 18C. A graceful double staircase with wrought-iron balustrade was ingeniously adapted to fit the hall, to give access to the low-ceilinged first-floor rooms with their delicate Louis XV woodwork, and Louis XVI garland and ribbon motifs.

The formal French garden contains parterres and statues, and "Mme Roland's mound" (butte de Mme Roland) where the wife of the future minister – at that time Inspector of Factories in Picardy – used to take her lunch.

The botanical park contains a large and varied collection of plants, some rare.

Musée d'histoire de France 1940 (Museum of the History of France in 1940) ⊙ – Dioramas, photographs, armaments and uniforms evoke the fierce and bloody battles fought on the Somme.

EXCURSIONS

Monts de Caubert (Caubert Heights) – *5km - 3 miles west. At the first sharp bend prior to a junction, take the small road to the left, following the crest for 1.5km - 1 mile.* From the calvary there is a good view over the Somme valley, Abbeville and the plains of Ponthieu beyond.

The Vimeu Region – *Round trip of 35km - 22 miles – about 1 hour.* The Vimeu region of Picardy, between the Rivers Somme and Bresle, seems like an isolated plateau, grooved by green valleys with hedged meadows full of apple trees. This farming country also contains many châteaux and, in the villages hidden among the trees, locksmiths' and ironmongers' workshops; these are the traditional occupations of the area, which have been practised locally since the 17C.

Friville-Escarbotin – *26km - 16 miles west along D 925.*
The **Museum of the Vimeu Region's Industries** (Musée des Industries du Vimeu) ⊙ traces the history of small-scale metalwork: locksmithery, taps and fittings, ironmongery... The ground floor displays 19C machines (pedal-worked drill) and reconstructed workshops: locksmith's shop, keymaker's workshop, local foundry. Among the collections of locks, nails and bolts, note the display of 135 padlocks, the smallest of which is made from a gold Louis coin.

The first floor displays examples of modern production (diorama).

Return to D 925, going east; turn right into D 29 after Fresenneville and continue to St-Maxent.

St-Maxent Windmill – This timber windmill, which was in use until 1941, retains its post, its counterbalancing "tail", its roof of chestnut shingles, its three storeys for sifting, and its mechanism and millstones.

Continue north on N 28 for 3km - 2 miles.

Huppy – Pop 592. Home of the 17C sculptor J-B Poultier, this village also boasts a 15C and 16C **church** (Renaissance stained glass) and a 17C **château** *(private)*, where Colonel de Gaulle established his headquarters on 29 May 1940 *(plaque)*; he was promoted to General on 1 June.

Return to Abbeville by N 28.

ALBERT

Population 10 010
Michelin map 52 fold 9 or 236 fold 25

The town, which was originally called Ancre, from the river which flows through it, was the seat of a marquess; the title was acquired in 1610 by Marie de' Medici's favourite, Concino Concini. Following his tragic death in 1617, which heralded the queen mother's disgrace, Louis XIII offered Ancre to Charles d'Albert, Duc de Luynes, who gave it his name.

Albert was almost totally destroyed during the Battle of the Somme in 1916 and the Battle of Picardy in 1918 *(see Historical Notes, qv)* and is today a well-planned, modern town that makes a good base from which to explore the battlefields. Méaulte, a large suburb to the south, is the home of the French aviation industry.

Notre-Dame-de-Brébières Basilica – The basilica is a popular place of pilgrimage. The tower (70m - 230ft high) is surmounted by a poignant statue of the Virgin and Child. Inside, the 11C Miraculous Virgin is venerated.

Below Place d'Armes, a branch of the Ancre flows through the pleasant **public garden.**

BATTLEFIELDS *Round trip of 34km - 21 miles – 45 min.*

A circuit east and north of Albert commemorates the British and South African soldiers under Douglas Haig who fell during the Allied attack in summer 1916 (Battle of the Somme).

Take D 929 northeast towards Bapaume.

On the right lies a British cemetery.

La Boisselle – Traces of explosions still suggest some of the violence of the fighting which occurred in this village.

Take D 20 on the right.

Cross Bazentin and Longueval, around which lie several British cemeteries, then turn left.

South African Memorial and Commemorative Museum at Delville Wood ⊙ – The battle of Delville Wood in July 1916 saw, over five days and nights, some of the fiercest fighting and worst devastation which resulted in the deaths of over 1 000 South African men, who were attached to the 9th Scottish Division. The original dense wood was blasted out of existence, apart from a single hornbeam which is now carefully tended.

A memorial (1926) and a museum (1986) commemorate the 12 000 and more South African soldiers who died in the First World War, and the 6 000 plus who fell in the Second World War, all of them volunteers. A lawn bordered by oaks grown from acorns picked in the Cape Province leads to the memorial arch, above which stands a sculpture of Castor and Pollux, hands clasped in friendship, who symbolise the English and Afrikaans communities in South Africa united in fighting for their country. The museum is housed in a replica of Cape Town Castle and features paintings, bronze panels, uniforms and relics relating to the South African sacrifice.

Return to D 20 and turn right into D 107; turn left into D 929.

Pozières – This British cemetery is encircled by columns which give it a majestic air. The names of 14 690 men who went missing in action are engraved on the memorial.

Turn right into D 73.

Thiepval British Memorial – The village of Thiepval was fortified by the Germans and withstood a long siege in the summer of 1916; it is now the site of a commanding memorial.

The enormous, towering brick-built triumphal arch overlooks the Ancre valley and is visible from afar. The memorial, surrounded by a lawn, bears the names of 73 367 British soldiers who went missing in action and have no known grave.

Continue on D 73.

The **Belfast Tower** (right), which was built in memory of the 6 000 Ulstermen who were killed or injured in July 1916, is a replica of Helen's Tower at Clandeboye, Northern Ireland, where the 36th Ulster Division were in training.

The road then crosses the Ancre valley.

★**Parc-mémorial de Beaumont-Hamel (Beaumont Hamel Memorial Park)** – This winds-wept plateau was the site of a battle fought by the Newfoundland Division in 1916 on the opening day of the Battle of the Somme. Some 700 Newfoundlanders were killed or wounded that first day. The area has been preserved and developed, and now displays trenches, outposts, "The Danger Tree", firing parapets, twisted iron rods suggesting bullet-blasted bushes...

At the base of the monument – a huge, bronze New World Caribou (the emblem of the Regiment) – tablets bear the names of 820 men with no known grave. A platform provides good **views** over the battlefield. It stands in the largest of the Memorial Parks, and was opened by Earl Haig in 1925.

Return to the Ancre valley and turn right into D 50 to Albert.

AMIENS ★★★

Agglomeration 156 120
Michelin map 52 fold 8 or 236 fold 24 – Facilities p 10

Amiens, the capital of Picardy, is an important communications centre and the setting for a beautiful cathedral. Devastated during the two World Wars, it is now largely a modern town, sheltering the precious remains of its past in picturesque areas. The ramparts were replaced in the 18C by circular boulevards; a lively shopping street runs from Gare du Nord to the Maison de la Culture.

The town has always been an economic, artistic and intellectual centre, and a university was founded there in 1964.

The delicious gastronomic specialities include chocolate wafers, macaroons, pancakes filled with ham and mushrooms with a white sauce ("ficelles Picardes") and the famous duck patés baked in a pastry case (pâtés de canard en croûte).

HISTORICAL NOTES

St Martin's Cloak – In Gallo-Roman times Amiens was the capital of a Belgian tribe, the Ambiens; in the 4C the town was converted to Christianity by Firmin and his companions. At that time a horseman in the Roman legion stationed here met a beggar shivering in the north wind: he sliced his cloak in two with his sword and gave half to the poor man. This episode is recalled in a low-relief by J Samson (1830) on the north wall of the law courts (Palais de Justice), Place d'Aguesseau. The soldier was later ordained, became Bishop of Tours and was subsequently canonised as **St Martin**, patron saint of France.

Birth of an Industry: Textiles – Affiliated to the Hanse of London (a merchants' guild), Amiens was very prosperous in the Middle Ages. The cloth business and wine trade, the port, and the influx of pilgrims who came to worship the relic said to be the head of John the Baptist, all contributed to the bustling atmosphere. *Guède* or *pastel*, a precious tinctural plant found locally and in the Santerre area, was treated here where it was known as *"waide"* (woad); when milled the plant produces a beautiful blue, which was exported to England. The late 15C saw the production of a woollen serge mixed with silk, *"sayette"*, which gave the products of Amiens *("Articles d'Amiens")* a far-reaching reputation. The famous "Amiens Velvets" were introduced during Louis XIV's reign.

Steely Assaults – The valleys of the Somme and the Aisne rivers are major obstacles to invaders from the north, and being the bridgehead, Amiens has suffered many attacks. In 1918, during the Battle of Picardy, the town was attacked by Ludendorff and bombarded with 12 000 shells. It was set ablaze in 1940 during the Battle of the Somme. In 1944 its prison was the target of a dangerous aerial attack aimed at helping the imprisoned Resistance members to escape.

Post-War Changes – As sixty per cent of Amiens was destroyed it had to undergo considerable reconstruction, the most prominent of which is around Place Alphonse-Fiquet (the station and Perret Tower), in the area around the Maison de la Culture, the Pierre-de-Coubertin Sports Centre and the Faidherbe district (**BY**). The town's edges are being redefined by other new buildings.
Traditional industries still hold sway in the city – knitting wools and the famous velvets – though the Longpré industrial zone is home to substantial metallurgy and chemical products businesses, major alternatives to the textile business. Factories producing tyres, car parts and electronic equipment have also been established.

Local Heroes – Amiens was the birthplace of several writers including **Choderlos de Laclos** (1741-1803), famous for *Les Liaisons Dangereuses*, Paul Bourget (1852-1925) and **Roland Dorgelès** (1885-1973), author of *Les Croix de Bois*, as well as the physician **Édouard Branly** (1844-1940) who invented the coherer, a device for detecting radio waves.

Jules Verne (1828-1905) was born in Nantes but spent most of his life in Amiens where he wrote his *Incredible Journeys (20 000 Leagues under the Sea, Around the World in Eighty Days)*. He was a town councillor and responsible for the building of the Amiens circus (cirque d'Amiens) (**BY**). He is buried among the mausoleums under the trees in the Madeleine cemetery. The Jules Verne Documentation Centre (**CZ M³**) stores a wealth of information on his life and work.

In Place René-Goblet a monument commemorates another local hero: Marshal Leclerc de Hauteclocque who distinguished himself during the Second World War.

★★★CATHEDRALE NOTRE-DAME (CATHEDRAL OF OUR LADY) (CY) ☉
1 1/2 hours

Amiens cathedral is the largest Gothic building in France (145m - 475ft long with vaults 42.50m - 139ft high).
In 1218 the Romanesque church on the site was destroyed by fire. Bishop Evrard de Fouilloy and the people of Amiens immediately decided to build a replacement, something exceptional worthy of sheltering the "head of John the Baptist", the precious relic brought back in 1206 from the fourth crusade by Wallon de Sarton, Canon of Picquigny.
The plans of the church were entrusted to Robert de Luzarches who was succeeded by Thomas de Cormont and then his son Renaud. The cathedral was begun in 1220 and the speed with which it was built explains the remarkable unity of style, though the towers remained uncrowned until the beginning of the 15C. The cathedral was later restored by Viollet-le-Duc; it miraculously escaped damage in 1940.

The nave, Amiens Cathedral

S Chirol

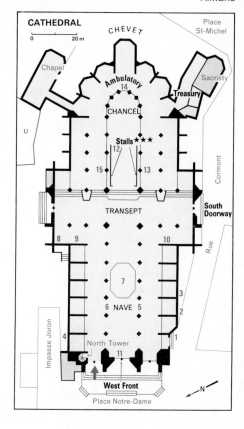

Each year a *son et lumière* show ⊙ in five acts presents the history of the cathedral, its construction and its role throughout the centuries.

Exterior

Unusually for a Gothic building, the west front of Amiens cathedral has a horizontal emphasis, consisting of several bands: the three doorways; the two galleries including the Kings' Gallery (galerie des rois) with its enormous figures; the great Flamboyant rose window (renewed in the 16C) framed by twinned open bays; and the small bell-ringers' gallery (galerie des sonneurs) topped by light arcading between the towers. Elegant sculptures – some damaged by pollution – further enhance the ensemble.

The **central doorway** is framed by the Wise and Foolish Virgins who, together with the Apostles and the Prophets on the piers, escort from a respectable distance the famous **Beau Dieu**, a noble and serene Christ standing on lavender and basil. He is the focal point of this enormous carved Bible. The tympanum portrays the Last Judgment presided over by a more archaic and severe God with a procession of virgins, martyrs, angels and damned souls in the arching above. The lower sections have quatrefoil low-reliefs framing the Virtues (women with shields) and Vices.

The **left doorway** is dedicated to **St Firmin** the evangelist of Amiens and to the Picardy region.

The quatrefoils on the base enclose lively representations of a **Calendar** symbolised by the signs of the Zodiac and the corresponding Labours of the Months.

Above, St Ulphe, a virgin hermit, stands ranged with various local bishops and martyrs including the decapitated St Acheul and St Ache, holding their heads in their hands.

The **right doorway** is dedicated to the **Mother of God.** On the central pier, the crowned Virgin presides over scenes from Genesis. In the embrasures, the large statues portray the Annunciation, the Visitation, and the Presentation in the Temple *(right)*, the Magi visiting Herod, Solomon and the Queen of Sheba *(left)*. The quatrefoils show the life of the Virgin and of Christ; the tympanum celebrates the Assumption. Go round the cathedral to the right, passing a giant St Christopher (1), an Annunciation (2), and, between the 3rd and 4th chapels, a pair of woad merchants with their sack (3).

The **south doorway,** known as the Golden Virgin Doorway because of the statue which used to adorn the pier, is dedicated to St Honoré who was bishop of Amiens.

Follow Rue Cormont to Place St-Michel.

From here there is a fine view of the east end with its pierced flying buttresses, and the soaring lead-covered chestnut spire (112.70m - 370ft high).

Return to Place Notre-Dame.

Before entering the cathedral by the left doorway, note the statue of Charles V (4) on the northern side, on the 14th buttress supporting the tower.

Interior

The sheer size and the amount of light inside the cathedral are striking.

The **nave** is the highest in France, reaching 42.50m - 139ft. Its elevation consists of large and exceptionally high arcades surmounted by a band of finely detailed foliage, a blind triforium and tall windows.

13C recumbent bronze effigies of the cathedral's founding bishops lie in the third bay: Evrard de Fouilloy (5) and Geoffroy d'Eu (6); the latter faces towards the St-Saulve chapel which shelters a figure of Christ in a long gold robe.

On the flagging, renewed in the 19C, the meandering lines of the labyrinth (7) have been restored. In the past the faithful would follow the lines on their knees, as a

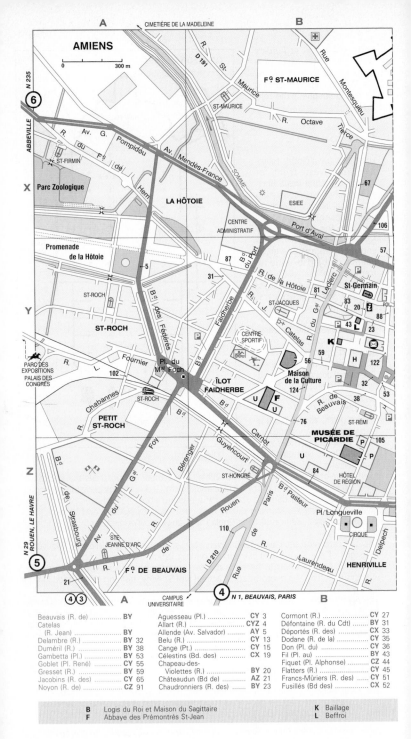

AMIENS

0 — 300 m

(map of Amiens with streets and landmarks)

B	Logis du Roi et Maison du Sagittaire	**K**	Baillage
F	Abbaye des Prémontrés St-Jean	**L**	Beffroi

Way of the Cross. At the centre, the names of those responsible for the cathedral are inscribed: Robert de Luzarches, Thomas and Renaud de Cormont (the original stone is in the Picardy Museum).

The **north transept** is pierced by a 14C rose window with a star-shaped centre. The font (8), to the left of the door, dates from 1180 and may originally have been used to wash the dead. On the west wall a painted sculpture in four parts represents Christ and the money-lenders in the Temple (9) (1520).

The **south transept arm**, which is illuminated through a Flamboyant rose window, bears on its west wall four scenes in relief (10) portraying the conversion of the magician Hermogene by St James the Great (1511).

The perspective back down the nave reveals its elegance and the boldness of the organ loft supporting the **great organ** (11) (1442) with its delicate golden arabesques, crowned by the majestic rose window at the west end.

The **chancel** is enclosed within a beautiful 18C choir-screen, wrought by Jean Veyren. The 110 Flamboyant oak **stalls★★★** ⊙ were created between 1508 and 1519 by the master cabinet-makers Arnould Boulin, Antoine Avernier and Alexandre Huet. They are arranged in two rows and surmounted by wooden tracery, and are presided over by

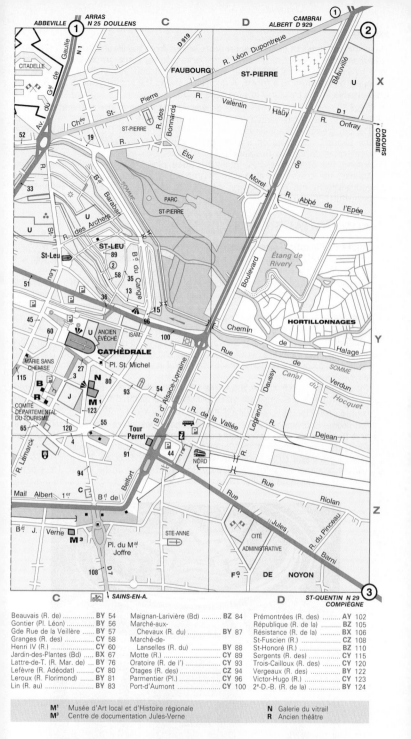

Beauvais (R. de)	**BY** 54	Maignan-Larivière (Bd)	**BZ** 84	Prémontrées (R. des)	**AY** 102
Gontier (Pl. Léon)	**BY** 56	Marché-aux-		République (R. de la)	**BZ** 105
Gde Rue de la Veillère	**BY** 57	Chevaux (R. du)	**BY** 87	Résistance (R. de la)	**BX** 106
Granges (R. des)	**CY** 58	Marché-de-		St-Fuscien (R.)	**CZ** 108
Henri IV (R.)	**CY** 60	Lanselles (R. du)	**BY** 88	St-Honoré (R.)	**BZ** 110
Jardin-des-Plantes (Bd)	**BX** 67	Motte (R.)	**CY** 89	Sergents (R. des)	**CY** 115
Lattre-de-T. (R. Mar. de)	**BY** 76	Oratoire (R. de l')	**CY** 93	Trois-Cailloux (R. des)	**CY** 120
Lefèvre (R. Adéodat)	**CY** 80	Otages (R. des)	**CZ** 94	Vergeaux (R. des)	**BY** 122
Leroux (R. Florimond)	**BY** 81	Parmentier (Pl.)	**CY** 96	Victor-Hugo (R.)	**CY** 123
Lin (R. au)	**BY** 83	Port-d'Aumont	**CY** 100	2e-D.-B. (R. de la)	**BY** 124

M¹	Musée d'Art local et d'Histoire régionale	**N**	Galerie du vitrail
M³	Centre de documentation Jules-Verne	**R**	Ancien théâtre

two master-stalls destined for the king and the dean of the chapter. Over 4 000 figures on the misericords, stall ends, canopies, pendentives and brackets realistically and spiritedly evoke Genesis and Exodus, the life of the Virgin, scenes of 16C life in Amiens such as craftsmen at work, and comical episodes culled from medieval fables. One worker carved himself holding his mallet (12) and inscribed his name: Jehan Turpin.

In the **ambulatory** on the right, on the choir-screen above two recumbent effigies, eight remarkable carved and coloured stone groups (1488) under delicate Gothic canopies evoke the **life of St Firmin** (13), his martyrdom and his exhumation by St Saulve three centuries later. The highly expressive figures are wearing 15C dress: the nobles in sumptuous attire, the humble poorly dressed and the executioner in curious breeches.

Behind the main altar, facing the central chapel containing a 19C gilded statue of the Virgin, the tomb of Cardinal de la Grange (1402) lies under the monument to Canon Guislan Lucas, famous for its **Weeping Angel** (14) carved by Nicolas Blasset (1628).

In the apsidal chapels vestiges of the 13C stained-glass windows remain.

AMIENS

The choir screen north of the chancel bears scenes from the **life of St John** (15) (1531) – *read from right to left*. Executed with less verve than the scenes of the life of St Firmin, they nevertheless reveal a striking wealth of detail and imagination: the desert is strangely represented as a forest. A quatrefoil shows the arrival of John the Baptist's head *(visible in the treasury)* in Amiens in 1206.

Trésor (Treasury) ⊙ – The collection was put together in the 19C and 20C; it is housed in the cloister and a room next to the sacristy.

The old treasure disappeared during the Revolution apart from the "face of John the Baptist", displayed on a silver gilt platter made in 1876 to replace the one confiscated during the Revolution.

Among the other treasures, note the three pieces from Paraclete Abbey near Amiens: the cross decorated with filigree work and engraved stones (13C), the votive crown and the reliquary vase (14C), as well as St Firmin's reliquary, a beautiful 13C work.

ADDITIONAL SIGHTS

★★**Musée de Picardie (Picardy Museum)** (BZ) ⊙ – The building was constructed between 1855 and 1867 for the Picardy Society of Antiquaries and is an imposing example of Napoleon III architecture.

Basement – Egyptian and Greek antiquities are displayed, together with archeological collections assembled from excavations in Amiens and the region (St-Acheul and Belloy-sur-Somme). There are numerous Gallo-Roman artefacts, glass and ceramics from Samarobriva, the former name for Amiens.

Ground floor – The main central room, restored to its original décor, displays large 18C and 19C paintings. The medieval collections contain *objets d'art*, gold and silver plate, religious sculptures in wood or stone, and architectural elements from local Gothic buildings, particularly Amiens cathedral (recumbent effigy, tombstone, the labyrinth's central stone).

The sculptures date from the 16C to the 19C: Rodin, Bourdelle, Barye are represented. In the rotunda the American artist **Sol Lewitt** has painted a huge mural, entitled Wall-Drawing no 711, using a technique involving washes of indian ink.

First floor – Enormous murals by Puvis de Chavannes adorn the main stairway and first-floor rooms. The Notre-Dame du Puy gallery and part of the following room house the works of art of the Confrérie du Puy Notre-Dame d'Amiens.

Originally a poets' circle known under the name « **Puy d'Amour** », this literary society became religious and dedicated itself to the glorification of the Virgin. The head of the society, elected annually, had to offer the cathedral a votive painting accom-

Wall-Drawing no 711 by Sol Lewitt

panied by a poem or palinode. Some of these paintings on wood have retained their sumptuous frame, fashioned by those who carved the cathedral stalls. François I is recognisable in the panel with a Renaissance canopy (1518) entitled "Au juste pois, véritable balance" ("True scales, just weight"); Henri IV appears under the Gothic canopy sheltering the palinode entitled "Terre d'où prit la vérité naissance" ("Land where Truth was born") (1601).

The remarkable *Virgin with Palm Tree* (1520) in its high openwork wood frame shows the Virgin surrounded by saints and the donors and their family, with Amiens Cathedral in the background.

The Nieuwerkerke gallery presents 17C paintings from the Spanish School (Ribera: *Miracle of St Donatus of Arezzo* and El Greco: *Portrait of a Man*), the Dutch School (Frans Hals: *Portrait of Langelius the pastor*) and the French School (Simon Vouet: *Repentant Magdalene*).

Subsequent rooms exhibit 18C French painting including works by Oudry, Chardin, Fragonard and Quentin de La Tour, as well as the nine *Hunts in Foreign Lands* (Chasses en pays étrangers) by Parrocel, Pater, Boucher, Lancret, Van Loo and De Troy for Louis XV's small apartments at Versailles. Italian masters (Guardi, Tiepolo) express the charm of Venetian painting.

The Charles-Dufour gallery is dedicated to 19C French landscape painters and in particular to the Barbizon School (Millet, Isabey, Corot, Rousseau).

Modern art is represented by Balthus, Masson, Fautrier, Dubuffet, Picabia.

Musée d'Art local et d'Histoire régionale (Museum of Local Art and Regional History) (**CY M¹**) ⊙ – The **Hôtel de Berny★** was built in 1634 to accommodate the meetings of the treasurers of France, and is a good example of the Louis XIII style with its exterior of red brick and stone trimmings. It derives its name from the last owner, Gérard de Berny (1880-1957), who dedicated himself to creating the refined interior on view today and then bequeathed the building to Amiens as a museum of local art.

The furniture and woodwork come from other residences in the region. The dining room features an immense chimney attributed to Jean Goujon and elegant 18C panelling which used to adorn the entrance hall of Grange-Bléneau Château, owned by the Marquis de La Fayette. On the first floor, note the Louis XVI gilded room which came from a local mansion, with furniture from an Abbeville residence, and the panelling from the library of the old abbey at Corbie *(qv)*.

Paintings show Amiens as it used to be, while several portraits present local celebrities: M and Mme Choderlos de Laclos, Jules Verne, Branly and Parmentier, the "inventor" of the potato in France.

Hortillonnages, Amiens

★**Hortillonnages** (**DY**) ⊙ – These little marshland market gardens (**aires**) have been cultivated since the Middle Ages by the **market gardeners** or *hortillons* (from the latin *hortus* meaning garden), who supplied the people of Amiens with early fruit and vegetables. They stretch over 300 ha - 740 acres within a network of canals fed by the Somme and Avre rivers; the silt cleaned out of the drains is used to renew the soil which would otherwise return to marshland.

At one time an entire population lived here; the vegetables have now been replaced by flowers and fruit trees, and the marshlanders' huts have become weekend cottages. The black boats, which have inclined prows *(cornets)* to allow them to be easily moored, were used to transport the vegatables to the old "market on the water".

Tour Perret (Perret Tower) (**CZ**) – The reinforced concrete "lookout tower" (26 floors, 104m - 340ft high), stands on Place Alphonse-Fiquet. Its architect, **Auguste Perret** (1874-1954), the man who rebuilt Le Havre, was also responsible for the railway station.

Logis du Roi et Maison du Sagittaire (Kings Lodging and Sagittarius House) (CY B) – The King's Lodging (1565), featuring a pointed-arch door decorated with a Virgin with a Rose, is the seat of the **Rosati** *(qv)* of Picardy, a society with the motto "Tradition, Art and Literature". Attached to the building is the **Sagittarius House** (1539) with its Renaissance front, which owes its name to the sign of the Zodiac embellishing its two arches.

Old Theatre (CY R) – The Louis XVI façade was the work of Rousseau in 1780; the building behind it is now a bank. Three large windows are framed by elegant low reliefs depicting garlands, medallions, muses and lyres.

Galerie du Vitrail (Stained-glass Gallery) (CY N) ⓥ – A master glassmaker, who may be watched working, displays his collection of stained glass including 13C pieces.

Maison de la Culture (BY) ⓥ – This construction by Sonrel and Dutilleul, supported by a blind tower, presents large glazed façades mounted on piles. A walkway adorned with sculptures by Étienne Martin surrounds it. It houses large and small theatres (1 050 and 300 seats), a 200-seater cinema, two contemporary art galleries, an archive centre, a restaurant, and studios belonging to the Music Centre.

Abbaye des Prémontrés St-Jean (Premonstratensian Abbey of St John) (BY F) – The beautiful 17C and 18C classical buildings have been restored and now house the University of Amiens. The main courtyard is flanked by two wings at right angles, built of brick and stone. The front is decorated with a wrought-iron balcony and sculptures.

Bailliage (Bailiwick) (BY K) – The restored front is all that remains of the edifice built under François I in 1541, presenting mullioned windows, Flamboyant gables and Renaissance medallions. On the right, note the "fool" wearing a hood with bells.

Belltower (BY L) – The enormous belltower in Place au Fil consists of a 15C base and an 18C belfry surmounted by a dome.

St-Germain (St Germanus' Church) (BY) – The church was built in Flamboyant Gothic style in the 15C; its tower leans slightly.

St Leu District (CY) – The 15C **Church of St Leu** contains three aisles, with a 16C Flamboyant belfry at the entrance. Several half-timbered houses remain beside the aisles (Rue Motte, Rue des Granges). The area has benefited from an important renovation project aimed at preserving its distinctive character. Antique shops, restaurants and craft shops now line the streets. From Rue Belu there is good **view** of the cathedral.
Pont du Cange (CY 15), a bridge built under Louis-Philippe (19C), leads to Place Parmentier where the "market on the water" is located.

Parc zoologique (Zoo) (AX) ⓥ – The zoo is pleasantly located by the **Promenade de la Hôtoie**, laid out in the 18C, and its lake. The lawns are encircled by branches of the River Selle where swans, pelicans, cranes and pink flamingoes flutter. A large number of animals includes giraffes, lions, panthers, elephants...

EXCURSIONS

South of Amiens – 24km - 15 miles round trip – *1 hour. Leave Amiens by D 7 south.*

Sains-en-Amiénois – The **church** ⓥ contains a 13C **tomb** and recumbent effigies of St Fuscien and his companions, Victoric and Gentien, who were martyred in the 4C; below, a low-relief portrays their decapitation.

Leaving Sains turn left (west) into D 167 to Boves.

Boves – Pop 3 146. The **ruins** of the 12C castle overlook this small town, which from 1630 was the seat of a marquess. The D 167 leads to the grassy courtyard, and from there to the mound *(motte)* bearing two imposing sections of wall from the keep.
From the summit there is an extensive **view**: south over the lakes of Fouencamps, north to Amiens.

Conty – Pop 1 450. *22km - 14 miles south of Amiens by D 210 then right into D 920.* **St Anthony's Church** (Église St-Antoine) is a 15C and 16C monument in a unified Flamboyant style; its right side offers a curious view of the projecting gargoyles. The tower is crowned with a pyramid-shaped roof, like the collegiate church in Picquigny, and bears traces of cannonballs dating from the 1589 siege of Conty by the Catholic League *(qv)*; in the corner, a statue of St Anthony the hermit. On the left of the west front, steps descend to St Anthony's fountain.

Every year
the Michelin Red Guide France
revises its selection of starred restaurants
which also mentions culinary specialities and local wines.
It also includes a selection of simpler restaurants
offering carefully prepared dishes which are often regional specialities...
at a reasonable price.
It is well worth buying the current edition.

ARRAS ★★

Agglomeration 79 607
Michelin map 53 fold 2 or 236 fold 15

Arras, the capital of the Artois region, hides its little-known artistic beauties behind a serious, reserved appearance. The city, a religious, military and administrative centre, is surrounded by boulevards that replaced the old Vauban-like fortifications. Small sausages (andouillettes) and chocolate hearts are the local gastronomic specialities.

HISTORICAL NOTES

Influence in the Middle Ages – The Roman town of Nemetacum, capital of the Atrebates, was founded on the slopes of Baudimont hill, which is still known as La Cité today. In the Middle Ages the town developed around the Benedictine abbey of St Vaast, forming the district known as La Ville. From that time on, Arras grew from being a grain market and the centre of woollen cloth manufacture to being a cradle of art, patronised by bankers and rich Arras burghers.

In terms of literature, the town is famous for its troubadours (trouvères) such as Gautier d'Arras, **Jean Bodel,** author of Le Jeu de saint Nicolas, and particularly the 13C **Adam de la Halle** who created French dramatic art with his play Le Jeu de la Feuillée.

From 1384 the manufacture of high-warp tapestries, under the patronage of the dukes of Burgundy, brought Arras widespread fame – such that in Italy today the term "arazzi" is used for all old tapestries.

It was at this time that the workshops in Arras, competing with those in Tournai, made delightfully realistic hangings, such as the Life of St Piat and St Éleuthère (1402) which today hangs in Tournai Cathedral.

Youth of "The Incorruptible" – **Maximilien de Robespierre,** whose father was an Artois Council barrister, was born in Arras in 1758. Orphaned at an early age, the young man went to school in Arras from 1765 to 1769; as the protégé of the bishop, he received a scholarship to attend the Louis-le-Grand School in Paris. Robespierre became a barrister on his return to Arras, pleading most notably for a citizen of St Omer accused of having put a lightning rod at the top of his house. Not only accepted by the Arras Academy but also affiliated with the **Rosati** (an anagram of "Artois") poetic society, Robespierre met Carnot, who was garrisoned in Arras at the time, and Fouché, a schoolteacher. During this period the pale young man, later the spirited leader of the Revolution, courted young ladies for whom he wrote verse.

In Arras Robespierre knew **Joseph Lebon** (1765-95), who was mayor of the town during the "Terror". During this time the former priest presided over the destruction of the town's churches and regularly sent aristocrats and rich farmers to the guillotine set up in Place du Théâtre. Lebon himself was later to perish under the blade in Amiens.

Arras and the Battles of Artois – During the First World War, the front was until 1917 constantly near Arras which suffered heavy shelling as a result. The most violent conflicts took place in the strategically-important hills north of the town. After the Battle of the Marne the retreating Germans fought to hold on to them, their backs to the rich coal basin, clinging to Vimy Ridge and the slopes of Notre-Dame-de-Lorette Hill (qv). In the autumn of 1914 they emerged to attack Arras, but were stopped during the battles at Ablain-St-Nazaire, Carency and La Targette.

In May and June 1915 General Foch, in command of the French forces in the north, attempted to pierce the German ranks; his troops took Neuville St-Vaast and Notre-Dame-de-Lorette. The attack failed at Vimy (qv), however, which was won only in 1917, by the Canadians.

★★MAIN SQUARES 1 hour

The two main squares in Arras, the theatrical-looking Grand' Place and Place des Héros, which are joined by the short Rue de la Taillerie, are extremely impressive. They existed as early as the 11C but have undergone many transformations through the centuries. Today's magnificent façades are remarkable examples of 17C and 18C Flemish architecture.

The local council of the period was careful to control the town's development, permitting citizens to construct only "in stone or brick, with no projecting architectural elements". The houses in these squares, though of different heights and widths, décor and details, form a rhythmical whole: this is largely due to the consistent use of walls laid in brick and stone; pilasters and ties; scrolled gables and curvilinear pediments.

The façades, formerly embellished with carved shop-signs, a few of which remain, rest on monolith-columned arcades which protected market stallholders and customers alike from inclement weather.

Today the squares hold their colourful market on Saturdays; as evening comes they take on a different charm when the gables, discreetly floodlit, stand out against the night sky.

Although badly damaged during the First World War, the squares have undergone extensive restoration with impressive results.

★★**Place des Héros** (CY) – The smaller and livelier of the two squares, Place des Héros is surrounded by shops and overlooked by the belfry. Note the shop signs at no 9, The Three Cockerels; no 11, The Mermaid; no 15, The Admiral; no 17, The Salamander; no 23, The Unicorn; and no 62, The Whale.

ARRAS

B	Hôtel de Guines
D	Ancien hospice St-Éloi
E	Demeure de Robespierre
H	Hôtel de ville et beffroi
J	Palais de Justice
T	Théâtre

★**Town Hall and Belfry** (Hôtel de ville et beffroi) (**BY H**) ⊙ – The town hall was destroyed in 1914 and rebuilt in the Flamboyant style. The beautiful front with its uneven arches rises on the western side of Place des Héros, while the graceful 75m - 246ft **belfry** rises over the more severe-looking Renaissance wings. It is possible to climb to the top (326 steps), but the view from even the first balcony *(access by lift)* is interesting, looking out over the squares and the cathedral's east end.

On the ground floor, the Gothic-vaulted lower room called the **Guards' Hall** (salle des Gardes) displays the giant town mascots, Colas and Jacqueline, together with chilling photographs of Arras in ruins in 1918.

Upstairs, the **Banquet Hall** (salle des fêtes) offers a view of the square through eight Flamboyant bays. A fresco by **Hoffbauer** which recalls Breughel's style runs above the carved wainscoting; it describes daily life in 16C Arras (notice the 12C cathedral from which a procession issues; the building was destroyed in 1799). Downstairs, an audio-visual presentation on the history of Arras is an excellent introduction to the town. The tour of the underground passages starts here.

Tour of the Underground Passages (Circuit des souterrains) ⊙ – *Entrance in the basement of the town hall.*

As early as the 10C galleries were cut into the limestone bank on which the town stands. Since then a complex network has been created, consisting of vast rooms supported by sandstone pillars, recessed staircases leading from one level to another (up to 13m - 42ft in difference), corridors etc.

This "underground city" has served as a refuge in times of trouble, a shelter during wars (during World War I the British set up a country hospital here) and above all as an enormous wine cellar, as the famous **caves** *("boves")* are at the ideal temperature for storing wine.

★★**Grand' Place** (**CY**) – This square covers a 2 ha - 5 acre area. The moderate height of the surrounding houses emphasises the vastness of this open space, empty except for market days *(the car park is underground)*.

The oldest house, dating from the 15C (no 49, north side), has three Gothic arches surmounted by a great stepped gable.

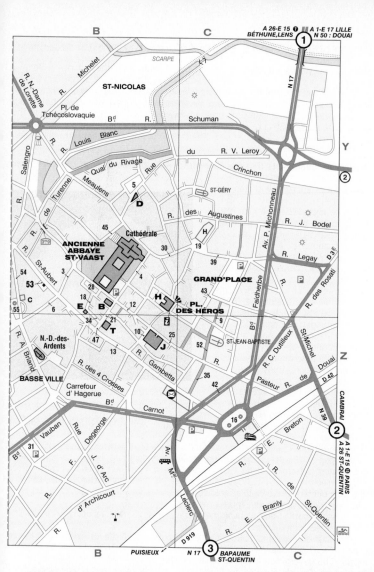

Grand'Place, Arras

To plan a special itinerary:

- consult the Map of Touring Programmes which indicates the recommended routes, the tourist regions, the principal towns and main sights.
- read the descriptions in the Sights section which include Excursions from the main tourist centres.

Michelin Maps nos 51, 52, 53, 55, 56, 60, 61, 101, 106, 236 , and 237 indicate scenic routes, interesting sights, viewpoints, rivers, forests...

★★ANCIENNE ABBAYE ST-VAAST (ST VAAST ABBEY) (BY) *1 hour*

The old abbey was founded in the 7C by St Aubert on the hill overlooking a tributary of the Scarpe River, and was entrusted with the relics of the first bishop of Arras, St Vaast. **Cardinal de Rohan**, commendatory abbot, began reconstructing the abbey buildings in 1746; they were deconsecrated during the Revolution, then restored after 1918. The gardens offer a view across to the austere west front. The porch of the main entrance (in Place de la Madeleine), surmounted by the abbey's arms, opens into the main courtyard. The central part of the abbey, straight ahead, contains the museum; wings to the side house the library and administration.

★**Musée des Beaux-Arts (Fine Arts Museum)** ⓥ – On the **ground floor**, the **Italian Room** (salon italien) serves as the entrance hall (1); it is adorned with the lion from Arras' original belfry (1554). Enter the **small cloister** (petit cloître), the so-called Well Court (cour du Puits). The surrounding galleries contain sculptures, a 14C funerary mask of a woman with delicate features, and 15C statues of St George and St Sebastian. The recumbent skeleton-effigy on Guille Lefrançois' tomb is an example of the Gothic style in the 15C, while Saudémont's charming angels exemplify 13C art: the delicately curling hair, mischievous almond-shaped eyes, faintly smiling lips, tapering fingers and the garments' graceful folds show them to be the work of a master. The 12C tombstone of Bishop Frumauld is late Romanesque.

14C funerary mask of a woman, Arras

Bellegambe's triptych (*Adoration of the Christ Child by the Abbot of St Vaast*, 1528) as well as Vermeyen's *Entombment* are also on display.

The small room (2) leading to the refectory is devoted to the town's history. It contains a relief map of 18C Arras and paintings by Desavary depicting the town around 1880.

The **refectory** (réfectoire) on the east side is of pleasing proportions and contains a great marble fireplace surmounted by a tapestry bearing the arms of Cardinal de Rohan.

The **main cloister** (grand cloître) adjoined the abbey church via a peristyle adorned with garlanded capitals and carved rosettes.

Two small rooms (3 and 4) near the entrance hall contain particularly fine Gallo-Roman archeological collections.

The **first floor** is devoted to 16C, 17C and 18C paintings. A canvas from one of Pieter Breughel's workshops (original in Brussels) represents *The Census-Taking in Bethlehem*. The gallery south of the small cloister houses *The Fruit Seller* by P Van Boucle and *The Macaw and the Bullfinch* by Adrien Van Utrecht. The east gallery contains 17C and 18C sculptures. It leads to the **Mays de Notre-Dame Room** (salle des Mays de Notre-Dame), so called as it presents great paintings by La Hire, Philippe de Champaigne, Jouvenet and others, which the goldsmith's guild formerly offered

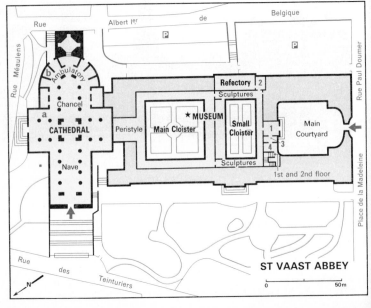

ST VAAST ABBEY

each spring to Notre-Dame Cathedral in Paris. Works by the local painter D Doncre as well as 18C paintings (Boullongne, Vien, M G Bouliar's *Aspasia*) are in the rooms along the façade.

Return to the first floor stairway to reach the small rooms where the 17C French School is represented by Claude Vignon *(The Martyrdom of St Matthew)*, Largillière *(Portrait of P de Montesquiou)* and La Hire *(The Mothers of the Children of Bethel* and *Dog Guarding Its Quarry)*.

The **second floor** features 19C paintings, and beautiful Bohemian glass is displayed in the Louise Weiss Room. Various early 19C schools of landscape painting are represented along the small cloister's edge: Barbizon, Lyon and especially Arras, with works by Corot and Constant Dutilleux. A separate room houses the larger 19C canvases, such as Delacroix's *Disciples and Holy Women Raising the Body of St Stephen* and Chassériau's *Young Shepherd*.

The ceramic collection in the front rooms is exceptional: in addition to the mid-17C glazed pottery, note the porcelain from Arras (1770-90) and especially the richly decorated 18C-19C Tournai pieces ("Buffon birds" service).

Cathédrale (Cathedral) (**BY**) — The old abbey church of St Vaast was built according to plans prepared by Contant d'Ivry in the 18C. It was finished in 1833 and elevated to a cathedral, to replace Notre-Dame-de-la-Cité *(see below)*. The Classical façade is graced by a monumental flight of steps; the luminous interior presents an Antique splendour. A line of lofty columns bearing Corinthian capitals flank the nave, transept and chancel. Enormous 19C statues of saints, from the Panthéon in Paris, adorn the side aisles. A poignant 15C wooden **Head of Christ** (a) is in the left transept; in the ambulatory's second chapel stands the beautiful 17C **Christ Bound** (b); the fourth chapel contains the kneeling figures of Philippe de Torcy (1652) and his wife. The right transept is decorated with large frescoes, in which St Vaast may be seen taming a bear.

ADDITIONAL SIGHTS

Place du Théâtre (**BZ 47**) — It was in this lively square that the guillotine stood during the darkest hours of the Revolution. The **theatre** (**BZ T**) dates from 1784 (though its façade is restored), and was built where the fish market once stood; it faces the **Ostel des Poissonniers** (1710), a narrow Baroque house carved with sea gods and mermaids.
In Rue des Jongleurs, note the majestic 18C **hôtel de Guines** (**BY B**); at no 9 Rue Robespierre (**BY E**) the former residence of the famous revolutionary *(see above)* may be seen.

Palais de Justice (Law Courts) (**BZ J**) — This former seat of the Artois government (1701) is embellished with Corinthian pilasters, while its side entrance (1724) is decorated with Regency shells.

Place du Wetz-d'Amain (**BY 53**) — The square is graced by a pretty Renaissance house, to which a Classical stone porch was added later. It served as refuge to the monks of Mont St-Éloi.

Place de l'Ancien-Rivage (**BY 5**) — The square-turreted house (D) was the former St-Éloi hospice, founded in 1635 by one of the town's goldsmiths.

Basse-ville (**BZ**) — This slightly run-down district lies between the town and the citadel. It is arranged regularly around the lovely, octagonal **Place Victor-Hugo** (**AZ 51**), built in 1756.

Notre-Dame-des-Ardents Church ☉ safeguards fragments of the Holy Taper. This miraculous candle was entrusted by the Virgin to two minstrels, to cure ergotic poisoning in the 12C. The silver reliquary is to the left of the main altar, in a latticed recess *(lighting below, to the right)*.
A stele has been erected along **Promenade des Allées** (**AZ**), under a peristyle decked with roses. It honours the Rosati and depicts a marquess and a 20C man watching a procession of muses.

Citadel (**AZ**) — This pentagonal-shaped citadel, built to plans by **Vauban** between 1668 and 1672, is encircled by grassy ditches. It was built less to protect the town from Spanish troops than to keep a watch on the inhabitants, and its nickname was "The Great Useless". Today it is occupied by an Army regiment.
The tour takes in a model of the citadel, the old arsenal and the Baroque Chapel (1675), now a memorial.

Mémorial britannique (British Memorial) (**AZ**) — *Access by Boulevard Charles-de-Gaulle.* The monument was erected in memory of the many British soldiers lost in the Battles of Artois (1914-18).

Mur des Fusillés — *Access by the road between the memorial and the citadel.* Plaques line the ditches southwest of the fort, in memory of the Resistance members martyred here.

Place de la Préfecture (**AY**) — This square was the heart of medieval Arras. Today the local authority (préfecture) occupies the former bishop's palace, finished in 1780. The 19C **St-Nicolas-en-Cité Church** rises on the site of Notre-Dame-de-la-Cité Cathedral, which was destroyed by angry mobs after the Revolution. It houses a triptych depicting *The Climb to Calvary*, painted in 1577 by P Claessens of Bruges.

ASTERIX PARK ★★

Michelin map 106 fold 9

Access – *By car: A1 motorway, exit "Parc Astérix". By train: RER line B to Roissy-Charles-de-Gaulle, then by shuttle bus to the park.*

TOUR ⓥ *allow a day*

Asterix the Gaul, hero of the famous cartoon strip by Goscinny and Uderzo known throughout the world and translated into several languages, provides the theme for this 50 ha - 123 acre fun park; it is a fantasy world for all ages which offers a journey into the past, presenting carefully reconstructed 'historic' sections, various attractions, shows and audio-visual displays.

On **Via Antiqua**, patrolled by Roman soldiers, houses of various architectural styles symbolise the different places visited by Asterix on his journeys through Europe (Germany, Helvetia, Spain...). The road leads to an enormous rock, from the top of which the likeable hero waves to visitors.

The **Asterix Village** is a Gaulish village with thatched huts, peopled with familiar figures – Obelix with his menhirs, Panoramix, the bard Cacofonix *(Assurancetourix)* in his tree-house – while all around scenes of feasting, hunting or scuffles take place.

The **Roman City** includes an arena where gladiators stage impressive, apparently merciless combats with each other.

Rue de Paris describes Paris through the centuries: each period is represented with typical shops brought to life by inhabitants in period costume. The Middle Ages is relived with tumblers, jugglers and acrobats, and dark and mysterious alleyways in which Quasimodo fleetingly appears. The 17C reveals the author La Fontaine writing fables while a rook recounts them... The 19C section introduces the *Commune* of Paris (rue Gavroche), its first big shops, the early days of the cinema. The thrilling attractions include the **Descent of the Styx**★ (Descente du Styx), a white water raft ride; the turbulent **Flying Carpet** (Tapis Volant); the **Big Splash** (Grand Splash) ride through a 15m - 49ft waterfall; the **Galley Ship** (galère), which undergoes breathtaking dips and swings through waves; the roller-coaster **Goudurix**, which twists, turns, loops and spins at terrifying speed.

There is also a dolphinarium, in which dolphins perform tricks.

AUVERS-SUR-OISE ★

Population 6 129
Michelin map 106 fold 6 or 55 fold 20

This village stretches over 7km – 4 1/2 miles from the River Oise to the escarpment edging the Vexin plateau. The old path, now a series of narrow streets winding their way from Valhermeil to Cordeville, still carries the memory of the artists who brought it fame. Here and there, panels indicate the scenes portrayed by painters ranging from Daubigny to Vlaminck. It is the district around the church, however, which constitutes the favourite "place of pilgrimage" for art lovers.

Doctor **Paul Gachet** (1828-1909) moved to Auvers in 1872, although he retained his surgery in Paris. An enthusiastic painter and engraver, with an unquenchable thirst for novelty and an extremely wide and varied medical experience – in epidemics, war wounds and mental disorders – he was the centre of attraction for a new generation of painters, known as the "Impressionists" *(qv)* who came to stay and paint locally.

Auvers Church by Van Gogh

The 1870s were therefore an exciting period for a great many artists who were stimulated by Pissarro's presence at Pontoise. Cézanne's talent blossomed during his three visits to Auvers and Pontoise (1873, 1877 and 1881), when he painted about a hundred canvases, working both outdoors and in the doctor's studio. In May 1890 **Van Gogh** was invited here by Paul Gachet. The Dutch painter managed to find spiritual relief by throwing himself into work but this state of well-being was only a brief interlude: overcome by another bout of madness and guilt over his financial dependence on his brother Theo, Van Gogh shot himself in an open field and died in his room at the Ravoux café on 29 July 1890.

SIGHTS

Église (Church) – The best view is from the back of the terrace, near the east end. The well-proportioned east end and 12C belltower were depicted by Van Gogh in one of his expressive paintings, now in the Orsay Museum in Paris. A bust portraying the painter Charles-François Daubigny stands at the foot of the church.

Monument de Van Gogh (Van Gogh Monument) – In the Van Gogh Park (Tourist Information Centre), located in Rue du Général-de-Gaulle. Van Gogh's statue is the work of the sculptor Ossip Zadkine.

Tombe de Van Gogh (Van Gogh's Grave) – The famous Dutch painter is buried in the cemetery that lies on the plateau *(directions from the church)*. His tomb stands against the left hand wall. His brother Theo, who gave him moral support all his life and who died soon after him, rests by his side. **View** of Auvers' belltower.

The AVESNOIS REGION★★

Michelin map 53 folds 6, 7 or 236 fold 29

The Avesnois region, which lies south of Maubeuge and extends along the Belgian border, is known for its undulating countryside of orchards, woodlands and pastures dotted with black-and-white dairy cows (the local cheese is the sharply-flavoured *boulette d'Avesnes*) and its pretty villages of brick, slate and stone.
The **Helpe-Majeure River** (58km - 36 miles long) drains the area, making its way through the Ardennes shale, outcrops of which can be seen downstream from Eppe-Sauvage.
The vast forests and the cluster of ponds around Liessies and Trélon are traces of a period when the great abbeys – Maroilles, Liessies and St-Michel – dominated the region, constructing mills and forges on every river. Some of the local churches contain works of art from these abbeys.
Many small industries developed in the 18C and 19C: glassmaking at Sars-Poteries, Trélon and Anor, wood turning at Felleries, spinning at Fourmies, marble quarrying at Cousoire...
Today the museums at Sars-Poteries, Felleries, Trélon and Fourmies recall the time when the region was highly populated and active.

AVESNES TO FOURMIES 70km - 43 miles – about 4 hours

It is advisable to follow this itinerary in the afternoon, when the museums are open.

Avesnes-sur-Helpe – Pop 5 108. The quiet town which gave the region its name stands on the south bank of the river; it has preserved some of its Vauban-like fortifications. From March to September 1918 the German army's Chief of Staff, **Hindenburg**, with his deputy Ludendorff, made his headquarters here. **Place du Général-Leclerc** is the town's main square, surrounded by old houses with high slate roofs. It is here that in June 1918 Kaiser Wilhelm II reviewed his troops, which included Jenny, the famous elephant mobilised by the Germans to move logs for trench shelters. A graceful bulb tops the 60m - 197ft belfry-porch of **St Nicholas' Church** (1534), inside which the hall-church contains two monumental Louis XV altarpieces with paintings by Louis Watteau. A double staircase with wrought-iron balustrades fronts the 18C Classical **town hall** in blue Tournai stone. The **Square de la Madeleine** *(behind the church)* provides a bird's eye view of the Helpe Valley.

Leave Avesnes by D 133 (east) towards Liessies.

Just outside Avesnes there is a good view *(right)* of the town's beautiful site and its ramparts.

At Sémeries turn right into D 123 towards Etrœung, then left into D 951.

Sains-du-Nord – The **Maison du Bocage** ⊙, a branch of the Fourmies-Trélon Regional Museum, has been established in a farm. Exhibitions present life and work in the woodlands and pastures of the Avesnois (stock farming, cheese-making...).

Take D 80 to Ramousies.

Ramousies – The 16C **church** ⊙ shelters two beautiful Renaissance altarpieces, from Antwerp workshops, which once belonged to Liessies Abbey. One depicts the life of St Sulpice, the other represents the Passion.
The 13C Christ was from the oldest calvary in northern France.

Continue along D 80 to Felleries.

On leaving the village there is a lovely view of the region.

Felleries – Since the 17C the town's inhabitants have specialised in "Bois-Joli": turned wood and cooperage. These workshops developed at the same time as the textile industry, the former making bobbins and spools for the latter.

Musée des Bois-Jolis (Museum of "Bois-Jolis") ⊙ – This museum, housed in an old water mill, brings together a wide variety of treen (wooden) items made in Felleries: butter moulds, tops, salt boxes, spools...

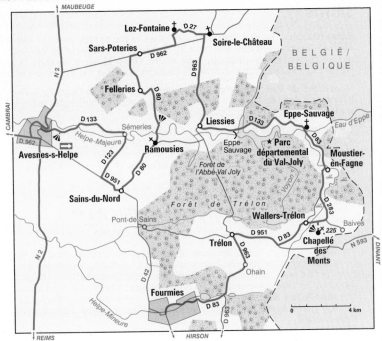

Sars-Poteries – Since the 15C the earth around Sars has been used by potters, and many small pottery workshops exist locally. In the 19C two glassworks were established here; all that remains of them is a **Glass Museum**★ (Musée du Verre) ⊙ containing an unusual collection of imaginative glassware made by the workers out of hours: carefully-worked lamps, great dishes, "revenge inkwells" (so-called because although they could not write, glassmakers owned the most beautiful inkwells... curious bottles... Recent local digs have added a collection of grey sandstone items (17C-18C) with cobalt blue decoration.

The **watermill** ⊙ north of the village was built in 1780 and still contains its great wheel and workings.

Take D 962 east, then turn left.

Lez-Fontaine – In the 15C church ⊙ the wooden vaults are decorated with paintings dating from 1531.

Solre-le-Château – The seigneurial château no longer stands but there are still many 17C and 18C houses. The sober Renaissance **town hall** (late 16C) has an austere belltower.

The lovely 16C Gothic **church** ⊙ is made of local blue stone. The powerful **belfry** was part of the fortifications; its base forms a most unusual porch, open on three sides. The mauve spire (1612) is crowned by a large bulb with openings where the watchman stood. Inside there is a double transept, wooden barrel-vaulting with carved tie-beams in the nave and diagonal vaulting in the chancel. The church also contains an 18C organ, 16C stained glass and Renaissance woodwork.

From Solre-le-Château, take D 963 south towards Liessies.

Liessies – The village originated with an 8C Benedictine abbey which had exclusive use of the surrounding woods. The monks drained the boggy marshlands by creating ponds for breeding fish. The abbey prospered and by the 17C the abbots were powerful lords, but the Revolution led to the break up of the 13C abbey church and the monastic buildings.

Liessies was declared the regional **Religious Heritage Centre** (Conservatoire du Patrimoine Religieux de l'Avesnois) ⊙, part of the Fourmies-Trélon Regional Museum *(qv)*: monastic buildings and a park are open to the public. The 16C parish **church** stands near the site of the old abbey. It contains beautiful 15C to 18C statues and remnants of the abbey, including a precious Romanesque cross of gilded copper decorated with chased enamels and stones.

Just outside the village, the 18C **Château de la Motte** was formerly a monks' retirement home; it is now a hotel.

Traditional Avesnois butter moulds

From Liessies follow D 133 and the Helpe Valley, which becomes more winding, narrower and wilder, while its undulating slopes are increasingly dotted with ponds and thick woods.

The waters of the River Helpe (originally Eppe) used to operate small forges.

★Parc départemental du Val Joly (Val Joly Park) – The construction of the arch dam at Eppe-Sauvage on the Helpe-Majeur created a magnificent 180 ha - 445 acre reservoir surrounded by the wooded slopes of the River Helpe and its tributary, the Voyon. The 200ha - 494 acre park has many leisure facilities including watersports, fishing, riding, footpaths and cycle tracks, a bathing area and a camp site. An old farm has been converted to hold exhibitions on the region.

Eppe-Sauvage – This village, close to the Belgian border, nestles in a pretty location in the hollow of a basin formed where the Helpe and the Eau d'Eppe rivers meet. In **St Ursmar's Church** (église St-Ursmar), with its 16C chancel and transept, there are two remarkable 16C painted wood triptychs. One is dedicated to the Virgin; the other to St Ursmar of Lobbes, patron of the Hainaut region.

After Eppe-Sauvage, the valley opens out and becomes less wooded; marshes, called "*fagnes*", are frequent along its floor. A beautiful manor-farm may be seen.

Moustier-en-Fagne – This small village derives its name from a 16C priory, or "*moustier*", which was a dependant of Lobbes Abbey. Olivetan Benedictines, who devote themselves to painting icons, live in the monks' quarters. They are near the **church** dedicated to St Dodon, the hermit invoked for back ailments, who was originally from this village. A handsome **manor-house** is visible (left) on entering Moustier-en-Fagne. Known as the Spanish House (Maison Espagnole), it was built of brick and stone in 1560 in a Gothic style: its features include a crow-stepped gable and an ogee arch over its door, ornamented by two angels bearing a crown.

Continue south and fork left into D 283, then turn right.

The top of a knoll (225m - 738ft high) affords a clear **view** of Trélon Forest (about 4 000 ha - 10 000 acres) and the Helpe Valley.

Chapelle des Monts – *15 mins by foot over wild heath.*
This 18C chapel is surrounded by a grassy terrace and hundred-year-old lime trees. The quarries and lime oven date from the 19C.

Wallers-Trélon – Built entirely in blue stone, this beautiful village owes its unique appearance to the numerous quarries nearby.

The **Maison de la Fagne** ☉, a branch of the Fourmies-Trélon Regional Museum *(see p 137)* established in the old presbytery, presents exhibitions on rural architecture, the quarrying of blue stone, stone carving and the riches of the natural environment.

Paths around the Maison de la Fagne allow visitors to discover the unusual flora of the Baives hills, which flourishes owing to the chalky soil.

Take D 83 south; turn right into D 951 to Trélon.

Trélon – Formerly known for its glass industry, Trélon is today the location of the **Glass Workshop-Museum** (Atelier-musée du verre) ☉, a branch of the Fourmies-Trélon Regional Museum. In the heart of the old hall of the 19C glassworks, which still contains two ovens from 1889 and 1924 together with their equipment, glassworkers demonstrate the blowing and shaping of glass. Through objects and photographs, the exhibitions present the history of the industry locally, as well as today's techniques for flat and hollow glass.

South beyond Olhain the route follows the Helpe-Mineure Valley, and is bordered by a sprinkling of ponds.

Fourmies – See Fourmies.

AZINCOURT

Population 228
Michelin map 51 fold 13 or 236 fold 13 - 6km - 4 miles south of Fruges

On 25 October 1415 Agincourt (Azincourt) was the scene of a bloody battle between the English and the French in the middle of the Hundred Years War which saw certain defeat for England transformed into a resounding victory.

Henry V had invaded France from the Seine estuary and captured Harfleur, and was moving eastwards and northwards with his 7 000 troops. By the time the mighty, 40 000-strong French army caught up with them at Agincourt, the English were weary, hungry and sick from their 250 mile march.

Despite little hope of success, the English managed to overcome enormous odds through astute tactical use of their skilled longbowmen. The waterlogged terrain was more advantageous to the lightly-clad and so more mobile archers, whereas the horses of the tightly-massed French squadrons became bogged down and their knights were obliged to fight on foot in heavy armour. Despite their substantially lesser number, the English archers, who were sheltering behind a hedgerow, and their supporting army of footsoldiers with axes and lead clubs decimated the French attack: 6 000 French men died within the first 3 hours of battle. This disaster for the French – total losses amounted to 10 000 dead and 1 500 taken prisoner – greatly encouraged Henry and his claims on the French crown.

Up to 1734 this fateful spot was known locally as Carrion (La Carogne).
A calvary erected in 1963 recalls this historic episode, as does, at the junction of D 104 and the road to Maisoncelle, an inscription at the foot of the pine-encircled menhir.

Musée de Traditions populaires et d'Histoire locale ⊙ – Documents, photographs, copies of arms and armour, and small models depict the weaponry of the time. The events of the battle are evoked in a video presentation. Some of the 14C paving found on the site of the old castle are also on show.
A round trip (map provided) leaving from the museum leads to the battlefield where an orientation table and various maps are displayed.

Medieval Centre ⊙ – *1km - 1/2 mile east, beside the battlefield.* Slide shows and film clips of the most famous moments of the battle are shown, and there are guided tours of the scene.

BARBIZON★★

Population 1 407
Michelin map 106 fold 45 or 61 folds 1, 2
10km - 6 miles northwest of Fontainebleau – Local map Fontainebleau Forest

The village of Barbizon, which was part of Chailly until 1903, was a popular spot with landscape painters *(see p 37)* and still carries memories of the artists who made it famous. The Bas-Bréau coppices, greatly cherished by the Goncourt brothers, are nearby.

The Barbizon Group – Breaking the rules of studio work and official art, the Barbizon artists were landscape painters who perfected the technique of working directly from nature after two great masters: Théodore Rousseau (1812-67) and Jean-François Millet (1814-75). The local people were happy to welcome these nature-loving artists who rose at dawn and whose genius and mischievous nature enlivened local feasts and banquets. Next came the writers, seduced by the beauty of the forest and the congenial atmosphere of this small, international community: George Sand, Henri Murger, the Goncourt brothers, Taine etc.
Millet, a patriarch with nine children, died after a life of hard work, his eyes forever riveted on the landscapes of the Bière plain. Like Rousseau, he was buried at **Chailly Cemetery** *(plan of graveyard at entrance)*.

HIGH STREET *1 hour*

From the Chailly road (D 64) to the forest.
Barbizon is a long high street (Grande Rue) lined with hotels, restaurants and villas. Many of these buildings bear commemorative plaques of the artists who stayed there.

Ancienne Auberge du Père Ganne (Father Ganne's Old Inn) ⊙ – This former inn run by "Father Ganne" offered lodgings to artists and soon became an important meeting place for contemporary painters: it was already shown to tourists in 1850. The communal living room still evokes the carefree, but nonetheless hardworking, existence of Father Ganne's guests, their mischievous sense of humour and their inclination to paint every inch of surface available, like the wooden dresser. The second room is devoted to contemporary landscape painters.

Musée de l'école de Barbizon (Barbizon School Museum) ⊙ – The museum is located behind the war memorial, in the old barn which Théodore Rousseau used as a studio. The small adjoining church was built at a later date.
The museum presents documents relating to the old part of the town and a number of original works by Rousseau, along with engravings by Diaz, Troyon and Charles Jacque.

Monument de Millet et Rousseau (Monument to Millet and Rousseau) – A bronze medal embedded in the rock is the work of Henri Chapu.
Behind this monument, a plaque set into another rock commemorates the 100th anniversary of the proposal to create protected forest zones, an early step towards nature conservancy: the first one was created in 1853 at the instigation of Rousseau *(see Description of the Country-Forrests).*

MICHELIN GREEN GUIDES

Art and Architecture
History
Geography
Ancient monuments
Scenic routes
Touring programmes
Plans of towns and buildings

A selection of guides for your holidays at home and abroad.

BAVAY ★

Population 3 751
Michelin map 53 fold 5 or 236 folds 18, 19

Bavay was originally the capital of the old Belgian tribe the Nervii; today it is a small town with low houses, known for its confectionery called "chiques de Bavay".

Bagacum during the Roman Peace – At the time of Augustus, Bagacum was an important town in Roman Belgium. The town, a judicial and administrative centre, seat of a curia, military post and supply centre, was at the junction of seven roads that led to Utrecht, Boulogne, Cambrai, Soissons, Rheims, Trèves and Cologne, this last being the busiest. The routes, still recognisable in the present road network, were furrowed by the pedestrians and carts which dug these ruts, traces of which can be found in the forum.

Ravaged at the end of the 3C, Bagacum never regained its former splendour.

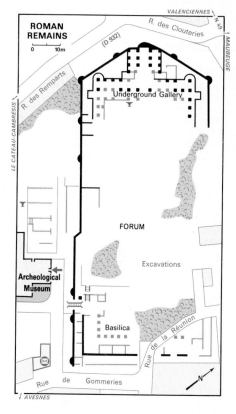

SIGHTS

Remains of the Roman City – In 1942 Canon Biévelet began searching around ground loosened in the bombing of 17 May 1940, during which Bavay had been badly damaged. Excavations revealed the remains of a large group of monumental buildings: a civil basilica, a forum, a portico above a horseshoe-shaped underground gallery *(cryptoportique)* and a room over a deep cellar stand along an east-west axis. A few houses have also been found south of the walls built after the invasions of the second half of the 3C.

Musée Archéologique (Archeological Museum) ⊙ – Installed in a large modern building, the museum exhibits various objects found during excavations. An audio-visual show presents daily life, trade, religious life and craft activities at the time of Bagacum. The numerous pots, dishes and vases with busts of divinities on them are a reminder that Bavay was an important pottery production centre. Delightful bronze figurines are among the treasures from a bronze-founder's hoard.

Grande Place (Main Square) – The brickwork of the 17C belfry contrasts with the 18C town hall, built of granite, next to it. A fluted column in the square supports a statue of Brunhilda, Queen of Austrasia, who took a great interest in road networks.

EXCURSION

Bellignies – *3km - 2 miles north of Bavay on D 24.*
In the 19C Bellignies-les-Rocs, in the middle of the Hogneau Valley, developed a marble industry. Over 1 000 people worked there: the men cut, the women polished. It was an important business right up to the Second World War.

Musée du marbre (Marble Museum) ⊙ – The tools traditionally used to cut and polish marble are displayed, together with typical examples of the workshops' output: clocks, socles etc.

Statue of Jupiter, Bavay

67

BEAUVAIS ★★

Population 57 704
Michelin map 55 folds, 9, 10 or 236 fold 33
Town plan in the current Michelin Red Guide France

Beauvais was ravaged by the bombing of June 1940 but despite this retained its striking cathedral, an architectural masterpiece almost defying the laws of gravity.

Bishops and Burghers – Beauvais, the Gallic capital of the Belgian tribe the Bellovaci, was destroyed by the Romans to create a fortified camp. The city was rebuilt and enclosed within walls during the Middle Ages; today boulevards straddle its ditches. From the 11C the city had as its lord a bishop, who was often in conflict with the town's wealthy merchants and jealous of their franchises. One of the bishops, Pierre Cauchon, bears a dubious fame: while the town wanted to support Charles VII, Cauchon rallied to the English. Chased out of Beauvais in 1429 by the burghers, he took refuge in Rouen where, on 30 May 1431, he sent Joan of Arc to the stake.

Jeanne Hachette – On 27 June 1472 Beauvais was besieged by Charles the Bold, Duke of Burgundy, who was marching on Paris with 80 000 men. The town had no troops so men and women ran to the ramparts and watched in horror as ladders were laid against the fortifications. Jeanne Laîné, the daughter of a humble craftsman, saw an assailant appear at the top of the wall, a standard in hand. She threw herself on him, tore away his banner and struck him with a hatchet, sending him flying into the ditch below. This example fired the brave few: the resistance was reaffirmed, giving time for reinforcements to arrive. Charles lifted the siege on 22 July.
Each year, at the end of June, Beauvais honours Jeanne "Hachette" *(see Calendar of Events)*.

Tapestries, stained glass and ceramics – In 1664 Colbert founded the National Tapestry Works (Manufacture nationale de Tapisserie). The artisans worked on horizontal looms producing low-warp tapestries in wool and silk which are noted for being extremely fine; they are more usually seen covering furniture. The great days of Beauvais tapestries date from when the painter Oudry was directing the works, from 1734 to 1753. The workshops, which were evacuated to Aubusson in 1939, were unable to return to Beauvais after the buildings were destroyed in 1940. The looms were relocated to the Gobelins Works in Paris, where they stood until 1989.
Beauvais' 16C stained glass is also famous, particularly that by the Leprince family. Glazed earthenware and stoneware, manufactured locally since the 15C, have made the Beauvais region one of the great ceramic centres of France.

★★★CATHÉDRALE ST-PIERRE (ST PETER'S CATHEDRAL) *1 hour*

The history of the cathedral has been tumultuous. Its unique appearance is due to the great technical drama of its construction and the desperate efforts of the bishops and chapters to raise the necessary funds: an exhausting struggle which was prolonged over four centuries but finally abandoned before the enormous project was completed.

Basse-Œuvre and Nouvel-Œuvre – During the Carolingian period a small cathedral, Notre-Dame, was erected; known as the Basse-Œuvre, now only three of the nave's bays remain complete, adjoining the newer building.
In 949 another cathedral was begun, but it was destroyed by two fires.
Subsequently, in 1225, the bishop and chapter decided to erect the biggest church of its day, a New Work *("Nouvel-Œuvre")* dedicated to St Peter.

A ruinous plan – While building a grandiose cathedral might seem a reasonable ambition in the Gothic period, in this case aspiration overcame sense. When the construction of the chancel was started in 1238, the clergy and the master builders wanted to better both past and future architects: the height to the vault's keystone was to be slightly above 48m - 158ft, making the roof (68m - 223ft high) about the height of the towers of Notre-Dame in Paris.
It took twenty five years to achieve this feat but for once the medieval architects had over-estimated their ability. The piers were too widely spaced and the buttresses too weak. In 1284 the chancel collapsed: forty more years of work and an enormous amount of money went into saving it. The three large arches of the chancel's right bays were reinforced by the addition of intermediary piers, the flying buttresses multiplied, the abutments strengthened.
No sooner had this task been finished than the Hundred Years War prevented any continuation. The cathedral was still only a chancel and its dependent parts. In 1500 the bishop decided to resume work and entrusted the construction of the transept to Martin Chambiges, assisted by Jean Vast; the first and most important thing, however, was to obtain funds.
The sale of exemptions from Lenten fasting, donations from the clergy, collections and François I's gift of part of the revenue from the royal monopoly of the sale of salt were not enough to cover the mounting costs. The citizens of Beauvais appealed to Pope Leo X, patron of Michelangelo and Raphael, who understood only too well having financial problems of his own, and a solution was found: the sale of indulgences. This scandalised the German monk Luther and partly triggered the Reformation. Leo X authorised the bishop of Beauvais to sell indulgences and the work continued. In 1550 the transept was finally completed.

Unfortunately, instead of building the nave next, it was decided to erect an openwork tower over the transept crossing, surmounted by a spire. The cross at the top of the spire was positioned in 1569, at a height of 153m - 502ft (Strasbourg's is 142m - 466ft). As there was however no nave to buttress the thrusts, the piers gave way, on Ascension Day in 1573 just as the procession had left the church.

After that, despite tremendous efforts and sacrifices, the clergy and people of Beauvais were able to restore only the chancel and the transept: the unfinished cathedral would never again have a spire, and would never have a nave.

★**East end** – The chancel dates from the 13C. Like the Flamboyant transept arms, it is shored up by flying buttresses with high piers which rise up to the roof. The transept arms were to have been very long and framed by towers.

South transept façade – The façade is richly decorated and bears two high turrets flanking **St Peter's Doorway** (portail de St-Pierre), the embrasures, tympanum and arching of which are adorned with niches sheltered by openwork canopies. It is topped with a high gable crossing a gallery. A large rose window with delicate tracery surmounts them, and is crowned by a gable with colonnettes. The door's **panels**★ are good examples of early, Italian-influenced Renaissance sculpture. They are the work of Jean le Pot: on the left, St Peter healing a lame man at the door of the Temple; on the right, the Conversion of St Paul (in the background, the walls of Damascus and St Paul's escape, lowered in a basket).

★★★**Interior** – The dizzying height of the vaults (almost 48m - 157ft high) is immediately apparent: they are nearly as tall as the Arc de Triomphe in Paris. It is here that the possibilities opened up by Gothic art become clear. The generous transept is almost 59m - 193ft long, and the chancel is extremely elegant. There is an open triforium. The windows are as tall (18m - 59ft) as the vaults of the Church of St-Germain-des-Prés in Paris. Seven chapels open off the ambulatory. The right bays' large arches, doubled in the 14C after the catastrophe of 1284, can be seen on the approach to the railings of the chancel enclosure. Traces of the early broken arches are visible.

★★**Stained-glass windows** – The transept features most of the 16C compositions. The south rose window, the work of Nicolas Leprince (1551), is dedicated to the Creation, with the Eternal Father occupying the central medallion; note the wonderful green tones. Underneath, ten prophets and ten apostles, or doctors, stand in two rows. Opposite, in the north transept, ten Sibyls reply to the Prophets (1537). The rose window and the lower gallery (parable of the Wise and Foolish Virgins) are by Max Ingrand (1954). In the chapel of the Sacred Heart (chapelle du Sacré-Cœur) (1) the "Roncherolles" window (1552) offers a close-up view of Renaissance stained-glass technique.

Ambulatory and radiating chapels – The radiating chapels which were devastated in 1940 and are currently undergoing restoration have had their windows replaced by contemporary glass masters.

The apsidal chapel still retains three 13C windows: the life of an unidentified saint (left); the Tree of Jesse and the Childhood of Christ (centre); scenes from the religious drama by Rutebeuf, the *Miracle of Theophilus (right)*.

A 16C altarpiece (3) from Marissel Church (see below) shelters in a side chapel. A Crucifixion scene is portrayed above the Death of the Virgin.

★**Astronomical Clock** (Horloge astronomique) ⊙ – This monumental clock, based on the one in Strasbourg, was made by the engineer Louis-Auguste Vérité from 1865 to 1868. It comprises 90 000 parts and has been reassembled several times. The lower part resembles a fortress with numerous windows at which appear an assortment of figures, among them Vérité, the prefect, the bishop... In the glazed openings 52 dials show the length of the days and nights, the seasons, the time of the Paris meridian etc.

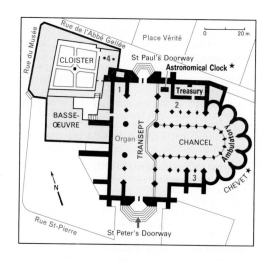

The Last Judgment unfolds in the upper part of the clock, which represents the Celestial City: a cock flaps his wings and crows, and Christ seated in His glory signals the angels to blow their trumpets. Then the Judgment takes place, and Virtue is led to heaven while Vice is dragged to hell by the Devil.

To the right of the astronomical clock is an old 14C clock (2) with chimes that play canticles corresponding to the different periods of the year.

Cloister – Two early-15C galleries have wooden ceilings; one of them extends into a sort of vaulted shelter which dates from the 16C and supports the Chapter room (4) above.

Return to the cathedral and leave by the north door, known as St Paul's Doorway.

North transept façade – This side is less ornate than the south façade, with unadorned buttresses. The doorway's tympanum features a tree bearing thirteen coats of arms: it is likely they represent the genealogy of François I, the cathedral's great benefactor.

The door's panels were again sculpted by Jean le Pot, but in the Gothic style: the four Evangelists *(right)*, and the four great Doctors of the Church *(left)*.

Return to the south doorway by going westwards around the cathedral.

Basse-Œuvre – Traces remain of the old 10C cathedral built from salvaged Gallo-Roman quarry stones known as *"pastoureaux"*. It served as the parish church until the Revolution.

ADDITIONAL SIGHTS

★**Église St-Étienne (St Stephen's Church)** – The nave and the transept are Romanesque. Their restraint, softened by the "Beauvais style" bracketed cornices, contrasts with the architectural richness of the chancel, rebuilt a little after 1500 in a refined Flamboyant style. The chancel, which is higher than the nave, is encircled by chapels. The tower flanking the west front, built from 1583 to 1674, served as the town belfry.

The left aisle gives on to a Romanesque doorway with a finely carved tympanum and arching; the wall, with three hollowed-out arcades above, features an unusual brick and stone mosaic. From this side a good view is offered of the north transept's lovely Wheel of Fortune, symbolising the frailty of earthly things: a rose window, showing ascending figures *(right)* who, on reaching the height of their climb, are brought down by Destiny *(left)*.

The Romanesque nave possesses rib-vaulting and blocked galleries. The transept crossing offers a good view over the aisles and their archaic Gothic vaulting: note that the arc of the transverse arches is slightly too generous; when seen from an angle, the rounded or faceted ribs of the pointed arches appear to rise crookedly.

Detail from the Tree of Jesse
in St Stephen's Church, Beauvais

★★**Stained-glass windows** – The chancel's stained-glass windows, by Angrand Leprince, are among the most beautiful preserved from the Renaissance period: among them is the extraordinary **Tree of Jesse**★★★ with its stunning design, colours and translucency.

On the left at the beginning of the ambulatory, a very low, late-15C former funerary chapel with finely interwoven ribs serves as the baptistry.

A 16C wooden statue of St Wilgefortis hangs in the right aisle: the crucified young Portuguese girl is shown with the beard which grew after she had implored the Virgin to save her from a heathen marriage as she had made a vow of chastity.

Ancien palais épiscopal (Old bishop's palace) – The fortified doorway is flanked by two large towers with pepperpot roofs. It was built by Bishop Simon de Clermont de Nesle with 8 000 *livres* of fines that the town had to pay after the riot of 1306 during which the bishopric was pillaged. At the far end of the courtyard stands the main body of the palace: set ablaze in 1472 by the Burgundians, it was rebuilt by Louis Villiers from L'Isle Adam *(qv)* around 1500 and retains an elegant Renaissance façade which was restored in the 19C.

★**Musée départemental de l'Oise** (Oise Department Museum) ☉ – The vaulted rooms of the entrance block contain the sculpture collections. The left tower houses wooden carvings from churches and abbeys (a 16C St Barbara by Jean Le Pot) and sculpted fragments from some of Beauvais' timber-framed houses, numerous in the town until 1940 (sign from a spice and mustard shop). In the right tower, with its frescoes of sirens playing musical instruments, there are stone carvings from the Middle Ages (tympanum from St Giles' church, a king's head, St James).

On the upper floor hangs one of the three series of tapestries bequeathed to the cathedral by Nicolas d'Argillères, *The Legend of the Gauls* (16C). The two other series *(not on display)* are Flemish tapestries by "Guillaume de Hellande" (15C) and 17C Gobelins works depicting the battles of Alexander.
Cross the garden.

The basement, halls and upper reaches of the palace are devoted to archeology, fine arts, decorative arts and regional ceramics. The 12C and 16C cellars house the archeological collections from recent excavations at local sites: Chevincourt, Verberie, Tartigny, Bulles. Note the Gallic warrior from St-Maur, the 1C AD bronze *tôle* statuette and the stele carved with a bearded Mercury (3C).

Remarkable local ceramics (16C to 18C) are exhibited on the first floor: large pieces of glazed earthenware including a piece known as "The Passion Dish" *(plat "de la Passion")*; a decorative roof tile (the hurdy-gurdy player). The painting galleries present the 16C French School, in particular *The Resurrection of Christ* by Antoine Caron (1521-99), and the 17C and 18C Italian and French Schools. The French landscape artists of the 19C include Corot *(The Fountain from the French Academy in Rome* and *The Old St-Michel Bridge, Paris).*

The law courts' old assizes room houses the enormous unfinished painting by Thomas Couture (1815-79), *The Enlisting of the Volunteers of 1792*, surrounded by preparatory sketches.

The second floor recreates France at the turn of the century and during the Roaring Twenties (the *"Belle Époque"* and *"Années folles"*) through a collection of paintings (decorative panel by Édouard Vuillard and spectacular stairway decor by Maurice Denis, *The Golden Age*), and through exceptional groups of furniture: two *Art Nouveau* dining rooms, the Parrot Salon *(salon Les Perroquets)* with Beauvais tapestry-work.

Works by the local master potter Auguste Delaherche (1857-1940) also reflect this turbulent period.

Some 600 ceramics from the Pays de Bray (19C and early 20C) are displayed under the imposing 16C roof: dishes, jugs and pitchers, salt cellars, decorative tiles, sweet-dishes, fountains, funerary monuments...
Reconstruction of a Pays de Bray potter's workshop.

Galerie nationale de la tapisserie (National Gallery of Tapestry) ⊙ – Housed in a building beyond the cathedral's east end, the gallery stages exhibitions giving an overview of French tapestry from the 15C to the present day. Building work revealed the walls of the old Gallo-Roman fortified town *(castrum)*; the important remains have been left exposed within the gallery.

Manufacture nationale de la tapisserie (National Tapestry Works) ⊙ – After over 40 years' exile, the Works returned to the town in 1989 thanks to the redevelopment of the old slaughter-houses by the local architect Desgroux. Today the factory contains about a dozen looms. The weavers work under natural light and follow the artist's cartoon, weaving on the reverse side and surveying their work with a mirror. The entire production is reserved for the State.

Église de Marissel (Marissel Church) ⊙ – *1.5km - 1 mile east.*
The village is now almost a suburb of Beauvais and its restored church rises on a terrace from where the cathedral's huge mass is visible, 2km - 1 1/4 miles away. A painting by Corot from 1866, now in the Louvre, made the church famous.
The building is the result of sporadic construction from the 11C to the 16C; the spire dates from only the last century.
The 16C west front with its Flamboyant doorway was inspired by the cathedral. The east end, the oldest and most surprising part, has a Romanesque chapel wedged between the Gothic transept and flat-ended chancel. To get an impression of the earlier sanctuary, imagine greater height on the tiny Romanesque belltower, ignoring the high roof of the nave against which it now abuts.

EXCURSIONS

★Gerberoy – *21km - 13 miles northwest of Beauvais by D 901. After Lachapelle-sous-Gerberoy, turn left.*
This fortified town perched on a knoll was forgotten from the 17C until the painter Le Sidaner (1862-1939) settled here, seduced by its charm. Since then numerous figures from the worlds of justice, the arts and letters have come to live in the old, timber-framed houses (restored) which line the cobbled streets.
The gateway which gave access to the castle leads to the modest 16C collegiate church. A shaded walk now follows the line of the old ditches.

Join us in our constant task of keeping up-to-date.
Please send us your comments and suggestions.

Michelin Tyre
Public Limited Company
Tourism Department - The Edward Hyde Building
38 Clarendon Road - WATFORD Herts WD1 1SX
Tel: 01923 415000 - Fax: 01923 415250

BERGUES ★

Population 4 163
Michelin map 51 fold 4 or 236 fold 4

Bergues is now a wealthy little Flemish town leading a peaceful life within ramparts which overlook a region famous for its pastures, butter and cheese. It grew rich on the wool trade and rivalled Dunkirk.

The warm tones of the buildings' yellow-ochre bricks are reflected in the waters of the moat which partly surrounds the town. Despite having been badly damaged in 1940, Bergues has retained its old character through the sympathetic rebuilding of the bombed districts. The winding streets, the large squares and the silent quays along the edge of the River Colme bear similarities with Bruges.

SIGHTS *1 1/2 hours*

Town Walls – The walls, pierced by four gateways and surrounded by a deep moat, date partly from the Middle Ages (Bierne Gate, Beckerstor, curtain wall east of Cassel Gate) and partly from the 17C, when the defences were developed by Vauban after the Treaty of Aix-la-Chapelle (1667), which gave Bergues to France (eastern hornwork, Cassel Gate, Hondschoote Crown). These fortifications were used by the French troops during the 1940 defence of Dunkirk, and the Germans had to use Stukas to intervene and flame-throwers to breach the walls.

★**Couronne d'Hondschoote** (Hondschoote Crown) – On the north side of the walls, Vauban used the branches of the River Colme to build an important system of bastions and demilunes completely surrounded by large moats filled with carp, pike-perch and tench: viewed from above, this defensive system outlines a sort of crown, hence its name.

Porte de Cassel (Cassel Gate) – This gateway was built in the 17C; its triangular pediment features a carved sun, Louis XIV's emblem. From the outside, there is a view to the right over the medieval curtain wall towards the towers of St Winnoc.

Ancienne abbaye de St-Winoc (St Winnoc's Abbey) – Only ruins remain of this famous Benedictine establishment founded by St Winnoc on the Groenberg, a rise surrounded by marshes. Most of the buildings were destroyed during the Revolution; the 18C front door, the pointed tower (rebuilt in 1815) which marks the site of the abbey's façade and the 12C-13C square tower of the transept crossing, supported by reinforced buttresses, survive.

Beffroi (Belfry) ⊘ – Built in the second half of the 16C, set ablaze in 1940 and dynamited by the Germans in 1944, the belfry was rebuilt by Paul Gélis who sought to preserve the main structure of the former edifice while simplifying the exterior decoration. The belfry (54m - 177ft high) is made of yellow bricks known as "sand bricks" and is surmounted by the lion of Flanders; the carillon comprises 50 bells. From the top there is a good view over the Flemish plain.

On the façade of the town hall (**H**) nearby, a bust of **Lamartine** recalls that the writer, brother-in-law to M de Coppens of Hondschoote, was elected Deputy of Bergues in 1833, after a first, unsuccessful attempt two years earlier.

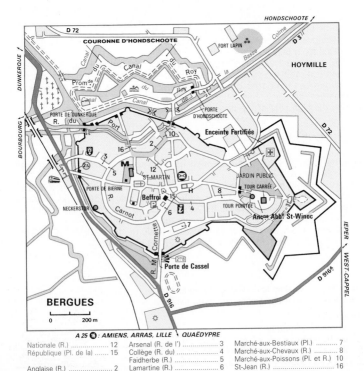

BERGUES

0 _____ 200 m

A 25 **18** : AMIENS, ARRAS, LILLE \ QUAÉDYPRE

Nationale (R.) 12	Arsenal (R. de l') 3	Marché-aux-Bestiaux (Pl.) 7
République (Pl. de la) 15	Collège (R. du) 4	Marché-aux-Chevaux (R.) 8
	Faidherbe (R.) 5	Marché-aux-Poissons (Pl. et R.) 10
Anglaise (R.) 2	Lamartine (R.) 6	St-Jean (R.) 16

Mont-de-Piété (M) – Sensitively restored after the War, like St Martin's church nearby, this building is the work of **Wenceslas Coebergher** (1561-1634), an extraordinary character who was painter, architect, economist and engineer: in the Flanders region he occupied himself with the draining of the Moëres, the marshes near Hondschoote *(qv)*, and introduced the first pawnshops *(monts-de-piété)*. This pawnshop was inaugurated in 1633 and its activities continued until 1848. The elegant building with a Baroque gable is constructed of brick and white stone, and presents an inventive composition of decorative elements: pilasters, niches, cartouches, pediments.

A museum is housed inside.

Musée municipal (Municipal Museum) ⊙ – The pride of the collection is **Georges de la Tour's** large painting *The Viola Player* (17C), though there are many other fine canvases among the 16C and 17C Flemish collection of paintings, including the curious *Peasants' Interior* by Breughel the Elder, a sketch by Rubens, portraits by Van Dyck, Cossiers and Simon de Vos, *Chaste Susanna* by Jan Massys and still-lifes by Ghysbrecht and Van Son.

On the second floor, the natural history section contains birds and butterflies. The collection of 16C and 17C drawings (1 430 items) is exhibited in rotation.

EXCURSION

Round trip of 12km – 7 1/2 miles – *About 45min. Leave Bergues by D 916 south and after 4km – 2 1/2 miles turn left into D 37.*

Quaëdypre – This village, located on a slight incline, has a **hall-church** ⊙ with three equal aisles and an interior decorated with 17C carved woodwork: main altar with a painting by Goubau, Largillière's tutor; communion table, pulpit and confessional from the Dominican church in Bergues; organ loft and stalls formerly in St Winnoc's Abbey, Bergues.

West-Cappel. This is a peaceful village on a rise. **St Sylvester's Church** ⊙, rebuilt in the 16C in "sand bricks", boasts a mighty porch-belfry, three aisles and a taller chancel. The interior features stained-glass windows, some dating from the 16C; a 17C communion table; an interesting pulpit; the reclining effigy of Ludwine Van Cappel (15C) *(back of the left aisle)*.

Den Leew Windmill ⊙ – *8km - 5 miles south via D 916 then turn right into D 110.* On the outskirts of **Pitgam** stands a wooden post mill dating from 1776 and named after the last miller here.

BLÉRANCOURT

Population 1 268
Michelin map 56 fold 3 or 236 folds 36, 37

Only a few sections survive from the former château of the dukes of Gesvres, built in the 17C by Salomon de Brosse and abandoned during the Revolution. In 1917 a group of American women led by a Miss Ann Morgan moved into the remaining parts in order to save them.

Musée national de la coopération franco-américaine (National Museum of Franco-American Cooperation) ⊙ – Two monumental doorways lead into the main courtyard surrounded by a moat. Pavilions frame the second doorway: the right one contains the library, documents and archives, the left one is filled with souvenirs of Miss Morgan.

The two wings of the museum itself partly recreate the château's ground floor. The left wing *(temporarily closed)* is dedicated to the War of Independence. The right wing (Florence Gould pavilion) displays paintings and sculptures executed between 1800 and 1945 by French artists in the United States and by American artists in France.

Finish the tour with a stroll through the garden planted with American species and the arboretum.

BOULOGNE-SUR-MER ★

Agglomeration 95 930
Michelin map 51 fold 1 or 236 fold 1
Town plan in the current Michelin Red Guide France

Boulogne, once a Roman city, is situated where the Liane Valley opens up after running between steep hills. The town has a lively port that thrives on its important and varied roles, and has a rough but appealing look and busy streets. St Beuve was born here in 1804; another local figure was the engineer Frédéric Sauvage (1786-1857), the inventor of the propeller used in steam navigation (statue on Marguet bridge opposite the tourist office).

The town itself is divided into an upper town, which is the administrative and religious centre enclosed within ramparts and overlooked by its basilica, and the lower town, the commercial and maritime heart, which was rebuilt after the war.

The Miracle of Our Lady – In 636 under Dagobert, a boat with neither crew nor sails came aground on the shore at Boulogne, carrying a statue of the Virgin. At the same time, the faithful praying in the chapel (which stood on the site of the present basilica) were notified of the event by an apparition of the Virgin. This miracle led to the establishment of a famous **pilgrimage** which has been undertaken by fourteen kings of France and five kings of England.

Boulogne's religious prestige was sometimes used for political gain: Louis XI awarded himself the realm – which then belonged to the Duke of Burgundy – declaring that, as the vassal of the Virgin on earth, he had to have a hand in local matters.

"Imperial" Boulogne – Boulogne is linked to Bonaparte because from 1803 to 1805 he kept his troops mustered at the **Boulogne Camp** *(camp de Boulogne)* for a possible invasion of England. On 26 August 1805 Napoleon I, crowned a year earlier, finally abandoned his project in order to set his Grande Armée against the Austrians.

In August 1840 the future Napoleon III tried to raise the town against Louis-Philippe, but the attempt floundered and he was imprisoned in Ham Fort (southwest of St Quentin) for six years before making his escape.

THE PORT

The foremost **fresh fish port** on mainland Europe, Boulogne is also the European centre of the fish trade and the home of an international industrial fish processing complex (freezing, canning, smoking and salting). About fifteen industrial trawlers, 90 small-scale fishing boats and 40 coastal boats, together with foreign ships, supply the port.

Boulogne ranks 9th as a **commercial port** in France with 5 million tonnes of traffic, comprising imports of manganese ore, paper and paper pulp, woods and veneers, frozen foods, and exports of iron alloys, cement and flour.

As a passenger port it specialises in ferrying people to Great Britain. The Boulogne to Folkestone crossing is made by Hoverspeed, in one of their vehicle and passenger carrying catamarans.

Completely destroyed during the war, the harbour installations have since been reconstructed and enlarged, and now extend beyond Boulogne to Le Portel where the commercial port is located. The **outer harbour** is protected by two

The harbour, Boulogne

jetties, one of which, the Carnot jetty, is 3 250m – over 2 miles long. The main part of the harbour is the Sarraz-Bournet deep-water dock with a western pier for large cargo ships, and an eastern pier for the ore ships supplying the metallurgical complex.

The **inner harbour** consists of a tidal dock reserved for travellers, small trawlers and pleasure boats, and the Napoleon and Loubet docks for the big fishing boats. The harbour railway station (gare maritime) (Y) has 4 quays and 3 gangways. At night the sorting of the trawled fish takes place in the refrigerated markets alongside Loubet dock. Gambetta Wharf (quai Gambetta) (Y), overlooked by tall buildings, is busiest when the trawlers unload their catch, some of which is sold on the spot.

Plage (Beach) (Y) – Already quite well known in the 18C, this beach of fine, white sand became very fashionable from the second Empire (mid 19C) onwards. An equestrian statue of San Martin *(see below)* stands on the promenade.

★★NAUSICAA (Y) ⊙

Nausicaa, the National Sea Centre (Centre National de la Mer), is a recent development on the site of the old casino, opposite the harbour railway station (gare maritime) on the edge of the beach.

The complex – the world's largest sea centre – presents the worlds of warm water and cold water fish, and man's different links with the sea.

Different Sea Worlds – On entering, visitors are plunged into the Deep through special effects, into a world of whale cries and of plankton, which is vital to marine life. The first aquariums concentrate on mimicry among fish (catfish, stone fish) and the way they can change colour depending on age or environment (angel fish).

Three big portholes look out into the deep sea, while fish that live at less than 1 000 metres - 3 280ft can be observed through periscopes. In complete contrast, exotic multicoloured fish can be seen swimming among the corals of the "**tropical lagoon**" (lagon corallien). The cold waters are home to fewer species of fish than warm waters, although in greater abundance which makes for good fishing. Shipwrecks harbour conger eels and moray; finally, the fish and invertebrates of the Boulogne coastal marshes are introduced.

Man's sea – The "**tuna fish diamond**" (espace diamant des thons) is an enormous upturned-pyramid shaped aquarium in which shoals of tuna fish swim; special effects give the visitor the impression of being caught in a large net along with the tuna. On the deck of a reconstructed trawler, the realistic effects follow nocturnal drag-net manœuvres in a stormy North Sea. Different fishing methods are explained.

New techniques of fish breeding are presented through models showing the different aquicultural sites. In a "touch tank" visitors can stroke thorn-back rays and approach urchins and starfish. An area is reserved for Blue Europe (l'Europe Bleue), created in 1983 by the EEC for better management of the sea. The journey ends with the spectacular **shark tank**, a panoramic basin in which huge sharks swim.

The 40m - 131ft long test pool which is part of the French National Underwater Exploration Institute (Institut Français de Recherche pour l'Exploitation de la Mer – IFRE-MER) is used by professionals and scientists to simulate the workings of fishing devices. The large entrance hall gives access to an information centre, a projection room, a conference room, a souvenir shop, a cafeteria and a restaurant.

★★LA VILLE HAUTE (UPPER TOWN) *3 hours*

The upper town, enclosed by ramparts, stands on the site of the old Roman *castrum* or fortified town. It is overlooked by the enormous dome of Notre-Dame Basilica and is popular with tourists in summer, offering pleasant strolls along the ramparts or within the walls, among the streets and sights.

Ramparts – The fortifications were built in the early 13C by Philippe le Hurepel, Count of Boulogne and son of Philippe-Auguste, on the foundations of the Gallo-Roman walls and were strengthened in the 16C-17C. The ramparts form a rectangle (325m – 1 066ft by 410m - 1 345ft) reinforced by the **castle** to the east, and are pierced by gates – Gayole, Dunes, Calais and **Degrés** (**X**) which is pedestrian only – flanked by two towers. The sentry walk is accessible from each gateway and offers lovely **views★** of the town and the port.

At the western corner the **Gayette tower** (tour Gayette) (**X B**), a former gaol, was the site of the take-off for the balloon flight in 1785 by **Pilâtre de Rozier** and Romain who were attempting to cross the Channel; they crashed near Wimille, just north of Boulogne.

A pyramid-shaped monument (**V K**) surmounted by a statue stands in the garden between Boulevard Auguste-Mariette and the ramparts: it is dedicated to another local figure, **Mariette** the Egyptologist, whom the statue shows in Egyptian costume.

Stroll through the Upper Town (**VX**) – Enter the ramparts through the western Dunes Gate (porte des Dunes) into Place de la Résistance, around which stand:
– The **library** (bibliothèque) in the old Annonciades Convent. The 17C buildings and the cloisters house study and exhibition rooms, while the main reading room occupies the 18C chapel with its superb coffered ceiling, visible through the windows from the square.
– The **law courts** (Palais de Justice) (**J**) dating from 1852, with a neo-Classical façade, a statue òf Charlemagne and Napoleon in two niches.
– The 13C Gothic **belfry** (beffroi) *(access from the town hall ⊙, see below)*, with a 12C base (the former keep from the castle of the counts of Boulogne) and an 18C octagonal section at the top.
It houses Gallo-Roman statues and regional antique furniture as well as a beautiful stained-glass window portraying Godefroy de Bouillon.

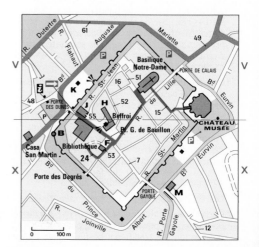

BOULOGNE-SUR-MER VILLE-HAUTE

B	Tour Gayette
F	Hôtel Desandrouins
H	Hôtel de ville
J	Palais de Justice
K	Monument à Mariette
M	Musée d'Histoire naturelle

BOULOGNE-SUR-MER

Faidherbe (R.)	Y	Aumont (R. d')	Z 7	Marquet (Pont)	Z 38
Grande-Rue	Z	Beaucerf (Bd)	Z 8	Perrochel (R.)	Z 47
Lampe (R. de la)	Z 32	Bras-d'Or (R. du)	Z 13	Porte-Neuve (R.)	Y 49
Thiers (R. Adolphe)	YZ 60	Dutertre (R.)	Y 20	Puits-d'Amour (R.)	Z 53
Victor-Hugo (R.)	Z	Entente-Cordiale (Pont de l')	Z 23	Résistance (Pl.)	Y 55
		Lattre de Tassigny (R. de)	Y 33	St-Louis (R.)	Y 56
		Lille (R. de)	Y 37	Tour-Notre-Dame (R.)	Y 61
				Voltaire (Bd)	Z 63

H Hôtel de ville **J** Palais de justice **M** Musée d'Histoire naturelle

The top of the belfry (183 steps) offers an extensive **view**★ of Boulogne and its surroundings.

Place de la Résistance leads into **Place Godefroy-de-Bouillon** located at the junction of the four main streets. The square owes its name to the leader of the first crusade, who was a member of the House of Boulogne.

The 18C façade of the **town hall** (Hôtel de Ville) (**H**) of red brick with stone dressings, contrasts sharply with the primitive Gothic belfry. Opposite the town hall stands the Louis XVI **Hôtel Desandrouins** (**F**): Napoleon stayed here several times from 1803 to 1811.

Follow Rue de Puits-d'Amour alongside Hôtel Desandrouins and turn right.

Rue Guyale (**X 24**) – The merchants' guildhall used to stand on this street, which has been restored and reveals the back of the Annonciades Convent and the rough stone façades of the old houses, one of which is occupied by the Tourism Development Office.

From Place Godefroy-de-Bouillon take Rue de Lille.

Notre-Dame Basilica (**V**) – The basilica was built from 1827 to 1866 on the site of the old cathedral (destroyed after the Revolution) and has preserved the Romanesque crypt. It is a popular place of pilgrimage *(see above)*. Inside, a powerful Corinthian colonnade supports the building. The superb, soaring **dome**★ with its circle of large statues rises behind the chancel; beyond it, in the central chapel, stands the wooden statuette of Our Lady of Boulogne (Notre-Dame de Boulogne), crowned with precious stones. Every year the statuette is carried in a procession *(see Calendar of Events)* during which the traditional sun-shaped head-dresses, bonnets and shawls of the region are worn.

★**Crypt and Treasury** ⊙ – *Access from the doorway on Rue de Lille.*
Under the basilica, a labyrinth of underground passages links 14 chambers. One of them houses the Treasury which contains religious statues and objects (chalices, shrines) from various churches in the region, and the relic of the Holy Blood offered by Philippe the Fair to Our Lady of Boulogne.
Continue through several rooms, among them St Luke's Hall adorned with 19C *grisaille* and another containing traces of a 3C Roman temple, to the **crypt of the painted pillars** dating from the 11C, discovered during the construction of the new basilica. Close by, near the foundations of the chancel, lies the tomb of Monsignor Haffreingue, who built the basilica.

Leave by the south transept and take Rue du Château opposite.

★**Castle-Museum** (Musée-Château) (**V**) – Formerly the residence of the counts of Boulogne, this powerful-looking polygonal building was the first in western Europe to abandon the traditional keep. Flanked by round towers, it protected the most vulnerable part of the ramparts towards the plateau; in the 16C a horseshoe bastion was added on one side. The castle is separated from the ramparts by a moat, which was crossed by a drawbridge.

Tour of the museum ⊙ – The varied collections are displayed in rooms throughout the four floors of the castle, including the count's hall, the towers, the chapel, the guard's room...

The archeology of the Mediterranean is represented by an Egyptian section – sarcophagi and numerous funerary objects, the gift of Mariette the Egyptologist – and also by a beautiful group of **Greek vases**, among them a black-figure jug portraying the suicide of Ajax.

Continue into rooms containing ceramics and earthenwares from the main French and foreign manufacturers (Rouen, Nevers; Delft) and remarkable pieces of porcelain (St-Cloud, Sèvres, Vincennes). The Boulogne Camp and Napoleon (bust by Canova, twin-cocked hat) are evoked on the stairway and landing of the 3rd level. In the next room, works by painters of the Opal coast reveal the artistic talent that flourished around Boulogne in the 19C.

Among the ethnographic collections, the **Eskimo and Aleutian masks** brought back from a voyage to North America by the anthropologist Pinart, and the objects from the South Sea Islands including a Maori battle canoe from New Zealand, are particularly interesting. Three rooms are devoted to 17C, 18C and especially 19C painting: Corot, Boudin and Fantin-Latour, together with sculptures by Rodin, Pompon and Carpeaux.

The enormous guard room displays collections from the Middle Ages and the Renaissance: copper and brassware, wood and stone sculptures, Gothic furniture and woodwork, an exceptional glazed earthenware roof ornament, paintings, coins. The archeological collections are exhibited in the underground rooms which rest largely on the 2C and 3C Gallo-Roman walls, and in La Barbière, a superb Gothic room.

ADDITIONAL SIGHTS

Église St-Nicolas (St Nicholas' Church) (Z) – The church, standing in Place Dalton where the market is held *(Wednesdays and Saturdays)*, is the oldest in Boulogne despite its Classical façade. It was built from 1220 to 1250, and underwent many alterations at the beginning of the 16C (apse, transept, chancel vaults, chapels) and in the 18C when the nave was rebuilt. The 17C main altar features spiral columns and a fine painting of *The Flagellation* by Lehmann, a pupil of Ingres.

Musée d'Histoire naturelle (Natural History Museum) (Z M[1]) ⊙ – The museum, which is in the process of expanding, presents collections of stuffed animals, beetles with metallic silvery reflections and exotic butterflies. Note the largest cricket in the world from Malaysia, and the skeletons of 3 whales which were beached locally several years ago.

Libertador San Martin Museum (X M[2]) ⊙ – From 1848 to 1850 this house was inhabited by the Argentinian general San Martin who, in 1816, freed his country from Spanish rule and then also liberated Chile (1817) and Peru (1821). He died in a room on the second floor, in 1850: mementoes of the illustrious soldier.

Calvaire des marins (Sailors' calvary) (Y) – *From Nausicaa, access by Rue des Signaux and Rue de la Baraque-de-l'Empereur.*
The calvary stands on the site of Odre tower, a Roman lighthouse destroyed in the 17C, near the crenellated walls of the sailors' chapel. From the calvary's surroundings and the platform of the neighbouring blockhouse there is a plunging **view★** over the beach, Nausicaa, the channel entrance, the bridges over the Liane, and St Peter's district to the left. Not far from here, following the cliff, a marker indicates the site of the Emperor's barracks and the Napoleonic powder magazine.

EXCURSIONS

★Colonne de la Grande Armée (Grande Armée Column) ⊙ – *3km - 2 miles north by N 1* (Y) *and an alley to the left.*
Designed by the architect Eloi Labarre (1764-1833) to commemorate the Boulogne Camp *(qv)*, the column was started in 1804 but finished under Louis-Philippe. The column is of marble from nearby Marquise, rises 54m - 177ft high and is 4m - 13ft in diameter. On its base, a bronze low-relief portrays Field Marshal Soult offering the plans of the column to the Emperor. A staircase *(263 steps)* leads to the square platform (190m - 623ft above sea level) from where the **panorama★★** extends over the lush countryside of the Boulogne region and, on a clear day, across the Channel as far as the white cliffs of Dover. Other sights include Cap Gris-Nez *(north)*, the jetties of Boulogne's port, the rocks of Le Portel, Alprech Point lighthouse, the Upper Town *(west and south)* and the triumphal avenue which leads to the column *(east)*.

Légion d'honneur (Monument to the Legion of Honour) – *2km - 1 1/4 miles north by D 940* (Y) *and a path to the right.*
This obelisk marks the site of the throne on which Napoleon I sat on 16 August 1804, for the second distribution of the Legion of Honour decorations (the first took place on 14 July 1804 at the Invalides in Paris). The troops were deployed in a

huge semicircle on the slopes of Terlincthun Valley; 2 000 of these men received their crosses, arranged for this ceremony in the shields and helmets of the ancient military heroes Du Guesclin and Bayard.

Pont de Briques Château – *5km - 3 miles south on N 1(Z)*. This modest 18C château *(private)* is one of the places where Napoleon stayed when he came to visit the troops at the Boulogne Camp; his apartments were in the right wing. The emperor apparently conceived his plan of campaign against Austria – which ended with his victory at Austerlitz in December 1805 – in the salon here.

Le Portel – *5km - 3 miles southwest (Z)*. The town has a sandy beach dotted with rocks and bordered by a raised promenade, facing the small isle on which stands **Heurt Fort** (fort de l'Heurt), built by Napoleon in 1804. A statue of Our Lady of Boulogne watches over the Epi jetty.
Alprech Point lighthouse perches on the cliff, to the south.

Hardelot-Plage – *15km - 9 miles south by D 940 (Z) and D 113E*.
This elegant seaside and sporting resort features a magnificent, gently-sloping beach of fine sand. Leisure facilities include paths for walking, riding and cycling; golf; sailing; a country club with tennis courts and a swimming pool.
The **château** ⊙ north of the village, by the Lake of Mirrors (lac des Miroirs), retains some of its 13C fortifications. In the 19C it was bought by an Englishman who had the château rebuilt in the style of Windsor Castle with crenellations and turrets. It is now the setting for local shows and pageants.

Boulogne Forest – *10km - 6 miles east by N 42 (Y) and D 341*.
The route climbs the slopes of **Lambert Hill** (Mont Lambert) (189m - 620ft); a television aerial rises from the top.
The forest covers 2 000ha - 4 940 acres and contains trails, bridleways, parking facilities and picnic areas.
The lush Liane Valley borders the forest to the south and east; the village of **Questrecques** nestles in its surroundings.

The BOULONNAIS REGION★

Michelin map 51 fold 1, 2 or 236 fold 1, 2

The Boulonnais (Le Boulonnais) is the region of lush countryside around Boulogne. Its complex relief is due to the juxtaposition of differing geological formations: marble in Marquise, sandstone in Outreau and chalk in Desvres and Neufchâtel, where it lies under a layer of clay, and crags of it sometimes rise over 200m – 656ft in altitude.
The plateau between Guînes and the River Aa is intermittently bare or dotted with copses and affords an unrestricted view in all directions; here and there great farms surrounded by thickets and pastures grow cereals and sugar beet.
The Wimereux, Liane, Hem and Slack Valleys are deep and narrow, providing fertile ground for orchards (cider apples) and meadows. A local breed of cow grazes peacefully here, in addition to the Northern Blue and the Flemish Red cows; sheep are put out to pasture with Boulonnais draughthorses, which are powerful grey animals capable of pulling as much as a ton in weight.
The modest villages with their low, white-washed stone houses are devoted to stock farming; they are scattered around the manor houses, which were Royalist dens during the Revolution.

ROUND TRIP STARTING FROM BOULOGNE

75km - 46 miles – about 3 hours

★**Boulogne** – *See Boulogne. 1 1/2 hours*.
Take N 42 east; 3km - 2 miles on, beyond the roundabout, turn off to D 232 north.
This picturesque road, edged with beeches and old elms, descends sharply into the freshness of the **Wimereux Valley** which is carpeted with meadows and scattered with copses.

Souverain-Moulin – The château and its outbuildings look very attractive in their leafy setting.
Take D 233 (east) to Belle, then turn left into D 238 and right into D 251 after the river. Turn right at D 127.

Le Wast – Many local people take walks which end at this charming village. The **church** ⊙ features a Romanesque portal with Eastern-looking festoons, and rounded arches supported by capitals decorated with waterleaves which curve to form scrolls. St Ide, the mother of Godefroy de Bouillon and the founder of the priory, was buried here in the 12C.
The **Boulonnais Regional Park Centre** (Maison du Parc national régional du Nord-Pas-de-Calais, zone du Boulonnais) is situated in **Huisbois Manor** (manoir du Huisbois) ⊙, a beautiful 17C house of local grey stone. The information centre provides documentation, a library, a video centre and exhibitions all relating to the Boulonnais. A trail starting here leads through typical countryside: farmland criss-crossed by hedges and trees.

Château de Colembert – *(Private)*. This vast 18C building stands out from its lush surroundings at the foot of Dauphin Hill (Mont Dauphin) (201m - 659ft high).

Join N 42 going east and take D 224 left to Licques.

Licques – All that remain of the Premonstratensian abbey (Abbaye de Prémontrés), founded in the 12C and rebuilt in the 18C, are the abbey church's tall nave (late-18C) and a few buildings from the same period, now occupied by the presbytery, the town hall and the school. 2km - 1 1/4 miles along D 224 north towards Ardres, the road offers a good **view** over Licques and the Hem River basin.

From Licques, follow D 191 west through Sanghem and Hardinghen.

Beyond Le Ventu the road begins to climb, overlooking the entire region. There are beautiful **views★** over the verdant, undulating Boulonnais countryside.

At Hardinghen, take D 127 southwest and D 127E (north) to Réty.

Réty – The small Flamboyant **church** ⊙ (late 15C; 12C tower) has decorative stone-work which creates a chequered effect. Inside, note the chancel's carved keystone in the centre of a stone crown. The cemetery has been transformed into a garden.

Turn left beyond Réty into D 232. After crossing D 127E, turn right.

Hydrequent – The **Maison du Marbre et de la Geologie** ⊙ is a centre concentrating on the formation of marble and coal in the Boulonnais. 26 different types of marble exist. During the Primary era this region was covered by a lush forest (model showing the giant animals and plants whose decomposition eventually formed coal). The Marquise quarry yields a type of "marble" which has been used for many buildings, among them Canterbury Cathedral in England; granules of the rock were used more recently for the vaults of the Channel Tunnel. The plaster cast of a dinosaur skeleton found locally (during the building of the motorway in 1991) and an audio-visual show may also be viewed.

Return to D 232.

Almost immediately, a pretty mill beside the River Slack comes into view (left).

Continue on D 232 to Wierre-Effroy; take D 234 (south) to Conteville-lès-Boulogne, then take D 233 west, following the Wimereux River.

Wimille – The graves of the aeronauts Pilâtre de Rozier *(qv)* and Romain are in the old cemetery.

Le BOURGET AIRPORT

Michelin map 101 folds 7 and 17 or 106 fold 20 – Michelin plan 20

Le Bourget airfield was created in 1914 and rapidly became an important airport and military air base. It was from here that Nungesser and Coli set off in their *White Bird* on 8 May 1927 in a doomed attempt to reach the American coast. Thirteen days later, in the early hours of 22 May, Lindbergh successfully landed his *Spirit of St Louis* in Paris, after achieving the first Atlantic crossing in the history of aviation. Costes and Bellonte were the first to accomplish this feat in the opposite direction when *Question Mark* landed on 1 September 1930.

Since the Charles-de-Gaulle airport at Roissy became operational, Le Bourget now caters mainly for private aircraft and business flights.

Every two years, Le Bourget hosts the International Air and Space Fair *(see Calendar of Events, qv)*.

★★Musée de l'Air et de l'Espace (Aeronautics and Space Museum) ⊙ – The former air terminal, now called the Great Gallery, traces the early years of aviation. 45 items are exhibited; among the oldest are the nacelle belonging to the balloon *La France* (1884), and the first glider *Le Biot* which flew for the first time in 1879. Many aircraft belonged to early 20C pioneers: Vuia's I-bis (1906), Henri Fabre's hydroplane (1910), the great Guynemer's Spad 13 and the Breguet 14 evoke the First World War, the first war to be fought in the air. Six exhibition galleries house an outstanding collection of civil and military aeronautical equipment from France and

Aeronautics and Space Museum, Le Bourget

abroad: over 100 rare aircraft, miniature models, engines, coloured slides and documents cover the conquest of the skies since 1919, including the pioneering flights between the continents in interwar years. After the fighters of the Second World War, modern history is represented by the first jet planes and by the space capsules *Apollo 13* (USA) and *Soyouz T6* (USSR). The heavier aircraft, like Concorde and the Ariane rocket, are exhibited on the esplanade.

CALAIS

Agglomeration 101 768
Michelin map 51 fold 2 or 236 fold 2
Map of conurbation in the current Michelin Red Guide France

Calais is divided into two distinct districts: the administrative and industrial centre, Calais-Sud, and the maritime centre, Calais-Nord, which was rebuilt after the last war. The town gave its name to the Pas de Calais, the strait known on the north side of the Channel as the Straits of Dover. The history of the town has been enormously influenced by its proximity to the English coast, only 38km - 23 1/2 miles away, and on a clear day the white cliffs of Dover are visible from the promenade and the vast sandy beach west of Calais harbour's entrance.

The Burghers of Calais – After his success at Crécy *(qv)* **Edward III** of England needed to create a powerful base in France. He began the siege of Calais on 3 September 1346 but eight months later had still not been able to breach the valiant defence led by the

CALAIS

Fontinette (R. des) .... **CDY** 24	
Gambetta (Bd Léon) .... **CY**	
Jacquard (Bd) .... **CDY**	
Lafayette (Bd) .... **DY**	
Pasteur (Bd) .... **DY**	
Royale (R.) .... **CX** 63	
Amsterdam (R. d') .... **DXY** 3	
Angleterre (Pl. d') .... **DX** 4	

Barbusse (Pl. Henri) .... **DX** 5	
Bonningue (R. du Cdt) .... **DX** 7	
Bruxelles (R. de) .... **DX** 10	
Chanzy (R. du Gén.) .... **DY** 13	
Commune de Paris	
(R. de la) .... **CDY** 16	
Escaut (Quai de l') .... **CY** 21	
Foch (R. du) .... **CXY** 22	
Georges V (Pont) .... **CY** 31	
Jacquard (Pont) .... **CY** 36	
Jean-Jaurès (R.) .... **DY** 37	
Londres (R. de) .... **DX** 42	
Mer (R. de la) .... **CX** 45	

Notre-Dame (R.) .... **CD** 46	
Paix (R. de la) .... **CX** 48	
Paul-Bert (R.) .... **CDY** 49	
Prés.-Wilson (Av. du) .... **CY** 54	
Quatre-Coins (R. des) .... **CY** 55	
Rhin (Quai du) .... **CY** 58	
Richelieu (R.) .... **CY** 60	
Rome (R. de) .... **CY** 61	
Soldat-Inconnu (Pl. du) .... **DY** 64	
Tamise (Quai de la) .... **CDY** 66	
Thermes (R. des) .... **CY** 67	
Varsovie (R. de) .... **DY** 70	
Vauxhall (R. du) .... **CY** 72	

B Tour du guet	**M¹** Musée des Beaux-Arts et de la Dentelle
H Hôtel de ville	**M²** Musée de la Guerre

town governor, Jean de Vienne; in fact, it was famine that forced the inhabitants to capitulate in the end.

Six burghers, led by **Eustache de Saint-Pierre,** prepared to sacrifice themselves in order that the other citizens of Calais would be spared the sword. In thin robes, "barefoot, bare-headed, halters about their necks and the keys to the town in their hands", they presented themselves before the king to be delivered to the executioner. They were saved by the intercession of Queen Philippa of Hainault who pleaded for mercy for them.

Calais was in the hands of the English for over two centuries and was liberated only in 1558, by the Duke of Guise. This was a mortal blow to **Mary Tudor,** Queen of England, who said: "When I am dead and opened, you shall find 'Calais' lying in my heart."

Port Activity – Calais is the leading passenger port in France and continental Europe. It has always had a close association with England and is today the starting-point for continental Europe's railway system, providing rapid access to Paris and Lille, as well as Basle, Germany and Italy.

In 1992 14 million passengers passed through the port (and 16.8 million tonnes of freight); to cope with this traffic, Calais has a bus and coach station leading directly to and from the gangways. This also allows two companies (P&O European Ferries and Sealink) to operate a convenient Calais-Dover service to England. These harbour facilities give immediate access, via a rapid dual-carriageway, to the A 26 motorway and the coastal bypass road. The Hoverspeed company operates a Calais-Dover service from the hoverport.

Traditionally, Calais has always been a leading commercial port, for the most part importing minerals and aggregates, wood, paper pulp and liquid sulphur, and exporting sugar, coke, sulphuric acid and various other products. A new tidal basin east of the harbour is large enough to handle three Panama-size vessels (60 000 tons dead weight); it also welcomes giant catamarans transporting 450 passengers and 80 vehicles.

Lace – Together with Caudry-en-Cambrésis, Calais is the great centre of machine-made lace, employing over 3 000 workers. Englishmen from Nottingham introduced the industry at the beginning of the 19C; quality was improved around 1830 when the first Jacquard looms were used.

Today 500 looms are used, mostly of English manufacture.

English terminology is also employed: work is counted by "racks" divided into "motions"; bobbin-winding is called "wheelage".

75 % of Calais' lace is exported, to 140 different countries. 80 % of it is used for lingerie, 20 % for dresses (wedding gowns, cocktail and evening wear...).

The town has also diversified into textiles, wood, paper pulp, chemicals and foods.

SIGHTS *3 hours*

★★Monument des Bourgeois de Calais (Monument to the Burghers of Calais) (**DY**) – This famous work by Rodin is located in a shady spot between the town hall (Hôtel de Ville) and St Peter's Park (Parc St-Pierre). It dates from 1895 and exemplifies the sculptor's brilliance: the bronze group is simultaneously full of vitality and pathos.

Each of the six lifesize figures should be admired separately: their veins and muscles exaggerated, their forms tense and haughty, they express the heroic nobility of the men obliged to humiliate themselves before the king of England.

The Burghers of Calais

Hôtel de ville (Town Hall) (**DY H**) – This beautiful and graceful building is built in brick and stone in the 15C Flemish style. The belfry (75m - 246ft) can be seen for miles in all directions; the sound of its bell is very appealing. Inside, a **stained-glass window** which recalls the departure of the English diffuses the sunlight over the grand staircase.

Le port (Harbour) – Walk around the old Paradise Basin (Bassin du Paradis), where the Louis XVIII Column recalls the king's landing in 1814; follow the quays (Monument to the Lifesavers) to the end of the harbour entrance.

The Courgain district *(right)*, which was rebuilt after the war, is where many sailors live. The lighthouse is located behind this area.

Le phare (Lighthouse) (**DX**) – The lighthouse (53m - 174ft tall; 271 steps) was built in 1848 to replace the watchtower lantern. From the top there is a surprisingly wide and splendid panoramic **view★★** over Calais, the harbour, the basins, the town's stadium, Place d'Armes and the Church of Our Lady.

Place d'Armes (**CX**) – Before the devastation of the war, this was the heart of medieval Calais. Only the 13C **watchtower** (tour de guet) (**B**) has survived. The belfry and the town hall beside it are popular subjects for artists.

★Musée des Beaux-Arts et de la Dentelle (Lace and Fine Arts Museum) (**CX M¹**) ⊙ – The history of Calais and its artistic development, from the 16C to the 20C, is presented here.

Ground floor – 19C and 20C sculpture includes works by Rodin, Carrier-Belleuse, Bourdelle, Lardera, Hajdu.

One room is devoted to the history of lace, illustrated through the various techniques used in France and abroad: needles, bobbins and industrial methods. There are samples of various types of lacework in addition to shawls, head-dresses and handkerchiefs, hand tools and a late-19C lacemaking loom.

First floor – The painting gallery presents a wide range of works: Flemish primitives, canvases by the 17C Dutch and Flemish schools, 16C and 17C Italian and French works, and English and French landscapes of the 18C and 19C. Works by European artists reflect the 20C.

Calais lace – Blériot crossing the Channel

Musée des Beaux-Arts et de la Dentelle, Calais

Musée de la Guerre (War Museum) (**CY M²**) ⊙ – Opposite the town hall, in the middle of St Peter's Park, there lurks a large blockhouse where switchboard operators directed telephone communications to the Germans during the Second World War. Posters, tracts, memorabilia and letters in some of the rooms evoke the Resistance, the occupation of Calais and the 1940 aerial battle over London. The documents and the museum's simplicity make this a moving visit.

Notre Dame Church (**CDX**) – Construction of the church started at the end of the 13C, when the nave was built. The building was finished during the English occupation at the end of the 14C, which explains the surprising look of the tower, chancel and transept: despite being in France, they recall the English perpendicular Gothic style.

In 1691 Vauban had a large cistern built on the north side.

The marriage of Captain Charles de Gaulle with a young Calais woman was celebrated here in 1921.

*Travel with **Michelin Maps** (scale 1:200 000) which are revised regularly.*

CAMBRAI★

Population 33 092
Michelin map 53 fold 3, 4 or 236 fold 27

Cambrai stands in the centre of a rich cereal and sugar beet region, on the east bank of the River Escaut (or Scheldt). Traditionally cambric linen was made here, bleached in the sunny meadows then used to make up handkerchiefs and fine lingerie. In gourmet terms, Cambrai is known for its small sausages *(andouillettes)*, its tripe and its mint-flavoured sweets *(bêtises de Cambrai)*.

The town is built of white limestone and is overlooked by the belfry's three towers, the cathedral and St Gery's Church. Once military and archiepiscopal, Cambrai today looks peaceful, boulevards having taken the place of the ramparts.

The "Swan of Cambrai" – In 1695 François de Salignac de La Mothe-**Fénelon** (1651-1715), a great lord, man of the Church and famous writer, was invested as archbishop of Cambrai. Fénelon was venerated by his flock for his gentleness and charity, and learned while in Cambrai that Rome had condemned his *Maximes des Saints*; this work defended quietism, a doctrine made fashionable by Mme Guyon, which exalted the "Pure Love of God". In response the former tutor of the Duke of Burgundy first climbed into the pulpit to preach obedience to the Church's decision and then wrote a pastoral letter to the same effect, thus showing an admirable humility.

The charity of the "Swan of Cambrai" was often called upon during the Spanish War of Succession; starving peasants from the surrounding Cambrai region poured into the archdiocese, where Fénelon welcomed them. On one occasion a cow was lost on the way to the archbishop, who immediately set out on foot with a servant to find the animal; he found the cow and was able to return it to its poor owner. Fénelon died at Cambrai after a carriage accident.

OLD TOWN *1 1/2 hours*

Porte de Paris (Paris Gate) (**AZ**) – This town gate, a vestige of the medieval fortifications, is flanked by two round towers dating from 1390.

Follow Avenue de la Victoire towards the town hall, visible at the end of the street. Place du St-Sépulcre appears shortly on the left.

Cathédrale Notre-Dame (Cathedral of Our Lady) (**AZ**) ⊙ – Originally dedicated to St Sepulchre, the abbey church was elevated to a cathedral dedicated to the Virgin after the Revolution. It was built in the 18C and has been remodelled several times since; the tower dates from 1876. An 18C convent building stands to the right. The rounded chapels terminating the transept arms are decorated with *trompe-l'œil* **grisailles**, executed in 1760 by the Antwerp painter Martin Geeraerts. They represent the Virgin *(south)* and Christ *(north)*. Fénelon's tomb, sculpted by David d'Angers in 1826, is in the apsidal chapel: the prelate raises himself, turning heavenward in a Romantic burst of emotion; the hands are particularly fine.

Chapelle du Grand Séminaire (Seminary Chapel) (**AZ B**) – The chapel is set back from the square where Auricoste's statue of Fénelon was placed in 1947. It was completed in 1692 and formerly belonged to the Jesuit school; its lively and theatrical Baroque façade nevertheless retains a symmetry through the regular arrangement of windows, pilasters and its scrolled and flame decoration *(illustration p 29)*.

Among the richly carved decor, note the high-relief of the Assumption, which was added in the 19C during restoration.

Maison espagnole (Spanish House) (**AZ E**) – *Tourist Office*. This wooden house, its gables sheathed in slate, dates from the late 16C. The beams have been carved in great detail, with monsters below and *putti* above. Note the 17C and 18C private residences along Rue du Grand-Séminaire, Rue de l'Epée and Rue de Vaucelette.

Place Fénelon (**AY 16**) – The square is located on the site of the old cathedral, which was a splendid Gothic structure built by Villard de Honnecourt and demolished after the Revolution. The 17C entrance porch still remains from Fénelon's **archiepiscopal palace** (palais archiépiscopal).

St-Géry (St Gery's Church) (**AY**) ⊙ – Overlooked by a tower (76 m - 249ft tall), the old church of St Aubert's Abbey rises on the site once occupied by a temple dedicated to Jupiter Capitolinus. Construction of this sober Classical building lasted from 1698 to 1745. The ambitious plans called for a chancel with an ambulatory and radiating chapels, preceded by a monumental canopy resting on four colossal Baroque columns.

The beautiful **roodscreen** (1632), which formerly closed off the chancel entrance, was moved to the west end of the nave. It is a good example of the Baroque style with its contrasting red and black marble and its carved decoration by Gaspard Marsy, creating an impression of movement or even agitation: *putti* on the wing, alabaster statues and

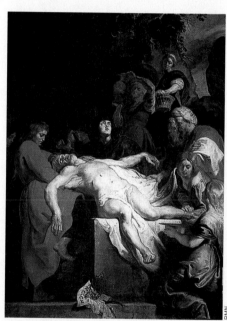

Entombment by Rubens, St Gery's Church

high-reliefs relating the miracles of Christ. The monumental pulpit, installed in 1850, was the work of Cambrai craftsmen. The chancel contains 18C furniture: altar and, in particular, the wood panels with medallions depicting the lives of St Augustine and St Aubert.

The north transept houses Rubens' enormous dramatic painting, **The Entombment★★**. The 14C painted **statue** in the right transept was discovered in 1982 during excavations in the crypt and represents a bishop.

Cross Place du 9 Octobre to reach Place Aristide Briand.

Place Aristide-Briand (**AYZ 6**) – The square was entirely rebuilt after the First World War and is dominated by the cold and majestic lines of the **town hall** (hôtel de ville) (**H**) which was rebuilt at the end of the 19C but was set ablaze during the First World War. Its reconstruction in the 1920s, together with that of the square itself, respected the old façade and its Louis XVI peristyle; this was largely due to the commitment of the Parisian architect, Antoine. The hall is surmounted by a colum-

CAMBRAI

B Chapelle du Grand Séminaire	**H** Hôtel de ville	**M** Musée municipal
E Maison espagnole	**K** Beffroi	**R** Château de Selles

ned belltower, flanked by the town's two Jacks o' the clock, Martin and Martine. According to legend these two individuals, who appear in parades as giants, were 14C blacksmiths who dealt with the lord ravaging the region by felling him with hammer blows. The bronze figures (2m - 6 1/2ft tall), dressed as turbanned Moors, date from 1512; they strike the town bell with their hammers to sound the hour.
The southwest corner of the square marks the beginning of a long avenue, Mail St-Martin, which offers a good view of the 15C-18C **belfry** (beffroi) (**AZ K**) (70m - 230ft tall), which is all that remains of St Martin's Church.

ADDITIONAL SIGHTS

Musée municipal (Municipal Museum) (AZ M) ⊙ – The museum is housed temporarily in the Falleur building, at no 39 Rue St-Georges, while restoration work on the 18C building in Rue de l'Épée is being completed.
The museum consists of archeological collections and rich sculptures, the remains of destroyed Cambrai monuments: 12C statue columns from St-Géry au Mont des Bœufs; a group of late-16C and early-17C alabasters from the old cathedral together with the 15C tomb of Pierre d'Ailly and J-B Lemoyne's bust of Fénelon (18C). A painting by Van der Meulen recalls the siege of Cambrai by Louis XIV in 1677.
Numerous Flemish paintings are on display (*Still Life* by Fyt, *The Card-Players* by T Rombouts, a church interior by Steenwyck) as well as several from the Dutch School (still-lifes by David de Heem and Van der Ast, a portrait of a man by Mierevelt).

Jacques de Lajoue's *Astronomy*, Roland de la Porte's *Still Life* and P-A Wille's *The Beloved Wife's Last Moments* all represent the French School in the 18C; works by Ingres, Chasseriau, Boudin, Marquet and Utrillo show 19C and 20C developments. Sculptures by Carpeaux, Rodin, Bourdelle and Camille Claudel are also exhibited.

Jardin public (Park) (BZ) – The park was laid out in the late 19C when the ramparts were destroyed, on the old military grounds alongside the 16C-17C **citadel** (citadelle) built by Charles V of Spain and later enlarged by Vauban. Only the principal gate and a barrack remain, while the countermine galleries lie underground.

Porte Notre-Dame (Our Lady's Gate) (BY) – This piece of the old fortifications was built at the beginning of the 17C; it owes its name to the statue of the Virgin which adorns the outer face. The gate is unusual for its diamond-shaped stones and its grooved columns. The sun representing Louis XIV was added to the pediment after the town was captured from the Spanish by France.

Château de Selles (AY R) ⊙ – This castle dates back to the 13C; its construction was attributed to Nicolas de Fontaine, bishop of Cambrai. It allowed the owner to keep watch on the artisans' quarter and the windmills belonging to the bishop. The five projecting corners were reinforced by round towers; each originally had three storeys with ogival vaulting. The castle is unusual in having a corridor ("gaine") running all the way around inside the walls, connecting the towers. This corridor, which was used as a prison in the 16C, is covered with period graffiti.

CASSEL ★

Population 2 177
Michelin map 51 fold 4 or 236 fold 4

Cassel is a small town that is Flemish in both its customs and appearance: an enormous cobbled main square (Grande Place), narrow, winding street and low whitewashed houses. It stands on a **site★** at the top of Cassel Hill, the green slopes of which, formerly dotted with windmills, overlook the flat Flanders region.
Local traditions are still celebrated: the religious fête *(ducasse)* with its Mass, parades, traditional games and competitions; archery; the carnival; the procession of the Reuze giants *(illustration see Folklore)*. Two regional specialities may be sampled here: Cassel butter and cheese from Cats Hill (Mont des Cats).

"Cassel Hill" – The highest point of the region (176m - 577ft high) and a link in the Flemish hill-range, it is surprisingly large rising in the middle of the Flemish plain: although about 30km - 18 miles from the coast, it is used as a beacon by sailors. Its peak is made up of a very hard ferruginous layer. To the east, **Recollect Hill** (Mont des Récollets) (159m - 521ft high) owes its name to a convent of Recollect nuns which existed there from 1615 to 1870.

Two World Wars – From October 1914 to June 1915 **General Foch** had his headquarters at Cassel. From here he followed the progress of the battle of Flanders which was raging in Yser. He stayed at the Hôtel de Schoebecque at no 32 of what is now Rue du Maréchal Foch. In May 1940 members of a British expeditionary corps retreating towards Yser and Dunkirk fought a fierce rearguard action at Cassel, which resulted in 2 000 dead and 1 000 prisoners on the battlefield.

SIGHTS *1 hour*

Public Gardens – The gardens at the top of the hill occupy the site of a medieval castle which once incorporated a collegiate church, the crypt of which remains. An equestrian statue of General Foch stands in the garden's centre, together with an 18C wooden **windmill** ⊙ from Arneke which was re-erected here to replace the castle's original windmill.
A tour of the terrace offers an excellent **panorama★★** *(viewing platforms)* over the picturesque jumble of Cassel's old rooftops, and beyond to the hills of Flanders and the plain, as far as the North Sea and the belfry of Bruges: a local saying maintains that "From Cassel you can see five kingdoms: France, Belgium, Holland, England and, above the clouds, the Kingdom of Heaven".

Grande Place (Main Square) – The square, irregularly shaped and cobbled, extends along the slope of the hill near the church. It retains an attractive group of 16C, 17C and 18C houses on its south side, among them the Hôtel de la Noble Cour.

Hôtel de la Noble Cour – Under the Ancien Régime this 16C-17C house was the seat of the court in which the local lord dispensed justice. A high roof dotted with dormer windows crowns the façade, which is entirely of stone – unusual in the North – pierced by large windows with alternately triangular and curvilinear pediments; the elegant Renaissance doorway, flanked by grey marble columns, is decorated with Fames in the spandrels and with Sirens and foliate scrolls on the frieze.
The **museum** (musée municipal) ⊙ contains through to the Archive Room with its Louis XV woodwork, the Grande Salle (Flemish furniture and 17C and 18C objects), the Court Room (collection of faiences and Northern porcelain), the Salon de la Châtellenie (Louis XV woodwork, Louis XVI furniture), and Foch's desk, preserved as it was in 1915. The ground floor houses reconstructions of a Flemish interior and a bar.

Collégiale Notre-Dame (Collegiate Church of Our Lady) ⊘ – This is a Gothic Flemish church with three gables, three aisles, three apses and a square tower over the transept crossing. Foch often came here to pray and meditate.

Ancienne chapelle des Jésuites (Old Jesuit Chapel) – Pleasing 17C brick and stone façade.

EXCURSIONS

Steenvoorde – *8km - 5 miles east by D 948*. This typical small Flemish town with painted houses under red tiled roofs was once famous for its sheets; today it is the home of one of the most important dairies in the area.

The town celebrates the legend of its giant, Yan den Houtkapper: he was a woodcutter who made a pair of everlasting boots for Charlemagne; in return he was given a suit of armour, which he always wears for the processions in which he is the hero.

Windmills ⊘ – Three well-preserved windmills can be seen near the town. The first, the Steenmeulen at Terdeghem *(on D 947 south – illustration under Architecture)*, is a truncated brick mill; the other two, the Drievemeulen *(private) (on D 948 west)* and the Noordmeulen *(on D 18 northwest)*, are wooden windmills on pivots.

Wormhout – *10km - 6 miles north via D 218 and D 916*.

La Briarde Windmill ⊘ – This wooden post mill is the last of 11 windmills which stood in the region in 1780.

Jeanne Devos Museum ⊘ – This charming Flemish house, flanked by a dovecote and set within lovely gardens, is the old Wormhout presbytery (18C). It was inhabited by Jeanne Devos who collected, until her death in 1989, a multitude of objects from daily life.

A photographer by profession, she left thousands of photographs portraying the ordinary and extraordinary lives of the villagers nearby.

CHAALIS ABBEY★

Michelin map 106 fold 9

The estate lies on the edge of Ermenonville Forest and, until the 19C, it evoked the gentle, romantic charm suggested by religious contemplation. Later, and up to 1912, Chaâlis inspired its last owners to collect works of art and to entertain some of the most notable personalities of their time.

A prosperous abbey – Chaâlis was a Cistercian *(qv)* abbey, built on the site of a former priory in 1136 by Louis the Fat. The monks led a modest country life, husbanding the land, cultivating vines, keeping bees and fishing in the lakes. St Louis paid frequent visits to the abbey: he took part in the monks' prayers and duties, even waited on them, cared for the sick and watched over the dying.

Decline – During the 16C the abbey was held *in commendam* and the abbots were appointed by the king.

The first was Cardinal Ippolito d'Este, son of Alfonso d'Este and Lucrezia Borgia, a distant cousin of François I (the Cardinal's brother, Ercole II d'Este, married Renée of France, the second daughter of Louis XII). Better known as Cardinal of Ferrara, this enthusiastic art lover had his private chapel decorated with murals and commissioned fine gardens but he nevertheless preferred his Tivoli residence, the Villa d'Este, where he died in 1572.

Chaâlis Abbey

In the 18C the ninth abbot, one of the Great Condé's grandsons, attempted a costly operation to restore the abbey to plans by Jean Aubert, the architect who designed the Hôtel Biron in Paris and the Great Stables at Chantilly. It was a disaster: after only one side of the building had been completed (1739, currently the Château-Museum) work stopped owing to lack of funds. This financial crisis prompted Louis XVI to close down the abbey in 1785.

During the upheaval of the French Revolution, Chaâlis was badly pillaged and the greater part of the building destroyed.

Restoration – The estate frequently changed hands. Romantic painters and poets appreciated the melancholy charm of the old walls and their lush, verdant setting. In 1850 the highly distinguished Mme de Vatry bought the abbey ruins: she converted the 18C building into a château, had the park refurbished and entertained lavishly.

These efforts were continued by Mme de Vatry's heirs and by the last owner, Mme Jacquemart-André, who founded the Paris museum which bears her name. She died in 1912 and bequeathed the estate to the Institute of France. Its first curator was the art critic Louis Gillet (1876-1943); his successor, the Art Historian Émile Mâle, died here in 1954.

★FORMER ABBEY *1 hour*

★**Church Ruins** – Ready for consecration in 1219, Chaâlis Abbey was the first Cistercian church built in the Gothic style. Of the original buildings there remain a staircase turret, the northern transept arm surrounded by radiating chapels – an unusual feature – and a section of wall from the north aisle with blind arcades.

Chapelle de l'abbé (Abbot's Chapel) – Built around 1250, the chapel is a fine example of Gothic splendour from the time of the Sainte-Chapelle in Paris. On the right, a bronze bust portraying Mme Jacquemart-André marks the site of her grave. Beyond the chapel a strange 16C crenellated wall with asymmetrical merlons *(qv)* sets the boundaries of the rose garden. Above the heavy archway the coat of arms of Cardinal Louis d'Este, nephew of Cardinal of Ferrara, is displayed. From north of the château there is a fine perspective of the park with its flower beds and dazzling lake, restored in the 19C.

Château-Musée (Château-Museum) ⓥ – The typical **Monks' Room** (Salle des Moines) houses miscellaneous 15C and Gothic furniture, miniatures, two panels painted by Giotto (St John the Evangelist and St Lawrence), works of art (mainly Italian), religious figures (14C-16C French), ceramics, stained-glass windows etc. The fireback bears the letter K, symbolising the coat of arms of the abbey.

The first-floor gallery opens onto a reference room (detailed plans of the abbey), the **Jean-Jacques Rousseau Chamber** (this collection on the French philosopher was donated to the Institute of France by the last Marquis de Girardin in 1923) and the **private apartments of Mme André:** silvered leather double doors lead to the Eagles' Room decorated in Empire style, and past a pair of imposing columns into the bedroom (huge giltwood canopied bed dating from the Louis XV period). The water-green bathroom and the boudoir, with its tapestry after a design by Boucher, lie beyond.

EXCURSION

Ermenonville – *2km - 1 mile south on N 330.* In May 1778 Jean-Jacques Rousseau was invited to stay at Ermenonville Château *(private)* by the Marquis de Girardin, who had acquired the estate in 1763, and it is here that Rousseau rekindled his passion for nature: he walked, daydreamed in the park and taught music to his host's children, until his sudden death on 2 July from a stroke.

The **park★**, which the marquess had transformed from sandy, swampy land into a superb landscaped garden in the French style with shaded paths, graceful vistas, elegant rockeries and charming brooks, still contains some strategically-sited monuments.

Mer de Sable ⓥ – *0.5km - 1/4 mile south on N 330.* The sand deposits date from the Tertiary Era and at the end of the Ice Age this region was probably one vast sandy moor covered with wild heather.

The landscape has been developed into themed areas evoking China, the Wild West or Morocco through characteristic scenery. Various scenes – of Indians attacking trains, scuffling by a ranch, or displays of horsemanship – animate the different areas. The small train tour of the desert and the shows are complemented by various thrilling attractions (white-water rides, head-first slides etc) and more peaceful games.

Ermenonville Forest – After 1840 the clearings in the vast heather-covered moor were planted with maritime and Scots pines, and country lanes have now been marked out as suitable for walks. Cars are not allowed on the forest roads except along the Long Road leading to the crossroads and on the section linking Baraque de Chaâlis to the commemorative monument marking the crash of the Turkish Airlines DC 10 on 3 March 1974, in which 346 people died.

The southwest of the forest, which enchanted Corot, is not accessible though the road from Mortefontaine to Thiers offers views of the lake and the wilder landscape.

CHAMPS CHÂTEAU ★

Michelin map 101 fold 19 or 106 fold 21 – Michelin plan 20

Champs, built with the funds of two unfortunate financiers at the end of Louis XIV's reign, is characteristic of 18C architecture and decoration. In 1934 the last owner M Cahen d'Anvers offered his residence to the State.

TOUR *about 1 1/2 hours*

★★**Park** ⊙ – The park is a masterpiece of French gardening. Originally created by Claude Desgots, one of Le Nôtre's nephews, it was redesigned by Duchêne in the early 20C according to a plan drawn up in the early 18C, featuring a sweeping perspective of the formal French gardens with elaborate boxwood patterns, fountains and groves.

★**Château** ⊙ – When the construction of Champs was completed by J-B Bullet in 1708, his contemporaries were struck by the many changes made in the name of comfort. The rooms no longer communicated, the corridors were improved, each bedroom had its own closet and boudoir and a proper dining room was designed (until then the tables were laid in an antechamber). Mezzanines connecting with the ground floor by means of hidden staircases were built at the end of each wing: they provided accommodation for the guests' domestics.

On the ground floor, visitors are shown round the great salon, the dining room and the smoking room, with its portrait of Louis XV by a representative of the Van Loo School. The **Chinese Salon**★★ (Salon Chinois) is decorated with ornamental panels painted by Huet. The armchairs are upholstered with Beauvais tapestry depicting scenes from the *Fables* of La Fontaine: one of the collections executed after the cartoons of Oudry, director of the National Tapestry Works at Beauvais *(qv)*.

The Boudoir is tastefully decorated with attractive pastoral scenes in monochrome blue.

On the first floor, the Music Room offers a superb view of the park. Mme de Pompadour's Bedroom may be visited – the marquise rented the château in 1757 – and the corner drawing room, embellished by superb rococo **wainscoting**★ and a portrait by Drouais of Mme de Pompadour.

The CHANNEL TUNNEL

Michelin map 51 folds 1, 2 or 236 fold 2

Men have schemed since the mid 18C to create a permanent link between Britain and mainland Europe, as there had been in the prehistoric era. By the late 20C the technology existed to exploit the layer of impermeable chalk beneath the English Channel. The Channel Tunnel was inaugurated on 6 May 1994.

History – Over 242 years there have been 27 proposals, the oldest of which was made in 1751 by a M Desmarets, who wanted to rejoin Britain to the mainland by a bridge, a tunnel or a causeway. In 1802 a serious project was presented by Albert Mathieu, a mining engineer, although it was actually Aimé Thomé de Gamond who became known as the father of the tunnel, thirty-two years later, when he put forward several different solutions *(see the **National Museum of Channel Crossing** at Cap Blanc-Nez, qv)*. In 1880 an attempt was made at Sangatte to bore a hole, which was named the Well of the Ancients (puits des Anciens). 1840m - 6 036ft were dug on the French side and 2 000m - 6 561ft on the British before the project was abandoned. Almost a century later, in 1971, the French and British governments signed an agreement on a tunnel and work began but the project was aborted within a couple of years.

Finally in September 1980, during the Franco-British Summit, the project for the construction of a tunnel was relaunched by the British Prime Minister Margaret Thatcher and the French President François Mitterand. In October 1985, following an international competition, four proposals were selected and on 20 January 1986 the Eurotunnel project was chosen. A Franco-British treaty concerning its construction was signed in Canterbury, England, on 12 February 1986.

Facts and figures – The Channel link consists of two single-track rail tunnels (7.60m - 24ft in diameter) for passenger and freight transport, and one service tunnel (4.80m - 15ft in diameter) for safety and ventilation. The tunnels are 50.5km - 31 miles long 37km - 23 miles of which are under the Channel, 3.7km - 2 miles under French soil (beginning at Sangatte) and 9.8km - 6 miles under English soil (beginning at Folkestone). Most of the tunnel is 40m - 131ft under the sea-bed, in a layer of blue chalk. The 5 boring machines in France and 6 in England tunnelled an average 800m to 1 000m - 2 624ft to 3 280ft into the rock each month. These enormous machines have been tunnelled into a siding under the Channel where they will be left indefinitely.

LE SHUTTLE

The train service running between France and Britain is called Le Shuttle. The passenger "carriages" are 775m - 2 542ft long and include two levels for cars and one for coaches and caravans; there are separate carriages for heavy goods vehicles. Le Shuttle operates 24 hours a day throughout the year. The frequency of departures depends on the volume of traffic (2-4 trains per hour during the day, hourly at night). The trip takes 35 min, 28 of which are in the tunnel.

THE TERMINAL

The terminal is located at Coquelles, 3km - 2 miles from the coast. It covers 700ha - 1 729 acres.

Information Centre ⓘ – *Access from junction 12*. This bold piece of architecture sits next to the terminal itself. Inside, a diorama traces the history of the Channel Tunnel, a video follows the construction of the tunnel and the working of the transportation system, and an audio-visual laser projection reveals another view of the link with Great Britain. From the tower (15m - 50ft), there is a panoramic view over the terminal and the town of Calais.

CHANTILLY CHÂTEAU★★★

Michelin map 106 fold 8 or 56 fold 11.

The name Chantilly brings to mind a château, a forest, a racecourse and the world of horse racing in general. Because of its remarkable setting, its park and the treasures in its museum, Chantilly Château is considered one of the major sights in France.
Chantilly is also rapidly becoming an important cultural centre thanks to the activities of the Centre des Fontaines with its library boasting 600 000 titles (philosophy, art, religion etc).

HISTORICAL NOTES

From Cantilius to the Montmorency – Over the past 2 000 years, five castles have occupied this part of the Nonette Valley.
Above the ponds and marshes of the area rose a rocky island where Cantilius, a native of Roman Gaul, built the first fortified dwelling. His name and achievement gave birth to Chantilly. In the Middle Ages the building became a fortress belonging to the Bouteiller, named after the hereditary duties he carried out at the court of the Capetians: originally in charge of the royal cellars, the Bouteiller de France was one of the king's close advisers.
In 1386 the land was bought by the chancellor of Orgemont, who had the castle rebuilt. The feudal foundations bore the three subsequent constructions. In 1450 the last descendant of the Orgemont married one of the Barons of Montmorency and Chantilly became the property of this illustrious family. It remained in their possession for 200 years.

Constable Anne, duc de Montmorency – Anne de Montmorency (1492-1567) was a devoted servant to a succession of six French kings from Louis XII to Charles IX. This formidable character gained a reputation as warrior, statesman, diplomat and art enthusiast. For forty years, apart from a few brief periods, he remained the leading noble of the land, second to the king. Childhood friend and companion-in-arms to François I, close adviser to Henri II, he even had some influence over Catherine de' Medici, who looked favourably upon the man who had advised her on cures for her infertility.
Constable Anne owned 600 fiefs, over 130 castles and estates, 4 mansions in Paris and numerous posts and offices. He was immensely wealthy. When he went to court he was escorted by 300 guards on horseback. Through his five sons and the husbands of his seven daughters he controlled most of the country's highest duties and had connections with Henri II, as well as with a number of other distinguished French families.

View of Chantilly by the 17C French School (c 1680)

Chantilly Château

In 1528 the feudal castle of the Orgemont was demolished and the architect Pierre Chambiges replaced it with a palace built in the French Renaissance style. On a nearby island Jean Bullant erected the charming château which still stands today: the Little Castle (Petit Château). It was separated from the Great Castle (Grand Château) by a moat – now filled in – which was spanned by two superimposed bridges. An aviary was set up in the tiny garden on the island. Constable Anne ordered great loads of earth and built the terrace which bears his statue. Plans were made for new gardens and the best artists in town were hired to decorate the two palaces. Chantilly had become one of the most celebrated sights of France and even Charles V expressed his admiration when he was shown round the estate.

In 1567 Montmorency, aged 75, engaged in hostilities against the Protestants and perished in the Battle of St-Denis. It was no easy task to kill this energetic soldier: five strokes of the sword cut his face to ribbons, two blows of the bludgeon smashed his head and an arquebus caused his spine to snap. Before collapsing, Constable Anne broke his opponent's jaw with the pommel of his sword.

The last love of Henri IV – Henri IV often stayed at Chantilly, with his companion-in-arms Henri I de Montmorency, the son of Constable Anne. At the age of 54 the king fell in love with his host's ravishing daughter Charlotte, aged only 15. He arranged for her to marry Henri II de Bourbon-Condé, a shy and gauche young man, whom the king hoped would prove an accommodating husband. The day after the wedding, however, Condé left the capital with his wife. Henri IV ordered them to return to Paris.

The young couple fled to Brussels, where they stayed under the protection of the king of Spain. Henri IV raged, implored, threatened and even went as far as to ask the Pope to intervene, but he was murdered by Ravaillac. Only then did the two fugitives return to France.

Sylvie and her poets – Henri II de Montmorency, the godson of Henri IV and the most brilliant and extravagant knight at court, married Marie-Félicie Orsini, god-daughter to Marie de' Medici. A charming, generous and highly-educated young woman, she was a close friend of the poets Mairet and Théophile de Viau. The latter – to whom she extended her protection when he was pursued by the Parlement de Paris – addressed her as Sylvie. The name remained associated with the pavilion built for Henri IV in 1604, a retreat where Marie-Félicie spent many enjoyable hours. Encouraged by Louis XIII's brother, the scheming Gaston d'Orléans, Henri de Montmorency plotted against Richelieu. He was defeated at Castelnaudary near Toulouse and made a prisoner after receiving eighteen wounds, including five by bullets. The last of the Montmorency was beheaded in Toulouse in 1632. By way of an apology, Henri II de Montmorency bequeathed to Cardinal Richelieu the two *Slave* statues by Michelangelo, now in the Louvre; those at Chantilly and Écouen are replicas. Beside herself with grief, Marie-Félicie withdrew to the Visitation convent in Moulins and remained there until her death.

The Great Condé – Charlotte de Montmorency and her husband the Prince of Condé – the couple persecuted by Henri IV – inherited Chantilly in 1643 and the château remained family property until 1830. Descendants of Charles de Bourbon, like Henri IV, the Princes of Condé were of royal blood and the heir apparent to the throne was called the Duke of Enghien. The Great Condé was the son of Charlotte and Henri II. He applied himself to renovating Chantilly Château with the same energy and efficiency he had shown in military operations. In 1662 he commissioned Le Nôtre to redesign the park and the forest. The fountains at Chantilly were considered the most elegant in France and Louis XIV made a point of outclassing them in Versailles. The work lasted twenty years and the result was a splendid achievement, part of which still stands today.

All the great writers of the 17C stayed at Chantilly including Bossuet, Fénelon, Bourdaloue, Boileau, Racine, La Fontaine, Mme de la Fayette, Mme de Sévigné, La Bruyère (who was tutor to the prince's grandson) and Molière, to whom Condé granted permission to perform *Tartuffe*.

The last of the Condé – The Prince of Condé died in Fontainebleau in 1686, to the king's great dismay. During the religious ceremony preceding the burial, Bossuet delivered a funeral oration which became famous.

The great-grandson of the Great Condé, Louis-Henri de Bourbon, alias "Monsieur le Duc", was an artist with a taste for splendour, who gave Chantilly a new lease of life. He asked Jean Aubert to build the Great Stables (Grandes Écuries), a masterpiece of the 18C, and set up a porcelain factory which closed down in 1870.

The Château d'Enghien was built on the estate by Louis-Joseph de Condé in 1769. His grandson the Duke of Enghien, who had just been born, was its first occupant.

The father of the newly-born baby was 16, his grandfather 36. The young prince died tragically in 1804: he was seized by the French police in the Duchy of Baden and shot outside the fortress of Vincennes on the orders of Bonaparte. During the French Revolution the main building was razed to the ground though the smaller château was spared. Louis-Joseph was 78 when he returned from exile. His son accompanied him back to Chantilly and the two of them were dismayed: their beloved château was in ruins and the park was in a shambles. They decided to renovate the estate. They bought back the plots of their former land, restored the Little Château, redesigned and refurbished the grounds. The prince died in 1818 but the duke continued the work. He was an enthusiastic hunter and at the age of 70 he hunted daily. Thanks to his efforts, Chantilly became the lively, fashionable place it had been in the years preceding the Revolution. As in former times, the receptions and hunting parties attracted crowds of elegant visitors. The renovation and restoration work was a source of income for the local population. The duke was worried by the Revolution of 1830, which raised his cousin Louis-Philippe to the throne, and considered returning to England. A few days later, he was found hanging from a window at his castle in St-Leu. He was the last descendant of the Condé.

The Duke of Aumale – The Duke of Bourbon had left Chantilly to his great-nephew and godson the Duke of Aumale, the fifth son of Louis-Philippe. This prince gained recognition in Africa when he captured Abd el-Kader and his numerous relations. The Revolution of 1848 forced him to go into exile and he returned only in 1870; in 1873 he presided over the court martial which sentenced Marshal Bazaine.

From 1875 to 1881 the duke commissioned Daumet to build the Grand Château in the Renaissance style. This castle, the fifth, still stands today. Back in exile between 1883 and 1889, he died in 1897 and the Institute of France inherited his estate at Chantilly, together with the superb collections that constitute the Condé Museum.

The first races – The first official race meeting was held in Chantilly on 15 May 1834 at the instigation of the members of the Société d'Encouragement, an association founded in 1833. The patronage of both the Duke of Orléans and the Duke of Nemours, and the fashionable trends introduced by the Jockey Club dandies, appreciative of the soft lawns, combined to make these races a major social event (*Prix du Jockey-Club* in 1836, *Prix de Diane* in 1843); before the opening of Longchamp in 1857, Parisian races used to be run on the hard ground of the Champ-de-Mars. The hunting parties, concerts, firework displays and aquatic entertainments at Chantilly delighted racegoers and socialites.

By the end of the 19C the races had attracted huge crowds of visitors and the Northern France Railways set up a transport system whose efficiency has never been matched. In 1908 it became necessary to introduce 40 to 50 special trains composed of 16 carriages. On a rare occasion, regulations were seriously infringed when a group of trains taking passengers back to Paris (leaving every three minutes) were running on the wrong side of the track between Chantilly and St-Denis.

The riding capital – With a total of over 3 000 horses trained on the tracks in and around Chantilly, the city of the Condé may be considered the capital of French thoroughbreds. Jobs for 1 000 stable-lads and a number of related occupations employ 10 % of the farming population of the Oise *département*. Each stable-lad rides three horses every morning.

The racecourses – *Private*. 100 trainers attend to their respective charges from sunrise to noon, either on the sandy or grassy tracks of the four courses, or along the sand-covered paths of the forest (in particular the constable's road, also known as Lions' Way or Piste des Lions). Numerous race meetings take place during the racing season in June.

ACCESS

Several roads lead to the château. From Chapelle-en-Serval, crossing Chantilly Forest, the château suddenly rises into view from Lions' Crossroad (carrefour des Lions); it appears to be floating on the water in a superb setting of rocks, ponds and stately trees. From Paris, take N 16; do not drive through the town but turn right after the lower road and into the shady Route de l'Aigle which skirts the racecourse. The road from Senlis through Vineuil offers a good view of the château and its park; leaving Vineuil, turn left at each junction.

THE CHATEAU

Try to picture Chantilly Château at the time of the Condé *(illustration see above)* when the two main buildings were still divided by an arm of water: the 16C Petit Château (also called Châtelet) and the Grand Château, for which Daumet used the foundations of the former stronghold.

Cross the constable's terrace, which bears the equestrian statue of Anne de Montmorency, and enter the main courtyard through the main gateway, flanked by the two copies of Michelangelo's *Slaves*.

★★MUSÉE (MUSEUM) ⊙

The museum contains a superb collection which according to Raoul de Broglie, former curator, would be impossible to put together today, even with unlimited purchasing power. The layout of the museum may surprise visitors. Unlike contemporary collections, the works of art are not classified according to their period or their artist. Italian and Flemish Primitive paintings are found next to 19C works, and illuminated manuscripts side by side with oil paintings. This was due to works being hung chronologically as they were acquired, though favourite works were sometimes placed in a separate room.

From 1852 onwards the Duke of Aumale, then in exile, turned collector and amassed his collection (the Standish library, paintings from the Dukes of Sutherland and Northwick) with a view to embellishing his future residence, emptied at the Revolution. He was more interested in compiling an impressive collection than in founding an educational museum, and the curators have respected this layout.

According to the terms of the duke's legacy, the Institute must agree "to make no changes to the interior and exterior architecture of the château". Moreover, it is not allowed to lend any of the exhibits.

The reception hall is the starting point for guided tours of the Chapel and the various apartments – if a group has already formed, it is best to join it – as well as for unaccompanied tours of the collections. It is advisable to interrupt a visit to the collections if the custodians announce a guided tour of the apartments.

★**Appartements des Princes (Princes' Suite)** ⊙ – Situated in the Little Castle, this suite, occupied by the Great Condé and his descendants, was embellished with Regency and rococo **wainscoting★★**, especially in the 18C thanks to the Duke of Bourbon. It was not occupied by the Duke of Aumale who had taken up residence on the ground floor. The antechamber and part of the library, the work of the Duke of Aumale, are located on the site of the old moat.

Library (Cabinet des Livres) (**1**) – It contains a splendid collection of manuscripts, including **The Rich Hours of the Duke of Berry** *(Les Très Riches Heures du duc de Berry)* with 15C illuminations by the Limbourg brothers.

This extremely fragile document is not permanently exhibited but visitors may see a facsimile by Faksimile Verlag of Luzern. Another interesting reproduction is Gutenberg's Bible, formerly the property of Cardinal Mazarin.

Among the ornamental motifs feature the monogram of the Duke of Aumale (H O for Henri d'Orléans) and the Condé coat of arms (France's "broken" coat of arms with a diagonal line symbolising the younger branch of the family).

Prince's Chamber (Chambre de Monsieur le Prince) (**2**) – This title referred to the Condé Prince who was on the throne, in this case the Duke of Bourbon (1692-1740), who had wainscoting installed at the far end of the room, into which were embedded panels painted by C Huet in 1735.

The famous Louis XVI commode was designed by Riesener and made by Hervieu.

Monkey Room (Salon des Singes) (**3**) – A collection of Monkey Scenes *(Singeries)* dating from the early 18C is a masterpiece by an anonymous draughtsman; note the fire screen: the Monkey's reading lesson.

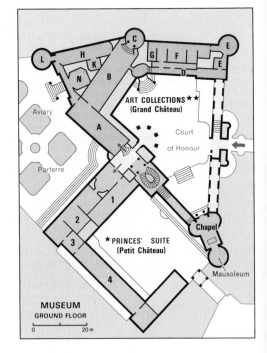

MUSEUM
GROUND FLOOR
0   20 m

Prince's Gallery (Galerie de Monsieur le Prince) (**4**) – The Great Condé had ordered his own battle gallery, which he never saw completed (1692). The sequence was interrupted from 1652 to 1659 during his years of rebellion. A painting conceived by the hero's son portrays him stopping a Fame from publishing a list of his treacherous deeds and asking another Fame to issue a formal apology.

Chapelle (Chapel) – An **altar**★ attributed to Jean Goujon and 16C wainscoting and stained-glass windows from the Chapel at Écouen were brought here by the Duke of Aumale. The apse contains the **mausoleum** of Henri II de Condé *(see above)* (bronze statues by J Sarrazin taken from the Jesuit Church St-Paul-St-Louis in Paris) and the stone urn which received the hearts of the Condé. Up to the Revolution, the Condé necropolis was at Vallery in Burgundy, where another sepulchral monument celebrating Henri II still stands.

★★**Grand Château (Art Collections)** – Cross the **Deer Gallery** (Galerie des Cerfs) (**A**), a reception area furnished for the Duke of Aumale.

Painting Gallery (Galerie de Peinture) (**B**) – It offers a medley characteristic of 19C work: Poussin *(The Massacre of the Innocents)*, Corot *(A Pastoral Concert)*, Fromentin *(Hawking)*, along with De Troy's *Oyster Lunch* and Lancret's *Ham Lunch*, formerly at Versailles, in the dining room of Louis XV's private apartments... In addition note the portraits of Mazarin and Richelieu by Philippe de Champaigne.

Rotunda (Rotonde) (**C**) – The *Loreto Madonna* by **Raphael**, **Piero di Cosimo's** portrait of the ravishing Simonetta Vespucci, who is believed to have been Botticelli's model for his *Birth of Venus*, and Chapu's kneeling statue of Joan of Arc listening to voices are exhibited here.

Logis Gallery (Galerie du Logis) (**D**) – Minor portraits painted in the French style of the 16C and 17C (Biencourt bequest) include Constable Anne, Henri II and Charles IX.

Smalah Hall and Minerva Rotunda (Salle de la Smalah et Rotonde de la Minerve) (**E**) – Family portraits of the Orléans (17C, 18C and 19C) and of Louis-Philippe's relations in particular: Bonnat's picture of the Duke of Aumale at the age of 68.

Orléans Chamber (Salle d'Orléans) (**F**) – The glass cabinets contain **soft-paste Chantilly porcelain** manufactured in the workshops founded in 1725 (armorial service bearing the Condé coat of arms or the Duke of Orléans' monogram).

Clouet Collection (Cabinet des Clouet) (**G**) – A precious collection of small and extremely rare paintings executed by the Clouets, Corneille de Lyon etc, portraying François I, Marguerite of Navarre (stroking a little dog), Henri II as a child etc.

Psyche Gallery (Galerie de Psyché) (**H**) – The 44 **stained-glass windows** (16C) that tell the story of the loves of Psyche and Cupid came from Constable Anne's other family home, Écouen Château. Opposite are the **Clouet drawings**★★, exhibited in rotation as the museum possesses a total of 363 portraits.

★★★**Sanctuary** (Santuario) (**K**) – It houses the museum's most precious exhibits: Raphael's *Orléans Madonna*, named after the noble family, *The Three Ages of Womanhood*, also known as *The Three Graces*, by the same artist; *Esther and Ahasuerus*, the panel of a wedding chest painted by Filippino Lippi and forty miniature works by Jean Fouquet, cut out of Estienne Chevalier's book of hours, a splendid example of French 15C art.

Jewel Room (Cabinet des Gemmes) (**L**) – It contains jewels of stunning beauty. The Pink Diamond (Diamant Rose), alias the Great Condé (a copy of which is permanently on show) was stolen in 1926 and subsequently found in an apple where the thieves has hidden it. The room also boasts an outstanding collection of enamels and miniatures.

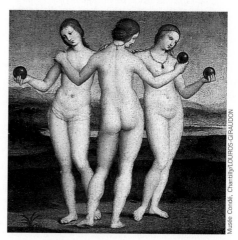

Musée Condé, Chantilly/LOUROS-GIRAUDON

The Three Graces by Raphael, Chantilly

Gallery (Tribune) (**N**) – Above the cornice of this polygonal room are painted panels representing family homes and other buildings (Aumale, Palais-Royal, Écouen, Guise, Villers-Cotterêts and Twickenham) connected with the Duke of Aumale and the house of Orléans.
The paintings include *Autumn* by **Botticelli**, *Love Disarmed* and *Pastoral Pleasures* by **Watteau**, a portrait of Molière by **Mignard**, and on the "Ecouen Wall", three superb works by **Ingres**: a self-portrait, *Madame Devaucay* and *Venus*. Amidst the portraits note Philippe de Champaigne's *Angelique Arnauld*, Abbess of Port-Royal *(qv)*.

Château d'Enghien – *Climb the ramp.* The 18C château is set back to the right; access to it is limited to the curators whom the Institute chooses from among its own members.

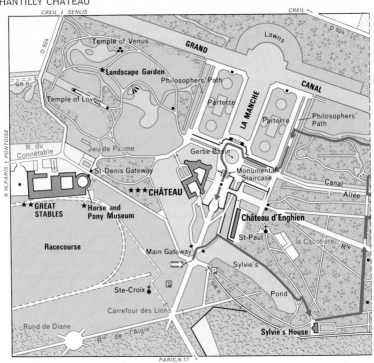

★★PARK ⓣ *about 1 hour*

Follow the route indicated on the plan and walk past Sylvie's Pond.

Maison de Sylvie (Sylvie's House) – *(Private)* This is a small garden pavilion where Marie-Félicie enjoyed meeting her close friends, surrounded by pleasant grounds. The Duke of Aumale added on a rotunda and decorated it with Louis XV panelling of hunting scenes which he had brought back from his retreat in Dreux Forest, which also belonged to the Orléans family.

Chapelle St-Jean (St John's Chapel) – The chapel was erected by Constable Anne in 1538, with six other chapels, in memory of the seven churches of Rome he had visited in order to gain the favours accorded by this pilgrimage. He obtained from the Pope the same privileges for the chapels at Chantilly.
Two other chapels still stand on the estate: St Paul's, located behind Enghien Château, and Ste-Croix, on the lawns of the racecourse.
Take Allée Blanche, lined with chestnut trees, to the falls.

La Chute (Falls) – These tiered waterfalls mark the start of the Grand Canal.
Return along Allée Blanche; cross the Canal des Morfondus at the footbridge.

Hameau (Hamlet) – Dating from 1775, it was built before the more famous Trianon at Versailles *(qv)*. Under the influence of Jean-Jacques Rousseau, French princes used to seek new horizons by creating miniature villages.
The mill and a few half-timbered buildings may be seen. These used to accommodate a kitchen, a dining room and a billiards room. The barn provided a living room that was restored by the Duke of Aumale. All the big parties included supper in this charming spot in the park. Skirt the brook by the small village.

Parterres – The parterres are framed by two avenues of stately lime trees, called "The Philosophers' Path" because the great writers who visited Chantilly used to pace up and down the shaded avenue, exchanging their views and ideas.
Le Nôtre diverted the course of the River Nonette to make the Grand Canal and La Manche.
The circular Vertugadin lawns lie in the axis of La Manche, flanked by delightful stretches of water. Between La Manche and the round Gerbe basin stands Coysevox's statue of the Great Condé, framed by the effigies of La Bruyère and Bossuet (statues of Molière and Le Nôtre, both seated, may be seen in the near distance). A monumental stairway (Grand Degré) leads from the parterres up to the terrace: on either side of these imposing steps are grottoes, their carved decoration representing rivers.

★★GRANDES ÉCURIES (GREAT STABLES)

Jean Aubert's masterpiece constitutes the most stunning piece of 18C architecture in Chantilly *(illustration see Architecture)*. The St-Denis Gateway – built astride the road leading to town – marks the site of an uncompleted pavilion. The most attractive façade of the stables overlooks the racecourse.
At the time of the Condé, this architectural complex housed a total of 240 horses, 500 dogs and around 100 employees (grooms, drivers, whips etc.)

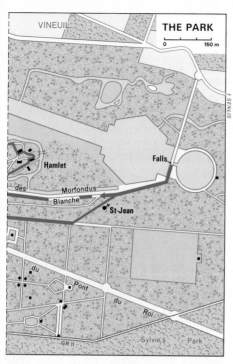

THE PARK

VINEUIL

0   150 m

Hamlet

Falls

des   Morfondus

Blanche

St-Jean

du

Pont

du

Roi

GR 11

Sylvie's   Park

SENLIS

★ **Musée Vivant du Cheval et du Poney** (Horse and Pony Museum) ⊙ – This museum is brought to life by the 28 saddle and draught animals – 18 horses and 10 ponies – bred in France or in the Iberian peninsula which occupy the stalls and boxes built under the Duke of Aumale.

In the central rotunda, 28 m - 92ft high, admire the water playing in the **fountain**, the basin of which was once used as a trough.

The exhibition in the east gallery focuses, through paintings and models, on the harness, the rider's costume and the general atmosphere of the competition in 30 equestrian events throughout the world.

Twenty-five rooms set up in the former sheds present the art of horse riding and a number of related professions: the blacksmith's trade, a veterinary's operating theatre etc.

The tour ends with a demonstration of **dressage** *(about 30min)*. The excellent acoustics, the riding master's smart costume and the comments on the various exercises make it a delightful experience. Equestrian entertainments on the theme "Riding and the Arts" take place in the kennels' quarry at night.

★LANDSCAPE GARDEN ⊙

The garden was laid out on the surviving relics of Le Nôtre's park in 1820. Its charm derives from the pleasant groves (plane trees, swamp cypresses, weeping willows) rather than from the symbolic monuments: remains of a Temple of Venus and a Temple of Love.

CHANTILLY FOREST

The vast wooded area covers about 6 300 ha - 15 500 acres and has been reshaped by hunting enthusiasts over 500 years. Tree species include oaks, hornbeams, lime trees and Scots pines in copses and groves, with more recent additions of oak and beech seedlings. The network of paths through the forest is suitable for country walks, and the light soil favours riding activities: training sessions take place at Carrefour du Petit Couvert every morning. From Route de l'Aigle a road south leads to the ponds.

Étangs de Commelles (Commelles Ponds) – They were used as fishponds by the monks from Chaâlis Abbey *(qv)*. The road provides access to the car parks and to the causeways that crisscross the water, which makes it possible to explore the area around the ponds on foot.

Château de la Reine Blanche (Queen Blanche's Castle) – In 1825 this old mill was restored in the troubadour style by the last of the Condé, the Duke of Bourbon, who used it as a hunting pavilion. It stands on the site of a legendary château believed to have been built by Queen Blanche of Navarre, wife of Philippe VI of Valois, after her husband's death around 1350.

An avenue of noble beeches completes this delightful site★.

MICHELIN GREEN GUIDES

Architecture
Fine Art
Ancient monuments
History
Geography
Picturesque scenery
Scenic routes
Touring programmes
Places to stay
Plans of towns and buildings

A collection of regional guides for France.

Population 39 595
Michelin map 106 folds 37, 38 or 60 folds 7, 8.
Town plan in the current Michelin Red Guide France

Chartres is the capital of Beauce, France's famous corn belt, but for tourists the town is known mainly for the magnificent Cathedral of Our Lady, which reigns supreme over a picturesque setting of monuments and old streets.

★**A bird's-eye view** – To get a good view of the cathedral dominating the Eure Valley, walk round the aviation memorial which rises above the east bank of the Eure: the **vista**★ is most impressive.

HISTORICAL NOTES

A town with a destiny – Since ancient times Chartres has always had a strong influence over religious matters.

It is believed that a Gallo-Roman well, located on the Chartres plateau, was the object of a pagan cult and that in the 4C this was transformed into a Christian cult by the first evangelists. Adventius, the first known bishop of Chartres, lived during the middle of the 4C. A document from the 7C mentions a bishop Béthaire kneeling in front of Notre-Dame, which points to the existence of a Marian cult.

In 876 the chemise said to belong to the Virgin Mary was offered to the cathedral by Charles the Bald, confirming that Chartres was already a place of pilgrimage. Up to the 14C the town of Chartres continued to flourish. Three representations of the Virgin are the subject of a special cult which has survived through the ages: Notre-Dame de Sous-Terre, Notre-Dame du Pilier

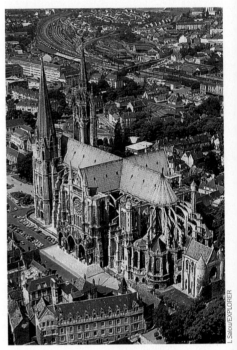

Aerial view of Chartres Cathedral

and Notre-Dame de la Belle-Verrière, but the cathedral features altogether 175 different illustrations portraying Mary.

Note that neither the cathedral nor the crypt contains any tombs: Chartres is a temple devoted exclusively to the Virgin, who remains protected from corruption.

The Pilgrimage – Chartres Cathedral was consecrated to the Assumption of the Virgin in 1260; in the Middle Ages it attracted huge crowds of pilgrims. The sick were housed in the northern gallery of the crypt. When the cathedral was thronged with visitors, the nave served as a shelter and provided night-time accommodation. A second statue – Notre-Dame du Pilier – was placed in the church for the adoration of the faithful.

In 1912 and 1913 the writer and poet **Charles Péguy** *(qv)* made the pilgrimage to Chartres. The strong influence it had on his work inspired a small group of enthusiasts after the First World War to follow suit and led later, in 1935, to the establishment of the "Students' Pilgrimage" *(see Calendar of Events)*.

An exceptional man – In the town's Church of **St John the Baptist** (Église St-Jean-Baptiste), in the Rechèvres district to the north, lies the body of the abbot **Franz Stock**, whose tomb is still a place of pilgrimage.

This German priest, chaplain to the prisons of Paris from 1940 to 1944, refused to fall in with the Wehrmacht and was taken prisoner. At the Morancez prison camp near Chartres he founded a seminary for the prisoners of war and was the Superior there for two years. He died in February 1948 at the age of 43.

★★★CATHEDRAL *1 1/2 hours*

The 4 000 carved figures and the 5 000 characters portrayed by the stained-glass windows demanded a lifelong commitment from the specialists who studied them. The most famous expert is probably Étienne Houvet, a custodian who died in 1949: he photographed the building in minute detail.

A neat, swift construction – The building rests upon the Romanesque cathedral erected by Bishop Fulbert in the 11C and 12C: there remain the crypt, the towers and the foundations of the west front, including the Royal Doorway, and fragments of the Notre-Dame de la Belle-Verrière stained-glass window. The remaining sections of the cathedral were built in the wake of the Great Fire of 1194: princes and dignitaries contributed generously to the work, while the poor offered their labour.

These efforts made it possible to complete the cathedral in 25 years, and to add on the north and south porches 20 years later, with the result that the architecture and decoration of Notre-Dame form a harmonious composition almost unparalleled in the history of Gothic art. By some miracle, the Wars of Religion, the French Revolution and the two World Wars spared the famous basilica, which Rodin referred to as "The Acropolis of France" on account of its aesthetic and spiritual value. Only the cathedral's "forest" – the superb roof timbers – were destroyed by flames in 1836, and subsequently replaced by a metal framework.

EXTERIOR

West front – The two tall spires and the Royal Doorway form one of the most perfect compositions encountered in French religious art. The New Bell Tower on the left was in fact built first; the lower part dates back to 1134. Its present name dates from the 16C, when Jehan de Beauce erected a stone spire (115m - 377ft high) to replace the wooden steeple which had burned down in 1506. The Old Bell Tower (c1145 to 1164) (106 m - 384 ft) is a masterpiece of Romanesque art, severe in the extreme.

The Royal Doorway and the three large windows above date from the 12C. Everything above this ensemble was built at a later date: the rose window (13C), the 14C gable and the king's gallery featuring the Kings of Judah, the ancestors of the Virgin. On the gable, the line of descendants ends with the Virgin offering her son to the flat expanses of the Beauce.

The **Royal Doorway★★★** (Portail Royal), a splendid example of late Romanesque architecture (1145-1170), represents the life and triumph of the Saviour. The Christ in Majesty on the central tympanum and the statue-columns are famous throughout the world. The elongated features of the biblical kings and queens, prophets, priests and patriarchs study the visitors from the embrasures. While the faces are animated, the bodies remain rigid, in deliberate contrast to the figures adorning the arches and the capitals. Statues were primarily designed to be columns, not human beings.

North porch and doorway – The main part of the cathedral is extremely high and unusually wide. The problem of how to support it was brilliantly resolved with the construction of three-tiered flying buttresses: the lower two arcs were joined together by colonnettes. The elegant Clock Pavilion (Pavillon de l'Horloge) near the New Bell Tower is the work of Jehan de Beauce (1520).

The ornamentation of the north porch is similar to that of the doorway, executed at an earlier date. The characters – treated more freely than those on the Royal Doorway – are elegant and extremely lively, illustrating a new, more realistic approach to religious art. The statue of St Modesta, a local martyr who is pictured gazing up at the New Bell Tower, is extremely graceful.

Once again, the decoration of the three doors refers to the Old Testament. The right door pays tribute to the biblical heroes who exercised the virtues recommended in the teachings of Christ. The central panel shows the Virgin and the Prophets announcing the coming of the Messiah. The door on the left presents the Annunciation, Visitation and Nativity, together with the Vices and Virtues.

In the bishopric's garden, the raised terrace commands a view of the town below standing on the banks of the Lower Eure River. Before reaching the garden gate, look left and note the archway straddling a narrow street and communicating with the walls of the Notre-Dame cloister.

East end – The complexity of the double-course flying buttresses – reinforced here as they cross over the chapels – and the sweeping disposition of the radiating chapels, chancel and arms of the transept are stunning. The 14C St Piat Chapel, originally separate, was joined to Notre-Dame by a stately staircase.

South porch and doorway – Here, the high stonework is concealed by a constellation of colonnettes. The perspective of these planes, stretching from the arches of the porch to the gables, confers to this arm of the transept a sense of unity that is lacking in the north transept.

South transept doorway, Chartres Cathedral

The theme is the Church of Christ and the Last Judgment. In the Middle Ages, these scenes would usually be reserved for the west portal but in this case the Royal Doorway already featured ornamentation. Consequently, the scenes portraying the Coming of a New World, prepared by the martyrs, were destined for the left door embrasures, while those of the Confessors (witnesses of Christ who have not yet been made martyrs) adorn the right door.

Christ reigns supreme on the central tympanum. He is also present on the pier, framed by the double row of the 12 Apostles with their lean, ascetic faces, draped in long, gently folded robes.

Among the martyrs, note the statues standing in the foreground: St George and St Theodore, both admirable 13C representations of knights in armour. These figures are quite separate from the columns – the feet are flat and no longer slanted – and are there for purely decorative purposes.

The most delightful feature of the sculpted porch is the display of medallions, grouped in sets of six and placed on the recessed arches of the three doorways: the lives of the martyrs, the Vices and Virtues etc.

Returning to the west front, note the Old Bell Tower and its ironical statue of a donkey playing the fiddle, symbolising man's desire to share in celestial music. At the corner of the building, stop to admire the tall figure of the sundial Angel.

★**Access to New Bell Tower** ⊘ – The tour (195 steps) leads round the north side and up to the lower platform of the New Bell Tower. Seen from a height of 70m - 230ft, the buttresses, flying buttresses, statues, gargoyles and Old Bell Tower are most impressive. It is still possible to recognise the former Notre-Dame Cloister thanks to the old pointed roof. Enclosed by a wall right up to the 19C, this area was frequented by clerics - especially canons.

INTERIOR

Enter the cathedral by the Royal Doorway. The main nave (16m - 52ft) is wider than any other in France (Notre-Dame in Paris 40ft, Notre-Dame in Amiens 46ft), though it has single aisles. The vaulting reaches a height of 37m - 121ft and the interior is 130m - 427ft long. This nave is 13C, built in the style known as early or lancet Gothic: the gallery has disappeared but has been replaced by a blind triforium.

As Notre-Dame was a noted place of pilgrimage, the chancel and the transept had to accommodate large-scale ceremonies; they were therefore wider than the nave. In Chartres, the chancel, its double ambulatory and the transept form an ensemble 64m - 210ft wide, stretching from north to south.

Note the gentle slope of the floor, rising slightly towards the chancel; this made it easier to wash down the church when the pilgrims had stayed overnight.

The striking state of semi-darkness in the nave creates an element of mystery which was not intentional: it is due to the gradual dimming of the stained glass.

★★★**Stained-glass windows** – *Restoration in progress*. The 12C and 13C stained-glass windows of Notre-Dame constitute, together with those of Bourges, the most important collection in France. The Virgin and Child and the Annunciation and Visitation scenes at the far end of the chancel produce a striking impression.

West front – These three 12C windows used to throw light on Fulbert's Romanesque cathedral and the dark, low nave that stood behind, which explains why they are placed so high. The scenes *(bottom to top)* illustrate the fulfilment of the prophecies: *(right)* the Tree of Jesse, *(centre)* the childhood and life of Our Lord (Incarnation cycle) and *(left)* Passion and Resurrection (Redemption cycle). Visitors may feast their eyes on the famous 12C "Chartres blue", with its clear, deep tones which are enhanced by reddish tinges, especially radiant in the rays of the setting sun. For many years, people believed that this particular shade of blue was a long-lost trade secret. Modern laboratories have now established that the sodium compounds and silica in the glass made it more resistant to dirt and corrosion than the panes made with other materials and in other times. The large 13C rose window on the west front depicts the Last Judgment.

Transept – This ensemble consists of two 13C rose windows, to which were added a number of lancet windows featuring tall figures. The themes are the same as those on the corresponding carved doorway: Old Testament (north), the End of the World (south).

The Three Kings (detail)
Central Window of West Front,
Chartres Cathedral

The north rose (ròse de France) was a present from Blanche of Castile, mother of St Louis and Regent of France, and portrays a Virgin and Child. It is characterised by the fleur-de-lis motif on the shield under the central lancet and by the alternating Castile towers and fleurs-de-lis pictured on the small corner lancets. The larger lancets depict St Anne holding the infant Virgin Mary, framed by four kings or high priests: Melchisidek and David stand on the left, Solomon and Aaron on the right. The centre roundel of the south rose shows the risen Christ, surrounded by the Old Men of the Apocalypse, forming two rings of medallions. The yellow and blue chequered quatre-foils represent the coat of arms of the benefactors, the Comte de Dreux Pierre Mauclerc and his wife, who are also featured at the bottom of the lancets.

The lancets on either side of the Virgin and Child depict four striking figures – the Great Prophets Isaiah, Jeremiah, Ezekiel and Daniel – with the four Evangelists seated on their shoulders. The morality of the scene is simple: although they are weak and lacking dignity, the Evangelists can see further than the giants of the Old Testament thanks to the Holy Spirit.

★★**Notre-Dame de la Belle-Verrière** (1) – This is a very famous stained-glass window. The Virgin and Child, a fragment of the original 12C window, has been mounted in 13C stained glass *(qv)*. Admire the superb range of blues.

Other stained-glass windows – The aisles of the nave and the chapels around the ambulatory are lit by a number of celebrated stained-glass windows from the 13C verging on the sombre side. On the east side, the arms of the transept have received two works of recent making, in perfect harmony with the early fenestration: St Fulbert's window (south crossing 2), donated by the American Association of Architects (from the François Lorin workshop – 1954), and the window of Peace (north crossing 3), a present from a group of German admirers (1971). The Vendôme Chapel (4) features a particularly radiant 15C stained-glass window. It illustrates the development of this art, which eventually led to the lighter panes of the 17C and 18C.

★★**Parclose** – The screen was started by Jehan de Beauce in 1514 and finished in the 18C. This fine work consists of 41 sculpted compositions depicting the lives of Christ and the Virgin. These Renaissance medallions, evoking Biblical history, local history and mythology, contrast sharply with the Gothic statues of the doorways.

Chancel – The marble facing, the Assumption group above the high altar and the low-reliefs separating the columns were added in the 18C.

Organ (5) – The case dates from the 16C.

Vierge du Pilier (Virgin of the Pillar) (6) – This wooden statue (c1510) stood against the roodscreen, now sadly disappeared. The richly clothed Virgin is the object of a procession celebrated annually.

Treasury ⊘ – St Piat Chapel was designed to receive the cathedral's treasure. The reliquary – presented in a glass cabinet – displays the Virgin's Robes, which the faithful pilgrims of the past saw as a "Sacred Chemise". There are also beautiful liturgical objects, engraved belts from the 17C threaded with sea shells by converted Indians, and remains of the 13C roodscreen, destroyed in the 18C.

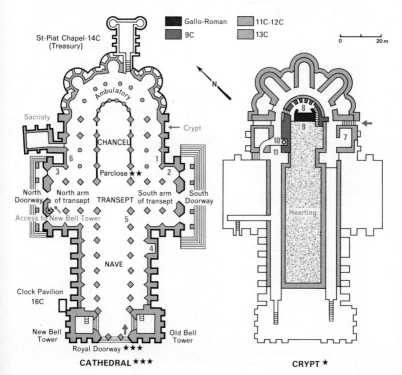

CATHEDRAL ★★★   CRYPT ★

★**Crypt** ⊙ – *Entrance outside the cathedral, on the south side (see plan above).* This is France's longest crypt (220m - 722ft long). It dates largely from the 11C and features Romanesque groined vaulting. It is a curious shape: the two long galleries joined by the ambulatory pass under the chancel and the nave and give onto seven chapels. The central area, which has been filled in, remains unexplored. Of the seven radiating chapels, only three are Romanesque. The other four were added by the master architect of the Gothic cathedral to serve as foundations for the chancel and the apse of the future building.

St Martin's Chapel (7), by the south gallery, houses the originals of the statues on the Royal Doorway: the sundial Angel etc. A staircase, starting from the ambulatory and leads down to a lower crypt.

St Lubin Crypt (Crypte St-Lubin) (8) – This served as the foundations of the 9C church. A thick, circular column with a visible base is supported by a Gallo-Roman wall (9), its bond easily recognisable by the alternating bricks and mortar. The crypt was a safe place that protected the cathedral treasures in times of social unrest or natural disaster. Thus, the Chemise of the Virgin survived the Great Fire of 1194.

Saints' Well (Puis des Saints-Forts) (10) – The lower part of this 33m - 108ft-deep shaft has a square section characteristic of Gallo-Roman wells. The coping is contemporary. The name dates back to 858: it is believed that several Christian martyrs from Chartres were murdered during a Norman attack, and their bodies thrown down the well.

Our Lady of the Underground Chapel (Chapelle Notre-Dame de Sous-Terre) (11) – A sacred retreat where pilgrims indulge in fervent praying. Since the 17C the chapel, together with the north gallery of the crypt, has played the part of a miniature church. It originally consisted of a small alcove where the faithful came to venerate the Virgin.

The interior of the chapel and its decoration were refurbished in 1976. On this occasion, the 19C statue of the Virgin was replaced by a more hieratic figure, based on the Romanesque model, enhanced by a Gobelins tapestry.

ADDITIONAL SIGHTS

★**Old Town (St Andrew's district and banks of the Eure)** – *Follow the route indicated on plan below.* This pleasant walk leads past the picturesque hilly site, the banks of the Eure River, an ancient district recently restored and the cathedral which is visible from every street corner. In season, a small tourist train ⊙ tours the old town.

St Andrew's Church (Église St-André) – This Romanesque church *(deconsecrated)* was the place of worship of one of the most active and densely-populated districts in town. Most of the trades were closely related to the river: millers, dyers, curriers, cobblers, tanners, drapers, fullers, tawers, serge makers etc. The church was enlarged in the 13C, and in the 16C and 17C it received a chancel and an axial chapel resting on arches that straddled the Eure River and Rue du Massacre. Unfortunately, both these structures disappeared in 1827.

Cross the Eure by a footbridge (**B**): there is a good **view**★ of the old humpback bridges. At the foot of the dilapidated nave of St Andrew's lie the remains of the arch that once supported the chancel. Wander upstream: the wash-houses and races of former mills have been prettily restored. Rue aux Juifs leads through an ancient district which has recently been renovated, featuring paved streets bordered by gable-ended houses and old-fashioned street lamps.

Rue des Écuyers – This is one of the most successful restoration schemes of the old

CHARTRES

B	Passerelle
E	Maison à pans de bois
F	Escalier « de la Reine Berthe »
M	Musée des Beaux-Arts
S	Grenier et cellier de Loëns (Centre International du Vitrail)

town. At nos 17 and 19 the houses have 17C doorways with rusticated surrounds, surmounted by a bull's-eye window. Stroll along the street to Rue aux Cois. The corner building is a delightful half-timbered villa (**E**), with an overhang in the shape of a prow. Opposite stands Queen Bertha's stairturret (**F**), a 16C structure, also half-timbered.

Grenier de Loëns (Loëns Loft) (S) ⊙ – From the 12C onwards, this half-timbered barn with treble gables in the courtyard of the old chapter house was used to store the wine and cereals offered to the clergy as a tithe. Renovated to house the International Stained Glass Centre, which organises stained glass exhibitions, the building now features a large hall with beautifully-restored roof timbering and a magnificent 12C cellar with three aisles.

Musée des Beaux Arts (Museum of Fine Arts) (M) ⊙ – The museum is housed in the old bishop's palace and occupies the first terrace of the bishopric's gardens. The large, handsome edifice which was built over four centuries consists of a 15C section arranged around an interior courtyard, a 17C and 18C façade, and an early 18C wing overlooking the garden.

On the ground floor note the hallway with its wrought-iron staircase, the chapel and the Italian Parlour with a late-14C wayside cross showing the death of St Francis and a superb 16C St Paul attributed to François Marchand.

The 18C collection is housed in a series of salons and includes works by Boucher, Fragonard, Watteau and Chardin, together with tapestries, earthenware, pewterware and a fine collection of old musical instruments. Note also the St Lucy by Zurbaran.

Paintings from the primitives to the 19C are displayed on the first floor (Holbein, Teniers, Cardi, Corot...) as are an important group of painted and carved wooden statues.

The medieval collections occupy several of the ground-floor rooms.

The old sacristy, close to the chapel, houses 12 unusually large **enamels**★ representing the Apostles, by Léonard Limousin. They were commissioned by François I in 1545 and offered by Henri II to Diana of Poitiers, for her residence at Anet. The museum's new rooms exhibit the permanent modern art collections (works by Vlaminck, Sérusier, Malavar) and a collection by the glass artist Navarre. Temporary exhibitions are also held here.

Rue du Cygne – The street has been widened into a little square planted with trees and shrubs (flower market on Tuesdays, Thursdays and Saturdays) and is at present an oasis of calm in this lively shopping district in the town centre.

At the end of Rue du Cygne, on Place Marceau, a monument celebrates the memory of the young local general who died at Altenkirchen (1796) at the age of 27. His ashes have been shared among Chartres (funeral urn under the statue on Place des Epars), the Panthéon and the Dome Church of the Invalides in Paris *(qv)*.

★**St-Pierre (St Peter's Church)** – *Southern end of Rue St-Pierre.* This 12C and 13C Gothic church used to belong to the Benedictine abbey of St-Père-en-Vallée. The belfry-porch dates from pre-Romanesque times. The Gothic **stained-glass windows**★ can be traced back to a period that is not represented in Chartres Cathedral: the late 13C and early 14C, before the widespread introduction of yellow staining.

The oldest stained glass is that in the south bays of the chancel, portraying tall, hieratic figures from the Old Testament. The windows in the semicircle of the chancel, with the most vivid tones, were mounted around 1300. Here the characters have been treated more freely.

The last windows to be installed were those of the nave (*c*1305-15). They feature an alternation of medallions and religious figures (apostles, bishops, abbots).

Monument de Jean Moulin (Jean Moulin's Memorial) – Jean Moulin was *préfet* (chief administrator) of Chartres during the German invasion; on 17 June 1940, despite having been tortured, he resisted the enemy and refused to sign a document claiming that the French troops had committed a series of atrocities. As he was afraid of dishonouring his country, he attempted to commit suicide.

Moulin was dismissed by the Vichy government in November 1940 and, from then on, he planned and coordinated underground resistance, working in close collaboration with General de Gaulle. Arrested in Lyons on 21 June 1943, he did not survive the harsh treatment received from the Gestapo. In December 1964 he was honoured in the Panthéon *(qv)*.

★**Le COMPA: Conservatoire du Machinisme et des Pratiques Agricoles (COMPA: Agricultural Museum)** ⊙ – *West of the town by D 24.* The museum is located in a strikingly-converted, semicircular former railway hangar near the station.

The spacious, modern-looking building, encircled by neat lawns offering a good view of Chartres and the cathedral, contains splendid, gleaming old machines and tools of leather, wrought iron or wood.

An **audio-visual display** *(in French)* introduces the development of agriculture through time and space.

Tools and machines – At the museum's core stands an assortment of machines of all ages grouped according to function: seeders, binder-harvesters, combine-harvesters... Note the American MOLINE tractor, from 1910.

Land, men and methods – A comparison of two farming concerns in different regions of France, in 1860 and today, provides a better understanding of rural life. Handsome ploughs and carts from around the world illustrate the diversity in methods used by workers on the land.

Inventors and inventions gallery – The 80m – 262ft long gallery introduces the figures responsible for major agricultural developments over the centuries.
The ideas and innovations of Pliny the Elder, Olivier de Serres, Henri de Vilmorin and, more recently, Ferguson and others are explained through information panels and fascinating interactive displays.

Tractor Room – The tour ends with an exhibition of eight tractors, the oldest dating from 1816, the most recent from 1954.

Musée de l'École (School Museum) Ⓥ – *Rue G Lelong, southwest of the town.* A classroom belonging to the old École Normale (teachers' training college) houses educational material and furniture evoking the schools of yesteryear: abacuses, magic lanterns using paraffin, books advocating humanist ethics, a collective money-bank with a separate compartment for each pupil etc.

Maison Picassiette (Picassiette House) Ⓥ – *East of the town.* Built and decorated by Raymond Isidore (1900-64), this house offers an amazing medley of naive art. A number of monuments and numerous religious scenes are suggested by mosaic compositions made with extremely diverse materials: pieces of crockery, fragments of tinted glass, dollops of cement etc. Visitors are given a complete tour of the house, including the "chapel", the Black Courtyard (tomb crowned by a replica of Chartres Cathedral), the summer house (frescoes); the garden is dotted with statues and features a large-scale mosaic depicting the town of Jerusalem.

CHEMIN DES DAMES

Michelin map 56 fold 5 or 236 fold 38

Chemin des Dames, which means Ladies' Way, follows the ridge of a cliff separating the Aisne Valley from the Ailette Valley. It derives its name from the daughters of Louis XV, known as "*Mesdames*", who followed this route to get to Bove Château, home of their friend the Duchess of Narbonne.

Nivelle's Offensive – In 1917, after the Battle of the Marne, the retreating Germans stopped here, having realised that the location was an excellent defensive spot which they fortified by making use of the caves ("*boves*" or "*creuttes*"), hollowed out of the ridge.
General Nivelle, commander of the French armies from December 1916, searched for a way of penetrating their defence along Chemin des Dames. In spite of the difficult terrain, riddled with machine gun nests, on 16 April 1917 he sent an army under Mangin to assault the German positions. The French troops occupied the ridges following the first assault but the Germans clung on to the slopes of the Ailette Valley: the terrible French losses that ensued, together with the failure of the venture, caused a crisis of morale which provoked mutinies in parts of the French army.

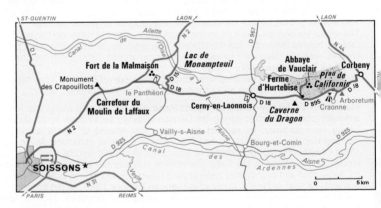

FROM SOISSONS TO CORBENY

52km - 32 miles – about 2 1/2 hours

★**Soissons** – *See Soissons. 2 hours.*
Take N 2 northeast towards Laon.

Carrefour du Moulin de Laffaux (Laffaux Windmill Crossroads) – On this hill, which marks the western extremity of the Chemin des Dames, stands the Monument to the Dead (Monument aux Morts des Crapouillots) killed by trench mortar shells *(behind the restaurant).* Laffaux windmill used to stand here.
Turn right into D 18 (Chemin des Dames).

Fort de la Malmaison (Malmaison Fort) – This fort was taken by the colonial troops of the 38th Regiment from the Prussian guard in 1917. Malmaison Cemetery: German graves (1939-45).
At Panthéon turn left into D15 which leads into the Ailette Valley.

Monampteuil Lake ⊙ – Formed by the waters of the River Ailette, the lake lies in a lush setting near Monampteuil. The lakeside area boasts many tourist facilites.

Return to Chemin des Dames.

Cerny-en-Laonnois – Near to the crossroads with the D 967 stand the Chemin des Dames memorial, chapel, French military cemetery (5 500 graves) and ossuary (2 800 dead).

Caverne du Dragon ⊙ – The **Chemin des Dames Museum**, installed in this "Dragon's Cave" contains mementoes of the First World War. Several chambers may be visited.

This "cave" (over 2.5ha - 6 acres) extends beyond the spine of the hill under the D 18; there are entrances to the north and south. The Germans made it a shelter, arsenal, command post and place of safety all in one; over 6 000 men lived here. Even though the French troops reached its southern exits on 16 April, it was not until 25 June that the 152nd Regiment gained complete control of the cave.

D 18 follows the top of the ridge known as Hurtebise's Isthmus, which extends to the northeast on the Craonne plateau formed by the Vauclair and Californie plateaux.

Hurtebise Farm – In 1814 the farm was fought over in the battle of **Craonne** in which Napoleon, newly-arrived from Corbeny, was victorious over Blücher. A hundred years later in September 1914 the same farm was the object of fierce fighting in which the Basques of the 36th Division excelled themselves. Commemorative monument to both battles.

Turn left into D 886 which descends into the Ailette Valley.

Vauclair Abbey ⊙ – The ruins of this Cistercian monastery, founded in 1134 by St Bernard, were uncovered in 1966. The best-preserved parts of the abbey are the storeroom (cellier), the refectory (réfectoire), the chapter-house (salle capitulaire) and the monks' room (salle des moines). The foundations of the abbey church and the guest house are also visible. A herb garden with medicinal plants has existed since 1976 and an exhibition gallery stands nearby.

All around, the ancient monastic forest of Vauclair covers 1 000ha - 2 471acres.

Return to Chemin des Dames and continue east; take first left into D 895.

Californie Plateau – First an observatory *(right)* comes into view, from where Napoleon directed the battle of Craonne in 1814 (statue of the Emperor). Further away, opposite a large car park, a viewing table explains the 1917 offensive. An arboretum has been planted on the former village of Craonne where the road rejoins the D 18.

Corbeny – Kings came to Corbeny Abbey the day after receiving the Sacrament, in order to venerate the relics of St Marcou who had the power to cure the king's evil (scrofula).

COMPIÈGNE★★★

Agglomeration 67 057
Michelin maps 56 fold 2 and 106 fold 10 inset or 236 fold 35 – Local map overleaf
Town Plan in the current Michelin Red Guide France

Compiègne, which was a royal residence long before it hosted the brilliant parties and receptions of the Second Empire, is bordered by one of the most beautiful forests in France. The town has become one of the busiest in Picardy, owing largely to its industry and its university (Benjamin Franklin University of Technology, Royallieu Research Centre).

Origins – Charles the Bald had a palace built to resemble Charlemagne's in Aix-la-Chapelle, which the former had lost to his brother Louis in 843 when the Treaty of Verdun divided up the Carolingian Empire. He also founded an abbey which from the 10C preserved the relics of St Cornelius. The town developed around this royal abbey of St Cornelius (today only the 14C cloister remains), which preceded St Denis as the royal necropolis and centre of culture. Ramparts were built around Compiègne in the 13C; Charles V reinforced them and in 1374 added a castle that was the foundation for today's palace.

Joan of Arc Imprisoned – In May 1430 the Burgundians and the English were camping in the shadow of Compiègne's town walls, on the north side of the River Oise. Joan of Arc came to examine the enemy position and returned on the 23rd after a few days' absence, entering the town from the south. That same evening she attempted an assault, crossing the river and chasing the Burgundian advance guard from their Margny encampment. However, reinforcements came to the aid of the Burgundians from Clairoix and Coudun, while the English came from Venette, stealing along the Oise to attack from the rear; the French had no choice but to give ground. The Maid of Orléans covered the retreat with a handful of men. She reached the moat just as the commanding officer in Compiègne gave the order to raise the drawbridge, fearing the enemy would slip inside with the last of the French soldiers. A short skirmish ensued. A Picardy archer toppled Joan of Arc from her horse and she was immediately taken prisoner. The place of capture is located near Place du 54ème-Régiment-d'Infanterie, where Frémiet's equestrian statue of the Maid of Orléans stands.

The Palace of Louis XV – All the kings of France enjoyed staying in Compiègne which they often visited. Yet, with four main buildings haphazardly arranged around a central courtyard, the château was not an obvious royal residence. Louis XIV said, "At Versailles, I am lodged like a king; at Fontainebleau, like a prince; and at Compiègne, like a peasant." He had new apartments built facing the forest. His 75 visits here were marked by sumptuous feasts and, in particular, great military camps. The most important of these was in 1698, the last time the King stayed at Compiègne.

When Louis XV ordered the complete reconstruction of the palace in 1738 he was less interested in outdoing his predecessor, who had built so much, than in having a place where he could reside with his court and ministers. The architect Jacques Gabriel and his successor Jacques-Ange Gabriel were limited by the town and its ramparts, which obliged them to rebuild on the old foundations. As a further inconvenience, they could not destroy an old building until a new one had been completed, as the King refused to cease his visits to Compiègne during the work.

Louis XV's master plan of 1751 was brought to a halt by the Seven Years War.

Louis XVI continued the project and achieved a great deal but left it unfinished. In fact, it was not until 1785 that he was finally able to occupy the royal apartments, which would later accommodate Napoleon I.

The south wing was finished that same year. Marie-Antoinette had personally overseen its arrangement, decor and furnishing but never actually stayed here herself. A great terrace was built in front of the palace's façade, which looked out onto a park. This terrace was connected to the gardens by a monumental central flight of steps, replacing the moat that had formerly been part of Charles V's fortifications.

From 1789 to 1791 the work continued, though at a slower pace, as the King hoped to withdraw to Compiègne. In 1795, in the aftermath of the Revolution, the furnishings were completely dispersed through auctions which lasted five months.

Various Installations – After the Revolution the palace served first as a military school, then as a college of arts and industry. In 1806 it became an Imperial residence and Napoleon I had the palace entirely restored by the architect Berthaut, the painter Girodet and the decorators Redouté and the Dubois brothers.

Wedding Palace – It was in Compiègne Forest that, on 14 May 1770, the future Louis XVI was introduced to Marie-Antoinette of Austria for the first time; the young Dauphin was paralysed with shyness.

On 27 March 1810 the great-niece of Marie-Antoinette, Marie-Louise of Austria, was to arrive in Compiègne. She had married Napoleon I by proxy and this time the groom was impatient. Despite torrential rain, the Emperor ran to meet the princess and threw himself soaking wet into her carriage, smothering the terrified Marie-Louise with demonstrations of affection. The dinner planned in Soissons was cancelled and instead the Emperor and his bride had supper at Compiègne. Some days later the wedding ceremonies were celebrated at St-Cloud, serving only as the consecration of a union imposed at Vienna and willingly accepted at Compiègne.

In 1832 Louis-Philippe, who transformed the tennis court into a theatre, married his daughter Louise-Marie to the first king of Belgium, Leopold of Saxe-Coburg.

The Second Empire "Series" – Compiègne was the favourite residence of Napoleon III and Empress Eugénie. They came every autumn for four to six weeks to enjoy the hunting season, receiving the kings and princes of Europe. They also received the celebrities of the time, arranged in "series" of about 80 people, grouped by "affinities". Lodging the guests often posed great difficulties and many distinguished individuals had to content themselves with rooms under the eaves. The hunts, theatrical evenings, "living tableaux" and balls left the guests with little free time. Romantic and political intrigue mixed freely. One rainy afternoon, to amuse the Imperial couple and their guests, the writer Mérimée composed his famous dictation, comprising the words with the greatest spelling difficulties in the French language. The Empress made the highest number of mistakes, 62; Pauline Sandoz, Metternich's daughter-in-law, had the least with 3. The luxuries and endless frivolities intoxicated the courtiers, who delighted in waltzes and long forest outings. The events of 1870 interrupted this joyous life and the work on the new theatre.

The World Wars – From 1917 to 1918 the palace was the general headquarters of generals Nivelle and then Pétain. In 1919 a fire damaged the royal apartments. The armistices of 11 November 1918 and 22 June 1940 were signed in the forest. Compiègne suffered heavy bombing during the Second World War. **Royallieu**, a district south of the town, served from 1941 to 1944 as a centre from which prisoners were sent to various Nazi concentration camps (a commemorative monument stands at the entrance to the military camp as well as in Compiègne railway station).

★★★ PALACE 2 hours

Viewed from the square the palace is paradoxically "a Louis XV château built almost entirely from 1751 to 1789".

This austerely Classical château covers a vast triangle (3ha - 7 1/2 acres); indeed, the regularity of its arrangement is even rather monotonous. The decoration inside and the collection of 18C and First Empire tapestries and furnishings is, however, exceptional. Among the many details unifying the various apartments are fine *trompe-l'œil* paintings by Sauvage (1744-1818) over the doors.

The Second Empire Museum and the Transport Museum are also in the palace.

★★Historic Apartments
(Appartements Historiques) ⓘ

The Historic Apartments of the palace begin with rooms devoted to its history; beyond them rises the Queen's Grand Staircase, or Apollo Staircase, which led directly to the queen's apartments and further still is the entrance hall or Gallery of Columns which precedes the Grand Staircase (**1**). Climb the staircase with its beautiful 18C wrought-iron balustrade to the landing where a great Gallo-Roman sarcophagus lies; it served as the font in the vanished abbey church of St Cornelius and is a relic of very early Compiègne.

The first-floor Guard's Room (1785) (**2**) leads into the antechamber or Ushers' Salon (**3**), which gave access to both the King's apartment *(left)* and the Queen's *(right)*.

The main courtyard and the principal body of the château are on different levels: the sovereigns' apartments were built on the old ramparts and are therefore on the ground floor facing the garden (on the same level as the terrace), but on the first floor on the side facing the courtyard.

Napoleon I's bedroom, Compiègne Palace

King's and Emperors' Apartment (Appartement du Roi et des Empereurs)

This apartment houses exceptional groups of objects, works and memorabilia.

Emperor's Dining Room (Salle à manger de l'Empereur) (**4**) – The décor and furnishings are First Empire (early 19C). Pilasters and doors, surmounted by *grisailles* by Sauvage, stand out against the rose-pink false onyx. One of Sauvage's paintings is an extraordinary *trompe-l'œil* representing Anacreon. It was here that on 1 May 1814 Louis XVIII entertained Tsar Alexander, who was still hesitating about returning the Bourbons to the throne of France. Under the Second Empire a private theatre was established here, with those close to the empress taking part in charades and revues.

Card Salon (Salon des cartes) (**5**) – First designated as the Nobles' Antechamber under Louis XVI, then as the Senior Officers' Salon under Napoleon I, this room ended up as the *Aide-de-Camp* Salon or the Card Salon under Napoleon III. The furnishings comprise elements from the First Empire (chairs covered in Beauvais tapestry) and the Second. Note the games: quoit and a pin table.

Family Salon (Salon de famille) (**6**) – This room was once Louis XVI's bedchamber (large mirrors hide the alcove).
The **view★** onto the park extends the length of the avenue to the Beaux Monts.
The furnishings recall Empress Eugénie's taste for mixing styles: Louis XV armchairs, unusual little seats for two (called "*confidents*") or for three ("*indiscrets*")...

Council Chamber (Salle du Conseil) (**7**) – Unfortunately only the original table has been returned, the rest of the furniture being lost. Together with Versailles and Fontainebleau, Compiègne was one of the three châteaux where the king held counsel. Representatives of the Republics of Genoa and France signed two successive treaties here (1756 and 1764) which accorded France the right to garrison troops in the maritime areas of Corsica. An immense tapestry illustrates *The Crossing of the Rhine by Louis XIV*.

Emperor's Chamber (Chambre de l'Empereur) (**8**) – This room has been restored to its appearance during the First Empire, with Jacob-Desmalter furnishings and eagle friezes.

Emperor's Library (Bibliothèque de l'Empereur) (**9**) – Formerly the King's Great Cabinet, this room was used as a library during the First Empire. The bookcase and the furnishings are by Jacob-Desmalter; the painted ceiling is the work of Girodet.

Empress' Apartment
(Appartement de l'Impératrice)

These rooms comprised the queen's principal apartments, the only ones in which Marie-Antoinette ever stayed; later, they were particularly favoured by Empresses Marie-Louise and Eugénie.

Breakfast Salon (Salon du Déjeuner) (**10**) – The delightful breakfast room, with pale blue and yellow silk hangings, was prepared for Marie-Louise in 1809.

Music Salon (Salon de musique) (**11**) – This was one of Empress Eugénie's favourite rooms; she furnished it herself. The Louis XVI pieces, from the apartment of Marie-Antoinette at St-Cloud, recall that the last sovereign consort of France was keeping the memory of the unfortunate queen alive.

Empress' Bedchamber (Chambre de l'Impératrice) (**12**) – The majestic canopied bed is enclosed by white silk curtains and gold-embroidered muslin. Paintings by Girodet represent the seasons and the Morning Star appears in the centre of the ceiling. The round boudoir leading to the bedchamber, also built for Marie-Louise, served as a dressing-room and for taking baths.

The last three of these interconnecting rooms form a decorative First Empire ensemble. Seats are arranged formally around a couch in the **Great Salon** (Grand Salon) (**13**); the **Flower Salon** (Salon des Fleurs) (**14**) owes its name to the eight panels painted with lily-like flowers, after Redouté; the **Blue Salon** (Salon Bleu) (**15**) strikingly contrasts blue walls and seats with a red marble fireplace and console tables. These rooms belonged to the imperial prince at the end of the Second Empire.

Empress' Dining Room (Salle à manger de l'Impératrice) (**16**) – The walls of this modestly-sized room are stucco-marble, of a caramel colour more elegantly known as "antique yellow". It was here that the Archduchess Marie-Louise dined with the Emperor for the first time.

Louis XV's Hunting Gallery (Galerie des chasses de Louis XV) – The room is hung with Gobelins tapestries, which were woven as early as 1735 in accordance with sketches by Oudry. One represents a hunt along the River Oise and includes the silhouettes of Compiègne and the old Royallieu abbey. The series continues in the **Stags Gallery** (Galerie des Cerfs)(**17**), formerly the Queen's Guards' Room, then the Empress' Guards' Room.

Ball Gallery (Galerie du Bal) – The room (39m by 13m - 128ft by 43ft) was constructed within a few months for Marie-Louise's arrival, by gutting two floors of small apartments.

The ceiling paintings glorify the Emperor's victories; the mythological scenes at the end of the room are by Girodet.

Throughout the Second Empire the gallery served as a dining room at the time of the "series", the sovereigns presiding from the centre of an immense table set up for the occasion.

Natoire Gallery (Galerie Natoire) – The room was built by Napoleon III to lead to the Grand Theatre (Grand Théâtre) (built in the courtyard on the other side of Rue d'Ulm but never finished). The gallery is decorated with *The Story of Don Quixote*, a series of **paintings★** by Natoire (1700-77) in the heroic style. These were copied at Beauvais to create the tapestries hanging today in the Aix-en-Provence Tapestry Museum.

Coypel Room (Salle Coypel) – In this room a second series of episodes, by Coypel, continue the Don Quixote story (1714-34) in a more light-hearted style. These paintings were also recreated by the Gobelins tapestry weavers.

1st FLOOR

★★ TRANSPORT MUSEUM

Cour de l'Orangerie

Louis XV's Hunting Gallery

EMPRESS' APARTMENT

Great Hall

Ball

Natoire Gallery

Gallery

Chapel

Cour de la Chapelle

KING'S AND ← EMPERORS' APARTMENT

MUSEUM OF THE SECOND EMPIRE ★★

Main Courtyard

Prince's Double Apartment

King of Rome's Apartment

HISTORIC APARTMENTS

Chapel (Chapelle) – The First Empire room is surprisingly small for such a vast château, as the great chapel planned by Gabriel was never built. It was here on 9 August 1832 that the marriage took place between Princess Louise-Marie, eldest daughter of Louis-Philippe, and Leopold I, King of Belgium. Princess Marie of Orléans, the French king's second daughter, conceived the design for the stained-glass window.

Prince's Double Apartment and King of Rome's Apartment (Appartement double du Prince et appartement du roi de Rome)

Prince's Double Apartment – Napoleon I had this apartment arranged to receive two foreign sovereigns. This excellent group of Empire rooms comprises a dining room, four salons and a great bedchamber (wallpaper, silk hangings, furniture).

King of Rome's Apartment – The apartment has been restored to its appearance in 1811, when Napoleon I's son (five months old at the time) stayed in it for one month. All the original furnishings adorn the salon-boudoir, bathroom, boudoir, bedchamber and principal salon. In the middle of the apartment a room (**18**) has been restored to appear as it did at the end of the 18C (Queen Marie-Antoinette's games room).

Museum of the Second Empire (Musée du Second Empire)

The museum is located in a series of small, quiet salons and presents life at Court and in the outside world, and the arts, during the Second Empire.

Beyond the first room, displaying Daumier's humorous drawings, a space is devoted to the "beauties" of the period. Princess Mathilde (1820-1904), one of the reign's great figures, has pride of place here. She was for a brief time the fiancée of Louis-Napoleon, her close cousin. After her Spanish marriage she devoted herself entirely to her salon in Rue de Courcelles, which was much frequented by the important writers and artists of the day, and to her St Gratien château.

The museum owns the famous Winterhalter painting, *The Empress with her Ladies-in-Waiting* (1855).

Among the many sculptures by Carpeaux in the last rooms, note the bust of Napoleon, aged by the fall of the Empire, and the statue of the Imperial Prince with his dog.

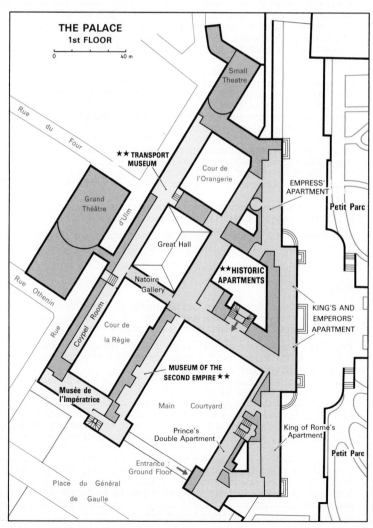

Musée de l'Impératrice (Museum of the Empress) – This collection was bequeathed by M and Mme F Ferrand and includes memorabilia of official life and life in exile, as well as the more popular objects associated with Empress Eugénie. Among the more moving items are those evoking the Empress and her son, the Imperial Prince, who was massacred by the Zulus.

★★Transport Museum (Musée de la voiture) ☉

The museum was created in 1927 on the initiative of the Touring Club of France. None of the authentic royal carriages has been preserved in France. The collection of antique carriages features berlin coaches for travelling or ceremonial use in particular; these carriages were mounted on a base with two shafts, safer than a single shaft, to which the horses were harnessed.

Grand Hall (Great Hall) – About fifty carriages are on display in what was formerly the kitchen courtyard, now covered over: the oldest, travelling berlin coach, which belonged to the kings of Spain, dating from c1740; the berlin coach used by the pope in Bologna, and the one in which Bonaparte made his entrance to the town in 1796; 18C and 19C travelling carriages, including one used by Napoleon in Russia; the travelling brougham used by the Duke of Angoulême for the Trocadero campaign, and that of Field Marshal Maison.

A mail-coach, a carriage with benches, a Madeleine-Bastille omnibus and Orsay broughams are also on show, as well as the gala berlin coaches used by Napoleon III and the president of the Republic.

The collection includes the 1878 Mancelle de Bollée vehicle and a strange steam stage-coach by the same builder, which it is hard to imagine running without horses; a tracked vehicle, a 1924 Citroën from the Croisière Noire (the first trans-African car expedition), and the salon-coach (Compagnie du Nord) used by Napoleon III to travel between Paris and Compiègne.

Kitchens and Outbuildings – The evolution of the two-wheeler, starting with the heavy ancestors of the bicycle (*draisiennes*) which the rider set in motion by pushing off, can be seen in the former pantries. Pedals appeared with the 1863 Michaux velocipede. The great penny-farthing, built out of iron tubing, had an unusually large front wheel to increase its speed. Developments such as the invention of the chain belt, which first appeared on the English tricycle, rendered wheels of disproportionate size unnecessary. The true bicycle became possible in about 1890. The army took advantage of the idea by developing a folding velocipede just before the First World War.

The exhibition in the large former kitchens of the palace follows the development of the **automobile**, from De Dion and Trépardoux's steam car to Guynemer's 1914 Sigma-Ballot open touring-car, the form of which already shows the technical efforts made to increase speed.

Between these two extremes in the evolution of the car there is the Panhard No 2, the first car equipped with a four-stroke Daimler engine; the 1895 car made by Bollée & Son, with facing seats, which was one of the entrants in the race from Paris to Marseille-en-Beauvaisis (north of Beauvais); the De Dion-Bouton series; the large 1897 wagonette belonging to the Duchess of Uzès, the first woman driver; the 1899 "Never-satisfied" on Michelin tyres, which was the first car to attain speeds of 100 kilometres per hour; and the little 1900 4-CV Renault, the first saloon car.

Steam, combustion and electric motors are also exhibited, showing the various ideas of the researchers and creators of the automobile industry.

First Floor – These rooms are devoted to foreign vehicles and their accessories: Dutch and Italian cabriolets, a Sicilian cart, palanquin, sleighs, coachmen's clothes etc.

Park

From a crossroads, three avenues lead into the forest. The gardens are known as the Petit Parc; the main entrance gate is to the left, when facing away from the town. The Grand Parc surrounds it and is part of the forest.

Petit Parc – Cross the trench which, at the time of Napoleon's investiture, was the only trace of the formal French gardens planned by Gabriel, together with the terraces planted with lime-trees alongside it.

The Emperor's guiding idea was "to link the château as soon as possible to the forest, which is the true garden and the real beauty of this residence". The enclosing wall which blocked the perspective to the woods was taken down and replaced by iron railings. Beyond, the openness of Avenue des Beaux-Monts creates a magnificent linear perspective (4km - 6 miles long), which was originally to have been closed with a monumental gateway to remind the Emperor's young bride of Shönbrunn.

Impatient to reach the forest without having to go through the town, Napoleon had a central ramp built for carriages between the terrace and the park; this was unfortunately at the expense of the glorious flight of steps by Gabriel.

From then on the Petit Parc was replanted as a formal English garden and lost its importance.

The present layout dates from the Second Empire.

ADDITIONAL SIGHTS

★Hôtel de ville (Town Hall) – This remarkable building was constructed under Louis XII in the late-Gothic style. It was restored during the last century and the façade statues date from this period. They represent, from left to right around the central equestrian statue of Louis XII: St Denis, St Louis, Charles the Bald, Joan of Arc, Cardinal Pierre d'Ailly who was born in Compiègne, and Charlemagne.

The belfry consists of two floors and a slate-covered spire, flanked by four pinnacled turrets. At the base of the spire, three figures, called "*picantins*" and dressed as Swiss foot-soldiers from the period of François I, ring the hours and the quarter-hours.

Two wings were added to the old building during its restoration.

Musée de la Figurine historique (Museum of Historic Figurines) ⓒ – *In Hôtel de la Cloche, right of the town hall.*

The museum houses over 100 000 model figures in tin, lead, wood, plastic, paper and cardboard; they are sculpted wholly or partly in the round, or are flat. A visit here offers an interesting retrospective of the development of dress, along with an evocation of historical events throughout the ages. The presentation, in rooms lit only by the display, allows leisurely contemplation of the various scenes. Note in particular *The Review of French Troops at Betheny* in 1901 in front of the Tsar of Russia and President Loubet (12 000 figures made by A Silhol, who participated in the parade himself); *The Battle of Waterloo* created by Charles Laurent from 1905 to 1923, which is completed by an audio-visual presentation; and *The Return of the Emperor's Ashes* with the veterans of the Napoleonic wars.

Église St-Jacques (St James Church) – The church features a 15C tower, the highest in the town, at one of the corners of its façade. St James' was the parish of the king and the court, which provided the funds for the chancel to be reworked in marble in the 18C and for the addition of carved wood panels at the base of the nave's pillars. The harmony of the Gothic style at the time of St Louis is particularly evident in the chancel with its narrow, clerestory-lit triforium and the 13C transept. An ambulatory was added in the 16C.

The 14C stone Virgin and Child in the left transept arm, known as "Our Lady of the Silver Feet" ("Notre-Dame aux pieds d'argent"), is the subject of much veneration. A chapel in the left side aisle houses three 15C painted and gilt wooden statues. They came from the calvary which surmounted the old roodscreen.

Tour de Beauregard (Beauregard Tower) – This former royal keep or "Governor's Tower", now in ruins, is located on the site of Charles the Bald's palace. The tower is all that remains from the time when Joan of Arc *(see above)* made her last, fatal military assault, which she began by leaving the town via the old St Louis bridge on 23 May 1430.

Musée Vivenel (Vivenel Museum) ⓒ – Compiègne's municipal museum is located in the Hôtel de Songeons; it is a pleasant building dating from the early 19C, the garden of which is now a public park.

The ground floor is devoted to Antiquity: Greek and Roman marbles and bronzes; Antique ceramics including a remarkable group of **Greek vases★★** discovered in Etruria and Southern Italy *(Magna Graecia)*; Egyptian sculptures and funerary objects (mummified sacred animals) dating largely from the New Empire (1580 to 1085 BC) and the Saitic Period (663 to 525 BC).

France's successive civilisations, from prehistory to the end of the Gallo-Roman period, are evoked through the tools, weapons and various objects found at excavation sites; archeological activities have been conducted in the region from the time of Napoleon III's campaigns. Note the three bronze helmets dating from *c*600 BC. In the room devoted to the Gallic sanctuary at Gournay-sur-Aronde, two great showcases display weapons and iron objects, and bones from animals which were ritually sacrificed.

The first-floor rooms have preserved their Directoire wainscoting. The painting collections are displayed here (large altarpiece representing the Passion by Wolgemut, Dürer's teacher), together with ceramics (pitchers in "Flemish stoneware", Italian majolicas), ivories, Limousin enamels etc.

COMPIÈGNE FOREST★★

Michelin map 106 fold 10 (inset) or 237 folds 7, 8

The State forest of Compiègne (14 500ha - 35 800 acres) is a remnant of the immense Cuise forest which extended from the edge of Ile-de-France to the Ardennes. It embraces delightful beech groves, magnificent avenues, valleys, ponds and villages.

The forest occupies a sort of hollow with the Oise and Aisne river valleys on two sides. A series of hills and promontories sketches a sharply defined crescent to the north, east and south. These peaks rise on average 80m - 262ft above the sandy base of the hollow, which is grooved with numerous rivulets. The largest of these, the Berne Stream, links a series of ponds.

1 500km - 930 miles of roads and footpaths cross the forest. François I first cut great rides through the trees, with Louis XIV and Louis XV later contributing more routes in order to create an ideal place for hunting.

The grounds, once the lands of Frankish kings, are today used by three different hunts.

Types of trees – The most common species in the forest are beech (40 %), oak (30 %) and yoke-elms (15 %). Beech in particular occupies the south plateau and its slopes, and the area immediately surrounding Compiègne itself. Oak, which was planted long ago, thrives in the better-drained clay soil, as well as on the Beaux Monts.

Since 1830 Norway pine and other conifers have grown in the poor, sandy soil.

A paved cycling path runs between Compiègne (east from Carrefour Royal along Route Tournante) and Pierrefonds.

Fishing regulations – A board in front of the forest warden's house at St Peter's Ponds (Étangs de St-Pierre) *(see above)* lists the clubs and organisations which issue permits and licences.

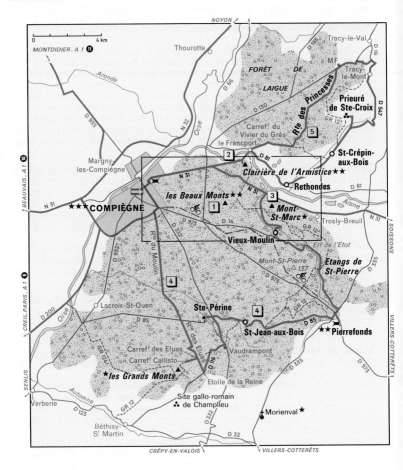

★★①BEAUX MONTS

Tour starting from Compiègne *18km - 11 miles – about 1 hour*

★★★**Compiègne** – *See Compiègne.*

Leave Compiègne southeast by Avenue Royale. At Carrefour Royal, turn left into Route Tournante and left at Carrefour Gabriel; the road crosses the long perspective of Avenue des Beaux-Monts. At Carrefour du Renard turn right into Route Eugénie and cross Carrefour des Vineux. The road rises to offer a good view of Avenue des Beaux-Monts from about halfway up the hillside. Continue as far as Carrefour d'Eugénie.

Carrefour d'Eugénie – Some of the forest's oldest **oak trees★★** stand at the side of this junction. The most ancient ones date from the time of François I.

Take the winding road on the left which climbs to Beaux Monts.

★★**Beaux Monts** – Stop at the summit, near the Beaux Monts viewing-point (point de vue); from here the view stretches along the straight line of the avenue through the forest all the way to the palace, barely visible 4km - 2 1/2 miles away.

Continue to the junction for Precipice Viewing Point.

Point de vue du Précipice (Precipice Viewing Point) – Here the extensive **view★** overlooks the woody stretches of the Berne River Valley and St Mark's Mount.

Return to the junction and turn right to descend the Beaux Monts.

The road heads down through a magnificent grove of oaks and beeches and reaches a straight road.

Turn right; cross Route Eugénie and take the first road on the right.

Chapelle St-Corneille-aux-Bois (Chapel of St-Cornelius-in-the-Woods) – The secluded chapel was founded in 1164; it later passed to the Abbey of St Cornelius in Compiègne. Later François I added a hunting lodge but its appearance today dates only from the time of Viollet-le-Duc (19C); the Gothic construction of the 13C chapel, however, has remained intact.

The wardens of Compiègne Forest came here during the Ancien Régime to hear Sunday mass.

Continue to D 14; turn right to return to Compiègne.

★★ 2 ARMISTICE CLEARING (CLAIRIÈRE DE L'ARMISTICE)

Direct road

6km - 3 1/2 miles northeast of Compiègne – 1 hour visit

By N 31 go straight over at Carrefour d'Aumont and continue to Carrefour du Francport; fork left to the Monument to the liberators of Alsace and Lorraine and the nearby car park.

★★**Clairière de l'Armistice** (Armistice Clearing) – In this shaded grove, on 11 November 1918, the armistice was signed, bringing to an end the hostilities between the Allies and Germany.

A site where a network of tracks existed for heavy artillery installations was cleared to make room for the private train of the allied forces' commander-in-chief, Field-Marshal Foch, and for that of the German plenipotentiaries. The tracks were linked to the Compiègne-Soissons line at Rethondes Station. Today, on the site of the two stationary railway carriages, rails and flagstones surround a memorial commemorating the date.

On 14 June 1940, 22 years later, during the Second World War, the German Army entered Paris; on 21 June, the French armistice delegation was received by Hitler and government dignitaries in the same car of the same private train, then located in its 1918 position. The leaders withdrew together and the representatives of the German high command gave their interlocutors the detailed document commanding the victors' terms for an armistice.

Wagon du maréchal Foch (Field Marshal Foch's Carriage) ⊙ – The original, historic dining-car which was transformed into an office for Field Marshal Foch was transported to Berlin as a trophy in 1940 but has since disappeared (probably after 1942 in a bombing raid).

In 1950 it was replaced by another carriage from a similar series. The actual objects used by the delegates in 1918, put aside safely at the time, are now back in place in the carriage.

★ 3 ST-MARK'S MOUNT AND ST PETER'S PONDS

From Compiègne to Pierrefonds

26km - 16 miles – about 1 1/2 hours

Leave Compiègne by N 31.

Pont de Berne (Berne Bridge) – It was here that the Dauphin, the future Louis XVI, met Marie-Antoinette for the first time; the future queen had just arrived from Vienna.

Turn right towards Pierrefonds. At Vivier-Frère-Robert turn left into Route du Geai.

★**Mont St-Marc** (St Mark's Mount) – The slopes of this flat-topped hill are covered with beeches. On reaching the plateau, turn left into the forest road which follows the edge: there are good views of the Berne and Aisne River valleys, Rethondes and Laigue Forest.

The road follows the northern promontory of the hill. 2.5km - 1 1/2 miles further along, Carrefour Lambin offers a particularly fine **view** of the Aisne Valley.

Return by the same road and fork left into the first road suitable for vehicles; descend Route du Geai and continue towards Pierrefonds. Turn right and continue through to Vieux-Moulin.

Vieux-Moulin – This former woodcutters' village has recently become a wealthy community of weekend homes. The little church, with a belfry resembling a Chinese hat, was rebuilt in 1860 at Napoleon III's expense.

Turn left at the junction with the war monument and take Route Eugénie (on the south bank) to Étot Pond (Étang de l'Étot).

Étangs de St-Pierre (St Peter's Ponds) – These ponds were created to stock fish; they were dug by members of the Celestine community from the priory of Mont-St-Pierre, to the west.

Empress Eugénie's former chalet is now a forest warden's house with exhibitions on the forest.

1km - 1/2 mile beyond the last pond, at a fork near the edge of the forest, take the small road left to reach Pierrefonds (qv).

★④ GRANDS MONTS

From Pierrefonds to Compiègne

27km - 17 miles – about 1 1/2 hours

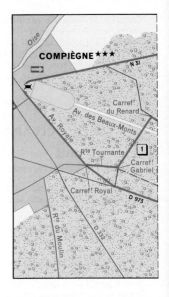

★★Château de Pierrefonds (Pierrefonds Château) – *See Pierrefonds. 1 hour*

Leave Pierrefonds by D 85, heading west.

The road first rises to a wooded plateau, where the beautiful beech groves were largely destroyed during storms in 1984; it then descends into St-Jean-aux-Bois.

St-Jean-aux-Bois – This charming village was appropriately renamed "Solitude" in 1794. The 12C monastic buildings which were at the heart of the village can be seen along one side of it, marked by a moat filled with water. The Benedictine recluses who settled here in the 12C left their abbey for Royallieu *(qv)* in 1634 as the forest was no longer safe; for a while Augustine canons took their place but in 1761 St-Jean was abandoned by its religious inhabitants.

The old fortified gate leads to the esplanade and the last vestiges of the abbey: the church, the chapter room and the doorway to the "Small Courtyard" (formerly workhouses). The architectural purity of the 13C **church★** is remarkable. Inside, the sober harmony of the transept and chancel create an impression of grandeur. The slenderness of the columns separating each transept arm into two bays emphasises the church's height. The arrangement here – which was common later, in the 16C – is the only example in the region from that period. The *grisailles* recall the interior's luminous atmosphere in the 13C.

The **chapter-house** (salle capitulaire) is located on the south side of the church; dating from 1150, it is the oldest part of the structure. It serves today as an annexe chapel and is generally open only for worship.

Continue along D 85.

Ste-Périne – The pond surrounded by plane trees and poplars, and the woodland house in an old priory form an attractive sight.

The nuns of Ste-Périne (a linguistic contraction of Pétronille) occupied this hermitage from 1285 to 1626. Lack of safety forced them to move first to Compiègne, then to Paris, then la Villette, Chaillot and finally Auteuil, where a retirement home still bears their name.

Turn round; turn right into D 332 towards Crépy-en-Valois and at Vaudrampont turn right into D 116. At Etoile de la Reine roundabout turn sharp right into Route des Éluas and first left into an unpaved road; park at Carrefour Callisto.

★Grands Monts – This southern part of the forest is divided into the plateau and the swamps. The short trip described below *(30min Rtn on foot)*, along an overhanging path shaded by beech groves, introduces some of the area's characteristics.

Descend Route des Princesses on foot; immediately after the barrier turn left into the well-maintained path marked with yellow indicators which goes around the promontory. Turn back when the path, less well cleared, reaches the bottom of the gully.

Turn round; continue along Route des Éluas and beyond the hairpin bend.
Return to Compiègne by following the long Route du Moulin.

A further intinerary ⑤ might take in the village of **Rethondes**, the church at **St-Crépin-aux-Bois**, and the 16C ruins of the beautiful priory church of the old **Prieuré Ste-Croix-d'Offémont**; Route des Princesses is a popular starting point for rambles.

CORBIE

Population 6 152
Michelin map 52 fold 9 or 236 fold 24

Corbie is a small town between the Somme and the Ancre rivers; it developed around the Benedictine abbey, where the powerful abbots held the title of Count and were allowed to print money.

A Cradle for Saints – The monastery was founded in 657 by St Bathild, wife of the Frankish king Clovis II, and in Carolingian times became a centre of Christian civilisation under the direction of St Adalard, Charlemagne's cousin. More than 300 monks there assured the constant worship of the Lord, day and night; St Paschase Radbert wrote the first theological treatise on the Eucharist; apostolic activity developed. The abbey spread to Corvey in Westphalia, which was to become the main centre of evangelism in northern Europe under the impetus of St Anschaire (or Oscar), who was born in Corbie in 801.

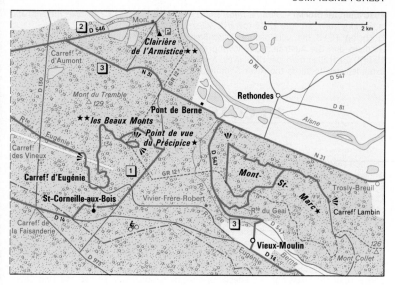

CORBIE

In the 11C St Gerard, a monk from Corbie, retreated to the area between the Garonne and the Dordogne, founding the Monastery of the Redemption. **St Colette** (1381-1447), the daughter of a local carpenter, lived as a recluse and was favoured with several visions. She came out of seclusion to establish several convents of Colettines, a branch of the Poor Clare nuns.

SIGHTS

From Place de la République go through the 18C **monumental doorway** to the abbey; the cloisters and convent buildings were razed during the Revolution.

Église St-Pierre (St Peter's Church) ⊙ – The construction of the former abbey church lasted from the 16C to the 18C but in 1815 the transept and chancel were knocked down, being by then almost in a ruined state.

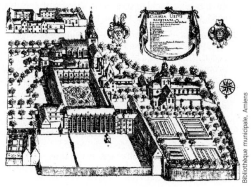

Corbie Abbey in the 17C

The stylistic unity of the remaining buildings is due to the architects' continued use of the Gothic style throughout the Renaissance and Classical periods: this accounts for the ribbed vaults in the three aisles, the rose window and the twin towers pierced by twin bays, and the west front featuring three doorways with broken arches, all following the style of Gothic cathedrals. Part of the decoration borrows from the Classical repertory, notably the cartouches on the porch coving.

The **interior** is now only about 36m - 118ft long, as opposed to 117m - 384ft originally (see the model of the church before the Revolution). The Treasury at one time contained 113 reliquaries which were often venerated by the French kings and some of which have been preserved. The works of art include:
– 15C statue of Our Lady of the Door *(right aisle, last pillar)*;
– St Bathild, an example of majestic 14C statuary *(back of right aisle, right of altar)*;
– a head of St Peter (13C) *(a pillar of left aisle)*;
– 15C tomb of Abbot Raoul de Roye, the tutor of St Colette *(left aisle)*.

Chapelle Ste-Colette – The chapel was built in 1959 on the site of the house in which St Colette was born and contains a 16C statue of the saint kneeling.

EXCURSIONS

La Neuville – *2km - 1 mile northwest, on right bank of the River Ancre.*
Above the doorway of the early-16C church is a large, interesting **low-relief** showing Christ's entry into Jerusalem on Palm Sunday. The relief is remarkable for its clarity and wealth of detail: spectators perched in the trees, in the background a miller wearing a cotton bonnet at the window of his mill...

Australian Memorial – *3km - 2 miles south. Leave Corbie by D 1 (towards Amiens) and in Fouilloy turn left into D 23 towards Villers-Bretonneux.*
In spring 1918 the hills around **Villers-Bretonneux** were fiercely fought over by the Germans and the Australians, following the German offensive on Picardy: more than 10 000 Australian men lost their lives. A memorial and a cemetery recall their sacrifice. Extended **view** towards the River Somme and Amiens.

La CÔTE D'OPALE ★

The OPAL COAST

Michelin map 51 folds 1, 2 or 236 folds 1, 2

The **Opal Coast** (Côte d'Opale) extends from the Somme Bay all the way round to the Belgian frontier; its name is derived from the creamy colour of the waves washing against the coast.
The most spectacular part of the coastline is between Boulogne and Calais, where the cliffs skirt the Boulonnais hills: between the sea and the sky there is only the Opal Coast bluff, characterized by promontories separating the small, dry valleys **(crans)** between the cliffs, which are similar to the *valleuses* of the region around Dieppe, Le Havre and Rouen. A strong north-south sea current wears away the base of the cliffs, sometimes causing large parts to collapse. Research has shown that the cliff is eroded by about 25m - 27yds each century.

This part of the coast has been declared a major national site, named the Two Capes Area *(Site des deux Caps)* ⊙; it offers enjoyable rambles and nature trails.

FROM BOULOGNE TO CALAIS *49km - 30 miles – about 2 1/2 hours*

★**Boulogne** – *See Boulogne. 1 1/2 hours.*

Leave Boulogne by D 940.

D 940 is a winding coastal road offering glimpses of the sea, the ports and the beaches, leading across hill crests which are intermittently bare or covered with closely cropped meadows. To the north the road comes to the Escalles *cran*, a mountainous-looking pass at an altitude of only 100m - 328ft. Car parks flank the road, allowing access to the sea or to walks among the dunes.

⌂⌂ **Wimereux** – The opening to the Wimereux Valley is the site of a large and popular seaside resort for families. A walk on the promenade edging the sand and pebble beach affords views of the strait, the Grande Armée Column *(qv)* and Boulogne. The promenade narrows to a path leading to **Pointe aux Oies** (Goose Point), where on 6 August 1840 the future Napoleon III set out in his attempt to win over the garrison stationed at Boulogne.

Between Wimereux and Ambleteuse the road runs beside tall dunes.

Ambleteuse – This picturesque village stands on a hillside above the mouth of the River Slack, which forms a beaching harbour. Ambleteuse was formerly a military port protected by the recently restored, 17C **Mahon Fort** (fort Mahon). Napoleon based part of his flotilla here at the time of the Boulogne Camp *(qv)*. Today it is a beach among the coastal dunes, from which Boulogne's harbour entrance and, in clear weather, the English coast, are visible.

Museum of the Second World War (Musée historique de la Deuxième Guerre mondiale) ⊙ – The museum on the edge of Ambleteuse traces the history of the conflict, from the Invasion of Poland in September 1939 to the Liberation. About a hundred different uniforms are exhibited, together with equipment worn or used by the armies involved in the war.

3km - 2 miles after Audresselles, turn left into D 191.

★★**Cap Gris-Nez** – This "grey-nose cape" marks the meeting point between the North Sea and the English Channel. Facing the English coast 30km - 19 miles away, the gently sloping cliffs rise to 45m - 148ft. The lighthouse (28m - 92ft tall) with beams visible 45km – 28 miles away, was rebuilt after the war. It stands at the tip of a flat peninsula which is exposed to the winds and scattered with the debris of demolished German blockhouses. The Gris-Nez branch of CROSS (Centre Régional d'Opération de Secours et de Sauvetage) is located underground: the organisation is responsible for watching over these waters, where maritime traffic is the heaviest in the world, and provides aid of any kind when needed. The crumbling debris from the cliffs mingles with the rocky reef known as "the Whales" *(Les Épaulards)* because, seen from a distance, it looks hump-backed and throws up spray.
Straight ahead, the **view**★ extends to the English cliffs which appear white next to the blue of the sky, while on the French side the folds of the coastline, including the characteristic dry valleys between the cliffs, are visible. Cap Blanc-Nez *(right)* and Boulogne *(left)* may also be seen.
A stele recalls that on 25 May 1940 the naval officer Ducuing and his sailors died here, defending the signal station against Guderian's armoured tanks.
The **Museum of the Atlantic Wall** (Musée du Mur de l'Atlantique) ⊙ is in the Todt battery, a Second World War blockhouse which served as a German missile launching base; missiles 2m – 6ft long were fired on England from here. There are collections of arms and uniforms inside the museum.

⌂ **Wissant** – This splendid beach of fine, firm sand is well sheltered from the eastern winds and currents. It forms a vast curve between Cap Gris-Nez and Cap Blanc-Nez. Villas stand among the dunes overlooking the shore.

The **Mill Museum** (Musée du Moulin) ☉ is housed in a flour mill driven by hydraulic power. It is well preserved and features pinewood parts, cast-iron waterwheels and a conveyor belt to lift the goods.

★★Cap Blanc-Nez – The "white-nose cape" is a vertical mass of chalk cliffs rising 134m - 440ft above the waves, offering extensive **views★** over the English cliffs and the French coast from Calais to Cap Gris-Nez. The **National Museum of Channel Crossing** (Musée National du Transmanche) ☉, located on Mont d'Hubert, faces Cap Blanc-Nez; it retraces the turbulent history of the strait, which scientists and scholars have always used to promote their ideas. The story began in 1751 with Nicolas Desmarets, who was the first to think of linking France to England. Later, Aimé Thomé de Gamond suggested a variety of options: a tunnel constructed of metal tubes, a concrete undersea vault, a pontoon, an artificial isthmus, a mobile bridge and a viaduct-bridge. He even dived to the bottom of the strait several times to collect numerous geological samples. Channel crossings were eventually achieved by balloon (Blanchard), plane (Blériot), steamboat (the first regular line was established in 1816), raft, on skis... Just over 400 braver characters since the first success in 1875 have breached the 21-mile stretch of water by swimming.

Lower down, near D 940, stands the monument to **Latham** (1883-1912), the aviator who attempted, unsuccessfully, to cross the Channel at the same time as Blériot.

Between Sangatte and Blériot-Plage, the bungalows are built directly on the sea-washed dunes. It is here that the Channel Tunnel *(qv)* emerges.

Blériot-Plage – The beautiful beach extends along to Cap Blanc-Nez. At Baraques (500m - 550yds west of the station), near D 940, a monument commemorates the first aerial crossing of the Channel, by **Louis Blériot** (1872-1936). On 25 July 1909 he landed his airplane in a valley in the Dover cliffs, after a flight of approximately half an hour.

Calais – *See Calais.*

Cap Blanc-Nez on the Opal Coast

COUCY-LE-CHÂTEAU-AUFFRIQUE ★

Population 1 058
Michelin map 56 fold 4 or 236 fold 37

Coucy extends along a promontory overlooking the Ailette valley on an impressive defensive **site★**, further sheltered by its medieval walls which used to incorporate 28 towers. Unfortunately, during the First World War the upper town suffered greatly from being in the front line of battle and in 1917 the Germans blew up the castle's keep.

The Lord of Coucy – "I am not a king, nor a prince, a duke or a count either. I am the Lord *(Sire)* of Coucy" was the proud boast of the castle's owner, Enguerrand III (1192-1242) who, after fighting loyally and valiantly at Bouvines *(qv)*, sought to take possession of the French throne during Blanche of Castille's regency.

SIGHTS

Castle ⊙ – A bailey is entered before the castle proper. To the right of the bailey's entrance a Guard Room (Salle des Gardes) contains a model and documents relating to Coucy.

The foundations of a Romanesque chapel are visible on the approach to the castle, which stands as an irregular quadrilateral at the end of the promontory. The great round towers which used to surround it were over 30m - 98ft high and were stronger than even the royal keeps.

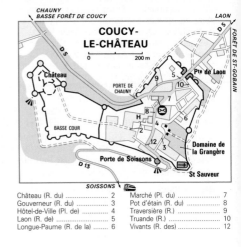

The round keep measured 31m - 101ft in diameter and 54m - 177ft high; its walls, faced with limestone, were 7m - 23ft thick; the whole was protected by an additional external defence, the "shirt". The interior contained three levels covered by Gothic vaults; a well, 65m - 213ft deep, provided water for the inhabitants.

The dwellings had been rebuilt by Enguerrand VII at the end of the 14C, then finished at the end of the 15C by Louis of Orléans, Charles VI's brother, who had bought back Coucy from Enguerrand VII's daughter. Remains of the Noblewomen's Chamber (Salle des Preuses) and the Noblemen's Chamber (Salle des Preux) exist, with a cellar underneath. From the west tower there is a good view over the Ailette and Oise river valleys.

Château (R. du)	2	Marché (Pl. du)	7
Gouverneur (R. du)	3	Pot d'étain (R. du)	8
Hôtel-de-Ville (Pl. de)	4	Traversière (R.)	9
Laon (R. de)	5	Truande (R.)	10
Longue-Paume (R. de la)	6	Vivants (R. des)	12

Porte de Soissons (Soissons Gate) – This gate, which was built in the 13C, is reinforced by the Coucy tower.

Historical Museum (Musée historique) ⊙ – A model of the town and the castle are among the exhibits, together with engravings and old photographs, and figures dressed in period costumes. From the platform there is a good view over the Ailette Valley.

Église St-Sauveur (St Saviour's Church) – This church nestles at the edge of the ramparts. Apart from the Romanesque west front (12C) and the 14C Gothic aisles, the building was almost totally rebuilt after the First World War.

Domaine de la Grangère – This garden belonged to the Governor's house where in 1594 César, Duke of Vendôme, was born, the bastard son of Henri IV and Gabrielle d'Estrées, Duchesse de Beaufort.

The lip of the garden's well is made from a keystone from the castle keep.

Porte de Laon (Laon Gate) – This entrance dates from the 13C and plays a major defensive role at the promontory's base; it is the only entrance with easy access and is therefore guarded by two important round towers, with walls 8m - 26ft thick at their base.

EXCURSION

Basse Forêt de Coucy (Coucy Forest) – *Leave Coucy by Porte de Chauny; at the junction at the foot of the promontory, take D 934 towards Noyon, through Montoir Woods.*

Montoir Woods (Bois de Montoir) – The "Big Bertha" which fired on Paris for the first time on 23 March 1918 was hidden in these woods; the shell covered the 120km - 74 miles in 3 minutes and 6 seconds.

Turn right into D 1 and right again into D 133 to Folembray.

Folembray – The kennels of the Rallye-Nomade Hunt are located here; the hounds are used for deer hunting. François I enjoyed staying in the château with his favourite Françoise de Châteaubriand.

The annual Michelin Red Guide France
revises its selection of establishments which
- *serve carefully prepared meals at a reasonable cost,*
- *include service on the bill or the price of each dish,*
- *offer a menu of simple but good food at a modest price,*
- *provide free parking.*

It is well worth buying the current edition.

COURANCES CHÂTEAU★★

Michelin map 106 fold 44 or 61 fold 1

The luxuriant vegetation and rippling waters surrounding Courances Château make this setting one of the most attractive sights in Ile-de-France.

Built around 1550 by Gilles le Breton for Cosme Clausse, Secretary of Finance to Henri II, the château acquired its present appearance in the 17C. It is a good example of the Louis XIII style: a brick building with sandstone quoins and window trims, pointed roofs and a sparsely-decorated exterior. In the 19C the entrance front was embellished with a replica of the horse-shoe staircase at Fontainebleau *(illustration Architecture)*. The château is still surrounded by a moat and a splendid avenue on the opposite side of the road completes this sweeping perspective.

★★**Park** – The approach to the château is very grand. Walk through the gate and cross the "forecourt", a vast stretch of lawn divided by a central path and flanked by two canals reflecting the noble plane trees.

The park, designed by Le Nôtre, extends behind the château and the rear façade gives onto a lush, green lawn. A path leads to the Grand Canal, which receives the waters of the École. Another path, set at right angles, skirts the small cascades and leads to the flower beds, offering a lovely view of the château mirrored in the crystal-clear water.

Before returning to the gate, turn right (when level with the château) towards the ruins of an old fuller's mill and its gushing stream. From the embankment on the left, admire the Japanese garden and, further back, the falls of an old mill.

Château ⊙ – The tour includes a number of living-rooms, low-ceilinged chambers and annexes. Note the corner dining room, tastefully decorated with walnut wainscoting and ornamental plates, and the Monkeys' Gallery, named after three 16C tapestries with scenes of monkeys mimicking man.

Rear view of the château

EXCURSION

Fleury-en-Bière Château – *4km - 2 1/2 miles northeast on N 372 and right into D 11.* The château *(private)* dates from the 16C and was designed for Cosme Clausse *(see above).* The stately proportions of the courtyard, sealed off from the street by a stout wall, can be glimpsed from the entrance. At the far end, surrounded by a moat, stands the brick and stone château, flanked on its right side by a large stone tower. Several huge out-houses stand either side of the building. The gracious Romanesque chapel *(set back to the right)* serves as parish church to the community.

CRÉCY-EN-PONTHIEU

Population 1 491
Michelin map 52 fold 7 or 236 fold 122

Crécy is today a peaceful little town on the edge of a farmed basin at the source of the River Maye, facing the plateau on which Crécy Forest stands; its name, however, still evokes the famous victory by Edward III of England over Philip VI of France on 26 August 1346, at the beginning of the Hundred Years War.

Church – The interior houses four large canvases from the Poussin School presenting the story of Moses. The paintings came from the now-ruined Dommartin Abbey *(near Tortefontaine on D 119, north of Crécy).*

117

Moulin Edouard III (Edward III's Windmill) – *1 km - 1/2 mile northeast on D 111.*
Beside the road *(right)* stands an observation tower on the site of the windmill from
where the King of England directed the battle. From the top there is a good **view** over
the undulating plain *(viewing table)*.

A memorial just off the battlefield marks the spot where the Prince of Wales took a
bunch of ostrich feathers from the body of the Duc de Luxembourg; the feathers
became the personal crest of the monarch's son and are still used to this day.

Edward III had landed in Normandy with 4 000 men-at-arms and 10 000 longbowmen;
they rampaged through Normandy as far as Poissy. When Philip VI advanced with
12 000 men-at-arms and thousands of other troops, Edward took up a defensive
position at Crécy. An attack was then launched by the French cavalry, in a spirited but
ill-planned move. The assault disintegrated under the hail from the English archers,
backed up for the first time in European history by bombardments; in the resulting
carnage, 20 000 Frenchmen fell on the battlefield. Philip's ally John the Blind, the old
king of Bohemia, was killed while being carried to his badly-wounded son at the heart
of the battle; the spot where he fell is marked with the Bohemia Cross (Croix de
Bohême) *(on D 56 southeast of Crécy)*. Edward went on to besiege Calais *(qv)*.

*A "ficelle picarde" consists of a rolled pancake, filled with ham and chopped
cooked mushrooms; covered in Béchamel sauce and browned in the oven.*

CRÉPY-EN-VALOIS

Population 12 277
Michelin map 56 folds 12, 13

Crépy is in the heavily-forested Valois, one of the oldest regions in France. The upper
part of the town is strategically placed on a plateau between two streams.

The Valois dynasty – For over two and a half centuries, from 1328 to 1589, the
French throne was occupied by the descendants of Charles I, comte de Valois and
brother of Philip IV the Fair. The last representatives of this dynasty, Charles VIII,
François I, Henri II and III, contributed to the development of Italian – therefore
Renaissance – art in France, while giving kingship a new, authoritarian stamp.

Capital of the Valois – The Counts and subsequently the Dukes of Valois made Crépy
their new capital. A 10C castle, as well as several monasteries and churches, testify to
the importance Crépy had acquired between the 11C and the 14C. It was only after
Henri II's reign that the princes showed a preference for Villers-Cotterêts.
In 1790 the reorganisation of the French *départements* split the old Valois territory
between the Oise and the Aisne. Crépy's golden age was over.

★OLD TOWN *1 1/2 hours*

Place Gambetta – This square has retained its quaint medieval charm. Among the
18C buildings, the **Maison des Quatre Saisons** (no 15) features four Rococo grotesque
masks representing the four seasons.
Follow Rue des Ursulines, then turn right into Rue du Lion.
At no 5, note the 14C mansion **Hôtel du Lion** with its crow-stepped gables.

Église St-Denis (St Denis' Church) – The majestic 16C transept consists of two bays.
The nave was built in the 12C, the aisles in the 15C. The south aisle presents several
small stone slabs celebrating the memory of the Ursuline nuns *(see below)*.

Abbaye St-Arnould (St Arnould Abbey) ⊙ – The ruins of this abbey – the necropolis of
the counts of Valois – are at their most impressive when seen from the edge of the
walls they dominate. On the opposite side stand the remains of a Gothic church.
Excavations have uncovered a series of 11C colonnettes with their capitals, belonging to a former crypt.
Take the opposite direction to St-Denis and return to the town centre along a
cobbled street; after a bend it leads to the **House of the Ursulines' Intendant** (Maison de
l'Intendant des Ursulines), a superb 18C building and further along, to the entrance
of the Ursuline convent, occupied by nuns who taught in Crépy from 1623 to 1791.
Return to Place Gambetta and turn right into Rue Gustave-Chopinet.

Vieux Château (Old Castle) – This building houses some charming collections from the
Museum of Archery and Valois.

Museum of Archery and Valois (Musée de l'Archerie et du Valois) ⊙ – Archery is a
traditional sport in the Valois area. Groups originated from part-civil, part-military
associations set up in the Middle Ages to train the militia in peacetime.
Wary of the strong religious and loyalist views of the archers, the members of the
1789 Constituent Assembly incorporated them into the National Guard. Archers'
associations reappeared in the 19C, for social and sporting purposes.
The main exhibition room of the museum presents the history and traditions:
documents depicting St Sebastian, the patron saint of archers, the internal hierar-
chy of the Guild, the "provincial bouquet" ritual, (formal procession around a

bouquet of honour in a commemorative vase). The glass cabinets display a great variety of bows and crossbows, ranging from early primitive weapons to the sophisticated models of today's competitions and consisting of metal, fibreglass and exotic woods...

The high-ceilinged rooms in the castle and the chapel contain a **collection of religious works★**: an early-16C Virgin and Child from Le Luat, a 15C nursing Virgin from Nanteuil-le-Haudouin, and several other figures representing St Martin, St Sebastian, the Virgin and a St John from Gilocourt.

ADDITIONAL SIGHT

Église St-Thomas (St Thomas' Church) – *Approach from Rue St-Lazare.* These distinguished ruins are the remains of a Gothic church built outside the ramparts in 1182 in memory of Thomas Becket, Archbishop of Canterbury, twelve years after he was murdered in his own cathedral. The ruins include the west front, the first bay of the nave, the truncated tower and its 15C spire. The rest of the grounds are now a garden.

Le CROTOY ☖

Population 2 440
Michelin map 52 fold 6 or 236 fold 21

Le Crotoy is reached by a scenic route (D 940) which runs alongside grass-covered sandbanks (*"mollières"* – *qv*). The town was once a strongpoint, with a castle in which Joan of Arc was imprisoned in 1430 before being taken to St Valery and then to Rouen. Today it is an attractive and popular seaside resort overlooking the Somme Bay.

The Port – The port is not far from Place Jeanne d'Arc, the resort's lively centre, and is used by small coastal fishing trawlers (which catch shrimps, flatfish and herrings); casting on the Somme's bed brings in plaice and eel.

Butte du Moulin (Mill Hill) – The hill is reached from the church by Rue de la Mer and offers an extensive **view★** from the terrace over the Somme Bay, St Valery, Le Hourdel and the open sea.

Chemin de fer de la baie de Somme (Somme Bay Railway) ⊙ – A train comprising old carriages with viewing platforms pulled by steam or diesel engines runs between Le Crotoy, Noyelles, St Valery and Cayeux-sur-Mer providing a journey (16km -10 miles) of discovery through this lush area bordered by the River Somme's grassy sandbanks.

DAMPIERRE CHÂTEAU ★★

Michelin map 101 fold 31 or 106 fold 29

Dampierre, situated in the narrow upper part of the Chevreuse Valley, is closely associated with two distinguished families, the Luynes and the Chevreuse.

Château★★ ⊙ – From 1675 to 1683 Jules Hardouin-Mansart rebuilt Dampierre Château for Colbert's son-in-law the Duke of Chevreuse, a former student at Port-Royal (*qv*) and the mentor of the Duke of Burgundy. The château – restored by Félix Duban during the reign of Louis-Philippe – remains the property of the Luynes family.

Dampierre Château

119

TOUR *40min*

The main body of the château, surrounded by a moat, opens onto a courtyard which is overlooked by two buildings with arcades. The pinkish tones of the brick harmonise with the sober stonework trims and columns, contrasting sharply with the darker hues of the park.

On the ground floor, visitors may admire Cavelier's statue of Penelope in the hall leading to the living-rooms embellished with Louis XV wainscoting, the suite occupied by Marie Leczinska, and an imposing dining room decorated with Louis XIV panelling. The first floor houses the Royal Suite, which welcomed Louis XIV, Louis XV and Louis XVI. The splendid 17C and 18C furnishings are beautifully preserved and reminiscent of the King's Suite at Versailles: the furniture, portraits, wainscoting, medallions and overdoor panels.

The most amazing achievement stands at the top of the great staircase. The Minerva Room (Salle de la Minerve) is a formal reception room by Duban from the Restoration period. Ingres was commissioned to paint a fresco representing the Golden Age; it was never completed. The duc Honoré de Luynes, who conceived the whole project, ordered a colourful 3m - 10ft statue of Minerva, a miniature replica of the legendary gold and ivory Parthenon Minerva executed by Phidias in the 5C BC.

Park ⊙ – The estate walls surrounding the grounds – where wild deer may be seen running freely – circle a 30ha - 74 acre garden featuring hundreds of flowers and plant species. In season, banks of colour are provided by tulips, hyacinths, irises, poppies, roses, azaleas and rhododendrons. The river and ponds are edged with aquatic plants.

EXCURSION

Vaux de Cernay – *4km - 2 1/2 miles south by D 91, 1/2 to 2 hours' walk.* The road (D 91) weaves up the wooded narrow valley, past a restaurant and across a brook by a mill, Moulin des Roches.

Park near the Chalet des Cascades ⊙

The slopes surrounding the undergrowth beneath oaks and beeches are dotted with sandstone boulders, little falls and whirlpools.

Cernay Pond (Étang de Cernay) – The pond was created by the monks of the local abbey to stock fish. A memorial to the 19C landscape painter Léon-Germain Pelouse stands at the top of the embankment, near a stately oak tree.

The walk may be continued for another 1/2 or 1 hour by following the wide path which veers right and leads straight up to the wooded plateau. From the ledge of the plateau turn back, bear right and return along the cliff path that skirts the promontory.

★**Vaux-de-Cernay Abbey** (Abbaye des Vaux-de-Cernay) – The abbey was founded in the early 12C. It came under Cistercian rule but was abandoned in 1791 by its last twelve monks and sold. The Rothschild family who bought the abbey in 1873 restored and preserved it until the Second World War. It has now been converted into a hotel.

In the **grounds** ⊙, the ruins of the abbey church may be seen (late-12C façade with rose window), and the monks' building, now a concert hall.

DISNEYLAND PARIS★★★

Michelin map 106 fold 22 – Michelin Green Guide Disneyland Paris

Standing on the Brie plain about 30km - 18 miles east of Paris is a unique development in Europe: Disneyland Paris.

The enormous site, which was conceived as a complete holiday resort and will continue to develop until the year 2017, already consists of the **Disneyland Paris theme park** and a resort complex offering accommodation and other recreational facilities.

The **Disneyland Hotel**, built in the style of a turn-of-the-century American mansion from a seaside resort, stands at the entrance to the theme park. Five other hotels stand beside Lake Disney or along the Rio Grande, each bringing to life a different American theme: the **Hotel New York** (Manhattan), the **Newport Bay Club** (a 19C New England beach resort), **Sequoia Lodge** (the National Parks), **Hotel Santa Fe** (New Mexico) and the **Hotel Cheyenne** (a small western town).

Not far from the hotels, the main entertainment centre, **Festival Disney**, recreates the American way of life with shops, restaurants and a nightclub. An evening spectacular, **Buffalo Bill's Wild West Show★★** – complete with horses, bison, cowboys and Indians – evokes the epic days of the Wild West. At a slight distance from the complex lies **Golf Disneyland Paris** with its 27 hole course. The **Davy Crockett Ranch** is a caravan and camp site in the woods 4.5km - 3 miles away, with wooden cabins recalling the life of the trappers.

A magician called Walt Disney – Walt Disney's name is linked to innumerable cartoon strips and animated cartoons which have entertained children throughout the world, and the heroes of his creations – Micky Mouse, Minnie, Donald, Pluto, Pinocchio, Snow White etc – no-one can forget.

He was born Walter Elias Disney in Chicago in 1901, the fourth child of Flora and Elias Disney. Walt soon showed great ability in drawing. After the First World War, in which he served as an ambulance driver in France, he returned to the United States where he met a young Dutchman called Ub Iwerks, who was also passionate about drawing. In 1923 the pair produced in Hollywood a series of short films called **Alice Comedies**. In 1928 Mickey House, the future international star, was created. There next followed the era of the Oscar-winning, full-length animated cartoon films: **The Three Little Pigs** (1933), **Snow White and the Seven Dwarfs** (1937), **Dumbo** (1941). Disney productions also developed to include films starring real people, such as **Treasure Island** (1950) and **20 000 Leagues Under the Sea** (1954), and some mixing the two, for instance **Mary Poppins** (1964) which won six Oscars.

On 15 December 1966 the man who had spent his life trying to bring dreams to life died; the Walt Disney Studios continued to make films, however, remaining faithful to Walt's ideas: **The Aristocats, Who Killed Roger Rabbit?** (which won four Oscars), **The Little Mermaid** (two Oscars), **Beauty and the Beast** (1991), **Aladdin** (1992) and **The Lion King** (1994).

★★★DISNEYLAND PARIS THEME PARK ⊙

This theme park, like those in the United States (opened in California in 1955 and in Florida in 1971) and Japan (Tokyo, 1983), is a realisation of Walt Disney's dream of creating "a small, enchanted park where children and adults can enjoy themselves together".

The large Disneyland Paris site (over 55ha - 135 acres) is surrounded by trees and comprises five territories or "lands", each with a different theme. As well as the spectacular shows featuring amazing automatons (Audio-Animatronics), each region has shops, bars, restaurants and food stalls.

Every day, the **Disney Parade★★**, a procession of floats carrying all the favourite Disney cartoon characters, takes place. On some evenings and throughout the summer the **Main Street Electrical Parade★★** adds extra illuminations to the fairytale setting. The **Fantasy in the Sky★** fireworks display spectacularly rounds off an eventful day.

Listed below are descriptions of the main attractions only; for more detailed information and plans refer to the **Michelin Green Guide Disneyland Paris.**

Main Street USA

The main street of an American town at the turn of the 20C, bordered by shops with Victorian-style fronts, is brought to life as though by magic. Horse-drawn street cars, double-decker buses, limousines, fire engines and Black Marias transport visitors from Town Square to Central Plaza (the hub of the park) while colourful musicians play favourite ragtime, jazz and Dixieland tunes. On each side of the road are **Discovery Arcade** and **Liberty Arcade** (exhibition on the famous Statue of Liberty at the entrance to New York harbour).

From Main Street station a small steam train, the **Euro Disneyland Railroad★**, travels across the park and through the **Grand Canyon Diorama**.

Main Street Motors – Enthusiasts of classic cars can peruse the cars exhibited here, and even have their photo taken in front of one of them.

Frontierland

The conquest of the West, the gold trail and the Far West with its legends and folklore are brought together in Thunder Mesa, a typical western town, and Big Thunder Mountain which rises on an island washed by the Rivers of the Far West. The waters here are plied by two handsome **steamboats★**, the *Mark Twain* and the *Molly Brown*.

★★★**Big Thunder Mountain** – In the bowels of this arid mountain lies an old gold mine which is visited via the mine train: this turns out to be a runaway train which hurtles out of control to provide a thrilling ride.

★★★**Phantom Manor** – A dilapidated house stands not far from Thunder Mesa, overlooking the Rivers of the Far West. Inside, a strange atmosphere hangs in the air: a spine-chilling tour of the house reveals hundreds of mischievous ghosts...

★**The Lucky Nugget Saloon** – This horseshoe-shaped saloon – every western town had its saloon – is richly decorated. Dinner show: **Lilly's Follies.**

Adventureland

This is the land of exotic adventure: waterfalls, an oriental bazaar, African drumbeats, a treasure island, swashbuckling pirates... Access is from Central Plaza, through Adventureland Bazaar.

★★★**Pirates of the Caribbean** – In the tropical Caribbean seas, marauding pirates attack and loot a coastal fort and village in this famous and action-packed encounter.

★★**Indiana Jones et le Temple du Péril** – In the jungle lies a ruined temple; courageous archeologists in wagons enter it and defy the laws of gravity. This is not for the faint-hearted.

★★**La Cabane des Robinson** – A giant tree (27m - 89ft high) offering panoramic views serves as the ingeniously-furnished home of the shipwrecked Swiss family Robinson from J D Wyss' novel.

Fantasyland

This area, based around Walt Disney's familiar trademark, Sleeping Beauty's castle, recalls favourite fairy tales by authors such as Charles Perrault, Lewis Carroll and the Brothers Grimm. Here familiar figures – Mickey Mouse, Pinocchio, Captain Hook – will happily pose for photographs.

★★**Le Château de la Belle au Bois Dormant** – The fairytale castle with its blue and gold turrets crowned with pennants is at the very heart of Disneyland. Inside, Aubusson tapestries recount episodes from this famous story. Below, in the depths of the castle, a huge scaly dragon appears to be sleeping...

★★**It's a Small World** – The delightful musical cruise is a celebration of the innocence and joy of children throughout the world.

★**Blanche-Neige et les Sept Nains** – Enjoyable tours lead through the mysterious forest in mining cars from the dwarfs' mine – just watch out for the wicked witch...

★**Les Voyages de Pinocchio** – Lively scenes based on Carlo Collodi's enduring tale present the lovable puppet Pinocchio and his friends.

★★**Peter Pan's Flight** – Fly – in a boat – through the skies above London and in Never-Never Land reliving the adventures of Peter Pan and the sinister Captain Hook who is relentlessly pursued by a hungry crocodile.

★**Alice's Curious Labyrinth** – At the end of this maze guarded by playing cards stands the Queen of Hearts' Castle where the queen from Lewis Carroll's classic story awaits those brave enough to visit...

★**Le Carrousel de Lancelot** – This is an enchanting merry-go-round of brightly-painted horses.

Discoveryland

This is the world of past discoveries and dreams of the future with the great visionaries such as Leonardo da Vinci, Jules Verne and H G Wells and their wonderful inventions.

★★★**Star Tours** – This is a breathtaking inter-planetary experience full of special effects inspired by the film *Star Wars:* voyage into space, piloted by a robot!

★★★**Space Mountain** – Fantastic journey through space, based on Jules Verne's novel *From the Earth to the Moon* (1873).

★★**Ciné Magique** – Enjoy rhythm, music and dance in a three-dimensional film about the adventures of Captain EO, played by Michael Jackson.

★★**Le Visionarium** – A 360° screen reveals the wonders of Europe.

DOUAI ★

Population 42 175
Michelin map 51 fold 16 or 236 fold 16

Douai stands on either side of the River Scarpe, which flows through its centre; despite the bomb damage of 1940, the town has preserved the 18C arrangement and buildings that gave it the aristocratic look Balzac evoked in his *Recherche de l'Absolu*.
Despite the number of large industrial firms – comprising metallurgy (Arbel, Renault), chemicals and food, a national printing works and France's fourth-ranking river freight trade – Douai appears as more of a legal centre, with a Court of Appeals, a relic of the Flanders Parliament which sat here from 1713 to the Revolution.
The town also enjoys a distinguished reputation for intellectual activity, which began with the elegiac poetess **Marceline Desbordes-Valmore** (1786-1859) who was born here, and is maintained by the many educational institutions which have taken the place of the university, founded in the 16C but transferred to Lille in 1887.

Parade of the Gayants – On the Sunday after 5 July, five giant figures of the Gayant family are paraded through the town in medieval costume, accompanied by folklore groups singing songs associated with this family: Gayant, the father (7.50m - 25ft tall, weighing 370kg - 816lbs), his wife Marie Cagenon (6.50m - 21ft tall) and their children Jacquot, Fillion and Binbin. They are escorted by a wheel of fortune and the artillerymen's mascot, a skirted horse. The giants appear in the town during the two days that follow, then return on Tuesday night to their house. Gayant, the oldest giant in the north (1530), is also the most popular. The week before his appearance is enlivened with concerts, ballets, folklore evenings, organ recitals and bell-ringing.
After the giants retire, a torch procession takes place, preceding the regattas, parade and fireworks display of 14 July. These popular rejoicings bring together the citizens of Douai, who refer to themselves in jest as "Gayant's children".

Bellegambe, painter of Douai and its region – The artist Jean Bellegambe (1470-1534), who seems to have lived his entire life in Douai, appears to have been a likeable character with wide-ranging artistic talent.

He mastered the transition from the Gothic tradition (religious subjects treated with realistic detail and harmonious colours) to the Italian influence of the Renaissance (works decorated with columns, pilasters, shells and garlands) which he linked with the objective, intimate realism of the Flemish school and the intellectualism of the French school, which is marked by a choice of subjects which are sometimes difficult to understand.

Bellegambe worked a great deal for the abbeys of the Scarpe Valley, and Douai's site and buildings can often be recognised in his works: the belfry and town gates, the towers of the abbey church of Anchin, Flines woods and the watery landscapes of the Scarpe and Sensée rivers. These representations testify to the painter's deep love for his region.

★BELFRY AND SURROUNDING AREA *1 hour*

Start from Place d'Armes, a part-pedestrian zone with terraces and fountains. L'**Hôtel du Dauphin** is the only remaining 18C house here; its façade is adorned with emblems. It now houses the Tourist Centre.

Walk along Rue de la Mairie.

Douai's belfry is one of the best known in northern France and has been made famous not only by Victor Hugo's description of his passage through the town in 1837, but also by Corot's fine painting, now in the Louvre. It is an imposing square Gothic tower, sombre and grim, and was built from 1390 to 1410; it stands 64m - 210ft tall (40m - 131ft from the ground to the platform).

The top of the belfry bristles with turrets, dormer windows, pinnacles and weather-vanes, and is crowned with a Flemish lion "that turns with a flag in its paws" (Victor Hugo).

The current chimes, consisting of 62 bells, are on the fourth floor. They replaced the famous ones which were destroyed by

Douai belfry

the Germans in 1917. They play the tune of the Scottish Puritans on the hour; on the half-hour, a boating air; at quarter past and quarter to the hour, a few notes of Gayant's tune.

From the top of the tower (192 steps), Douai and its industrial suburb may be seen through the louvre-boarding.

Inside the **town hall** (hôtel de ville) the Gothic Council Chamber (15C), the old chapel (now the main hall), the White Salon with 18C wood panels over the old partitions, and the festival hall are open to visitors.

Follow the vaulted passageway and cross the courtyard of the town hall to Rue de l'Université.

This street passes beside the old 17C **pawnshop** (mont-de-piété) (**BZ E**), now a food and agriculture research laboratory; it then leads to the 18C **theatre** (**BZ T**) with its Louis XVI façade.

On the other side of Rue de la Comédie stands the **Hôtel d'Aoust** (**ABZ L**), a beautiful example of Louis XV architecture. Note the *rocaille* door and the allegorical statues representing the four seasons decorating the façade. It is today the headquarters of the Northern Collieries Board (Direction des Houillères du Nord); indeed, Douai was formerly the heart of the French mining basin *(qv)*.

Continue on Rue de la Comédie and turn right into Rue des Foulons.

The **Hôtel de la Tramerie** (**AYZ K**) is another example of Louis XIII architecture. Take the tiny, curious Ruelle des Minimes almost exactly opposite, which leads back to the town hall.

Continue to Place d'Armes.

The 18C **Maison du Dauphin** (**BZ**) houses the Tourist Office.

★MUSÉE DE LA CHARTREUSE (CHARTERHOUSE MUSEUM) (AX) ⊙ *1 hour*

The museum is installed in an interesting group of 16C, 17C and 18C buildings, which were once the old charterhouse. On the left is the Flemish Renaissance Hôtel d'Abancourt, where the first Carthusian monks settled in the 17C. They built the small cloister, the refectory, the chapter-house and the church, which was completed in 1722. The great cloister and the monks' cells were destroyed during the Revolution. The museum is in two parts: Fine Arts Section, and Archeology and Natural History Section.

Fine Arts Section – The collections consist principally of fine early paintings but among the other works of art there is the astonishing 18C relief map of Douai.

Room 1 – Early Flemish, Dutch (the Master of Manne, the Master of Flemalle) and Italian paintings.

Passage – Plan of the Charterhouse convent.

Room 2 – Large 16C altarpieces from other abbeys are on display here, in the old refectory. The **Anchin Polyptych★** by Bellegambe portraying the Adoration of the Cross

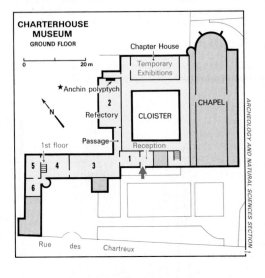

or the Adoration of the Holy Trinity, depending on whether the leaves are open or closed, and the Marchiennes Polyptych by Van Scorel (Utrecht School, 16C), dedicated to St James and St Stephen, are especially noteworthy.

Room 3 – The room includes two masterpieces of the Italian Renaissance: Veronese's portrait of a Venetian woman and Carracci's *Scourging of Christ* in which the *chiaroscuro* effect was used to create a work of rare intensity. The bronze *Venus of Castello* recalls the work of the famous sculptor and architect Giambologna (Jean de Bologne). Although he conducted most of his career in Italy, in Rome and particularly Florence, he was born in Douai in 1529 and trained in Flanders.

Rooms 4-5-6 – 16C Flemish and Dutch Mannerism is exhibited: works by Rolandt Savery *(Village Brawl)*; the Antwerp artists Jean Matsys, son of Quentin *(The Healing of Tobias)*, and Frans Floris; the Dutchmen Van Hemessen *(The Outrages Against Christ)*, Van Reymerswaele *(St Jerome)*, Goltzius *(The Young Man and the Old Woman)* and Cornelis Van Haarlem *(Baptism of Christ)*.

Take the staircase in Room 6 to the first floor.

Rooms 7-8 – Works by Rubens and Jordaens; landscapes by Momper and Govaerts; a witchcraft scene by David Teniers.

Rooms 9-10 – These rooms feature an interesting series of lesser 17C Dutch masters: still-lifes by Van der Ast and Abraham Mignon; *The Child* by Cuyp; a view of Haarlem by Berckheyde; a landscape by Ruisdaël; *The Young Musician* by Duyster.

Rooms 11-12 – The French school (17C-19C) is well represented here by portrait painters: Le Brun *(Louis XIV on Horseback)*, Vivien, Largillière, Nattier, François de Troy *(The Franqueville Family)*, Boilly, Chardin *(Still Life)*, David *(Mme Tallien)*.
Works by Impressionist painters are also on show: Renoir, Sisley and Pissaro and Post-Impressionists including Bonnard and Maurice Denis *(qv)*.

Return to the ground floor.

Cloister (Cloître) – The cloister vaults are pointed despite having been built in 1663, in the middle of the Classical period. The red brickwork contrasts pleasantly with the white stone of the ribs and the framing, carved with Baroque designs.

Chapter-house (Salle capitulaire) – The chapter-house was built in the same year as the cloister (1663) and in the same style; it now holds temporary exhibitions.

Archeology and Natural History Section – *Turn left on leaving the Charterhouse and left again into Rue St-Albin.*

The evolution of man is traced from the Paleolithic Age to AD 400 through the findings of excavations in the north of France (first floor). The collection includes a cast of Biache Man's skull, discovered at Biache-St-Vaast, about 13km - 8 miles southwest of Douai; the man is supposed to have lived *c*250 000 BC.
The Gallo-Roman period is illustrated through material found at Bavay (statuettes) and at Lewarde (busts). There are some interesting models of the merovingian village of Brebières and the necropolis at Hordain.
On the ground floor, an **aquarium** includes freshwater and saltwater fish from around the world (from African lakes and tropical oceans...). There are also collections of exotic butterflies and stuffed birds.

The pages on art in Flanders, Picardy and the Paris Region
give a general idea of artistic tradition in the area,
so that visitors can place in context the local art and architecutre.

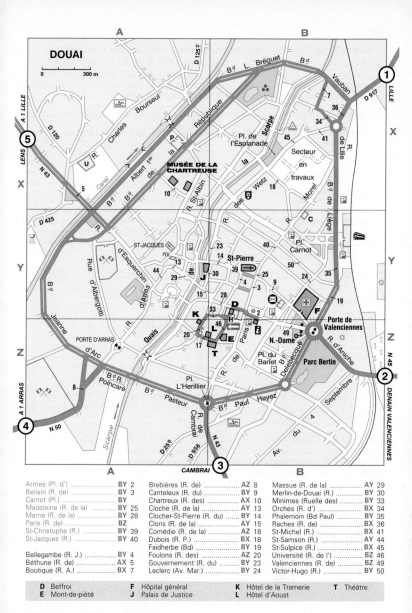

Armes (Pl. d')	BY 2	Brebières (R. de)	AZ 8	Massue (R. de la)	AY 29
Bellain (R. de)	BY 3	Canteleux (R. du)	BY 9	Merlin-de-Douai (R.)	BY 30
Carnot (Pl.)	BY	Chartreux (R. des)	AX 10	Minimes (Ruelle des)	BY 33
Madeleine (R. de la)	BY 25	Cloche (R. de la)	AY 13	Orches (R. d')	BX 34
Marne (R. de la)	BY 28	Clocher-St-Pierre (R. du)	BY 14	Phalemoin (Bd Paul)	BY 35
Paris (R. de)	BZ	Cloris (R. de la)	AY 15	Raches (R. de)	BX 36
St-Christophe (R.)	BY 39	Comédie (R. de la)	AZ 18	St-Michel (R.)	BX 41
St-Jacques (R.)	BY 40	Dubois (R. P.)	BX 18	St-Samson (R.)	AY 44
		Faidherbe (Bd)	BY 19	St-Sulpice (R.)	BX 45
Bellegambe (R. J.)	BY 4	Foulons (R. des)	AZ 20	Université (R. de l')	BZ 46
Béthune (R. de)	AX 5	Gouvernement (R. du)	BY 23	Valenciennes (R. de)	BZ 49
Boutique (R. A.)	BX 7	Leclerc (Av. Mar.)	BY 24	Victor-Hugo (R.)	BY 50

D	Beffroi	F	Hôpital général
E	Mont-de-piété	J	Palais de Justice
K	Hôtel de la Tramerie	T	Théâtre
L	Hôtel d'Aoust		

ADDITIONAL SIGHTS

Église St-Pierre (St Peter's Church) – The main features of this former collegiate church are the 16C-17C stone belltower, the 18C brick nave and chancel faced with stone, and the 18C apsidal chapel surmounted by a graceful bulb.

Inside, the chancel is as long as the nave; it was reserved for canons and members of the Parliament. Note the 18C organ case originally from Anchin Abbey, and the three 18C paintings in the right transept arm.

The Modern Style boutique in Rue Bellegambe *(opposite the church)* features a shop front decorated with sunflowers.

Palais de Justice (Law Courts) (J) ⊙ – The Courts date from the early 16C but were almost entirely rebuilt in the 18C; they were once the refuge of Marchiennes Abbey and then became the seat of the Flanders Parliament. The brick façade overlooking the Scarpe still bears traces of its original Gothic pointed arches. The main front, rebuilt under Louis XVI by the architect Lillois Lequeux has a severe-looking central porch.

The first-floor courtroom, called the **Parliament's Great Hall** (grande salle du parlement) (1762), is furnished with a vast marble fireplace, carved Louis XV woodwork, a portrait of Louis XIV and allegorical paintings by Brenet (1769). In 1972 buildings were constructed on the site of the old tribunal; they contain two courtrooms. The old cells (access from the quayside) have been transformed into **exhibition rooms** tracing the history of the town and the Law Courts.

In season, **boat cruises** ⊙ depart from the jetty outside the Law Courts.

Scarpe River Quays – The quaysides along the Scarpe River, no longer frequented by the barges, provide a pleasant walk. Old houses can be seen.

Porte de Valenciennes – This monumental gateway today stands alone, 15C Gothic on one side and late-17C Classical on the other.

Notre-Dame Church – The church, formerly abutting the ramparts, has always been part of Douai's history. The sandstone and brick nave was built in the 12C. The 14C Gothic chancel has five bays; the ribs of the pointed vaults are stone, the segments between them brick. The five-sided apse is pierced by tall lancet windows. The church has been restored since the damage of 1944.

General Hospital (F) – This vast building was built between 1752 and 1756.

Parc Bertin – The landscaped park (5ha - 12 acres) laid out in 1904 lies on the site of an old bastion.

EXCURSIONS

Flines-lez-Raches – *11km - 7 miles north by exit (1), on D 917 and D 938.*
The village has a curious church, which is entered through a very old brick and sandstone porch-belfry (some say as old as AD 800). The narrow nave opens onto chapels dating from various periods. In the first two chapels on the right, the roof beams are decorated with historiated corbels; they bear the arms of Philippine Torck, Abbess of Flines from 1561 to 1571.

★★**Lewarde Mining Heritage Centre** – *See Lewarde Mining Heritage Centre.*

DUNKERQUE
DUNKIRK
Population 73 618
Michelin map 51 folds 3, 4 or 236 fold 4
Map of conurbation in the Michelin Red Guide France

The "heroic town" of Dunkirk (Dunkerque) was 80 % destroyed during the Second World War. Since its rebuilding it has expanded rapidly, both commercially and industrially, owing to the enormous growth of its port.

Church of the Dunes – Until the 7C the site on which Dunkirk stands was covered by sea. Its name, which means "church of the dunes", did not appear until 1067. Until the end of the 17C, possession of this poorly-defended market town specialising in fish was fought over by Spanish, French, English and Dutch alike. In 1658 it was taken by Turenne after the Battle of the Dunes and fortified shortly after by Vauban.

A Corsairs' Lair – During Louis XIV's wars the Dunkirk corsairs destroyed or captured 3 000 ships, took 30 000 prisoners and wrecked Dutch trade.
The most fearless of these corsairs, **Jean Bart** (1651-1702), was a plain, rough-mannered man. Accomplishing exploit after exploit, he earned the rank of Fleet Commodore. According to local history Louis XIV himself announced Bart's nomination to him, saying: "Jean Bart, I name you Fleet Commodore," to which the daring seaman is said to have answered: "Sire, you have done well."
The following year, while entrusted to take the Prince of Conti to Poland, Bart evaded nine enormous vessels. The danger over, the prince remarked: "If attacked, we would have lost and been taken prisoner." "Never," answered Jean Bart, "We would all have been blown up together: my son was in the magazine under orders to set light to a barrel of powder as soon as he received the signal."

Evacuation of Dunkirk (May-June 1940) – From 25 May to 4 June Dunkirk was the prize in a bloody battle at the time of the evacuation of Allied forces who were cut off from their bases after the German breakthrough at Sedan towards of the sea.
The boats at the Dunkirk's port and on the beaches from Malo to Bray-Dunes made the journey back and forth between the French coast and England. Despite the mines, torpedoes, bombs and the pounding of heavy German shells, almost 350 000 men were rescued, about two-thirds of them British.

★★THE PORT

Dunkirk is classed as France's third most important port, having had over 40 million tonnes of traffic in 1992. Imports are high (30 million tonnes) and include minerals, chemical and petroleum products, coal, sand and gravel, metallurgical products, wood, oils, textiles and oil-yielding seeds. The exports (a quarter of the total traffic) encompass petroleum and metallurgical products, early vegetables and fruit, cement, sugar, fertilizer, cereals, heavy goods and prefabricated materials.
Since 1987 the eastern and western ports have been linked by a **deep-water canal**. The port installations cover 7 600ha - 18 800 acres and extend along 15km - 9 miles of coastline.

Eastern Port (Port-Est) – The port has a **harbour basin** (bassin maritime) 6km - 4 miles long, and 385ha - 950 acres of wet docks, divided into six open basins and specialised industrial basins, in addition to storage installations. It is serviced by an outer harbour (80ha - 198 acres) and three locks, the largest of which, the Charles-de-Gaulle Lock (365m by 50m - 400yds by 55yds) can receive 125 000 tonne vessels.

DUNKERQUE

H Hôtel de ville	**M¹** Musée des Beaux-Arts	**M³** Musée portuaire
L Beffroi	**M²** Musée aquariophile	**N** Leughenaer

Well-equipped for naval repairs, the port has four dry docks and two floating docks. The quays extend north to the entrance of the deep-water canal and handle heavy-cargo ships as well as the local metallurgical production, cereal traffic (three silos) and steel traffic.

Western Port (Port-Ouest) – This port, in use since 1975, has the advantage of a very deep (20.50m - 67ft) and very large (560 ha - 1 380 acres) harbour entrance with a wharf which can receive 300 000-tonne oil tankers.

It contains a rapid-transit port to which ships gain access without having to pass through any locks, 2km - 1 1/2 miles of quays and two harbour stations. The car and train ferries handling traffic to England leave from here to Ramsgate for passengers only and to Dover. In order to receive the largest container vessels, this rapid-transit port has a series of quays equipped with storehouses, powerful hoisting equipment (three cranes) and 80 ha - 198 acres of marshalling yards.

Metallurgical industries are established on the west side of the harbour basin, near the crude oil reserves and the power station at Gravelines. The coal and minerals terminal is accessible to 180 000-tonne ships.

The Industrial Complex – Dunkirk's port activity is largely linked to the size of the industrial complex established here.

The **iron and steel industry** is represented by Sollac, Dunkirk's "factory on the water", which produces a large percentage of France's steel. On the other hand, French **fine-grade iron and steel** is well known owing to the Ascométal firm's Dunes works (between Malo-les-Bains and Bray-Dunes). The plant specialises in making round bars, wheels, rail axles and oil drilling pipes.

The **petroleum industry** is represented by the presence of the BP, Elf and Total installations; **petro-chemical** industry is especially important, with the Copenor plant producing ethylene and polyethylene here, among other products; the Stocknard port terminal is equipped to handle deliveries of liquid chemical products.

Other companies include GTS Industries (large pipes), Air Liquide, Lafarge (cement works) and, at Coudekerque-Branche, the Lesieur factory (cooking oil).

Tour of the Port on foot – *About 1 hour.* Start from Place du Minck (**CY 53**) (fish market) between the Commercial Basin (Bassin du Commerce) and the "fishermens' dock" and go west. Cross the old citadel district, where the transit agencies are established today. The channel and the marina are on the right. Cross Trystam Lock and head towards the **lighthouse**. The tower is 59m - 194ft tall and its 6 000 watts produce beams which can be seen 48km - 30 miles away. Beyond the floating docks *(left)* the route reaches Watier Lock. The eastern port's control tower stands at its entrance, to the right on the blockhouse; there is a good view of the port and harbour entrance from the eastern length of the long jetty where the French troops embarked in 1940.

Tour of the Port by boat ☉ – Boats leave from the Commercial Basin (Bassin du Commerce), the largest of the three old basins, and cruise the entire length of the port. The textile depot (**X**), sugar depot (**Z**), storage tank area, cranes, workshops (dry docks), locks, BP refinery and petroleum wharfs, the power station cooled by sea water, the Sollac steelworks, the old coal basin and the Break jetty are all clearly visible.

Musée portuaire (Harbour Museum) (**M³**) ☉ – This new museum is installed in an old 19C tobacco warehouse; it recounts the evolution of the different harbour activities. Dunkirk used to be a trading and fishing port but since the 1960s it has become a major industrial port. Piloting, access to the port, naval repairs, handling produce, coastal fishing and trawling off Iceland are all evoked in dioramas, models of ships, maps and plans, paintings, prints and old tools once used by the dockers. Dunkirk was at the heart of the wars during the 17C, and its waters were defended by Jean Bart, the corsair: *The Battle of Texel* (a reproduction of the original painting in Paris), and prints by Ozanne recount Bart's combats in 1675 and 1676. Each year there is a different exhibition highlighting some aspect of the port. On leaving the museum, note along the quayside two disarmed fire-ships; they were once used to signal sandbanks but have now been replaced by illuminated buoys.

ADDITIONAL SIGHTS

★★**Musée d'Art contemporain (Museum of Contemporary Art)** (**CDY**) ☉ – The museum stands in the middle of a **sculpture park**★ (jardin de sculptures) designed by landscape gardener Gilbert Samel. The paths climb outcrops and run down slopes, leading past great stone pieces by the sculptor Dodeigne, metal structures by Féraud and

Museum of Contemporary Art, Dunkirk

compositions by Viseux, Arman and Zvenijorovsky, all against the backdrop of the port's cranes and the North Sea. Architect Jean Willerval bore in mind the existing garden when he built his modern concrete building sheathed in white ceramic. This rather sober structure is preceded by a fine porch by Philippe Scrive; it is made of azobe, an African wood.

Inside, temporary exhibitions adorn the vast hall; stairs lead to the first floor which opens into eight rooms where the collections are exhibited.

★**The Collections** – The collections were largely put together by a passionate contemporary art collector, Gilbert Delaine, to whom the museum owes its existence. In 1974 he created the Contemporary Art Association, then appealed to artists for donations and persuaded industrialists to buy works by invoking the Malroix Law. This law allows tax deductions on up to a thousandth of a business' turnover against purchases of works of art. In this way over 700 works were brought together in the museum. They cover paintings and sculptures from 1950, including works by Karel Appel (17 colourful sculptures make up *The Circus*), by Mathieu, Alechinsky, César, Soulages, Kijno, Télémaque, Vasarely, Christoforou...

Belfry (L) ☉ – Built in the 13C and heightened in 1440, it served as the belltower to St Eligius' Church, which burnt down in 1558. This high tower (58m - 190ft) shelters a carillon of 48 bells which play "Jean Bart's tune" on the hours and other popular tunes on the quarter hours. The tourist office is housed on the ground floor.

A monument to the dead has been erected under the arch opposite St Eligius' church.

Église St-Éloi (St Eligius' Church) ☉ – The church was built in the 16C and remodelled in the 18C and 19C. It has a neo-Gothic west front and a pyramid roofline along the sides aisles and apse. The proportions appear odd since the suppression of the transept.

Note the size of the five aisles with quadripartite vaulting supported by elegant piers, and its apse with radiating chapels. The restored pointed windows feature stained glass by the master glassworker Gaudin. On the north side of the chancel, a white marble slab marks the tomb of **Jean Bart**.

Place Jean-Bart – On this square at the centre of the town stands a statue of the famous corsair, Jean Bart, by David d'Angers (1848).

★**Musée des Beaux-Arts (Fine Arts Museum) (M¹)** ☉ – This museum (rebuilt 1973) houses beautiful collections of 16C to 20C paintings and documents tracing Dunkirk's history. In the entrance hall, a panel of 540 Delft tiles portrays the bombardment of the port in 1695.

On the **ground floor** a strange trunk shaped liked a chained captive, which was used in the 17C when buying back slaves, comes from St Eligius' Church. Models of boats are displayed in a gallery overlooking the garden.

On the first floor the 16C and 17C **Flemish school** is well represented: F Pourbus the Younger *(Head of a Child)*, Snyders *(Fruit and Vegetables)*, Jean de Reyn (several portraits), Francken *(The Feast of Herod)*, Robert van der Hoecke *(Snow Effects)*, Teniers the Younger *(Village Fête)*, Van Dyck *(Head of a Bearded Man)*.

The **Dutch school** offers interesting portraits of women by Morelse, Aert de Gelder and Bylert, still lifes by Van der Poel and Claez. Among the 18C Italian painters, note the work of Magnasco *(Adoration of the Magi)*.

The **French school** from the 17C to the 20C contains canvases by Largillière, Vignon, Riguaud, Lesueur, de La Fosse, Hubert Robert, Vernet, Corot, Boudin, Carrier-Belleuse, Forain.

There is a natural history section in the basement, together with an exhibition on the Second World War. An audio-visual show with a model follows the development of the Battle of Dunkirk.

Hôtel de ville (Town Hall) (H) – Built in 1900 by Louis Cordonnier, who designed the Peace Palace in the Hague, it includes a 75m - 246ft high central belfry. Inside, a stained-glass window by Félix Gaudin commemorates Jean Bart's return following his victory at Texel (off the Netherlands) in 1694.

Leughenaer (N) – The liar's tower (Leughenaer is Flemish for a liar) is the only vestige of the Burgundian walls and 28 towers which encircled the city in the 14C. It owes its name to a watchman's mistake.

Notre-Dame-des-Dunes Chapel – The chapel was rebuilt in the 19C; it shelters a wooden statue of the Madonna which has been worshipped by sailors since 1405.

Église St-Jean-Baptiste (John the Baptist Church) ☉ – This modern, brick-built church (1962), shaped like the prow of a ship, stands separately from its wooden belfry which rises like a mast. Inside there is a lovely Christ surrounded by four angels.

⌂ MALO-LES-BAINS (DY)

Founded before 1870 by a local shipowner named Malo, this seaside resort has become the residential district of Dunkirk. The large, gently sloping beach of fine sand extends east of the port: it is flanked by a promenade beside which stands the casino. Avenue du Casino leads to the Park and aquarium.

Musée aquariophile (Aquarium) (M²) ☉ – The aquarium's 21 tanks hold 150 species of fish of various origins, some of them from the Dunkirk region.

EXCURSIONS

Gravelines – *13km - 8 miles west.*
The town is enclosed within classic, Vauban-style ramparts with brick bastions and stone courses; it was an important part of Dunkirk's defence in 1940. The 1742 powder magazine, now set within pleasant gardens, houses the **Prints and Engravings Museum** (Musée de la Gravure et de l'Estampe originale) ⊙ and temporary exhibitions.
The town also boasts a large sports centre ("Sportica"), a harbour full of yachts and sailings boats, and a Flamboyant church with a Renaissance front portal.
To the northeast rise the towers of the Nuclear Power Station.

From Malo-les-Bains to Bray-Dunes – *13km - 8 miles northeast by D 79 and D 60.*

The road bypasses Dunes Fort which gave its name to the Battle of the Dunes (1658), then continues past the Ascometal company's Dunes plant.

Zuydcoote – The town found literary fame with the novel *Weekend in Zuydcoote* by Robert Merle, on which a film was based evoking the tragic episodes of the 1940 embarkations. The great sanatorium, transformed into a hospital, was at that time the setting of dramatic scenes, with an influx of wounded whose number reached 7 000.

Bray-Dunes – A promenade runs alongside the sandy beach which stretches all the way to la Panne in Belgium; it is a popular spot for sailing boats.
On the promenade, a stele commemorates the sacrifice of the soldiers who fought until 4 June 1940.

ÉCOUEN CHÂTEAU ★★

Michelin map 101 fold 6 or 106 fold 7

Access is through the forest, on foot; cars must be parked at the entrance to the forest.
The château, nestling in a park (17ha - 42 acre), overlooking the plain was originally intended for Constable Anne de Montmorency *(qv)* and his wife Madeleine of Savoy, who lived here from 1538 to 1555.
When Constable Anne's grandson Henri II de Montmorency was beheaded in 1632, the château reverted to the Condé family but was later confiscated during the Revolution. Napoleon I salvaged the estate in 1806 by founding the first school for the daughters of members of the Légion d'Honneur. In 1962 the château and its grounds were ceded to the Ministry of Culture, who undertook to turn it into a state museum devoted to Renaissance art.

TOUR *1 hour*

Exterior – Écouen Château reflects the transition of French art from the Early Renaissance period (Châteaux of the Loire) to the High Renaissance during Henri II's reign *(illustration p 28)*.

Courtyard – The buildings feature square pavilions at each corner and are surmounted by elaborate dormer windows. The beautiful east range was destroyed in the 18C and replaced by a low entrance wing.
The porticoes bearing replicas of ancient columns on the south wing which housed the constable's suite feature a frontispiece by Jean Bullant, designed to receive replicas of Michelangelo's famous *Slaves* (originals in Louvre) in the lateral niches at ground-floor level. They were a present from Henri II to Anne de Montmorency.

North Terrace – Sweeping **view** of the surrounding cereal-growing countryside.

★★**Musée de la Renaissance (Renaissance Museum)** ⊙ – The exhibits on display belonged to the Renaissance collections of the Cluny Museum in Paris. Écouen Museum presents a wide range of works dating from the 16C and early 17C, which introduce visitors to the various branches of the decorative arts: furniture, wainscoting, tapestries and embroideries, ceramics, enamels etc. Most of the exhibits were made in France, Italy or the Netherlands. They represent a small selection but the ambience they create is in keeping with the life of the rich during the Renaissance. The original interior decoration consists mainly of grotesques, painted on the friezes below the ceiling and the embrasures of the windows. But it is for its **painted fireplaces** that Écouen is famed. Created during the reign of Henri II, these chimneypieces are representative of the first Fontainebleau School *(qv):* the central biblical scene is painted on an oval or rectangular-shaped medallion, surrounded by grotesques, garlands of fruit and motifs in leather; the hazy landscapes depicting antique ruins, fortresses and humble cottages are in imitation of Niccolo dell'Abbate.

Ground Floor – The monograms A and M (Anne de Montmorency and Madeleine of Savoy) have been included in the decoration of the chapel, built in 1544 and covered by painted vaulting resting on diagonal arches. This heraldic motif reappears in different places (musicians' gallery, panelling in the oratory, the vaulting in the sacristy). The Altarpiece of the Passion is adorned with enamelling and a copy of Michelangelo's *Last Supper*.

Several rooms are devoted to a particular trade or technique: note a clock of German origin in the shape of a nave, thought to date from the time of Charles V of Spain, now shown incorporated into a 16C collector's cabinet and, in the reconstruction of a 16C goldsmith's workshop, a drawing frame set in an inlaid chest. The northwest pavilion was formerly occupied by Catherine de' Medici.

First Floor – In the south wing, visitors are shown round the constable's bedroom and Madeleine of Savoy's suite, both interesting on account of the period furniture. The west wing is almost exclusively taken up by the **Tapestry of David and Bathsheba★★★** (1510-1520). The 75m - 246ft hanging divided into ten sections tells of the romance between King David and Bathsheba. The outstanding quality of the tapestry – woven with wool and silk threads, as well as silver braid – is equalled only by that of *The Hunts of Maximilian* in the Louvre, without doubt the two most precious examples of 16C Brussels tapestry work existing in France.

The hanging starts in Abigail's Chamber, continues in Psyche's Gallery and ends in the King's Apartment, situated in the northwest pavilion. For explanations of the monograms read the paragraph entitled "Henri II's Château" in the chapter on Fontainebleau *(qv)*.

Musicians' scene in the Tapestry of David and Bathsheba, Écouen

The king's suite occupied the northern wing: the floor tiles were made specially for the château in 1542 by the Rouen potter Masséot Abaquesne. The winged victory on the central panel of the monumental fireplace was taken from a similar design in the François I Gallery at Fontainebleau *(qv)*.

Second Floor – In the northeast pavilion, many pieces of Isnik pottery (mid 16C to early 17C) are exhibited in glass cabinets, illustrating the exotic tastes of 16C collectors. The first room in the north wing presents religious stained glass painted in *grisaille*: admire the *Virgin and Child*, dated 1544.

The second hall deals entirely with French ceramics and there is a reconstruction of another floor designed specially for the château, showing the arms of the Constable, those of his wife, of Henri II and Catherine de' Medici.

The fifteen marriage chests *(cassoni)* on show in the northwest pavilion form a remarkable ensemble: these painted panels are taken from wooden chests that were presented to newlyweds in sets of two.

The cabinets in the west gallery contain enamels (pieces by Léonard Limosin), tin-glazed pottery or majolica from Deruta in Italy and glasses (goblets belonging to Anne de Bretagne and Catherine de' Medici).

The southwest pavilion concentrates on silverware (cutlery, jewellery), mainly of German origin. Above the chapel is the former library of Constable Anne – admire the beautifully restored wainscoting.

ADDITIONAL SIGHT

Église St-Acceul (St Acceul Church) – The chancel by Jean Bullant is the most interesting part of the building. The complex rib patterns of the vaulting *(temporarily concealed by supporting timber)* date it to the 16C. St Acceul features several Renaissance **stained-glass windows★**; those in the left side aisle are dated 1544: *Dormition and Assumption of the Virgin, Annunciation and Visitation, Nativity and Adoration of the Magi.*

FERRIÈRES★

Population 1 340
Michelin map 101 fold 30 or 106 folds 21, 22

The shooting parties on Ferrières estate, the luxurious furnishings of the château and the precious collections gathered by the members of the Rothschild dynasty were the talk of the town for over 100 years. The landscape park – created at the same time as the Bois de Boulogne – is extremely attractive especially in the vicinity of the lake.

A Challenge to Tradition – In 1829 James de Rothschild, founder of the French line of the family, acquired 7 500 acres of hunting grounds formerly belonging to Fouché, with a view to building a villa which would accommodate his invaluable collections and satisfy his taste for splendour. The baron did not choose a professional architect: he broke with tradition and hired **Joseph Paxton**, the English glasshouse and garden designer with a penchant for modern materials such as iron and glass. Already famed for his London Crystal Palace (destroyed in 1936), Paxton erected a rectangular building flanked by square towers, with a central hall equipped with zenithal lighting. Construction work was completed in 1859. The decoration, left in the hands of the baroness, was entrusted to the French specialist Eugène Lami.

On 16 December 1862 Napoleon III paid an official visit to the Rothschilds in their new residence. Delighted by the splendid apartments and the 800 head of game for his day's shoot, the Emperor planted a sequoia tree as a commemorative gesture.

Less than 10 years later, Jules Favre – in charge of Foreign Affairs in the new National Defence government – turned up at the gates of the château on 19 September 1870. In his capacity as Minister, Favre came to see Chancellor Bismarck, who was staying at Ferrières with King William I of Prussia, to ask him to agree to an armistice. The chancellor however made this conditional on the surrender of Strasbourg, Toul and Bitche, and further implied that the cession of Alsace and part of Lorraine was inevitable. Jules Favre left the premises the following morning but it was only on 28 January 1871 that Paris fell to the hands of the enemy. In 1977 Baron Guy de Rothschild and his wife Marie-Hélène donated their château and part of the estate to the Confederation of Paris Universities.

CHÂTEAU ⊙ *2 hours*

Exterior – Its architecture reflects the various styles of the Renaissance period, including the odd eccentricity that occurred in those times.

Although balusters, galleries and colonnades reigned supreme, the façades were each different. The most striking and the most typically English is the main front overlooking the lake, with its centrepiece flanked by turrets and its display of superimposed galleries. Step back to take in the tall decorative stone chimneys, reminiscent of Chambord Château.

Interior – A pavilion sporting a large clock is fronted by the main entrance porch which bears the baron's monogram (J R) and the family coat of arms (the five Rothschild arrows). The main staircase leads to the central hall – 40m - 130ft wide and 12m - 40ft high under the glass ceiling – now stripped of its paintings and tapestries. Above the main door, a row of telamones and caryatids in bronze and black marble support a musicians' gallery, a popular decorative feature under the Second Empire. The Blue Salon, overlooking the park, has busts of the Empress Eugénie and Bettina de Rothschild, the first proprietress of the château.

The Louis XVI salon is the most typical example of Eugène Lami's work: it features off-white wainscoting with pinkish hues, a ceiling mural inspired by Boucher and reproduction Louis XVI furniture. Opposite is the Red Salon, in which the 1870 negotiations took place. It now presents an exhibition on the history of the estate.

Museum of Figurative Art ⊙ – *Housed here until late 1996 before moving to Fontainebleau.* The collection includes works by about a hundred artists, among them Dunoyer de Segonzac, Lucien Fontanarosa, Brayer and Buffet.

★**Park** ⊙ – The park designed by Paxton boasts a number of superb compositions, mainly consisting of ornamental coniferous trees: cedars of Lebanon, numerous Atlas cedars – including the highly decorative blue form – and sequoias, introduced into France around 1850.

Several individual trees also deserve a mention: a cedar of Lebanon with unusually long, spread-eagled branches, swamp cypresses, with twigs which turn deep russet and drop off in winter, copper beeches, groves of plane trees and, on the far side of the lake, feathery weeping species, adding an autumnal touch to the tableau.

Outside the park, the Lions' Avenue (Allée des Lions) presents an imposing driveway of stately sequoias.

*Michelin Maps (scale 1:200 000) which are revised regularly
provide much useful information:*
- *latest motorway developments and changes;*
- *vital data (width, alignment, camber, surface) of motorways or tracks;*
- *the location of emergency telephones.*

*Keep current **Michelin Maps** in the car at all times.*

FOLLEVILLE

Population 63
Michelin map 52 fold 18 or 236 fold 34

This modest village located on a hill at the end of the Noye Valley was once the seat of an important fief. The ruins of a castle (13C-16C), once owned by the illustrious Lannoy and Gondi families, stand as testimony to the town's former importance.

A Valiant Knight – Raoul de Lannoy, the son of a Flemish family, was Chamberlain and Counsellor to Louis XI, Charles VIII and Louis XII. He achieved great glory in 1477 at the siege of Le Quesnoy, and Louis XI presented him with a gold chain saying: "Because, my friend, you are too furious in combat you must be chained to contain your ardour, as I do not want to lose you." This chain is exhibited in Folleville church. During the Italian wars Lannoy was named Governor of Genoa by Louis XII, and died there in 1513.

Monsieur Vincent's First "Mission" – In January 1617 a humble, wise old priest – Vincent de Paul – travelled through the lands of Françoise de Gondi, heiress of the fief of Folleville through her mother Marie de Lannoy. The region was in an advanced state of secularisation. Horrified, the priest entered the pulpit and spoke in such an eloquent way that a general confession ensued. Following this experience, in 1625 Vincent founded the Congregation of the Priests of the Mission, later known as Lazarists.

CHURCH ⊙ *1 1/2 hours*

The exterior of this early-16C church is decorated with remarkable carvings: 16C statue of St James on the corner of the west front and a Virgin and Child in the niche of a buttress.

Nave – A Renaissance font stands near the entrance: the white Carrara marble basin is carved with the symbolic chain and the coat of arms of the Lannoy family. In the right hand nave the pulpit from which Vincent de Paul preached still stands.

★Chancel – The chancel is constructed in a largely Flamboyant architectural style but also features numerous Renaissance decorative elements. Note the finely-carved ribbed vault.

The first **tomb★★** on the left is that of Raoul de Lannoy and his wife Jeanne de Poix. The white marble sarcophagus was made in Genoa in 1507, when Raoul de Lannoy was still alive, by the Milanese sculptor Antonio Della Porta and his nephew Pace Gaggini; the recumbent effigy of Lannoy is portrayed wearing the gold chain he was given by Louis XI. The base is adorned with graceful weeping children, the family coat of arms and an epitaph. The recess in which the tomb lies is a masterpiece of French art with its delicate sculptures and carvings. The background is garlanded with sweet pea flowers *(fleurs de poix)*, a reference to de Lannoy's wife. It is

The tomb of Raoul de Lannoy
and Jeanne de Poix, Folleville

crowned by a double ogee framing a graceful Virgin and Child emerging from a fleur-de-lis and surmounted by a tent-shaped canopy; a trellised enclosure, a daisy chain, little angels and the symbols of the Evangelists complete the composition.
The second **tomb★** shows the progress of funerary art, moving in 50 years from recumbent effigies to kneeling stone figures. Among those kneeling are François de Lannoy, Raoul's son who died in 1548, and his wife Marie de Hangest. The base of the white marble surround is decorated with figures of the Cardinal Virtues (Prudence, Temperance, Fortitude and Justice).

Recess and piscina – A pointed arch beyond the altar opens on to a large garlanded recess. Inside the arch a sculpted Christ appears to Mary Magdalene; on either side angels carry the instruments of the Passion. This recess housed a white marble tomb by Antonio della Porta and Pace Gaggini which the Gondi family, the inheritors of Lannoy, had transferred to Joigny (in the Yonne valley, southwest of Fontainebleau).
On the right of the altar, a pretty piscina is decorated with statuettes of St Francis and John the Baptist, the patron saints of François de Lannoy and Jeanne de Poix.

*For historical information on the region
consult the table and notes in the introduction.*

FONTAINEBLEAU ★★★

Population 15 714
Michelin map 106 folds 45, 46 or 61 folds 2, 12

It was not until the 19C that Fontainebleau – which long remained a hamlet of Avon – started to develop, owing to the growing popularity of country residences and the general appreciation of its unspoilt forest.

This residential area has also become an important centre for regional industry; the area includes various workshops and laboratories, a research centre for mining engineers, the European Institute of Business Management and a contemporary archive library, a branch of the National Archives.

Military and riding traditions – Throughout French history, whether under monarchic or republican rule, independent units have been posted to Fontainebleau. Tradition, it seems, favoured the cavalry, present in the 17C with the king's bodyguard. A number of racecourses and riding schools were created under Napoleon III: the National Centre of Equestrian Sports perpetuates this tradition *(see Calendar of Events, qv)*, while the forest caters for riding enthusiasts.

The history of the town has been marked by several military organisations, notably the Special Military Academy (1803 to 1808, before St-Cyr), the polygon-shaped School of Applied Artillery and Engineering (1871 to 1914) and the SHAPE (Supreme Head-quarters, Allied Powers, Europe) headquarters of NATO, which gave the town a cosmopolitan touch from 1947 to 1967.

At present Fontainebleau houses the Army Sports School, an officers' training centre for members of the Gendarmerie Nationale, a Ground Forces Depot, the Service Corps, the Ordnance Corps and a riding centre for the army.

PALACE ★★★

Fontainebleau Palace (Le Palais de Fontainebleau) owes its origins to royalty's passion for hunting; it owes its development and decoration to the kings' delight in amassing works of art and displaying them in their "family house". This palace has an extremely distinguished past: from the last of the Capetians up to Napoleon III, it was designed for and occupied by French rulers.

A hunting seat – A spring – called Bliaud or Blaut fountain in the middle of a forest abounding in game – prompted the kings of France to build a mansion here. The exact date is not known but it was probably before 1137 as a charter exists issued under Louis VII from Fontainebleau, dating from that year. Philippe-Auguste celebrated the return of the Third Crusade here during the Christmas festivities of 1191 and St Louis founded a Trinitarian convent, whose members were called Mathurins; Philip the Fair was born here in 1268: unfortunately he also died here following a serious riding accident.

The Renaissance – Under François I almost all the medieval buildings were pulled down and replaced by two main edifices, erected under the supervision of Gilles Le Breton. The oval-shaped east pavilion – built on the former foundations – was linked to the west block by a long gallery. To decorate the palace, François I hired many artists: he dreamed of creating a "New Rome" furnished with replicas of Antique statues.

The actual building consisted of rubble-work as the sandstone taken from the forest was too difficult to work into regular freestones. The harled façades are enlivened by string-courses of brick or massive sandstone blocks.

The Fontainebleau School – 16C – The teams of painters and stucco workers were supervised by Rosso, one of Michelangelo's pupils and a native of Florence, and by Primaticcio, a disciple of Giulio Romano who came from Bologna. They developed a decorative technique strongly inspired by allegories with hazy implications. Attention to detail, which typified late Gothic architecture, was no longer in vogue beyond the Loire Valley as it had been during the Early Renaissance.

The Fontainebleau artists were more intent on depicting a dreamy form of elegance, characterised by the representation of human bodies arched into arabesque poses.

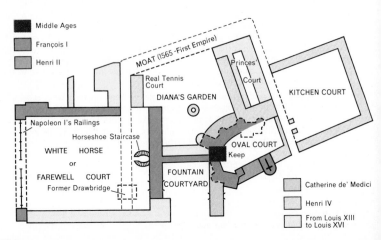

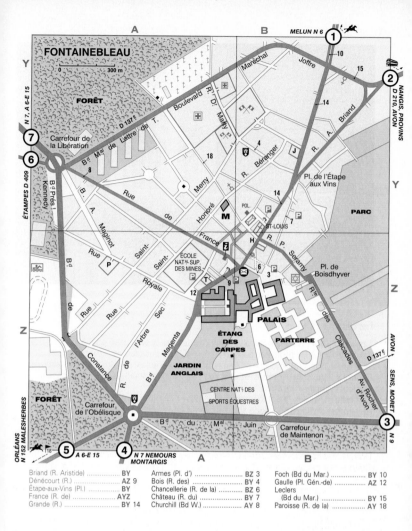

These painters formed the First Fontainebleau School, which blossomed under the reign of François I. The school created a style of decoration incorporating both stucco and paintings – exemplified by the François I Gallery – a semi-miniature genre referred to as "French style" by the Italians.

Rosso died in 1540. Primaticcio was sent to Rome to make moulds of famous Antique statues – the *Laocoon*, the *Belvedere Apollo* – which were brought back to Fontainebleau and cast in bronze.

In his private suite (Appartement des Bains), the king could feast his eyes on masterpieces by Raphael and Leonardo da Vinci *(The Mona Lisa)*, while the Arms Pavilion housed the silver cutlery, jewellery and other miscellaneous curios that delighted contemporary royalty.

Henri II's château – Henri II pursued the efforts undertaken by his father. He gave orders to complete and decorate the ballroom, which remains one of the splendours of Fontainebleau Palace. The monograms – consisting of the royal H and the two intertwined Cs of Catherine de' Medici – were legion. It has now been accepted that the three superimposed letters form a double D, the monogram of the King's mistress Diane de Poitiers.

When Henri II was killed in a tournament, his widow sent her rival to Chaumont-sur-Loire *(see the Michelin Green Guide Châteaux of the Loire)* and dismissed the foreman Philibert Delorme, who was Diane's protégé. He was replaced by the Italian Primaticcio: those working under him, including Niccolo dell'Abbate, favoured light, cheerful colours.

Henri IV's palace – 17C – Henri IV, who adored Fontainebleau, had the palace enlarged quite significantly. The irregular contours of the Oval Court were corrected and he gave orders to build the Kitchen Court and the Real Tennis Court (Jeu de Paume). These he had decorated by a new group of artists of largely Flemish, and not Italian, inspiration: frescoes were replaced by oil paintings on plaster or canvas. In the same way, the plain wood panelling highlighted with gilding gave way to painted wainscoting. This was the Second Fontainebleau School, whose representatives moved in Parisian circles.

The House of Eternity – Louis XIV, XV and XVI undertook numerous renovations aimed at embellishing their apartments. The Revolution spared the château but emptied it of its precious furniture. Napoleon, who became consul, then emperor, thoroughly enjoyed staying at the palace. He preferred Fontainebleau to Versailles, where he felt haunted by a phantom rival. He called the palace "The House of Eternity" and left his mark by commissioning further restoration work. The last rulers of France also took up residence in this historic palace. It was eventually turned into a museum under the Republic.

The Pavilion on Carp Lake, Fontainebleau

Exterior *1 hour*

★★**Farewell Court (Cour des Adieux)** – This former bailey was used only by domestics but its generous size soon earmarked it for official parades and tournaments. It was also called the White Horse's Court the day Charles IX set up a plaster cast of the Capitol's equestrian statue of Marcus Aurelius: a small slab in the central alley marks its former location.

The golden eagles hovering above the pillars of the main gate remind visitors that the Emperor had this made into his main courtyard. He gave orders to raze the Renaissance buildings that lay to the west of the court but kept the end pavilions. It is clear, walking between the two long wings that only the one on the left with its brick courses has retained the elegance that characterised the work of Gilles Le Breton, François I's favourite architect. The right wing – which boasted the Ulysses Gallery decorated under the supervision of Primaticcio – was dismantled by Louis XV and rebuilt by Jacques Ange Gabriel.

At the far end of the court the main block, fronted by a balustrade marking the site of the former moat, was completed in several stages from the reign of François I to that of Louis XV. Nonetheless the façades show a certain unity of style. The large horizontal planes of the blue slating are broken by the white façades, the trapezoidal roofs and the tall chimneys of the five pavilions. The celebrated horseshoe staircase executed by Jean Du Cerceau during the reign of Louis XIII is a harmoniously-curved, extravagant composition showing clearly royalty's taste for splendour. The staircase served as a majestic backdrop on many occasions. Saint-Simon described the arrival of the 11-year-old Princess Marie Adélaïde of Savoy at Fontainebleau on 5 November 1696 for her betrothal to the Duke of Burgundy. "The entire Court was assembled waiting to receive them on the horseshoe staircase, with the crowd standing below, a magnificent sight. The King led in the princess, so small that she seemed to be emerging from his pocket, walked very slowly along the terrace and then to the Queen Mother's apartments...".

The Farewell – On 20 April 1814 the Emperor Napoleon Bonaparte appeared at the top of the horseshoe staircase; the foreign army commissioners in charge of escorting him away were waiting in their carriages at the foot of the steps. Napoleon started to walk down the staircase with great dignity, his hand resting on the stone balustrade, his face white with contained emotion. He faltered a moment while contemplating his guards standing to attention, then moved forward to the group of officers surrounding the Eagle, led by General Petit. His farewell speech, deeply moving, was both an appeal to the spirit of patriotism and a parting tribute to those who had followed him throughout his career. After embracing the general, Bonaparte lowered the flag, threw himself into one of the carriages and was whisked away amid the tearful shouts of his soldiers.

★**Cour de la Fontaine (Fountain Courtyard)** – The fountain at the edge of Carp Lake used to yield remarkably clear water. This was kept exclusively for the king's use and to that end the spring was guarded by two sentinels night and day. The present fountain dates back to 1812 and is crowned by a statue of Ulysses. The surrounding buildings feature stone masonry and the whole ensemble forms a pleasant courtyard. At the far end, the François I Gallery is fronted by a terrace: it rests on a row of arches which once opened onto the king's bathroom suite.

The **Pavilion of the Fine Fireplace** on the right was built by Primaticcio around 1565. The name originated from the fireplace that adorned the vast first-floor hall until the 18C. At that point in history Louis XV – who had arranged the room as a theatre stage rechristening it Aile de l'Ancienne Comédie – dismantled the chimney, and the carved low-reliefs were scattered in all directions. The imposing staircase is in the Italian manner. On the left the Queen Mothers' and Pope's Suite ends in the Grand Pavilion built by Gabriel.

★Étang des Carpes (Carp Lake) – In the centre of the pond – alive with shoals of carp – stands a small pavilion built under Henri IV, renovated under Louis XIV and restored by Napoleon I. It was used for refreshments and light meals.

★Porte Dorée (Golden Gate) – Dated 1528, this doorway is part of an imposing pavilion. It was the official entrance to the palace until Henri IV built the baptistry door. The paintings by Primaticcio have all been restored and the tympanum sports a stylised salamander, François I's emblem. On the two upper levels are Italian-style loggias. The first floor – its loggia sealed off by large bay windows – used to house Mme de Maintenon's suite.

The ballroom wing is lined by an avenue of lime trees. The view from the glass front is splendid and it is regrettable that the initial plans to build an open-air loggia were changed on account of the climate. The east end of the two-storeyed St Saturnin Chapel can be seen in the distance.

Porte du Baptistère (Baptistry Doorway) – The doorway opens onto the Oval Court. Its foundations were provided by the Farewell Court's old drawbridge door, made of carved sandstone, and it was the work of Primaticcio. It is crowned by a wide arch surmounted by a dome. The door is named after the christening of Louis XIII and his two sisters, Élisabeth and Chrétienne, celebrated with great pomp on a raised platform on 14 September 1606.

The Golden Gate, Fontainebleau

E Berne/FOTOGRAM STONE

★Cour Ovale (Oval Court) Ⓥ – This is by far the most ancient and the most interesting courtyard of Fontainebleau Palace. The site where it stands was the bailey of the original stronghold: of the latter there remains only the keep, called St Louis, although it was probably built prior to his reign. François I incorporated it into the structure he had erected on the foundations of the old castle, shaped like an oval or rather a polygonal form with rounded corners. Under Henri IV, the courtyard lost its shape, although not its name: the east side was enlarged, the wings were aligned and squared by two new pavilions framing the Baptistry Doorway. The general layout of the palace was preserved.

Cour des Offices (Kitchen Court) – Its entrance, the Hermes Gate, faces the Baptistry Doorway and is guarded by two arresting sandstone heads depicting Hermes, sculpted by Gilles Guérin in 1640. The Kitchen Court was built by Henri IV in 1609: it is a huge oblong, sealed off on three sides by austere buildings alternating with sturdy pavilions. With its imposing porch executed in the style of city gates, it bears

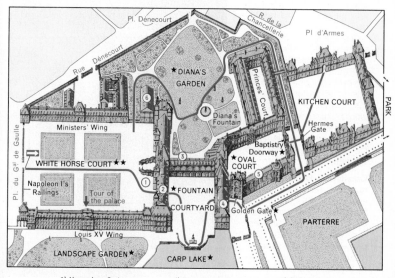

1) Horseshoe Staircase
2) Queen Mothers' Wing
3) François I Gallery
4) Fine Fireplace Wing
5) Ballroom
6) Real Tennis Court

a strong resemblance to a square. Walk through the gate and admire its architecture from Place d'Armes: the sandstone front presents rusticated work and has a large niche as centrepiece.

Continue the tour around the palace. The east and north wings of the Princes' Court are two functional buildings designed or redesigned under Louis XV to provide further accommodation for members of the court.

★**Jardin de Diane (Diana's Garden)** – The queen's formal garden created by Catherine de' Medici was designed by Henri IV and bordered by an orangery on its northern side. In the 19C the orangery was torn down and the park turned into a landscape garden. Diana's fountain, an elegant display of stonework dated 1603, has survived in the middle of the grounds. It has now resumed its original appearance: the four bronze dogs formerly exhibited in the Louvre Museum sit obediently at the feet of their mistress, the hunting goddess.

★★★Main Apartments (Grands appartements) ⊙

The main apartments are reached by the Stucco Staircase (**a**), the Hall of Splendour (**b**) and the Gallery of Plates (**c**) which features 128 beautifully decorated pieces of Sèvres porcelain.

★**Chapelle de la Trinité (Trinity Chapel)** – It takes its name from the Trinitarian convent set up on the premises by St Louis. Henri IV had the sanctuary reinforced by vaulting and then decorated. Martin Fréminet (1567-1619), one of the lesser-known followers of Michelangelo, painted the arches with strong, vigorous scenes characterised by daring perspective and foreshortening. These represent the mystery of the Redemption and a number of figures from the Old Testament.

It was in this chapel that Louis XV was wedded to Marie Leczinska in 1725 and that Louis Napoleon, soon to be Napoleon III, was christened in 1810.

★★★**Galerie de François Ier (François I Gallery)** – This gallery was built from 1528-30 and was originally open on both sides, resembling a covered passageway. When Louis XVI enlarged it in 1786, he filled in the windows giving onto Diana's garden. A set of false French windows was fitted for reasons of symmetry. The greater part of the decoration – closely combining fresco and stucco work – was supervised by Rosso, while the wood panelling was entrusted to the Italian master carpenter Scibec from Carpi. François I's monogram and his mascot the salamander were widely represented.

The scenes are difficult to interpret and there are no enlightening documents, though they seem to split into two groups, one on either side of the central bay which is adorned with an oval painting depicting two figures: Danaë by Primaticcio and the Nymph of Fontainebleau (1860) after Rosso.

The east side, near a bust of François I, features mostly violent scenes, referring to the recent misfortunes of the French king (the defeat of Pavia, the king's captivity in Madrid), the fatality of war and death (the battle between the Centaurs and the Lapiths, Youth and Old Age, the Destruction of the Greek fleet). Beneath the vignette depicting Venus and Love at the edge of a pond, note the miniature picture set in a tablet, representing the château around 1540 with both the François I Gallery and Golden Gate clearly visible.

On the west side, near the entrance, the decor exemplifies the sacred qualities of the royal function – Sacrifice, the Unity of the State – and the concept of filial piety in the old-fashioned sense of the word (the twins Cleobis and Biton): the king, his mother Louise of Savoy and his sister Marguerite d'Angoulême were devoted to one another. The most striking scene is the portrait of an elephant whose caparison bears the royal monogram; the pachyderm was considered the symbol of Science and Wisdom.

★★**Escalier du Roi (King's Staircase)** – It was built in 1749, under Louis XV, in the bedroom that once welcomed the Duchess of Étampes, François I's favourite. The murals – the history of Alexander the Great – were by Primaticcio (note Alexander taming Bucephalus above the door) and

The Ballroom Fireplace in Fontainebleau Palace

Ch Sappa/CEDRI

dell'Abbate (Alexander placing Homer's books in a chest, on the far wall). The stucco work of the Italian master is highly original: the upper frieze is punctuated by caryatids with elongated bodies.

★★★**Salle de Bal (Ballroom)** – This room (30m – 100ft long and 10m – 33ft wide) was traditionally reserved for banquets and formal receptions. It was begun under François I and completed by Philibert Delorme under Henri II. A thorough restoration programme has revived the dazzling frescoes and paintings by Primaticcio and his pupil dell'Abbate. The marquetry of the parquet floor, completed under Louis-Philippe, echoes the splendid coffered ceiling, richly highlighted with silver and gold.

The monumental fireplace features two telamones in the form of satyrs, cast after Antique statues in the Capitol Museum in Rome.

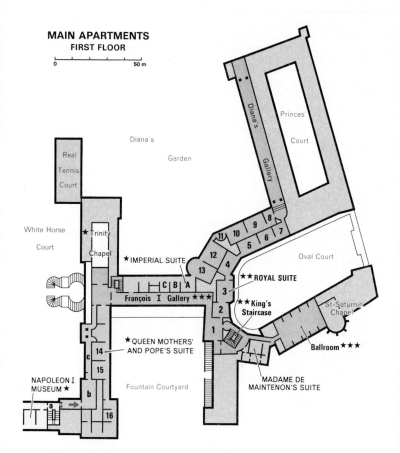

MAIN APARTMENTS
FIRST FLOOR

Appartements de Mme de Maintenon (Mme de Maintenon's Suite) – Note the delicate wainscoting in the Grand Salon, most of which was executed in the 17C.

★★**Appartements royaux (Royal Suite)** – At the time of François I, Fontainebleau Château featured a single suite of apartments laid out around the Oval Court. Towards 1565, the regent Catherine de' Medici gave orders to double the curved building between the Oval Court and Diana's Garden. Subsequently, French rulers installed their bedrooms, closets and private salons on the side of Diana's Garden. The original suite now houses antechambers, guardrooms and the salons where the king used to entertain his guests.

Guardroom (1) – The first room of the King's Suite. Late-16C ceiling and frieze.

Keep (Salon du Donjon) – A long triumphal arch leads from the Buffet Hall (Salle du Buffet) (2) to a chamber in the oldest tower of the castle. Until the reign of Henri IV these sombre quarters were occupied by French kings, who used them as a bedroom (3) hence its other name, the St Louis Bedroom. The equestrian low-relief (c1600) portraying Henri IV came from the Fine Fireplace (see above).

Louis XIII Salon (4) – It was here that Louis XIII was born on 27 September 1601. His birth is evoked by the coffered ceiling which depicts Cupid riding astride a dolphin (the word 'dauphin' means both dolphin and heir to the throne). The panel with painted wainscoting is crowned by a set of 11 pictures by Ambroise Dubois: the Romance between Theagenes and Chariclea, executed soon after the king's birth.

François I Salon (5) – Of Primaticcio's work there remains only the fireplace.

Tapestry Salon (6) – This room, having been the queen's chamber, the guardroom and the queen's first antechamber, became the empress's principal drawing room in 1804, the guardroom once more in 1814 and finally the Tapestry Salon in 1837.

The fireplace dates from 1731 and the Renaissance ceiling in pine-wood is the work of Poncet (1835). The furniture was made during the Second Empire. The tapestries telling the story of Psyche were manufactured in Paris in the early 17C.

Empress' Antechamber (7) – Formerly the queen's guardroom, this chamber was built on top of the old royal staircase: the ceiling and panelling are both dated 1835. The Gobelins tapestries, executed after cartoons by Le Brun, illustrate the four seasons. The Second Empire furniture features a console, a carved oak writing desk (Fourdinois, 1865) and a set of armchairs of English inspiration. Note the two Indian-style enamel vases produced by the Sèvres factory.

Diana's Gallery ☉ – This long gilt passageway (80m – 263ft) was decorated during the Restoration and converted to a library under the Second Empire. The painted ceiling portrays Diana and other allegorical figures and eight of the original twenty-four scenes from French history.

White Salon. Queen's Parlour (8) – In 1835 the room was decorated with furnishings from an earlier period: Louis XV wainscoting, Louis XVI fireplace inlaid with bronze etc. The furniture is Empire: chairs in gilt wood by Jacob Frères, settee, armchairs and chairs from St-Cloud Château, mahogany console and heads of fantastic animals in bronzed, gilt wood (Jacob Desmalter).

Empress' Grand Salon (9) – This salon, formerly the queen's gaming room, features a ceiling painted by Berthélemy: the scene is Minerva crowning the Muses. The Empire furniture includes chairs and consoles by Jacob Desmalter and a "four seasons" table made of Sèvres porcelain and hand-painted by Georget in 1806-1807. The furniture has been upholstered with material woven to the design of the carpet.

Empress' Bedchamber (10) – This used to be the queen's bedroom. The greater part of the ceiling was designed for Anne of Austria in 1644, the fireplace and the top of the alcove were created for Marie Leczinska in 1747 and the doors with arabesque motifs were installed for Marie-Antoinette in 1787.

The brocaded silk was rewoven according to the original pattern in Lyon at the end of Louis XVI's reign.

Among the furniture note Marie-Antoinette's bed, designed in 1787 by Hauré, Séné and Laurent, a set of armchairs attributed to Jacob Frères and several commodes by Stöckel and Beneman (1786). The vases are Sèvres porcelain.

Queen's Boudoir (11) – This delightful room was designed for Marie-Antoinette. The wainscoting was painted by Bourgois and Touzé after sketches by the architect Rousseau. The ceiling – representing the tender rays of sunrise – is the work of Berthélemy. The roll-top writing desk and the work table were executed by Riesener in 1786.

Throne Room (12) – This was the king's bedroom from Henri IV to Louis XVI; Napoleon I converted it into a throne room. The ornate mural paintings, dating from several periods, were harmonised in the 18C. Above the fireplace is a full-length portrait of Louis XIII, painted in Philippe de Champaigne's studio.

Council Chamber (13) – This room featured in François I's château but was given a semicircular extension in 1773. The ceiling and panelling are splendid examples of Louis XV decoration.

Five pictures by Boucher adorn the ceiling, representing the four seasons and Phoebe, supreme mistress of the starlit skies. The wainscoting presents an alternation of allegorical figures painted in blue or pink monochrome by Van Loo and Jean-Baptiste Pierre.

★**Appartement Intérieur de l'Empereur (Imperial Suite)** ☉ – *Undergoing restoration.* Napoleon had his suite installed in the wing built by Louis XVI, on the garden side running parallel with the François I Gallery.

Napoleon's Bedchamber (A) – Most of the decoration – dating from the Louis XVI period – has survived. The furniture is typically Empire.

Small Bedroom (B) – A little private study which Bonaparte furnished with a camp-bed in gilded iron.

Abdication Room (C) – According to tradition, this is the room in which the famous abdication document was signed on 6 April 1814. The Empire furniture of this red salon dates back to that momentous time.

The François I Gallery leads to the Horse-shoe Hall, at the top of the curved steps of the same name. This was the official entrance to the palace from the late 17C onwards. Both the gallery of Trinity Chapel and the Queen Mothers' Suite give onto this hall.

★**Appartements des Reines Mères et du Pape (Queen Mothers' and Pope's Suite)** ☉ – *Undergoing restoration.* Built in the 16C and redesigned under Louis XV following the completion of the end pavilion – now called the Great Pavilion – the suite was named after Catherine de' Medici, Marie de' Medici, Anne of Austria and Pope Pius VII, who stayed here in 1804 and 1812-14. Napoleon III and Eugénie applied themselves to harmonising, renewing and restoring the decoration and furniture of these apartments.

The ceiling in the Grand Salon **(14)** was taken from the former bedroom of Henri II (1558) and placed here on the orders of Anne of Austria. The decoration – attributed to one of Philibert Delorme's collaborators – represents the Sun and revolving Planets of the Universe.

The state bedchamber (**15**) has a Gobelins tapestry – The Triumph of the Gods – matching the grotesque-style wainscoting executed by the master decorator Jean Cotelle the Elder (1607-76). The bedroom of the Duchess of Orléans (**16**), previously occupied by the Pope, presents a highly distinguished set of Louis XVI furniture, set off by a superb decor of deep crimson damask.

★Napoleon I Museum (Musée Napoléon Ier) ⊙

The museum is dedicated to the Emperor and his family: it occupies 15 rooms on the ground level and first floor of the Louis XV wing. Exhibits include portraits (paintings and sculptures), silverware, arms, medals, ceramics (Imperial service), clothing (Coronation robes, uniforms) and personal souvenirs. Thanks to the numerous works of art and furniture adorning their interior, these apartments have kept their princely character.

The rooms on the first floor evoke the Coronation (paintings by François Gérard), the Emperor's various military campaigns, his daily life (remarkable folding desk by Jacob Desmalter), the Empress Marie-Louise in formal attire or painting the Emperor's portrait (picture by Alexandre Menjaud) and the birth of Napoleon's son, the future King of Rome (cradles).

The ground floor presents the Emperor's close relations. Each of the seven rooms is devoted to a member of the family: Napoleon's mother, his brothers Joseph, Louis, Jérôme and sisters Elisa, Pauline and Caroline.

★Small Apartments and Deer Gallery
(Petits appartements et galerie des cerfs) ⊙

These rooms are located on the ground floor below the François I Gallery and the Royal Suite range giving onto Diana's Garden.

Petits Appartements de Napoléon Ier (Small Imperial Suite) – These rooms comprise François I's former bathroom suite (located beneath the gallery), converted into private rooms under Louis XV for the king. Mme de Pompadour and Mme du Barry, and the ground floor of the new Louis XVI wing, situated under the Imperial Suite. The rooms opening onto Diana's Garden have been decorated with Louis XV wainscoting and Empire furniture.

★**Appartements de l'Impératrice Joséphine (Apartments of the Empress Joséphine)** – This suite of rooms adorned with Louis XV panelling was designed for Joséphine in 1808. It lies beneath the grand royal suite.

The study, with its large rotunda, is located beneath the Council Chamber (1st floor).

The Empire furniture here has a feminine touch: Marie-Louise's tambour frame, her easel etc.

The Yellow Salon constitutes one of the palace's most perfect examples of Empire decoration. The gold-coloured silk hangings provide an elegant setting for Jacob-Desmalter's choice furniture pieces, set off by a large Aubusson carpet with a white background.

★**Galerie des Cerfs (Deer Gallery)** – The gallery is decorated with numerous deer heads (only the antlers are genuine). The mural paintings were renovated under Napoleon III: they show palatial residences at the time of Henri IV, seen in perspective. It was in this gallery that Queen Christina of Sweden had her favourite, Monaldeschi, assassinated in 1657. The original casts used to make Primaticcio's 1540 replicas of Antique statues are on display in the gallery.

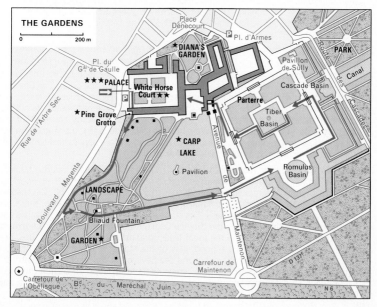

★Gardens

These consist of Diana's Garden *(see above)*, the Landscape Garden, the parterre and the park.

Follow the route indicated on the map below.

★**Grotte du Jardin des Pins (Pine Grove Grotto)** – This rare ornamental composition carved in sandstone reveals the popular taste, copied from the Italians, for nymphs and bucolic landscapes in vogue towards the end of François I's reign. The rusticated arches are supported by giant telamones. The frescoes have disappeared.

★**Jardin Anglais (Landscape Garden)** – The garden was created in 1812 on the site of former gardens – featuring a pine grove – redesigned under Louis XIV and abandoned during the Revolution. The Bliaud or Blaut fountain – which gave its name to the palace – plays in a small octagonal basin in the middle of the garden.

Parterre – This formal garden was started under François I, redesigned under Henri IV and eventually renovated by Le Nôtre. The Tiber and Romulus Basins take their name from a sculpture, based on the Antique model, which adorned them in the 16C and then the 17C. The Tiber – melted during the Revolution – was cast after the original (in the Louvre) a second time and is now back in the place Louis XIV had assigned it. Skirt Bréau Canal to get a broad view of the palace.
Until the 18C, a series of cascades marked the end of this first group of tiered fountains. At present there remains only a basin of the same name, its ornate niches adorned with marble statues.

Park – The park was created by Henri IV, who filled the canal in 1609 and had the grounds planted with elms, pines and fruit trees. Sixty years before the installation of the Grand Canal at Versailles, this dazzling sight was a great novelty for the *Ancien Régime*, as were the aquatic displays.

ADDITIONAL SIGHTS

Musée Napoléonien d'Art et d'Histoire Militaire (Napoleonic Museum of Military Art and History) (AY M¹) ⊙ – The museum contains around one hundred figures, complete with full equipment and arsenal: swordsmen and veterans from the Imperial Grand Army, soldiers who fought for the conquest of Algeria and the Second Empire.
The first floor houses a **collection** of statutory **swords and sabres**★ dating from the 19C.

Musée d'Art Figuratif (Museum of Figurative Art) – *Undergoing redevelopment.* Temporarily transferred to Ferrières *(qv)*.

EXCURSIONS

Croix du Calvaire (Calvary) – *5km - 3 miles from the Palace. Leave by Boulevard Maréchal-Leclerc. Just before the swimming pool, take the second turning on the left and proceed along Route de la Belle Amélie.*
Almost a mile after the road starts to rise, turn left to reach the esplanade and calvary: admire the fine **view** of the town nestling amidst woodlands.

Avon; By-Thomery – *Leave Fontainebleau by Boulevard du Maréchal Juin (see above); at the junction, Carrefour de Maintenon, fork left to D 137ᴱ (BZ).*

Avon – Built in the 11C, **St Peter's Church** (Église St-Pierre) features a Romanesque nave surmounted by diagonal arches. The belltower was erected in the 13C, the Renaissance door dates from the 15C. The Gothic chancel, the work of architect Jean du Montceau, was completed in 1555. Note, among the funerary stones, that of the marquess of Monaldeschi, the favourite of Queen Christina of Sweden who had him assassinated at Fontainebleau in 1657. The recently-restored porch was erected in the 18C.

Leave Avon and proceed along D 137 then turn right on entering By-Thomery.

Rosa Bonheur's Studio (Atelier de Rosa Bonheur) ⊙ – Rosa Bonheur (1822-99), a painter of animals widely acclaimed by her contemporaries, bought By Château in 1859 to satisfy her need for space (she had numerous pets) and quiet. The Empress Eugénie paid her a visit when she was awarded the French order of merit, the Légion d'Honneur. Another famous visitor, Buffalo Bill, gave her one of his outfits, presently exhibited in the corridor. The tour includes the study (portrait of the artist by Achille Fould, painter and close adviser to Napoleon III), the studio (stuffed animals, deer antlers, her last, uncompleted picture) and a closet furnished with her bed, her wardrobe and a glass cabinet of souvenirs.

Château de Bourron (Bourron Château) ⊙ – *7km - 4 1/2 miles south. Michelin map 237 fold 37. Leave Fontainebleau by ④ the N 7 and turn left at Bourron-Marlotte.* Built on the remains of a medieval stronghold in the late 16C, the château consists of a large central block flanked by two perpendicular pavilions: these are fronted by two low wings (stables). The stone and brick patterns of the façades and the horse-shoe staircase evoke the Kitchen Court at Fontainebleau. On the northern side, a swivel bridge spanning the moat leads to another horse-shoe staircase. The parterre to the south affords a good view of the stately and harmonious proportions of the château. Note the delightful Ste-Sévère spring, which flows into the Grand Canal to the north of the park. Louis XV came to Bourron Château to meet his father-in-law Stanislas Leczinski, the dethroned King of Poland, who was staying on the estate.

FONTAINEBLEAU FOREST★★★

Michelin map 106 folds 44, 45, 46 or 61 folds 2, 11, 12

This lovely (25 000ha – 62 000 acres) forest is largely State-owned and has always provided magnificent hunting grounds. It is immensely popular with ramblers and climbing enthusiasts.

GENERAL APPEARANCE OF THE FOREST

Geological formation – The relief of the forested area comprises a series of parallel sandstone ridges running in an east-west direction.

These ridges are thought to be the result of a tropical spell during the Tertiary Era, when strong winds gradually accumulated sand deposits in this part of the Paris Basin. The sand dunes subsequently solidified into a hard sandstone matrix and were then buried beneath deposits of Beauce limestone, which resulted in the preservation of the area's rolling landscape.

Where the upper layer of Beauce limestone was spared from erosion, the valley sides culminate in small **hillocks**. They reach a maximum height of 144m – 475ft and bear some of the forest's most charming groves.

Where the limestone has eroded revealing the sandstone, the resultant rocky areas are known locally as **platières**.

These **moorlands** consisting of heather and other shrubs are often cracked and dotted with ponds. When the sandstone layer has many crevices and holes, water seeps through and starts to wash away the underlying sands. The upper sandstone strata is no longer supported and crumbles as a result, producing picturesque rocky clusters, the famous Fontainebleau "**rochers**".

Vales or **plains** averaging 40-80m – 130-260ft in height are found where the sandstone layer has been eroded away, exposing the sand or the Brie marl and limestone beneath. The planting of conifers fertilises the soil, making it possible to grow beeches. These produce humus and are eventually replaced by oaks, the ideal tree species for a forest *(qv)*.

The forest itself is nine-tenths wooded: mainly oaks, Scots pines and beeches, with hornbeams, birches, maritime and Corsican pines, spruce, acacias, chestnuts and wild service trees.

The **Denecourt-Colinet Paths** *(1)* cover 150km – 94 miles; they were begun in the 19C by Sylvain Denecourt who cleared caves, opened up the most attractive sites and marked out paths. His work was continued by Sylvain Colinet. The routes are marked in blue on selected rocks or trees. More interesting sights bear a blue star or reference letter (explained in the guide by *Les Amis de la Forêt* – see 1). The signposting was finished in 1975: each major junction has a white, enamel-coated sign with a green border.

Long-distance footpaths are marked in red and white; white and green signs refer to a 65km – 40 mile long Grand Tour of Fontainebleau (TMF) marked out by the French Forestry Commission (ONF = Office National des Forêts).

Climbing is now quite common in the area; over a hundred climbing itineraries have been marked out by small arrows painted on the rocks.

★★FRANCHARD GORGE

① Round tour starting from Croix de Franchard
1/2 to 2 hours Rtn on foot

Franchard Hermitage (Ancien ermitage de Franchard) – A hermitage developed here in the 12C, and in the 13C a community moved in to look after the pilgrims. Today only the chapel walls remain, incorporated into the forest cabin.

★**Viewpoint** (Grand Point de vue) – *1/2 hour Rtn on foot*. Beyond the cabin's fence, skirt the sandy track on the left and climb towards the rocks without changing direction. This leads to a very sandy road; after 300m – 330yds a mushroom-shaped rock will appear ahead. At the plateau turn right and on reaching the rock bear left to a bench overlooking the ravine. The view of the gorge is breathtaking.

To return to the hermitage, walk down three steps and bear left; to pursue a longer walk, bear right after the three steps.

★★**Druids' Tour** (Circuit des Druides) – Follow the blue markings of path no 7. At the bottom of a first dip in the ravine, cross a sandy

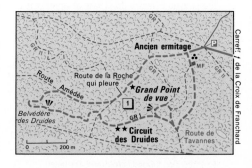

(1) The "Guide des Sentiers de promenades dans le Massif forestier de Fontainebleau", published by the Société des amis de la Forêt de Fontainebleau – based at no 31 Place Napoléon Bonaparte in Fontainebleau – includes a comprehensive list of signposted footpaths (on sale at the Office du Tourisme and in bookshops).
For long-distance footpaths and short-distance routes consult the Topo Guides published by C.N.S.G.R. (see Practical Information).

track (isolated oak) and climb the rocks again. Follow the climb (↔) signs up to the second belvedere, marked with a star. Continue along the edge of the plateau to the **Druids' Belvedere** (Belvédère des Druides). Take the signposted lane below going east; at the bottom of the gorge turn right into Route Amédée. At the next fork turn left into a steep rise known as Route de la Roche qui Pleure (avoid the zigzag route marked in blue, on the left), which returns to the hermitage.

★APREMONT GORGE

② Round tour starting from Barbizon
10km - 6 miles – about 3 1/2 hours on foot

Leave Barbizon *(qv)* by Allée aux Vaches, the continuation of Grande Rue, as far as the crossroads known as Carrefour du Bas-Bréau.

★**Apremont Boulders** (Chaos d'Apremont) – *3/4 hour Rtn on foot from the crossroads; take a torch.* Follow the path marked in blue left of the refreshment chalet (buvette) and continue up amid the rocks; at the top bear right and follow the edge of the plateau. Views are over the wooded slopes of the gorge and the Bière plain. The path veers left: a clump of acacia and pine trees marks the entrance to the **Robbers' Cave** (Caverne des Brigands).

Return to the car and drive along Route de Sully to the car park at Cul-de-Chaudron junction.

★**Great Belvedere of Apremont** (Grand Belvédère d'Apremont) – *1/4 hour Rtn on foot.* Walk onto the plateau and turn left into the path marked in blue. At the fork with the Denecourt-Colinet signpost, turn right; the lane follows a downward slope in the midst of a *chaos* (French geological term for a group of irregular rocks and boulders). Bear left while remaining at the top of the *chaos*. The gorge, its slopes dotted with boulders, with the Bière plain to the west, soon comes into view.
Return to the car and to Carrefour du Bas-Bréau.

★★**Desert Tour** (Circuit du Désert) – *3 1/2 hours on foot.* This part of the forest is famous for its barren and desert-like appearance.
Take the old route from Barbizon to Fontainebleau; after a mile turn south into Route du Clair Bois. Take the first lane on the right, Route de la Chouette, over a pass and down to Apremont Desert, a valley dotted with oddly-shaped boulders. Bear left into path no 6 marked in blue. On reaching the rock resembling an animal with two snouts (reference P), bear right. At the junction (Carrefour du Désert) take the blue-marked path which lies between Route du Clair Bois and Route de Milan: it leads to a ravine framed by boulders, then along a rocky ledge.
Immediately after the Dryads' Cave (Grotte des Dryades), marked with a star, bear left and walk down path "6-6" and up the far side of the valley to the raised platform; Boars' Pond (Mare aux Sangliers) lies to the left. The prominent part of the plateau offers a good **view** of Apremont Desert and the Bière plain.

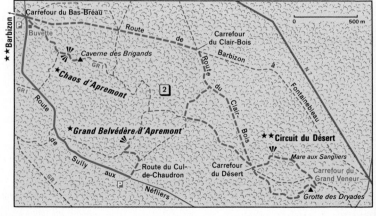

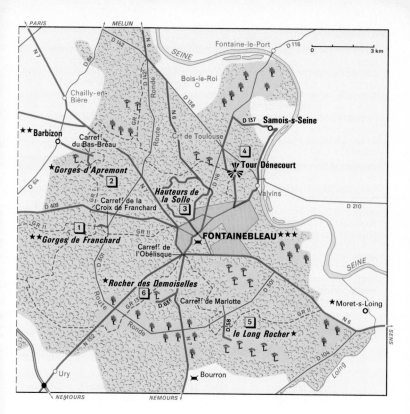

***LONG ROCK

③ Round tour starting from Marlotte junction
(Carrefour de Marlotte)
1.5km - 1 mile – then 2 hours Rtn on foot

Along Route Ronde branch off towards Marlotte.

After 1/2 mile, before reaching a steep slope, turn left into Route du Long Rocher, a sandy forest lane (ONF board: "Zone de Silence de la Malmontagne").

Park at the next crossroads (barrier).

Walk into Route des Etroitures (first turning on the right).

After 100yds, turn right into path no 11, marked in blue.

Narrow Belvedere (Belvédère des Étroitures) – Reference U. Admire the view of Marlotte and the Loing Valley.

Return along path no 11 and continue weaving through the boulders and pine trees to the top of a plateau called Restant du Long Rocher.

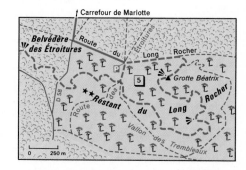

⋆⋆Restant du Long Rocher – The edge of the plateau, strewn with uneven-sized boulders, offers several good views of the forest. Return to path no 11 and continue in an easterly direction. Leave the plateau via the precipice which houses Beatrix's Cave (Grotte Béatrix). Walk past a series of boulders used for exercise by mountaineering schools (red arrows). Further along, the path rises slightly: branch off left and take the steep, clearly-marked track down. This leads back to Route du Long Rocher; bear left to return.

⋆THE THREE GABLES

④ Round tour starting from Arbonne
2.5km – 1 1/2 miles – then 3 hours Rtn on foot

Leave Arbonne to the south (D 64) towards Achères-la-Forêt.

After 1 mile the road veers towards the motorway; turn right under it. Park the car. The Three Gables (les Trois Pignons) massif is an unusual extension of Fontainebleau Forest: it is a stony, barren site, unique in Ile-de-France, with dry valleys, eroded peaks and other peculiarities which are common to sandstone landscapes.

From the car park go straight ahead and follow the road past two houses on the right. At the corner of the fencing, bear right and walk to the edge of a sandy depression, to the starting point of Denecourt-Colinet path no 16.

On the other side of the depression, in straight alignment with the plaque, is the first blue mark. The path crosses a flat stretch of land dotted with boulders and leads past the platform of the old Noisy telegraph transmitter to the plateau. After an hour's walking, a chestnut grove is reached. The path follows the recesses of the impressive Cats' Canyon (Gorge aux Chats) and continues southeast and then south, crossing a sandy, rocky area cleared of trees.

★★**Viewpoint of Close Valley** (Point de vue de la Vallée Close) – The edge of the plateau offers a good **view**★★ of the massif. In the foreground, a monument crowned by a cross of Lorraine honours the local Resistance network.

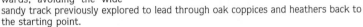

The blue path then turns north and descends eastwards, avoiding the wide sandy track previously explored to lead through oak coppices and heathers back to the starting point.

Suggestions for additional tours:

– north of Fontainebleau ③ along **Route Louis-Philippe**★ and **Route du Gros-Fouteau**★ through ancient groves and then to the **Rochers du Mont Ussy**★ where a pleasant path leads through pine trees;

– a round trip northeast of the town ④ taking in **Tour Dénecourt**, a 19C tower offering **panoramic views**★, and **Samois-sur-Seine**, an attractive and once-important town on the banks of the river;

– Carrefour de Marlotte (Marlotte crossroads), south of Fontainebleau, near which numerous footpaths lead through the picturesque pinewoods of the **Long Rocher**★ ⑤ ;

– to the southwest ⑥ , pleasant rambles through the Cirque des Demoiselles and to the **Rocher des Demoiselles**★.

FOURMIES

Population 14 505

Michelin map 53 fold 16 or 236 fold 29. Local map p 61

Fourmies is a busy town which developed an important textile industry in the 19C; it is surrounded by huge forests and a series of lakes. The lakes were created by monks from Liessies (qv) and it is from them that the best-known of these, the **Monks' Lake** (Étang des Moines) with its fishing, boating and swimming facilities, derives its name.

Écomusée de la région Fourmies-Trélon (Fourmies-Trélon Regional Museum) – The museum's aim is to preserve and promote the different economic and cultural aspects of life, past and present, in the region. Established with the help of the locals, the museum includes several satellites specialising in different areas: industrial activity is featured at the Textile and Social Life Museum (see below) and at the Glass Workshop-Museum, Trélon (qv); rural activities at the Maison du Bocage in Sains du Nord (qv); the religious heritage in Liessies (qv).

The environmental heritage can be seen in the natural setting of the Baives Hills (Monts de Baives), in the Maison de la Fagne at Wallers-Trélon (qv) and along the **Observation trails** in the **Wignehies area** (Sentiers d'Observation sur la Commune de Wignehies) ⊙. An audio-visual presentation (15min) in the textile museum presents an overall view of the region and the museum satellites.

★**Musée du Textile et de la Vie sociale** (Textile and Social Life Museum) ⊙ – The museum, which is housed in an old spinning mill, displays a collection of textile machines from the late 19C to the present day, all in working order.

Photographic records, reconstructions – of a textile laboratory, a hosiery workshop, and a street with a bar and shops – evoke the life of the locals over a century and retraces the events which marked their history (the strike of 1 May 1891).

Join us in our constant task of keeping up-to-date.
Please send us your comments and suggestions.

Michelin Tyre
Public Limited Company
Tourism Department - The Edward Hyde Building
38 Clarendon Road - WATFORD Herts WD1 1SX
Tel: 01923 415000 - Fax: 01923 415250

FRANCE MINIATURE ★

Michelin map 106 folds 28, 29 – Outskirts of Élancourt

France Miniature ⊙ stretches across a 5ha – 12 acre site, bordered by lakes representing the sea, and consists of almost 2 000 models of the most famous and characteristic buildings and monuments in France; these models (scale 1:30) make up an entire relief map of the country and provide a simple way of getting acquainted with the geography and architecture of this varied country.

A tour might start with a climb to the top of the Alps (9m - 29ft high) from which there is a panorammic view over this map of France. Paths beside the "mountains", "plains" and "rivers" trace a journey of discovery through the country, taking in the Roman Theatre at Nîmes, the Eiffel Tower, the Palace of Versailles, the Futuroscope in Poitiers etc, complete with miniature boats, trains and planes.

GUÎNES

Population 5 105
Michelin map 51 fold 2 or 236 fold 2

Guînes, now a busy cereal market town, was the seat of a powerful earl, a vassal of the English crown for more than 200 years, from 1352 to 1558.

The Field of the Cloth of Gold – The famous encounter between **François I** of France and **Henry VIII** of England took place near Guînes, on the road to Ardres, in 1520. The 17-day meeting from 7 June now known as the Field of the Cloth of Gold (Camp du Drap d'Or) was convened to discuss a possible Anglo-French alliance; however, it developed into a competition of one-upmanship.

François was staying in Ardres, Henry stayed with the earl at Guînes castle; each was accompanied by his queen and a substantial court: the gentlemen of the Knight King (Roi Chevalier) were so sumptuously dressed that the contemporary writer Martin du Bellay was moved to note that "They carried their mills, their forests and their fields on their backs."

The camp was arranged around jousting rails. On one side the English king occupied a "crystal palace" which sparkled in the sun, on the other François I sheltered under a tent of gold brocade: the surroundings had been arranged by the painter Jean Bourdichon. This luxurious display proved fruitless however: Henry was irritated by the French king's extravagance, the crystal palace was damaged by the wind and he was toppled by his royal adversary during a contest. Humiliated and angry, Henry returned to Gravelines *(qv)* and two weeks later made an alliance with the Emperor Charles V of Spain, undertaking not to enter into any fresh partnership with François for two years.

E Villez Municipal Museum ⊙ – Numerous archeological remains, documents, objects, maps (atlas of 1609), engravings and paintings evoke the history of the town from its origins to the 20C.

Forêt de Guînes (Guînes Forest) – The road from Guînes enters this hilly area which is densely covered with varied species (oaks, beech, hornbeam, birch) and extends (785ha – 1 940 acres) to the northern edge of the Boulonnais region. The road

The Field of the Cloth of Gold by Bouterwek, Guînes

ends at **Balloon Clearing** (Clairière du Ballon). To the left and slightly set back, Blanchard's Column (Colonne Blanchard) in marble marks the spot where, on 7 January 1785, the balloon flown by Jean-Pierre Blanchard (1753-1809) and the American physician John Jeffries landed, having achieved the first aerial crossing of the Channel.

EXCURSION

Forteresse de Mimoyecques (Mimoyecques Fort) ⊙ – *10km - 6 miles southwest by D 231 and D 249 from Landrethun-le-Nord.*
Because of its position 8km - 5 miles from the coast and 150km - 93 miles from London, Mimoyecques was chosen as the launching site for the formidable V3 howitzer, invented after the V1 and V2, to bombard London. To fire these shells the Germans had developed enormous, 130m - 426ft long cannons. Work began in September 1943 when thousands of prisoners were forced to dig the 600m - 1 968ft rail tunnel under 30m - 98ft of chalk, and the ditches where the cannons were to be installed. The Allied forces bombed Mimoyecques from November 1943, and in July 1944 a Tallboy bomb pierced the cement covering; this resulted in flooding which put an end to the works.
The huge scale of the project can still be seen, including the impressive tunnel where over 40 trains daily brought materials from Germany.

Ardres – *9km - 5 1/2 miles east on D 231.*
This pleasant and peaceful market town, where François I stayed during the Field of the Cloth of Gold, was prosperous in Gallo-Roman times and later became a frontier town coveted by the English and the Spanish. The town lake (swimming, fishing, sailboarding facilities) was formed over the old peat bogs, out of which turfs were cut for fuel from Antiquity until the 19C.
The triangular, paved main square is bordered by picturesque old houses with pointed roofs. The old 17C Carmelite chapel stands opposite the east end of the 14C-15C church.

GUISE

Population 5 976
Michelin map 53 fold 15 or 236 fold 28

Guise (pronounced Gu-ize) lies in a pleasant setting at the bottom of the Oise Valley; despite its modern appearance the town has preserved an old district, near the church at the foot of the hillside.
Elevated to a duchy by François I, Guise gave its name to an illustrious family – an offshoot of the House of Lorraine – whose most famous members were: **François de Guise** (1519-63) who defended Metz against Charles V of Spain, retook Calais from the English and who was assassinated; and **Henri de Guise** (1550-88), head of the Catholic League *(qv)* during the Wars of Religion, who was assassinated at Blois Château on the orders of Henri III.
Guise was the birthplace of **Camille Desmoulins** (1760-94), the son of a lieutenant in the bailiff's court. The most famous French journalist at the time of the Revolution, Desmoulins publicly denounced the violence and injustices being committed in its name and was guillotined as a traitor for saying so.
In 1914 General de Lanzerac's army defended the passage through the Oise valley against the Germans, allowing the French troops time to regroup for the Battle of the Marne.

SIGHTS

★Château Fort des Ducs de Guise (Castle) ⊙ – *Access from the town, beyond St Peter's church.*
The castle was built in medieval times (11C) from Ardennes sandstone. Later, in the 16C, it was one of the first fortresses in France to have bastions added to it, at the instigation of the first Dukes of Guise, Claude and François. Situated in the path of invaders of the Oise Valley, the castle was further reinforced by Vauban the following century. The buildings cover an area of 17ha – 42 acres. One of the targets during the First World War, it was subsequently used as a quarry for materials and later as a rubbish tip.
In 1952 Maurice Duton, a local man, decided to save the castle with the help of young volunteers who were brought together under an organisation which they named the Club du Vieux Manoir.
Enter the castle through the restored 16C Ducal Gate (Porte Ducale) which faces the town. From the Upper Town Bastion (Bastion de la Haute Ville) cross the medieval passageway – which leads to the vaulted alley of the carriage entrance – to reach the Prison Building (bâtiment des Prisons) and the large storeroom in which 3 000 men were garrisoned during sieges; continue along the vaulted alley to the remains of the Governor's Palace (Palais du Gouverneur) and the medieval keep. The foundations of the Collegiate Church of St Gervase and Protase are also visible. The great Guard Rooms in la Charbonnière and l'Allouette Bastions have been

converted into a museum exhibiting finds from excavations, including the coat of arms of François de Guise, the second Duke, and of his wife the Duchess of Este and Ferrara. Follow a series of underground passages to return to the Upper Town Bastion and the Lepers' Gallery (Galerie des Lepreux).

Familistère Godin (Godin Workers' Co-operative) – The creation of a co-operative was the brainchild of Jean-Baptiste André Godin (1817-88), the founder of factories producing heating and cooking appliances.

Godin was a daring business chief and one of his ideas was to establish a phalanstery for a co-operative community, following the system put forward by the social theorist Fourier. As well as this "Social Palace", built between 1859 and 1883, he created a co-operative for capital and labour.

Museum (Musée) ⊙ – Installed within the co-operative, next to the library, the museum presents the town's history together with souvenirs of famous figures, including Camille Desmoulins and especially J-B A Godin who devoted his life to improving workers' morale and physical conditions. A model shows the importance of the co-operative's factories, dwellings and other facilities (shops, school, swimming pool, theatre, garden...).

The dwellings, built around courtyards with glazing supported on wooden or metal frameworks, can still be seen today. On each floor, walkways allow public access. On the other side of the River Oise, the Godin factories are still active.

EXCURSION

Round trip of 17km - 10 miles – *About 1/2 hour. Leave Guise by D 946 north and after 3km – 2 miles turn left into D 693.*

The route offers a good **view** *(left)* over the Oise Valley.

Follow D 693 into the valley of the Sambre canal (Canal de la Sambre à l'Oise) – which joins the Sambre to the Oise and the Noirieux, a tributary of the Oise – crossing it at Tupigny.

Turn left into D 66 beside the northern side of the valley.

Vadencourt – Popular with anglers, Vadencourt sits in a pleasant spot at the junction of the Oise and the Noirieux rivers. The 12C **church** has beautiful capitals.

From D 66 turn left beside the church; D 960 returns to Guise.

L'HAŸ-LES-ROSES

Population 29 591
Michelin map 101 fold 25 or 106 north of fold 31 – Michelin plan 22

The town is famed for its spectacular rose garden, located on the edge of a pleasant **park.**

★★Roseraie (Rose Garden) ⊙ – The garden was created in 1892 and subsequently embellished by Jules Graveraux, a man passionately fond of roses who also helped design the famous Parisian department store Le Bon Marché.

The flower beds are planted with thousands of wild and grafted roses from all over the world. The gardens also feature a display of arches, trellises and colonnades for the climbing varieties which will delight visitors. The selection of roses is enriched every year.

Musée de la Rose (Rose Museum) – It houses a collection of miscellaneous works of art inspired by this noble flower: engravings by Redouté, embroideries, costumes, curios, ivory ornaments, ceramics, bindings etc.

The Rose Garden, L'Haÿ-les-Roses

The star ratings are allocated for various categories:
- *regions of scenic beauty with dramatic natural features*
- *cities with a cultural heritage*
- *elegant resorts and charming villages*
- *ancient monuments and fine architecture*
- *museums and picture galleries.*

HONDSCHOOTE

Population 3 654
Michelin map 51 fold 4 or 236 folds 4, 5

This Flemish-speaking town, which is bedecked with flowers in summer, centres on its main square (Grand-Place). Until the 17C the town produced a lightweight serge cloth *(sayes)* which was made in 3 000 workshops by 28 000 workers.

Hôtel de ville (Town Hall) ⊙ – The building, which is dated 1558, was built on the main square in a Gothic-Renaissance style. The stone front is articulated by high mullioned windows linked by fine mouldings of curves and counter-curves. The rear façade is brick and stone, with a pointed tower crowned with an onion dome.

On the ground floor, a display of inscriptions by the writer Lamartine show his affection for the local Coppens family, and a large painting portrays the 1793 Battle of Hondschoote in which the French triumphed over the English and the Austrians. On the first floor, an exhibition room displays ten 17C paintings showing nine noblewomen and Joan of Arc, together with works by Dutch painters. The inn beside the town hall dates from 1617.

Église (Church) – This hall-church type of building, with a tower at the west front and parallel aisles of equal height, is common in the maritime region of Flanders. The 16C tower (82m – 269ft high) dominates the town: it was the only thing to survive the fire of Hondschoote in 1582. The aisles were rebuilt in the early 17C. Inside, the lyre-shaped organ case and the pulpit are 18C Flemish Baroque.

The savings bank (Caisse d'Épargne) opposite is installed in the former manor house of the Coppens family, the lords of Hondschoote.

Moulin (Windmill) ⊙ – *500m - 550yds north of Hondschoote, near D 3.*

This windmill, known as the Noord-meulen, is the oldest windmill in Europe – its foundation dates back to 1127 – and was in use until 1959. The wooden cabin rests on a timber pivot and brick base.

To commemorate the bicentenary of the Battle of Hondschoote a new post mill was built in 1993.

Hondschoote windmill

EXCURSION

Les Moëres – The name, which means marshes, relates to the old lagoon which was drained in the 17C by Coebergher *(qv)*, using dams, canals and 20 windmills equipped with Archimedean Screws to pump the water.

The marshes – which extend as far as Furnes in Belgium – are below sea-level and flooded over from 1645 to 1746 and again in 1940. Reclaimed from the sea and protected by dykes, the marshes now provide fertile stretches of land which are dotted with large farms and criss-crossed by canals full of tench, bream and pike. On the horizon stand the belfry, factories and cranes of Dunkirk.

Leave Hondschoote by D 947 and turn left into D 3 towards Bergues, along Basse Coline canal; turn right into D 97, then take the small road leading to the village of Moëres. Return to Hondschoote by D 947.

L'ISLE-ADAM

Population 9 979
Michelin map 106 fold 6 or 55 fold 20

In 1014 a castle built on one of the River Oise isles was ceded to Adam de Villiers by Robert II the Pious, Hugh Capet's son. The former erected a priory on the estate. In 1364 the fief was acquired by Pierre de Villiers, whose descendants gained widespread recognition: Jean (1384-1437), Maréchal de Bourgogne, served two Dukes of Burgundy, John the Fearless and Philip the Good, before becoming one of the king's followers; Philippe (1464-1534), Commander of the Order of St John of Jerusalem, and subsequently Grand Master of the Order of Malta, heroically defended Rhodes against Suleiman the Magnificent for five months, and succeeded in obtaining Malta as headquarters for the order. In the 19C Villiers de L'Isle-Adam, the author of *Cruel Tales*, was to become one of the great names of French literature.

In the 16C the land came into the hands of Constable Anne de Montmorency. Louis XIII later offered the estate to Henri II of Bourbon, Prince de Condé. In 1646 Armand de Bourbon, Prince de Conti, moved in with his lavish court.

Honoré de Balzac was a regular visitor at L'Isle-Adam and several of his novels are set in the area. L'Isle-Adam was also home to Henri Prosper Breuil (1877-1961), the renowned archeologist.

The site – The château belonging to the Conti was razed during the Revolution. The old bridges – in particular Cabouillet Bridge, a 16C stone construction with three arches – command a pleasant view of the Oise, which is still frequented by pleasure boats as in former times *(booking office on the beach)*.
L'Isle-Adam has France's largest inland beach, now a popular water sports centre: it features numerous facilities for yachting, sailing, rowing, canoeing etc.

Église St-Martin (St Martin's Church) ⊙ – Like St-Martin's, Montmorency *(qv)*, this church is typical of 16C architecture and presents highly intricate vaulting. It was consecrated on 1 October 1567, in the presence of Constable Anne. The tower erected in 1869 is a replica of the one adorning Trinity Church in Paris.
The interior offers an important collection of well-preserved furnishings. The 1560 **pulpit**★ – of German origin – features inlaid panels and portrays numerous statues, grouped in sets of four: Great Prophets, Evangelists, Doctors of the Church, Cardinal Virtues (also the three Theological Virtues).
On the northern side stands the funeral chapel of Louis-François de Bourbon (1717-76), the penultimate descendant of the Conti dynasty, Grand Prior of France of the Order of Malta. The remains of the original monument (1777), including the prince's medallion, have been reassembled.

Pavillon chinois de Cassan (Cassan Pagoda) – *To the northeast, along Rue de Beaumont. Enter through the main gateway of the former park.*
This quaint pavilion rising out of a lake was built to adorn the landscape park of Cassan. The estate used to belong to the financier Bergeret (1715-85), an enthusiastic art lover and patron of Fragonard; the rest of the estate has been parcelled out into plots.
The pagoda, brightly decorated in red, green and saffron tones, stands on a stone base resting upon arches that house the spillway for the waters of the park (ponds and canals). The pagoda-shaped roof is supported by a peristyle of eight wooden pillars. It conceals the elaborate network of imbricated domes which act as a lantern and crown the room, decorated with painted hangings. The mast at the top of the pavilion features several tiers of rings adorned with small bronze bells.

Forêt de L'Isle-Adam (L'Isle-Adam Forest) – Up to 1783 this 1 500ha - 3 800 acre forest was carefully maintained for hunting purposes by the Princes de Conti; it is now State-owned.
Two-thirds of the forest is oak, the remaining third is made up of elms, birches, chestnuts and lime trees. The estate also features several massifs divided by main roads: the N 184 and D 64. Altitude varies from 27m to 193m - 89ft to 634ft.
The area near L'Isle-Adam is quite flat, but near Maffliers – known as Parc de la Tour under the *Ancien Régime* – the landscape is higher and hillier.

J-P Nacivet/EXPLORER

The Cassan Pagoda at L'Isle-Adam

Michelin Maps (scale 1:200 000) which are revised regularly, indicate:
- *golf courses, sports stadiums, racecourses, swimming pools, beaches, airfields,*
- *scenic routes, public footpaths, panoramas,*
- *forests, parks, interesting sights...*

*The perfect complement to the **Michelin Green Guides** for planning holidays and leisure time.*

*Keep current **Michelin Maps** in the car at all times.*

JOUARRE ★

Population 3 274
Michelin map 106 fold 24 or 56 fold 13

Jouarre stands on the upper ridge of a hillside dominating the last loop of the Petit Morin River before it flows into the Marne.

The town already featured two abbeys in the 7C. The one for men was short-lived but the one for women adopted the Benedictine rule and survived. It soon acquired a prestigious reputation and the great ladies of France, among them Madeleine d'Orléans, François I's half-sister, were flattered to receive the title of Abbess.

Badly damaged during the Hundred Years War, the abbey was rebuilt several times, particularly in the 18C. When the abbey was seized during the Revolution, it was the residence of a fervent, united religious community, close observers of monastic rules and widely praised by Jacques Bossuet. The monastery resumed its activity c1837. The **principal offices** are celebrated according to Benedictine liturgy.

ABBEY and CRYPT *1 hour*

Tour (Tower) ⊙ – Only the tower remains from the old medieval sanctuary; it once served as belltower and porch to the 12C Romanesque church. The interior has been carefully restored: three vaulted rooms, furnished by Madeleine d'Orléans in the 16C, house souvenirs of the abbey (note the armorial bosses).

★**Crypte (Crypt)** ⊙ – It lies behind the parish church, at the far end of Place St-Paul. This square presents an imposing 13C cross resting on a stone base with the Virgin and Child in the centre of a four-lobed medallion. The crypt consists of two formerly underground chapels which were linked in the 17C.

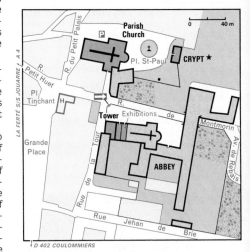

St Paul's Crypt, the mausoleum of the founding family, is considered to be one of the oldest religious monuments in France. It dates from the 7C.

The crypt is divided into three aisles by two rows of columns dating from Gallo-Roman times, made of marble, porphyry and limestone. It is believed that the 7C capitals were made of white marble from the Pyrenees. The famous Merovingian wall near the entrance presents a primitive stone mosaic with geometric motifs (oblongs, squares, diamonds etc). The most striking sarcophagus is the Tomb of St Agilbert, Bishop of Dorchester and later of Paris, the brother of Theodechilde: Christ sits enthroned, surrounded by a crowd of praying figures with upraised arms. One of the galleries affords a good view of the low-relief at the head: Christ circled by the four Evangelists' symbols (man, lion, bull, eagle). The tomb of St Osanne – an Irish princess who allegedly died in Jouarre – presents a 13C recumbent figure. The most elaborate decoration is that of the sarcophagus of Theodechilde, the first abbess of Jouarre. A display of large cockleshells adorns a Latin inscription.

St Ébrégésile's Crypt is a small Romanesque church of lesser interest, separate from the first crypt. Recent excavations have revealed the nave of the modest St-Ébrégésile Church, along with several Merovingian sarcophagi.

Above these two crypts, a large room houses the **Brie Museum** ⊙, presenting exhibits relating to regional folklore and history: costumes, tools, paintings...

ADDITIONAL SIGHT

Église Paroissiale (Parish Church) – *Enter by the south transept (see plan).* It was rebuilt after the Hundred Years War and completed in the early 16C. The north arm of the transept features a 16C Entombment (studio of Michel Colombe), 15C *Pietà* and two shrines (12C and 13C) covered in silver-gilt with enamels, cabochon and filigree work. The south side contains a 16C statue of Our Lady of Jouarre.

The Practical Information section at the end of this guide lists:

- information on travel, motoring, accommodation, recreation
- local or national organisations providing additional information;
- calendar of events
- admission times and charges for the sights described in the guide.

JOUY-EN-JOSAS

Population 7 687
Michelin map 101 fold 23 or 106 fold 30 – 6km – 3 1/2 miles southeast of Versailles –
Michelin plan 22

This town has retained a noble aspect owing to the neat, tidy houses and the substantial properties, partly preserved after being ceded to various research and academic centres. The village was once a secluded spot favoured by frequent visits from Victor Hugo. The former French President Léon Blum and the bacteriologist Professor Albert Calmette are buried in Jouy cemetery.

A textile centre – In 1760, at the age of 22, **Christophe-Philippe Oberkampf** founded his first textile workshop, specialising in a type of printed calico known as *toile de Jouy*. In 1783 the factory became the Royal Works; business thrived. Oberkampf recruited his first skilled workers in Switzerland, and they in turn trained new apprentices. He showed a great interest in scientific advancement and modern machinery, and during the Continental Blockade he obtained permission from Napoleon to despatch several envoys to Switzerland, Alsace and even England. This gifted manufacturer employed up to 1 300 workers, a remarkably high number for the time.

Musée de la toile de Jouy, Jouy-en-Josas

The commercial losses sustained during the Napoleonic Wars, the foreign invasion (in which Oberkampf perished) and the advent of competition (over 300 firms in 1815) dealt a deathblow to the Royal Works. In 1843 the company was forced to file a petition for bankruptcy.

SIGHTS

Musée de la toile de Jouy (Toile de Jouy Museum) ☉ – *54 Rue Charles de Gaulle*. This former residence of Field Marshal de Canrobert, who distinguished himself during the Crimean campaigns, was built in the late 19C. Seven rooms house displays of printed cloths, clothing fabrics and hangings (note two bedcovers), together with delightful period engravings, portrayals of the Oberkampfs' patriarchal life and Jouy in the past.

Toile de Jouy, Jouy-en-Josas

Église (Church) – *Place de la Division-Leclerc*. The 13C base of the belltower is the oldest part of the building. Inside, at the far end of the single aisle, note the **Diège★**, a restored 12C painted wooden Virgin.

Fondation Cartier (Cartier Foundation) – *3 Rue de la Manufacture*. The former estate of Baron Oberkampf houses this prestigious foundation, exclusively devoted to modern art. A 15ha - 38 acre landscape park designed by Mme Oberkampf presents an imposing collection of sculptures, among them *Long Term Parking* by Arman (1982), César's *Tribute to Gustave Eiffel*, the *Greenhouse* by J P Raynaud (1985) and Bernard Pagès' brightly-painted *Totem* (1983). The Bunker – formerly the Luftwaffe headquarters – has been converted into an exhibition hall. Lastly, the Village constitutes a creative forum for artists from all over the world.

Musée Léon-Blum (Léon Blum Museum) ☉ – *4 Rue Léon-Blum*. The estate which the former French president acquired in 1945 and on which he lived until his death in 1950 provides an interesting vignette of his life and political career.
Several of the rooms contain documents relating to his early days, his literary work (essays, reviews) and his role in both the socialist movement and French current affairs. The main room houses his writing desk and his private collection of books.

Maison de Victor Hugo (Victor Hugo's House) – *Rue Victor-Hugo*. *Private*. A plaque indicates the small house rented by the poet for his mistress Juliette Drouet in 1835. His stay here inspired the writing of *Olympio*.

EXCURSION

Bièvres – Pop 3 950. The **French Museum of Photography★** (Musée Français de la Photographie) ☉, at no 78 Rue de Paris, in the direction of Le Petit Clamart, presents a history of photography from technical and artistic viewpoints. The many interesting exhibits range from Da Vinci's studies to the very latest apparatus, relying on sophisticated technology. The crucial discoveries of Nicéphore Niepce, who took the first photograph on 5 May 1816, are explained, Daguerre and his photographic process, the advent of amateur photography in 1888 (George Eastman-registered trademark "Kodak"), the invention of the miniature cameras (Leica) in 1925...

The museum highlights the continuous, sometimes naïve quest for technical advancement, together with the craftsmanship involved: the large-format cameras are masterpieces of cabinet-making and leatherwork. The first-floor collections are devoted to the bygone industry of amateur photography: plate cameras from the golden years (1910-1945).

15 000 apparatuses, including 300 Kodak cameras, and about a million photographs are on show.

LAON ★★

Population 26 490
Michelin map 56 fold 5 or 236 fold 38.
Access map in the current Michelin Red Guide France.

Laon occupies a splendid site★★, perched (over 100m - 328ft high) like an acropolis on a rock, crowning a tall outcrop of land which overlooks the plain. The Carolingian town is a celebrated tourist destination incorporating a famous cathedral, interesting sights and houses in medieval streets, and 13C ramparts overlooking a wide horizon. Below the old, Upper Town lies the modern town.

There are two districts in the Upper Town (Ville Haute): the Cité, Laon's original heart around the cathedral; and the Bourg. An automatic cable railway, the Poma, links the old town to the railway station in the modern town at the base of the mount. The Le Nain brothers (17C), born here, evoked the life and people of Laon in their paintings.

HISTORICAL NOTES

Tertiary Age "Island" – At the northeastern edge of the Parisian Basin, following a line linking the towns of Monterau, Épernay, Rheims, Corbeny and Bruyères, there rises sharply a chalky promontory; this is known by geologists as the "Ile-de-France cliff". The rise on which Laon stands is a kind of island, set slightly apart from the other Tertiary Age formations and now strangely eroded. Once covered with grapevines, the land is today pitted with natural caves (creuttes).

Carolingian Capital – Ancient Laudunum was the capital of France for a time during the Carolingian period (9C-10C). Berthe au Grand Pied, Charlemagne's mother, was born in Samoussy (northeast of Laon) and Charles the Bald, Charles the Simple, Louis IV d'Outremer, Lothaire and Louis V all lived on "Mount Laon" in a palace near the Ardon Gate. The reign of the Carolingians finally came to an end with the arrival of Hugh Capet, who took Laon by treachery; Charlemagne's descendants were driven out and Capet established himself in Paris.

Cathedral City – St Remigius, who was born in Laon, founded the first bishopric in the 5C; under Hugh Capet the bishops became dukes and peers with the privilege of assisting the king during sacred rites at Rheims.

From the Carolingian period on, Laon became a renowned religious and intellectual centre, thanks to Jean Scot Erigène and Martin Scot in the 9C; to Anselm and Raoul of Laon in the 11C, under whose auspices the "Laon school" flourished; and to Bishop Gautier de Mortagne in the 12C, who had the cathedral built. In the 13C the town was surrounded with new ramparts and from the 16C Laon was a powerful military stronghold which was besieged on several occasions, once by Henri IV in 1594. In 1870 the munitions magazine exploded; over 500 people were injured.

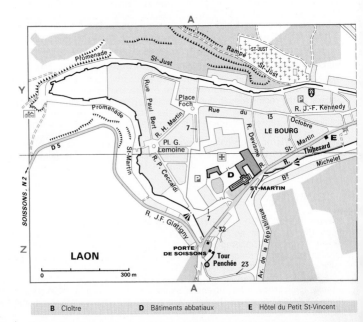

| B | Cloître | D | Bâtiments abbatiaux | E | Hôtel du Petit St-Vincent |

★★CATHEDRAL DISTRICT 2 1/2 hours

★★Cathédrale Notre-Dame (Cathedral of Our Lady)

(BY) – Laon boasts one of the oldest Gothic cathedrals in France; it was begun in the 12C and completed in about 1230. The cathedral's main feature is the traces of Romanesque architecture evident in its structure, in common with Noyon and Soissons cathedrals. These traces may be seen in the lantern tower and galleries, in the shape of some of the rounded arches and in the style of several capitals. There were originally seven towers: two on the west front, one over the transept crossing and four on the transept arms, two of which were destroyed during the Revolution.

The west front is one of the loveliest and most unusual in existence. The beautifully balanced appearance is due to the three deep porches decorated with majestic statuary (reworked in the 19C) and in particular to the famous towers (56m - 184ft tall). Their supposed creator, **Villard de Honnécourt**

Cathedral tower, Laon

(qv) said: "I have been in many lands but nowhere have I seen more beautiful towers than those of Laon." These towers, imposing yet light in appearance, are pierced by large bays and framed by slender turrets. They bear great oxen on their corners, recalling the legend of the ox which appeared miraculously to help a struggling team of yoked oxen working on repairs to the cathedral. The two towers of the transept arms are built in the same way (60m - 196ft and 75m - 246ft).

Interior – The dimensions are 110m - 360ft in length, 30m - 98ft in width and 24m - 78ft in height (Notre-Dame de Paris: 130m - 426ft, 45m - 147ft, 35m - 114ft). The **nave★★★**, roofed with sexpartite vaulting, rises to a magnificent height through four levels: great arches, galleries, a blind triforium and a tall clerestory. Beyond the nave, the wide chancel terminates in a flat east end, as in Cistercian churches. The chapter numbered 80 canons assisted by 50 chaplains.

The transept crossing offers a good view of the nave, chancel, transept arms and the lantern tower (40m – 131ft high) of Norman influence. Beautiful 13C stained-glass windows grace the apse's lancet bays and rose window, dedicated to the Glorification of the Church; the rose window in the north transept also contains 13C stained glass, evoking the Liberal Arts.

The chancel railings and the organ date from the 17C. The south transept leads to the 13C **chapter-house** (salle capitulaire); the bays look out onto a pretty cloister (BY **B**) from the same period.

Leave the cathedral by the south transept and follow the outer wall of the cloister, which is decorated with a frieze of sculpted foliage; on the corner is a Sundial Angel.

Hôtel-Dieu (BY) – In the past the bays and wide pointed arches of the 12C two-storey former hospital opened onto the street; today they are bricked up. The building has retained its great Gothic sick room with three aisles which now houses the tourist office, and the room on the ground floor called the Passers-by Room.

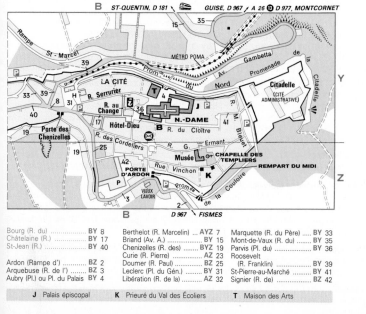

Bourg (R. du) .... BY 8	Berthelot (R. Marcelin) ... AYZ 7	Marquette (R. du Père) ..... BY 33
Châtelaine (R.) .... BY 17	Briand (Av. A.) .... BY 15	Mont-de-Vaux (R. du) .... BY 35
St-Jean (R.) .... BY 40	Chenizelles (R. des) .... BYZ 19	Parvis (Pl. du) .... BY 36
	Curie (R. Pierre) .... AZ 23	Roosevelt
Ardon (Rampe d') .... BZ 2	Doumer (R. Paul) .... BZ 25	(R. Franklin) .... BY 39
Arquebuse (R. de l') .... BZ 3	Leclerc (Pl. du Gén.) .... BY 31	St-Pierre-au-Marché .... BY 41
Aubry (Pl.) ou Pl. du Palais BY 4	Libération (R. de la) .... AZ 32	Signier (R. de) .... BZ 42

J Palais épiscopal	**K** Prieuré du Val des Écoliers	**T** Maison des Arts

Palais épiscopal (Bishop's Palace) (BY J) – The palace, today used by the law courts, is preceded by a courtyard offering a view of the east end of the cathedral. The 13C building on the left rests on a gallery of pointed arches, its capitals decorated with leaves and fruit. Upstairs, the Great Hall of the Duchy (over 30m – 98ft long) today serves as the Assize Court.

The building at the far end was built in the 17C; it contains the bishop's apartments which lead directly to the two-storey 12C chapel. The lower chapel was reserved for servants and was used for eucharistic celebrations in particular; the upper chapel (visible through the glass door), in the form of a Greek cross, served for religious ceremonies in the bishop's presence.

The **Arts Centre** (Maison des Arts) (BY T) ☉, opposite the palace, opened in 1971. It stands on the site of the third hospital founded in the 13C. The cultural centre comprises an exhibition hall, reading room, theatre, meeting rooms and a function or conference room.

In Rue Sérurier (BY) no 53 has a 15C entrance and no 33 bis incorporates the 18C door of the old town hall. The 16C-17C old Dauphin Inn, at no 7-11 Rue au Change (BY), has preserved its beautiful wooden gallery.

ADDITIONAL SIGHTS

★**Rempart du Midi et porte d'Ardon (South Ramparts and Ardon Gate)** (BZ) – The 13C Ardon Gate, or Royée (King's) Gate, stands at the end of the South Ramparts, flanked by watchtowers with pepperpot roofs; it overlooks a picturesque old public wash-house. The ramparts offer good **views**★ over St Vincent's plateau crowned by the Arsenal *(right)*, once St Vincent's Abbey, and the hills separating the Laon plain from the Ailette Valley *(ahead)*. The South Ramparts end in a **citadel** built for Henri IV by Jean Errard *(qv)*; it can be circled on foot along Promenade de la Citadelle which offers views of the plain dotted with other, small Tertiary Age hillocks.

★**Musée (Museum)** (BZ) ☉ – The archeological collection is remarkable: Greek figure vases, baked clay figurines, 3C BC Greek head of Alexander the Great. Local finds are displayed on the mezzanine: bronzes and ceramics, Merovingian and Gallo-Roman jewellery. The first-floor rooms are devoted to painting: a 15C diptych fragment by the Master of the Rohan Hours; the Le Nain brothers; 17C still-life paintings; 18C works by the Laon painter, Berthélemy.

★**Chapelle des Templiers (Knights Templar's Chapel)** (BZ) ☉ – The building recalls the Temple commandery founded here in the 12C which, after the order was suppressed, passed to the St John's Knights of Jerusalem. A peaceful flower garden has replaced the Knights Templar's cemetery but the Romanesque chapel has been preserved: it is octagonal with a gabled belltower and a small chancel with an oven-vaulted apse. The porch and the gallery were added in the 13C and 14C. The interior houses two statue-columns of prophets from the west front of the cathedral and the 14C recumbent effigy of Guillaume de Harcigny, Charles VI's doctor.

On leaving, turn right into Rue G Ermant and round into Rue Vinchon.

Rue Vinchon is lined with old houses (BZ K): no 44 was the 13C Val des Écoliers Priory (15C chapel and 18C portal) and no 40 the Val-St-Pierre Abbey refuge (15C-16C).

★**Église St-Martin (St Martin's Church)** (AZ) ☉ – This 12C-13C former Premonstratensian abbey church, restored after 1944, is a beautiful example of the early Gothic style. The square offers a good general view: note the long, Romanesque-looking nave, the height (35m – 114ft) and arrangement of the two towers over the transept, the tall south transept with its rose window and arcades.

The west front soars up, pierced by a great bay; its gable is decorated with a high-relief of St Martin *(qv)*. The tympana over the side doors depict the Decapitation of John the Baptist and the Martyrdom of St Lawrence, who was roasted alive.

Interior – The chancel and the transept chapels have flat east ends, following Cistercian custom. Recumbent figures lie near the entrance: Raoul de Coucy, a Laon knight (late 12C) and Jeanne de Flandre, his sister-in-law, abbess of Sauvoir-sous-Laon (14C). The wooden panels in the nave are in the Louis XV style and those in the chancel Louis XIII. A 16C Christ of Compassion stands to the right of St Eligius' chapel (chapelle St-Eloi), separated from the church by a Renaissance stone screen.

Abbey Buildings (AZ D) – The restored 18C section, visible from the cloister, houses the **library** (bibliothèque). A fine elliptical stone staircase leads to the first floor.

★**Porte de Soissons (Soissons Gate)** (AZ) – The gate was built in the 13C from quarried stone and reinforced with round towers. It stands in a park containing a monument to Marquette (1637-75), a Jesuit from Laon who discovered the Mississippi River. A curtain wall links the gate to the great Lady Eve's Tower, known as the **Leaning Tower** (Tour Penchée) following subsidence.

Rue Thibesard (AYZ) **et Porte des Chenizelles (Chenizelles Gate)** (BY) – Rue Thibesard follows the sentry path along the ramparts, offering good **views**★ of the cathedral: its towers rise above the old slate roofs with their red brick chimneys.

Continue into Rue des Chenizelles, an old, cobbled street, to the 13C **Chenizelles Gate:** the two towers create a narrow passageway through to Rue du Bourg.

Hôtel du Petit St-Vincent (**AY E**) – The building was constructed in the first half of the 16C as the town refuge for St Vincent's Abbey, which was outside the ramparts. The main body of the Gothic building by the road is surrounded by turrets and flanked with an entrance vault surmounted by a chapel. A later wing has an enclosed stairway framed by pilasters and surmounted by the figure of a drunk.

LEWARDE MINING HERITAGE CENTRE★★

Michelin map 53 fold 3 or 236 fold 16 (8km – 5 miles southeast of Douai)

The Lewarde Mining Heritage Centre (Centre Historique Minier de Lewarde) ⊙ is housed in the converted buildings of the Delloye Colliery which closed in 1971. The museum's design has adapted the original structure to provide exhibition rooms, a restaurant, a lecture room etc. An exhibition presents mining work in both economic and technical terms as well as social and human terms: the discovery and mining of coal over three centuries, the development of different techniques, daily life for the families... The tour, partly guided

Tour of the mine, Lewarde

by ex-miners, follows the miners' different activities up to the descent in the cage: from cloakroom, shower room – or "hanging room" (salle de pendus) because of the hooks on which the clothes, boots and helmets were hung – lamp room, infirmary... A small train leads to Pit no 2, where the descent to the seams is by lift. A 450m – over 3/4 mile long circuit incorporating an audio-visual show and reconstructions of mining scenes traces the evolution of mining work since the 1930s.

A tour of the processing building (extraction machines, coal-screening room) and the pit stables completes the visit. A vast collection of fossils is also on display, shown in the context of the formation of the mining basin 300 million years ago.

LILLE★★

Population 174 034 – Urban area 950 265
Michelin map 51 fold 16 or 236 fold 16
Map of conurbation of Lille-Roubaix-Tourcoing in the Michelin Red Guide France

Lille, the lively capital of French Flanders, today enjoys a role as a regional and European metropolis owing to its location on major north-south and east-west routes. The city's handsome appearance is due to successful efforts over several years to preserve and restore the lovely 17C and 18C buildings and monuments of the old district; at the same time, much modernisation has taken place: the rebuilding of St Saviour's district; the construction of the **Forum** (**FYZ**), a new business centre; the creation of Villeneuve-d'Ascq *(qv)*, a new town 8km - 5 miles east.

"Station Triangle" – Right at the heart of the city a new district is being developed. In September 1993 Lille Railway Station was renamed Lille-Flandres; this is where the TGV (Trains à Grande Vitesse – High-Speed Trains) from Paris arrive. Nearby, construction is under way on another station: Lille-Europe, which will receive the TGV Eurostar trains travelling between Paris and London, and London and Brussels via the Channel Tunnel. Two tall landmarks, the twenty-five storey World Trade Center and the twenty-storey Crédit Lyonnais building, tower above the business district. To the south, the elliptical Palais des Congrès is being built to host major events in the metropolis. To the north, an urban park covering 10ha - 24 acres is also scheduled.

LIFE IN LILLE

The typical Lille citizen is sensible and hardworking but also a *bon vivant* who likes his food and appreciates a beer or two in one of the city's many brasseries. Place du Général-de-Gaulle, the pedestrianised Place Rihour and nearby streets, particularly Rue de Béthune with its numerous cinemas, are always lively.

Cultural Activity – Lille is now a major cultural centre following the establishment of a philharmonic orchestra, the opening of Opéra du Nord (which brings together the lyric workshop and the ballets of the north) and the institution of several theatre companies (including La Métaphore, the national company). Several cultural festivals take place here every year; the autumn festival includes concerts, fine arts, and theatre and dance performances.

Folklore – Folklore *(qv)* still plays an active part in the city, as it does in much of northern France: every district of Lille has its own feastday *(ducasse)*.

La Grande Braderie – *First Sunday and Monday in September*. From Sunday evening (8pm) to Monday afternoon (1pm) the whole of Lille – it is a city-wide holiday – celebrates the Braderie.

Miles of pavement are taken over by professional and amateur traders and stallholders who may sell whatever they like, wherever they like. The pedestrian zone around Place Rihour is by far the busiest area.

The restaurants and cafés traditionally serve mussels and white wine, competing with each other to build the highest pile of shells on their doorsteps.

The Giants – Lille's giants, **Phinaert** and **Lydéric,** are paraded on holidays. According to legend, in about AD 600 a highwayman called Phinaert lived in a château where Lille stands today. One day the highwayman attacked the Prince of Dijon and his wife as they were on their way to England; the prince was killed but his wife was able to escape. Some time later she gave birth to a boy whom she put into hiding, before being caught herself by the highwayman. The baby was taken in by a hermit who baptised him Lydéric and had him suckled by a doe.

Once grown to manhood, Lydéric vowed to avenge the death of his parents; he challenged Phinaert to a fight and slew the highwayman. He then married the sister of King Dagobert and was entrusted with the Flemish forests which had belonged to Phinaert.

HISTORICAL NOTES

Lille has had a turbulent history having been sometimes Flemish, sometimes French, sometimes under Austrian or Spanish control. The city has faced 11 sieges and has been destroyed several times.

The Counts of Flanders – The name "I'Isle" (pronounced Lille) first appeared in 1066, in the charter of a donation to the collegiate church of St Peter by Baudoin V, Count of Flanders, who owned a château on one of the islands in the Deule River. The town developed around this château and a port which existed on the site of the present Avenue du Peuple-Belge.

In 1205 Count Baudoin IX, crowned Emperor of Constantinople during a crusade, died leaving two daughters, Jeanne and Marguerite. The young heiresses were raised by Philippe Auguste; Jeanne, the elder daughter, was married to Ferrand of Portugal and the couple was then sent to Lille.

Although a French vassal, Flanders began by being linked, at least economically, with England and the Holy Roman Empire. Owing to Philippe Auguste's claims on the northern regions, a coalition was formed which included the counts of Boulogne, Hainault and Flanders, King John of England and the Holy Roman Emperor Otto IV. The **Battle of Bouvines,** the first great French victory, concluded this war on 27 July 1214. Ferrand was imprisoned in the Louvre, while Jeanne governed Lille.

The Dukes of Burgundy and the Spanish – The marriage of Marguerite of Flanders to Philip the Bold in 1369 made Flanders part of the duchy of Burgundy. The presence of the dukes stimulated trade. Philip the Good (1419-67) had Rihour Palace built, where he made the "Pheasant Vow" in 1454 promising to leave for the crusades. His glittering court included the great painter Jean van Eyck.

The marriage of Marie of Burgundy, daughter of Charles the Bold, to Maximilian of Austria in 1477 brought the duchy of Burgundy, including Flanders, under Hapsburg control; the duchy later became Spanish when Charles V of Spain became emperor.

After the Wars of Religion, owing to Spanish domination the situation deteriorated: gangs of peasants in revolt devastated the countryside and sacked the churches. Lille escaped the assault of the "Howlers" *(Hurlus)* thanks only to the inhabitants' energetic defence, led by the inn-keeper **Jeanne Maillotte.**

Lille becomes French – Following his marriage to Maria-Theresa of Spain in 1663, Louis XIV laid claim to the Low Countries, taking advantage of the rights of his wife to a part of Spain's heritage.

In 1667 he personally directed the siege of Lille and triumphantly entered the city after only nine days of resistance, after which Lille became capital of the Northern Provinces. The Sun King hastened to have a citadel built by Vauban and enlarged the town, laying down regulations on the height and style of the houses.

Lille under Siege – In September 1792, 35 000 Austrians laid siege to Lille which was defended by only a small garrison. Cannonballs rained down on the town and many buildings were destroyed; nevertheless, the courageous inhabitants held on and the Austrians eventually raised the siege. It is said that a barber who was shaving clients in the street used the fragment of a shell as a shaving dish.

In early October 1914, when six Bavarian regiments tried to breach the fortifications, Lille was very poorly defended. The town was obliged to submit after three days of bloody resistance during which time 900 buildings were destroyed. Prince Ruprecht of Bavaria, receiving the surrender, refused the sword of Captain de Pardieu "in recognition of the heroism of the French troops".

In May 1940 during the Second World War, 40 000 French soldiers defending Lille held out for three days against seven German divisions and Rommel's tanks. The French troops finally capitulated on 1 June 1940.

ECONOMY

Owing to its location at the crossroads of major routes and waterways, Lille has always been industrially and commercially important.

Past – During the Middle Ages Lille became famous for its clothmaking; later the high-warp weavers which Louis XI had forced to leave Arras came to establish their tapestry workshops here.

Lille devoted itself to cotton and linen milling in the 18C, whereas Roubaix and Tourcoing nearby specialised in wool. Large-scale industry came to Lille at the end of the 18C, creating an urban proletariat with its accompanying miseries: by 1846 the rate of infant mortality in St Saviour's slums reached 75 % and the cellars where workers laboured achieved a notoriety which Victor Hugo evoked in tragic verse.

Another of Lille's specialities was the milling of linseed, rapeseed and poppyseed to produce oil, and the production of lace and ceramics.

Present – Lille's urban area is more than ever the economic centre of northern France. Business facilities (trade fairs, conference centres), traditional industries (textiles, mechanics), computer and technology giants, food production companies and research concerns all co-exist here, side by side with the universities.

The urban area of Lille-Roubaix-Tourcoing is the centre of mail-order selling and also of business, with the Forum business centre, the Chamber of Commerce and Industry, and the Stock Exchange. The metropolis of Lille is at the heart of a highly-developed network of motorways leading to Paris, Brussels, Dunkirk and Antwerp; further, it has the fourth-ranking river port in France and an international airport at Lesquin. Lille is also a retailing centre with shops lining the streets in the pedestrian zone. The city boasts the world's most modern metro, the **Val**, an entirely automatic system linking Lille to Villeneuve-d'Ascq and Lomme.

★★OLD LILLE *2 hours*

The real renewal of Lille's old district began in 1965, when a few architecture enthusiasts decided to do something to recover the beauty of the 17C and 18C façades, hidden under unsightly rough-rendering. The restorations progressed well and whole blocks of buildings changed completely in appearance. Luxury shops, interior decorators and antique dealers settled in the area which is today a attractive place to explore.

The distinctiveness of the **Lille style** is due to the particular mix of bricks and carved stone. Façades decorated with quarry stones shaped into lozenges (Place Louise-de-Bettignies) first appeared in the early 17C; then came the period of the Flemish Renaissance (Old Exchange, the House of Gilles de la Boé) where the wealth of ornamentation reached its limit. By the end of the 17C the French influence began to be felt in the decoration of the houses and in their arrangement in aligned rows. Ground floors consist of arcades in a close-grained sandstone which prevents humidity reaching the upper floors. The brick above alternates with limestone carved into cherubs, cupids, cornucopias, sheaves of wheat...

Leave from Rihour Palace which houses the Tourist Office.

Palais Rihour (Rihour Palace) (EY) ⊙ – This Gothic palace was built between 1454 and 1473 by Philip the Good, Duke of Burgundy. Outside, note the beautiful mullioned windows and the graceful octagonal brick turret. The guardroom, with its tall, pointed arches, still exists on the ground floor. The chapel, known as the Conclave Room, is upstairs; the chapel for the Duke's private worship, reached by an elegant stone staircase, has traceried vaults.

A monument to those who died during the two world wars flanks the northeast side of the chapel.

Place Rihour (EY) – Note the 17C houses on the left: their style is a mix of Flemish and French culture, characteristic of the architecture that developed in Lille after the victory by Louis XIV.

Walk to Place du Général-de-Gaulle.

Grand' Place (Place du Général-de-Gaulle) (EY 66) – The Grand' Place or main square has always been the busy centre of Lille; as early as the Middle Ages it was a market place. The jewel in the square is the Old Exchange. *La Voix du Nord*, a daily newspaper, has its offices in the building with a stepped pediment beside the **Grand' Garde** (T¹) (1717), which is surmounted with pediments and once housed the king's guard.

"Furet du Nord" (B), located in a copy of a 17C house opposite the Old Exchange, is the largest bookshop in France. The Column of the Goddess (1845) rises in the middle of the square, a symbol of the city's heroic resistance during the siege of 1792 *(see above)*.

Among the beautiful, restored houses at the top of Rue Esquermoise note the furrier's (the Galliaerde shop) on the left; opposite, at nos 4 and 6, little cupids on the façades kiss or turn their backs on each other, depending on whether or not they belong to the same house.

★★**Vieille Bourse (Old Exchange)** (EY) – The exchange was built in 1652-53 by Julien Destrée, at the request of the tradesmen of Lille who wanted an exchange to rival those of the great Netherlandish cities. It consists of 24 mansard-roofed houses around a rectangular court which served in the past for commercial deals; today they house second-hand bookshops.

The profusion of decoration on the façade is due to the fact that Destrée was a wood sculptor. The caryatids and telamones on two storeys, the garlands and masks above the outer windows, the fruit and flowers carved on the inner court are all reminiscent of a big Flemish cupboard. Bronze busts, and medallions and tablets honouring learned figures and the sciences, shelter under the arcades.

The Old Exchange, Lille

Place du Théâtre (EY) – The square is dominated by the imposing New Exchange (Nouvelle Bourse) and its neo-Flemish belltower. The Exchange is home to the Chamber of Commerce (**C**) and stands beside the Louis XVI Opera (**T**). These two buildings date from the beginning of the century and are the work of architect Louis Cordonnier.
Opposite the New Exchange stands **"Beauregard Row"** ("Rang de Beauregard") (**D**), comprising houses adorned with pilasters surmounted by elegant cartouches. The row, built in 1687, is the most characteristic and most interesting example of late-17C Lille architecture.

Rue de la Grande-Chaussée (EY **73**) – The old sandstone houses with their arcades have been renovated and now contain shops selling luxury goods. Some of the wrought-iron balconies and the upper part of the windows are very intricately worked. Note the first house on the right and nos 9, 23 (ship on the window's keystone) and 29.

Rue des Chats-Bossus (EY **27**) – The curious name ("Street of the Humpback Cats") derives from an old cooper's sign.
"L'Huîtrière", a famous seafood restaurant, has a typical Art Deco front dating from the 1930s.
"Nord Antiquités" (nos 23 and 25) combines several antique dealers. The façade is decorated with a beautiful frieze. Inside, a second façade is visible: 17C Lille was so crowded it was necessary to build additional houses in the gardens of those which looked out on the street.

Place du Lion-d'Or (EY) – At no 15 "Golden Lion Square", the Olivier Desforges shop occupies the 18C Maison des Poissonniers.

Place Louise-de-Bettignies (EY **16**) – The square bears the name of a First World War heroine. The **House of Gilles de la Boé★** (demeure de Gilles de la Boé) (**E**), at no 29 on a corner, was built in about 1636 and is a superb example of Flemish Baroque. The abundant ornamentation includes cornices and prominent pediments. In the past this building stood on the edge of the Basse-Deûle port, in the days when there was a great deal of river traffic.
In 1936 the Basse-Deûle, an important port until the 18C, was filled in to make way for Avenue du Peuple-Belge; the modern tower houses the law courts.

★**Rue de la Monnaie** (EY **120**) – The Mint once stood in this street where the restored houses now attract antique dealers and interior decorators. On the left there is a row of 18C houses (note the apothecary's shop sign of a mortar and distilling equipment at no 3). The houses at nos 5 and 9 are decorated with dolphins, wheat-sheaves, palms...
At no 10 a statue of Notre-Dame de la Treille adorns the front and at nos 12 and 14 the crow-stepped gable has been rebuilt. Neighbouring houses date from the first third of the 17C and flank the lozenge-decorated main door (1649) of the Hospice Comtesse.

★**Hospice Comtesse (Countess Hospital)** (EY) ⓥ – The hospital was built in 1237 by Jeanne de Constantinople, Countess of Flanders, to ask for divine intervention on behalf of her husband Ferrand de Portugal, taken prisoner at Bouvines *(see above)*. It was destroyed by fire in 1468 but was rebuilt and enlarged in the 17C and 18C. It became a hospice during the Revolution, then an orphanage. It changed use in 1939 and is today a museum of history and ethnography which also holds concerts and exhibitions.
The monumental 17C main entrance is built from beautiful sandstone worked into lozenges.

Sick Room (Salle des malades). – A long, sober building, rebuilt after 1470 on the old 13C foundations, flanks the main courtyard. Inside, the immense proportions of the interior and its panelled timber **vault★★** are striking. It contains two beautiful tapestries, woven in Lille in 1704. One represents Baudouin of Flanders with his wife and two daughters; the other portrays Jeanne, the founder of Flanders, flanked by her first and second husbands. The chapel, which extends the length of the interior, was enlarged and isolated by a rood screen after the fire of 1649. The old 15C window and traces of mural paintings have been revealed on the right wall. The vault is decorated with the heraldic arms of the hospital's benefactors.

Museum – Furniture and artworks evoking the atmosphere of a 17C religious establishment are displayed in the right wing, which was built by the community in the late 15C and heightened in the 17C: the kitchen features blue and white tiles from Holland and Lille; the Baroque overmantel in the refectory frames a 16C Nativity, the sombre Louis XIV panels of the parlour are decorated with a series of 17C votive offerings. The prayer room is lined with Louis XV wood panelling. One room contains interesting paintings by Louis and François Watteau portraying 18C Lille, and a beautiful 16C Christ from Picardy where the arms and shaft of the cross bear medallions of the Evangelists. The old dormitory *(first floor)* with its ceiling of carved beams is the setting for temporary exhibitions.

★★MUSÉE DES BEAUX-ARTS (FINE ARTS MUSEUM) (EZ) ⊙

Among the sculptures, two works in particular are of special note: the famous 17C **Head of a Young Girl**, attributed to F Duquesnoy, in wax on a terracotta base; and Herod's Feast, a marble by Donatello. Other fine pieces in the *objets d'art* section include the 12C engraved bronze **Lille Incense-Burner** from the Meuse region; seals dating from the 12C to the 16C; Gothic statues in wood; beautiful 18C **Lille glazed earthenware**; Delft ceramics; pottery, stoneware and European porcelain.

Primitives Gallery – Exhibits include J Bellegambe's *Mystic Fountain* triptych, two leaves of a triptych by **Thierry Bouts** (Heaven and Hell) and a delicately embroidered silk altar frontal from 1420, representing the Annunciation.

17C Flemish School – Several characteristic canvases by Jordaens are displayed, ranging in themes from the religious *(The Temptation of Mary Magdalene)* to the mythological *(The Abduction of Europa)* to the rustic *(The Huntsman)*; his study of cows was later taken up by Van Gogh. There are important paintings by Rubens and from his workshop: *The Descent from the Cross* (1617), a variation of that in Antwerp, and the original sketch; *The Ecstacy of Mary Magdalene; The Martyrdom of St Catherine; St Francis and the Virgin; St Bonaventure*. Other paintings include Van Dyck's moving *Christ on the Cross*, David Teniers II's beautifully-coloured *Temptation of St Anthony* and lively scenes by Snyders, the animal painter.

17C Dutch School – Dutch masterpieces by Van Honthorst *(Portrait of a Woman)*, de Witte *(Nieuwe Kerk in Delft)* and Ruysdael *(The Wheat Field)* hang with still-life paintings by Van der Ast and Van Duynen, Van Goyen's *The Skaters* and Pieter Codde's *Melancholy*.

17C French School – Works by Lille artists Wallerand Vaillant *(The Young Draughtsman)* and Monnoyer, Le Sueur, Philippe de Champaigne, La Hyre and Largillière *(Jean-Baptiste Forest)*.

18C and 19C French School – Remarkable works by Boilly (1761-1845), born at La Bassée near Lille, adorn the walls: *Le Jeu du Pied de Bœuf, Marat's Triumph* and numerous portraits, including Jules Boilly as a child and sketches of heads for Isabey's studio. Note Quentin de La Tour's portrait of Madame Pèlerin, the charming paintings by Louis Watteau, who adopted Lille as his permanent home *(Lille Shaving Dish, View of Lille)* and the work by his son François *(Alexander's Battle)*. Other great painters represented include David *(Belisarius Begging for Alms)*, Delacroix, Géricault, Corot and Courbet.

Italian and Spanish Schools – Italy is represented by Mainardi's *Young Virgin with Wild Roses, The Martyrdom of St George*, Liss' *Moses Saved from the Waters* and a sketch of Heaven by Veronese. The few Spanish paintings are of a rare quality: *Time or The Old Women* and *The Letter or The Young People* by **Goya**, kind and cruel satirist of his period; and El Greco's *St Francis Praying*.

Impressionists – The end of the 19C is represented by works from the Masson Bequest. The pre-Impressionist paintings include canvases by Boudin *(The Port of Camaret)*, Jongkind *(The Skaters)* and Lépine. Impressionism itself is embraced in works by Sisley *(Port Marly, Winter: Snow Effects)*, Renoir *(Young Woman in a Black Hat)* and Monet *(The Disaster, The Houses of Parliament)*. Paintings by Vuillard, Carrière, Lebourg and several Rodin sculptures complete the collection.

Contemporary Artists – Figurative and abstract works on show are by Dufy *(Figures from the Comédie Française)*, Marie Laurencin *(Heads of Young Girls)*, Léger *(Women With a Blue Vase)*, Gromaire *(Landscape of the Coalmining Region)*, Poliakoff *(Composition)* and Da Silva (the blue-toned *Frozen Canal Lock*). Picasso's tapestry, *Jacqueline*, dates from 1964.

OTHER SIGHTS

★**Église St-Maurice (St Maurice's Church) (EY)** – This vast Gothic edifice was built from the 15C to the 19C. It is a beautiful example of a hall-church, with five aisles of equal height, five roofs and five gables. A 16C Christ of Compassion, often dressed in a long velvet mantle, stands in the chapel of the false left transept; it is venerated as "Jesus Scourged".

South of the church stand two restored houses: the Croix de St-Maurice bakery (1729) and the Fox House (1660); opposite *(at no 74 Rue de Paris)* is the House of the Three Graces.

Béthune (R. de) .... EYZ
Esquermoise (R.) .... EY
Faidherbe (R.) .... EY
Gambetta (R. Léon) ..... EZ
Gaulle (Pl. Gén.-de–)
(Grand Place) .... EY 66
Grande-Chaussée
(R. de la) .... EY 73
Monnaie (R. de la) .... EY 120
Nationale (R.) .... EYZ
Neuve (R.) .... EY 124

Anatole-France (R.) ...... EY 3
Arsenal (Pl. de l') .... EY 6
Barre (R. de la) .... EY 9
Bettignies (Pl. L. de) .... EY 16
Bigo-Daniel (Bd) .... DZ 18
Canonniers (R. des) ..... FY 19
Chats-Bossus (R. des) . EY 27
Comédie (R. de la) .... EY 34
Debierre (R. Ch.) .... FZ 43
Delesalle (R. E.) .... EZ 45
Déportés (R. des) .... FY 46
Dr-Calmette (Bd) .... FY 51
Faubourg-de-Roubaix
(R. du) .... FY 55
Fosses (R. des) .... EYZ 61
Hôpital-Militaire
(R. de l') .... EY 78
Jacquart (Pl.) .... EZ 79
Jacquemars Giélée (R.) EZ 81
Jardins (R. des) .... EY 82
Jeanne-d'Arc (Pl.) .... EZ 84
Lebas (Bd J.-B.) .... FZ 93
Lefèvre (R. G.) .... FZ 100
Loyer (R. H.) .... DZ 103
Maillote (R.) .... EZ 105
Manuel (R.) .... DZ 106
Mendès-France (Pl.) ..... EY 115
Pasteur (Bd. L.) .... DZ 123
Philippe-le-Bon (Pl.) ...... EZ 126
Plat (R.) .... EZ 127
Réduit (R. du) .... FZ 132
Roisin (R. Jean) .... EY 135
Roubaix (R. de) .... EFY 138
St-Génois (R.) .... EY 139
St-Venant (Av. Ch.) ..... FYZ 141
Ste-Catherine (R.) .... DY 142
Sec-Arembault (R. du) . EY 144
Tanneurs (R. des) ...... EYZ 147
Tenremonde (R.) .... EY 148
Théâtre (Pl. du) .... EY 150
Voltaire (R.) .... EY 162

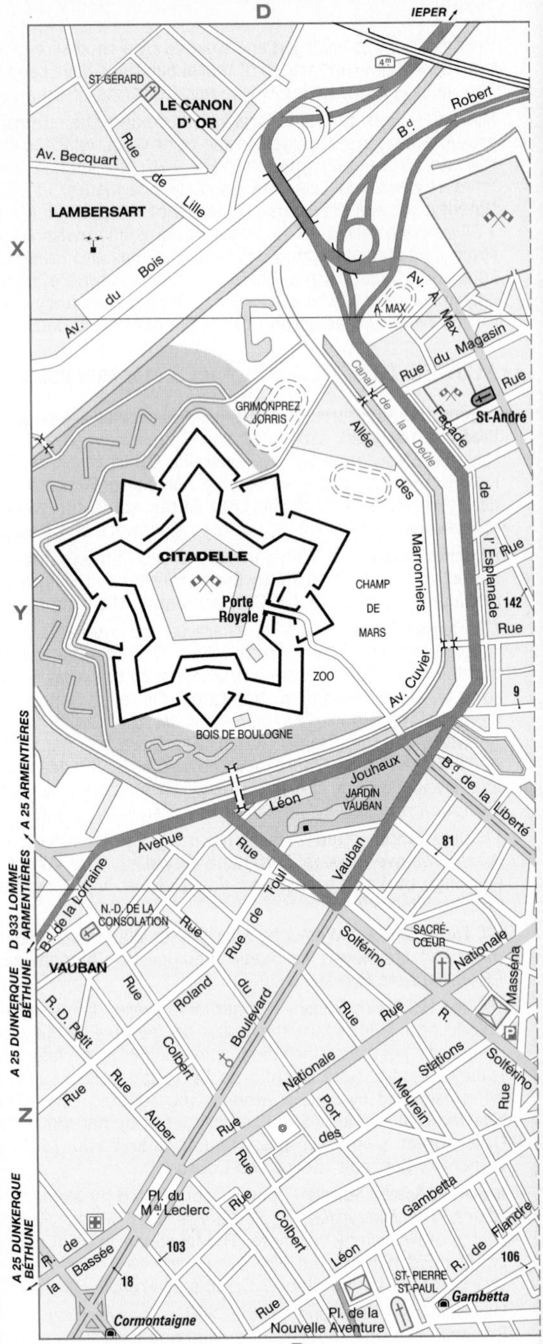

B « Furet du Nord »
C Chambre de commerce
D « Rang de Beauregard »
E Demeure de Gilles de la Boé
F « L'Huîtrière »
H Hôtel de Ville
K Monument aux Fusillés
L Hospice Ganthois
M Musée d'Histoire naturelle
N Pavillon St-Sauveur
Q Noble Tour
R Chapelle du Réduit
S Hôtel Bidé-de-Granville
T[1] Grand'Garde
V Ancien Hôtel de l'Intendance
W Maison natale du Général de Gaulle

★**Citadelle (Citadel)** (DY) ⓥ – This citadel is the largest and best preserved in France. It was Louis XIV's first project after the conquest of Lille and is a fine example of Vauban's genius; it is still occupied by the army today.

It took three years to build (1667-70) using 2 000 men who first undertook an enormous levelling project then handled 60 million bricks (manufactured in four brickworks created for the purpose) and 3 1/2 million blocks of stone. The result was this stone-faced brick construction comprising five bastions and five demilune fortifications *(see Military Architecture)*, which protect the moats formerly fed by the Deûle River. These defences enclosed an entire town.

The **Royal Gate** (porte Royale), which bears a Latin inscription praising Louis XIV, gives onto a vast pentagonal parade ground surrounded by buildings by Simon Vollant: the Classical chapel, the officer's quarters and a superb restored arsenal. These stone and brick buildings are representative of the Franco-Lille style which developed during this period.

The citadel could be completely self-sufficient as it has its own wells, bakery, brewery, tailors, cobblers...

During the last two world wars many French patriots were executed by firing squad in the outer moats.

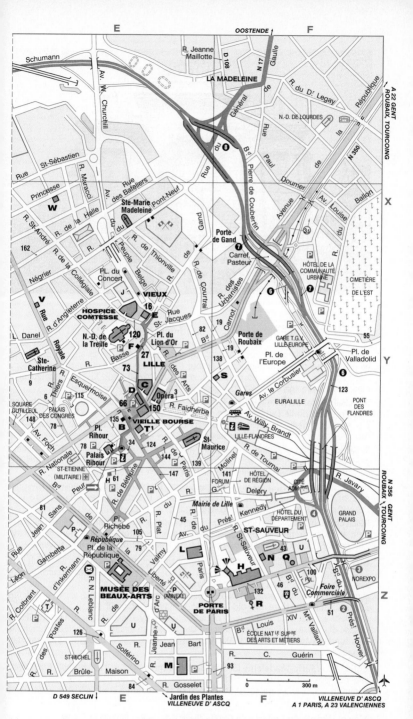

A zoo has been established in the Bois de Boulogne, near the Champ de Mars; there is also a tropical house and a playground. The Vauban garden on the Deûle Canal bank is typical of Second Empire country gardens, with its clumps of trees, sinuous paths, beds of flowers and ponds. A statue of the Lille poet Albert Samain (1859-1906) stands within it.

A **Monument to the Dead** (Monument aux Fusillés) (**DY K**) by Félix Desruelle stands in neighbouring Square Daubenton; it dates from 1915 and commemorates the Lille citizens executed by firing squad.

Quartier St-Sauveur (St Saviour's District) (**FZ**) – This former working-class district was known for the misery of its slums which inspired Emile Desrousseaux, author of the famous French lullaby *Le P'tit Quinquin*. The area has today been completely remodelled into a business centre around the town hall. Relics of the past remain dotted among the modern buildings.

Ganthois Hospital (Hospice Ganthois) (**L**) – The hospice was founded in 1462 by Jean de la Cambe, known as Ganthois, and is still in use. The original sickroom has been preserved; its gable, on Rue de Paris, is flanked on either side by 17C buildings. Note the sculpture on the door panels, dated 1664.

The Paris Gate, Lille

★**Paris Gate** (Porte de Paris) – This gate, built from 1685 to 1692 by Simon Vollant in honour of Louis XIV, is the only example of a town gate which also served as a triumphal arch; it was formerly part of the ramparts. It appears as an arch decorated with the arms of Lille (a lily) and of France (three lilies) on the outward side. Victory stands at the top, honoured by Fames, about to crown Louis XIV represented in a medallion. From the inner side the gate has the appearance of a lodge.

Town Hall (Hôtel de Ville) (**H**) ☺ – The town hall was built from 1924 to 1927 by the Lille architect Emile Dubuisson and is overlooked by a tall belfry (104m – 341ft). The two Lille giants, Lydéric and Phinaert *(see above)*, are sculpted at its base. The top of the belfry offers a lovely **view**★ over the region.

St Saviour's Pavilion (Pavillon St-Sauveur) (**N**) – This is the wing of an 18C cloister, preserved when a hospice was demolished in 1959. The brick and stone arches are surmounted by clerestory windows decorated with flowered medallions.

Noble Tower (Noble Tour) (**Q**) – This keep with its "cut-off" appearance is the only relic of the 15C fortifications; it has become a Resistance memorial. There is a beautiful work by the sculptor Bizette-Lindet.

Réduit Chapel (Chapelle du Réduit) (**R**) – This chapel is all that remains of Réduit Fort, built at the same time as the citadel to serve as its counterpart elsewhere in the city. The pretty Louis XIV front is decorated with the arms of France and Navarre.

Rue Royale (**DEY**) – This was the main route through the elegant district which was built during the 18C between the citadel and the old town. **St Catherine's Church** (Église Ste-Catherine), with its austere 15C tower, stands on the left at the beginning of the street. The handsome private houses bordering Rue Royale show a definite French influence. Note the old *Intendance* building at **no 68** (**V**), built by the Lille architect Lequeux in 1787; it is occupied today by the bishop. **St Andrew's Church** (Église St-André), a Carmelite chapel in the 18C, is an example of the Jesuit style. It was topped with a tower in 1890. Charles de Gaulle was baptised here on the day he was born.

Église Ste-Marie-Madeleine (St Mary Magdalene Church) (**EY**) – The church's main body and its high dome (50m - 164ft) recall Les Invalides in Paris. The building was begun in 1675 and completed at the end of the regin of Louis XIV; the west front was reworked in 1884.

Maison Natale du Général de Gaulle (General de Gaulle's Birthplace) (**EY W**) ☺ – *9 Rue Princesse.* Charles de Gaulle was born on 22 November 1890 in this lime-washed brick house in Lille, where his grandfather had a lace works. The old workshop and the house have been turned into a small museum exhibiting photographs and memorabilia. On display are de Gaulle's christening robe and the car in which the General and his wife were riding on the day of the attempt on their lives in Petit-Clamart.

Portes de Gand et de Roubaix (Gand and Roubaix Gates) (**FY**) – These massive gates from the 1621 Spanish fortifications are composed of a sandstone base surmounted by a dripstone and a layer in brick. They were pierced in 1875 to create a tramway passage and their moats have been turned into gardens.

Hôtel Bidé-de-Granville (**FY S**) – The industrialist A D Scrive Labbe established the first carding machine here in 1821. The building was constructed in 1773 and today houses the offices of the Regional Administration of Cultural Affairs.

Musée d'Histoire naturelle (Natural History Museum) (**EZ M**) ☺ – Numerous mammals, local and exotic birds, reptiles and insects are exhibited in the zoological part. The geological section consists of minerals, rock formations and fossils which together explain the formation of the region's soil and the coal basin in particular.

Jardin des Plantes (Botanical Garden) ⊙ – *From Boulevard J-B-Lebas* (**EZ**) *take Rue de Douai, Rue Armand-Carrel and turn right after Boulevard des Défenseurs-de-Lille.*
Among the 12ha - 27 acres of lawns, trees and rare flowers stands a modern concrete and glass conservatory sheltering tropical and equatorial flora.

EXCURSIONS

★Vert-Bois Château ⊙ – *11km - 7miles north. Leave by* ① *on N 17; at Bondues turn right into D 952, then right again to the château.*
This charming 18C residence, surrounded by water-filled moats, contains beautifull collections of ceramics (Persian and Hispano-Moorish plates, 18C Delft), Impressionist and contemporary paintings (Renoir, Bonnard, Picasso, Dufy, Gromaire, Rouault, Chagall) and a stunning collection of rare minerals collected by Anne and Albert Prouvost during their travels.

Septentrion Foundation (Fondation Septentrion – Anne et Albert Prouvost) ⊙ – An old farm on the Vert-Bois estate holds temporary exhibitions of paintings, ceramics and civilizations.
Septentrion also consists of a gallery of contemporary art, a restaurant, a second-hand goods shop, a craft village, shops selling minerals, embroidered goods, masks, wooden toys...

LONGPONT ★

Population 298
Michelin map 56 southwest of fold 4 or 237 fold 8

The village lies on the edge of Retz Forest and is overlooked by the ruins of the church and the buildings of the Cistercian abbey founded by St Bernard in the 12C. A picturesque 14C fortified gate, with four conical turrets, remains from the original fortifications.

★Abbey ⊙ – The important ensemble formed by the ruined abbey church and the buildings, restored in the 18C, is complemented by internal gardens opening onto a park. The abbey's former size is evoked in a model showing the 14C buildings.

Abbey Church Ruins – The pure Gothic church was consecrated in 1227 in the presence of the young Louis IX and Blanche of Castille. The abbey's possessions, deemed to be national property, were sold during the Revolution. The new owners of the church demolished it little by little, selling its stones until 1831 when it was bought by the Montesquiou family, which still owns it today.
The west front remains but the tracery of the rose window has disappeared. The ruined walls and pillars standing among the vegetation inside give a clear idea of the church's size: 105m - 115yds long and 28m - 92ft high (Notre-Dame de Paris: 130m - 142yds by 35m - 115ft high).

Abbey Buildings – The great cloister's south gallery (remodelled in the 17C) still exists and leads to the unique 13C **calefactory** (chauffoir des moines), preserved intact with its central hooded fireplace. The west building was transformed in the 18C by the commendatory abbots, who had tall windows with large wrought-iron balconies set into the façades, providing a Classical elegance. Inside, the vast entrance hall features a staircase with a beautiful 18C wrought-iron balustrade; the 13C monks' cellars with Gothic vaults have been transformed into reception rooms.

Parish Church (Église paroissiale) – *Entrance from the square.* This church takes up four arches of the old cellar. Two 13C reliquaries have been preserved: Jean de Montmirail, councillor to Philippe Auguste, and the head of St Dionysius the Areopagite.

MAINTENON ★

Population 4 161
Michelin map 106 fold 26 or 60 fold 8

This charming town on the banks of the Eure River is renowned for its château, irrevocably linked to the incredible destiny of **Françoise d'Aubigné**: she was born in 1635 to a family with Calvinist views, was orphaned at the age of 12, became the widow of the burlesque poet Paul Scarron at the age of 25, the clandestine governess of Mme de Montespan's children by the age of 34 and, in a secret ceremony, the wife of Louis XIV at the age of 48.

The corridors of power – When her clandestine charge, the duc de Maine, was legitimised, Françoise Scarron made a public appearance at court. Louis XIV, who was extremely fond of his son, used to see her every day. Initially, he found her a trifle pedantic but soon revised his opinion of "the Scarron widow" and succumbed to her charm, intelligence and strong temperament. In 1674 Françoise Scarron bought the Maintenon estate for 250 000 livres, paid by the King, who then publicly christened her "Madame de Maintenon".

MAINTENON

After the Queen's death, Louis XIV secretly married Mme de Maintenon in the chapel at Versailles during the winter of 1683-84. The morganatic queen acceded to the rank of peer and marquise in 1688 – a privilege bestowed on her directly by the King – and from then on she became an extremely powerful figure in the country's political life. When the King died in 1715, she withdrew to St-Cyr, where she died in 1719.

A Herculean task – Between 1685 and 1688, the area around Maintenon saw one of the century's most ambitious projects: the diverting of the waters of the Eure River to the fountains of Versailles. François Louvois acted as supervisor: he left Sébastien Vauban *(qv)* in charge of the plans and entrusted him with the construction of an 80km – 50 mile long aqueduct linking Pontgouin *(Michelin map 60 fold 6)* to Tower Pond (L'Étang de la Tour), which was already linked with the Versailles reservoirs by rivulets from the Trappes plateau.

The Maintenon aqueduct was a colossal enterprise, involving a total length of 4 600m - 15 000ft and three superimposed rows of arches, placed 72m - 237ft above the level of the Eure River. In fact, it was only possible to fit in one row of arches. The link with the canals on the plateaux was to be implemented by pressurised pipes acting as a battery of pumps.

The operation was carried out like a military campaign: 20 000 soldiers took part in the excavation work, in addition to the 10 000 skilled workers summoned from remote villages and the local peasants who helped cart the materials. The Voise and Drouette rivers were canalised and used to convey the freestones and sandstone rubble from Gallardon and Épernon quarries. The shipments of Newcastle coal needed to work the lime and brick kilns, and the pipes and iron bars despatched from Champagne, Belgium and Pays d'Ouche were carried along the Seine and Eure rivers.

In 1689, the wars triggered off by the Augsburg League interrupted the work. The French troops, in poor physical condition, were sent off to the borders to defend their country. The work was never resumed.

From then on, Mme de Maintenon ceased her visits to the château: she was offered the impressive but unfinished aqueduct to compensate for the damage to her estate.

SIGHTS

★**Château** ⊙ – The present château occupies the site of a former stronghold circled by the waters of the Eure. The construction work was undertaken by Jean Cottereau, Minister of Finance to Louis XII, François I and Henri II, and completed around 1509. The building is Renaissance.

The estate then came into the hands of the d'Angennes family. In 1674 Louis XIV bought the château from Françoise d'Angennes and offered it to the future Marquise de Maintenon. The Marquise left it to her niece, who was married to the Duke of Ayen, son of the first Maréchal de Noailles. The château has remained in this family ever since.

Exterior – Decorative details such as elaborate dormer windows, stonework tracery and lace-like roof cresting give the entrance front its Renaissance character.

The archway, flanked by two protruding turrets and bearing Jean Cottereau's arms (three lizards), leads to the inner court which is the starting-point for tours. The square 12C keep, now crowned with an elegant roof, is all that remains of the original stronghold. The adjoining wing was built by Mme de Maintenon and the narrow door set in the tower still sports the Marquise's emblem, a griffin's head.

Maintenon Château

Interior – A door depicting St Michael and bearing the lizard emblem gives onto a staircase leading to Mme de Maintenon's suite. It consists of an antechamber, a bedroom – where Charles X spent the night on 3 August 1830 when he fled Rambouillet – and a small cabinet.

After leaving the main block, visitors are shown round the first floor of the Renaissance pavilion, redesigned to accommodate the apartments of Mme de Montespan and her royal charges.

The tour ends with the reception rooms furnished by the Noailles family in the 19C. The Grand Salon bears portraits of the two royal rivals, Mme de Montespan and Mme de Maintenon. In the Portrait Gallery, a collection of paintings represents the illustrious members of the family. The mortal remains of the Marquise rest in the chapel of St-Cyr Military Academy. A memorial was erected in her honour in 1980.

Parterre – The parterre is flanked by charming canals fed by the waters of the Eure. The bench at the far end offers an extensive view of the Grand Canal and three of the arches of Maintenon aqueduct. Turn round and enjoy the superb **vista**★ of the château with its elegant towers and grey and pink stone and brickwork.

★ **Aqueduct** – The fifty-odd arches that remain, many of which are crumbling and overgrown with plants and weeds, stretch from Maintenon station – Hôtel de l'Aqueduc marks the start of the bridge – to the D 6, leading to St-Piat. On the way to Gallardon, the road runs under a curious arch of four ribs of archstones hanging suspended in mid-air.

EXCURSION

St-Piat; L'Arche de la Vallée – *12km - 7 1/2 miles southwest, then 1 hour Rtn on foot. Leave Maintenon by D 6 south towards Chartres.*

St-Piat – Pop 836. The village has developed around its 16C church and one of the big mills of the area (now disused).

After leaving St-Piat, turn right; cross Chartainvilliers and D 906.

The road to Théléville and Berchères-la-Maingot passes a wooded mound on the right which marks the scene of a major excavating operation aimed at diverting the waters of the Eure. The project, called Les Terrasses, was to raise the canal to the upper level of the aqueduct; it was doomed. After leaving Théléville, the road to Berchères descends into a wooded area. At the foot of the incline, park the car at a large crossroads.

L'Arche de la Vallée – *1 hour Rtn on foot.* In the dip of the valley, bear right of the bridge and take the cart track which follows the gully of the stream to reach the artificial embankment dividing the valley.

This depression was one of the greatest obstacles lying in the way of the canal (save the interruption of the river at Maintenon). A stonework aqueduct had initially been planned but, desirous of cutting costs, Vauban installed a closed gallery supported by a ramp, working on the principle of a pump.

Proceed along the foot of the embankment, to the left. This leads to l'Arche de la Vallée, a tunnel supported by intricate brick vaulting, remarkably well-designed for such a small watercourse. *Avoid crossing the river as the ground tends to be muddy.* Go back and turn left into a wide path trodden by horses' hooves leading onto the embankment and to the west funnel: a gallery running to the bottom of the well which was designed to receive the waters from the canal *(bring a torch).* The passageway used to extend along the upper ridge of the embankment – then much higher – and join up with an east funnel *(private property).*

MAISONS-LAFFITTE CHÂTEAU ★

Michelin map 101 fold 13 or 106 fold 18 – Michelin plan 18

The Longueil Supremacy – The château was built between 1642 and 1651 for René de Longueil, President of the Parlement de Paris, appointed Governor of the royal châteaux at Versailles and St-Germain.

The plans were drawn up by the architect **François Mansart**, a difficult man known to be extremely conscientious: he would not hesitate to knock down one of his own pavilions and rebuild it if he considered it inadequate. The château was designed to receive royalty as it was one of the official places of residence assigned to French rulers. The palace was inaugurated during a brilliant reception celebrated in honour of Anne of Austria and Louis XIV, then aged 13. The Sun King subsequently took up residence at St-Germain and paid frequent visits to Maisons, as did his successors.

From D'Artois to Lannes – The Comte d'Artois, brother of Louis XVI, acquired the estate in 1777 and gave orders to build the famous racecourse. His extravagant parties were attended by everyone at court. In July 1789 he went into exile, accompanied by a staff of 200, and had to wait 25 years before returning to France. He was crowned King of France in 1824, under the name Charles X, but was exiled a second time in 1830 and died in 1836 at the age of 79. The estate was sequestered during the Revolution and sold to Marshal Jean Lannes, Duke of Montebello, in 1804. Napoleon I, who enjoyed the Marshal's company, was a regular visitor to the château.

Maisons-Laffitte – In 1818 the famous banker **Jacques Laffitte** (1767-1844) bought the estate, where he entertained the adversaries of the Restoration: General Foy, the Marquis de Lafayette, Casimir Périer, Benjamin Constant etc. Laffitte did much to secure Louis-Philippe d'Orléans' accession to the throne during the revolution of July 1830 which overthrew Charles X.

This shrewd financier was made Prime Minister to the new king in 1830 but proved unable to calm the disturbances that had broken out in the capital: mistrusted by both the Orleanists and the moderates, Laffitte was forced to resign in March 1831.

Ruined, in debt to the tune of 50 million francs, he sold and dismantled the imposing stables and with these funds had the Grand Park parcelled out to accommodate two oblong pavilions.

Mansart erected these two beautiful wings along Avenue du Château – presently renamed Avenue du Général-Leclerc – where they formed a very grand entrance to the Longueils' residence.

The château frequently changed hands and was bought by the State in 1905.

TOUR ⊙ *1 hour*

The château dates from the early part of Louis XIV's reign and has always been considered a model of French architecture.

From the main driveway, formerly called the king's entrance – royal visitors generally approached from St-Germain Forest, ie from the west – there is a splendid view of the high-pitched roofs.

The façade facing the Seine is fronted by a wide moat, a terrace and the main staircase. The stone exterior presents classical ornamentation: Doric on the ground floor, Ionic on the first floor and Corinthian on the attic storey level with the dormer windows. The alternating fluted columns and engaged pilasters form a pleasing, well-balanced composition *(illustration under Civil Architecture)*.

Interior – *Enter through the pavilion on the right.* Although the comte d'Artois made a number of alterations in the 18C, there are no obvious discrepancies between Mansart's austere work, executed around 1650, and the sober stamp of neo-Classicism.

Comte d'Artois' Apartments – The corner dining room provides a good example of the neo-Classical carved decoration commissioned by the comte. He hired two experts on Antiquity, Bélanger and Lhuillier, who produced a splendid coffered ceiling, an overdoor representing a group of Fames, a fireplace decorated with bacchantes.

Principal Vestibule – Lying in the centre of the château, it constitutes a perfect entrance articulated by eight Doric columns. It was originally enclosed by two imposing wrought-iron gates. They were installed in 1650 and later moved to the Apollo Gallery in the Louvre. A group of mythological figures by Jacques Sarrazin incarnate the four Elements: Jupiter (fire), Juno (air), Neptune (water) and Cybele (earth).

The eagles are not those associated with the emperor: their "long eye" *(long œil)* is merely a pun on the first proprietor's name.

Grand Staircase – The staircase, one of Mansart's major accomplishments at Maisons, is characteristic of the period: square plan with straight flights of stairs. Groups of cherubs executed by Philippe Buyster symbolise Music and Singing, Science and Art, War and Peace, Love and Marriage.

Royal Suite – 1st floor. A suite of rooms built in the Italian style, featuring domed or barrel-vaulted ceilings with no painted decoration. Walk down the Grand Gallery and enter Hercules' Salon (formerly the king's antechamber), which leads through to the **King's Bedroom.** Admire the domed ceiling, the original parquet floor and the handsome bed.

Chamber of Mirrors – The parquet floor and panelling are master-pieces of marquetry inlaid with wood, bone and tin.

Maréchal Lannes' Bedroom – The passage leading to the bedroom houses a collection of figurines portraying various corps of the Grand Army.

The queen's former bedchamber was redesigned to receive Marshal Jean Lannes. The furniture, chandelier and decoration are all Empire. In the centre stands a magnificent Restoration table inlaid with elm wood. The paintings include a scene which shows Napoleon's ashes being carried past Sartrouville Bridge in 1804. A display of miniature figures re-enacts in minute detail the Battle of Wagram and Napoleon's farewell at Fontainebleau *(qv)*.

RACECOURSE AND PARK

The racecourse at Maisons-Laffitte, located on the banks of the River Seine, is well known to Paris racegoers.

The training stables and the tracks, second only to Chantilly *(qv)* in importance, lie to the north of the park, on the edge of St-Germain Forest.

A walk in the park early in the morning (0700) will reveal the morning training of the various "charges": mounted by stable hands, they will be walking or trotting along the sandy lanes. The most prestigious route, however, for exercising thoroughbreds is a circular ride known as the Cercle de la Gloire (Circle of Glory). The wider tracks used for galloping are not open to the public.

Agglomeration 189 103
Michelin map 106 fold 15 or 55 fold 18
Town plan in the current Michelin Red Guide France

This extremely active town has grown considerably with the industrial development of its suburbs.

Henri IV's Conversion – Henri IV, who had delivered Mantes from the Catholic League *(qv)* in 1590, returned to the town on account of the ravishing Gabrielle d'Estrées. During one of his stays in May 1593 he decided to renounce Protestantism a second time (he had already done so once to escape the Massacre of St Bartholomew). In view of the ceremony, a number of meetings took place between the king, supported by the Protestants Duplessis-Mornay and Sully, and Cardinal Duperron, the Abbot of St-Denis, as well as various other leading ecclesiastic figures. It was during one of these encounters that Henri IV is believed to have pronounced the famous adage "Surely Paris is worth a Mass". The abjuration ceremony took place in the Basilica of St-Denis *(qv)* on 25 July 1593.

★★COLLÉGIALE NOTRE-DAME
(COLLEGIATE CHURCH OF OUR LADY) *1/2 hour*

This church – which inspired Corot to paint one of his most beautiful works (now in the Musée des Beaux-Arts, Reims) – would compare favourably with many of France's cathedrals. It was built by the chapter of a collegiate church which owned a fair amount of land in the area. The funds for this ambitious project were provided by the municipality, William the Conqueror and several Capetian kings.
The construction of the church, started in 1170, ran into the 13C in the case of the nave and the chancel. The chapels were added in the 14C. The church stood within the precincts of the fortified bailey that defended the old royal castle (behind the east end, on the site now occupied by the public gardens).

Exterior – The west front is the oldest part of the church. The tower on the left and the narrow gallery linking it to the right tower were renewed in the 19C.
Three badly-damaged doorways adorn the exterior. The one in the centre is dedicated to the Virgin and was executed between 1170 and 1195. Like the north doorway on the left, it features foliated scrolls on the piers and bases of the colonnettes.
A walk round the right side leads to the protruding 14C Navarre Chapel. Note the unusual east end, with its gabled apses crowned by a gallery and built onto a high wall circling the ambulatory. This open-work structure admitting large, round bays is surmounted by hefty buttresses. Above the fortified wall, the upper part of the chancel is supported by a series of sturdy flying buttresses.

Interior – The light, elegant nave (33m - 108ft tall) is almost as high as that of Notre-Dame in Paris (35m - 114ft). Its elevation of wide arches, brightly-lit galleries and clerestory windows marks the transition from Romanesque to early Gothic. The splendid rose window (early 13C) in the west front features the original stained glass. Walking down the nave, note the arrangement of the sexpartite vaulting. The heavier supporting arches at each end rest on thick pillars, while the lighter ones end in round columns.
The deep, well-lit galleries above the aisles – a feature of Romanesque architecture – open onto the nave by a series of bays with triple arcades. Observe the old-fashioned structure of the galleries in the apse and the north part of the chancel, surmounted by barrel vaulting.

The **Navarre Chapel** (Chapel of the Blessed Sacrament), built onto the right side of the chancel, forms a separate ensemble. It resembles a sort of shrine featuring early-14C windows with Radiant Gothic roundels. It is thought the name comes from the kings of Navarre, who belonged to the ruling house of Évreux (the comtes d'Évreux held the lordship of Mantes from 1328 to 1364).
The entrance to the chapel is graced by four dainty statuettes dating from the 14C. The crowned women carrying a miniature church model are probably the founders of Notre-Dame: Jeanne de France, comtesse d'Évreux (1312-49) and Jeanne d'Évreux, Queen of France by her marriage to Charles IV the Fair in 1324. The other two young women are probably Jeanne de France's daughters. Queen Blanche, who married Philip VI of Valois, and Agnès, wife of the famous Gaston Phoebus, comte de Foix.

*The current edition of the annual **Michelin Red Guide France***
offers you a selection of pleasant and quiet hotels in convenient locations.
Their amenities are included (swimming pools, tennis courts,
private beaches and gardens...)
as well as their dates of annual closure.

The selection also includes establishments which offer excellent cuisine: carefully prepared meals at reasonable prices, Michelin stars for good cooking.

*The current annual **Michelin Camping Caravaning France**, lists the facilities offered by many campsites (shops, bars, restaurants, laundries, game rooms, tennis courts, miniature golf courses, playgrounds, swimming pools...)*

MARLY-LE-ROI ★

Population 16 741
Michelin map 101 fold 12 or 106 fold 17 – Michelin plan 18

Although a number of important new housing estates have spread across the Grandes Terres plateau since 1950, stretching towards Le Pecq, the name of Louis XIV remains firmly attached to this town.

Marly was the Sun King's favourite residence. Unfortunately, its golden age lasted barely twenty years. After the First Empire only the park remained, an impressive display of greenery bordering the old village, which has welcomed many writers and artists: the two Alexandre Dumas, Alfred Sisley, Camille Pissarro, the sculptor Maillol and the tragedienne Mlle Rachel, to name but a few.

The early stages – Marly's construction was due to Louis XIV's desire to retreat from the formal etiquette of Versailles. After the Treaty of Nijmegen in 1678, at the summit of his glory, tired by the continual entertaining at Versailles, the king dreamed of a peaceful country residence, far from the madding crowd. His barony at Marly offered a deep, lush valley which seemed to suit the purpose and he entrusted Jules Hardouin-Mansart with the plans. Mansart came up with an ingenious idea: instead of designing one huge single pavilion, he conceived a series of 13 separate units. The royal pavilion would stand on the upper terrace, while the other twelve, smaller in size and all identical, would be arranged along a stretch of water. To promote his idea, Mansart explained that the decoration of the king's pavilion could symbolise the sun – Louis XIV's emblem – and that the surrounding buildings could represent the twelve signs of the zodiac.

To cut down on costs, it was agreed to replace the carved low-reliefs by *trompe-l'œil* frescoes. The King, delighted, gave orders to start building in 1679. It took nine years for the whole project to be completed. After working relentlessly all his life, Mansart died at the château in 1708.

1714 watercolour of the Great Cascade at Marly

Further embellishments – Right until the end of his reign, Louis XIV applied himself to the improvement of his Marly residence and kept a close watch on the various works under way. He would even show gardeners how to trim the hedges properly.

Behind the royal pavilion rose the steep, wooded slopes of the hillside. The Sun King gave orders to build the River, also called the Great Cascade (*illustration above*), the Wonder of Marly, which was served by the famous "Machine" *(see below)*: starting from the top of the hill, an impressive series of falls poured down a flight of fifty-two steps of pink marble set into the terraced slope. The whole ensemble – adorned with statues, portices and rockeries – was completed in 1699.

The same year, the King decided to clear the main perspective and raze the ground that stood in the way, an enterprise that occupied 1 600 soldiers for a period of four years.

Life at Marly – Apart from his close relatives, Louis XIV brought very few guests to Marly: the facilities for accommodation were limited to 24 apartments. It is estimated that 500 lords and 300 ladies altogether were invited to the château over a period of 30 years. The King himself drew up a list of the guests and he personally determined where they should stay: the nearer they were to the royal pavilion, the greater the honour. The "happy few" were not necessarily members of the aristocracy or high dignitaries, but lively, intelligent personalities whose wit and charm would enliven the king's stays.

The formal etiquette of Versailles was dropped at Marly. The King shared his meals with his guests, with whom he conversed in a free, casual manner. Hunts, forest walks, outdoor games, card games, games of chance, balls and concerts were a regular feature of life here. The standard of comfort at the palace, however, left something to be desired: in summer the guests caught fever, in winter they shivered with cold or choked with smoke because it was too damp to start a fire. Louis XIV – who personally undertook to tackle the heating problem – introduced new systems every year, in vain. On 9 August 1715, the King suffered a bout of exhaustion after following the hunt in his carriage. He was taken to Versailles, where he died on 1 September, aged 77.

★MARLY PARK

Enter Marly Park by the Double Gateway (Deux Portes). Take the first right turn through the woods to the car park near the presidential pavilion.

A large esplanade flanked by lime trees in the centre of the park marks the former site of the royal pavilion. A series of slabs defines the plans of the building: the large octagonal salon is surrounded by four corner rooms, separated by vestibules. The decoration in the King's rooms was red, the Dauphin's rooms were green (they were originally intended for the Queen but she never occupied them); the apartments for "Monsieur" (Louis XIV's brother) were yellow and those of "Madame", his second wife Elisabeth of Bavaria, were blue.

This is where the two perspectives of the park meet: across to the drive leading to the Royal Gates, and along the route running from St-Germain and the Seine Valley up to the Grand Mirror fountains and the green "carpet" of lawn.

The plans for one of the guests' pavilions are marked out by the slabs lying behind the car park.

The present grounds are suggestive of old Marly, with its terraces, fountains and trimmed hornbeam hedges. Further information can be obtained from the museum in the annexe near the Royal Gates.

Grille Royale (Royal Gates) – Louis XIV would use this entrance when he approached from Versailles. Admire the perspective of the steep road climbing up the hillside and its continuation on the opposite slope, slicing its way through the trees.

Marly-le-Roi-Louveciennes Promenade Museum (Musée-Promenade) ⊘ – The museum contains precious material on the 13 pavilions and the garden statues which no longer exist: the plans drawn up in 1753 and a miniature model of the whole project give a fair idea of what the king's country residence looked like. Note the interesting approach to 18C ornamental gardening.

The corner of the main pavilion houses the casts of the statues sculpted by Coustou and Lepautre, a painting of the château and its fountains by Martin le Jeune (1723) and numerous line drawings of former copses and spinneys.

The room dedicated to Louveciennes displays a number of items related to Mme du Barry: Pajou's statue of *Loyalty*, a drawing by Moreau le Jeune portraying a banquet held in the Music Pavilion in honour of Louis XV in 1771. It also features the only religious work by Mme Vigée-Lebrun, as well as her two paintings *Summer* and *Autumn*, which were hung at Marly in 1755. Admire one of Desportes' hunting scenes and a Lamentation (1516) from St-Vigor Church.

Before leaving the museum, visit the small chamber presenting the "Marly Machine": it contains drawings and plans, together with a model. The mural painting depicts the waterworks of Versailles.

Return to the car and leave the park by Avenue des Combattants. Drive down to the horse-pond.

Abreuvoir (Horse-Pond) – After a steep descent – known as Côte du Cœur-Volant – N 386 leads to the horse-pond, once used as a spillway for the waters of Marly park. From here, the water was conveyed back to the Seine by a system of pipes and drains. The terrace flanked by yew trees above the pond used to bear Coysevox' *Winged Horses* and, at a later date, Guillaume Coustou's *Rearing Horses*. Two replicas stand in their place. The original statues once adorned Place de la Concorde in Paris and have now been moved to the Louvre. Two reproductions have also been installed on the Parisian square.

ADDITIONAL SIGHTS

The Marly Machine – It was decided to divert the waters of the Seine to supply the fountains of Marly and, subsequently, those of Versailles.

Colbert succeeded in finding a Belgian engineer, Arnold Deville, and a master carpenter, Rennequin Sualem, who agreed to take on the daring project of raising the water 150m - 493ft above the level of the river. The work started in 1681, took three years and involved a considerable amount of equipment: 13 hydraulic wheels with a diameter of 12m - 40ft operated 225 pumps ranged in three ranks, by which the waters were conveyed from the water tower – set at a height of 163m - 535ft above the Seine – to the Louveciennes reservoirs via an aqueduct with a capacity of 5 000m³ a day. From there they were channelled to Marly or Versailles. Since the 19C, several pumping devices have occupied the site; the last disappeared in 1967.

The site – The road bridge of Ile de la Loge affords a good view of the 18C buildings (*Quai Rennequin-Sualem at Bougival*) that made up the Marly Machine, and the pipes lining the hillside. At the top of the rise stands a white lodge by Ledoux: **Mme du Barry's Music Pavilion.** It was inaugurated on 2 September 1771, during a sumptuous banquet attended by Louis XV. The building was moved to this site and raised a storey in 1934 by the famous perfumer René Coty.

Château de Monte-Cristo (Monte-Cristo Château) ⊘ – To the right of the steep road down to Port-Marly stands the extravagant folly built by **Alexandre Dumas** *(qv)* in 1846, which mingles Gothic, Renaissance and Oriental styles. It became an object of curiosity among fashionable circles in Paris but Dumas' later debts forced him to sell it. The building (largely restored) features medallions depicting Dumas and his favourite authors. The tour includes the ground floor (19C decoration) and the superb Moorish bedroom featuring sculpted panels, stained glass and furniture of Moorish inspiration. The **Alexandre Dumas Museum** (Musée Alexandre Dumas) displays various mementoes of the writer and his family. On the hillock opposite the château note the small pavilion, known as Yew Castle (Château d'If); the titles of Dumas' works are engraved in the freestone.

EXCURSIONS

Louveciennes – This small residential town on the edge of Marly Forest still features several substantial properties.

The **church** (12C-13C) on the village square retains a Romanesque look, but the polygonal belltower is 19C. The interior boasts an interesting collection of stone piscinae, resting against the east end.

Walk through the public gardens, along Rue de l'Étang and down Rue du Pont for a pleasant view of the 16C **Château du Pont** *(private)*, the groves of trees and the moat's rippling waters. Follow Rue du Général-Leclerc to the town hall, opposite which stand arches of the disused aqueduct that used to convey the waters of the Seine to Versailles.

From the church, follow Rue du Professeur-Tuffier, then Rue du Maréchal Joffre as far as Chemin des Gressets to reach **Field Marshal Joffre's Tomb** (tombeau du Maréchal Joffre). The rotunda-shaped temple seen from the gates of the property which used to belong to the marshal, at the beginning of Chemin des Gressets, contains his relics and those of his wife. Joffre, who died in 1931, was extremely fond of Louveciennes and insisted on being buried here rather than at Les Invalides in Paris.

★**Bougival** – In the 19C Bougival was a centre of art, fêtes and bohemian life. Bizet, Corot, Meissonier and Renoir lived here. The "boaters" – fun-loving, young Parisian men and women – who flocked to the dances at La Grenouillère had their carefree lives evoked by Maupassant in his novels and short stories, and captured on canvas by Impressionists (Renoir, Berthe Morisot, Monet).

Turgenev Museum (Musée Tourgueniev) ⊙ – *16 Rue Ivan-Tourgueniev. Access on foot via a small alleyway off N 13 level with the Forest Hill hotel.*

Built on the heights, the house where Turgenev lived in his exile was part of the property owned by his friends Louis Viardot and his wife Pauline, a singer like her sister La Malibran.

On the ground floor, various of the writer's documents, photographs of family and friends, engravings, and his piano are displayed. His works are evoked through extracts from novels and essays, among them the *Récits d'un Chasseur* published in 1852, in which he predicted the abolition of serfdom in Russia. On the first floor, atmospheric reconstructions show the writer's study and the room where he died on 3 September 1883. His body was transferred to St Petersburg on 1 October: a photograph captures Ernest Renan giving a speech at the Gare du Nord in Paris (the "Adieu to Paris"); another shows the funeral procession in St Petersburg.

MARLY-LE-ROI FOREST

The state forest – once royal hunting grounds, jealously guarded by high walls – covers a rough but picturesque plateau planted with oaks, beeches and chestnut trees. The total area is estimated at 2 000ha - 5 000 acres.

The thicker groves, featuring some beautiful trees, lie west of the roads from St-Germain to St-Nom-la-Bretèche, and in the vicinity of Joyenval crossroads. *Consult Michelin map 101 to see which lanes are closed to traffic (barriers). These may however be recommended as cycling paths.*

Désert de Retz (Retz Wilderness) ⊙ – *In Chambourcy, take Rue Francis-Pedron then Rue de Joyenval which becomes Rue de la Cafetière and Allée Frédéric-Passy. Park near Ferme de Retz.*

The park was created by Monsieur de Monvule, usher to the king's chamber, in the second half of the 18C. It lies on the edge of Marly forest and is adorned with seventeen buildings (Tartars' tent, Greek temple dedicated to Pan, Chinese house, ice-house in the shape of a pyramid etc), an Anglo-Chinese garden, two lakes, an open air theatre... Famous figures such as Marie-Antoinette and the King of Sweden visited the Wilderness.

Abandoned for many years, the park, where rare species and hundred-year-old trees cluster, is being transformed into a nature reserve over about 40ha – 99 acres. The main residence *(undergoing restoration)* resembles a truncated column.

The MARQUENTERRE RESERVE★★

Michelin map 51 fold 11 and 52 fold 6 or 236 fold 11

The Marquenterre area is an alluvial plain reclaimed from the sea; it lies between the Authie and Somme estuaries and its name derives from "mer qui entre en terre" (sea which enters the land).

The stretches of land are made up of briny marshes, salt-pastures and sand dunes secured to the land by vegetation, and are of fairly recent origin. The town of Rue was a seaport in the Middle Ages.

The Marquenterre lands, particularly around the Somme Bay where vast reaches of sand are uncovered twice a day at low tide, have always been an important stopover for migratory birds and a place of hibernation for many others. It was a paradise for hunters who, from hides, could fire on the hundreds of ducks, geese and sandpipers of all types, to the extent that many species disappeared.

As a result of the decimation, in 1968 the Hunting Commission (Office de la Chasse) created a reserve on the maritime land, to ensure the protection of the birds along 5km – 3 miles of coastline. The owners of the Marquenterre lands, who supported the reserve, then decided to set up a bird sanctuary within it to allow the general public to watch the extraordinary variety of birdlife in its natural habitat.

★★**Parc Ornithologique (Bird Sanctuary)** ⊙ – *It is advisable to visit on a rising tide when the birds leave the stretches of the Somme Bay, and during the spring and autumn migration periods.*

The Bird Sanctuary was created in 1973 and covers 150 ha – 370 acres at the edge of the Somme Bay reserve. Over 300 bird types have been identified, among them many ducks including the red-beaked sheld-duck, geese, tern, waders such as the avocet with its delicately-curved beak, seagulls, ash-grey herons, sandpipers, spoonbills...

Two different trails are signposted:

– The tour of the lakes and aviaries at the foot of an old hill-dune, offering a close-up view of the birds which live here permanently: ducks, seagulls, geese and herons. Some of these birds have had their wings clipped in order to attract wild birds of the same species with their cries.

An avocet, Marquenterre Reserve

D'après photo by Antony/JACANA

– The 2km – 1 1/4 mile walk (*allow 2 1/2 hours, binoculars recommended*) follows a path through the dunes to various observation hides, a heronry and a large aviary, from where the development of numerous species in their natural habitat, can be studied.

MEAUX ★

Agglomeration 63 006
Michelin map 106 folds 22, 23 or 56 folds 12, 13 – Local map p 135
Town plan in the current Michelin Red Guide France

Formerly the property of the house of Champagne, Meaux was an agricultural centre lying between the Petit Morin and Grand Morin rivers, on the edge of the Multien cereal-growing plains and the famous dairy pastures of Brie. It is now an average-sized town, in rapid expansion since the 1960s.

In the summer months, a **son-et-lumière performance** featuring a cast of 2 100 re-enacts Meaux's moments of glory in the charming setting of the Episcopal Precinct *(see Calendar of Events, qv)*.

Jacques Bossuet, Bishop of Meaux – Having completed his tutorial commitments towards the Dauphin, **Bossuet** was made Bishop of Meaux in 1682 at the age of 55.

The man later known as the "Eagle of Meaux" exercised his ecclesiastic duties with the utmost assiduity: he kept an attentive eye on catechism, was often seen preaching in his own cathedral and assumed full command of the religious communities in his diocese. For instance, despite his great esteem for Jouarre Abbey *(qv)*, he did not hesitate to have the place besieged when the abbess refused to dismiss two nuns whose conduct he considered improper.

Bossuet enjoyed working in the huge library of the Episcopal Palace, or in his study at the back of the garden: it was there that he composed five of his most famous sermons, including those dedicated to Louis XIV's wife Marie-Thérèse and the Great Condé. He also wrote a number of books defending Gallican orthodoxy. He died in Paris in 1704, aged 77, at the height of his intellectual pursuits. As was his wish, his relics rest in his cathedral in Meaux.

★**EPISCOPAL PRECINCT** *1 1/2 hours*

★**Cathédrale St-Étienne (St Stephen's Cathedral)** – The construction of the church continued from the late 12C to the 16C, covering the entire gamut of Gothic architecture. The façade (14-16C) is pure Flamboyant. Only the left tower was completed. The one on the right – a plain belltower – is called the Black Tower on account of its dark-coloured shingles. The limestone used for the stonework has crumbled in several places and the exterior decoration is badly damaged. The Wars of Religion brought further destruction.

The south transept façade is an elegant example of Radiant Gothic. The south doorway – in poor condition – is dedicated to St Stephen.

Enter the cathedral through this doorway.

The interior of the cathedral – last restored in the 18C – contrasts sharply with the badly weathered exterior. The lofty, well-lit nave is an impressive sight. The double side aisles are unusually high owing to the suppression of the upper galleries as in Notre-Dame in Paris. These were removed around the middle of the 13C, which had the effect of heightening the aisles.

The two bays of the nave next to the transept date from the early 13C: their austere appearance typifies early Gothic. The west bays were completed in the 14C and the pillars redesigned in the 15C.

The transepts – in particular the south arm – are superb examples of 14C architecture: the elegant, generous proportions characterise the golden age of Radiant Gothic. Below the huge stained-glass window runs an open-work triforium so fine that it allows a full view of the lancets. The chancel – also Radiant Gothic – is a pleasing sight with its double aisles and its five apsidal chapels. Note the pretty 15C Maugarni doorway to the left of the choir. A walk round the ambulatory leads to Bossuet's tomb, marked by a slab of black marble, visible through the parclose enclosing the chancel.

Vieux Chapitre (Old Chapter-House) – This is believed to have been the chapter's 13C tithe barn. The external staircase is roofed over and dates from the Renaissance period. The ground floor, linked to the cathedral by a wooden gallery, is used as a sacristy and a spare chapel.

Ancien Évêché (Episcopal Palace) ☉ – The old palace houses a **museum** largely dedicated to Bossuet. The building was completed in the 12C and renovated in the 17C. The main front gives onto the garden. The two magnificent Gothic rooms facing the park on the ground floor, the nearby crypt and the upstairs chapel are the oldest parts of the palace. The chapter-house contains some of the museum's archeological collections, dating from prehistoric, protohistoric and especially Gallo-Roman times. The amazing brick ramp was designed by Bishop Briçonnet in the 16C in order that the mules loaded with grain might reach the attics.

Enter the palace through the Synod's Chamber which together with the western salons has been made into a Fine Arts Museum (15C to 19C). Among the many artists feature Floris, Boullogne, De Troy, Bouchardon, Millet and Courbet. The donation made by Annie and Jean Pierre Changeux in 1983 has considerably enriched the collections of 17C and 18C French painting. The exhibition presents a striking display of medals and counters evoking the 1848 Revolution, the War of 1870 and the Paris Commune.

Bossuet's apartment, located in the east wing, has retained its original layout but the decoration was renewed in the Louis XV style. Admire Mignard's portrait of the bishop and a splendid Cressent commode (early 18C).

The former library contains an anonymous 17C portrait of Henrietta Maria of England, for whom Bossuet composed his famous sermon. The room also offers a variety of documents and personal souvenirs. The chapel houses the museum's religious works (medieval sculptures, reliquaries and robes), which include several interesting holy-water stoups of the type designed for the east end. The head of Ogier the Dane – jack of spades in our modern pack of cards – the fragment of a 12C recumbent statue, deserves a special mention. The history of the town is also presented: 1738 plan by Monvoisin, pictures of the old bridge spanning the Marne with its picturesque mills (sadly disappeared), apothecary's shop of the former hospice, Moisan's electric oven (1892) for studying artificial diamonds.

Gardens – The gardens, shaped like a bishop's mitre, were designed by Le Nôtre in the tradition of French formal gardens. A staircase leads to the terrace, the former watchpath of the old ramparts.

At the top of the steps stands the humble 17C pavilion which Bossuet used as a study. The bishop would retire here to collect his thoughts or to write in the peaceful hours of the night.

Anciens remparts (Ramparts) – *Turn back towards the museum.* When level with the first tower (yew tree trimmed into a conical shape), lean over the edge of the terrace. The Gallo-Roman part of the wall (4C) is easily recognisable on account of the fine stonework, crossed by thin layers of brick. The centre of the terrace affords a good **view★** of the gardens, the Episcopal Palace and St Stephen's Cathedral.

EXCURSION

Montceaux-les-Meaux Château ☉ – *8.5km - 5 miles east. Leave Meaux by N 3 (east). Beyond Trilport, in Montceaux Forest, turn right into D 19. The lane to the château is on the right.*

Montceaux was known as the Château of the Queens. Catherine de' Medici had it built and Philibert Delorme almost certainly worked on it between 1547 and 1559. Henri IV later gave it to Gabrielle d'Estrées who had work continued by J A du Cerceau (1594-99). On the death of the one who was "almost Queen", the king gave the château to his bride Marie de' Medici who entrusted the works to Salomon de Brosse before he started to build the Luxembourg Palace (1608-22 in Paris). The château fell into disrepair and after 1650 became uninhabitable. Handsome ruins lurk among the trees: from the roofless entrance pavilion, there is an especially good view of a section of wall with gaping windows. The oblong-shaped moat has remained intact.

The town is located on the slopes of the plateau which bears Meudon Forest. In the mid-18C Mme de Pompadour acquired **Bellevue** estate and gave orders to build the château. Louis XV paid frequent visits to the estate and in 1757 he bought Bellevue from his favourite. He embellished the house, refurbished the grounds and installed a hot water heating system under the flooring. The last occupants were the two unmarried daughters of Louis XV, the aunts of Louis XVI. They added a botanical garden and a charming hamlet. The estate was pillaged during the Revolution and sold as State property. In the 19C it was parcelled out into building plots.

All that remains of the former estate is part of the terrace and its balustrade at the junction of Rue Marcel-Allégot and Avenue du 11-Novembre. The wonderful panorama *(belle vue)* of the past has been replaced by a view of modern Paris with, in the foreground, Boulogne-Billancourt and the Seguin islet.

On 8 May 1842, the small station on the left was the scene of a train accident in which the explorer **Admiral Dumont d'Urville** died (he had just discovered Adélie Coast in the Antarctic), together with 40 other passengers who had been locked in the compartments according to regulations.

CHÂTEAU AND TOWN

The stately Avenue du Château is lined with four rows of lime trees. Half-way down the street, a plaque on the left marks the little house (no 47) where **Richard Wagner** composed the score for the *Flying Dutchman* in 1841.

Château of the House of Guise – A manor house in Meudon dating from the early 15C became the property of the Duchess of Étampes, former mistress to François I, whose generosity graced the estate with two new wings and a beautiful park. The domain was subsequently sold to Cardinal de Lorraine, who belonged to the House of Guise. He commissioned the sumptuous grotto from Primaticcio, as well as the two superimposed orangeries. For a hundred years Meudon remained in the hands of the Guise. The family later sold the estate to Abel Servien in 1654 owing to financial difficulties.

Meudon at the time of Servien – The wealthy Abel Servien, marquis de Sablé and Minister of Finance, commissioned Le Vau to renovate the château at great expense and gave orders to build the terrace, a large-scale project. Servien led a life of luxury but his fortune soon ran out: when he died in 1659, he was in debt to the tune of 1 600 000 livres. Abel's son sold the estate to Louvois, the lord of Chaville.

Meudon at the time of Louvois – The new owner pursued the efforts of his predecessor, renewing the decoration and embellishing the park. He asked Trivaux to create the perspective and entrusted the plans of the gardens to Le Nôtre, then to Mansart. After Louvois' death, his widow agreed to give Louis XIV her domain in exchange for Choisy Château, which belonged to the king's son, the Grand Dauphin.

Meudon at the time of the Grand Dauphin – Of the Sun King's six legitimate children, Monseigneur was the only one who did not die in early childhood. He retained little of the worthy principles his tutor Bossuet *(qv)* imparted to him; it was for the Grand Dauphin that Bossuet had written his *Discours sur l'Histoire Universelle*. The king's son delighted in hunting and his favourite reading matter was the obituary page of the *Gazette de France*. He was however an enthusiastic art lover and made considerable changes in the interior decoration of the Old Château. In 1706 he dismantled the grotto and replaced it with a new pavilion for his private apartments. This New Château was Mansart's last major accomplishment. In 1711 Monseigneur died of smallpox and the following year his son the Duke of Burgundy succumbed to the disease. The château came into the hands of a two-year-old boy, who was to become Louis XV. His great-grandfather Louis XIV administered the estate up to 1715.

Meudon abandoned by Royalty – Until the Revolution, Meudon fell into disrepair. In 1793 the chemist Berthollet and Général Choderlos de Laclos – who wrote *Les Liaisons Dangereuses*, recently adapted for the cinema by Stephen Frears as *Dangerous Liaisons* and by Milos Forman as *Valmont* – set up an artillery research centre in the Old Château. Unfortunately it was so badly damaged by a fire that the whole building had to be razed in 1804. Only the columns of pink marble still adorn the Luxembourg Palace and the Carrousel Arch, both in Paris *(qv)*.

The flames spared the New Château, which housed a workshop for military balloons. The famous aerostats which contributed to the victory of Fleurus (1789) were manufactured in Meudon. Napoleon I renewed the furniture in the New Château, which was occupied by Marie-Louise and the King of Rome during the Russian campaign.

In 1870 the terrace was turned into a redoubt for a Prussian battery intent on bombarding Paris. When the Germans withdrew the following year, Meudon was burned down along with St-Cloud. Only two small wings still stand. The central section of the building was restored and made into an observatory.

★**Terrace** – The terrace (450m - 1 480ft long and 136m - 447ft wide) is planted with handsome trees and sweeping lawns. It lies at an altitude of 153m – 502ft and commands an extensive **view**★ of Meudon, the Seine Valley and Paris. One of the most impressive trees of the forest stands to the left of the gates. The pedestal-like pilasters adorning the breast wall of the upper terrace date from the 16C and 17C.

The far end of the esplanade rests on the foundations of the old orangeries of the château. From here, visitors may discover Le Nôtre's beautiful perspective with the modern complex of Meudon-la-Forêt in the far distance.

Observatoire (Observatory) ⊙ – On the right stands the observatory, housing the astrophysics section of the Paris Observatory. A large revolving dome with a diameter of 18.5m – 60ft crowns the central block of the New Château. Note the astronomical telescope dating from 1893.
Founded in 1876 by the astronomer Janssen, this observatory is considered the most important in France. It is also the leading aerospace research centre in France. A mushroom-shaped tower was added in 1965: its 35m – 115ft shaft attracts the rays of the sun, which are then broken down and analysed under a spectroscope.

Musée d'Art et d'Histoire (Art and History Museum) ⊙ – *11 Rue des Pierres, at the foot of the terrace (drive there from the town centre).*
The museum, in the house which Molière's wife Armande Béjart bought in 1676, three years after the writer's death, centres on the history of the town, the celebrities who lived there and the châteaux of Bellevue and Meudon (reference library). It also presents the municipal art collections: Dunoyer de Segonzac, Magnelli, Pape etc. The formal gardens are dotted with contemporary sculptures by Arp, Bourdelle and Stahly.

Musée Rodin (Rodin Museum), Villa des Brillants ⊙ – *19 Avenue Auguste-Rodin.*
An indispensable complement to the Rodin Museum in Paris *(see Michelin Green Guide Paris)*. The museum stands next to Villa des Brillants, Rodin's residence and studio from 1895. It contains moulds, drawings and rough sketches by the great sculptor, together with a number of original plaster casts *(The Gates of Hell, Balzac, The Burghers of Calais)*. The façade of the museum was taken from the old château at Issy-les-Moulineaux. Rodin died in 1917 and his grave was laid out in front of the museum. Sitting pensively on the tombstone is his famous statue *The Thinker.*

MILLY-LA-FORÊT★

Population 4 307
Michelin map 106 fold 44 or 61 north of fold 11

The locality of Milly-la-Forêt developed around the old covered market and it is now an important starting-point for many of the forest lanes crisscrossing the Three Gables *(qv)* and Coquibus massifs.
Milly has been a long-standing centre for the growing of medicinal plants, including one variety still considered a local speciality: peppermint. Lily of the valley and a wide range of aromatic herbs for cooking purposes are also grown.

Halles (Covered Market) – Located on the town square, the market building – made entirely of oak and chestnut wood – dates back to 1479.

Chapelle St-Blaise-des-Simples (St Blaise-des-Simples Chapel) ⊙ – *On the way out of the village, along the road to Chapelle-la-Reine.*
In the 12C the chapel was part of the St Blaise leper house. More recently, Jean Cocteau decorated the walls in 1959: a huge line-drawing above the altar depicts Christ with a crown of thorns and a mural represents the Resurrection of Christ. The walls of the nave are adorned with illustrations of medicinal herbs or simples (mint, belladonna, valerian, buttercup and aconite).
The chapel houses a bust of Cocteau by the German sculptor Arno Breker, and the poet's grave. The epitaph on the tombstone simply reads: "I remain with you". The garden surrounding the chapel is planted with common medicinal herbs.

MONTFORT-L'AMAURY★

Population 2 651
Michelin map 106 north of folds 27, 28 or 60 folds 8, 9

This old town is built on the side of a hill dominated by castle ruins. Under the *Ancien Régime*, Montfort was an important county town enjoying far more power than nearby Rambouillet *(qv)*.
The district was founded and fortified in the 11C by the builder Amaury de Montfort. The most famous descendant of this illustrious family was Simon IV, the leader of the Albigensian Crusade, who waged a fierce war against the heretical Cathars of Languedoc *(see Michelin Green Guide Gorges du Tarn, Cévennes, Languedoc)*. Simon de Montfort was killed by a stone in 1218, during an assault on the town of Toulouse.

A Breton outpost in Ile-de-France – In 1312 the marriage of the Breton Duke Arthur to one of the Montfort daughters made this citadel a part of Brittany.
Subsequently, when Anne of Brittany, comtesse de Montfort married Charles VIII and then Louis XII, Montfort-l'Amaury became a French fief. The duchy was made royal territory when Henri II, the son of François I and Claude de France – herself the daughter of Louis XII – came to the throne.

SIGHTS

★**Église St-Pierre (St Peter's Church)** – The renovation of the church was undertaken by Anne of Brittany in the late 15C. The decoration work continued through the Renaissance and was completed in the early 17C: the nave was elevated and levelled, and the belltower and the façade were both remodelled.

Walk round the church, surrounded by quaint old houses. Observe the striking gargoyles that adorn the walls of the apse and the high flying buttresses supporting the chancel. The pretty doorway on the south front bears medallions portraying the benefactors whose generosity made it possible to carry out the renovation work in the Renaissance: André de Foix and his wife.

The interior of St Peter's features a superb set of Renaissance **stained-glass windows**★ in the ambulatory and around the aisles *(read description in "Montfort-l'Amaury" booklet published by the tourist information centre)*. The vaulting above the aisles features many hanging keystones. The historiated bosses in the nave include a low relief bearing the emblem (ermine) of Anne of Brittany.

★**Ancien charnier (Old Ossuary)** – Admire the beautifully-carved Flamboyant doorway. This old cemetery is enclosed within an arcaded gallery surmounted by splendid timbered roofing. The left gallery is 16C, the two others date from the 17C. These galleries were intended to receive the bones of the buried when it became necessary to empty the graveyard.

Castle Ruins – Take the narrow, twisting road to the top of the hill. Two sections of wall overgrown with ivy are all that remain of the 11C keep. The stone and brick turret belonged to the building commissioned by Anne of Brittany.

The summit offers a good **view**★ of the town, the old-fashioned roofs and the first groves of the forest.

Maurice Ravel Museum ⊙ – In 1920 the French composer Ravel bought a tiny villa in Montfort-l'Amaury. It was in this house – called Le Belvédère – that he wrote most of his music: *L'Enfant et les Sortilèges, Boléro, Daphnis et Chloé* etc. The composer developed a brain tumour but stayed on in Montfort, despite doctor's orders to stop working in 1934. He was forced to move back to Paris in 1937, where he died soon afterwards.

The rooms are somewhat cramped and Ravel – who was a short man – had several of them made even smaller. The interior decoration has remained intact: much of the painting was done by Ravel himself and featured dark, sombre tones. The museum exhibits include the composer's piano, his record player and numerous mementoes reflecting his taste for refinement.

EXCURSIONS

Maison Jean Monnet (Jean Monnet's House, Houjarray): Information Centre on Europe ⊙ – *4.5km - 3 miles east. Leave Montfort by D 13 towards Tremblay-sur-Mauldre. Cross N 191 and turn right to Houjarray before Bazoches-sur-Guyonne.*

Jean Monnet (1888-1979), the political economist and diplomat, bought this country retreat in 1945; it has a thatched roof and a large, gently sloping garden which overlooks the surrounding countryside.

Monnet was instrumental in the successful modernisation and strengthening of the tattered French economy after the Second World War, and is also famous for being one of the founders of the European Community. The declaration text of his Schuman Plan of 1950 (embodied in a treaty that same year) was conceived and written here; it led to the creation of the European Coal and Steel Community (ECSC).

Monnet would return to this haven of peace after his frequent trips around the world and had many famous figures and heads of state to stay. He retired here in 1975, writing his memoirs until his death. His ashes were transferred to the Panthéon in Paris on 9 November 1988.

Some of the original furnishings remain, together with various possessions: Monnet's *Memoirs*, letters from Schuman, Roosevelt, Adenauer and de Gaulle, various publications with Monnet on the cover, paintings by his wife Sylvia, a bust of Marianne (1945) by the sculptor Paul Belmondo. Display panels recount the important moments of his career.

★**Round tour of Rambouillet Forest** – *21km - 12 miles then 1/2 hour Rtn on foot. See Rambouillet.*

Étang de la Porte Baudet ou des Maurus (Porte Baudet Lake or Maurus Lake) – *4km - 2 1/2 miles southwest then 45min Rtn on foot. Leave Montfort by D 112 and D 138, towards St-Léger.*

Go past the turning to Gambais *(right)* and turn left into Rue du Vert-Galant. Follow the plateau along the winding route which enters the wood (the road surface rapidly deteriorates).

Park the car at the "Zone de Silence de la Mare Ronde". Certain forests have silent areas *(zones de silence)* where motor bikes, radios etc are prohibited.

Use the Map of Principal Sights to plan a special itinerary.

MONTMORENCY ★

Population 20 920
Michelin map 101 fold 5 or 106 fold 19 – Michelin plan 18

This charming town, set on hilly ground, consists of a town centre surrounded by wealthy residences. Its main claim to fame is to have been the home of the celebrated author and social theorist Jean-Jacques Rousseau (1712-78) for a period of his life.

The "First Christian Barons" – The Bouchard family, who held the lordship of Montmorency, had the reputation of being difficult vassals and it was only after the 12C that they served the French court loyally. Over a period of 500 years, the Montmorency family produced 6 constables, 12 marshals and 4 admirals. Moreover, their land was made a duchy by Henri II. They had connections with every ruler in Europe and chose to call themselves the "first Christian barons". One of their most celebrated descendants was Constable Anne *(qv)*, companion-in-arms to François I, Henri II and Charles IX.

The oldest branch of the family died out when the constable's grandson Henri II de Montmorency, governor of Languedoc, was beheaded at the age of 37 for having plotted against Cardinal Richelieu. Despite the numerous appeals made to Louis XIII, the King refused to pardon the Duke and ordained that the execution take place. The duchy passed into the hands of Henri de Bourbon-Condé but the title was given to a member of the Montmorency-Boutteville family by Louis XIV.

During the Revolution, the town was called Émile in honour of Rousseau's famous treatise on education. It recovered its former name in 1832.

Jean-Jacques Rousseau's literary retreat – The author lived in Montmorency from 1756 to 1762. Invited by Mme d'Épinay, a society woman who moved in literary circles, Rousseau took up residence in the Hermitage, a small garden pavilion which has since been taken down. He was 44 years old. His short temper and bouts of melancholic depression annoyed the other house guests. He was living with Thérèse Levasseur, a linen maid whom he later married, but fell passionately in love with his hostess's sister-in-law Mme d'Houdetot, who was nearly 20 years his junior.

His romantic involvements caused him to fall out with Mme d'Épinay in 1757, at which point he moved to Montlouis where he completed *La Nouvelle Héloïse* and published *Émile* and *Du Contrat Social*. These were his three major works.

The owners of Montlouis – the Maréchal de Luxembourg and his wife – took Rousseau under their wing. Their admiration for the writer, who would read them his latest chapters, helped them put up with his changing moods. The stately grounds of their estate have survived but the château has been replaced by a modern building.

In 1762 *Émile* was qualified as subversive literature by the Parlement de Paris and an order was issued for Rousseau's arrest. Fortunately, the author was forewarned: he fled Montlouis in the marshal's carriage and sought refuge in Switzerland. He returned to France in 1767.

Country outings – From the late 18C to the Second Empire, the area around Montmorency was a popular resort among writers, artists, politicians and young Parisian socialites. Informal picnics and lunches at the Auberge du Cheval Blanc – on the marketplace now called Place Roger Levanneur – were a common feature of life at Montmorency. Visitors were known to sample the local cherries and donkey rides were very much in vogue. Visitors, some of whom were to become leading personalities, engraved their name, together with that of their loved one, on the bark of the chestnut trees or on the mirrors at the inn.

Even the crowned heads of France forgot about protocol when they stayed at Montmorency. Queen Hortense, the Duchess of Berry, Napoleon III and the Condé princes would run about the meadows like carefree children, astride their little donkeys.

SIGHTS

★**Collégiale St-Martin (St Martin's Collegiate Church)** – *Rue de l'Église*. Started in the 16C by Guillaume de Montmorency and completed by his son Constable Anne, St Martin's is characteristic of Flamboyant Gothic. It was originally designed to be the mausoleum of the Montmorency family.

Walk round the church to appreciate its **site** which dominates the new town of Montmorency, spread out in the valley. The view extends to the heights of Sannois and the Orgemont hill (tower).

The nave features complex ribbed vaulting in keeping with 16C architecture, except for the two ribs in the choir that present ornamental brackets at the point where they meet the pillars.

Certain bosses and bands crowning the columns bear variations on the Greek word *APLANOS* (straight ahead), which was the Constable's motto.

The chapel was specially designed to receive the remains of the Montmorency and, in the 18C, the relics of several Condé descendants. The family tombs were destroyed during the Revolution. Some were salvaged and moved to the Louvre, including those of Constable Anne and his wife Madeleine. The others have disappeared save for the funeral slab of Guillaume de Montmorency and his wife Anne Pot, of the famous Burgundian family: it rests on the upper level on the south aisle.

★**Stained-glass windows** – *Explanatory plans are attached to the corresponding pillars.* The 14 windows that adorn the apse and the five nearest righthand bays of the chancel provide a fine example of Renaissance decoration, tastefully restored in the 19C. The family connections of the Montmorency are illustrated by the effigies of their ancestors, the brightly-coloured coats of arms and the saints they worshipped. Above the glass cage of the side doorway is a magnificent window representing the famous emblem of this illustrious family: alerions or eagles without beaks or feet painted in blue against a yellow background.

The other windows in the nave – executed in the 19C – harmonise well with the earlier Renaissance windows. They evoke the joys and sorrows of the dynasty up to the execution of Henri II de Montmorency in 1632, which heralded the start of a new era for the Condé *(see Chantilly, qv)*.

The Polish heritage – The south side features a number of busts, recumbent figures and plaques relating to the members of an aristocratic community from Poland who moved to Montmorency in the wake of the failed national insurrection (1831). They were attracted to the town by the fresh, vivifying countryside – reminiscent of their own homeland – and by the literary connections with Rousseau. In the chancel is a copy of the painting, Our Lady of Czestochowa or the Black Madonna, the patron saint of Poland.

Detail of stained-glass window
in St Martin's Collegiate Church, Montmorency

Musée Jean-Jacques Rousseau (Jean-Jacques Rousseau Museum) ⊙ – *5 Rue Jean-Jacques-Rousseau*. This is the house where the French writer lived from 1757 to 1762 and where he wrote his major works. The museum evokes the daily life of Thérèse and Jean-Jacques. The old part of the house affords a good view of the valley. The "Hall of Greenery" planted with lime trees leads through to the small garden pavilion Rousseau used as a study, which he sardonically called his "keep".

The exhibition hall and audio-visual room in the modern part of the museum present particular aspects of Rousseau's life and work. The 18C house at the edge of the grounds contains a library with numerous studies on Rousseau.

EXCURSION

Collégiale St-Martin de Groslay (St Martin's Collegiate, Groslay) – *2km - 1 1/4 miles east.* This 12C and 13C church which was altered and enlarged in the Renaissance features a lovely series of stained glass, among which note the **Tree of Jesse** inspired by that in Beauvais Cathedral *(qv)*.

Montmorency Forest – *3km - 2 miles north.* The area west of Domont and N 309 is the more interesting section of the forest, with deep wooded vales and patches of moist undergrowth. Oaks and chestnut trees are the dominant species, with the occasional birch. The forest boasts several footpaths, a cycle route which cuts through the forest, and the Caesar's Camp recreational area.

MONT NOIR

Michelin map 51 southwest of fold 5 or 236 fold 5 (4km – 2 1/2 miles north of Bailleul)

The Black Hill (Mont Noir) with its dark wooded slopes is part of the Flemish hill range and stands on the border between France and Belgium. The hill (131m – 429ft high) gives good views across to Ypres, Red Hill (Mont Rouge) and Cats Hill (Mont des Cats), with its abbey and signal post, and over a pleasant landscape of hop-fields, poplars and red roofs.

Mont Noir is a busy summer resort offering a choice of hotels and bars, and boasts many tourist facilities (go-carting, camping, play areas etc).

EXCURSION

Mont des Cats – *7km - 4 1/2 miles west by D 318 and D 10 north.* Cats or Catsberg Hill (158m - 518ft high) is also part of the Flanders hill-range and is known for its fine cheese similar to Port-Salut. It is crowned by a neo-Gothic Trappist abbey founded in 1826 and subsequently restored. St Bernard's **parish church** ⊙, right of the monastery's entrance, contains interesting stained-glass windows by Michel Gignon (1965).

Return to D 10 and turn left to Boeschepe.

Moulin de Boeschepe (Boeschepe Windmill) ⊙ – At the foot of Cats Hill, the village of Boeschepe boasts a restored windmill *(illustration p 11)*, next to a charming café.

Return to Mont Noir by D 10 and D 318.

MONTREUIL ★

Population 2 450
Michelin map 51 fold 12 or 236 fold 12

Montreuil, which was once "on sea", occupies a **site**★ on the edge of the plateau overlooking the Canche Valley. This peaceful town preserves a certain slightly nostalgic charm in its old streets lined with 17C and 18C houses, and its shaded citadel and ramparts commanding vast horizons.

Montreuil developed around two buildings: the monastery founded in the 7C by St Saulve, Bishop of Amiens, from which the town derived its name; and the fortress built in about 900 by Helgaud, Count of Ponthieu. From the 11C Montreuil became part of the royal domain and in the Middle Ages it comprised nearly 40 000 inhabitants.

In 1537 Charles V of Spain's troops forcibly seized the town, almost completely destroying it in the process. The ramparts were rebuilt by the engineers of François I, Henri IV and Louis XIII; and Montreuil included up to 8 churches. In 1804, at the time of the Boulogne Camp *(qv)*, Napoleon stayed in Montreuil and in 1916 Douglas Haig, commander of the British troops, made his headquarters here. Montreuil's proximity to the coast and particularly to Le Touquet attracts numerous tourists in summer.

A "Storm in the Mind" – Montreuil's setting and surroundings have seduced many writers, among them Laurence Sterne (1713-68), the English writer and author of *"A Sentimental Journey through France and Italy"*, and also **Victor Hugo**. Hugo visited Montreuil in 1837 and used the town as the setting for one of the main episodes in *Les Misérables*. The novel tells how the convict Jean Valjean, reformed by a life of generosity and sacrifice, becomes mayor of Montreuil; when, however, an innocent man is to be tried in his place, Valjean is subjected to a terrible moral dilemma, immortalised by Hugo under the heading "Storm in the Mind".

CITADEL AND RAMPARTS *1 hour*

★**Citadelle (Citadel)** ⊙ – Montreuil citadel was built in the second half of the 16C and was completely remodelled in the 17C by Errard *(qv)* and then by Vauban. Nevertheless, it still incorporates elements of the former castle (11C and 13C).

On the side of the town, one of Vauban's demilunes protects the entrance. Having crossed this, the tour encompasses:
– the two 13C round towers which flank the royal château;
– Queen Bertha's Tower (Tour Berthe) (14C) which was the entrance to the town until 1594. It is part of a 16C bastion and houses the emblems of the lords killed at Agincourt *(qv)* in 1415. The tower's name evokes Queen Bertha who was repudiated by her husband Philippe I – who wanted to marry the alluring Bertrade de Montfort – and locked in Montreuil château where she suffered such a fate that the people of Montreuil organised collections for her benefit, chanting "Give, give to your queen."
– the sentry walk, which offers attactive **views**★★ over the Canche valley: the old charterhouse of Notre-Dame-des-Près and the opening of the Course Valley *(right)*, the wetlands of the Canche, the estuary and Le Touquet marked by its lighthouse *(left)*.
– the casemates (pillboxes) built in 1840 and the 18C chapel.

★**Remparts (Ramparts)** – The red brick and white stone walls with bastions date largely from the 16C-17C, though some elements of the 13C walls have remained on the west front.

Leave the citadel by the bridge which crosses the ditch and turn right into the small path which runs alongside the walls; continue for 300m - 330yds towards the France Gate (Porte de France).

MONTREUIL

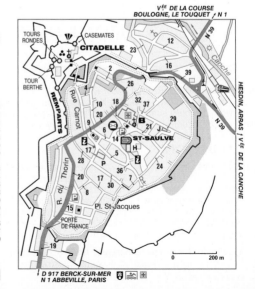

B Chapelle de l'Hôtel-Dieu

From the sentry walk there is a lovely perspective of the curtain walls with their series of 13C towers incorporated into the 16C walls; one side offers a view over the roofs of Montreuil, the other of the Canche Valley and the plateau of the Montreuil region. For those with time to spare, the entire circuit of the ramparts *(1 hour)* follows a shaded path offering extensive views over the surrounding countryside.

ADDITIONAL SIGHTS

Chapelle de L'Hôtel Dieu (Hospital Chapel) (**B**) ⊘ – The chapel was altered in 1874 by a follower of Viollet-le-Duc *(qv)* but retains its Flamboyant 15C chapel. It is adorned inside with rich 17C **furniture**★, including a unified set of woodwork (carved panels, pulpit, confessional) and a curious Baroque altar covered with gilding and mirrorwork.

★**Église St-Saulve (St Saulve Church)** ⊘ – This former Benedictine abbey church dates from the 11C (the northeasterly face of the porch-belfry in particular) but was remodelled in the 13C and again in the 16C following a fire which led to the collapse of the vaults. These were rebuilt lower than their original height, which accounts for the dim light in the church.
Inside, the frieze on the capitals to the right of the nave and two large 18C paintings are of particular note: on the main altar, *The Vision of St Dominic* by Jouvenet, and to the left, in the Lady Chapel (the old crossbowmen's chapel), *St Austreberthe taking the Veil* by Restout.

Rue du Clape-en-Bas – This charming paved street *(illustration: see Traditional Rural Housing)* is lined with low, lime-washed houses with mossy-tiled roofs – typical in the Canche Valley – where craftsmen are installed in their workshops (weavers, potters...).

*The annual **Michelin Red Guide France** offers an up-to-date selection
of hotels and restaurants
serving carefully prepared food at reasonable prices.*

MORET-SUR-LOING ★

Population 4 174
Michelin map 106 fold 46 or 61 northeast of fold 12

Moret is a charming riverside town nestling on the banks of the Loing, at a comfortable distance from the busy motorways.

A fortified town and a royal residence – Situated near the Champagne border, Moret and its fortified castle defended the king's territory from the reign of Louis VII up to Philip the Fair's marriage to Jeanne of Navarre, the daughter of the Comte de Champagne (1284), which put an end to the feud between the two families. Its keep and curtain wall – the two gates still stand – lost their strategic value, and Fontaine-bleau *(qv)* became the official place of residence for French rulers. These fortifications remained until the mid 19C and the part of town traversed by the River Loing kept its quiet, secluded character.
The history of Moret was marked by a number of famous women, including Jacqueline de Bueil (1588-1651), one of the last loves of Henri IV, who founded the Notre-Dame-des-Anges hospital and convent. Marie Leczinska was greeted in Moret by Louis XV on 4 September 1725: a commemorative obelisk marks the place where the betrothed met (at the top of the rise along N 5). The following day they were married in Fontainebeau.

SIGHTS

★**The site** – Branch off the road to St-Mammès and proceed towards the Pin meadow (pré de Pin) which runs along the east bank of the Loing. Admire the view of the rippling water, the shaded islets, the fishermen, the church and the ancient keep.

Bridge over the Loing – One of the oldest bridges in Ile-de-France, it was probably built around the same time as the town fortifications but was frequently torn down and then strengthened. On the approach to the Burgundy Gate (Porte de Bour-gogne) the ramparts and several houses with overhangs – one of which rises out of the Loing waters – come into view.

Notre-Dame Church – The building is reminiscent of many great churches in Ile-de-France.
The **chancel** is believed to have been consecrated in 1166. The original elevation is visible in the apse and on the south side; the main arches resting on round columns are crowned by a gallery opening onto triple arching, surmounted by clerestory windows. The arches and the bays on the left side were walled in to offer greater support to the unusually high belltower erected in the 15C. The elevation of the transept with its open-work design, and that of the nave with its crowned arches, were undertaken in the 13C and 14C.
The Renaissance organ case presents a coffered front with delicate carvings and painted decoration.

Ancien hospice (Old Hospital) – The corner post on Rue de Grez bears an effigy of St James. A few steps along Rue de Grez a modern cartouche bears the foundation date of the hospital (1638). The place became famous on account of the Moret barley-sugar sweets prepared by the nuns. Needless to say, this tradition was continued by the town's confectioners.

Sisley's House – Alfred Sisley (1839-99), the Impressionist painter of English parentage, spent the latter part of his life in Moret. His studio was at no 19 Rue Montmartre *(private)*. He turned his back on a life in commerce to paint, and belonged to the Impressionist group but never achieved fame in his lifetime and was continually beset by financial difficulties. A pure landscape painter, Sisley delighted in the scenery of Ile-de-France and showed feeling for portraying water, light and air.

Rue Grande – At no 24 a commemorative plaque marks the house where Napoleon spent part of the night on his way back from Elba (19 to 20 March 1815).

François I's House – *Walk through the town hall porch and into the small courtyard.*
Note the extravagant Renaissance decoration of the gallery, and the door crowned by a salamander.

Porte de Samois (Samois Gate) – Also known as the Paris Gate. A statue of the Virgin adorns the inner façade. Note the old-fashioned royal milestone that once marked out the highway leading from Lyon to Paris (now N 5).

Grange Batelière (Riverside Cottage) ⊙ – *Take Rue du Peintre Sisley east and then a private lane which strays from the towpath, on the right, just before the bridge spanning the Loing canal.*
Built in 1926, this was the residence of Michel Clemenceau (1873-1964), who personally supervised the finishing touches. Standing on the banks of the Loing, this charming cottage and its thatched roof was built in imitation of the traditional Vendée cottage. The house of the great statesman has been turned into a museum to his memory, which is tended by his daughter-in-law.

BOAT TRIPS ⊙

Embarkation: from St-Mammès, north of Moret.

MORIENVAL★

Population 1 040
Michelin map 56 fold 3, 106 fold 11 (inset) or 237 fold 7

This beautiful Romanesque church, nestling in the lush setting of the old abbey grounds and the surrounding valley, is best viewed from the northeast.

Take the road above the church square, below the school.

200m - 220yds from here the road to Fossemont offers an excellent view of the church and its east end. The ensemble has not changed since the 12C, except for some reconstruction above the chancel: the narrow windows date from the last restoration (1878-1912).

★**Église Notre-Dame (Church of Our Lady)** ⊙ – The church was a dependant of a convent which, according to tradition, was founded in the 7C by Dagobert and richly provided for in the 9C by Charles the Bald, but destroyed by the Normans in 885. The rebuilding of the church and convent began in the 11C. In the 17C Abbess Anne II Foucault undertook several alterations, which were marked with her monogram (keystones in the nave).

Exterior – The abbey church has a typical silhouette with its three towers, one adjoining the west front and two flanking the chancel: the north tower is marginally shorter and slimmer than the south tower.

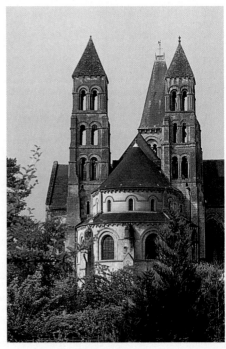

Morienval Church

The base of the porch-belfry is the earliest part (11C), then the transept, the chancel's right bay and the two east towers. Originally the porch-belfry stood apart from the Romanesque front and not attached to the extended aisles, an arrangement dating from only the 17C. The church's old porch has been reopened and the restored door reinstated.

Go northwards around the church to the apse: note the ambulatory which was squeezed onto the semicircle of the chancel at the beginning of the 12C, to give it extra strength as it was threatened by infiltration.

Interior – The extremely narrow ambulatory is a purely architectural element and is the most unusual part of the church. Its arches, dating from about 1125, are some of the oldest in France. Here for the first time ogee arches have been used in the curved part of a building; however, they are separate from the areas of vaulting that they support. The transition from groined vaulting to quadri-partite vaulting can be seen.

The nave and transept are not as old, having been vaulted in the 17C.

The 11C capitals in the nave (a, b, c, d) – with their spirals, stars, faces and animals, side by side – are the only certain remains of the Romanesque church.

An important series of memorial stones stands along the wall of the left aisle; one commemorates the great abbess Anne II Foucault (1596-1635) (1). On the wall of the opposite aisle 19C engravings show the church as it was before the last restoration: note the large apsidal windows. The most notable statues include Our Lady of Morienval (17C) (2), the 16C Crucifixion group (3) once mounted on a rood beam, and the large 17C terracotta St Christopher (4).

NAOURS CAVES *

Michelin map 52 fold 8 or 236 fold 24 (13km - 8 miles north of Amiens)

The old village of Naours contains excellent examples of white-washed Picardy architecture.

Below the surface of the plateau next to Naours there exists the largest number of refuge-caves dug out of limestone; there are many in Picardy and parts of Artois, known as *creuttes, boves* or, in Naours, **"muches"**. During times of trouble the men of the village would hide themselves *("musser")* there.

The history of the caves of Naours goes back to the 9C and the Norman invasions, although they are only mentioned in documents only from the 14C. They were much used during the Wars of Religion and the Thirty Years War; in the 18C salt-smugglers used them to avoid the collectors of the hated salt tax.

Forgotten for a while, they were rediscovered in 1887 by Abbot Danicourt, the local priest, who explored and cleared them with the help of the villagers. In 1905 treasure was found: 20 gold coins from the 15C, 16C and 17C. In 1942 the caves were occupied by the Germans.

Grottes (Caves) ⊙ – An amusement park stands nearby and it is also possible to climb to the top of the ridge, to the two reconstructed Picardy windmills; there were at one time up to seven windmills in Naours *(bird's-eye view over the town)*. The underground passages form a town which could shelter 3 000 people in its 2km - 1 1/4 miles of streets and squares, its 300 rooms, 3 chapels, stables, bakery with ovens, storerooms etc. Chimneys link the passages to the surface of the plateau, 30m - 98ft above.

During the tour the different layers of the soil are revealed: chalk, clay in fissures and pockets, flint in parallel bands. The small **Folklore Museum** is housed in a few of the chambers: local crafts are presented in enormous dioramas.

NOTRE-DAME-DE-LORETTE HILL *

Michelin map 51 fold 15 or 236 fold 15 (11km - 7 miles southwest of Lens)

Notre-Dame-de-Lorette is among many places (including Carency, Albain St-Nazaire, Souchez, Neuville St-Vaast, Vimy and La Targette – where **General Pétain** had his command post while the 33rd division pierced the German lines) mentioned in dispatches during the First World War, especially during the first battle of Artois from May to September 1915.

In a dramatically bleak setting, under an often grey sky, Notre-Dame-de-Lorette Hill (166m - 544ft high) is the culminating point of the Artois hill-range and overlooks the battlefield *(bronze orientation table left of the cemetery entrance)*.

The enormous cemetery contains 20 000 named graves; General Barbot's is first left of the main alley. The chapel, in a Romanesque-Byzantine style, is decorated with mosaics and marble.

The main ossuary with its lantern tower (52m - 170ft high) and the seven other ossuaries house the remains of 20 000 unknown soldiers. On the first floor, there is a **Remembrance Museum** (musée du Souvenir) ⊙: soldiers' letters, photographs, personal effects... and from the top floor, a vast **panorama**★ of the mining basin *(north)*, the Vimy Memorial *(qv) (east)*, the ruined church of Ablain St-Nazaire, the towers of Mont-St-Éloi and Arras *(south)*.

NOYON ★

Population 14 426
Michelin map 56 fold 3 or 236 fold 36

Noyon is an ancient religious town with a rich history; its buildings are overshadowed by its imposing cathedral.

Originally Gallo-Roman, Noyon was elevated by St Medard to a bishopric linked to Tournai in 581. A century later, St Eligius was one of its bishops. The town has witnessed the splendour of two coronations, Charlemagne's in 768 as King of Neustria and Hugh Capet's in 987 as King of France.

Noyon was one of the first French cities to obtain its own charter, in 1108. It was the homeland of Calvin (1509) and the sculptor Sarazin (1592).

The local industrial activity is varied (smelting, metal furniture, milling, printing works, food products); agriculture is favoured by the presence of local fertilizer businesses, food packing and grain storing.

★★CATHEDRAL *1/2 hour*

Four buildings preceded the present cathedral, which was begun with the chancel in 1150 and finished in 1290 with the west front, and is a remarkable example of the early Gothic style. It has a sober, solid Romanesque appearance combined with the breadth and harmony of the great masterpieces of the golden age of cathedral-building. It was restored after 1918.

Place du Parvis is edged with a semicircle of canons' residences; a representation of a canon's hat is over each entrance. The square has kept its old charm despite the fact that most of these buildings were rebuilt after 1918.

Exterior – The sparse front is preceded by an early-13C porch with three bays; it was reinforced in the 14C with two flying buttresses decorated with small gables. A gallery with tall, slender colonnettes surmounts the great central bay, framed by two belltowers with prominent corner buttresses. The more austere south tower is also the older; it was built in 1220.

The north tower is one of the loveliest types of belltowers built in northern France in the 14C: it is discreetly decorated with fine mouldings and twists of foliage on the gallery's arcades, and foliate friezes under the upper shoulders of the buttresses. The crowning of the two towers suggests that the original plan included spires which were never built.

The south transept ends in a beautiful semicircle. The east end is surrounded by gardens; the arrangement of the radiating chapels, the ambulatory and the tall windows produces a lovely effect in spite of 18C additions.

To the south lie the ruins of the bishop's private chapel and to the north stands the old **chapter library** *(private)* with its wooden-pillared gallery (16C). It is known for housing the precious Gospel Book from Morienval *(qv)* which dates from the 9C. The north transept arm, surrounded by canonic buildings, is barely visible.

★★**Interior** – The proportions of the nave and chancel are extremely pleasing. The nave has five double bays. The elevation rises through four storeys: great arches, large and elegant galleries with double arcading which are particularly striking viewed from the transept crossing, shallow triforium and clerestory windows.

Among the side chapels, the Lady Chapel (Chapelle de Notre-Dame du Bon Secours) *(right aisle)* contains lierne and tierceron vaulting forming a star, with hanging keystones representing sibyls.

The nave's severity is accentuated by the absence of stained-glass windows. The transept arms, like the chancel, are rounded at the end. This feature, found also at Soissons and Tournai cathedrals, was a result of Rhenish influence.

The chancel vault is as high as the nave's. The eight ribs of the apse radiate from a central keystone and develop into a cluster of small columns. Nine chapels open onto the ambulatory.

Among the furnishings, the Louis XVI high altar shaped liked a temple is of particular interest, as are some largely-18C grilles which enclose the chancel and the chapels off the nave.

Today only a single gallery remains of the **old cloister** *(off the left aisle)*; the bays with beautiful radiating tracery overlook the garden.

The opposite wall is pierced with wide pointed-arch windows and a door giving access to the 13C **chapter-house**. The pointed vaults rest on a series of columns.

ADDITIONAL SIGHTS

Musée du Noyonnais (Noyon Regional Museum) ⓥ – This small, brick and stone, Renaissance building (a remnant of the old bishop's palace), with a corner turret and a 17C wing which was rebuilt after the First World War, contains collections on local history. Many objects were discovered during excavations in Noyon and its surrounding area (Cuts, Béhéricourt): 12C chess pieces, a cache of Gallo-Roman money, ceramics. 12C and 13C coffers from the cathedral are exhibited upstairs.

Hôtel de Ville (Town Hall) – Despite several alterations the façade retains some 16C elements, among them the niches with carved pedestals which used to house statues. The lion-adorned pediment was added in the 17C.

Musée Jean-Calvin (Calvin Museum) ⓥ – The museum is installed in a house built in 1927 partly on the foundations, and following old plans, of the house where Calvin was born which was destroyed at the end of the 16C.
In the ground-floor entrance hall an audio-visual display *(10min)* presents Calvin and his time.
The great reformer's room has been recreated and contains authentic portraits and engravings, together with a letter written by Calvin.
On the first floor 16C Latin and French Bibles are displayed, including the famous Olivetan Bible and the Lefèvre d'Étaples Bible. There is also a model of a 16C printing house.
Works by Calvin and his contemporaries are on the second floor, together with models of the round Paradise temple in Lyon (1564) and the galley-ship *La Réale*. The library holds 1 200 books dating from the 16C to the 20C.

OLHAIN CASTLE FARM★

Michelin map 51 fold 14 or 236 fold 15
(6km - 3 1/2 miles southeast of Bruay-en-Artois)

This medieval **castle** farm (château-ferme d'Olhain) ⓥ is set in a romantic lake at the bottom of a vale. The castle dates from the 13C-15C and boasts a large bailey from the Middle Ages which has been transformed for agricultural use. A drawbridge gives access to the bailey and from there to a watchtower *(staircase with 100 steps)*, a Gothic room known as the Guardroom, cellars with walls 2 to 3m - 6 1/2 to 10ft thick, and a chapel.

Olhain Castle

Parc départemental de Nature et de loisirs (Regional Nature and Leisure Park) – *1km - 1/2 mile north on D 57E.* In this nest of greenery at the heart of the mining region, numerous facilities have been established: swimming, golf, tennis, games areas, picnic areas, trails etc.

Dolmen de Fresnicourt (Fresnicourt Dolmen) – *3km - 2 miles on D 57 and a little road to the right (signposted).*
The "Fairies' Table" is situated at the edge of a small, once-sacred oakwood. It is an impressive sight, even though its top stone has slipped.
The crest of the hill on which the megalith stands, separating Flanders from Artois, provides extensive views.

The River Ourcq rises in Villers-Cotterêts Forest, situated in the Aisne *département*. After La Ferté-Milon, it follows a winding course, which skirts the beds of hard coarse limestone of the Brie subsoil and used to flow into the Marne downstream from Mary-sur-Marne. In 1529 however the magistrates of the City of Paris embarked upon the construction of a canal which diverted the waters to the heart of the capital, where the first shipment of wood and cereals was delivered in 1636.

The Ourcq Canal – In 1802 Bonaparte decided to divert the course of the Ourcq by creating a canal-aqueduct to take the waters to La Villette basin, north of Paris. The canal was inaugurated seven years later and permitted navigation between Paris and Claye-Souilly in 1813. By 1821 it had joined up with the canalised river running from Ourcq to Mareuil-sur-Ourcq. Five locks were installed and those which already existed on the canalised watercourse were renewed. From 1920 to 1930 the canal was widened between La Villette basin and Les Pavillons-sous-Bois and a new lock set up at Sevran.

The Ourcq canal supplies the locks of the St-Denis and St-Martin canals in Paris; it also provides water for factories in Paris. Commercial navigation between La Villette and Meaux ceased in 1960: it has been replaced by pleasure boating. The navigable section of the Ourcq is 110 km - 68 miles long and may be divided into three parts. The canalised river (10km - 6 miles - 4 locks) starts upstream from La Ferté-Milon. The canal itself (90km - 54 miles - 4 locks) links Mareuil-sur-Ourcq to Les Pavillons-sous-Bois: it is 1.5m - 5ft deep and 11m - 37ft wide. Finally, a wide watercourse (no locks) flows into the "canal roundabout" in Paris (La Villette Basin).

Boat trips along the Ourcq canal are available in season.

BATTLE OF THE MARNE

The first Battle of the Marne originated with the Battle of the Ourcq, which in fact took place on the heights of the Multien plateau and not in the valley itself. The outcome of this battle did much to secure the success of the general offensive launched between Nanteuil-le-Haudouin, north of Meaux, and Révigny, northwest of Bar-le-Duc.

It is little known that this battle was triggered off – on both sides – by the confrontation between reserve units (55th and 56th French Divisions, 4th German Corps). Owing to the hazards of drafting and the movement of retreat, many of the French soldiers were in fact defending their native territory.

The retreat: 24 August to 4 September 1914 – After the invasion of Belgium (4 August) and the defeat of Charleroi (23 August), the Anglo French armies suffered heavy enemy pressure and were forced to withdraw.

Joffre, who had been appointed commander-in-chief, ordered his men to withdraw in good order. His troops re-formed and he hoped to be able to launch another attack as soon as possible. On 27 August, the 6th Army was created to contain the German advance on the Aisne river: it was led by General Maunoury. It was also to be used as a striking force against the left flank of the enemy pocket. Unfortunately, the retreat continued and by 1 September the Armies had taken up position along a line running west of Beauvais, Verberie, Senlis and Meaux. On the right, it was continued by the 4th British Division led by Sir John French. At this point in the battle, the Germans – who were marching towards Paris and the southwest – wheeled their flank southeast. Von Kluck's Army passed in front of Paris.

Gallieni, in charge of the Paris garrison and Maunoury's 6th Army, mistook the manœuvre: in his mind, Von Kluck wanted to capture the British Army which was withdrawing to the Grand Morin. After discussing the matter, Gallieni and Joffre decided to attack the enemy's flank and crush the powerful right wing of their invaders. The offensive was scheduled for 6 September.

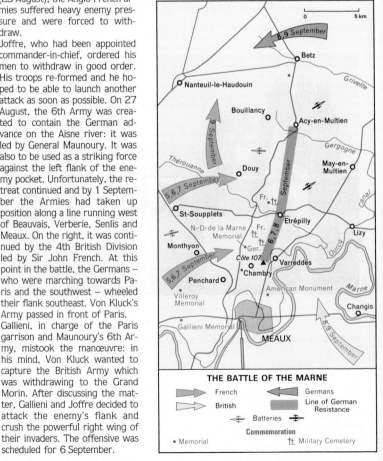

THE BATTLE OF THE MARNE

French — Germans

British — Line of German Resistance

Batteries

Commemoration

▪ Memorial   ✝ Military Cemetery

The check: 4 to 8 September – Gallieni and Maunoury's 6th Army prepared for combat on 4 September. The following day, they endeavoured to reach the position between Lizy-sur-Ourcq and May-en-Multien but ran up against the 4th German Corps. Despite their dominant position, the Germans were afraid of being outflanked and that night evacuated the wooded hills of Monthyon and the village of Penchard. Having suffered badly, the two French Divisions and the Moroccan Brigade – incorporating Lieutenant Juin, soon-to-be Marshal – were withdrawn in order that they might re-form. Along the Grand Morin line, Sir John French's Army, exhausted by the retreat, swung slowly towards the north.

On 6 September, from his headquarters in Châtillon-sur-Seine, Joffre launched a moving appeal to all his men: "On the eve of the battle on which the future of our Country depends, it is important to remind all that there must be no looking back". The French and British Armies advanced a further 200km - 120 miles: it was the start of a general attack. In the 6th Army sector, the French reached the Chambry-Douy-Bouillancy line. The day of 7 September was marked by the bloody confrontation with the German line. The toughest fighting took place in the villages of Étrépilly and Acy-en-Multien, the two bastions of the line, in the valleys of the Thérouanne and the Gergogne. A series of violent bayonet charges were delivered by d'Urbal's light infantry and the Zouaves of Colonel Dubujadoux. French's Army repulsed the German rear-guard and took up position along the road from La Ferté-sous-Jouarre and Montmirail.

On 8 September, the war of movement shifted north of Multien to the sector of Nanteuil-le-Haudouin. The previous night the town had received the 7th Division, despatched by Gallieni and transported by the famous "Marne taxis". It was there that Maunoury and Von Kluck were desperately hoping for a definitive solution, relying on a strategy of encircling movements.

The victory: 9 to 13 September – Wednesday the 9th was a turning-point in the Battle of the Marne. On the left, the French troops facing north in the Nanteuil-le-Haudouin sector suffered an assault of such violence that Maunoury began to fear for Paris. The British Army, however, succeeded in crossing the Marne.

In the centre, the French troops entered Étrépilly and Varreddes which had already been evacuated. Von Kluck's Army retired. The German commander-in-chief Von Moltke was astonished by the French recovery. An alarming gap separated Von Kluck's 1st Army from Von Bülow's 2nd Army, checked by Foch near the St-Gond marshes, and Von Moltke was afraid that his front line would not hold: he gave orders for a general withdrawal following a line passing north of Soissons, Rheims and Verdun.

This war of movement ended on 13 September. In October, the operations became bogged down and the battle developed into trench warfare.

The French offensive failed to fulfil its objective, ie to crush Von Kluck's Army but it halted the invasion at a critical moment. The official telegram sent by Joffre read: "The Battle of the Marne is an incontestable victory for us".

THE BATTLEFIELD AND THE OURCQ VALLEY

Round tour starting from Meaux
96km - 58 miles – allow 4 hours –
Local map below

★**Meaux** – *See Meaux.*

From Meaux take N 3 (west) towards Paris. After 6.5km - 4 miles, a memorial paying tribute to Gallieni stands on the left hand side of the road. Turn right into D 27, towards Iverny, then right again towards Chauconin-Neufmontiers.

Villeroy Memorial (Mémorial de Villeroy) – It stands on the site of the early operations of 5 September 1914. The funeral vault houses the remains of 133 officers and soldiers who died in the fields nearby. **Charles Péguy** (1873-1914) was buried with his comrades-in-arms belonging to the 276th Infantry Regiment (reserve). Their collective grave lies to the right of the vault. Facing it is a cross celebrating the memory of the writer, philosopher and social reformer.

The 19th Company of the 276th Regiment was called in to relieve the Moroccan Brigade who accompanied them and who were dangerously engaged in battle near Penchard. It launched an attack towards Monthyon, under the fire of the enemy, under cover in the valley around the Rutel brook. Péguy was the only surviving officer. He told his men to lie down and was inspecting the German positions when he was struck by a bullet.

At the next crossroads, turn left towards Chauconin-Neufmontiers. Drive through Penchard and follow directions to Chambry. Drive through the village.

The belltower of Barcy is visible to the left.

Chambry National Cemetery (Cimetière National de Chambry) – Most of the soldiers buried here died during the fighting that took place on 6, 7 and 8 September when they defended the village of Chambry, which was assaulted several times.

Located 500m - 500yds east of the crossroads, the German military cemetery marks the place where the main German line – which roughly follows the dirt track – met the road to Varreddes.

Turn back, towards Barcy.

Notre-Dame-de-la-Marne Monument – This was erected in 1914 on the orders of Monseigneur Marbeau, Bishop of Meaux, and dominates the whole battlefield. Turn to the north for a good view of the Multien plateau in the far distance.

Proceed towards Puisieux. At the crossroads after the old factory, turn right to Étrépilly. In the town centre, 200m - 220yds before reaching the church, turn left towards Vincy and Acy-en-Multien.

Étrépilly – The small national cemetery and the memorial evoke the fighting that took place during the night of 7-8 September, reaching a climax near the village graveyard.

Acy-en-Multien – This village nestling in Gergogne Valley was the scene of intensive warfare on 7 September 1914. The winding alleys, the hillsides planted with small spinneys and the garden walls of the château provided many opportunities for close combat, often ending in tragic death.

Turn left (west) out of Acy, to Bas-Bouillancy.

Bouillancy Church (Église de Bouillancy) – Located in the lower part of the village. In the quiet valley – rural life is concentrated in the village on the heights – lies an early Gothic church (12C-13C) of harmonious proportions. Note the belltower flanked by buttresses featuring numerous projections.

Turn back to Acy and take D 18 up to the plateau.

Enjoy the **view** of Acy and the elegant village spire. Beyond Étavigny, the route strays from the battlefield.

Beyond Boullarre take D 922, right.

The road leads to **Mareuil-sur-Ourcq**, marking the start of the canal.

Take D 936 south; turn left, through Varinfroy, to Crouy-sur-Ourcq bridge.

Crouy-sur-Ourcq – Just after the level crossing, the road skirts the ruins of the **Houssoy Stronghold** (Château Fort de Houssoy), now converted into a farmhouse. The keep has remained separate and can be approached by the left hand lane, leading to the courtyard gates.

Crouy Church features a Gothic interior with two 16C aisles. Admire the beautiful made panelling (1670) in the chancel. The patron saints of the church are represented above the retable: St Cyricus, who was made a martyr at the age of 3, and his mother, St Julitta.

Turn back, and after the bridge turn left towards May.

The twisting road affords extensive **views** of the surrounding landscape.

May-en-Multien – The village enjoys a privileged position, 100m - 330ft above the river Ourcq. It is visible from afar on account of its church tower, one of the highest landmarks in the area.

Drive down to Lizy. Do not cross the canal bridge but go up the right slope along the road to Congis (D 121).

View of the last loop of the Ourcq, overgrown with greenery.

Cross Congis and Varreddes and join D 405, south, following a steep upward slope.

On the left stands the huge American monument that pays homage to the Marne combatants. The road dips and leads straight into Meaux.

*Admission times and charges for the sights described
are listed at the end of this guide.
Every sight for which there are times and charges
is identified by the symbol ⊙ in the Sights section of the guide.*

Population 2 152 333
Michelin map 101 and plan 10 (single sheet) or 11 (atlas with street index)

Paris dominates France's intellectual, artistic, scientific and political life, and has done so since the 12C when the Capetian kings made it their capital. It is today a lively, handsome city with considerable charm, boasting a wealth of attractions. The map and descriptions on the following pages give an outline of the most important sights in Paris, so that the visitor with just a day or two may become acquainted with the capital's landmarks and treasures. Like any city with a rich and varied history, however, Paris needs a little time to get to know; for a comprehensive guide, consult the **Michelin Green Guide Paris.**

THE CITY'S MONUMENTS

Civil Architecture

★★★ The Louvre – The original Louvre was a fortress built in 1200 by Philippe Auguste on the banks of the Seine to protect the weakest point in his new city; it was used as treasure-house, arsenal and archive. In the 14C the fortress ceased its military functions with the erection of a new perimeter and Charles V converted it into a residence, installing his famous library in one of the towers.

In 1527 François I took up residence in the Louvre. The keep was razed and defences knocked down but it was not until 1546 that a new royal palace was commissioned, on the site of the old keep, which was to become the residence of the kings of France. It was the architect Pierre Lescot who brought the Italian Renaissance style to the banks of the Seine; Jean Goujon added the sculpture. Over the following centuries, almost all the French monarchs added to and altered the evolving Louvre. The Florentine **Catherine de' Medici,** as Regent for Charles IX, ordered Philibert Delorme to build the Tuileries Palace nearby for her while work continued on the Louvre. Charles XI and Henri III both lived in and added to the Louvre, as did Henri IV and Louis XIII who both added pavilions. In 1662 the young King Louis XIV celebrated the birth of the Dauphin with a great fête here.

The monumental, colonnaded façade facing the city was conceived by Perrault, aided by Le Brun and Le Vau. It was begun in 1667 but completed only in 1811. Both Napoleon I and Napoleon III continued with additions, alterations and restorations. In 1871 The Communards set the Tuileries Palace and some of the wings of the Louvre ablaze, most of which were subsequently restored and rebuilt. The Tuileries Palace was finally demolished in 1883.

In 1984 President Mitterrand chose the glazed pyramid designed by the American I M Pei as the contemporary entrance to the Louvre Museum.

The **Louvre Museum** (Musée du Louvre) ⊙ is one of the largest and most famous museums in the world. It is divided into seven main sections: Oriental Antiquities, Egyptian Antiquities, Greek, Etruscan and Roman Antiquities, Sculpture, Paintings, Graphic Art and Art Objects. Among its innumerable treasures are Mesopotamian statues; the Frieze of the Archers from Darius' Palace; the jewellery of Rameses II; the Winged Victory of Samothrace and the Venus de Milo; Michelangelo's *Slaves*; Renaissance master paintings by Giotto, Fra Angelico, Leonardo da Vinci *(Mona Lisa)*, through to Veronese, Caravaggio, Van Dyck, Rubens, Rembrandt, Watteau... There are Classical and Romantic works by the great French painters David, Ingres, Delacroix and Géricault.

The *objets d'art* include the Crown Jewels of France; Brussels and Gobelins tapestries; fine furniture, clocks etc.

★★★ Hôtel des Invalides (The Invalides) – Guns captured at Vienna in 1805 line the Esplanade leading to the huge building (designed 1671-76 to house old soldiers invalided out of service) with a front (200m - 650ft long) featuring dormer windows in the form of trophies. St Louis' Church within the precinct is the resting-place of some of France's great soldiers; it also contains flags captured from the enemy. Berlioz' *Requiem* was first performed here.

The **Dome Church★★★** (Église du Dôme) ⊙ was designed by Jules-Hardouin Mansart and begun in 1677; it is one of the great works of the Louis XIV style. The façade giving onto Place Vauban has Doric and Corinthian orders, topped with a pediment carved by Coysevox. The soaring, gilded dome stands on a great columned drum supporting a balcony; an elegant lantern rises above.

The church took on its role as military necropolis when Napoleon had Field Marshal Turenne (d 1685) buried here. There is also a memorial to Vauban, the great military architect, and the tomb of Field Marshal Foch. In an impressive crypt of green granite stands the unmarked red porphyry mausoleum, which is **Napoleon's Tomb★★★**.

★★★ Arc de Triomphe ⊙ – The great triumphal arch is one of Paris' main focal points; it stands in Place Charles de Gaulle – known as the Star (l'Étoile) owing to its 12 radiating avenues. The arch was designed in 1806 as one of the landmarks of Napoleon's imperial capital but was finished only in 1836, in the reign of Louis Philippe.

In 1920 the arch saw the burial of the Unknown Soldier; three years later the flame of remembrance was kindled for the first time. Sculpture on the arch includes Rude's 1836 masterpiece known as *La Marseillaise*, showing the departure of volunteers to fight the invading Prussians (1792).

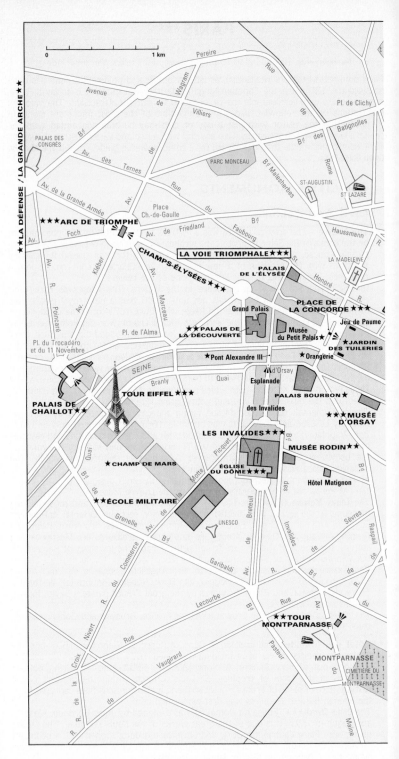

***Place de la Concorde** – This perfect expression of the Louis XV style was designed by Jacques-Ange Gabriel in 1755 and completed over 20 years. In January 1793 the guillotine was set up here for the execution of Louis XVI and other victims of the Terror.

The square features colonnaded buildings to the north, massive pedestals, magnificent marble sculptures and the pink granite Luxor Obelisk, 3 300 years old and covered with hieroglyphics, which was brought back from Egypt in 1836.

***Tour Eiffel** (Eiffel Tower) ⊙ – The tower is Paris' most famous symbol. The first proposal for a tower was made in 1884; construction was completed in 26 months and the tower opened in March 1889.

In spite of its weight (7 000 tonnes) and height (320.75m - 1 051ft) and the use of 2 1/2 million rivets, it is a masterpiece of lightness. The tower actually weighs less than the volume of air surrounding it and the pressure it exerts on the ground is that of a man sitting on a chair.

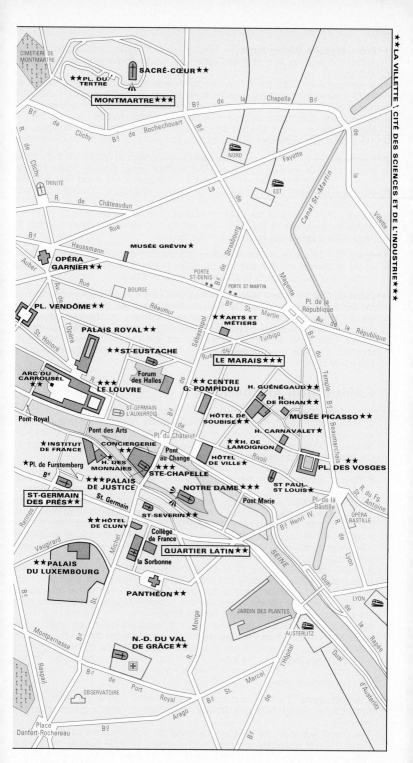

★★★**Palais de Justice (Law Courts)** – This, the main seat of civil and judicial authority, has been the residence of Roman governors, Merovingian kings and the children of Clovis, Dagobert's mint, Duke Eudes' fortress and the royal palace of the rulers of medieval France. The Capetian kings gave it a chapel and a keep and its 1313 Gothic halls were widely admired. Later, Charles V built the Clock Tower (Tour de l'Horloge), the first public clock in Paris.

The **Conciergerie**★★ Ⓥ served as antechamber to the guillotine during the Terror; it contains the Prisoners' Gallery, Marie-Antoinette's cell and the Girondins' Chapel.

★★**Palais-Royal** – In 1632 Richelieu commissioned the huge building which became known as the Cardinal's Palace when it was extended in 1639. On his deathbed Richelieu bequeathed it to Louis XIII who renamed it the Palais-Royal. The formal gardens at the rear and the surrounding arcades were laid out in 1783; the adjoining Théâtre-Français was added four years later. The 260 columns in the outer courtyard were designed in 1986 by Daniel Buren.

★★**École Militaire (Military Academy)** – Though lack of funds curtailed the original design, this work by Jacques-Ange Gabriel is an outstanding example of 18C French architecture.

It was begun in 1752, partly financed by Mme de Pompadour, and completed in 1773; various wings and buildings were added later. True to its original function, it houses the French Army's Staff College. The main front has a projecting central section with Corinthian columns rising through two storeys, crowned with a quadrangular dome and adorned with allegorical figures and military trophies. The superb **main courtyard★★** is lined by beautiful porticoes with paired columns.

★★**Panthéon** ⊙ – In 1744 Louis XV had made a vow at Metz to replace the half-ruined church of St Genevieve's Abbey: in 1758 Soufflot began building on the highest point of the Left Bank. Despite predictions of collapse, it has stood firm over the years but has been much remodelled. In 1791 it was closed to worshippers and converted into the last resting place of the "great men of the epoch of French liberty". The building, in the shape of a Greek Cross, is still crowned by Soufflot's dome; the pediment of the Corinthian portico was carved by David d'Angers in 1831. The crypt houses the tombs of the famous.

★★**Opéra** ⊙ – This is the National Academy of Music, the magnificent home of French opera. It opened in 1875 and was the work of Charles Garnier. The sumptuous interior is embellished with marble and a ceiling by Chagall.

★★**Palais de Chaillot (Chaillot Palace)** – These elegant inter-war buildings were constructed for the 1937 exhibition. The twin pavilions and wings framing gilded bronze statues house a theatre and four museums: Museum of Mankind (Musée de l'Homme), Navy Museum (Musée de la Marine), Museum of the Monuments of France (Musée des Monuments français) and the Cinema Museum (Musée du Cinéma). There is a **superb view★★★** over the Seine, the Eiffel Tower and the Champ-de-Mars.

Ecclesiastical Architecture

★★★**Notre-Dame Cathedral** – The metropolitan church of Paris is one of the triumphs of French architecture. People have worshipped here for 2 000 years and in many ways Notre-Dame is the cathedral of the nation. Work was begun by Maurice de Sully in 1163 on what turned out to be the last great galleried church and one of the first with flying buttresses.

The chancel was built under Louis VII and consecrated in 1182 in the reign of Philippe Auguste. The double ambulatory and the tracery reinforcing the wide windows set new trends, and the extended spouts of the flying buttresses formed the first gargoyles. By 1210 the first bays of the nave had been built; within 10 years it was completed and the 28 statues of the Kings' Gallery were in place. By 1245 the bulk of the work was complete: St Louis held a ceremony for the knighting of his son and placed the Crown of Thorns here until the Sainte-Chapelle was ready to receive it. In 1250 the twin towers were finished and the nave given side chapels.

In 1430 the young Henry VI of England was crowned King of France in the cathedral; in 1455 a ceremony was conducted to rehabilitate Joan of Arc; in 1558 Mary Stuart was crowned here on becoming Queen of France by her marriage to François II, and in 1572 the Huguenot Henri IV married Marguerite de Valois here; the king converted to the Catholic faith in 1594.

The cathedral square is the point from which distances along the main roads *(routes nationales)* radiating from Paris are measured. Emmanuel, the famous bell weighing 13 tonnes, hangs in the south tower; its pure tone is said to be due to the gold and silver jewellery thrown by the ladies of Paris into the molten bronze when the bell was recast in the 17C. The great rose window, above the Kings' Gallery, still contains medieval glass.

★★★**Sainte-Chapelle** ⊙ – This masterpiece of High Gothic is strikingly different from Notre-Dame, though built only 80 years later: lighter, with a greater clarity of structure.

The chapel was built for St Louis to house the recently-acquired relics of the Passion; it was completed in a record 33 months. Like other palatine chapels it is built on two storeys, the upper for the monarch, the lower for the palace staff. The upper chapel resembles a shrine with stained-glass walls; 720 of the 1 134 different scenes are still of original glass, some created by the masters who had worked on the windows at Chartres *(qv)*.

★★**St-Germain-des-Prés Church** – With the exception of Clovis, all the Merovingian kings were buried here. The church was subsequently destroyed by the Normans but restored in the 10C and 11C; the west tower has a fortress-like character. Around 1160 the nave was enlarged and the chancel rebuilt in the new Gothic style. From 1631 to 1789 the austere Congregation of St Maur made the church a distinguished centre of learning and spirituality. "Improvements" in the 17C were followed in 1822 by an over-zealous restoration.

★★**St Séverin Church** – This Latin Quarter church consists of the portal's lower part and the first three bays of the nave in High Gothic, with the rest largely Flamboyant – note the famous spiral pillar in the ambulatory. In the 18C the pillars in the chancel were clad in wood and marble.

★★**St Eustache** – St Eustache was once the richest church in Paris, with a layout modelled on Notre-Dame when building began in 1532, but it took over a hundred years to finish; tastes changed and the Gothic frame was padded out with Renaissance touches such as Corinthian columns and semicircular arches; the chancel windows and Colbert's tomb, designed by Le Brun with Coysevox and Tuby, are Classical.

★★**Val-de-Grâce Church** – After many childless years, Anne of Austria commissioned François Mansart to design a magnificent church in thanksgiving for the birth of Louis XIV in 1638. The church recalls the Renaissance architecture of Rome; the ornate dome is obviously inspired by St Peter's. Inside, the Baroque spirit prevails: polychrome paving, highly-sculptured vaults, massive crossing pillars and a huge canopy with six wreathed columns. The **dome**★★ has a fresco featuring 200 figures.

Urban Design

Since the sweeping away of much of medieval Paris in the 19C, three central districts have come to typify particular stages in the city's evolution.

★★★**The Marais** – This smart shopping and residential area has Renaissance, Louis XIII and Louis XIV architecture. Charles V's move to the Marais district in the 14C led to the incorporation of a suburban area into Paris; the area soon became fashionable and Rue St-Antoine the city's finest street. It was here that the characteristic French town house, the *hôtel*, took on its definitive form with the collaboration of architects and artists.

The **Hôtel Lamoignon**★★ (1584) is a typical example of a mansion in the Henri III style. It was the first time the Giant Order, with flattened pilasters, Corinthinan capitals and a sculpted string-course, was seen in Paris. The Henri IV style appeared in the symmetrical **Place des Vosges**★★ (completed 1612). The 36 two-storey houses of alternate brick and stone facings have steeply-pitched slate roofs pierced with dormer windows.

Louis XIII's reign heralded the Classical style; in 1624 the **Hôtel de Béthune-Sully**★ was built, with a gateway flanked by massive pavilions and a main courtyard with triangular and curved pediments and scrolled dormer windows. The early Louis XIV style is seen in Mansart's fine **Hôtel Guénégaud**★★ (1648) with its simple lines, majestic staircase and small formal garden; in the **Hôtel de Beauvais**★ with its curved balcony on brackets; in the **Hôtel Carnavalet**★ (now the Museum of Parisian History) built in 1655 by Mansart; and in Cottard's theatrical **Hôtel Amelot de Bisseuil**★ with its cornice and curved pediment decorated with allegorical figures. The Louis XIV style is seen in the **Hôtel de Rohan**★★ with its sculpture of the *Horses of Apollo* and the adjoining **Palais Soubise**★★ with its horseshoe-shaped courtyard and double colonnade; both have raised ground floors, massive windows, roof balustrades and sculpture on the projecting central sections.

★★★**La Voie Triomphale (From the Tuileries to the Arc de Triomphe)** – A great axis leading from the courtyard of the Louvre to St Germain had been planned by Colbert but today's "Triumphal Way" was laid out under Louis XVI, Napoleon III and during the years of the Third Republic.

★★**Carrousel Arch** (Arc du Carrousel) – This pastiche of a Roman arch is decorated with statues of Napoleonic military men. An impressive perspective runs from the Louvre through the arch to the obelisk in Place de la Concorde, then on to the Arc de Triomphe.

★**Tuileries Gardens** – The gardens were first laid out in the 1560s by Catherine de' Medici in the Italian style. A century later they were remodelled by Le Nôtre who created the archetypal formal French garden.

★★★**Place de la Concorde** – *See above.*

★★★**Champs-Élysées** – In 1667 Le Nôtre extended the axis from the Tuileries to a new focal point, the Rond-Point. The avenue was a service road at the back of smart houses but when refreshment stalls were set up along it crowds began to cluster. In 1724 the Duke of Antin planted rows of elms to extend the "Elysian Fields" up to the Étoile. In 1729 street lanterns lit the evening scene. Finally, in 1836 the **Arc de Triomphe**★★★ *(see above)* was completed. The Champs-Élysées became fashionable during the reign of Louis-Napoleon, when high society flocked to its restaurants.

★★**La Défense** – This modern business centre with skyscrapers and pedestrian terraces descending towards the Seine was planned as a whole, the individual buildings subordinated to the overall design.

The precincts are overlooked by the enormous cube of the marble-faced Grande Arche (1989) by Danish architect Johan Otto von Spreckelsen, which stands astride the axis of the Étoile and the Champs-Élysées. The area is also known for its public sculpture: works by Miró, Calder, Takis, Venet, Kowalski etc make it virtually an open-air museum.

THE POLITICAL CAPITAL

Élysée Palace – This has been the Paris residence of the President of France since 1873. It was built in 1718 and was once the property of the Marquise de Pompadour. During the Revolution it housed a public dance-hall, a gaming salon and a picture gallery. In Napoleon's time, Marie-Louise had a boudoir here and the young King of Rome, their son, a set of rooms.

Hôtel Matignon – The attractive town house (1721) has been the residence of the French Prime Minister since 1958.

★**Palais Bourbon** – This has been the seat of the Lower House of France's parliament, the Assemblée Nationale, for over 150 years. The Assembly consists of directly-elected deputies; it examines and where necessary amends all draft legislation.
The palace was built in 1722; during the Revolution it was the seat of the Council of Five Hundred. The decorative treatment of the façade (1804) which overlooks Place de la Concorde was chosen by Napoleon.

★★**Luxembourg Palace** – This is the seat of the Senate, the French Upper House. Its 283 members are elected for a period of 9 years but a staggered system ensures that a third of them face reselection every three years.
After the death of her husband the king, the regent Marie de' Medici decided to move from the Louvre: in 1615 she commissioned a palace, something to remind her of the Pitti Palace in Florence, from Salomon de Brosse. The result has an exterior with ringed columns and rusticated stonework; a courtyard with columns, semicircular windows, curved pediments, balconies and roof balustrades; a south front with a quadrangular dome, a massive pediment and garden terraces.

★**Hôtel de Ville (City Hall)** – Central Paris is governed from here. Municipal government was introduced in the 13C under the direction of leading members of the powerful watermen's guild appointed by Louis IX. The place has long been the hub of uprising and revolt: during the Revolution it was held by the Commune, in 1848 it was the seat of the Provisional Government. The Republic was proclaimed from here in 1870 and, in March 1871, the Communards burnt it down. It was rebuilt from 1874.

THE INTELLECTUAL AND ARTISTIC CAPITAL

Intellectual Life

The city as a whole functions as the capital of the country's intellectual life, though there is a particular concentration on the Left Bank, in the Fifth and Sixth *arrondissements*. The capital's most venerable institutions stand in the area around Mont Ste-Geneviève, in the Latin Quarter (so-called because Latin was the language of instruction right up to the French Revolution).

★**Institut de France (Institute of France)** – The institute originated as the College of Four Nations founded by Mazarin for scholars from the provinces incorporated into France during his ministry (Piedmont, Alsace, Artois and Roussillon). Its building, which dates from 1662, was designed by Le Vau and stands over the river from the Louvre; it is famous for its dome, its semicircular flanking buildings and the tomb of Mazarin in the vestibule. The Institute is made up of five academies:
The **French Academy** (Académie Française), the most prestigious of all, was founded in 1635 by Richelieu; its membership is limited to 40. The members, "Immortals", devote themselves to upholding the quality of the French language and enshrining it in the *Dictionnaire de la langue française*, the country's standard dictionary.
The **Academy of Fine Arts** (l'Académie des Beaux-Arts) dates from 1816. It has 50 members who cover painting, sculpture, architecture, engraving and music.
The **Academy of Literature** (l'Académie des Inscriptions et Belles Lettres) was founded by Colbert in 1663. It deals with literary history and maintains an archive of original documents.
The **Academy of Sciences** (l'Académie des Sciences), founded by Colbert in 1666, has 66 members working in astronomy, mathematics, medicine and natural science.
The **Academy of Moral and Political Sciences** (l'Académie des Sciences morales et politiques) was founded by the Convention in 1795. It has 40 members and is dedicated to philosophy, ethics, law, geography and history.

Collège de France – The college was founded in 1529 by François I under the name of the College of Three Languages (Latin, Greek, Hebrew) in order to combat the narrow scholasticism of the Sorbonne. The present buildings date from the time of Louis XIII, who renamed it the Royal College of France; it underwent major reconstruction in 1778. It was here, in 1948, that Frédéric Joliot-Curie formulated the laws controlling the process of nuclear fission and built a cyclotron to test his theories.

Sorbonne – This is the country's most illustrious university, the successor to the theological college founded in 1253 by Robert de Sorbon for 16 poor scholars. In 1469 France's first printing press was installed here by Louis XI. For many years, the university court constituted the highest ecclesiastical authority beneath the Pope.
The **Sorbonne Church★**, built by Lemercier from 1635, is a fine example of Jesuit architecture. **Richelieu's tomb★** (1694) by Girardon lies inside.

ENTERTAINMENT AND CULTURE

Paris remains a thriving cultural centre, with a large number of different shows, exhibitions and events on at any one time.

Entertainment – There are 58 **theatres** and over 650 **cinemas** in the capital. **Music-hall, variety shows** and **reviews** take place at the Crazy Horse, the Folies Bergère, the Moulin Rouge... There are numerous **concert halls**, some with resident orchestras, as well as the Opera and the Comic Opera. There are also nightclubs, jazzclubs, cabarets, café-theatres, circuses, concerts, recitals in churches...

Exhibitions – Paris boasts 87 museums and 120 art galleries, plus about another 30 places for temporary shows. Museums include the world-famous Louvre, the **Orsay Museum★★★** ⊘ (1848-1914 art), the Pompidou Centre (Museum of Modern Art), the **Hôtel de Cluny★★** ⊘ (Museum of the Middle Ages), the Military Museum at the Invalides and the fascinating **City of Science and Industry★★★** ⊘ at La Villette.

Tourist Paris – Certain parts of the city have come to be identified in the visitor's mind with the very essence of Paris itself.

★★★**Montmartre** – The "Martyrs' Mound" became the haunt of artists and Bohemians in the late 19C; its steep and narrow lanes and precipitous stairways still evoke the picturesque village it once was. The mound rises abruptly above the city's roofs and at its centre is **Place du Tertre★★** with its "art market".
The exotic outline of the **Sacré-Cœur Basilica★★**, a place of perpetual pilgrimage, rises nearby. The basilica offers an incomparable **panorama★★★** over the whole city.

★★★**Champs-Élysées** – *See above.*

★★★**Eiffel Tower** – *See above.*

★★★**Louvre Museum** – *See above.*

★★★ **Notre-Dame Cathedral** – *See above.*

★★★ **The Marais** – *See above.*

★★**St-Germain-des-Prés** – Antique dealers, literary cafés, smart shops and a lively night life may all be found in this former centre of international Bohemian life.

★★**Georges Pompidou Centre** ⊘ – The old Beaubourg district has been transformed by the construction of this cultural centre with its library, exhibitions and Museum of Modern Art.

★★**La Défense area** – *See above.*

★★ **Chaillot Palace** – *See above.*

PÉRONNE

Population 8 497
Michelin map 53 fold 13 or 236 fold 26

At the confluence of the River Cologne and the Somme stands the old fortified town of Péronne, stretching between fish-filled lakes and **"hardines"**, marshland vegetable gardens similar to the *hortillonages (qv)* of Amiens. This is an eel centre, which is reflected in the local gastronomy: eel pâté, smoked eels.
The commercial port, on the north canal, is flanked by a yacht harbour.

Miseries of War – In 1536 the town suffered a violent assault by the troops of Charles V of Spain; one heroic woman, however, saved the day: **Marie Fouré** managed to galvanise a resistance and the assailants were forced to lift their siege. Each July a procession through the town and a fête commemorate the occasion.
In 1870 Péronne was besieged by the Prussians who bombarded the town for 13 days.
During the Battle of the Somme in 1916 Péronne was occupied by the Germans. That year and the next saw the destruction of virtually the entire town.

SIGHTS

★**Historial de la Grande Guerre** ⊘ – The unusual and innovative Museum of the Great War is housed in a modern building standing on stilts behind the 13C castle, beside Cam Lake. Access to the museum is through an opening carved into the wall of the castle.
Louis XI was held prisoner by Charles the Bold in one of the towers here.
The museum presents an overview of the circumstances and unfolding events concerning the different countries involved on the eve of the First World War and throughout hostilities.
Maps, some of them illuminated, illustrate at regular intervals the development of battles on various fronts. A large collection of objects, works of art, documents, letters and postcards reveal the thoughts and the pattern of daily life for those caught up in the conflict.
Uniforms, arms and personal effects show the differences and the similarities between men of opposing sides.
Clips from archive films are shown on videos dotted around the museum; a flim by a British soldier shows the Battle of the Somme.

Hôtel de Ville (Town Hall) – *Place du Cdt Daudré.* This building presents a Renaissance façade flanked by turrets towards the square, and a Louis XVI front towards Rue St-Sauveur. Inside, the **Danicourt Museum** ⊘ contains a precious collection of ancient coins and Greco-Roman and Merovingian jewellery.

Porte de Bretagne – *Off Rue St-Sauveur.* This gateway dates from 1602 and was one of two entrances giving access through the town walls, which were destroyed before the First World War. It is now a freestanding brick pavilion with a slate roof, and is adorned with the emblem of Péronne.
Beyond the moat, walk through the gate of the demilune and follow the old brick ramparts with stone courses (16C-17C) for an attractive view over the Cologne lakes and the "hardines".

PIERREFONDS CASTLE ★★

Michelin map 106 fold 11 (inset) or 237 fold 8 – Local map Compiègne Forest

This famous castle rises above a pretty town which, in its heyday, was a fashionable spa resort. A small lake adds to the romantic image.
A **tourist train** ⓥ offers various rides across the town.

Louis of Orléans' Castle – A castle has stood on this site since the 12C. The Valois earldom – which was elevated to a duchy when Charles VI gave it to his brother, Louis of Orléans – consisted of the castellany of Pierrefonds together with Béthisy, Crépy and Ferté-Milon.
Louis of Orléans assumed the regency during the king's madness but was assassinated in 1407 by his cousin John the Fearless, Duke of Burgundy. Before his death he constructed a chain of fortresses on his Valois lands, of which Pierrefonds was the linchpin; to the south, barely 7 miles apart, stand the castles of Verberie, Béthisy, Crépy, Vez, Villers-Cotterêts and Ferté-Milon forming a barrier from the River Oise to the Ourcq. The Prince also had the medieval castle completely rebuilt by the King's architect, Jean le Noir, and Pierrefonds triumphantly withstood sieges by the English, the Burgundians and the royal troops. In the 16C the castle passed to Antoine d'Estrées, Marquess of Coeuvres and father of the beautiful Gabrielle. On the death of Henri IV the Marquess took sides with the Prince of Condé against the young Louis XII: besieged once again by the royal forces, the castle was finally seized and dismantled.

Viollet-le-Duc's Castle – In 1813 Napoleon I bought the castle ruins for a little under 3 000 francs. Napoleon III, an enthusiastic archeologist and since his days in the army passionate about the art of sieges, entrusted its restoration in 1857 to Viollet-le-Duc. It was only a matter of returning parts of it (the keep and annexes) to an inhabitable condition, leaving the smaller courtyards and towers as "picturesque ruins". At the end of 1861, however, the programme of works took on an altogether different, larger dimension: Pierrefonds was to be transformed into an Imperial residence. Work lasted until 1884 and cost 5 million francs, 4 million of which was deducted from the Emperor's civil list.
Fascinated by medieval life and Gothic art in particular, Viollet-le-Duc set about a complete reconstruction of the castle, following the basic shapes that were already outlined by the numerous walls and fragments remaining at the time.
Aiming at all times to "adapt the medieval architecture to modern needs" the architect nevertheless did not hesitate to invent parts of the building – encountering severe criticism from specialists in military architecture and purists when he did – and to give free rein to his ideas for the painted and carved decoration.

TOUR ⓥ

Leave the car in the town hall square (Place de l'Hôtel de Ville) and approach the main entrance to the castle at the foot of the Arthus Tower.

Exterior – The quadrangular castle (103m - 337ft long, 88m - 288ft wide) has a large defensive tower at each corner and in the middle of the walls. On three sides it overlooks the village, almost vertically; to the south a deep moat separates the castle from the plateau.
The walls have two sentry walks, one above the other: the lower, covered one is dressed with machicolations; the upper one only has merlons. The towers (38m - 124ft high with walls 5 to 6m – 16 to 20ft thick) are crowned with two storeys of defences: from the cart road *(route charretière)* they are a formidable sight. Eight statues of named military heroes *(preux)* adorn them, indicating the building's political significance: Arthus, Alexander, Godefroy, Joshua, Hector, Judas Maccabaeus, Charlemagne and Caesar.

Pierrefonds Castle

On the chapel roof stands a copper statue of St Michael. Having walked along the esplanade, cross a first ditch to reach the forecourt known as Les Grandes Lices. A double drawbridge (1) (one lane for pedestrians, the other for vehicles) leads to the castle doorway which opens into the main courtyard.

Interior – A permanent exhibition celebrates Viollet-le-Duc and his work (engravings, paintings, photographs of the ruins, history of the castle etc).

The main front appears with its basket-handle arcading forming a covered shelter, surmounted by a gallery. Neither of these existed in the original castle, but were created by Viollet-le-Duc, freely inspired by the courtyard at Blois Château. The equestrian statue of Louis of Orléans (2) by Frémiet (1868) stands before the monumental stairway.

ESCALIER VIOLLET-LE-DUC

The inside of the chapel, heightened by Viollet-le-Duc, presents a bold elevation with a vaulted gallery above the apse, which was another of the architect's inventions.

The doorway's pier incorporates a figure of St James the Great with Viollet-le-Duc's features.

The keep, where the lord had his living quarters, rises between the chapel and the entrance. Viollet-le-Duc accentuated its residential function by giving it an elegant open stairway. It is flanked by three towers: two of them round on the outside, the other square on the inside.

The provisions courtyard between the keep and the chapel communicates with the main courtyard by means of a postern gate and with the outside world by another postern, 10m - 30ft above the foot of the castle walls. To introduce food and other supplies into the fortress, a steeply-inclined wooden ramp was lowered; provisions were then dragged up.

Keep Rooms (Logis au donjon) – Reaching the first floor of the keep, the tour leads through the Imperial couple's rooms: the Great Room (3) with woodwork and a few, rare pieces of furniture designed by Viollet-le-Duc. Among the symbolic decorative motifs, notice the Napoleonic eagle, the thistle (Empress Eugénie's emblem) and on the chimneypiece the heraldic arms of Louis of Orléans (the "broken" arms of France) and another family emblem, the entwined staff. Beyond the Emperor's Room (4) (view down over the fortified entrance) the tour leads to the Hall of the Heroines, leaving the keep.

Hall of the Heroines (Salle des "Preuses") – This timber-ceilinged hall (52m by 9m - 170ft by 29ft) was created by Viollet-le-Duc. The mantelpiece of the double chimney (5), with its 15C base, is decorated with statues of nine women, heroines from chivalrous stories. The central figure of Semiramis, Queen of Assyria and legendarily of captivating beauty, has the features of the Empress whilst the others are portraits of ladies of the court.

Alexander Tower and north sentry walk (Tour d'Alexandre et chemin de ronde Nord) – The original walls on this side of the ruins still stand 22m - 72ft high: note the different colour of the stones. Along the sentry walk Viollet-le-Duc highlighted the last advance in defence systems before the arrival of the cannon: level walkways without steps or narrow doorways, which allowed the defenders (housed in nearby barracks) to muster quickly at critical points without blundering into obstacles. The view extends over Pierrefonds Valley.

Guardroom or Mercenaries' Room (Salle des gardes ou des mercenaires) – A double spiral staircase (6) leads down to this room which now houses beautiful lapidary fragments: remains of the original 15C statues of the heroic figures on each tower. The tour ends at the model of the castle.

Return to the town by the direct staircase (towards the car park).

Consult the Map of Places to Stay at the beginning of the guide to choose a suitable location.

POISSY

Population 36 745
Michelin map 101 folds 11, 12 or 106 fold 17
Town plan in the current Michelin Red Guide France

The town of Poissy, situated on the banks of the Seine, was a royal residence as early as the 5C. St Louis was christened here in 1214; the king's private correspondence was even signed Louis de Poissy. The château used to stand on Place Meissonnier but it was demolished by Charles V.

An abbey for Augustinian nuns founded in the 11C was offered to members of the Dominican order by Philip the Fair. From 9 September to 13 October 1561 the abbey refectory hosted the **Poissy Symposium**: Catholics and Protestants were invited to discuss their differences at the instigation of Chancellor Michel de l'Hôpital. The debate was attended by the papal legate, 16 cardinals, 40 bishops and the head of the Jesuits on the one side, and by an important group of theologians led by Theodore Beza on the other. The symposium lasted seventeen days. Unfortunately, these high-level talks proved vain and the divide between the two parties was even greater after the conference.

Up to the middle of the last century, Poissy was the main market town for the cattle that were sent to Paris. Today, it is the site of a large automobile plant (Talbot).

★Collégiale Notre-Dame (Collegiate Church of Our Lady) – The greater part of the building is Romanesque, dating from the 11C and 12C. Several chapels were added in the 15C and the whole church was restored by Viollet-le-Duc. The front tower, built in the Romanesque style, once served as a porch-belfry. The square base of the tower develops to an octagonal section on the highest level, ending in a stone spire. The central tower, also Romanesque, is eight-sided through two floors, and ends in a timberwork spire.

Interior – The vaulting of the nave now features ribbing. The capitals of the south columns in the first two bays were remodelled in the 17C. The other capitals feature interlacing, monsters and foliage motifs. Some of them are thought to be older than this building and were probably taken from another church. The nave is very well lit owing to the installation of a triforium by Viollet-le-Duc in the 3 bays nearest to the chancel, which is circled by an ambulatory with groined vaulting. The side chapels – added in the 15C – pay homage to the various trade guilds: butchers, fishermen, etc.

The first chapel to the right of the doorway contains fragments of the font used for St Louis' christening, displayed behind railings. For many centuries, the faithful would scrape the stone sides, dissolve the dust in a glass of water and drink the potion as a remedy for high fever. This explains why the font is in such bad condition. The central Lady Chapel is the work of Viollet-le-Duc. The statue of the Virgin and Child is attributed to the Duchess of Uzès (c1890).

The most impressive furnishings are in the first chapel on the right: majestic 15C statues of John the Baptist and St Barbara, and a superb 16C Entombment *(see below)* portraying Mary, John, Mary Magdalene, the Holy Women, Nicodemus and Joseph of Arimathea.

Musée du Jouet (Toy Museum) ⓥ – The toys and games exhibited cover the period until the advent of television, and are housed in a building flanked by towers, which used to be the fortified entrance to the "**Abbey**" (the old **St Louis Priory** – ancien Prieuré St-Louis) which hosted the Poissy Symposium.

The ground floor contains an important collection of dolls, including many made by the great 19C French manufacturers such as Jumeau; wax and wood gave way to porcelain and biscuit, which in turn were replaced by celluloid and developed with the introduction of pivoting heads and articulated limbs...

16C Entombment in Notre-Dame Church, Poissy

A cabinet on the first floor houses a number of magic lanterns for games with hand-painted glass plates, shadow pantomimes and other optical entertainments. A separate exhibition presents teddy bears and wooden animals, as well as scientific and technical toys.

On the second floor, the former attic houses a selection of figurines, inanimate and mechanical toys, ranging from ordinary items to the miniature car models manufactured in one of Citroën's special workshops between 1923 and 1940.

Musée d'Art et d'Histoire (Art and History Museum) ⊙ – *12 Rue St-Louis*. The history of Poissy from Merovingian times (sarcophagi) up to the present day (automobile industry) is presented in a simple, pleasing manner. One of the glass cabinets displays numerous seals, some of which date back to the 12C, other exhibits include a painting by Meissonnier depicting summer bathing in the Seine, a splendid 16C painted wooden statue taken from the Church of Our Lady etc.

Villa Savoye ⊙ – *82 Rue de Villiers*. This masterpiece of modern architecture was designed in 1929 by **Le Corbusier** and Pierre Jeanneret for the industrialist Savoye. The use of cylindrical piles made it possible to do away with the supporting walls and introduce huge glass surfaces. The main rooms are located on the first floor, at a height of 3.5m - 12ft. They are arranged around a large terrace which opens onto the countryside, as does the curved solarium occupying the top level of the house. The Villa Savoye – evocatively called The Daylight Hours – features a ramp leading to the upper levels and a spiral stair with vertical lines deliberately brought in to counter the horizontal configuration of the villa.

PORT-ROYAL-DES-CHAMPS ABBEY ★

Michelin map 101 fold 21 or 106 fold 29

Little remains of this famous abbey, which was the scene of a serious religious dispute for more than one hundred years of French history.

An abbess aged eleven – In 1204 an abbey for Cistercian nuns was founded in Porrois, a town later known as Port-Royal. Although this order is supposed to be strict, the rules grew extremely lax over a period of four centuries and by the turn of the 17C, the 10 nuns and 6 novices who resided at the abbey were leading a most unsaintly life: the cloister had become a promenade, fasting was a bygone practice and the vows of poverty were hardly compatible with the entertaining carried out at the abbey, including Carnival celebrations. In 1602 **Angélique Arnauld**, the 11-year-old daughter of an important family of lawyers was passed off as 17 and appointed Abbess of Port-Royal.

A reformer without mercy – Recovering from a bout of ill health, Mother Angélique realised where her duty lay and set about reforming her nunnery. She re-instated the enclosure and would not receive her mother, nor her father, except in the parlour, despite their repeated supplications and threats (1609). She introduced the perpetual adoration of the Blessed Sacrament, and imposed observance of the Cistercian rule, meditation and manual labour. The abbey was transformed and greeted an increasing number of novices. Mother Angélique chose Jean Duvergier de Hauranne, better known as the Abbot of St-Cyran, and Antoine Singlin to be the directors of Port-Royal-des-Champs. Like Angélique's parents and close relatives, many of whom were Calvinists, these austere confessors aspired to draw man away from earthly pleasures, make him see how corrupt he was and persuade him that divine grace alone could save him.

By 1625 it became necessary to find new premises for Port-Royal-des-Champs Abbey: the conventual buildings were too cramped and the surrounding marshes were ruining the nuns' health. The community moved to the capital, where it occupied new buildings and was renamed Port-Royal-de-Paris (now a maternity clinic).

The "Messieurs" of Port-Royal – One of Angélique's brothers was a theologian with great influence over his friends and relations, all of whom shared the pessimistic views propounded by the Abbot of St-Cyran. These men – known as the *Solitaires* or the *Messieurs de Port-Royal* – decided to withdraw from society in order to take up prayer and meditation. In 1637 they left Port-Royal-de-Paris and moved to Port-Royal-des-Champs, which had remained empty. There they applied themselves to the renovation of the abbey: they drained the land, raised the ground and enlarged the buildings. The following year, the Abbot of St-Cyran was incarcerated on the orders of Cardinal Richelieu, whom he had refused to serve. He died in 1643. Mother Angélique returned to Port-Royal-des-Champs in 1648 and from then on she and her flourishing community spent their time between this abbey and the one in Paris. The *Solitaires* were lodged in The Granges (barns) perched on top of a hill overlooking the old town of Porrois.

The Jansenist Movement – The growing influence that the Port-Royal *Messieurs* exerted over people at court and in Parliament, as well as over the younger generation, was resented by the Jesuits. They were especially indignant because the town of Port-Royal published the works of Cornelius Jansen, the former Bishop of Ypres, who had been entrusted by Louvain University with the task of refuting the doctrine advocated by the Jesuit Luis de Molina. Molina maintained that man could attain self-improvement through his own will-power, overcome all the problems in this world if he genuinely wished to do so and expect God to come to his assistance in any circumstances, simply on account of his merits; quite the opposite of the *Solitaires'* belief.

Cornelius Jansen died in 1638, soon after he completed his treaty *Augustinus*, unaware of the dramatic developments that were to follow its publication.

Problems of conscience – The theologians based at Port-Royal approved of *Augustinus* because it confirmed their views, many of which were close to the Calvinist theory. They had it published in France. The Jesuits retaliated by accusing the Jansenists of holding heretical views and produced a text of heretical "quotes" by Jansen.

The Church eventually took action with the result that, from 1653, nuns and priests were required to sign a document condemning Jansen; the nuns at Port-Royal agreed that the text was heretical but refused to sign the document on the grounds that the quotes were not Jansen's. The theological war raged on. In 1656 the celebrated mathematician and religious philosopher **Blaise Pascal**, who was in retreat near Port-Royal-des-Champs, published a series of pamphlets – the **Provinciales** – which attacked Jesuit theory and staunchly defended the cause at Port-Royal.

From 1661 Jansenists were again persecuted (the Pope's death in 1655 had produced a brief lull) and in that year Mother Angélique died. Eventually, with new publications and religious studies, the Jansenist question seemed to fade into oblivion.

In 1679 Louis XIV decided to settle the whole affair once and for all: the noviciate was forbidden, the *Solitaires* were dispersed and some went into exile. The nuns at Port-Royal-de-Paris disowned their counterparts at Port-Royal-des-Champs, who were the object of continual persecution. By 1705 they numbered only 25, the youngest being 60 years old. On 20 October 1709 the remaining nuns were expelled by 300 musketeers. The mortal remains of Jean Racine, who had been buried in the northern cemetery, were moved to St-Étienne-du-Mont, in Paris, and he now rests beside Blaise Pascal.

In 1710 the monastery buildings were razed to the ground. The graveyard was desecrated and the bones of the buried thrown into a communal grave in the cemetery of St-Lambert. The religious objects and furnishings went to a number of neighbouring parishes. The funeral slabs which once paved the church at Magny-les-Hameaux have now been re-assembled.

The Jansenist doctrine continued to arouse controversy under Louis XV. The Parlement de Paris refused to ratify royal edicts and ordinances, and priests refused to distribute the Blessed Sacraments. Clandestine publications began to circulate. Jansenism became a religious sect and it was only after the Revolution that its influence over French society started to decline.

RUINS AND MUSEUMS *2 hours*

The tour of Port-Royal estate comprises two parts. The pilgrimage to the abbey ruins is enhanced by a visit to the park (Longueville Gate, canal, view of the ruins). The Little Schools building is situated on a plateau, surrounded by pleasant, shaded grounds. It now houses a national museum, containing a wide range of documents on the former teaching colleges. The farmhouse where the hermits used to stay is a farming concern closed to the public.

Ruins and Abbey Museum ⓥ – The shaded path leading to the abbey branches off the Dampierre-Versailles road. *Park in the car park.*

The guided tour leads round a square area defined by avenues of lime trees, which was the site of the former cloister. The graveyard where the Cistercian nuns were buried after 1204 has been planted with grass. The church adjoined the cloister. Because the *Solitaires* had raised the floor level in an attempt to ward off the dampness, the building was razed down to the paving. When the original level was restored, the works uncovered the base of the pillars and the walls of the first building. An oratory built in 1891 stands on the site of the chancel.

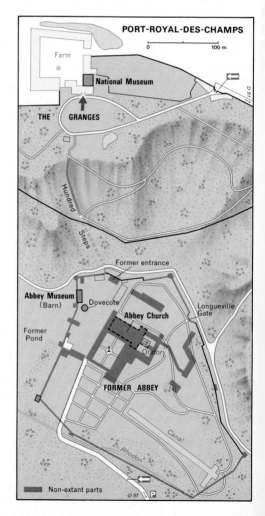

PORT-ROYAL-DES-CHAMPS

Farm

National Museum

THE GRANGES

Hundred Steps

Former entrance

Abbey Museum (Barn)
Dovecote
Abbey Church
Longueville Gate

Former Pond

Oratory

FORMER ABBEY

Canal

Rhodon

Non-extant parts

Next to the dovecote, a 17C barn houses a collection of paintings, engravings and souvenirs which illustrate and enliven the tour of the estate.

The Granges, where the *Solitaires* lodged, lies above the valley behind a cluster of trees. Ascending and descending the steep slope daily to attend Mass in the abbey must have required great effort; it is said that the Hundred Steps were designed by the *Messieurs* themselves. *The Hundred Steps may be climbed only during the summer, at weekends.*

Musée National des Granges de Port-Royal (Port-Royal Granges National Museum) ⊙ – The building was specially designed for the Little Schools (established by the *Messieurs* to provide religious education) in 1651-52 and presents a suitably austere front. In the 19C a Louis XIII-style wing was added.

Most of the rooms have been restored to their former condition and contain books, engravings and drawings on the history of the abbey and the Jansenist movement, the *Solitaires* and the Little Schools. Other exhibits include a series of portraits by Philippe de Champaigne depicting the principal Jansenist leaders. Note the touchingly naïve collection of 15 gouache paintings portraying the life of the Cistercian nuns.

Jean Racine lived at Port-Royal between the ages of 8 and 19, with a break at college in Paris. He was taught Greek and Latin and French versification, and was lectured on diction and rhetoric. The French poet learned much from his tutors and he soon became an outstanding reader. Louis XIV was spellbound by his beautiful voice and Racine's advice was sought by many as an actor.

Although the Jansenists were sceptical about the Arts, they accepted paintings inspired by authentic religious feelings. The exhibition hall dedicated to Philippe de Champaigne reminds visitors of the strong ties that linked this painter to the abbey: every day the nuns could admire his two works *Ecce Homo* and *Mater Dolorosa*.

Blaise Pascal *(see above)* was also a visitor; tradition has it that his knowledge of mathematics came in useful during his stay at the abbey when he produced the calculations for a new winch for the well: this enabled the nuns to draw a huge bucket as big as 9 ordinary buckets from a depth of 60m - 197ft with no extra effort.

ADDITIONAL SIGHT

St Lambert Church ⊙ – This small picturesque country church is perched above the village. A granite pyramid erected in the church cemetery in the early 20C marks the communal grave that received the remains of the Cistercian nuns and the *Solitaires*. To the right of the drive stands a cross bearing the words "To the human race" ("A la personne humaine"). It was set up in 1944 and celebrates the memory of all those who suffered during the Second World War, in particular in concentration camps, irrespective of race, nationality or creed.

PROVINS ★★

Population 11 608
Michelin map 61 fold 4 or 237 fold 33

Whether approaching Provins from the Brie plateau to the west or from Champagne and the Voulzie Valley, this medieval city presents the eye-catching vision of its distinctive silhouettes of the Caesar Tower and of the dome of St-Quiriace Church.

The lower town, a lively shopping centre, sits at the foot of the promontory and extends along the Voulzie and the Durteint rivers. The town is of monastic origin, developing from the 11C around a Benedictine priory.

The Provins fairs – Since the 10C Provins has been one of the economic capitals of the Champagne region, thanks to its two annual fairs which, with those of Troyes, were among the largest in the region. Traders from the north and from the Mediterranean came here for business.

Linens, silks, spices from the Orient and wine were traded, involving lots of other ancillary businesses: money agents and merchants among whom mingled the hard-working *bourgeoisie* of the region.

These fairs were prosperous until the early 14C, when the political and economical weight shifted to Paris, eclipsing the Champagne region.

Roses – According to tradition it was Thibaud IV the Troubadour who brought roses back from Syria and who planted them successfully here in Provins. Edmund Lancaster (1245-96), brother of the King of England, married Blanche of Artois and was for a while suzerain of Provins, at which time he introduced the red rose into his coat of arms. June is the best month to visit the banks of roses, at the **Pépinières et Roseraies Vizier** ⊙, Rue des Prés.

Common Rose of Provins,
by Pierre-Joseph Redouté

201

Bourreau (Sentier du) .... EZ 9
Capucins (R. des) .... EZ 12
Chapelle St-Jean (R.) .... DY 17
Clemenceau
  (R. Georges) .... DZ 22
Collège (R. du) .... EY 23
Couverte (R.) .... DY 28

Desmarets (R. Jean) .... DZ 29
Enfer (R. de l') .... EZ 32
Gambetta (Bd) .... EZ 38
Jacobins (R. des) .... EY 44
Madeleine (R. de la) .... DY 49
Moulin de la Ruelle (R.) .... DY 53
Opoix (R. Christophe) .... EZ 57
Ormerie (R. de l') .... DY 58
Palais (R. du) .... EY 59
Petits Lions
  (R. des) .... EY 62

Pie (R. de la) .... EZ 63
Pompidou (Av. Georges) ...... EZ 67
St-Quiriace (Pl.) .... EZ 77
Vieux Minage (R. du) .... DY 83

K Hostellerie
  de la Croix d'Or
L Hôtel des Lions
N Hôtel de Vauluisant
Q Maison de Saint Thibaud

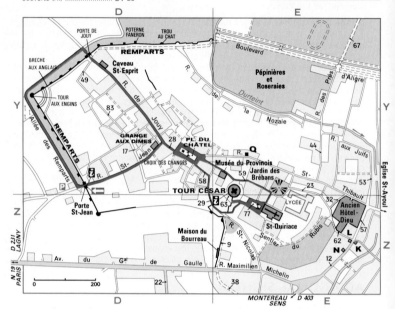

★★UPPER TOWN *1 1/2 hours*

It is advisable to park in the car park near Porte St-Jean. This is the location of the Tourist Office and the departure point for the small tourist train which tours the Upper Town and then returns to the Lower Town.

Porte St-Jean (DYZ) – St John's Gateway was built in the 13C. This stocky construction is flanked by two towers which are partially hidden by the buttresses which were added in the 14C to support the drawbridge.

Follow Allée des Remparts which overlooks the old ditches.

★★**Remparts** – These were built in the 12C and 13C along an existing line of defence, then altered on several occasions. They constitute a very fine example of medieval military architecture. The most interesting part runs between St John's Gateway and Jouy Gateway. The "Engine Tower" (Tour aux Engins), on the corner, links the two curtain walls; it derives its name from a barn nearby in which the war machines were housed.

In summer, on a space behind this tower, within the ramparts, the falconers of the "Aigles de Provins" company put on **a show** ⊙ of free-flying birds of prey; some raptors may also be viewed in cages.

Beyond the 12C Porte de Jouy take Rue de Jouy, which is lined by picturesque low houses with long tiled roofs or an overhanging upper storey. **Caveau St-Esprit** (open during events) was once the store of an old hospital which was destroyed by fire in the 17C.

★**Grange aux Dîmes** (DY) ⊙ – *Rue St-Jean.* This massive 13C building belonged to the canons of St-Quiriace, who hired out the space to merchants during the major fairs. When the fairs went into decline the barn became a store for the tithes *(dîmes)* levied on the harvests of the peasants.

Place du Châtel (DY) – This vast, peaceful square, rectangular in shape, is bordered by attractive old houses: the 15C House of the Four Gables (southwestern corner), the 13C House of Small-Chequerwork (northwest corner), the Shell Mansion to the north. The remains of St-Thibault Church (12C) stand on the northeastern corner. In the centre, next to an old well with a wrought-iron cage, stands the Croix des Changes, where the edicts of the Counts of Champagne were posted.

Musée du Provinois (EY) ⊙ – This local museum is housed in one of the oldest buildings in the town, "The Romanesque House". On the ground floor are displayed the sculpture and ceramic **collections**★, precious treasures of local medieval and Renaissance art. Exploiting the underground clay quarries enabled potters to produce pieces now noted for their remarkable variety and timelessness.

St-Quiriace Church (EZ) – The church was begun in the 11C, the transept and nave date from the 13C, the dome from the 17C. On the square in front of the church stands a Cross, on the site of the old belltower which collapsed in 1689.

★★Tour César (EYZ) ⊙ – This superb 12C keep, 44m - 144ft high and flanked by four turrets, is the emblem of the town. It was once part of the walls of the upper town. The pyramidal roof was built in the 16C. The "shirt" which encloses the base of the keep was added by the English during the Hundred Years War, in order to house the artillery.

The guard room on the first floor is octagonal and 11m - 36ft high; it is topped by vaulting formed of four arcades of pointed arches ending in a dome and pierced by an orifice through which the soldiers on the floor above were passed supplies. From the originally-open gallery which encircles the keep at the height of the turrets, the **view★** extends over the town and the surrounding countryside.

A very narrow stairway leads to the upper level. Under the fine 16C wooden roof are the bells of St-Quiriace, which have hung here since the church lost its belltower.

ADDITIONAL SIGHTS

St-Ayoul Church – In 1048 Thibaud I, count of Troyes and Meaux (and also count of Blois under the name Thibaud III), grand protector of the abbeys, installed the monks from Montier-la-Celle in the St-Ayoul district in the Lower Town.

Missing parts of the central doorway were replaced with new pieces by the sculptor Georges Jeanclos, who was responsible for the patinated bronze **statues★** which now harmonise well with the medieval reliefs.

Inside, in the north aisle, stand 16C **statues★★** of marble highlighted with gold: a graceful Blessed Virgin Mary and two musician angels with wonderfully draped clothes.

Underground Passages (EZ) ⊙ – *Entrance in Rue St-Thibault, left of the doorway to the old Hospice (Ancien Hôtel-Dieu).* There is a substantial network of underground passages around Provins, some marked with ancient graffiti. The section which is open to the public runs through a layer of a tufa which lies parallel to the base of the spur on which the Upper Town stands.

Maison du Bourreau (EZ) – The last occupant here was Charles-Henri Sanson who, together with his brother, the executioner *(bourreau)* of Paris, executed Louis XVI.

Le QUESNOY★

Population 4 890
Michelin map 53 fold 5 or 236 fold 18 - Town plan on following page

This quiet town of low, white-washed houses lying in a lush, lake-filled setting close to Mormal Forest is a fine example of French military architecture.

★FORTIFICATIONS *1 hour*

The perfectly-preserved fortifications still show clearly the unique qualities of the old strongpoint. Built of coarse stone and flint smothered in lime mortar then covered with bricks, they outline a polygon of defensive curtain walls along which jut out projecting bastions; despite apparently being in the style of Vauban *(qv)* these defences in fact date in part from the time of the Emperor Charles V (16C), for example the bastions with projecting towers. Various all-season paths offer pleasant walks, enabling enthusiasts of military architecture to study the layout of the defences *(information panels).*

Leave from Place du Général-Leclerc and head for the postern gate by Avenue d'Honneur des Néo-Zélandais.

The gateway gives access to the ditches, to the spot where the men of the New Zealand Rifle Brigade scaled the walls. The Monument to the New Zealanders (monument des Néo-Zélandais) commemorates their exploits.

Walk in the ditches around the south front of the ramparts.

From **Red Bridge Lake** (étang du Pont Rouge) ⊙ continue to **Vauban's Lake** (lac Vauban) which lies at the foot of the ramparts around Fauroeulx Gate (porte Fauroeulx). The bridge provides a lovely view of the red-brick curtain walls and their reflection in the blue-green waters.

Étang du Fer à Cheval (Horse-shoe Lake) ⊙ – Lying northwest of the town, the lake follows the original design by Vauban.
The calm and verdant setting is extremely peaceful.

EXCURSION

Potelle Castle – *2km - 1 mile east; take the road to Bavay and turn right beyond the railway.* In the 15C, this small medieval castle and chapel *(private)* were the property of Jean Carondelet, Chancellor to the Dukes of Burgundy.

LE QUESNOY

0 ___ 300 m

To choose a hotel, a restaurant or a campsite,
*consult the current edition of the annual **Michelin Red Guide France***
*and the **Michelin Guide Camping Caravaning France***

RAMBOUILLET ★

Population 24 343
Michelin map 106 fold 28 or 60 fold 9

The combination of attractive château, park and forest makes Rambouillet one of the main sights in Ile-de-France. Since 1897 it has been the official summer residence of the President of the French Republic.

HISTORICAL NOTES

The death of François I – At the age of 52, François I fell ill and his health started to decline. He became restless and left his St-Germain residence in February 1547. He went to stay with his major-domo at Villepreux, paid a visit to his treasurer's widow in Dampierre, spent Shrove Tuesday in Limours with his favourite the Duchess of Étampes and indulged in a three-day hunt in Rochefort-en-Yvelines.
On the way back, he dropped in to see the captain of his bodyguard Jacques d'Angennes at Rambouillet Château. The château was built in 1375 by Jean Bernier – a prominent court figure under Charles V – and had remained the property of the d'Angennes family since 1384. During his stay at Rambouillet François I's condition grew worse. Feeling that his end was drawing near, the King summoned his son Monseigneur le Dauphin and placed his servants and the French people in his hands. He died on 30 March 1547.

From Armenonville to Louis XVI – In 1706 Louis XIV bought Rambouillet for the Comte de Toulouse, one of Mme de Montespan's legitimated sons. He trebled the private apartments and added two perpendicular wings onto the main building. Under Louis XVI the estate came into the hands of the Comte de Toulouse's son the **duc de Penthièvre**. Like his father, he was a dedicated governor who applied himself to the improvement of his domain. He refurbished the grounds for his sister-in-law the Princesse de Lamballe. A close friend of Marie-Antoinette, the princess was butchered in the old La Force prison in Paris on 3 September 1792.
Louis XVI was an enthusiastic hunter who enjoyed staying at Rambouillet and he purchased the estate, and the opportunities it offered for hunting, in 1783.
The Queen was bored by life at the château, which she referred to as a "Gothic toad hole". In an attempt to divert her, the King gave orders to build the Dairy, a small pavilion reminiscent of the Trianon at Versailles *(qv)*. A landscape garden was started by Penthièvre and completed after plans by Hubert Robert.

A sense of destiny – In 1814 Marie-Louise met up with her father François II in Rambouillet: she decided to leave Napoleon and accompany the King of Rome to Vienna. A year later, on 29 June 1815, Napoleon made an unexpected stop here on his way from Malmaison *(qv)* to St Helena, to spend a night of melancholy reflection on his time here with Marie-Louise.

On 31 July 1830 Charles X arrived at Rambouillet, fleeing the insurrection at St-Cloud. For three days the ageing ruler debated what course of action to choose. The troops under his command disbanded and the rebellion was spreading towards Paris. He eventually abdicated and set sail for England.

It was in Rambouillet – where he stayed from 23 to 25 August 1944 – that General de Gaulle gave orders for the Leclerc Division to march towards Paris.

CHÂTEAU ⊘ *1 hour*

Leave from Place de la Libération, the site of the Town Hall *(if the car park is full, leave the car in the park – a number of exceptions are made)*.

The château presents a triangular shape owing to the fact that Napoleon dismantled the left wing. The large François I tower belonged to the 14C fortress. It is difficult to distinguish because of the numerous additions made by the Comte de Toulouse.

Mezzanine – The reception rooms commissioned by the Comte de Toulouse are embellished with superb rococo **wainscoting★**. Note the charming boudoir designed for the Comte's wife.

The corridor adjoining the François I tower leads through to the Imperial bathroom suite, adorned with Pompeian frescoes. This opens onto the Emperor's Bedchamber, where he spent the night on 29 June, and the study. It was in the dining room – the former ballroom – that Charles X signed the abdication document. The view of the park is stunning.

Ground Floor – The Renaissance-style Marble Hall, dating from the time of Henri II, is entirely lined with marble tiles.

★PARK ⊘

Parterre – The château is set in a pleasant formal garden. On the right stands a quincunx, surrounded by small clusters of trees. The perspective ends with the Rondeau Basin and a sweeping avenue of swamp cypresses planted in 1805.

Water gardens – These were remodelled by the duc de Penthièvre. The central canal is continued by a green carpet of lawn, the tapis vert. The other canals with their geometric lines enclose islets of greenery: Gourmet Island, Rock Island etc.

★**Laiterie de la Reine (Queen's Dairy)** ⊘ – Louis XVI had the dairy built to amuse his wife Marie-Antoinette. The small sandstone pavilion resembling a neo-Classical temple consists of two rooms. The first – which houses the actual dairy – features marble paving and a marble slab as table dating from the First Empire. The Sèvres porcelain bowls and jugs used for tasting have disappeared.

The room at the back was designed as an artificial grotto adorned with luxuriant vegetation. It presents a marble composition by Pierre Julien depicting a nymph and the she-goat Amalthea (1787).

★**Chaumière des Coquillages (Sea Shell Cottage)** ⊘ – The **landscape garden** in the park features a charming cottage built by Penthièvre for the Princesse de Lamballe. The walls of the rooms are encrusted with a variety of sea shells, chips of marble and mother-of-pearl. A small boudoir with painted panelling adjoins the main room.

Sea Shell Cottage, Rambouillet

ADDITIONAL SIGHTS

★**Bergerie Nationale (National Sheep Farm)** ⊘ – In 1786 Louis XVI decided to add to his amateur farming activities with the production of fine wool and so he purchased a flock of merinos from Spain. The sheep farm buildings were completed under the First Empire. Today it houses around 800 animals, including 120 merino sheep.

Musée Rambolitrain (Rambouillet Museum) ⊘ (**M**) – An astounding collection of toy trains and models explains the history of the railway from its early beginnings to the present day. A large O-shaped circuit occupies the whole of the second floor.

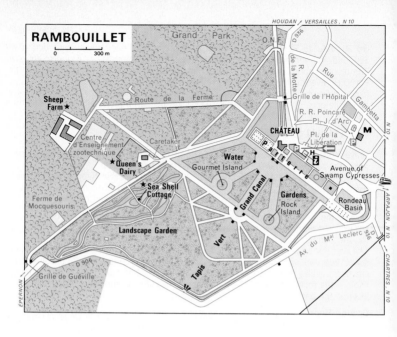

RAMBOUILLET

0   300 m

Grand Park   O.N.F.

Route   de   la   Ferme

Grille de l'Hôpital

Sheep
Farm ★

R. R. Poincaré
Pl. J. d'Arc
CHÂTEAU

Centre
d'Enseignement
zootechnique

Caretaker

Pl. de la
Libération

★Queen's
Dairy

Water
Gourmet Island

Avenue of
Swamp Cypresses

★Sea Shell
Cottage

Ferme de
Mocquesouris

Gardens
Rock
Island

Rondeau
Basin

Landscape Garden

Grille de Guéville

Av. du Ml Leclerc

★RAMBOUILLET FOREST

Rambouillet forest is part of the ancient Yveline forest; it covers a total area of 20 000ha - 50 000 acres, about two-thirds of which is State owned, and stretches over a clay plateau cut across by sandy vales. Trees were cleared in the Middle Ages and as a result the forest is divided into three large massifs by a number of clearings.

The forest, which is rich in game – deer, roe deer and wild boar – features mainly oaks (60 %) and pine trees (30 %), and is dotted with several ponds, lakes and rivers ⊙.

Cycling paths cross the forest – *see Michelin map 106 or 60.*

Round tour starting from Montfort-L'Amaury
21km - 12 miles - 1/2 hour Rtn on foot

Mormaire Château (Château de la Mormaire) – Built in stone and brick under Henri IV, this castle is reminiscent of the houses on Place des Vosges in Paris *(qv)*.

Gambaiseuil – Pop 31. A former woodcutter's village with a population now practically died out. There remain a few lived-in houses in the old church quarter.

New Lake (Étang Neuf) – Situated in a remote corner of the forest, this pond is a popular fishing haunt. It lies in pleasant surroundings planted with beech trees.

Grand Baliveau Crossroads – The road to the right of the sign "Route Forestière du Parc d'en Haut" offers a charming walk through a lovely green glade. One of the clearings affords a good **view★** of a secluded valley.

Round tour starting from Rambouillet
41km - 25 miles – about 1 hour then 1 1/2 hours Rtn on foot

Leave Rambouillet by D 906 (west). At Gazeran turn left into D 52; after 6.5km - 4 miles turn into the parking area in the dip of Drouette Valley.

Réserve Zoologique de Sauvage (Sauvage Wildlife Park) ⊙ – This 40ha - 100 acre park surrounded by oak groves contains free-roaming antelopes, deer and kangaroos, and many aquatic birds including rare swans and ducks together with a colony of flamingoes.

The Tropical Aviary features many tropical bird species: toucans, eclectus parrots, gouras, hornbills etc.

Return to Gazeran and continue north.

D'Angennes Rocks (Roches d'Angennes) – *Leave from the car park signposted "Zone de Silence des Rabières".* Walk 100yds up the steeper slope of the valley to find the real path leading to the summit. Go past an arena-shaped shelf circled by boulders to reach the crest: **view** of Guesle Valley and d'Angennes Pond, bordered by bulrushes, reeds and other aquatic plants.

Haut Planet Crossroads (Carrefour du Haut Planet) – The ledge of the Haut-Planet plateau – planted with birches and conifers – commands a sweeping **view★** of the northern St-Léger massif.

★**Haut Planet Belvedere** (Balcon du Haut Planet) – *Leave the car.* Bear right and take the straight path leading to Haut Planet, which crosses rough, hilly ground. After passing a spring fenced by wire netting on the right, the lane reaches a shaded terrace on the edge of the plateau (shelter for ramblers). The path – offering beautiful vistas all the way – eventually leads to a rocky promontory. *Return to the car.*

Étangs de Pourras et de St Hubert (Pourras and St Hubert Ponds) – *1/2 hour Rtn on foot. Leave from the large star-shaped St-Hubert crossroads. Follow the continuation of N 191, a rough track flanked by houses which leads to the road running between the two ponds.*

The ponds were part of one of Vauban's projects to create reservoirs for Versailles' water requirements. A series of six ponds separated by paths was laid out near the Dutch Pond (Étang de Hollande). Only the two end basins are filled with water. The two central ponds – known as Bourgneuf and Corbet – have been replaced by a rivulet overgrown with aquatic plants.

Yvelines Wildlife Park (Parc Animalier des Yvelines) ☉ – *Car park and entrance 500m - 550yds southwest of the road from Rambouillet to Rochefort (D 27).*

This 250ha - 650 acre reserve encloses a flat area of land populated with roe deer, wild boar and fallow deer, many of which are tame and may be approached.

RAMBURES CASTLE ★

Michelin map 52 fold 6 or 236 fold 22 (6km - 4 miles northeast of Blangy-sur-Bresle)

The **castle** (château) ☉ is an interesting example of 15C military architecture; during the Hundred Years War it played an important part, being a French enclave in the middle of the English-occupied territories, and it has been called "The key to the Vimeu". The castle has remained in the same family since the 15C.

From the outside the castle retains the look of a powerful fortress, with its enormous machicolated round towers and its rounded curtain walls (so that there were no level surfaces for the enemy to fire against), its deep moats and its tall watchtower. It was conceived to resist the artillery of the time and its brick walls are 3m - 10ft thick. In the 18C the castle was converted into a country residence and the courtyard façade was pierced with huge windows.

Inside, for many of the rooms the only source of daylight is still through loopholes, though the alterations begun in the 18C did provide reception rooms decorated with woodwork and marble chimneypieces *(first floor)*.

After a glance over the 15C sentry walk, the tour continues on the second floor, to the library-billiards room hung with a collection of portraits.

The kitchen is located in the old sentry post above the oubliettes; the cellars were used to shelter the villagers during invasions.

The English garden is planted with ancient trees.

La ROCHE-GUYON ★

Population 561
Michelin map 106 fold 2 or 55 fold 18

This village lies between the River Seine and the Vexin plateau. It developed at the foot of an old stronghold; its crumbling keep still dominates the steep, rocky ledge. Life at La Roche-Guyon has resumed its peaceful character since the bombings of July 1944 and the Battle of Normandy, when Marshal Rommel established his headquarters in La Roche-Guyon Château. In the 13C, a residential château was erected at the foot of the cliff not far from the fortress: it was linked to the keep by a flight of steps carved in the rock. François I and his numerous retinue took up residence here in 1546. Their stay was marred by an unfortunate incident; the young comte d'Enghien – whose glowing accomplishments in Ceresole two years earlier had earned him public recognition – died of a broken skull when a chest fell out of a window. La Roche-Guyon was made a duchy-peerage in 1621. Fifty-eight years later the title came into the hands of **François de la Rochefoucauld**, who wrote many of his famous *Maximes* at the château.

In 1816 Louis-François Auguste, **Duc de Rohan-Chabot,** acquired the estate. He lost his wife in 1819 and took holy orders at the age of 31. On his return, he continued to entertain at the château, combining acts of charity with the social favours of the *Ancien Régime*. Among the guests were fellow students at St-Sulpice Seminary and the young Romantic authors Victor Hugo, Alphonse de Lamartine, Hugues Lamennais, Henri Lacordaire and Abbot Dupanloup. They delighted in the grand but respectful services delivered in the underground chapel to the strains of a superb Italian organ. In 1829 the duke was appointed Archbishop of Besançon, and then Cardinal, and sold the château and its grounds to François de la Rochefoucauld-Liancourt. La Roche-Guyon has remained family property ever since.

★**The banks of the Seine** – The quayside promenade commands a good **view**★ of the sleepy countryside and the twisting river. Behind, the two castles stand side by side. The abutment pier of the former suspension bridge (dismantled in the 19C) provides a good observation point.

Château – *Private*. The splendid gates bearing La Rochefoucauld's coat of arms give onto a grassy courtyard surrounded by 18C stables. The main building stands on a terrace with arched foundations. It is set back slightly and believed to be 15C. It acquired its present appearance in the 18C, when the crenellations were taken down and a three-storey wing added onto the east side. The symmetrical square tower to the west was restored after the 1944 bombings. Much of the château was renovated in the 19C. The gates into the main court overlook the monumental entrance pavilion lying at the foot of the cliffs, among the remains of the 13C curtain wall and its crenellated turrets.

★Route des Crêtes (Ridge Road) – *Round tour of 4km - 2 1/2 miles.* Take the road to Gasny which passes the entrance to the famous troglodyte caves called **boves**, carved in the chalk. On reaching the pass, turn right into D 100, also known as "Route des Crêtes". When the estates no longer conceal the view of the river, park the car on a belvedere near a spinney of pine trees.

View★★ of one of the Seine's loops, circling the groves of Moisson Forest, and, further along the promontory, of the spurs of the Haute-Isle cliffs. In the foreground, down below, the truncated keep of La Roche-Guyon Château *(private).*
Continue along D 100. At the first junction, turn right into Charrière des Bois, which leads back to the starting point. The road follows a steep downward slope and passes under the 18C aqueduct that supplies water to the village and the château.

Arboretum de La Roche (La Roche Arboretum) – *On D 37 towards Amenucourt.* The arboretum, which spreads over 12ha - 29 acres, has been planted to define the Ile-de-France area. Each *département* is distinguished by a different species: oak for Seine-et-Marne, maple for Essonne, hornbeam for Val-de-Marne, ash for Val-d'Oise, cherry for Seine-Saint-Denis, lime for les Hauts-de-Seine, beech for Yvelines. The plane-trees in the middle represent Paris. They are all young trees, apart from the twenty-five-year-old Cedar of Lebanon at the central roundabout. Among the plantations, snaking stretches of lawn evoke the valleys.

ROYAUMONT ABBEY★★

Michelin map 106 fold 7 or 56 fold 11

Royaumont Abbey ☉ is an impressive symbol of the wealth that often accrued to the great French abbeys of the Middle Ages. A tour of this sanctuary is strongly recommended.
The abbey, founded in 1228 and completed in 1235, was occupied by members of the Cistercian Order. It was richly endowed by the king and his successors, which explains why it is graced with stately, elegant proportions. Six of St Louis' relatives – three children, a brother and two grandsons – were buried in the abbey. Their remains have since been moved to St-Denis *(qv).*
In 1791 Royaumont was sold as State property and the church dismantled. Since 1923 the abbatial palace and the grounds forming the estate have been separated from the abbey itself. In 1964 the last owners Isabel and Henri Gouïn (1900-77) created the Royaumont Foundation for the Advancement of Human Science, to which they offered their domain.

Royaumont Abbey

A cultural calling – In 1978 the abbey was assigned a new cultural mission. The international **Cultural Centre** set up on its premises ensures the preservation of the abbey; it also organises concerts, lectures, training seminars and exhibitions.

Church ruins – *See plan over.* Royaumont Church was consecrated in 1235. The fragments of columns that remain mark the foundations of this unusually large building (101m - 330ft long).
The chancel and its radiating chapels break with Cistercian tradition in that they do not feature a flat east end (eg Fontenay in Burgundy). A corner turret (1) belonging to the former north transept gives a fair idea of its elevation.

Abbey buildings – The cloisters surround a delightful garden. The east gallery (opposite the entry) is paralleled behind by a narrow, uncovered passageway known as the Lay Brothers Alley. This was built for the lay brothers in order that they might have access to their wing and to the church without passing through the cloisters, habitually reserved for the choir monks.

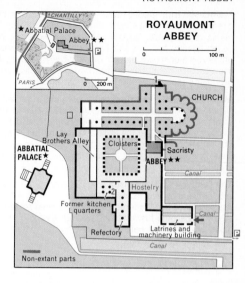

Refectory – This spacious dining hall – which consists of two aisles – is a masterpiece of Gothic architecture which could accommodate 60 choir monks without difficulty (note the monolithic shafts of the columns).

St Louis would take his turn at serving the monks at table while they sat in silence listening to the reader who stood erect in a pulpit carved out of the thick stone wall.

Former kitchen quarters – These house a statue of the Virgin of Royaumont (2), executed in the 14C.

The strange building resting on 31 semicircular arches astride the canal waters is the **latrines and machinery building.** In former times, the water reached a higher level and activated the machinery in the workshops. One of the water wheels has remained intact.

★**Palais Abbatial (Abbey Palace)** – Built on the eve of the Revolution for the last commendatory abbot of Royaumont, this white cubic construction is reminiscent of an Italian villa. In neo-Classical style, it is the work of Louis Le Masson, who trained at the Ponts-et-Chaussées Civil Engineering College. The façade facing the road to Chantilly is fronted by a charming pond.

RUEIL-MALMAISON★★

Population 66 401
Michelin map 101 folds 13, 14 or 106 fold 18 – Michelin plan 18

The town of Rueil is famed for Malmaison, the delightful estate that remains firmly attached to the name of Napoleon Bonaparte.

Malmaison during the Consulate – Marie-Joseph-Rose Tascher de la Pagerie, born in Martinique in 1763, the widow of Général de Beauharnais, married General **Bonaparte** in 1796. Three years later, while Napoleon was away on campaign, she bought Malmaison and the 260ha – 640 acres surrounding the château. The purchase was against her husband's wishes – although he liked the house, he had thought it too expensive – and, as a result, on his return, Napoleon passed a law forbidding married women from buying property without their husband's consent.

When Napoleon was First Consul he lived at the Tuileries, which he found "grand and boring". He decided to spend the end of each decade at Malmaison. These were the happiest moments of his married life. Elegant, lively **Josephine** – she had 600 dresses and would change five or six times a day – was the spirit of the party at Malmaison. Life was carefree and formal protocol was dropped.

The dining room at Malmaison

209

Malmaison in Imperial times – Crowned Emperor in 1804, Napoleon had no alternative but to stay at St-Cloud, Fontainebleau and the Tuileries, which were the official places of residence. Visits to Malmaison were too rare for the Empress' liking: she began to miss her splendid botanical and rose gardens, unparalleled in France. Josephine was a generous person with expensive tastes who spent money like water. When she ran into debt, her husband would complain bitterly but he invariably gave in, grumbling that this would be "the last time".

Malmaison after the divorce – Josephine returned here after her divorce in 1809. Napoleon had given her Malmaison, the Élysée and a château near Évreux. She fled the estate in 1814 but the Allied powers persuaded her to return. She behaved a little rashly by entertaining the Russian Tsar and the King of Prussia at Malmaison Château. She caught cold while staying with her daughter Queen Hortense at St Leu Château and died on 29 May 1814, at the age of 51. The debts she left behind were estimated at 3 million francs.

The farewell to Malmaison – Ten months after Josephine's death, Napoleon escaped from Elba and revisited Malmaison.
At the end of the Hundred Days he returned to the estate and stayed with Hortense, who had become his sister-in-law and was to give birth to Napoleon III. On 29 June 1815 the Emperor paid a last visit to the château and his family before leaving for Rochefort and St Helena.

★★MUSEUM ⊙

After Josephine's death, Malmaison Château and its 726ha - 1 800 acres of land passed to her son Prince Eugène, who died in 1824. The château was sold in 1828 and changed hands several times until it was bought by Napoleon III for the sum of one million francs. The Emperor undertook to restore the architecture and interior decoration to its former glory.

By 1877 the château was in a sorry state and the grounds reduced to a mere 60ha - 148 acres. Malmaison was sold as State property and saw yet another succession of owners.

The last proprietor, a Mr Osiris, acquired the estate – by now reduced to 6ha - 15 acres – in 1896, restored the château and bequeathed it to the State in 1904. The site of the Mausoleum of the Imperial Prince was donated to Malmaison by Prince Victor-Napoleon. Mr and Mrs Edward Tuck, an American couple who owned Bois-Préau Château, also gave their residence and its 19ha - 47 acre park, formerly part of Josephine's private gardens.

The entrance gate still sports its old-fashioned lanterns. The **château** was built around 1622 and when Josephine bought it in 1799 it featured only the central block; the square, jutting pavilions were added soon after and the veranda in 1801-02.

The museum was founded in 1906. It houses many exhibits which were purchased, donated or taken from either Malmaison, St-Cloud and the Tuileries, or from other national palaces connected with the Imperial family.

Ground Floor:
1) Vestibule built in the Antique style: busts of Napoleon's family.
2) Billiards Room: furniture belonging to the former gallery.
3) Salon: beautiful furniture, including Josephine's tapestry frame. Note the splendid fireplace, flanked by two paintings by Gérard and Girodet (based on the poems by Ossian).
4) Music Room: elegant furniture by the Jacob brothers, the Empress's harp, piano belonging to Queen Hortense.
5) Dining Room: walls adorned with delicate painted panels portraying dancers.
6) Council Chamber: tent-shaped décor, embellished with military furnishings. The armchairs were taken from the former château at St Cloud.
7) Library: original decoration by Percier and Fontaine (note how mirrored panels cleverly conceal heating vents), furniture by the Jacob brothers. The books and military maps come from Malmaison and the Tuileries.

FIRST FLOOR

GROUND FLOOR

ENTRANCE COURT

First Floor:
The first rooms were occupied by the Emperor when he spent his last days in Paris (June 1815), between the Battle of Waterloo and his departure for St Helena.
8) Imperial Salon: several large portraits of the Imperial family, painted by Gérard.
9) Emperor's Bedroom: Prince Eugène's bed and a private collection of furniture, both taken from the Tuileries. The Victory standing on a pedestal table is the same one the Emperor was holding at the top of the Grand Army column on Place Vendôme in Paris (it was torn down by the Commune in 1871). The walls are decorated with white hangings.

10) Marengo Room: paintings by David and Gros, ceremonial sabre and sword belonging to the First Consul.

11) Josephine's Room: portrait of the Empress, various personal souvenirs, porcelain services manufactured in Sèvres and Paris, picture representing the Emperor surrounded by the marshals who took part in the Battle of Austerlitz.

12) Exhibition Gallery: frieze taken from the Paris hôtel where the Imperial couple stayed, located in Rue Chanteraine, later renamed Rue de la Victoire. Josephine's dressing table, bust of the Empress by Chinard.

13 to 17) Josephine's Suite (antechamber, State bedchamber, ordinary bedroom, bathroom, boudoir): holy water stoup and sprinkle, portraits of the Empress by Gérard and Prud'hon, bed and travelling toilet case.

Pavilions – The **Osiris Pavilion** (Pavillon Osiris) contains all the collections that have been donated over the years: the works of art and Antique pieces belonging to Mr Osiris, a remarkable selection of snuff boxes, glass objects and caskets relating to the Napoleonic legend. The central area is dominated by Gérard's full-length portrait of Tsar Alexander I. The **Coach Pavilion** (Pavillon des Voitures) displays several Imperial carriages, including the landau that Blücher took to leave Waterloo in June 1815.

Park – In the park (now limited to 6ha - 15 acres) note the Marengo cedar tree planted soon after the victorious battle of 14 June 1800, the rose garden and a number of rare tree species.

At the end of an avenue of stately lime trees stands the **Summer House** (Pavillon de Travail d'Été) that Napoleon used in conjunction with the library.

Leave the estate on foot and skirt the park along Avenue Marmontel (gates). On the left lies the Mausoleum of the Imperial Prince, the son of Napoleon III, who was killed by members of the Zulu tribe in 1879.

The statue of the prince playing with his dog Nero is a replica of Jean-Baptiste Carpeaux' work; the original is in the Orsay Museum.

★**Bois-Préau Château** ⊙ – This château, bought by Josephine in 1810 and rebuilt in 1855, and its park were bequeathed by Mr and Mrs Edward Tuck. The exhibits displayed in Malmaison Museum include personal souvenirs left by Napoleon in St Helena, a number of items relating to the return of his ashes, and a wide selection of objects dedicated to the Napoleonic legend.

St Peter's and St Paul's Church – Built in the late 16C and completed under Richelieu, this church was restored thanks to the generosity of Napoleon III. The interior is Renaissance. The **organ case★**, made in Florence in the late 15C, is among the most beautiful in France and was a present from Napoleon III. To the right of the chancel lies the white marble tomb of the Empress Josephine. She is portrayed kneeling in formal attire, just as she was in David's painting of the coronation ceremony. Nearby stands a small mausoleum celebrating the memory of her uncle, governor of Martinique. The funeral monument to Queen Hortense – who died in 1837 – lies to the left of the chancel. The high altar features a beautiful 17C bronze low-relief representing the Embalming of Christ. It used to adorn the chapel of Malmaison Château.

Leave the church and bear left along D 39. Turn right into Rue Masséna to reach Rue Charles-Floquet, which becomes Chemin de Versailles. Enter the forest and continue to St Cucufa Lake. Park nearby.

Malmaison Forest – This 200ha - 500 acre forest is planted with oaks and chestnut trees; it is believed that a chapel was once built in the forest in honour of St Cucufa, who was made a martyr in 304 under the rule of Diocletian.

In a small, wooded vale lies **St Cucufa Lake★**, which is covered with water-lilies during the summer months. Josephine gave orders to build a dairy at the water's edge and it supplied the château with milk, butter and cheese. It has since disappeared. The wooden cottages lining the shores of the lake were built by the Empress Eugénie.

Return to the car. On leaving the forest, take the first turning on the right.

Avenue de la Châtaigneraie and Rue du Colonel de Rochebrune (D 180) cross the **Buzenval** district, where the heroes of the Paris Commune fought bravely in January 1871. A memorial has been erected on the top of the mound, which commands an extensive view of the northern lowlands.

MICHELIN GUIDES

The Red Guides (hotels and restaurants)
Benelux - Deutschland - España Portugal - Main Cities Europe - France - Great Britain and Ireland - Italia - Suisse

The Green Guides (fine art, historical monuments, scenic routes)
Austria - California - Canada - England: the West Country - France - Germany - Great Britain - Greece - Ireland - Italy - London - Mexico - Netherlands - New England - New York - Paris - Portugal - Quebec - Rome - Scotland - Spain - Switzerland - Washington

... and the collection of regional guides for France.

Population 16 776
Michelin map 51 fold 17 or 236 fold 17 – local map p 146 – Facilities p 10

The town is set on the west bank of the River Scarpe, which separates it from a vast forest; its name derives partly from St Amand, who was Bishop of Tongres in the 7C and founder of a Benedictine monastery here which became one of the most important abbeys in the north of France, and partly from its hot springs, used for the treatment of rheumatism and respiratory disorders.

Abbey – The last reconstruction of these monastic buildings was undertaken c1630 by Abbot Nicolas du Bois, with their solemn inauguration in 1673.

After the Revolution, only the impressive abbey tower and the priory or magistrates' buildings remained.

★Abbey Tower – Museum (Tour abbatiale – Musée) – This is a colossal building (82m - 269ft high) in a traditional Baroque style and was the narthex of a church with a nave (non-extant) which occupied part of what is now the public garden.

The façade is divided into five levels, each using a Classical order: from the bottom to the top the orders run through Tuscan, Doric, Ionic, Corinthian and Composite. The columns and mouldings set the rhythm for the arrangement with its curious "swollen" sculptures.

The damaged statues show God the Father, St Amand, St Benedict, St Martin and others.

At the centre of the first level, a *trompe-l'œil* depiction of a church sheltered a now-faint scene of Christ expelling the money-lenders from the Temple.

The tower above the balustrade is crowned with a vast dome surmounted by a generously carved lantern turret and lantern; inside hangs the 17C Great Bell, weighing 4 560kgs – nearly five tons.

Interior ☉ – The superb ground-floor chamber has carved stone vaulting around a central void to allow for the passage of the bells. Masks and scrolls, niches and stoups evoke the Antwerp mannerist style. Temporary exhibitions are held here. The first floor, with its lovely ribbed vault, houses a collection of 18C *faiences* from the two local potteries, Desmontiers and Fauquez; the collection includes over 300 pieces.

Climbing the tower *(362 steps)* gives a good **view** of the 17C timberwork. The workings of the 17C clock can be seen before reaching the bells themselves (48 of them), electrically operated each day between 12 noon and 1230. An outside gallery offers a wide **panorama** over the Scarpe Valley and Raismes Forest as far as Valenciennes.

Magistrates' building, St-Amand-les-Eaux

Priory or Magistrates' Building (Prieuré ou échevinage) ☉ – The priory was conceived by Nicolas du Bois as both the prior's residence and an entrance pavilion to the abbey, and was also used by the "magistracy" comprising the mayor and his judges.

The façade, flanked by towers with domes and a lantern, has a sandstone base and is in typically Flemish Baroque style: stone surrounds carved to suggest worm-tracks, ringed columns, sculpted cartouches. The door is surmounted by a proclamations balcony and the belfry houses the original "proclamations bell".

Inside, on the first floor, the Chamber of the Justice of the Peace (salle de justice de Paix) still has its original decor. On the second floor, two symmetrical rooms in the towers are covered by beautiful domed vaulting with radiating ribs. The magistrates' chamber, reserved for the local council, has been entirely redecorated; the **Watteau Salon**, so-named because in 1782 Louis Watteau of Lille, nephew of the great painter, adorned it with religious and allegorical paintings, has kept its period feel.

Établissement thermal (Spa) – *4km - 2 1/2 miles east by D 954 and D 151.*
The "Bubbling Fountain Spring" (les sources de Fontaine-Bouillon) was known to the Romans for its curative powers and was also a place of cult worship. When the exploitation of the waters began again in the 17C, under Vauban's direction, several ex-voto wooden statues left by those who had taken the waters in the past were found at the bottom of the basin.

The waters and mud, bubbling at a temperature of 26°C - 82°F, are among the most radioactive in France; they are used mainly for the treatment of rheumatism and for physical re-education.

The centre, which was rebuilt after the Second World War, also houses a hotel and a casino; its park (8ha - 20 acres) extends into the forest along Drève du Prince which was marked out on the orders of Louis Bonaparte, who took the waters here in 1805. A tall beech grove stretches nearby to the south.

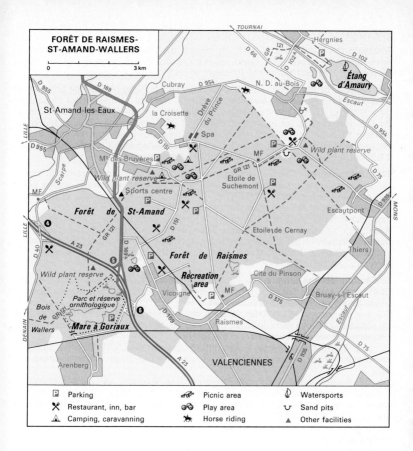

FORÊT DE RAISMES-
ST-AMAND-WALLERS

0 _____ 3 km

	Parking		Picnic area		Watersports
	Restaurant, inn, bar		Play area		Sand pits
	Camping, caravanning		Horse riding		Other facilities

In March 1793 Fontaine-Bouillon Château (since demolished) served as the head-quarters for **Dumouriez** after he was evacuated from Belgium. It is here that the victor of the battles of Valmy and Jemmapes received the commissioners of the Convention who had come to strip him of command; Dumouriez instead delivered them to the Austrian general Clairfayt. He then went over to the enemy with his staff, which included General Égalité, ex-duke of Chartres and future King Louis-Philippe.

★**Raismes-St-Amand-Wallers Forest** – This forest (4 600ha - 11 370 acres), an important section of a larger, 10 000ha - 24 710 acre Regional Nature Park (parc naturel régional), is however only a sliver of the great mantle which covered the Hainault region in the Middle Ages. The flat sand and clay soil, combined with the quarries of former mining works, has resulted in marshes and small lakes through-out the forest, which is made up of oak, beech, birch and poplar groves. Amenities include trails, bridleways, picnic areas, a recreation area (base de loisirs), a water-sports centre at the 100ha - 247 acre **Amaury Lake** (étang d'Amaury) and the **Goriaux Pool** (Mare à Goriaux) bird sanctuary (réserve ornithologique) where numerous bird species such as the crested grebe, the common coot and the little ringed plover live. A circuit in the area leads to several local dovecotes including that at **Bouvignies** ⊙ where documents and objects related to the breeding and training of pigeons are displayed.

ST-CLOUD★★

Population 28 597
Michelin map 101 folds 14, 24 or 106 fold 18 – Michelin plan 22

St-Cloud is situated on the west bank of the River Seine and belongs to the residential suburbs of the French capital. It is known mostly for its park, which once surrounded a splendid château.

Clodoald – Unlike his unfortunate brothers, Clodoald, the grandson of Clovis and Clotilda, escaped murder and became a disciple of the hermit Severin. He founded a monastery, where he died in 560; his tomb soon became a place of pilgrimage and the town of Nogent, which surrounded it, was subsequently renamed St-Cloud. The saint bequeathed his seignorial rights to the Bishops of Paris who, until 1839, held the title of Dukes of St-Cloud and Peers of France.

The assassination of Henri III – In 1589 Henri III launched an assault on Paris, which had fallen into the hands of the **Catholic League**: this religious alliance between members of the French nobility (led by the Guise and Montmorency families) and Spain had been formed in order to gain military and political power during a time of weak monarchy in France.

213

Following the King's alliance with his cousin, the Protestant Henri of Navarre, a vengeful young Jacobin friar called Jacques Clément gained admission to the King's presence and stabbed him in the abdomen. Henri III died two days later.

The Château of Monsieur – In 1658 the episcopal building became the property of Louis XIV's brother, known to all as "Monsieur". His first wife Henrietta of England died there in 1670. The Sun King's brother later married Charlotte-Elisabeth of Bavaria. He extended the grounds to 590ha - 1 460 acres and asked Jules Hardouin-Mansart to draw up the plans for a series of beautiful buildings. The park and its impressive cascade were conceived by **Le Nôtre.** Marie-Antoinette bought the estate in 1785 but it became State property during the Revolution.

The 18 Brumaire – When General Bonaparte returned from his campaigns in Egypt, the army troops and the French people saw him as the leader who would restore peace and order. On 18 Brumaire of the year VIII in the new French calendar (9 November 1799), the seat of the Consulate was moved to St-Cloud.
The following day, the Five Hundred held a meeting at the Orangery, presided over by Napoleon's brother Lucien Bonaparte. The General was greatly disconcerted by the hostile reception he got and was saved only by the swift intervention of this brother. Lucien summoned Joachim Murat, who cleared the assembly room instantly. The Directory was no longer.

St-Cloud under the Empire – In 1802 Bonaparte was appointed a consul for life and St-Cloud became his favourite official residence. He celebrated his civil wedding with Marie-Louise on the estate and followed it with a religious ceremony in the Square Salon of the Louvre (1810). Later, in 1814, the Prussian Marshal Gebhard Blücher took up residence at the château. In an act of vengeance, he cut the silk hangings to ribbons, and wrecked both the bedroom and the library.
It was at St-Cloud that Charles X signed the Ordinances of July 1830, which abolished the Charter and precipitated his fall. It was also from St-Cloud that he departed into exile.
On 1 December 1852 the Prince-President Louis-Napoleon was made Emperor. A meeting was held at St-Cloud Château on 15 July 1870, during which it was decided to declare war on Prussia. The building was badly damaged in a fire three months later; it was finally razed to the ground in 1891.

★★PARK ⊙

The 450ha - 1 110 acre park which spreads from the slopes of the Seine Valley to the Garches plateau has retained most of the original layout designed by Le Nôtre. In the former Guards' Pavilion, a **History Museum** (Musée Historique) ⊙ tells the story of the estate and its château, consumed by the raging flames in October 1870.

★**Grande Cascade (Great Cascade)** – Conceived in the 17C by Lepautre, these impressive falls were later enlarged by Jules Hardouin-Mansart. Dominated by allegorical statues of the rivers Seine and Marne, the waters of the cascade flow into a series of vases, basins and troughs before reaching the lower falls, from where they are channelled down to the edge of the park. The whole works are about 90m - 296ft long. At **Grandes Eaux★★** ⊙ the view is quite remarkable.

Grand Jet (Great Fountain) – Nestling in greenery near the Great Cascade, it is the most powerful fountain in the park and rises to a height of 42m - 138ft.

Terrace – A cluster of yew trees and a marble slab mark the former site of the château, which was also the start of the Tapis Vert lawns and their continuation, the Allée de Marnes perspective.
The private gardens used to spread on either side of this avenue.

★**Jardin du Trocadéro (Trocadero Gardens)** – These were laid out on the site of the former château; they date from the Restoration period. This beautiful landscape garden features numerous tree and flower species, a charming pond and an aviary. The far end of the terrace commands a view of Paris. In the foreground, note the Pavillon d'Artois, part of which was built in the 17C and which now houses the École Normale Supérieure (the prestigious teachers' training college).

Tapis Vert – Running from the Grande Gerbe Basin to Rond-Point des 24 Jets, these lawns command a lovely view of the parterres and the city of Paris.

Rond-Point de la Balustrade – On this site Napoleon erected a monument surmounted by a lantern which was lit when the Emperor was staying at the château. It was based on a model from ancient Greece, which is why the Parisians called it Demosthene's lantern. It was blown up by the Prussians in 1870. The terrace offers a superb **panorama★★** of Paris, stretching from the Bois de Boulogne to the woods of Clamart and Meudon.

Breteuil Pavilion – This 18C pavilion – St-Cloud's former Trianon – houses the International Bureau for Weights and Measures, the world centre of scientific meteorology, which still features the original standard metre.

La Fayette Memorial – *West of the park, along Boulevard Raymond-Poincaré (N 307).* The memorial was erected by an American foundation. It pays homage to the 209 pilots from the United States who volunteered to take part in the La Fayette Squadron during the First World War. The monument consists of an arch and a colonnade reflected in a small pond. The crypt beneath the terrace contains the mortal remains of the 67 pilots who perished, including the ace fighter Lufbery.

★**Pasteur Institute – Museum of Applied Research** ⊙ – *3 Boulevard Raymond-Poincaré*. In 1884 when **Louis Pasteur**, who had already done considerable research work, lacked space in Paris to pursue his studies on rabies, a decree ruled that he could move to the now State-owned Villeneuve-l'Étang estate; in 1885 he successfully invented the first vaccine for human use, crowning a lifelong career.

The museum is housed in the Hundred Guards' Pavilion, occupied by Napoleon III's soldiers in the 19C. It presents the history of the struggle against infectious diseases through the accomplishments of Pasteur and his disciples: Pierre Roux, Yersin, Gaston Ramon, Albert Calmette, Nicolle and Laveran, and concentrates on three major fields of research: serum therapy, vaccination and chemotherapy. The techniques used to overcome diseases such as diphtheria, tetanus, typhus, cholera, tuberculosis and polio are explained, together with the progress of modern research into hepatitis B, AIDS, immunology and artificial vaccines.

The room where Pasteur died in 1895 remains intact and features the family measuring rod bearing inscriptions made by Mme Pasteur. The study of Gaston Ramon, who discovered toxoids, has been reconstructed. The former drawing-room houses a collection of 19C instruments from medical laboratories: Elie Metchnikoff's microscope, Chamberland's sterilizer and Doctor Roux' optical bench.

TOWN

Overlooked by the spire of St-Clodoald Church (1865), the steep, narrow streets of the old town wind their way up the hillsides of the Seine Valley.

★**Stella Matutina Church** – *Place Henri-Chrétien along Avenue du Maréchal-Foch*. The church was consecrated in 1965: it is shaped as a huge circular tent made of wood, metal and glass. It is fixed to a concrete base by nine pivots and fronted by a porch roof in the shape of a helm. The converging lines of the copper roofing and the pine timbering create an impression of loftiness and soaring height.

Pont de St-Cloud (St-Cloud Bridge) – In the 8C a bridge was built across the River Seine. According to tradition, no King was to set foot on it, or he would die instantly. Until the middle of the 16C, French rulers would cross the river in a boat. However when François I died in Rambouillet, it was decided that the funeral procession would cross the famous bridge: no ill omens were feared as the King was already deceased. This put an end to the long-standing tradition. François' son Henri II replaced the old wooden bridge with a magnificent stone construction featuring 14 piers. The local villagers were astonished by such a massive display of stonework, which they claimed was the Devil's work, and the bridge had to be exorcised.

Michelin Maps, Red Guides and Green Guides are complementary publications - to be used together.

ST-DENIS CATHEDRAL★★★

Michelin map 101 fold 16 or 106 fold 19 – Michelin plan 20

In 1840 the locality of St-Denis numbered a few thousand inhabitants; the industrial revolution brought this number to 100 000 and made the town one of the main manufacturing centres of the northern suburbs.

The Gérard-Philipe Theatre and summer music festivals staged every year provide a wide range of intellectual and artistic activities. The most interesting sight in St-Denis, however, is its cathedral which houses the mausoleum of the Kings of France.

"Monsieur Saint Denis" – Legend has it that after being beheaded in Montmartre, the evangelist St Denis, the first bishop of Lutetia, started to walk, carrying his head in both hands. He was finally buried where he fell by a saintly woman, and an abbey developed on the site of his tomb, which soon became a popular place of pilgrimage. In actual fact, a Roman city Catolacus had existed here since the 1C AD as the site offered a commanding view of both the river and the Paris-Beauvais highway. It is believed that the man known as Monsieur (Monseigneur) St Denis was secretly buried in one of the fields around the city after his martyrdom.

In 475 a large village church was erected on the site. Dagobert I had it rebuilt and offered it to a Benedictine community who took charge of the pilgrimage. This abbey was to become the most wealthy and the most celebrated in France. Towards 750 the church was dismantled a second time and rebuilt by Pepin the Short, who set up a shrine under the chancel to receive the sacred remains of saints. The building as it stands today is principally the work of Abbot Suger (12C) and Pierre de Montreuil (13C).

Abbot Suger – The abbot's formidable personality dominates the history of the cathedral. He was born of a peasant family and was "given" to the abbey at the age of ten. His remarkable gifts caused him to gain ascendancy over one of his fellow novices, a young boy whose destiny was to become Louis VII. The King made friends with the monk, invited him to court and consulted him on numerous matters.

ST-DENIS CATHEDRAL

Elected Abbot of St-Denis in 1122, Suger personally drew up the plans for the abbey church. The minister of Louis VII, he was made Regent of France when the King took part in the Second Crusade. His wisdom and concern for public well-being were so great that when Louis VII returned, he gave him the name "Father of the Homeland".

The Lendit Fair – Lendit was an important trade fair founded by the abbot in 1109. It was held on St-Denis plain, on the site presently occupied by the Landy gasometers. It remained a major European event for over 600 years. A total of twelve hundred booths were placed at the disposal of the participants. Every year the University of Paris would travel to Lendit to buy the parchment used in the Montagne Ste-Geneviève faculties.

The Mausoleum of the Kings of France – Most of the kings of France from Dagobert I to Louis XVIII – a remarkable span of twelve centuries – were buried at St-Denis. In 1793 Barrère asked the Convention for permission to destroy the tombs. They were opened and the remains thrown into unnamed graves. Alexandre Lenoir salvaged the most precious tombs and moved them to Paris: he left them at the Petits-Augustins, later to become the Museum of French Monuments (Musée des Monuments Français). In 1816 Louis XVIII returned the tombs to the basilica.

Construction of St-Denis – This cathedral was a turning-point in the history of French architecture. It was the first large church to feature a chancel and many architects in the late 12C used it as a model for their own creations (eg Chartres, Senlis and Meaux). Suger supervised the construction of the west front and the first two bays of the nave from 1136 to 1140, the chancel and crypt between 1140 and 1144. The Carolingian nave was provisionally preserved and remodelled between 1145 and 1147. The amazing rapidity of the whole operation was due to Suger's dedication and to the help he received from his parishioners: they all teamed up to pull the wagons of stone from the limestone quarries of Pontoise.

In the early 13C the north tower was crowned by a magnificent stone spire. Work on the chancel was resumed and the transept, then the nave, were entirely restored. In 1247 Pierre de Montreuil was appointed master mason by St Louis: he remained in charge of the work until his death in 1267.

Decline – The basilica subsequently fell into disrepair. The French Revolution caused further ravages and in his *Genius of Christianity*, Chateaubriand lamented the sorry state of the church. Napoleon gave orders to repair the damage and reinstated public worship in 1806.

Restoration – Debret – the architect who took over in 1813 – aroused a wave of public indignation on account of his poor knowledge of medieval methods. For the spire, he used heavy materials which disrupted its gentle harmony. It collapsed in 1846 and had to be dismantled.

In 1847 Debret was succeeded by **Viollet-le-Duc**, who studied a number of original documents which guided him in his work. From 1858 up to his death (1879), he toiled relentlessly and produced the cathedral that stands today. A series of excavations in the crypt has revealed sections of the Carolingian martyrium and the remains of a Merovingian mausoleum (late-6C tomb of Princess Aregunde, the wife of Clotaire I, magnificent sarcophagi, splendid jewels). Foundations of earlier sanctuaries have also been uncovered.

Effigies of Marie-Antoinette and Louis XVI, St-Denis Cathedral

Recumbent figure of Jeanne de Bourbon, St-Denis Cathedral

TOUR *1 hour*

Exterior – The absence of the north tower mars the harmony of the west front. In the Middle Ages the building was fortified and some crenellations are still visible at the base of the towers. The tympanum on the central doorway represents the Last Judgment, that on the right doorway depicts the Last Communion of St Denis and on the left the Death of St Denis and his companions Rusticus and Eleutherus. All three doorways have been restored. The archshafts of the doorways feature the Wise and Foolish Virgins (*centre*), the labours of the months (*right*) and the signs of the Zodiac (*left*).

On the north side of the cathedral, the nave is supported by double flying buttresses. The transept, which presents a wonderful rose window, was initially to have had two towers but work stopped after the first floor. If the original plans had been carried out, the church would have had six towers altogether.

Interior – The cathedral is 108m - 354ft long, 38m - 125ft wide in the transept and 29m - 95ft high. These figures are slightly less than those of Notre-Dame in Paris.

The narthex is formed by the two bays beneath the towers. Part of its pointed vaulting, which rests on a series of sturdy pillars, was designed by Suger. The elegant nave is attributed to Pierre de Montreuil. The bays in the triforium open onto the exterior (one of the first of such arrangements). The stained-glass windows in the nave are modern.

★★★**The tombs** – *The following comments should help with the approximate dating of monuments simply from their appearance.* St-Denis Cathedral houses the remains of kings, queens and royal children, as well as those of leading personalities who served the French court, such as Bertrand du Gueslin (1). The mausoleum may be seen as a museum of French funeral art through the Middle Ages and during the Renaissance period (79 recumbent figures). The tombs have been empty since the Revolution.

After the 14C it was customary to remove the heart and viscera from the bodies of French kings before embalming them. The inner organs, the heart and the body were all buried in different places. The bodies were taken to St-Denis.

Up to the Renaissance, the only sculpture adorning tombs were **recumbent figures.** Note the funeral slab of Clovis (2) and Fredegunde (3), featuring a mosaic enhanced with copper lines, made in the 12C for St-Germain-des-Prés Church.

Around 1260 St Louis commissioned a series of effigies of all the rulers who had preceded him since the 7C. The figures were purely symbolic but they provide a telling example of how royalty was portrayed towards the mid 13C. They include the imposing tomb of Dagobert (4), with its lively, spirited scenes, the recumbent statues of Charles Martel (5) and Pepin the Short (6), and the female effigy carved in Tournai marble (7).

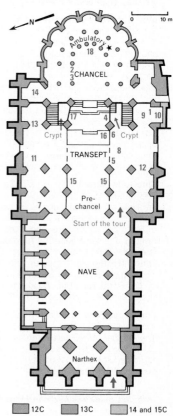

The statue of Philippe III the Bold (8), who died in 1285, shows an early concern for accurate portraiture and bears a strong resemblance to the living character.

Towards the middle of the 14C wellknown people had their tomb built when they were still alive. The effigies of Charles V by Beauneveu (9), Charles VI and Isabella of Bavaria (10) are therefore extremely lifelike.

Under the Renaissance, these **mausoleums** took on monumental proportions and were lavishly decorated. They were laid out on two levels, contrasting sharply with one another. The upper level featured the king and his wife, kneeling in full regalia. On the lower level, the deceased were pictured lying down as naked cadavers. Admire the twin monument built for Louis XII and Anne of Brittany (11), and that of François I and Claude de France (12), executed by Philibert Delorme and Pierre Bontemps.

Catherine de' Medici, who survived her husband Henri II by 30 years, gave orders to build the royal tomb. When she saw how she had been portrayed according to tradition, she fainted in horror and ordered a new effigy which substituted sleep for death. Both works are on display in the cathedral. Their making was supervised by Primaticcio (13), and Germain Pilon (14), respectively.

Chancel – The beautiful pre-Renaissance stalls (15), in the pre-chancel were taken from the Norman Château at Gaillon. On the right stands a splendid Romanesque **Virgin★** in painted wood (16), brought from St-Martin-des-Champs. The episcopal throne opposite (17) is a replica of Dagobert's royal seat (the original lies in the Medals and Antiquities Gallery at the Bibliothèque Nationale in Paris). At the far end, the modern reliquary of the Saints Denis, Rusticus and Eleutherius (18) stands on the edge of Suger's **ambulatory★**, characterised by wide arches and slim columns. The radiating chapels are decorated with several altarpieces and fragments of stained glass dating from the Gothic period.

★★Crypt – The lower ambulatory was built in the Romanesque style by Suger (12C) and restored by Viollet-le-Duc (acanthus capitals). In the centre stands a vaulted chapel known as Hilduin's Chapel (after the abbot who had it built in the 9C). Beneath its marble slab lies the burial vault of the Bourbon family, which houses the remains of Louis XVI, Marie-Antoinette and Louis XVIII, among others. The communal grave in the north transept received in 1817 the bones of around 800 kings and queens, royal highnesses, princes of the blood, Merovingians, Capetians and members of the Orléans and Valois dynasty.

ADDITIONAL SIGHTS

Ancienne Abbaye (Former Abbey) – *Private.* It adjoins the cathedral that was once the abbey church. The present conventual buildings date from the 18C and are the work of Robert de Cotte. In 1809 Napoleon I made the abbey the seat of a college for the daughters of holders of the French order of merit the **Légion d'Honneur.**

Musée d'Art et d'Histoire (Art and History Museum) ⊙ – *22 bis Rue Gabriel-Péri.* The museum is set up in the former Carmelite convent, part of which has been restored. The convent was founded by Cardinal de Bérulle in 1625 and occupied by Louis XV's daughter Madame Louise de France between 1770 and 1787. The refectory and the kitchen contain archeological exhibits discovered at St-Denis (fragments of medieval pottery). Many of the items on display come from the old hospital, including a superb apothecary's collection of ceramic phials and jars (17C and 18C).

The cells on the first floor contain many works of art, mementoes and paintings, including several by Guillot, evoking the daily life of the Carmelite nuns. Mystical adages have been inscribed on the walls.

On the second floor – where the king stayed when he visited his daughter – a host of documents present the Paris Commune of 1871 (audio-visual exhibition).

The **former Carmelite chapel** has a splendid Louis XVI dome. It was here that the prioress Louise de France died in 1787.

Christofle Museum ⊙ – *112 Rue Ambroise-Croizat.*

The famous gold and silverware manufacturing company – the first to apply the principle of electroplating – set up premises here in 1875. They became official supplier to Napoleon III and their silver pieces still adorn the tables of many heads of State and rulers throughout the world. The museum presents a number of rare exhibits and some beautiful reproductions crafted in the St-Denis workshops in the late 19C. The history of the silverware industry covers Antiquity, the Gallo-Roman period (Hildesheim treasure), the Renaissance (Henri II's ceremonial armour), the 18C (Vinsac ewer), the Second Empire and the present century up to 1960 (objects by Gio Ponti Sabattini, Wirkkala etc). The Design Department is currently run by Tony Bouilhet, grandson of the founder's nephew.

Courneuve Park – *2.5km - 1 1/2 miles east along Rue de Strasbourg and N 301 (on the right).*

This 440ha - 1090 acre stretch of greenery features a cycling track, riding lanes, a ski jump, a little train, sporting equipment, playgrounds for children and other facilities. Rowing boats and pedaloes may be hired to explore the 12ha - 30 acre lake *(bathing prohibited).*

*With this guide use **Michelin Maps** nos 51, 52, 53, 55, 56, 60, 61, 101, 106, 236 and 237.*

Population 39 925
Michelin map 101 fold 12 or 106 fold 17 – Michelin plan 18

St-Germain is both a residential district and a popular resort with many tourists, attracted by its château, its huge terrace and its forest.

HISTORICAL NOTES

The Old Castle – In the 12C Louis VI, the Fat, eager to exploit the strategic position of the St-Germain hillside, built a fortified stronghold on the site of the present château. In 1230 St Louis added a charming little chapel which still stands today. The fortress was destroyed during the Hundred Years War and restored by Charles V around 1368. In 1514 Louis XII married his daughter Claude de France to the duc d'Angoulème, who became François I the following year. The young ruler was acquainted with Italian culture and the ancient citadel was hardly suited to his taste for palatial comfort and luxury. In 1539 he had the whole building razed with the exception of Charles V's keep and the chapel built by St Louis. The reconstruction was entrusted to Pierre Chambiges, who produced the present château.

New Château – Even the new building presented itself as a fortified structure equipped with machicolations and defended by a garrison numbering 3 000. Henri II, who wanted a real country house, commissioned Philibert Delorme to draw up plans for a New Château on the edge of the plateau. The construction work was completed under Henri IV. The château became famous on account of its fantastic location and the terraces built along the slopes overlooking the River Seine. The area beneath the foundation arches has been arranged into artificial grottoes where hydraulically-propelled automatons re-enact mythological scenes: Orpheus playing the viola with a bow, Neptune's chariot in full motion etc. Henri IV was a mischievous man: he installed a system whereby fountains of water would spring out from all directions at the end of the show, drenching the King's guests. This wonderful mechanism was the work of the Francine, a family of Italian engineers, to whom Louis XIV later entrusted the waterworks of Versailles.

Chronology of court events – The court occupied both the New Château and the Old Castle which were used as a palatial residence, or a safe retreat when riots broke out in Paris.
Henri II, Charles IX and Louis XIV were all born at St-Germain. Louis XIII died here. Mary Queen of Scots lived here between the ages of 6 and 16. In 1558 she married the Dauphin François, aged only 15, and was crowned Queen of France the following year. Her husband died after a year, however, and she was forced to return to Scotland, where her tragic destiny led her to die on the scaffold.

Mansart's improvements – Louis XIV – who was born, christened and brought up at St-Germain – grew fond of the château. As king, he paid frequent visits to the estate. The apartments of the Old Castle had become too cramped for Louis' liking and he commissioned **Jules Hardouin-Mansart** to build five large pavilions as a replacement for the five corner turrets adjoining the outer walls. Le Nôtre conceived the plans for the park, the terrace and the forest: in 1665 the grounds were replanted with five and a half million shrubs. In 1682 the court moved from St Germain to Versailles. In 1689 the deposed King of England James II came to stay at the Old Castle, where he died, in great financial straits, in the Odour of Sanctity (funeral monument in St Germain Church, facing the château).
Maréchal Louis de Noailles (1713-93) subsequently became the important figure at St Germain as governor of the château and its estate, which was carved up and acquired the reputation of being the most fashionable residential area in town.

Final developments – In 1776 the badly dilapidated New Château was ceded to the comte d'Artois by his brother Louis XVI. The future king Charles X had the building dismantled, except for the Henri IV pavilion on the terrace and the Sully Pavilion, located near Le Pecq. He originally intended to reconstruct the building according to new plans but he dropped the work at St Germain when he purchased the château at Maisons *(qv)*. The remains, together with the park, were sold during the Revolution.
The Old Castle was stripped of its furniture. Under Napoleon I it was the seat of a cavalry college, under Louis-Philippe it housed a military penitentiary and in 1855 it was evacuated by Napoleon III. It was then entirely restored under the guidance of the architect Millet, succeeded by Daumet. In 1867 Napoleon III inaugurated the National Museum of French Antiquities which he had set up on the premises. The signing of the 1919 peace treaty with Austria took place in the château at St Germain.

THE CHÂTEAU AND ITS NEIGHBOURHOOD *3 1/2 hours*

The most striking approach to the château is from the north, along Avenue des Loges. The tour starts from the square beside the château, Place Charles-de-Gaulle. The express RER line (which runs underground at St-Germain and has an exit giving onto the square) has replaced the famous railway track between Paris and St-Germain: its inauguration between Le Pecq and the French capital on 26 August 1837 was an unprecedented landmark in the history of French railway services.

★Château (BZ) – The château is the shape of an imperfect pentagon; its surrounding moats were originally filled with water. The feudal foundations are distinguishable together with the covered watchpath and a series of machicolations restored by Daumet. The roof, laid out as a terrace fringed with vases and a balustrade and dominated by tall chimneys, was an innovative idea.

At the northern end of the façade overlooking Place Charles-de-Gaulle stands the quadrilateral keep built by Charles V, to which a belltower was added under François I.

Senior officers were housed on the ground floor while the mezzanine apartments were occupied by princes of the blood, ladies of honour, favourites and ministers, among them Mazarin, Colbert and Louvois.

The royal suites were on the first floor: the bedroom belonging to the king and the dauphin was in the wing facing the parterres, the queen's suite looked towards Paris and the children's rooms were in the wing which now faces Rue Thiers. Under Henri IV twelve of the fourteen royal infants, born to four different mothers, romped noisily in these quarters.

The château now houses the Museum of Antiquities.

★★Musée des Antiquités Nationales (National Museum of Antiquities) ⊙ – The museum contains many rare archeological exhibits relating to France's early history, ranging from the first signs of man's existence (Paleolithic Age) to the Middle Ages.

Ground floor – A life-size facsimile of the famous Bull's Hall in the caves at Lascaux evokes cave art in Paleolithic times. The cave's atmosphere has been faithfully recreated using special effects, allowing visitors to view one of the most stunning compositions of the prehistoric sanctuary of the Vézère Valley. It presents the concepts of confrontation and coupling between animals, expressed through a complex form of symbolism. In addition to the celebrated bulls, figures of stags and horses may also be seen, and a strange beast which, despite its leonine muzzle and two protruding horns, is know as the "unicorn".

Mezzanine (Prehistory and Protohistory) – The Paleolithic or early Stone Age goes back one million years before our era.

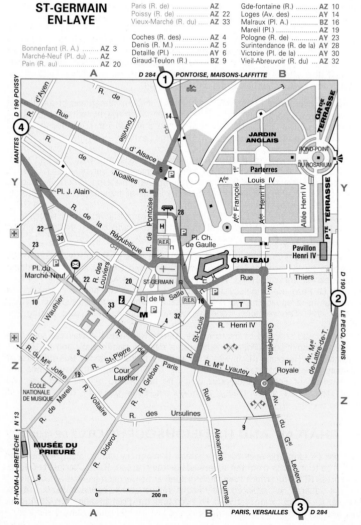

ST-GERMAIN EN-LAYE

The glass cabinets on the right provide general information on materials such as stone (flint), quartz, bone and horn belonging to the cervidae species, and displays tool-making techniques of that period. Note the traces of man's existence in prehistoric times: photographs of the handprints at Gargas, mould of the footprints found in a cave at Aldène. The lefthand cabinets displaying the results of the excavations are in chronological order. The major works of art dating from the Paleolithic Age are surprisingly small: the **Lady of Brassempouy** (height: 3.6cm – 1.44in), the oldest human face to date (c20 000 BC), a bison licking itself (Magdalenian – c16 000 BC), the Bruniquel baton in the shape of a jumping horse (c13 000 BC), the Mas-d'Azil head of a neighing horse (c10 000 BC) etc.

During the Neolithic Age, which originated in the Near-East (8 000 BC), man developed farming and cattle rearing, community life in huts and the use of ceramics. He produced arms and tools by polishing very hard stones (jadeite).

Lady of Brassempouy
from the National Museum of Antiquites
in St-Germain-en-Laye

The discovery of an alloy combining copper and tin led to the early stages of metallurgy (Bronze Age). Gold too was widely used and the museum displays several objects and pieces of jewellery made in solid gold or sheets of beaten gold. Note the numerous weapons (daggers, axes with curved blades) and the metal necklaces and other decorative objects (open bracelets) which give these particular collections the sparkle that characterised some of the so-called "primitive" civilisations of the modern world. The large iron sword is typical of the items from princely burial sites dating from the early Iron Age (the period known as Hallstatt). It was found together with clasps, ceramics, pieces of furniture (Magny-Lambert cist), horses' harnessing and even four-wheel funeral carriages.

The La Tène period that followed benefited from the contributions made by foreign civilisations and especially the increasingly important trade relations with the Mediterranean world. Most of the objects exhibited here come from excavation sites in Champagne and Burgundy (finery, vases). Gallic tribes still buried funeral chariots in their tombs, worked gold (jewellery) and coins. The fall of Alésia (52 BC) put an end to their own culture.

First Floor (Gallo-Roman and Merovingian Antiquities) – The lengthy period of Roman peace (Pax Romana), the indulgence of the victors and the deeply-rooted religious feeling for indigenous gods gave rise to a flourishing industry of mythological and funeral sculpture (until then the Celts had shown little interest in statuary art). Note the large collection of funeral slabs.

Ceramic pieces played an important role in domestic life: one of the cabinets offers a fairly comprehensive presentation of "sigillated" ceramics, decorated with stamped motifs, made in workshops at Lezoux, La Graufesenque, Banassac etc (1C-4C AD). Little is known about the following period (3C-8C AD), though its heritage consists mostly of Merovingian burial places rich in arms – swords with damascene blades – and items of finery: heavy flat buckles for belts, S-shaped clasps etc.

The large ballroom in the château – also called the Mars Hall (Salle de Mars) – is a beautiful vaulted room with ornate stone ribbing and a fireplace bearing François I's emblem, the salamander. It is dedicated to comparative archeology: a superb selection of objects from all five continents makes it possible to draw parallels between techniques and life-styles belonging to geographically distant civilisations, and to compare their evolution in time.

The displays are carefully arranged according to two thematic approaches: the transition from one continent to another can be followed by studying the cabinets lengthwise, while the items placed along the width of the room testify to the chronological evolution of technology.

Observe the splendid Egyptian collections dating from pre-Dynastic times, a set of bronze sculptures from Kodan and Armenian Talysh (Asia), **Mérida's Chariot** (6C BC), a masterpiece of Iberian workmanship. The impressive ethnographical exhibits from Oceania feature a magnificent wooden statue depicting the god Rao (Gambier Islands).

Return to the ground floor by the back stairs. At the end of the tour, enter the inner courtyard – note the ornamentation of the upper balustrade, François I's salamander and first initial F – to get a good view of the chapel.

★Ste-Chapelle – The church was built on the orders of St Louis between 1230 and 1238, about ten years before the Sainte-Chapelle in Paris. It is believed they were both the work of the same architect, Pierre de Montreuil. The clerestory windows in St-Germain do not, however, feature the superb set of stained glass which adorns the Parisian sanctuary. The beautiful rose window on the façade has been screened by a series of subsequent additions.

The bosses present carved figures thought to represent St Louis, his mother Blanche of Castile, his wife and other close relations. They are probably the most ancient images of French royalty in existence.

Parterres (BY) – Enter the gardens through the gate on Place Charles-de-Gaulle. Skirt the château. Built into the façade is the loggia opening onto the inner main staircase. The moat contains restored megalithic monuments and replicas of Roman statues.

The east esplanade – now the site of a blockhouse – was the scene of the last judicial duel during which the will of God was invoked. The duel opposed Jarnac and La Châtaigneraie and was attended by Henri II, accompanied by his retinue of courtiers. La Châtaigneraie, one of the finest swordsmen in Europe, was confident about the outcome of the battle. Jarnac, however, had learnt a new tactic: he severed the left hamstring of his adversary, who collapsed and slowly died.

Pavillon Henri-IV (Henri IV Pavilion) (BY) – The brick pavilion was built on the very edge of the escarpment; it is crowned by a dome, and, together with the **Sully Pavilion** set lower down on Le Pecq hillside, is all that remains of the New Château. It contains the Louis XIII oratory where Louis XIV was baptised on 5 September 1638, the day he was born.

The hôtel which opened in this historic building in 1836 became an important meeting-place for 19C writers, artists and politicians. Alexandre Dumas wrote *The Three Musketeers* and *The Count of Monte Cristo* while he was staying here, Offenback composed *The Drum Major's Daughter* and Léo Delibes produced the ballet *Sylvia*. The statesman and president Thiers died here in 1877.

**Terrace (BY) – The Small Terrace starts beside the hotel and extends to the Rosarium roundabout. There, a worn Touring Club of France viewing table is a reminder of past views over the lands stretching towards the western suburbs of Paris.

The Grand Terrace extends beyond the roundabout. It is one of Le Nôtre's finest accomplishments and was completed in 1673 after four years of large-scale construction work. Lined with stately lime trees, it is 2 400m - 8 000ft long and among the most famous promenades around Paris.

The vista from the terrace being the same all the way along, visitors pressed for time may return to their car through the lovely **landscape garden★**.

ADDITIONAL SIGHTS

★Priory Museum (AZ) ⊙ – The Priory was founded in 1678 by Mme de Montespan and was originally designed as a royal hospital. In 1914 it became the property of the painter **Maurice Denis** (1870-1943), who moved there with his numerous relatives and frequently entertained his friends of the Nabis movement *(qv)*.

The rooms are former dorters joined by stately staircases featuring flattened groined vaulting.

The museum explains the origins of the **Nabis** group – founded by Paul Sérusier in 1888 – and illustrates their passion for various forms of pictorial and decorative expression: painting, posters, stained glass etc.

The works assembled in the priory testify to the considerable influence the symbolic movement – the "search for the invisible" – had on the arts world at large: literature, decorative arts, sculpture, painting and music. The Pont-Aven School is represented by Gauguin, Émile Bernard, Filiger and Maufra; the Nabi group by Sérusier, Ranson, Bonnard, Vuillard, Maurice Denis and Verkade. The museum also displays works by Toulouse-Lautrec, Mondrian, Lalique etc. The ground floor houses a sculpture by Maillol called *Homage to Debussy*.

Chapel (Chapelle) – The chapel was entirely decorated by Maurice Denis between 1915 and 1925: stained glass, frescoes, liturgical furnishings,...

Studio (Atelier) – Maurice Denis had this studio built by his friend Auguste Perret in 1912 when he was working on the decoration for the ceiling of the Théâtre des Champs-Élysées, an undertaking which required a vast amount of space. Perret, Bourdelle and Maurice Denis worked on the project together.

Park – A series of terraced flower beds are pleasantly dotted with statues by Antoine Bourdelle. The park offers a charming vista of the priory façade and its elegant severity.

Maison Debussy (AZ M) – *38 Rue au Pain*. This house was the birthplace of the composer Claude Debussy on 22 August 1862. The restored building contains the Tourist Office on the ground floor and mementoes of the composer on the first floor.

Forest – Circled by one of the Seine's loops, St-Germain Forest was once part of the Forest of Laye. It is planted with oaks, beeches and hornbeams, with conifers on the poorer soil of the northern massif. 120km – 74 miles of footpaths and 60km – 37 miles of bridleways skirt hunting lodges, wayside crosses, old gates and clearings.

Gourmets...

The introductory chapter of this guide describes the region's gastronomic specialities and best local wines.

The annual Michelin Red Guide France offers you an up-to-date selection of good restaurants.

ST-GOBAIN FOREST★★

Michelin map 56 fold 4 or 236 fold 37

This beautiful forest (6 000ha - 14 000 acres) between the Oise and the Ailette rivers covers a plateau pitted with quarries and furrowed with vales which are dotted with pools. Tree species include oak and beech, with ash on the clay, birch over the sand and poplar in the valleys. The region is rich in deer and used to be the home of wolves and wild boar.

Deer-hunting, a tradition here since the time of Louis XV, still continues today: the Rallye Nomade Hunt and kennels are based at **Folembray** *(qv)*.

Signposted trails penetrate the forest; in season, the area provides a rich crop of mushrooms and lily of the valley.

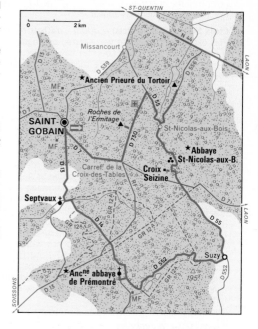

ROUND TOUR FROM ST-GOBAIN

23 km - 14 miles – about 2 hours 45min.

St-Gobain – The town was established as a consequence of pilgrims visiting the Irish hermit Gobain, and rises on the edge of a band of fossil-rich limestone which reaches a height of 200m - 656ft in parts.

St-Gobain is best known for its **Mirror Factory** (manufacture de glaces) founded by Louis XIV at Colbert's request, and established in 1692 in the ruins of the castle that had belonged to the Lords of Coucy. It was the first to use a method of casting which allowed the production of mirror glass in quantity. The factory's entrance has a monumental 18C gateway.

Take D 7 east for 3km - 2 miles; at the crossroads turn left into D 730.

The **Hermitage Rocks** (Roches de l'Ermitage) *(1/4 hour Rtn on foot)* are very picturesque.

Continue on D 730 beyond a training centre (Centre de rééducation) to the crossroads; turn right onto D 55 and first left onto D 556.

★**Ancien Prieuré du Tortoir (Le Tortoir Priory)** – The walls of Le Tortoir, a 14C fortified priory which was a dependent of St Nicholas-in-the-Woods Abbey, appear in a clearing surrounded by lakes where teal and moorhen are to be found.

Around the courtyard of the priory (now a farm) stand the guest-houses (28m - 91ft long) and the prior's residence with its elegant mullioned windows; the chapel dates from the early 14C.

Le Tortoir Priory, St-Gobain Forest

Return to D 55 and continue south.

Soon after the village of St Nicolas-aux-Bois, the ruins of the abbey become visible (*right*).

★**Abbaye St-Nicolas-aux-Bois (St Nicholas-in-the-Woods Abbey)** – The abbey, the remains of which have been incorporated into a private property, occupied a delightful setting here at the bottom of a valley. The road skirts first the moat which protected the abbey walls and then two pools encircled by greenery, beyond which the 15C abbey buildings appear.

Croix Seizine (Seizine Cross) – *400m - 440yds from D 55.*
This expiatory monument was erected by Enguerrand IV, Lord of Coucy, who was condemned in 1256 by St Louis for having executed four students from St-Nicholas-in-the-Woods Abbey who were caught hunting on his land.

Continue along D 55.

At the picturesque village of **Suzy** turn right into D 552.

★**Ancienne abbaye de Prémontré (Prémontré Abbey)** ⊙ – This former abbey nestling in a wooded valley was founded by **St Norbert**, who was born at the end of the 11C near the Rhine in the Duchy of Cleves. He lived a wordly life until one stormy day he was thrown from his horse like St Paul and a voice reproached him for his dissolute living. Touched by grace, Norbert sold all his possessions and retreated to Prémontré where he founded the abbey and the order which took its name.

The **Premonstratensian order**, which adopted St Augustin's rule, was recognised by the pope from 1126 and prospered – numbering 1 500 houses for men and women. The fathers wore the biretta (cap) and white habits.

The abbey was rebuilt in the 18C, converted to a glassworks in 1802 and is now a psychiatric hospital. Three buildings stand around the flowered parterres: they feature remarkable "colossal Ionic" pilasters which set the rhythm for the façade. The main body has a round outer porch with an unusual curved triangular pediment, with a cardinal's shield above. Note the wrought-iron balcony with the cardinal's arms and the finely-carved keystones of the windows.

The wings are simpler: their porches are topped with a shell framed by monumental urns. The lefthand building contains a stairway of advanced design, entirely supported by the walls of the oval well.

The abbey church was not built; a connecting building housed the canons' chapel.

Follow D 14 to Septvaux.

Septvaux – The Romanesque church with its two belfries was used by the Premonstratensians before the Revolution; it stands on a mound overlooking the lovely 12C wash-house *(on the road to Coucy).*

D 13 returns to St-Gobain.

ST-LEU-D'ESSERENT ★

Population 4 288
Michelin map 106 fold 8 or 56 fold 11 – northwest of Chantilly

The Archbishop of Sens, St Leu, who died in 623, gave his name to several French localities. St-Leu-d'Esserent, located on the banks of the River Oise, boasts a magnificent church which the philosopher and historian Ernest Renan once compared to a Greek temple on account of its pure, harmonious lines.

★CHURCH *1/2 hour*

Leave Chantilly and proceed towards St-Leu along D 44. The bridge over the Oise affords the best **general view** of the church from a distance. Nearby quarries produced the lovely stone which was used for the construction of many other churches and cathedrals as well as the palace at Versailles.

The Germans converted these quarries into workshops for their V-1 missiles. As a result, the town was repeatedly bombed and the church wrecked in 1944.

Exterior – The façade has been significantly restored since the 19C – in particular the sculpted furnishings – and is separate from the nave. It forms a Romanesque block (first half of the 12C) presenting a porch and, on the upper level, a gallery, each consisting of three bays. The belltower and its stone spire were to be balanced by a north tower: note the two lines of toothings on the left. Four centuries later, the west front gable above the nave, set back slightly, was given a Flamboyant Gothic rose window.

Skirt the right side of the church, then the left side, walking past the entrance to the former priory.

The chancel is dominated by two square towers with saddle-back roofs. It is surrounded by the ambulatory and its five radiating chapels which date back to the second half of the 12C. The flying buttresses were added to consolidate the buttresses which supported the transept crossing.

★**Interior** – The nave offers a superb perspective. It is filled with a golden light filtering through modern stained glass (1960). The chancel and the first two bays of the nave – square bay with four main arches and sexpartite bay *(see the chapter on Art and Architecture, qv)* – are Romanesque (12C) while the rest of the nave is 13C.

Originally the chancel was to be fitted with galleries, as is usual with Romanesque buildings. In the 13C, however, when the flying buttresses were added to support the east end, the architects realised that the galleries were no longer necessary and so replaced them with a single triforium. They decided to apply this principle to the whole building.

Before returning to the car, stroll to the nearby cemetery.

View of the upper part of the church.

ST-OMER ★★

Population 14 434
Michelin map 51 fold 3 or 236 fold 4
Town plan in the current Michelin Red Guide France

St-Omer is an aristocratic, wealthy and religious town which has largely retained its ancient appearance. It is characterised by quiet streets lined with 17C and 18C pilastered mansions and houses with sculpted bays. This refined atmosphere is in contrast to the simpler nature of the northern suburbs, where low Flemish houses line the quays of the River Aa.

Clerics Take Action – In the 7C Benedictines from Luxeuil evangelised the Morini region, a marshy land with Thérouanne as its capital. They were led by the future **St Omer**, joined by Bertin and Mommolin who founded a monastery on the island of Sithieu in the Aa marshes; it was named St Bertin's. Omer, for his part, had been named Bishop of Thérouanne and in 662 had a chapel built on the hill overlooking Sithieu island; a small market-town quickly formed around it.

St-Omer developed from the joining of the monastery and the chapel, by-then collegiate; the link between the two religious establishments is reflected in the town's layout.

★★CATHEDRAL DISTRICT *3 hours.*

★★**Notre-Dame Cathedral** – The cathedral is the most beautiful religious building in the region and is surprisingly large and majestic. It stands at the heart of a peaceful area which was formerly the canons' "Notre-Dame cloister".

The chancel dates from 1200, the transept from the 13C, the nave from the 14C and 15C; the powerful west front tower (50m - 164ft) with its network of vertical, English-style blind arcades is crowned by 15C watch-turrets. The pier of the large south door is ornamented with a 14C Virgin and the tympanum bears a Last Judgement in which the chosen are very few. In a corner of the chancel stands an octagonal Romanesque tower.

The complex arrangement of the vast interior (100m – 110yds long, 30m - 33yds wide, 23m - 75ft high) consists of a three-storey nave (arcades, a tall, blind triforium and clerestory windows) flanked by side aisles, a transept with aisles, and a chancel with ambulatory and radiating chapels. The chapels off the side aisle, formerly reserved for the canons, are screened by richly pierced and painted marble.

★★**Works of Art** – Among the numerous interesting pieces, note in particular:

– the 1717 organ case (1) surmounted by statues of King David and St Cecilia;

– the 13C cenotaph (2) of St-Omer *(left of the nave)*;

– the 16C mausoleum (3) of Eustache de Croy, Provost of the St-Omer Chapter and Bishop of Arras. This striking work by the Mons artist Jacques Du Broeucq presents the deceased kneeling in his episcopal costume and also lying nude in the Antique manner *(right of the nave)*.

– 15C engraved memorial stones and a *Descent from the Cross* attributed to Rubens *(first bay of the right aisle)* (4);

– 15C funerary monuments and 16C and 17C carved alabasters (5) with a charming Madonna with Cat *(right aisle)*;

– the 13C statue of Notre-Dame-des-Miracles (6), a highly venerated object of pilgrimage *(right transept arm)*;

CATHEDRAL

0   20m

Octagonal Tower

Ambulatory

CHANCEL

TRANSEPT

NAVE

Enclos Notre-Dame

N

– a 13C low-relief Nativity (7) with a Syrian inscription; the 8C tomb of St Erkembode (8), Abbot of St Bertin's *(ambulatory)*;
– the Astronomical Clock (9) with a mechanism dating from 1558 *(left transept arm)*;
– the "Great God of Thérouanne" (10), a famous 13C carved group which stood at a height of 20m - 65ft, over the portal of Thérouanne Cathedral which was destroyed by Charles V of Spain. The shapes, which seem deformed, were foreshortened by the artist to take into account the distorting effect of perspective *(left transept arm)*.

Take Rue des Tribunaux.

The street runs behind the east end of Notre-Dame and in front of the **old bishop's palace** (ancien palais épiscopal) (**J**), which dates from the 17C and is today the law courts, leading to Place Victor-Hugo. The square is the busy centre of St-Omer and features a fountain placed there to celebrate the birth of the Count of Artois, the future Charles X.

Rue Carnot leads to Hôtel Sandelin.

★★Hôtel Sandelin et musée (Sandelin Mansion and Museum) ⊙

The house was built in 1777 for the Viscountess of Fruges. It is set between a courtyard and a garden, with access through a monumental portal with an elegant Louis XV gate.

Ground Floor – The wainscoting and 18C fireplaces of the rooms overlooking the garden are set off by the beautiful collection of Louis XV furniture and paintings, donated by Mme du Teil-Chaix d'Est Ange. Paintings include *The Rising of Fanchon* by Lépicié, which recalls Chardin; Nattier's portrait of Mme de Pompadour as Diana; the *Portrait of a Man* by Greuze; five spiritual paintings by Boilly.

The chapel corridor leads to the Treasure Room where the famous gilded and enamelled **St Bertin's Base of the Cross** is exhibited; this 12C masterpiece of goldsmithery from the Meuse region is decorated with effigies of the Evangelists and enamels portraying scenes from the Old Testament. It came from St Bertin's Abbey, together with the beautiful carved ivory representing an old man of the Apocalypse.

St Bertin's Base of the Cross, St-Omer

Publications Filmées d'Art et d'Histoire

The series of rooms overlooking the courtyard contains an interesting group of Flemish primitives by lesser Flemish masters of the 17C: Pieter II Brueghel, or "Hell Brueghel" *(Flemish Village Fair)*, Abraham Diapram *(The Smoker)* and Dutch masters such as Van der Ast *(Lizard and Shells)*, Elias *(Portrait of an Old Woman)*, Keyser, Steen *(The Bawdy Woman)*.

First and Second Floors – The ceramics on display include local pieces made in St-Omer and an exceptional series of Delftware (750 pieces). Other rooms have been set aside for the history of the city, antique arms and a collection of clay pipes.

Continue along Rue Carnot and take the second turning right, into Rue St-Denis.

Église St-Denis (St Denis' Church) – This church, restored in the 18C, still preserves its proud 13C tower and the 15C chancel hidden by 18C wainscoting (rich canopy with a gilded coffered ceiling). A chapel left of the chancel houses an alabaster Christ attributed to Du Broeucq.

From Rue St-Bertin turn into the street which runs beside the Jesuit chapel.

★Ancienne chapelle des Jésuites (Old Jesuit Chapel) – This chapel, now a school, is an example of early Jesuit style. Gothic influences can be seen in the shape of the bays and the layout of the ambulatory. The chapel was conceived by Du Blocq, a Jesuit from Mons, and completed in 1639. Its height is striking, as are the alignment of the scrolling in the nave and the narrow square towers enclosing the chancel in the Tournai tradition. The most beautiful part of the buidling, however, is the monumental brick-and-white-stone **façade**, five storeys high and adorned with statues.

Turn left into Rue Gambetta.

Bibliothèque (Library) ⊙ – The collection contains 70 000 volumes including over 1 600 manuscripts (11C Life of St Omer) and more than 120 early printed books or "incunabula" (famous Mazarine Bible). They are presented in bookcases from St Bertin's Abbey.

Turn round and return up Rue Gambetta.

Rue Gambetta, which is lined with affluent homes, leads to **Place Sithieu.** The square has preserved its provincial charm which was described by Germaine Acremant in his novel *Ces Dames aux Chapeaux verts*.

Returning to the cathedral square, the "Canon's Door" in the south corner opens into Rue de l'Échelle which slopes down to the ramparts.

ADDITIONAL SIGHTS

★**Jardin public (Park)** – This vast park (10ha - 24 acres) is located on part of the old 17C ramparts. The moat has been turned into a formal French garden; the slope bears an English garden with winding paths shaded by beautiful trees. There are lovely views of the bastion, the roofs and the cathedral tower. The large moat south of the garden now contains a swimming pool.

Ruines de St-Bertin (Ruins of St Bertin's Abbey) – All that remains of the abbey are a few arches and the lower part of the tower (1460). The square in which the ruins lie contains a marble statue of Suger, who lived locally and was a benefactor to the abbey. Rue St Bertin provides a lovely view of the ruins surrounded by great trees.

Ancien Collège des Jésuites (Old Jesuit School) – The school was built in 1592 and became a military hospital. Remodelled in 1726, it features a beautiful front decorated with Corinthian pilasters and garlands.

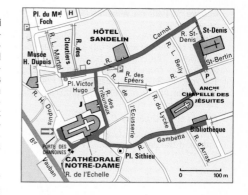

Musée Henri-Dupuis (Henri Dupuis Museum) ⊙ – The museum is housed in an 18C private residence with a beautiful period Flemish kitchen. It presents a large collection of birds from the Arctic to Indonesia in their natural habitat (films, information panels). On the first floor, across the courtyard – paved in the old style – an impressive collection of shells is on display.

Place du Maréchal-Foch – The massive town hall, built in 1840, contrasts with the **old bailey** (now a bank). This elegant Louis XVI building is decorated with sculpted garlands. The narrow, shop-lined **Rue des Cloutiers** connects the square to Place Victor-Hugo.

EXCURSIONS

Marais audomarois (St-Omer Marshes) – *4km - 2 1/2 miles northeast on D 209.*
The marshes sit in a vast depression (3 400ha - 8 401 acres) stretching from Watten in the north to Arques just south of St-Omer, and from Clairmarais Forest (northeast) to the Tilques watercress beds (northwest). They are the result of painstaking efforts begun in the 9C by St Bertin's monks to transform the area.
Today the marshes encompass a series of small parcels of land linked by **waterways** *("watergangs")*, which are used by large flat-bottomed boats known as *bacôves*. A large number of the plots are devoted to swamp gardening; their most famous vegetable is the St-Omer cauliflower. The marshes also provide good fishing: pike, eel, sauger, perch, roach... and bird-watching as they are a stopover for migratory birds (heronry).
From D 209 beside Neuffossé canal the circulation and drainage canals can be seen here and there, crossed by culverts and lift bridges; but for a proper **tour of the marsh** ⊙ it is necessary to hire a boat or join one of the tours in a *bâcove* or other vessel.

The **Grange-Nature** ⊙ in Clairmarais is the visitor centre for the St-Omer section of the **Regional Nature Park** (Parc Naturel Régional ; *qv*); it contains exhibitions and audio-visual presentations on nature and wildlife. The centre is also the starting-point for organised walks, some within the Romelaere nature reserve (observation and study paths).

Rihoult-Clairmarais Forest – *4.5km - 2 1/2 miles northeast on D 209.*
When he stayed at St-Omer, Charlemagne hunted here in the oak groves; in the 12C it was the property of Cistercian monks.
The forest (1 167ha - 2 884 acres) is now managed with tourists in mind *(picnic tables)*, especially around **Harchelles Pond** (étang d'Harchelles), the last of seven ponds dug by the Cistercians for peat or for fish. It is circled by a path *(1/2 hour on foot)*.

Arques – *4km - 2 1/2 miles southeast. Leave St-Omer by N 42.*
Arques, which is an industrial town known chiefly for its crystal glassware, is also an important port at the junction of the canalised Aa and the Neuffossé Canal, linking the River Aa to the River Lys.

In Arques, take N 42 east towards Hazebrouck; about 1km - 1/2 mile beyond the bridge over the Aa, turn right into a small road marked "Ascenseur des Fontinettes" which ends near a factory.

227

★Ascenseur à bateaux des Fontinettes (Fontinettes Barge Lift, Arques) ⊙ – The lift, which was in use from 1888 to 1967, is an interesting remnant of 19C technology. It was established on the Neuffossé Canal to replace the five locks needed to negotiate the 13.13m - 43ft drop in the canal. The principle is simple: the barges took their place in one of two water-filled basins, attached to two enormous pistons which were a kind of hydraulic balance; one went up while the other simultaneously went down.

A visit to the machine room and a working model help to understand how it functioned.

The lift was replaced by an impressive **giant lock**, 500m - 550 yards upriver. This can contain six barges and requires 20 minutes to operate.

★Eperlecques Blockhouse ⊙ – *15km - 9 miles northwest. Leave St-Omer by D 928 and turn left at Watten.*

This 22m - 72ft concrete mountain rising out of the forest is the largest blockhouse ever built: V2 bombs loaded with explosives with which to bombard London were to be launched from here. Its construction – in fact only a third of its planned size – involved over 35 000 French, Belgian, Dutch, Polish, Russian and other prisoners during 1943 and 1944. On 27 August 1943, 187 British "flying fortresses" bombed the blockhouse, disabling it at the cost of numerous lives of detainees working there. After this episode the blockhouse was enlarged to become a factory making liquid oxygen; a film inside evokes these tragic events.

Abbaye St-Paul de Wisques (St Paul's Abbey, Wisques) – *7km - 4 miles west. Leave St-Omer by N 42.*

Benedictine monks occupy the château which consists of both old buildings (15C tower, 18C house and portal) and modern buildings (chapel, cloister, refectory and belltower). The belltower houses Bertine, the bell from St Bertin's abbey church, which dates from 1470 and weighs 2 600kg - over 2 1/2 tons.

The road (D 212) continues past the Petit Château (1770) and climbs to a summit where the Abbey of Our Lady (abbaye Notre-Dame), the Benedictine monastery, stands.

Return to St-Omer by D 208.

The route offers pretty **views** over the town, dominated by the Cathedral of Our Lady and the Jesuit chapel.

ST-QUENTIN

Population 60 641
Michelin map 53 fold 14 or 236 fold 27
Town plan in the current Michelin Red Guide France

St-Quentin is perched on a limestone hill riddled with caves and underground passages, and overlooks the canalised Somme River which crosses the Isle marshlands. St-Quentin's waterways and railways link it to the north European capitals and the Ruhr, making it a transportation centre between Paris, the English Channel, the countries north of France and the Champagne region. It suffered terribly during the First World War but has since strengthened its industrial position: its heritage of textile works (mills, machine weaving, fine articles) has now been overtaken by chemicals, machinery and food products.

St-Quentin Canal – Before the Canal du Nord was built, this was the most important and busiest canal in France. It links the Somme and Oise river basins to the Escaut (Scheldt) River, flowing for about 100km - 62 miles between Chauny and Cambrai. Napoleon considered it one of the period's greatest achievements. It is made up of two sections: the Crozat Canal, running between the Oise and Somme rivers, which was named after the financier who had it constructed, and the St-Quentin Canal proper, which crosses the plateau between the Somme and Escaut rivers partly through tunnels at Tronquoy (1km - 1/2 mile long) and Riqueval. It is the St-Quentin Canal which assures the regular shipments of sand, gravel and especially grain to the Paris region. The enlargement of the canal, which is part of a long-term project, will improve the town's links with Dunkirk.

The Battle of St-Quentin – St-Quentin was the prize in a bloody battle in 1557: the army led by the Montmorency High Constable, which had come to the rescue of the beleaguered citizens of St-Quentin, was defeated by Spanish troops on St Lawrence's Day. A vow made by **Philip II** at this victory was the origin of the Escorial near Madrid.

SIGHTS

Musée Antoine-Lécuyer (Antoine Lécuyer Museum) ⊙ – The pride of the museum is the splendid **portrait collection★★** by the pastel artist **Quentin de La Tour** (1704-88), who was born and died in St-Quentin. La Tour, who painted all the important 18C society figures, is representative of an age marked by the importance of individuality. His works, both sensitive and honest, are "incomparable illustrations of moral anatomy": each smile has its own personality, whether spontaneous, ironic, mischievous, benevolent, embittered...

The main room is devoted to the 17C and 18C French schools. The next three rooms are set aside for La Tour and contain 78 remarkable portraits: princes and princesses, great lords, financiers, clerics, men of letters (Jean-Jacques Rousseau) and artists. The greatest are perhaps of Abbot Huber reading; of Marie Fel, a friend of the artist; and a self-portrait, which is an exceptional study, both introspective and penetrating.

A bust of the artist by J B Lemoyne stands in another room.

A room upstairs displays 19C painting, illustrating various artistic movements: works by Lebourg, Corot, Fantin-Latour and Renoir (pastel portrait of Mlle Dieterle). Another room presents 20C painting with works by Gromaire, Ozenfant and Lebasque.

Self-portrait by Quentin de La Tour
St-Quentin

There are also interesting collections of ceramics and glazed earthenwares, carved ivories and enamels; among the 18C furniture, note the 1750 harpsichord.

★Basilique (Basilica) – The Basilica of St Quentin is a mainly Gothic building which could rival many of the great cathedrals. It began as a collegiate church under the patronage of Quentin, who worked as a missionary in the region and was martyred at the end of the 3C; it became a basilica in 1876.

After the famous 1557 siege, a fire in 1669 and bombing in 1917, the basilica came close to total destruction in October 1918.

Exterior – The west front incorporates a massive porch-belfry; its lower part dates from the late 12C while the upper storeys were rebuilt in the 17C and the top after 1918.

Left of the church, Square Winston Churchill (cast-iron wells) offers a good view★ over the large and small transepts and the east end; note the soaring, triple flying buttresses.

A tour around the church continues to offer interesting views of this remarkable building. At the south arm of the small transept stands the St Fursy Chapel, which was tacked on in the late 15C. The pretty, Flamboyant Lamoureux porch can be seen on the left.

The spire dates from 1976 and reaches the height of the original one (82m - 269ft).

Interior – The impressively large 13C chancel consists of a double transept, double aisles, an ambulatory and radiating chapels. The vaulting of the chapels right of the ambulatory rests on two columns, following the elegant arrangement of the Champagne region. The Lady Chapel contains old stained-glass windows depicting the Life of the Virgin; a 13C statue of St Michael stands left of the chapel entrance. The chancel's screen, reworked in the 19C, portrays scenes from the life of St Quentin; on the left sits the stone chest (*sacrarium*) (1409) in which sacred vessels were kept. Note the great hieratic figures of the stained glass adorning the clerestory windows in the centre, and the 16C glass in the north arm of the small transept, portraying the Martyrdom of St Catherine and that of St Barbara. A restored Gothic crypt exists under the chancel; it contains the 4C tomb of St Quentin and the grooved shaft of a Gallo-Roman column.

The bold, 15C nave (34m - 111ft high) has a long Way of the Cross (260m - 284yds) traced on its floor, which the faithful followed on their knees.

The superb organ case (1690-1703) was designed by Bérain; the instrument itself, by Clicquot, was destroyed in 1917; it was replaced by a modern organ with 74 stops.

The sculpted Tree of Jesse, at the start of the right aisle, dates from the early 16C; the second chapel bears 16C mural paintings.

Champs-Élysées – Originally military grounds under the Restoration, this area has been transformed into a pleasant park (10ha - 24 acres): playground, sports field, flower garden.

Hôtel de Ville (Town Hall) ⊙ – This jewel of late Gothic art (early 16C) has a boldly designed front with a deep arcade, a windowed gallery and three gables; it is decorated with Flamboyant statues. The tower was reworked during the 18C and houses a famous bell. Inside, the **Marriage Room** (salle des Mariages) retains its old beam and a monumental Renaissance fireplace; the Council Chamber is fitted out in the Art Deco style.

Espace St-Jacques – *14 Rue de la Sellerie.*

This neo-Gothic building was built on the site of St James' Church and was formerly the seat of the Chamber of Commerce. Today it houses the tourist information office and temporary exhibitions on the ground floor, with an entomological museum on the first floor.

Entomological Museum (Musée entomologique) ☉ – This collection of butterflies and other insects, made up of bequests and donations, is the most important in Europe. It includes about 600 000 specimens, of which about a fifth are exhibited at any given time.

Door of the Hôtel des Canonniers – *21 Rue des Canonniers*. The door features beautiful 17C military emblems carved in low-relief.

Marais d'Isle (Isle Marshlands) This zone covering over 100ha - 247 acres has been provided with fishing and watersports facilities, and it also includes a **nature reserve** ☉ which lies along the route taken by migratory birds from Northern and Eastern Europe.

The flora of damp environments is very varied and includes rare species like water hemlock (also known as dropwort or cowbane) or strange ones like bladderwort, a carnivorous plant. Among the numerous birds here there are nest-building species (crested grebes) and overwintering species (ducks).

A small Centre (maison de la nature) presents an audio-visual show and documents relating to the ecosystem of the lake. A path around the reserve allows a view of some of the birds.

EXCURSION

North of St-Quentin *Round trip of 30km - 18 miles*

Take N 44 north for 15km - 9 miles.

Bellicourt American Memorial (Mémorial américain de Bellicourt) – The memorial stands north of the village over the Riqueval tunnels. It consists of a white stone cenotaph which commemorates the 1918 attack by the US Army's 2nd Division against Hindenburg's line. From the surrounding area there is a **panoramic view** of the plateau bearing traces of the German trenches (American cemetery at Bony).

Continue on N 44 and turn first right to Mont St Martin.

Mont St Martin – The ruins of an old Premonstratensian abbey may be seen here.

North of the village, a path gives access to the **Escaut (Scheldt) River Source** which is hidden in a quiet and mysterious spot, once a place of pilgrimage. The clear water flows between rows of aspens and ash trees which form a leafy vault in summer: this is the beginning of the river's 400km - 250 mile course through France, Belgium and Holland.

Drive north along D 71 to Gouy and turn right (D 28) to Beaurevoir.

Beaurevoir – This village has preserved a tower of the château where Joan of Arc was a prisoner from August to November of 1430. She was held by the Count of Luxembourg, who handed her over to the English.

ST-RIQUIER ★

Population 1 166
Michelin map 52 fold 7 or 236 folds 22, 23 (9km - 5 1/2 miles northeast of Abbeville)

The little town of St-Riquier grew around an ancient Benedictine abbey which boasts an imposing Gothic church to rival many cathedrals.

A Hermit and a Son-in-Law – The town was called Centule when, in 645, the hermit **Riquier** passed through Crécy Forest, near to what is now the village of Forest-Moutiers. This cenobite monk who came from a noble family had previously evangelised the Ponthieu region; after his death his body was transported to Centule where he became the object of an important pilgrimage.

A Benedictine monastery was founded as a result and prospered so much that in 790 Charlemagne gave it to his son-in-law, the poet **Angilbert,** the "Homer of the Palatine Academy". Angilbert, to whom the Emperor paid several visits, gave a new lease of life to the abbey and had the buildings rebuilt in more precious materials: Italian porphyry, marble and jasper. At that time the monastery also included a main church, which housed the tomb of Riquier, and two secondary churches (St Benedict and St Mary) united by a triangular cloister.

★CHURCH ☉ *45min*

Despite having been destroyed and rebuilt several times, the present, largely Flamboyant (15C-16C) church has nevertheless retained some 13C architectural elements (lower parts of the transept and chancel).

The ensemble was restored by Abbot Charles d'Aligre (17C) who also had the furniture renewed; it is the same in use today.

Exterior – The west front is essentially made up of a large square tower (50m - 164ft high) flanked by stairtowers and dressed with abundant, finely carved ornamentation. Above the central doorway, the gable bears a Holy Trinity surrounded by two abbots and the Apostles, as at St Wulfram's Church in Abbeville *(qv)*. Higher still stands a Crowning of the Virgin. Finally, between the two windows of the belfry, a statue of St Michael can be seen. Above the vaulting of the right doorway a St Genevieve holds a candle which, according to legend, the devil used to blow out and an angel used to relight.

**Interior – The beauty, size and simplicity of the architecture are worth admiring. The two storeys of the large central nave (13m - 42ft wide, 24m - 78ft high, 96m - 314ft long) are separated by a frieze as in Amiens Cathedral and by a balustrade. The chancel has preserved its 17C decoration and furniture: wrought-iron grilles, lectern and monks' stalls, marble screen surmounted by a large wooden Christ by Girardon.

The right transept is unusual: its end is cut off by the sacristy and the treasury above it which occupy three bays of the cloister gallery. The wall of the treasury is decorated with fine sculptures and statues.

In the first of the ambulatory's radiating chapels, on the right after the staircase, note the painting by Jouvenet *Louis XIV touching for the King's Evil*. The Lady chapel contains star vaulting with ribs running down to historiated corbels (Life of the Virgin); at the entrance, *The Apparition of the Virgin to St Philomena* (1847) is by Ducornet, an artist who painted with his feet as he had no arms. In St Angilbert's chapel the five coloured statues of saints are typical of 16C Picardy sculpture: they show *(left to right)* Veronica, Helen, Benedict, Vigor and Riquier.

The left transept contains a Renaissance font, its base carved with low-reliefs showing the Life of the Virgin and the Baptism of Christ.

Treasury (Trésor) ⊙ – This was the abbey's private chapel. The walls of the beautiful 16C vaulted chamber are decorated with murals from the same period; the best of them depicts the Meeting of the Three Dead and the Three Living, which symbolises Life's brevity.

The treasury contains a 12C Byzantine Christ, 13C reliquaries, a 15C alabaster altarpiece, a curious 16C hand-warmer and some 16C priests' ornaments.

ST-VALERY-SUR-SOMME *

Population 2 769
Michelin map 52 fold 6 or 236 folds 21, 22

St-Valery (pronounced Val'ry), the capital of the Vimeu region, occupies a lush setting overlooking the peaceful countryside of the Somme Bay. It consists of an upper town with a lower town beside the port.

The port, which is used by coasting vessels, handles numerous yachts and fishing boats known as *"sauterelliers"* (a *sauterelle* is a grey shrimp).

St-Valery began as an abbey founded by a monk called Valery from Luxeuil in Lorraine. In 1066 William the Conqueror stopped here before invading England; Joan of Arc passed through the town in 1430 as prisoner of the English, on the way from Le Crotoy.

The Somme Bay – Like all bays, the Somme suffers from the flow of water and silt which settles and tends to widen the sandbanks; these become covered with grass, creating the **"mollières"** or salt-pastures where lambs now graze.

The silting up combined with a gradual increase in the size of boats in general has considerably affected the formerly active traffic here; the development of the Somme canal from 1786 to 1835 and the creation of a sheltered port at Le Hourdel merely slowed its decline. It is worth noting, however, that during the First World War the bay served as a British base: in 1919, traffic reached an exceptional 125 000 tonnes.

Hunting and fishing – The bay's three fishing ports (St-Valery, Le Crotoy and Le Hourdel) specialise in shellfish and squid fishing.

When the tide is out fish are also caught in the channels, pools and ruts on the shore: cockles, mullet, eels and flatfish, either speared or just picked up by hand. Wildfowl hunters lie in wait either in special boats or in hides formed in grassy mounds pierced with firing holes, using domestic or artificial ducks as decoys. The Marquenterre reserve *(qv)* and bird sanctuary, northwest of the Somme Bay, nevertheless serve as a stopping-off place for migratory birds; 315 of the 452 species found in Europe have been identified in the area (the Camargue region is host to 360 species).

SIGHTS

Basse-Ville (Lower Town) – This extends for almost 2km - 1 1/4 miles, to the mouth of the River Somme where the port is located.

*Promenade – The promenade, which is shaded in summer by plane and lime trees, leads to a sheltered beach and offers lovely views over the Somme Bay to Le Crotoy and Le Hourdel point. Pleasant villas set in gardens stand inland; beyond the Relais de Normandie appear the ramparts of the upper town, overlooked by St Martin's church.

Sailors' Calvary (Calvaire des Marins) – Access from Rue Violette and Sentier du Calvaire, through the sailors' district which is full of charming painted cottages. **View** over the lower town and the estuary.

*Musée Picarvie ⊙ – This appealing little museum faithfully recreates regional life before the industrial age. Reconstructions of workshops and stalls show the work of cobblers, locksmiths, coopers, blacksmiths etc and there is also a village with a school, café and barbershop. An entire period farm has been recreated on the first floor, with the bedroom, kitchen, stable, cider-press and the barn where flax, grown in the surrounding villages, was beaten to make linen.

Haute-Ville (Upper Town) – Part of the fortifications have been preserved.

Nevers Gate (Porte de Nevers) – The name of this 14C gate, which was heightened in the 16C, harks back to the dukes of Nevers who owned St-Valery in the 17C.

St Martin's Church (Église St-Martin) – The exterior of this Gothic building bordering the ramparts is of flint and sandstone laid in a check pattern. In the left aisle, a Renaissance triptych portrays the Crucifixion, the Baptism of Christ and the Martyr-dom of John the Baptist.

William's Gate (Porte Guillaume) – The 12C gate stands between two majestic towers; extensive view over the Somme Bay.

Chapelle des Marins ou de St-Valery (Sailors' or St Valery's Chapel) – Take Rue de l'Abbaye beyond William's Gate: **St Vale-ry's Abbey** used to lie in the vale to the left. The abbey's brick and stone château survives, with a carved 18C pediment. From Place de l'Ermitage take the path to the chapel *(1/4 hour Rtn)*. The chequer-board sandstone and flint chapel houses the tomb of St Valery. Overlooking the Somme Bay, the chapel offers an ex-tensive **view★** of the salt-pastures and the estuary as far as the Marquenterre re-serve in the distance.

Sailor's Chapel, St-Valery

FROM ST-VALERY TO CAYEUX-SUR-MER

14km - 8 1/2 miles – about 2 hours.

Leave St-Valery by D 3 (west) and follow signs to Maison de l'Oiseau.

★**The Bird House** (Maison de l'Oiseau) ☺ – A superb collection of stuffed birds assembled by an inhabitant of Cayeux was the basis for the Bird House, which is fittingly located in the ornithologically-rich Somme Bay area. A building round a courtyard was especially constructed, following the layout of traditional farms.
Inside, displays highlight local birds in their natural habitat: cliffs, sand and mud-flats, dunes and gravel pits... In a room dedicated to ducks, a reconstructed hide looks out over a pond behind the house where wild duck, geese, waders etc live. Films, exhibitions and information for fledgling birdwatchers complete the presen-tation.

Return to D 3, turn left then right into D 102 to Le Hourdel.

Le Hourdel – The typical Picardy houses of this small fishing and pleasure port stand at the tip of an offshore bar which begins at Onivel. The bar forms a pebbly ring, stones from which are crushed to make emery powders and filtering materials. Views over the bay.

D 102 skirts the shingle beach and the dunes.

Brighton Lighthouse (Phare de Brighton) ☺ – The top of the lighthouse provides lovely views over the sea and Cayeux-sur-Mer.

Cayeux-sur-Mer – This windswept health resort is bordered by a 1 600m - 1 mile long promenade. The long beach of hard sand extends from the woods of Brighton-les-Pins (footpaths).

The **Somme Bay Railway** (Chemin de fer de la baie de Somme) ☺ *(qv)* offers excursions in the region.

SCEAUX★★

Population 18 052
Michelin map 101 fold 25 or 106 fold 31 – Michelin plan 22

In 1670 Louis XIV's building adviser **Colbert** commissioned Claude Perrault, Le Brun, Girardon and Coysevox to build a superb residence in Sceaux. The two groups of sculptures flanking the entrance pavilion were executed by Coysevox: the dog and the unicorn, representing loyalty and honesty, were Colbert's favourite emblems. The grounds were placed in the hands of Le Nôtre, who succeeded admirably in spite of the rough, uneven terrain. The canal, cascades and fountains were supplied by the waters diverted from the hillsides of Plessis-Robinson. The château was inaugurated in 1677 at a lavish reception attended by the Sun King in person: one of the many attractions that night was the performance of Jean Racine's famous tragedy *Phaedra*.
In 1685 Colbert's son Seignelay entertained Louis XIV and Mme de Maintenon at the château, an occasion for which Racine and Lulli composed their *Ode to Sceaux*.

Sceaux in the hands of the duc du Maine – In 1700 the estate became the property of the duc du Maine, the legitimated son of Louis XIV and Mme de Montespan. The King often came to stay with his favourite son.

The duchesse du Maine, the Great Condé's grand-daughter, surrounded herself with a large court of brilliant personalities. She entertained on a grand scale, providing opera, ballet, comedy and tragedy for her many guests. The dazzling "Nights of Sceaux", enhanced by superb displays of fireworks and twinkling lights, were the talk of all Paris and Versailles.

On the eve of the Revolution, the estate of Sceaux belonged to the duc de Penthièvre, the duc du Maine's nephew, for whom the fabulist Florian acted as librarian. The domain was confiscated and subsequently sold to a tradesman who had the château razed to the ground and the park made into arable land.

Sceaux today – In 1856 the duc de Trévise, which inherited the estate through his wife's family, built the château that stands today. The grounds gradually slipped into a state of neglect, providing the original setting for Alain Fournier's novel *Le Grand Meaulnes*. In 1923 the château was bought by the Seine *département*, which undertook to restore both the building and its park. The Ile-de-France Museum was installed in the premises in 1936.

★★PARK ⊙

Main Entrance – Designed for Colbert, the two entrance pavilions with sculpted pediments are flanked by two small lodges surmounted by Coysevox's groups of statues.

Orangery ⊙ – This conservatory (60m - 196ft long) was designed by Jules Hardouin-Mansart in 1685. It is decorated with a series of carved pediments. In summer it was used as the ballroom – note the interior decoration – and in winter it sheltered the 300 orange trees of Sceaux Park.

Today the Orangery is a venue for conferences, exhibitions and concerts *(see Calendar of Events, qv)*.

★**Musée de l'Ile-de-France (Ile-de-France Museum)** ⊙ – The museum is located in the former château of the duc de Trévise. Its collections of paintings, watercolours, drawings, models, ceramics and figures in local costume present a history of Ile-de-France, its attractive landscapes, its many royal palaces and stately mansions, its local crafts and many little-known aspects of the area around Paris. Note the magnificent 19C inlaid parquet flooring, two Gallo-Roman treasure-troves consisting of numerous coins discovered in the Val-de-Marne, local earthenware and porcelain (Sèvres, Sceaux, St-Cloud, Creil and Vincennes), a curious collection of ornamental glass objects (vases) made in St-Denis, printed calico, regional costumes and trappings, and the panelling from Mlle Guimard's private boudoir at Pantin. A display of wainscoting, models and portraits (Van Loo, F de Troy, Nattier) tells the story of Sceaux and the major châteaux of the province.

The painters who were inspired by the landscapes around the French capital are respresented at the museum (Hubert Robert, Camille Corot, Lebourg, Maurice Utrillo, Dunoyer de Segonzac and Fautrier).

The **Reference Library** (Centre de Documentation) ⊙ houses several million written documents about and illustrations of the Ile-de-France area.

Close to the library stands a beautiful 17C bronze compositon by Desjardins, representing the **Vanquished Nations★** ; Spain, Holland, Prussia and Austria. It was originally set up on Place des Victoires in Paris in honour of Louis XIV.

The Great Cascade, Sceaux Park

★**Grandes-Cascades (Great Cascade)** – The waters are approached from Allée de la Duchesse; they spring out of carved masks by Rodin and tumble down a series of ten terraces before flowing into the Octagonal Basin. The sight of these various fountains and cascades is particularly spectacular when all the fountains are playing during the **Grandes Eaux★** ☺. This perspective is continued by a green carpet of lawn, the Tapis Vert.

Octagonal Basin – The basin has kept its original design by Le Nôtre. Of ample proportions, circled by a row of plane trees, it exudes a gentle, peaceful atmosphere. The jets of water reach a height of 10m - 32ft.

Pavillon de Hanovre (Hanover Pavilion) – *Private*. The pavilion was built by the architect Chevotet in 1760 and moved from the Boulevard des Italiens in Paris to Sceaux in 1930. The pavilion provides the focal point for the Petit Canal.

★**Grand Canal** – It is as long as the Petit Canal at Versailles (1 030m - 3 380ft) and flanked by a double row of Lombardy poplars.

Terrasse des Pintades (Guinea-Fowls' Terrace) – From the canal, two ramps lead up to a terrace which is the starting-point for the park's two sweeping perspectives: one extends towards the château while the other follows the axis of the Grand Canal.

Petit Château – *Private*. An elegant early-17C building which was incorporated into the estate by Colbert. The children of the duchesse du Maine were brought up here.

Pavillon de l'Aurore (Pavilion of the Rising Sun) ☺ – This charming pavilion crowned by a dome is the work of Claude Perrault. It is approached by a series of staircases featuring dainty, neatly-arranged balusters. The interior decoration forms a harmonious ensemble: wainscoting, flooring, ceilings and a superb dome by Le Brun, reproducing the delicate tints of sunrise.
It was here that Colbert received the French Academy in 1677. For this momentous occasion the poet Quinault composed a poem of 900 verses on the subject of Le Brun's fresco. He read it out to the members of that prestigious assembly, who spent most of the evening craning their necks towards the ceiling to follow Quinault's detailed explanations. The audio-visual presentation in the basement gives visitors a history of the estate and points out the interesting sights in the park.

Intendance – *Private*. This is a splendid Louis XVI building, and was formerly the residence of the intendant of Sceaux.

Anciennes Écuries (Former Stables) – *Private*. The stables were built under Colbert, after studies made by Le Pautre. Facing the stables stands a horse-pond *(visible from the esplanade)*.

TOWN

Jardin des Félibres (Poets' Garden) – Florian, the celebrated Fabulist from the Cévennes, died in 1794 and was buried at Sceaux. In the 19C this garden became a place of pilgrimage for Provençal poets and writers – known locally as *Félibres* – who would come and pay their respects once a year (on a Sunday in June). The garden contains several busts of Provençal poets, including one of Frédéric Mistral.

Église St-Jean-Baptiste (John the Baptist Church) – The church was rebuilt in the 16C and was given a façade and a spire under Louis-Philippe. The 17C *Baptism of Christ* by Tuby behind the high altar was taken from the chapel of the former château. The altar in the north aisle is adorned with a medallion of the Virgin by Coysevox (18C).

Jardin de la Ménagerie (Menagerie Garden) – This menagerie used to belong to the duchesse du Maine and enshrines the remains of her canaries (beneath the columns) and her favourite cat (in a funeral urn). It was used to host popular dances under the Revolution: the famous *Bal de Sceaux*, attended by the *Muscadins* and the *Merveilleuses*, was very much in vogue at the time and gave its name to one of Honoré de Balzac's novels. Subsequently it went out of fashion and was replaced by dancing at Robinson.

Ancienne manufacture de céramique (Ceramics Works) – The old works were founded by the duchesse du Maine and lie at the corner of Rue des Imbergères. The ceramics production is on display at the Ile-de-France Museum.
The scientists **Pierre Curie** (1859-1906) and **Marie Curie** (1867-1934), and their daughter lived at Sceaux and lie buried in the cemetery here (Rue Houdan, on D 60).

Every year
the Michelin Red Guide France
revises its selection of starred restaurants
which also mentions culinary specialities and local wines.
It also includes a selection of simpler restaurants
offering carefully prepared dishes which are often regional specialities...
at a reasonable price.
It is well worth buying the current edition.

Population 14 432
Michelin map 56 fold 11 – Town plan in the current Michelin Red Guide France

Senlis derives its romantic charm from its picturesque old streets, its connections with Frankish rulers, enterprising bishops and abbots, the rich cornfields of Valois and the wooded horizons.

The election of Hugh Capet – The conquerors of Senlis incorporated a massive stronghold into the first Gallo-Roman ramparts of the town. The kings of the first two Frankish dynasties would often take up residence here, lured by the game in the nearby forests. The Carolingian line died out when Louis V suffered a fatal hunting accident. In 987 the Archbishop of Rheims called a meeting at Senlis Castle in which he and the local lords decided that Hugh Capet – the Duc des Francs – would be the next king. Senlis went out of fashion as a royal place of residence and was gradually replaced by Compiègne and Fontainebleau. The last French ruler to have stayed at the castle was Henri IV.

OLD TOWN *1 hour*

Jardin du Roy ☉ – These gardens occupy the former moat of the Gallo-Roman ramparts which, at their widest point, measured 312m - 1 024ft across and at their narrowest 242m - 794ft. Twenty-eight towers (7m - 23ft high and 4m - 14ft wide) defended the city walls; 16 remain today, some still intact, others badly damaged. There is a lovely **view**★ of the ramparts and the towers, the cathedral and the scattered buildings that once formed the castle.

Return to Rue de Villevert and proceed towards Place du Parvis.

★**Place du Parvis** – A charming little square beside the cathedral.

★★**Cathédrale Notre-Dame** – Its construction was started in 1153 - 16 years after St-Denis and 10 years before Notre-Dame in Paris – but progressed at a slow pace owing to insufficient funds. The cathedral was consecrated in 1191. In about 1240 a transept which had not originally been planned and a spire were added.

The building was struck by lightning in June 1504; as a result, the timbering and the transept walls needed to be rebuilt. A set of new side aisles was also added, giving the cathedral its present appearance. Initially, the two towers were identical. It was only towards the mid 13C that the right tower was crowned with the magnificent **spire**★★ *(illustration Art and Architecture)* with its distinctive silhouette, which was to have such a strong influence over religious architecture in the Valois area *(see below)*. The spire reaches a height of 78m - 256ft.

The **main doorway**★★ – dedicated to the Virgin and celebrating her Assumption into Heaven – is strongly reminiscent of the doorways at Chartres, Notre-Dame in Paris, Amiens and Rheims. The lintel features two famous low-reliefs representing the Dormition of the Virgin Mary and the Assumption. The realism and freedom of expression of the sculpture were unusual for the 12C: note the touching swiftness with which the angels raise Mary off the ground and remove her to the celestial skies.

The embrasures are adorned with eight figures from the Old Testament, depicted in a lively manner. The heads were smashed during the Revolution and remodelled in the 19C. On the left, Abraham is about to sacrifice his son Isaac, while an angel holds the sword in an attempt to stop him. The statues rest on square bases presenting a series of light-hearted panels sculpted into the labours of the months. The calendar starts with January, on the righthand side near the door.

South front – Executed by Pierre Chambiges in the 16C, the **south transept**★★ contrasts sharply with the west front. It is interesting to follow the evolution of Gothic architecture from the austere 12C to the 16C, when late Flamboyant already showed signs of Renaissance influence, introduced after the Italian wars. The clerestory and its huge Flamboyant windows were also completed in the 16C.

The lower part (12C) of the east end and the radiating chapels are intact. The axial chapel was replaced by a larger structure in the 19C. The galleries – dating from Romanesque times – support the nave and chancel with the help of Gothic flying buttresses.

Interior – Enter through the south doorway. The church interior is 70m - 230ft long, 9.2m - 30ft wide and measures 24m - 79ft to the keystone. Above the organ, the 12C vaulting which escaped the ravages of the fire in 1504 marks the original height of the church: 17m - 56ft. The nave and the chancel, comparatively narrow in spite of their height, are graced with an airy lightness. The triforium galleries above the aisles are among the finest in France.

South transept, Senlis Cathedral

D'après photo by Baciocchi/PIX

235

SENLIS

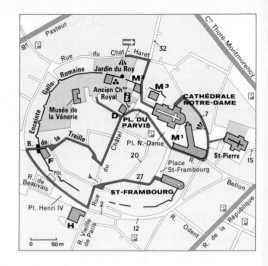

The first chapel to the right of the south doorway features superb vaulting with pendant keystones, a 14C stone Virgin and a lovely set of stained-glass windows. These are the only original panes to have remained intact. A statue of St Louis from the 14C is placed in the south aisle of the ambulatory. The north transept chapel houses a 16C Christ made of larch.

Leave through the northern side doorway.

The lefthand aisle features an elegant statue of St Barbara dating back to the 16C.

North doorway – The northern front is similar to the southern façade but less ornate. The gable surmounting the doorway bears François I's salamander and the capital F as a reminder of the 16C reconstruction campaign, financed by the generous contributions of the French King.

North front – The cathedral's setting on this side is much less solemn; it features several patches of greenery and is extremely picturesque. Skirt the little garden that follows the east façade of what was once the bishop's palace. The building rests on the ruins of the old Gallo-Roman ramparts: the base of one tower remains. Lovely view of the cathedral's east end.

Église St-Pierre ⊙ – The church was started in the 12C and drastically remodelled in the 17C. The small left tower and its stone spire are both Romanesque, while the heavier tower on the right dates from Renaissance times (1596). The badly-damaged but very elaborate façade is characteristic of Flamboyant Gothic. The church was abandoned during the Revolution. It is now used as a venue for a variety of cultural activities.

Musée d'Art et d'Archéologie (M¹) ⊙ – The Art and Archeology Museum is housed in the old bishop's palace, which is made up of a series of buildings dating from the 13C to the 18C.
The Gallo-Roman collections are exhibited on the ground floor: glass, merovingian jewellery, small bronze statues, strange votive offerings carved in stone from a small sanctuary in Halatte Forest *(see below)*, the **bronze base★** dating from AD 48 and engraved with a dedication to Emperor Claudius.
In the crypt there are traces of a house built on this site in the early 2C; the foundations of the Gallo-Roman wall (3C) are also visible, made up of fragments of columns, pilasters and carved stonework from buildings of the earlier town which stood here.
In the Gothic Room (late 14C) there are striking medieval sculptures including the **Head of a Bearded Man** (early 13C) and a majestic marble **Virgin and Child** (late 14C). Note also the entertaining series of small figures of painted and gilded wood which came originally from a depiction of the Passion on a late-15C altarpiece. At the bottom of the stairs the mid-12C stained-glass windows recount the creation of Eve and the Temptation of Adam and Eve.
17C to 20C paintings are on display on the first floor: Champaigne, Corot, Boudin, Sérusier, Thomas Couture (1815-79) who was born in Senlis.
Return to Place du Parvis and, before entering the castle courtyard, start to walk up Rue du Châtel to see the original fortified entrance to the stronghold (presently filled in). Adjoining the old doorway, the 16C Hôtel des Trois Pots (**D**) proudly sports its old-fashioned sign.

Musée des Spahis (M²) ⊙ – *By the entrance to the old Royal Castle.* This museum retraces 150 years of history of the North African cavalry, which held a special place in the French Army from 1880 to 1814 and from 1830 to 1964. It largely concentrates on the old Spahis (native Algerian horsemen), Goumiers (indigenous and tribal horsemen), Meharists (dromedary riders) and Saharans (cameleers).

Ancien Château royal (Royal Castle) ⊙ – This fortified site was occupied at least as early as the reign of the Emperor Claudius (AD 41-54). Throughout its history, up to the time of Henri II, it has featured a charming collection of stone ruins.

The sturdy square "praetorium" tower is the most striking piece of architecture that still stands today: the 4.5m – 15ft thick walls are further supported by a set of hefty buttresses. Although apparently dating from the Middle Ages, its history is not entirely clear.

In the 13C St Louis founded St-Maurice priory next to the Royal Castle. The relics of St Maurice of Agaune were kept here by the monks until the Revolution. A new building was built in the early 18C which now houses the Hunting Museum.

Musée de la Vénerie (Hunting Museum) ⊙ – The works presented here were chosen from among the many illustrations of stag hunts which have enriched French culture. Desportes (1661-1743) and Oudry (1688-1755) represent the *Ancien Régime*, while later painters of animals include Carle Vernet, Rosa Bonheur *(qv)*, Charles Hallo (the founder of the museum) etc. The walls are hung with numerous trophies and stags' heads.

The display of historical hunting gear renders the exhibition particularly interesting. The hunting costume of the Condé – fawn and amaranth-purple – can be seen on a figure representing a Chantilly forest warden, and in the painting depicting the young duc d'Enghien (1787).

Note the famous collection of hunting "buttons", which were the most highly prized trappings of a hunting outfit, chiselled hunting knives, horns (including a beautiful silver hunting horn made in 1817) etc.

★**Old Streets** – *Follow the route indicated on map above.* Rue du Châtel used to be the main street through Senlis for those travelling from Paris to Flanders. This is why its southern continuation is named "Rue Vieille de Paris". In 1753 it was succeeded by Rue Neuve de Paris, now called Rue de la République.

Take the charming **Rue de la Treille** and walk to the "False Doorway", which was the postern of the former Gallo-Roman ramparts. On the left stand the Chancellery Buildings (**F**), flanked by two towers. The **Town Hall** (Hôtel de Ville – **H**) on Place Henri-IV was rebuilt in 1495. The front bears a bust of Henri IV and an inscription conveying his affection for the town of Senlis. These date back to a visit by Charles X on his way back from his anointment at Rheims Cathedral (1825).

Chapelle Royale St-Frambourg ⊙ – Hugh Capet's wife the pious Queen Adelaide founded this chapel before 990 to house the relics of a recluse from the Bas-Maine, known as St Frambourg or St Fraimbault. The chapel was rebuilt by Louis VII after 1177 but abandoned during the Revolution.

The chapel was restored as the Franz Liszt Auditorium in 1977, through the efforts of the pianist Georges Cziffra. The Cziffra Foundation organises concerts and exhibitions for lovers of classical music.

The **church** and its single Gothic nave have been restored to their former grandeur. Descend to the archeological **crypt**. Excavations have revealed the floor of a sanctuary dating from about AD 1000 featuring fragments of columns, some of which have been reconstructed. Two fragments of pilasters belonging to the flat east end of this church still bear the mural paintings of bishops.

At the east end the crypt comes to rest on a sturdy round tower of fine brickwork and on the inner ramparts of the town, which follow the old Gallo-Roman wall.

ADDITIONAL SIGHTS

Ancienne Abbaye St-Vincent ⊙ – *Southwest of the town, via Rue l'Apport-au-Pain and Rue de Meaux.*
St Vincent's Abbey was founded in 1060 by Henri I's wife Anne of Kiev, following the birth of their son Philippe, heir to the throne. The child's christening marked the introduction into France of the Byzantine name Philippe. A 12C open-work belltower – one of the finest and the most delicate in Ile-de-France – dominates the church, the silhouette of which has been marred by successive building and reconstruction campaigns.

The former abbey buildings, rebuilt in the 17C, house a cloister with classical features: colonnettes with Doric capitals and coffered stone vaulting adorned with sunken panels.

Rempart Bellevue – *Start from St Vincent's. Turn right (east) into Rue de Meaux; just before the town gate, a staircase in a recess to the left leads up to the ramparts. Turn right and follow the walls.*
View of the countryside around St Vincent's, and the Nonette river.

Musée de l'Hôtel de Vermandois (**M³**) ⊙ – This small museum installed in a 12C mansion – a lovely example of Romanesque civil architecture – illustrates the history of the town and its cathedral. Sculpture plays a large part: 12C head of an angel from one of the doorways of Notre-Dame; carved capitals and consoles from the cathedral and from the priory chapel.

EXCURSIONS

★**Halatte Forest** – This large forest north of Senlis includes beech groves, cherished by the Capetians, and oaks, hornbeams, pine trees etc to the south.

Aumont-en-Halatte – This charming village houses a museum on the activist author Henri Barbusse (1873-1935), best known for his wartime novel *Under Fire* (1917) recounting life as a French soldier in the trenches.

★**Butte d'Aumont** – *1/2 hour Rtn on foot from Aumont church: towards Apremont take the first public lane on the left (chain), a sandy track flanked by wire fences*. The hillock offers a superb **panorama**★ over the wooded horizon and the towns.

Mont Pagnotte – *Northeast of the forest*. One of the heights of the Paris region, Mont Pagnotte reaches an altitude of 221m - 727ft (television transmitter). A footpath runs along the edge of the plateau at its summit.

Pont-Ste-Maxence – *11km - 7 miles north by N 17*. Because of its old bridge spanning the River Oise, the town has always been an important road post. It owes the second part of its name to an Irish saint who was martyred here in the 5C. East of the town stands **Moncel Abbey** (Abbaye du Moncel) ⊙ which Philip the Fair had built next to a royal castle, two towers of which still remain. The abbey, dedicated to the Order of St Clare, found favour with Philippe VI, the first ruler of the Valois dynasty (1328-50); in 1347 the abbey received the mortal remains of his wife Jeanne of Burgundy, and after Philippe's death, his second wife Blanche of Navarre withdrew there.

The main façade still looks medieval and offers two imposing chimneys. The **courtyard**★ is surrounded by three wings crowned with tall roofs of brown tiles (restored). Other elements of note include one of the galleries from the 16C cloister, the storeroom and its pointed vaulting, the Gothic charterhouse and the amazing 14C **timberwork**★ above the nuns' dorter, made with oak from Halatte Forest.

Château de Raray – *13km - 8 miles northeast by D 932A. At Villeneuve-sous-Verberie, turn right*.
Standing on the edge of a charming hamlet, the château (now part of a golf club) is famous for the striking decoration of its main courtyard, used in Jean Cocteau's film *Beauty and the Beast*. Its game pens alternate with a series of arcades, with recesses and niches housing busts of the gods of Antiquity and 17C historical figures. These are crowned by two lively hunting scenes carved in stone, a stag hunt and a boar hunt.

St-Vaast-de-Longmont – *16km - 10 miles northeast by D 932A*.
Seen from the village cemetery, the Romanesque belltower and its stone spire appear to be extremely ornate: cornices with billet moulding, arcades resting on colonnettes decorated variously with spiralling, zig-zag or torus motifs.

At **Rhuis** nearby (west on D 123), the 11C Romanesque church has an elegant belltower with a double row of twinned windows. The tower is believed to be one of the oldest in Ile-de-France. The interior features four bays and an apsidal chapel with no vaulting.

Tour of Valois Belltowers – *Tour of 48km - 29 miles. Allow 2 1/2 hours*. This tour leads across the arable plains which lie near the forest and through a string of small villages with charming 19C farmhouses. The route is dotted with belltowers, the slender spires of which feature crockets and open-work pinnacles.

Leave Senlis to the southeast, past St Vincent's abbey – the first belltower of the tour – and then the Meaux Gate. Turn left soon afterwards and turn right into D 330, towards Mont-l'Évêque. After passing over the motorway, take a right turning.

Villemétrie – The bridge spanning the Nonette river offers a pleasant vista of the old mill, an ancient stone cross and the shady grounds of the park.
Turn round and proceed along D 330ᴬ.

Baron – Note the **church** ⊙ and its crocketed steeple (45m - 148ft). The nave was rebuilt in the 16C and features many ornate embellishments on the exterior. The 14C stone Virgin and the 18C **panelling**★ inside were taken from Chaâlis Abbey *(qv)*.

Versigny – Presents a belltower typical of Senlis Cathedral. Observe the strange **château** ⊙ on the opposite side of the road. This long, low, U-shaped building of Italian inspiration was first started in the 17C and subsequently remodelled under Louis-Philippe: the balustrades, curved pediments, steps and columns date from the Restoration period.

Proceed towards Nanteuil-le-Haudouin but on reaching the edge of the château grounds take a right turning at the next junction and follow directions to Montagny-Ste-Félicité. Drive up to the isolated church.

Montagny-Ste-Félicité – Superb open-work **belltower**★, rising 65m - 213ft above the ground.

Turn round. At the crossroads north of Montagny, turn left to Baron and the road to Senlis. Do not follow the direct route. Instead, at the Fontaine-Chaâlis junction, turn right towards Montépilloy.

Fourcheret – A former **barn** ⊙ belonging to Chaâlis Abbey *(qv)* still stands, supported by 18 pillars. Built in the 13C, this monastic structure (65m - 213ft long and 18m - 60ft wide) features an impressive display of timberwork.

Montépilloy – The ruins of the old stronghold – presently occupied by a farmhouse *(private)* – are perched on top of the plateau that rises between the shallow valleys of the rivers Nonette and Aunette. On 15 August 1429 Joan of Arc spent the night at Montépilloy, having challenged the English troops of Bedford who occupied Senlis. A commemorative plaque has been affixed onto the church exterior. The 13C entrance gatehouse – itself a small castle – offers a view of the farmhouse and, in the background, the ruins of the 14C keep.

The **Manufacture Nationale de Porcelaine** (National Porcelain Factory) established here in the 18C has made the Sèvres district famous throughout the world. The present buildings date back to 1876.

SÈVRES PORCELAIN

Porcelain is a ceramic material which undergoes vitrification when fired in the kiln, emerging as a brittle product, translucent on its outer surface (as opposed to china, which is opaque).

Soft-paste porcelain – In the 16C European potters were intrigued by the discovery of porcelain from the Far East and many of them attempted to imitate these products. They had no idea, however, how the Chinese prepared their paste and were reduced to experimenting with several types of earthenware. They ended up using a finely-grained marl, which they combined with a variety of glass called "fritte", thus achieving vitrification.

This soft-paste porcelain was produced in Vincennes in 1740. Sixteen years later the factory – which enjoyed the patronage of Louis XV and Mme de Pompadour – moved into its new premises at Sèvres. Initially known for its wild-flower motifs, Sèvres porcelain later specialised in tableware, ornamental statuettes and even entire scenes in porcelain. The sophisticated techniques used for applying the hand-painted decoration onto the enamel glaze ensured a beautifully smooth finish.

Hard-paste porcelain – In the early 18C a deposit of kaolin – one of the basic compounds for making porcelain – was discovered in Saxony, but the trade secrets were well kept at Meissen, near Dresden. In France it was not until 1769 that a similar deposit was found at St-Yrieix in Limousin, permitting the production of hard-paste porcelain. From the Empire onwards the factory here concentrated exclusively on hard-paste ware.

The new product required firing at a high temperature (1 400°C - 2 550°F): it proved remarkably resistant but was more difficult to decorate. Only a small selection of colours were actually suitable for high-temperature firing, among them the famous Sèvres blue *(bleu de Sèvres)*, used on 18C soft-paste under the name *bleu lapis*. Light colours suitable for low-temperature firing, such as pinks, did not blend into the glaze as they did on soft-paste ware and could not be used by manufacturers.

From its beginnings, the factory enjoyed the exclusive right to gild the pieces it produced and this tradition has been continued. Except in a very few cases attributed to technical problems, all Sèvres pieces feature gilding. "Biscuit" was fired and decorated but left unglazed; it was used for statuettes to preserve the dainty, graceful forms of the figures.

★★Musée National de Céramique ⓥ – *Place de la Manufacture.*

The National Porcelain Museum, founded by Brongniart in 1824, houses an impressive selection of china and porcelain exhibits, classified according to the country and date of fabrication: glazed clay pieces from Europe and Asia, earthen wares from Renaissance Italy, 17C and 18C France and other European countries, 18C porcelain from the Paris region, Sèvres and Meissen. The exhibition hall left of the entrance displays part of the factory's present-day production of traditional and modern creations; all these wares are for sale.

The tour includes an audio-visual presentation of the various operations involved in making a porcelain piece: turning, firing, moulding, decoration etc. Each piece is handled by 20 craftsmen and is automatically destroyed if it does not meet the required standards.

The Thesmar Vase,
National Porcelain Museum, Sèvres

Maison des Jardies ⓥ – *14 Avenue Gambetta.*

This modest garden pavilion was once part of the Jardies estate, where Honoré de Balzac lived and attempted the cultivation of pineapples, unsuccessfully. Corot stayed here and Gambetta died here on 31 December 1882. Several of the politician's mementoes have been kept and are on show to the public. At the crossroads near the villa stands a memorial to Gambetta, by Bartholdi.

Consult the index to find an individual town or sight.

SOISSONS ★

Population 29 829
Michelin map 56 fold 4 or 236 fold 37
Town plan in the current Michelin Red Guide France

Soissons rises in the midst of rich agricultural land which is overlooked by the tall spires of the town's Abbey of St John of the Vines, visible from far around. Although the town was largely rebuilt after the First World War, it retains many old monuments.

The Frankish Capital – The town played an important role at the time of the Frankish monarchy: it was at this town's gates that Clovis defeated the Romans, ruining them for his own benefit. The famous story of the "**Soissons Vase**" took place after this battle: Clovis demanded that his booty include a vase which had been stolen from a church in Rheims. A soldier angrily opposed him, broke the vase and cried "You will have nothing, O King, but that which Destiny gives you!". The following year, while Clovis was reviewing his troops he stopped before the same soldier, raised his sword and split the soldier's skull saying, "Thus you did with the Soissons vase". This episode is illustrated in a low-relief on the war memorial.

Clotaire I, son of Clovis, made Soissons his capital as did Chilpéric, King of Neustria and husband of the notorious Frédégonde; the latter was famous for her rivalry with Brunhilda, whose sister she had had assassinated.

The election of Pepin the Short in the 8C, naming him successor to the fallen Merovingians, also took place in Soissons and in 923, following a battle outside the town walls, Charles the Simple lost his throne to the house of France.

★★ANCIENNE ABBAYE DE ST-JEAN-DES-VIGNES ⊙ *1 hour*

The old Abbey of St John of the Vines, which was founded in 1076, was one of the richest monasteries of the Middle Ages. The generosity of the kings of France, bishops, great lords and burghers allowed the monks to build a great abbey church and large monastic buildings in the 13C and 14C. In 1805, however, an imperial decree backed with the approval of the Soissons bishopric ordered the demolition of the church, so that its materials could be used to repair the cathedral: the resulting outcry led to the preservation of the west front.

West front – The cusped portals are delicately cut and surmounted with late-13C gables; the rest of the front dates from the 14C except for the belltowers which were built in the 15C. An elegant open-work gallery separates the central portal from the great rose window, which has lost its tracery. Statues of the Virgin and the saints are placed in pairs beside the towers' buttresses.

The two Flamboyant belltowers are extremely graceful. The **north tower** is the larger, taller and more ornate: the platform of the buttresses is finely worked; the spires of the pierced turrets bear prominent groins and crockets; on the western face, against the mullion of the upper window, a Christ on the Cross stands with statues of the Virgin and St John at his feet.

The back of the façade is much plainer, the north tower having been gutted from this side. The south portal shelters a 13C door which linked the church and cloister.

Cellier (Store) – This magnificent room, located under the refectory and of the same shape, has pointed vaulting resting on solid octagonal pillars.

The building opposite was rebuilt in the 16C to serve as the abbot's residence.

★Réfectoire (Refectory) – The refectory was built into the extension of the west front, at the back of the great cloister. The 13C construction has two naves with pointed vaulting. The transverse arches and ribs rest on seven slender columns with foliate capitals. Eight great lobed rose windows pierce the east and south walls. The reader's pulpit still exists.

Cloîtres (Cloisters) – All that remains of the **great cloister★** are two 14C galleries. The pointed arches separated by elaborate buttresses had a graceful blind arcade, remains of which can be seen in the south bays. The delicately-worked capitals represent flora and fauna.

The **small cloister** nearby has two Renaissance bays.

Maison franque (Frankish House) – The reconstruction of this 6C house was based on findings from excavations at Juvincourt, a village in the Aisne region.

★★CATHÉDRALE ST-GERVAIS-ET-ST-PROTAIS ⊙ *1 hour*

The pure lines and simple arrangement of St Gervase and St Protase Cathedral make it possibly one of the most beautiful examples of Gothic art.

Construction of the cathedral began in the 12C with the south transept; the chancel, nave and side aisles rose during the 13C; the north transept and the upper part of the façade did not appear until the early 14C. The Hundred Years War brought work to a halt before the north belltower was built; it was never to be.

After the First World War only the chancel and the transept remained intact.

Exterior – The asymmetrical front gives no hint of the beauty of the interior: some unfortunate 18C alterations, partly corrected in 1930, have disfigured the portals and today only their deep arching remains. The rose window, surmounted by a graceful gallery, is set within a wide pointed arch. Rue de l'Evêché offers a good view over the south transept which ends in a semicircle; Place Marquigny overlooks the solid and austere east end.

A portal with a soaring gable supported by two buttresses stands east of the north transept; the more ornate decorative art of the 14C may be seen here. The transept's façade is decorated with radiating blind arcades, also 14C, and is pierced by a great rose window set within a pointed arch, topped by a gable flanked by two pinnacles.

★★**Interior** – Excluding the transept arms, the cathedral (116m - 380ft long, 25.6m - 83ft wide and 30.33m - 99ft high) is perfectly symmetrical; no superfluous detail breaks the perfect harmony of the interior. Cylindrical columns separate the bays of the nave and chancel. Their sparsely-decorated capitals bear the weight of great arcades of wide, pointed arches. They also serve to support five shafts sustaining the vaulting, which are extended to their base by an engaged column. The arcades are surmounted by a triforium and twinned clerestory windows.

The **south transept**★★ presents an extremely graceful arrangement, due largely to the ambulatory and the gallery above it.

A beautiful keystone adorns the intersection of the vaulting's ribs, which rest on fine columns framing the windows and on two huge columns at the entrance. The upper chapel, similar to the lower one, leads to the transept gallery.

The **chancel** is one of the earliest examples of the decorated Gothic style. The five lancet windows are embellished with beautiful 13C and 14C stained glass. The main altar is framed by two white marble statues representing the Annunciation.

The pointed vaulting of the five radiating chapels links up with that of the ambulatory; the eight ribs of the vaulting intersect at the same keystone.

The **north transept** has the same arrangement as the nave; the rose window containing old glass was a 14C addition. The *Adoration of the Shepherds* on the left was painted by Rubens for the Franciscans, to thank them for their care at Soissons.

ADDITIONAL SIGHTS

Musée municipal de l'ancienne abbaye de St-Léger ⊘ – St Leger's Abbey was founded in 1152 but devastated in 1567 by Protestants who also demolished the nave of the church. An interesting museum is now attached.

Church – The 13C chancel and transept are lit by high and low windows. The chancel has a cant-walled east end. The west front and the nave with its double side aisles were rebuilt in the 17C. Note the tympanum and capitals from the old abbey at Braine.

Crypt – The crypt contains two galleries and two bays from the late 11C. The groined vaults are supported by pillars which are flanked by columns with square, foliate capitals. The nave leads into the 13C polygonal apse with pointed vaulting.

Chapter-house (Salle capitulaire) – The 13C chapter-house gives onto the cloister of the same date. The six quadripartite vaults rest on two columns.

Museum – The museum's various collections are housed in the old monastery buildings.

The prehistoric, Gallic and Gallo-Roman are on display on the ground floor. The first floor is devoted to 16C-19C painting: Northern school (Francken), Italian school (Pellegrini) and French school (Largillière, Courbet, Boudin and Daumier). The other room has maps, documents, paintings and models tracing the history of the town.

Avenue du Mail offers a view of both the east end of the church and the town hall (Hôtel de ville), which was the Intendancy under the *Ancien Régime*.

Abbaye de St-Médard ⊘ – This abbey was very well known during the Frankish period; today only the 9C pre-Romanesque crypt remains. It sheltered the tombs of St Médard and the founding Merovingian kings, Clotaire and Sigebert.

EXCURSION

Courmelles – *Pop 2 112. 4km - 2 1/2 miles by ⑤; take D 1 for about 2km - 1 1/2 miles then take the small road on the right.*

The 12C **church** with its squat belltower has preserved its rounded Romanesque east end. Four buttresses of slender columns with finely carved capitals separate the rounded-arch windows, which are decorated with stars and surmounted by blind arcades of pointed arches. The projecting central window was formerly a recess for the altar.

SOMME VALLEY ★

Michelin map 52 folds 6 to 10 or 236 folds 22 to 26

The slow-moving waters of the River Somme, "which made Picardy as the Nile made Egypt" (Mabille de Poncheville), often burst their banks to spill into silvery ponds or dark peat bogs and have formed a wide, lush valley in Picardy's chalky plateau.

As the Somme is a natural barrier and has long been a regional frontier, it has been the site of numerous encounters; it has given its name to two battles, one in 1916, the other in 1940.

The source of the river is upstream of St-Quentin, at an altitude of 97m - 318ft; from there it flows 245km - 152 miles westwards. The gentleness of this descent, together with the absorbent quality of the peat through which the river meanders, largely explains the lazy pace of the waters.

The regular flow of the river is, however, assured by the uninterrupted seeping from the chalk plateau, which produces numerous springs along the sides of the valley. This moisture is the reason for the fresh, green countryside.

Along the river bed, edged with willows and poplars, the waters are separated in places by small islands.

During their journey, the waters wind past peat bogs hidden under tall grasses, and meadows where laundry used to be spread out to bleach in the sun; past farmed fields and slopes pitted with quarries; past woods revealing shaded springs... In places, the bogs have been drained and turned into marsh gardens *(hortillonnages, qv)*.

The deep-looking, rectangular ponds were formerly peat bogs. In the past the dense, black **peat** *(la tourbe)* was used as a household

View over the Somme Valley

fuel in modest Picardy homes. It formed in the swamps when vegetation decomposed, producing 60 % carbon. The peat was cut out in bars with special shovels *(louchets)* and cut up into blocks; these were then dried in the meadows or in small barns *(hallettes)*. Navigation on the river has always been limited owing to the fords and the shallowness of the water, but the Somme River nevertheless once carried **"gribannes"** between Amiens and St-Valery: these heavy skiffs transported wheat from Santerre and wool from Ponthieu downstream; salt and wine were brought upstream. In the 19C a few steamboats joined this traffic.

The **Somme Canal** which was finally completed in the 19C links St-Quentin and St-Valery. Sometimes it follows the river bed itself, at other times it runs alongside it or takes shortcuts across the meanderings. The canal was hardly used, however, as there was never a true maritime port at the end.

Hunting and Fishing – Hunting here chiefly consists of lying in wait for wildfowl, in either a boat or the shelter of a hide *(see St-Valery)*. A great quantity of duck and snipe provide the game here; hunting wild swans, however, has not been allowed since the early 18C.

The river, ditches and ponds teem with fish, although the salmon and sturgeon which were so numerous in the 18C are rarely seen. Excellent pâté is made from the abundant swarms of eels which share the waters with pike, carp, perch, tench...

AMIENS TO ABBEVILLE

58km - 36 miles – about 3 hours

★★★**Amiens** – *See Amiens. 1 1/2 hours.*

Leave Amiens on N 235 (west) towards Picquigny; follow the road parallel to the Paris-Calais railway line.

Ailly-sur-Somme – The market town is overlooked by the sober lines of the modern church: its unusual design comprises a great slanting roof like the sail of a boat, which on one side rests on a stone wall and on the other, the ground.

Cross to the north bank of the Somme and turn left towards La Chaussée Tirancourt.

★**Samara** ⊙ – This park (25ha - 62 acres) lies at the foot of a Celtic settlement overlooking the Somme River. Footpaths lead to an arboretum, a botanical garden, the marshes at the bottom of the valley and reconstructions of dwellings from the Neolithic, Bronze and Iron Ages. The working of flint, wood and pottery is brought to life by demonstrations of prehistoric techniques. Peat extraction is also explained.

Daily life in Picardy from the Paleolithic era to the Gallo-Roman period is evoked in the **exhibition pavilion**: a reindeer hunter's house, a bronzesmith's and an Iron Age ironsmith's workshop, a Gallic village street, Gallo-Roman kitchen...

Picquigny – In 1475 Trève Island in the middle of the Somme was the setting for the Peace of Picquigny between **Louis XI** and **Edward IV** of England.

The town itself defends a passage across the Somme and is crowned by the ruins of a **castle** ⊙; its 14C fortifications include a massive keep with walls 4m - 13ft thick. A beautiful Renaissance kitchen, a great chamber, underground passages and prisons may all be seen. The château is early 17C. The church contains a 13C nave with 15C apse and tower.

Take D 3 (northwest) out of Picquigny.

Abbaye du Gard – Gard Abbey was founded in 1137 by the Cistercians; in the 17C Mazarin was its commendatory abbot. After the Revolution the buildings were used by the Trappists, the Fathers of the Order of the Holy Spirit and Carthusian reclusive nuns; it was then abandoned and fell into ruin.

In 1967 the Abbey was bought by the monks of St-Riquier *(qv)* who restored the beautiful main building and the abbey's role as a place of prayer and meeting.

Continue on D 3 to Hangest.

Hangest-sur-Somme – The village specialises in growing watercress. The 12C-16C church ⊘ contains 18C furniture from Gard Abbey.

After Hangest, the road climbs a hill offering extensive views of the valley.

In 1940 the German 7th Tank Division commanded by **Rommel** crossed the Somme River between Hangest and Condé-Folie using the only railway bridge that had not been blown up; large French military cemetery at Condé-Folie.

Longpré-les-Corps-Saints – The town derives its name from the relics which the church founder, Aléaume de Fontaine, sent from Constantinople during the Crusades.

The **church** features a portal with a tympanun depicting the Death and Resurrection of the Virgin. The reliquaries are on display at the far end of the chancel.

1km - 1/2 mile beyond Longpré, turn right at Le Catelet into D 32 towards Long.

The road crosses the floor of the valley, here dotted with ponds, offering a lovely view of Long Château.

Long – The great church in this pretty hillside village was rebuilt in the 19C, in the Gothic style, but retained its 16C spire; Cavaillé-Coll organ.

The elegant Louis XV **château** ⊘ with its slate mansard roof and red brick and white stone resembles Bagatelle Château *(qv)*. Note the unusual, rounded wings and the graceful openings surmounted by keystones carved with masks and other ornamentation.

Cross the Somme again and return to D 3.

Liercourt Church – The charming Flamboyant building with its gable tower stands just before the village. The fine basket-handled doorway is surmounted by the arms of France and a recess containing a statue of St Riquier.

Turn right into D 901, crossing the Paris-Calais railway line.

Pont-Remy Château – This château was built on an island near Pont-Remy in the 15C but was rebuilt in 1837 in the "Gothic Troubadour" style.

Return to D 3.

The road runs along the bottom of the hillside, skirting ponds and meadows, and approaches the Caubert Heights (Monts de Caubert) *(qv)*; at their base, turn right to Abbeville.

Abbeville – See Abbeville.

The THIÉRACHE REGION ⋆

Michelin map 53 folds 15 and 16 or 236 folds 28, 29, 39

The Thiérache region forms a green patch in the bare, chalky plains of Picardy and Champagne. The high altitude (250m - 820ft in the east) provides greater rainfall which, combined with the terrain's lack of porousness, creates a well-watered area, devoted to forestry and especially grazing. The deep valleys of the Oise and Serre Rivers and their tributaries cut through the region.

The woodland is interspersed with meadows, cider-apple orchards and a scattering of farms. For eight months of the year curly-coated black and white cows graze in the pastures. Their milk is dispatched throughout the region and to Paris; some of it is used to make butter, milk powder or the French Maroilles and Edam cheeses; the whey is kept for the pigs. Basket-making is a speciality around Origny owing to the presence of large quantities of osier.

⋆FORTIFIED CHURCHES

Until the reign of Louis XIV the Thiérache region was a frontier and so repeatedly invaded – by 14C mercenaries led by Du Guesclin, by German foot soldiers and by Republicans... particularly during the Hundred Years War, the Wars of Religion and the conflicts between France and Spain under Louis XIII and Louis XIV. From the late 16C and during the 17C, local inhabitants, lacking fortresses and ramparts, fortified their churches.

This accounts for the watch-turrets, round towers and square keeps pierced with arrow slits found on most of the 12C and 13C buildings, resulting in an uncomfortable architectural mix of brick and stone. Other fortress-churches, such as that at Plomion, date entirely from the turn of the 17C. The interiors of these churches were adapted to receive soldiers and shelter villagers: the naves have low ceilings owing to an extra room being included upstairs; fireplaces, a bread oven and a well allowed those taking refuge within to survive for some time.

About sixty of these curious churches still exist in the Thiérache region and the Oise river valley.

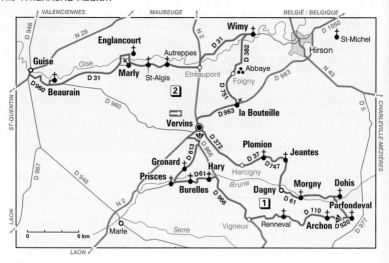

1 **Round Trip starting from Vervins**

65km - 40 miles – about 3 hours

Vervins – The charm of the town, which is the region's capital, lies in its ramparts, its cobbled and winding streets and its squares bordered by houses with steeply-pitched slate roofs. The **church** features a 13C chancel, 16C nave and imposing brick tower (34m - 111ft tall) with stone ties (note the double buttresses on the corners).
Inside, 16C mural paintings adorn the piers and a huge, brightly-coloured composition by Jouvenet (1699) portrays *Supper in the House of Simon*; 18C organ case and pulpit.
Leave Vervins by D 372 (southeast); at Harcigny take D 37 east.

Plomion – The 16C church features a fine west front flanked by two towers; note the square keep with its great hall leading up to the garret. A large covered market in front of the church testifies to Plomion's commercial activities.
Take D 747 east towards Bancigny and Jeantes.

Jeantes – The façade of the **church** is flanked by two towers.
Expressionist frescoes on the walls of the interior, representing scenes from the Life of Christ, are the work of painter Charles Van Eyck (1962). Note the 12C font.

Dagny – This old village has preserved its cob houses and half-timbered houses with brick courses.

Morgny-en-Thiérache – The chancel and nave of the church date from the 13C. Fortification mainly affected the chancel, which was raised by a storey to create a room of refuge.

Dohis – There are many half-timbered and cob houses here. The church (12C nave) is particularly interesting because of its porch-keep, added in the 17C.
Turn around from the church and take the first road on the left (south); fork left to Parfondeval.

Parfondeval – This lovely village stands perched on a hill, its warm-toned brick houses clustering around a broad green. The 16C **church** rises at the far end of the square, an indisputable fortress behind a fortification of neighbouring houses. The white stone portal is in the Renaissance style. On the walls, varnished bricks form a crisscross design.
Back at the entrance to the village take D 520 (west) to Archon.

The road offers a good view over Archon and the undulating countryside dotted with copses.

Archon – Cob-walled and brick houses encircle the church, which is guarded by two great towers; a footbridge between the towers also served as a lookout point. Follow D 110 west through **Renneval** (stone church with fortified chancel) to Vigneux.
At Vigneux take D 966 northwest to Hary.

Hary – A 16C brick keep rises above the chancel and nave of this 12C, white stone, Romanesque church.

Burelles – The 16C and 17C village **church** has a number of defences: arrow slits; a reinforced keep with watch-turrets; barbicans and watch-turrets on the left transept arm; the chancel flanked by a turret. The upper floor of the transept has been turned into a vast fortified room.

Fortified church at Burelles
in the Thiérache region

244

Prisces – The 12C chancel and nave of the **church** ☉ were given an enormous, square brick keep (25m - 82ft tall) with two turrets on diagonally-opposing corners. The four floors inside allowed about a hundred soldiers to take shelter with their arms and provisions.

Cross the Brune River and follow D 613 to Gronard.

Gronard – The façade of the church is almost hidden behind lime trees.
The keep is flanked by two round towers.

Return to Vervins along D 613 and D 966.

The route offers a picturesque view of Vervins and its surrounding area.

② **From Vervins to Guise**

51km - 32 miles – about 2 hours

This tour largely follows the Oise River valley which also features many nearby fortified churches.

Vervins – *See above.*

From Vervins take D 963 to La Bouteille.

La Bouteille – The church has thick walls (over 1m - 3ft) and seems divided by its four turrets. It was built by Cistercians from nearby **Foigny Abbey**, now in ruins.

D 751 and D 382 lead to Foigny. Cross D 38 and take the little road which runs beside the abbey ruins, to Wimy.

Wimy – The fortified church's enormous keep is flanked by two large, cylindrical towers. Two fireplaces, a well and a bread oven were added inside. The first floor has a vast room for refuge.

D 31 crosses Etréaupont and continues through **Autreppes**, a village of brick buildings. The road runs in front of the fortified church and continues past the village of **St Algis** which is overlooked by its church keep.

Marly – The 13C and 14C church has a beautiful, wide-arched portal to which two great watch-turrets were added. The large arrow slits near the base allowed crossbows to be used.

Take D 774 north to Englancourt.

Englancourt – The fortified **church**, in a pretty location overlooking the Oise River, has a west front flanked by watch-turrets, a square keep in brick and a chancel with a flat east end reinforced by two round towers.

Return to D 31 via D 26.

Beaurain – The **church** stands isolated on a hill which rises from lush surroundings. The beautiful fortress dates entirely from the same period. The great square keep is flanked by towers, as is the chancel. A Romanesque font stands by the entrance.

Follow D 960 to Guise.

Guise – *See Guise.*

*Day excursions to England can be made via
the ports of Calais (Dover) and Boulogne (Folkestone)
or through the Channel Tunnel.
Details available from Tourist Information Offices and travel agents.*

Le TOUQUET ≙≙≙

Population 5 596
Michelin map 51 fold 11 or 236 fold 11 – Facilities

Named "Paris Beach" (Paris-Plage) at its creation in the 19C, the resort was almost immediately adopted by the English and took the name Le Touquet Paris-Plage in 1912. Since then it has developed into an all-year European resort with a substantial hotel trade, year-round sporting activities and a centre offering saltwater cures.

The Town – Le Touquet lies between the sea and the forest, its parallel streets intersected by access roads to the beach. The liveliest area of the town – which boasts sporting facilities and a pony club – is around Rue St-Jean and Rue de Paris. Rue Jean-Monnet continues through the arch of the **covered market** (**AZ K**), a monumental, half-moon-shaped ensemble, to the town hall and church facing each other.

Église Ste-Jeanne-d'Arc (**AZ B**) – Joan of Arc's Church was built in 1912 and restored in 1955; it is decorated with clear figurative glass and with decorative ironwork by Lambert Rucki.

Hôtel de ville (Town Hall) (**AZ H**) – The town hall was built from local stone in 1931 in Anglo-Norman style and is flanked by a belfry (38m - 125ft tall).
Along the sea front, the **promenade** is edged by numerous gardens and parking spaces.

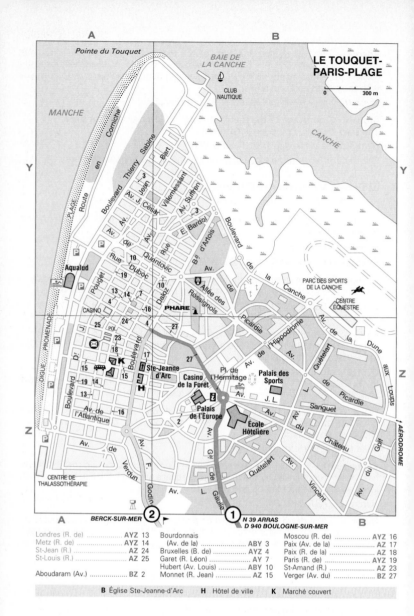

LE TOUQUET-PARIS-PLAGE

The Beach and Port – The gently sloping beach of fine, hard sand, which is uncovered for 1km - 1/2 mile at low tide and stretches as far as the mouth of the River Authie (12km - 7 1/2 miles), attracts many sailing boats. The coast road which follows the line of the dunes leads to the marina, well sheltered by Le Touquet Point (Pointe du Touquet).

Aqualud (AY) ⊙ – This lively aquatic leisure complex consists of an indoor section under a glass pyramid with a wave pool, a giant, snaking toboggan, an infant's pool, a sauna etc, and outdoor swimming pools and slides for warmer days.

Phare (Lighthouse) (BY) ⊙ – The lighthouse (53m - 173ft) which was rebuilt after 1945 stands on open ground between the town and the forest. Its hexagonal red-brick column is crowned with two white balconies. Ascent of the wide stairway to the first platform (214 steps) is rewarded with an exceptional **view★★** over the mouth of the River Canche, the English Channel, the town, the belfry, the tower of the catering college and the forest.

Forêt – The forest (800ha - 1 900 acres) was planted in 1855; its maritime pine, birch, alder, poplar and acacia trees protect about 2 000 cossetted villas – either Anglo-Norman in style or resolutely modern – from the wind. Near the attractive shopping galleries of the Hermitage district are the **Sports Centre** (Palais des Sports) (BZ) with its heated pool, horse show arenas and 38 tennis courts, the select **Forest Casino** (Casino de la Forêt) (BZ), the **Palais de l'Europe** (BZ) where conferences and cultural exchanges take place and the **Catering College** (École hôtelière) (BZ) which presents a curious external arrangement of reversed stars. Three golf courses extend south of the forest.

Along the River Canche are the racecourse, the equestrian centre and the **airport** from which there are regular flights to Lydd in England: from the observation terrace there is a good **view** over the bay, spanned by the road and rail bridges of Étaples, a small port where the railway station is located.

EXCURSIONS

Stella-Plage – *8km - 5 miles. Leave Le Touquet by ② on the map (south) and after 5km - 3 miles, turn right into D 144.*
Behind the dunes which extend along the beach, the woods shelter numerous villas before becoming part of Le Touquet forest.

St-Josse – *10km - 6 miles southeast by ① on N 39, D 143 and D 144* (views over Étaples).
St-Josse, which stands on a hill, was once the home of an abbey founded by Charlemagne in memory of St Josse, a 7C pilgrim and hermit whose shrine is venerated in the church's early 16C chancel.
About 500m - 550yds east, in the middle of a wooded close, stand St Josse's chapel (chapelle de St-Josse), which is a place of pilgrimage, and St Josse's fountain.

VALENCIENNES

Population 38 441
Michelin map 51 fold 17 or 236 folds 17, 18
Town plan and map of conurbation in the current Michelin Red Guide France

This busy commercial town, located on the River Escaut (Scheldt), is surrounded by boulevards which replaced the former ramparts.
The architectural variety in Valenciennes is a result of the damage inflicted on the town during sieges and wars over the centuries; the bombings of 1940 and 1944 completely destroyed the old, wood-built centre.
Valenciennes was once the capital of the steel industry and metallurgy in the north, while the coal basin nearby was fully active. Today these industries have decreased markedly but have been replaced by others: iron materials, car manufacturing, paints, pharmaceutical laboratories, fine mechanics, electronics etc. The presence of a scientific university has contributed to this growth.

Athens of the North – Valenciennes earned this nickname because of the town's long-standing interest in the arts and the many artists who were born here. Native sculptors include André Beauneveu (14C) – the "image-maker" of Charles V – who was also a painter; Antoine Pater (1670-1747); Saly (1717-76) who went to work for the court of Denmark; Philippe Dumont (18C), creator of the beautiful bust of his fellow citizen, actress Rosalie Levasseur, and in particular **Carpeaux** (1827-75), who brought new life to French sculpture and who created the famous group *The Dance* which stands in the Paris Opera.
Famous local painters are also numerous: notably Simon Marmion, who died in Valenciennes in 1489, among those of the 15C; in the 18C, the great **Antoine Watteau** (1684-1721) and Jean-Baptiste Pater (1695-1736) who both specialised in painting scenes of gallantry; Eisen (1720-78), painter, draughtsman and engraver; Dumont "the Roman"; Louis and François Watteau, nephew and great-nephew of Antoine; and in the 19C, the landscape painter Henri Harpignies (1819-1916) and the portrait painter Abel de Pujol (1785-1861).
In the 18C the citizens of Valenciennes, wishing to encourage the arts, founded an Academy, a Salon and a School of Fine Art. The granting of scholarships was also established with the same aim.
There are many treasures in the town's museum and the library is the home of *The Cantilena of St Eulalie*, the oldest known French poem, written in the dialect of northern France in about 880.

Traditions – Each year, in September, the **Tour du St-Cordon** takes place, a procession of the statue of the Virgin kept in the neo-Gothic Basilica of Notre-Dame-du-St-Cordon. This tradition dates back to the 11C when Valenciennes was threatened by the plague; the Virgin is said to have appeared uncoiling a long scarlet cord around the town to protect it.
In the 17C and 18C fine Valenciennes **lace** was particularly famous; lacemaking is once more taught today.

SIGHTS

★Musée des Beaux-Arts ⊙ – This vast Fine Arts Museum has a particularly rich collection of Flemish works from the 15C to the 17C (especially Rubens), sculptures by Carpeaux and 18C French paintings.

Flemish School, 15C to 17C – The first room contains a panel by Hieronymus Bosch portraying *St James and the Magician; The Tax Collector* by Marinus Van Reymerswaële; and *The Preaching of John the Baptist* by Frans Pourbus the Elder.
Several paintings by Rubens hang in the following rooms including a *Descent from the Cross* from a Valenciennes church; the *St Stephen Triptych*, formerly in St-Amand Abbey; and a landscape entitled *The Rainbow*. They are interspersed with portraits of Marie de' Medici and Isabelle of France by Pourbus the Younger and paintings by Martin de Vos *(Marriage of the Virgin)*, Jansens, a Rubens disciple, and Snyders, a great still-life painter *(The Store-Cupboard)*...

18C French School – A remarkable work by Watteau, his *Portrait of the Sculptor Antoine Pater*, dominates this section together with another work from his youth, *True Gaiety*, painted in Valenciennes in 1703. Other fine canvases include the *Portrait of Jean de Julienne and his wife*, friends of Watteau, by François de Troy; *The Pastoral Concert* and *Country Pastimes* by Jean-Baptiste Pater; small genre pictures by Louis Watteau and a view of *The Capitol in Rome* by Hubert Robert.

19C French School – This period is represented by Hardoin landscapes, portraits by Abel de Pujol and works by Chassériau, Ravier and Boudin.

Jean-Baptiste Carpeaux Room – The evolution of his art may be traced here through paintings, drawings, engravings and sculptures, among which note in particular *The Neapolitan Fisherman*, a bust of the graceful Anna Foucart and a statue of Watteau.

Maison espagnole – This 16C half-timbered, corbelled house was built during the Spanish occupation. It has been restored and is today the home of the tourist office.

Église St-Géry ⊙ – This old Recollect church was built in the 13C and remodelled in the 19C. Restoration has reinstated the original Gothic purity to the nave and chancel.

The fountain in nearby **Square Watteau** is overlooked by a statue by Carpeaux of Antoine Watteau, who lived at 39 Rue de Paris.

Bibliothèque municipale (Library) – The 100 000 volumes are located in the buildings of the old **Jesuit school**. It was founded in the early 17C, remodelled the following century, and restored in recent years. The pleasing brick and stone façade has Louis XVI garlands and bull's-eye windows on the ground floor. Next door, the Jesuit chapel, today **St Nicolas' Church**, has a pretty 18C front.

EXCURSIONS

St-Saulve – *2km - 1 1/4 miles northeast. Leave Valenciennes by Avenue de Liège, N 30.*

Chapelle du Carmel – *1 Rue Barbusse.* This Carmelite chapel, which was completed in 1966, was inspired by a model created by the sculptor Szekely and then built to plans prepared by the architect Guislain who favoured effects of mass and the use of simple materials. The chapel stands back from the road and is flanked by an asymmetrical belltower. The interior is bathed in a gentle light which filters in above the altar through stained-glass windows featuring geometric designs.

The Scarpe and Escaut (Scheldt) River Plain – *10km - 6 1/4 miles northwest on A 23.*
In 1968 this plain was declared the first **Regional Nature Park** in France, under the title St-Amand-Raismes. The area (10 000ha - 24 710 acres) incorporates various forests, including that of **Raismes-St-Amand-Wallers★** *(qv).*

Sebourg – *9km - 5 1/2 miles east. Leave Valenciennes by ③ D 934 towards Maubeuge, turn left at Saultain on D 59; beyond Estreux turn right into D 350.*
This little market town attracts people from Valenciennes owing to its still-rural aspect: it stretches over the verdant slopes of the Aunelle Valley.
The 12C-16C **church** ⊙ is the destination for pilgrimages to St Druon: the 12C shepherd-hermit is invoked to cure hernias. In the right aisle lie 14C recumbent effigies of Henri of Hainault, Lord of Sebourg, and his wife.

Bruay-sur-l'Escaut – *5km - 3 miles north by D 935.*
The **church** ⊙ contains the **cenotaph** of St Pharaïlde, the sister of St Gudule; the 13C block of white stone depicts a graceful woman's form.

VALLOIRES ABBEY★

Michelin map 51 fold 12 or 236 fold 12

The old Cistercian abbey is located on a solitary site in the Authie valley, surrounded by woods and orchards; it is a rare and beautiful example of 18C architecture.

War and Peace – The abbey was founded in the 12C by a Count of Ponthieu and became a burial place for his family. In 1346 the bodies of knights killed at Crécy *(qv)* were transported here.
In the 17C the abbey was ravaged by several fires, but the monks were wealthy and in 1730 the abbot ordered that huge amounts of wood be cut in order to begin rebuilding. Reconstruction, following plans by Coignard, took place from 1741 to 1756. The decoration is the work of Baron **Pfaff de Pfaffenhoffen** (1715-84) from Vienna who was forced to leave his city after a duel; he settled in St-Riquier in 1750.
From 1817 to 1880 the **Basiliens**, members of a lay congregation founded in Mons in 1800, lived in Valloires. All members of the community exercised their profession, scrupulously fulfilled their religious duties and wore an all-blue outfit: a cotton cap, loose shirt and leggings. The monastery is today a child-care centre.

ABBEY ⓥ

A 16C dovecote stands in front of the long building which is extended to the left and rear by the east front of the abbey lodgings; these in turn are surrounded by smaller buildings. The chapter-house is no longer near the church as in the Middle Ages, but is in the main building itself; Pfaffenhoffen's elegant decoration has given it the look of a salon.

The simple cloister gallery has groined vaulting. The refectory is located on the ground floor of the east wing; the abbot's rooms and the monks' cells are upstairs. The vestry is decorated with wood panels by Pfaffenhoffen and paintings by Parrocel.

★Church – "It would delight Mme de Pompadour yet St Bernard would see nothing to take exception to". This comment by an English traveller illustrates the balance between the building's architectural restraint and the elegant ornamentation of its decor.

Inside, the **organ** (1) is supported by a gallery carved by Pfaffenhoffen with musical instruments; the statues at each side symbolise religion. The balustrade and small organ case are decorated with *putti* and cherub musicians. Caryatids support the great organ case, which is crowned by a statue of King David accompanied by angel musicians.

The beautiful **grilles** (2) are of a graceful and light design: the central part is surmounted by the Valloires arms and Moses' brazen serpent (prefiguration of the Crucifixion), framed by baskets of flowers. The creator of the grilles, Jean Veyren, was also responsible for those in the cathedral in Amiens *(qv)*.

Two adoring angels in gilded lead by Pfaffenhoffen are located around the main altar (3), over which hangs a curious and rare eucharistic monstrance in the form of an abbot's crook, another masterpiece of ironwork by Jean Veyren.

Carved religious emblems adorn the stalls (4); those reserved for the abbot and the prior stand on either side of the entrance to the apsidal chapel, which is decorated with wood panels by Pfaff.

The right transept arm houses recumbent effigies of a Count and Countess of Ponthieu (5).

Gardens ⓥ – This 7ha - 17 acre landscaped park at the foot of the abbey contains 4 000 species of plants and trees. A stroll along the paths reveals a White Garden, the Golden Isle, the Cherry Tree Chamber, a Marsh Garden...

36 15 THE MICHELIN Minitel Service

Michelin Travel Assistance (AMI) is a computerised route-finding system offering integrated information on roads, tourist sights, hotels and restaurants

36 15 MICHELIN is one of the French Telecom videotex services.

36 15 MICHELIN: access code to connect with the service.

Route planning: give your point of departure and destination, stipulate your preference for motorways or local roads. Indicate the sights to see along the way and it will do the rest.

Lunchtime or overnight stops: now look for that special restaurant, secluded country hotel or pleasant campsite along the chosen route.

Where to find the Minitel terminals: public terminals are usually to be found in all post offices, some petrol stations and hotels (over 6 million terminals in France). The cost of consulting 36 15 MICHELIN is 1.27 F per minute. This user-friendly travel service is available round the clock.

Access for users outside: foreign subscribers can access Franch Telecom videotex services; consult your documentation.

Field of operation: this outstanding European and road tourist database covers most European countries.

VAUX-LE-VICOMTE ★★★

Michelin map 106 folds 45, 46 or 61 fold 2 – 6 km - 4 miles northeast of Melun

This château, built by Fouquet, remains one of the greatest masterpieces of the 17C.

The rise of Nicolas Fouquet – Born of a family of magistrates, Fouquet became a member of the Parlement de Paris by the age of twenty. He was made Procureur Général of this respectable assembly and was appointed Superintendent of Finances under Mazarin. Owing to the customs of the time and the example of Cardinal Mazarin, he acquired the dangerous habit of confusing the credit of the State with his own. He was forever surrounded by a large retinue of senior personalities whose services cost vast sums of money. Intoxicated with success Fouquet chose a squirrel as his emblem – in Anjou patois *fouquet* means a squirrel – and decreed his motto would be *Quo non ascendam* (How high shall I not climb?).

In 1656 Fouquet decided to grace his own seignory of Vaux with a château worthy of his social standing. He showed excellent taste when it came to choosing his future "collaborators": the architect **Louis Le Vau**, the decorator **Charles Le Brun** and the landscape gardener **André Le Nôtre**. He was equally discerning in other matters: the famous chef Vatel was hired as his major-domo and La Fontaine as close adviser. The builders were given carte blanche. A total of 18 000 workers took part in the project, which involved the demolition of three villages.

Le Brun created a tapestry works at Maincy to fulfil his commission. After Fouquet's fall it was moved to Paris, where it became the Manufacture Royale des Gobelins. The whole operation took five years to complete and the result was a masterpiece that Louis XIV wished to surpass with the construction of Versailles.

An invitation to royal vexation – On 17 August 1661 Fouquet organised a fête for the King and his court, who were staying at Fontainebleau. The reception was one of dazzling splendour. The King's table featured a service in solid gold: this detail annoyed him intensely as his own silverware had been sent back to the smelting works to meet the expenses incurred by the Thirty Years War.

After a banquet dinner at which Vatel had surpassed himself, the guests could feast their eyes on the garden entertainments, enhanced by 1 200 fountains and cascades. The programme included country ballets, concerts, aquatic tournaments and lottery games in which all the tickets won prizes. It also included the premiere of *Les Fâcheux*, a comedy-ballet by Molière, performed by the author and his troupe against a delightful backdrop of greenery.

The King was vexed by such an extravagant display of pomp and luxury, unparalleled at his own royal court. His first impulse was to have Fouquet arrested immediately but Anne of Austria managed to dissuade him.

The fall of Nicolas Fouquet – Nineteen days later, the Superintendent of Finances was sent to jail and all his belongings sequestrated. The artists who had designed and built Vaux entered the King's service and were later to produce the Palace of Versailles. At the end of a three-year trial, Fouquet was banished from court but this sentence was altered by the King to perpetual imprisonment.

Only a few close friends remained loyal to the fallen minister: Mme de Sévigné and La Fontaine, who composed *Elegy to the Nymphs of Vaux*. On account of her dowry, Fouquet's widow was entitled to recover the ownership of the château. After the death of her son, the estate was bought by the Maréchal de Villars in 1705, when it was made a duchy-peerage. It was sold in 1764 by one of Louis XV's ministers the duc de Choiseul-Praslin, and survived the Revolution without suffering too much damage.

In 1875 Vaux was bought by the great industrialist Mr Sommier, who applied himself to restoring and refurnishing the château, as well as refurbishing its grounds. This task has been continued by his heirs.

TOUR

★★**Château** ☉ – The château stands on a terrace surrounded by a moat. The impressive approach leads towards the château's imposing northern front, with its tall windows on a raised ground floor. The building is characteristic of the first period of Louis XIV architecture.

The glass doors in the entrance hall – presently covered up by tapestries – opened onto the Grand Salon and the perspective of the formal gardens. This vestibule leads up to the first floor, occupied by the suites of M and Mme Fouquet. Visitors are shown the superintendent's antechamber (large ebony desk inlaid with gilt copper), his study and his bedroom (superb ceiling decorated by Le Brun), followed by Mme Fouquet's boudoir (portrait of Fouquet by Le Brun), the Louis XV study and bedroom embellished with contemporary furniture (large canopied four-poster bed attributed to F Leroy) and the Louis XVI bedchamber.

Back on the ground floor, the Square Salon with its French-style ceiling decoration was the only addition made under Louis XIII.

Six reception rooms giving onto the gardens are laid out on either side of the main Grand Salon. The ceilings were decorated by Le Brun, who conferred a sense of unity to the ensemble. Admire his rendering of *The Nine Muses* in the Muses' Hall, *Hercules entering Mount Olympus* in Hercules' Hall. The latter houses an equestrian statue of Louis XIV by François Girardon. It is a miniature bronze of the monument set up on Place Vendôme in 1699 and destroyed during the Revolution.

★**Grand Salon** – This room, crowned by the central dome, was left unfinished after Fouquet's arrest and suffers from the absence of decoration (the various studies made by Le Brun are on display). The sixteen caryatids supporting the dome

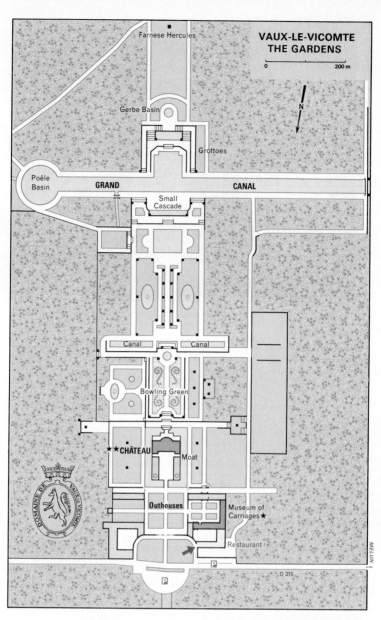

**VAUX-LE-VICOMTE
THE GARDENS**

0   200 m

N

Farnese Hercules

Gerbe Basin

Grottoes

Poêle
Basin

GRAND   CANAL

Small
Cascade

Canal   Canal

Bowling Green

★★ **CHÂTEAU**   Moat

Outhouses   Museum of
Carriages ★

Restaurant

DOMAINE DE VAUX-VICOMTE

MELUN

P

P   D 215

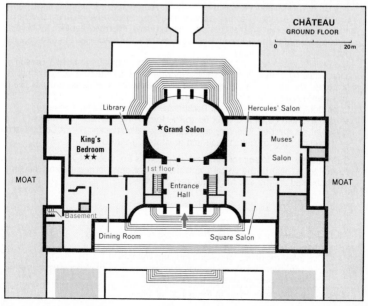

CHÂTEAU
GROUND FLOOR

0   20 m

Library

Hercules' Salon

★ Grand Salon

**King's
Bedroom**
★★

Muses'

Salon

MOAT   1st floor   MOAT

Entrance
Hall

Basement

Dining Room   Square Salon

251

Vaux-le-Vicomte Château

symbolise the twelve months and the four seasons of the year. The only remains of the original furnishings are two marble tables, as well as six statues and six paintings discovered by M Sommier when he moved in.

★★King's Bedroom – The room communicates with the former antechamber (now a library beautifully furnished in the Regency style).
Its decoration is characteristic of the Louis XIV style that was to leave its mark on the State Apartments at Versailles. The ceiling features stucco work by Girardon and Legendre, and a central painting by Le Brun representing *Time taking away Truth from the Skies*. Below the cornice is a frieze of palmette motifs alternating with tiny squirrels.
The Dining Room probably served a similar function in Fouquet's time. It gives onto a wood-panelled passageway hung with paintings, where a long row of dressers would receive the bowls of fruit and other dishes brought from the distant kitchens.
A tour of the basement shows a number of rooms (Map Room, Archive Hall) and the kitchen quarters, which were used up to 1956. Note the servants' dining hall, complete with a fully-laid table.

★★★Gardens ⊙ – M Sommier carefully restored Le Nôtre's masterpiece, of which the most striking feature is its sweeping perspective. The grounds offer several "optical illusions", including the discovery of basins which are not visible from the château. Walk to the far end of the upper terrace to get a good view of the southern façade. The central dome and its surmounting lantern turret, the square corner pavilions, heavier than on the north side, and the decoration of the frontispiece, crowned by statues form an impressive, if somewhat heavy, composition. Starting from the château, walk past the *boulingrin* or former bowling green, two oblong areas of greenery trimmed into ornamental lace motifs.
The three main water perspectives – the moat, the two rectangular canals and the Grand Canal – suddenly come into view in a most impressive manner. Owing to the prevailing customs of that period, the artificial grottoes appear to have been arranged around the edge of the very last square basin, as the Grand Canal is optically hidden from view.
The Grand Canal – known as the "frying pan" on account of its rounded extremity – is approached by a steep flight of steps level with the Small Cascade located opposite the grottoes. The niches at each end house two statues of river gods, some of the most important examples of 17C sculpture at Vaux; these Mlle de Scudéry fondly imagined to be the Tiber and the Anqueuil (local name given to the Almont stream).
Skirt the Grand Canal and walk up to the foot of the Farnese Hercules which ends the great perspective. The very last basin aptly called the spray – La Gerbe – affords an extensive view of the château and its stately grounds.

Outhouses – The **Museum of Carriages★** (Musée des Équipages) ⊙ lies in the western outbuildings, next to the visitors' entrance. It presents harnessing and saddlery, an old-fashioned smithy and fully-equipped carriages.

Michelin Maps (scale 1:200 000) which are revised regularly
provide much useful information:
      - *latest motorway developments and changes;*
      - *vital data (width, alignment, camber, surface) of motorways or tracks;*
      - *the location of emergency telephones.*
Keep current Michelin Maps in the car at all times.

VERSAILLES ★★★

Population 87 789
Michelin map 101 folds 22, 23 or 106 folds 17, 18 – Michelin plan 22
Town plan in the current Michelin Red Guide France

Versailles was created during the golden age of French royalty and, except under the Regency, it remained the government headquarters and the political centre of France from 1682 to 1789. It owes its reputation to the outstanding royal residence consisting of the palace, its grounds and the Trianons. The town was built as an annexe with a view to housing the numerous titled and untitled people who served the French court: dukes, ministers, craftsmen, civil servants etc. Owing to its former duties, the town has retained a certain austere charm.

Versailles will delight all those interested in the Bourbons' penchant for splendour and the insurrectionary beginnings of the French Revolution.

Louis XIII's Château – In the 17C the locality of Versailles was the seat of a medieval castle perched on a hillock. At the foot lay the village, surrounded by marshes and woodland abounding in game. Louis XIII used to come hunting here fairly often and in 1624 he bought part of the land and gave orders to build a small country residence. In 1631 the Archbishop of Paris Monseigneur Gondi granted him the lordship of Versailles, and he commissioned Philibert Le Roy to replace the manor with a small château built of brick, stone and slate.

The glorious task of taming nature – 1661 marked the year of Louis XIV's accession to the throne. The King hired the various artists, builders, designers and landscape architects who had produced Vaux-le-Vicomte *(qv)* and entrusted them with an even more challenging task.

Louis was wary of settling in Paris following the Fronde uprisings and so searched for a site in the outskirts of the capital. He chose Versailles as he had spent many happy days there as a boy. It was by no means an ideal site: the mound was too narrow to allow Louis XIII's château to be enlarged. Although the surrounding land was swampy, and therefore unsuitable for growing ornamental plants, it did not yield enough water to supply the many fountains and canals that were an essential part of 17C gardens. The King ruled that nature be tamed and gave orders to divert the waters of nearby rivers, drain the land and cart heavy loads of earth to consolidate the site.

In the early stages, **Louis Le Vau** built a stone construction around the small château in 1668: it was reminiscent of Italian architecture and was aptly named the "Envelope". André Le Nôtre designed the new gardens and created his celebrated perspectives. By 1664 the first receptions were held at the new château.

A massive operation – In 1678 **Jules Hardouin-Mansart**, aged only 31, was appointed head architect, a position he kept until he died in 1708. From 1661 to 1683 **Charles Le Brun** supervised a team of accomplished painters, sculptors, carvers and interior decorators. **Le Nôtre** applied himself to the embellishment of the grounds. When designing the waterworks, he joined forces with the Francine, a family of Italian engineers. Louis XIV kept a close watch on the various works under way, leaving strict instructions when he marched to war. He was a critical overseer who made numerous comments aimed at altering, rectifying and improving the plans of his new residence. In 1684, two years after the King and his elegant courtiers had moved to Versailles, the *Journal de Dangeau* reported that a total of 22 000 labourers and 6 000 horses were at work on the different sites.

It was necessary to build a hill to accommodate the entire length of the château (680m - 2 230ft). Whole forests were transplanted and the King's gardeners produced 150 000 new flowering plants every year. The orangery housed around 3 000 shrubs: orange and myrtle trees, oleanders...

The problem of water supply was of great concern to Colbert, and later Louvois. The waters of Clagny Pond – located near the present Rive Droite railway station – proved insufficient and the builders were forced to divert the course of the Bièvre and drain the Saclay plateau. The Marly Machine conveyed the waters pumped from the river Seine but the diversion of the Eure *(see Maintenon)* was a fiasco.

Louis XIV entering Dunkirk,
tapestry after Charles Le Brun

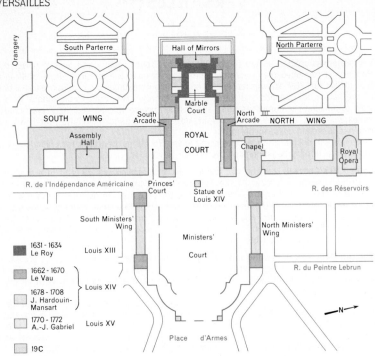

It took fifty years to complete the shell of the palace at Versailles, allowing for the interruptions and slack periods attributed to contemporary wars. It was only in 1710 that the last chapel was finished. By that time, Louis XIV had reached the age of 72.

Life at Court – When the King and his entourage moved to Versailles, the palace and the adjacent outbuildings were required to lodge at least 3 000 people. The Fronde movement had been a humiliating experience for the King, who had witnessed many intrigues involving men in high places. Consequently, his main concern was to keep the aristocracy with him at court, in an attempt to stifle opposition that might threaten the stability of the throne. The lavish entertainments suited his extravagant tastes and served to keep the nobility in subjection.

For the first time in French history, the royal suites in the palace were given fixed, permanent furnishings. Thanks to Colbert's efforts to encourage the production of luxury goods (tapestries, furniture, lace etc) on a national scale, the palace – which remained open to the public – offered a standing exhibition of arts and crafts in France. Strict etiquette governed the visits that the French people would pay Versailles. The famous chronicler Saint-Simon described a day at court as a "clock-work ceremony" consisting of a series of banquets, audiences and entertainments. After 1684, the pious Mme de Maintenon put an end to these large-scale festivities: the court had to find other ways to overcome its boredom.

When Louis XIV died in 1715 his successor was still a young boy. The Regent Philippe d'Orléans administered the king's affairs from the Palais-Royal, his Paris residence. During this time, the court left Versailles and moved to the Tuileries.

In 1722 Louis XV, aged twelve, decided to settle at Versailles. In order that royal etiquette might not interfere with his private life, he gave orders to convert several of the private apartments. He dreamed of having the front of the palace remodelled, a task he entrusted to Jacques-Anges Gabriel. Unfortunately, no major alterations could be carried out owing to insufficient funds but the Petit Trianon was built. Louis XVI – a man of simple tastes – and Marie-Antoinette commissioned no further works. The Queen was perfectly happy to stay in the Petit Trianon: it was for her that the hamlet and the present grounds were conceived in 1774. On 6 October 1789, the national insurrection forced the royal family to return to Paris: after that date, Versailles ceased to be a place of residence for the kings of France.

To the glory of France – After the storming of the Tuileries and the fall of the Monarchy on 10 August 1792, most of the furniture was removed and auctioned. The major works of art – paintings, carpets, tapestries and a few items of furniture – were kept for the art museum which opened in the Louvre in August 1793. After the renovation work undertaken by Napoleon and Louis XVIII, Versailles was threatened once more: it was spared demolition by Louis-Philippe, who contributed a large part of his personal fortune to found a museum of French history in 1837.

More recently, Versailles was restored following the First World War, thanks to the generosity of the Academy of Fine Arts and the handsome contributions made by a number of wealthy patrons, including the American J D Rockefeller.

Restoration – An important restoration campaign was launched in the early 1950s, permitting the renovation of the Royal Opera, the installation of central heating and electric lighting, and the completion of various refurnishing and maintenance projects. In 1980 the King's Bedroom and the Hall of Mirrors were both restored to their 18C splendour.

Phases of construction and other historical events

1631   Completion of Louis XIII's château.
1643   Death of Louis XIII. Five-year-old **Louis XIV succeeds to the throne**. France is ruled by the Regent Anne of Austria and Cardinal Jules Mazarin.
1661   Louis XIV comes of age. After Mazarin's death, he decides to reign without the assistance of a Prime Minister.
1664   The first sumptuous receptions are held.
1666   The Versailles fountains play for the first time.
1668   Louis Le Vau starts work on the château.
1671   Charles Le Brun and his team of artists begin the interior decoration.
1674   Louis XIV's first major stay at Versailles.
1682   The court and government officials take up residence at the palace.
1683   Death of Marie-Thérèse of Austria. Louis XIV is secretly married to Mme de Maintenon.
1684   The Hall of Mirrors is completed.
1687   The Porcelain Trianon is replaced by the Marble Trianon.
1710   Birth of Louis XV, great-grandson of the Sun King.
1715   Death of Louis XIV. Five-year-old **Louis XV succeeds to the throne**. France is ruled by the Regent Philippe d'Orléans. The court leaves Versailles.
1722   The court returns to Versailles.
1729   Birth of the Dauphin, later father to Louis XVI, Louis XVIII and Charles X.
1745   Mme de Pompadour becomes Louis XV's favourite. Her "reign" was to last fifteen years.
1754   Birth of Louis XVI.
1770   Marriage of Louis XVI to the Austrian Archduchess Marie-Antoinette.
1774   Death of Louis XV. **Louis XVI succeeds to the throne.**
1783   The Treaty of Versailles is signed, granting independence to 13 American States.
1789   The States-General meet in the town. The royal family leaves Versailles for good.

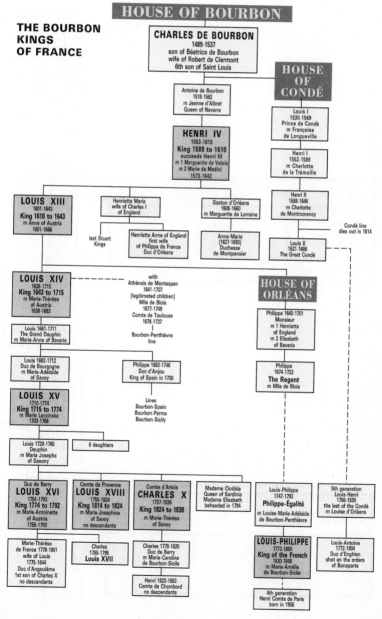

THE BOURBON KINGS OF FRANCE

HOUSE OF BOURBON

CHARLES DE BOURBON
1489-1537
son of Béatrice de Bourbon
wife of Robert de Clermont
6th son of Saint Louis

HOUSE OF CONDÉ

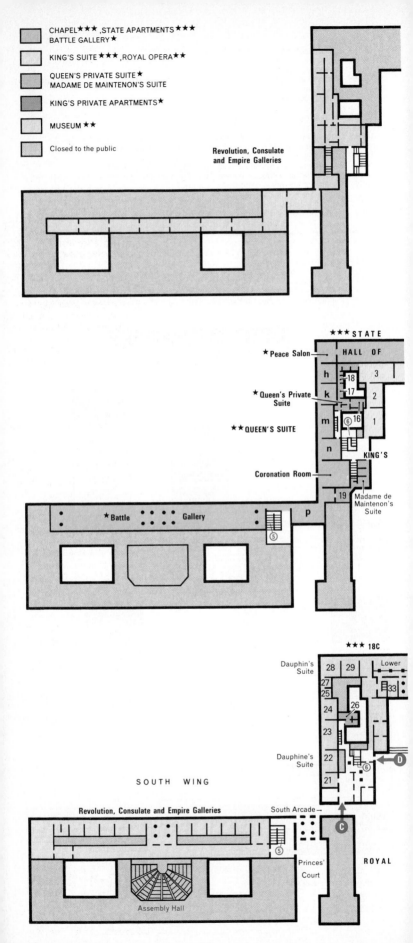

CHAPEL★★★, STATE APARTMENTS★★★
BATTLE GALLERY★

KING'S SUITE★★★, ROYAL OPERA★★

QUEEN'S PRIVATE SUITE★
MADAME DE MAINTENON'S SUITE

KING'S PRIVATE APARTMENTS★

MUSEUM★★

Closed to the public

Revolution, Consulate
and Empire Galleries

★★★ STATE

HALL OF

★Peace Salon

h   18   3
          17   2
★Queen's Private
Suite   k

★★QUEEN'S SUITE   m   ⑥ 16   1

n

KING'S

Coronation Room

19   Madame de
                   Maintenon's
                   Suite

★Battle   Gallery   p
                    ⑤

★★★ 18C

Dauphin's   28   29   Lower
Suite
          27   33
          25
          24   26
          23
Dauphine's   22   ⑥ ←D
Suite
          21

SOUTH   WING

Revolution, Consulate and Empire Galleries

South Arcade→

⑤

Princes'   C   ROYAL
Court

Assembly Hall

256

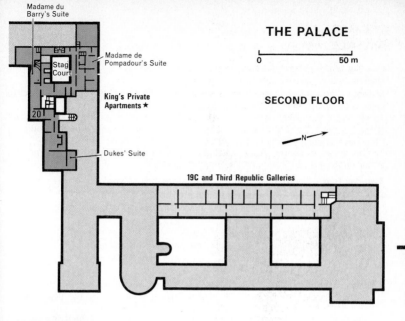

THE PALACE

0 — 50 m

SECOND FLOOR

N →

Madame du Barry's Suite

Stag Court

Madame de Pompadour's Suite

King's Private Apartments ★

20

Dukes' Suite

19C and Third Republic Galleries

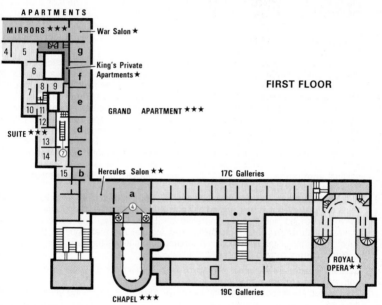

APARTMENTS

MIRRORS ★★★ — War Salon ★

4 | 5

g

6

f — **King's Private Apartments ★**

7 | 8 | 9

e

FIRST FLOOR

10 | 11

GRAND APARTMENT ★★★

12

d

13

c

SUITE ★★★

14

⑦

15 | b

Hercules Salon ★★

17C Galleries

a

④

ROYAL OPERA ★★

19C Galleries

CHAPEL ★★★

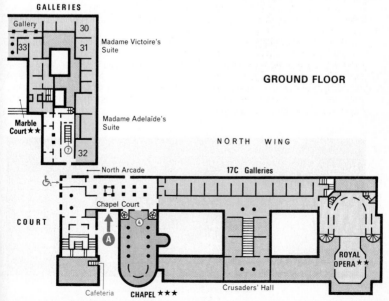

GALLERIES

Gallery | 30

33 | 31 — Madame Victoire's Suite

GROUND FLOOR

Marble Court ★★

Madame Adelaïde's Suite

⑦ | 32

NORTH WING

North Arcade

17C Galleries

♿

Chapel Court

④

COURT

Ⓐ

ROYAL OPERA ★★

Cafeteria

CHAPEL ★★★

Crusaders' Hall

PALACE ★★★ ⊙

One-day tour – Programme for visitors pressed for time:
Morning: Palace (exterior and State Apartments).
Afternoon: King's Suite and Royal Opera, the gardens (the main perspective and the south groves) up to the Apollo Basin and the Grand Canal.
By car: from the Grand Canal to the Trianon (arrange to be picked up by the driver when you reach the Grand Canal – for access by car see map of the park, below).
The Grand Trianon (exterior), the gardens of the Petit Trianon.
The North Parterre of the palace, starting from the Neptune Basin (*park the car nearby, either on Avenue de Trianon or Boulevard de la Reine*).

Two-day tour – Tourists with more time to spare may proceed as follows:
Day 1 – **Morning:** Tour of the palace as indicated above.
       Afternoon: Complete tour of the palace gardens and boat trip along the Grand Canal.
Day 2 – **Morning:** King's Suite and Royal Opera.
       Afternoon: Complete tour of the Trianon (châteaux and gardens).

PALACE EXTERIOR *Quick tour: allow 1 hour*

Place d'Armes – This huge square was the meeting-point for the three wide avenues leading to Paris, St-Cloud and Sceaux, separated by the **Royal Stables★** (Écuries Royales) built by Jules Hardouin-Mansart. Identical in size, the Petite and the Grande Écuries were so named for reasons of convenience: the former housed the various carriages and equipages, while the latter was used for saddle horses: its ring was often the scene of impressive equestrian entertainments.

Courtyards – The wrought-iron railings date from the reign of Louis XVIII. Beyond them stretches a series of three courtyards.
The forecourt or **Ministers' Court** is flanked by two long ranges housing the four blocks in which the king's ministers would take up residence. An equestrian statue of Louis XIV, commissioned by Louis-Philippe, stands in the middle of the drive.
The **Royal Court** was separated from the outer courtyard by railings through which only persons of high rank (peers, princes of the blood, noblemen etc) might pass in carriages. The two wings lining this court were originally separate from the palace and used as outhouses. They were joined to the main building and fronted by a set of colonnades under Louis XV and Louis XVIII. Beyond the North Arcade – leading through to the park – and the South Arcade stand three gilded gates marking the entrance to the State Apartments. On the left rises the Queen's Staircase. The original entrance lay to the right but it was blocked up after the Ambassadors' Staircase was destroyed in 1752.
The **Marble Court★★** – paved with slabs of black and white marble – has been raised to its original level. It is surrounded by Louis XIII's old château, the façades of which were remodelled and greatly improved by Louis Le Vau and Jules Hardouin-Mansart: balustrades, busts, statues, vases etc. On the first floor of the central pavilion, the three arched windows belonging to the king's bedroom are fronted by a gilded balcony resting upon eight marble columns.

★★★**Garden Façade** – *Walk under the North Arcade, skirt the main part of the palace and step back to get a good view.*
The huge building occupies a total length of 680m - 2 230ft and yet its general appearance is not monotonous: the central body stands proud from the wings, and the length of the façade is articulated with intermittent rows of sculpted columns and pillars to break the rigidity of the horizontal lines. The flat roof, built in the Italian style, is concealed by a balustrade bearing ornamental trophies and vases. The statues of Apollo and Diana, surrounded by the Months of the Year, surmount the central body which housed the Royal Suite. Certain members of the royal family, including several of the king's children, stayed in the South Wing.
The terrace extending in front of the château commands an extensive view of the park and its many perspectives. It bears two **giant vases★**, one at each end: the one to the north was executed by Coysevox and symbolises War, while the south vase, attributed to Tuby, is a representation of Peace. They are placed outside the respective bay windows of the War and Peace Salons.

The entrance front by night, Versailles

At the foot of the main building lies a row of four sculptures, the very first to be executed by the Keller brothers *(see also the Water Gardens, below)* who drew inspiration from the antique model: Bacchus, Apollo, Antinoüs and Silenus.

The terrace offers a general view of the grounds and their distinctive features *(description below):* in the foreground the Water Gardens (Parterres d'Eau), with a sweeping perspective as far as the Grand Canal; on the left the South Parterre; on the right the North Parterre and the North Groves, cut across by another canal leading to the Neptune Basin.

Return to the Marble Court through the South Arcade in the South Wing.

PALACE INTERIOR

Restoration work under way at the palace is mentioned only when it affects the programme of the tour.

The visitors' entrance   leads through to a vestibule which houses the ticket office. From there, go up to the Chapel (**a**) on the first floor, either by using the circular staircase   or by crossing the 17C galleries of the Museum of French History.

★★★CHAPEL

Dedicated to St Louis (Louis IX), the chapel at Versailles is an elegant display of stonework decorated in white and gold tones. This masterpiece is the work of Mansart and was completed by his brother-in-law Robert de Cotte in 1710.

The pillars and arches bear exquisite low-reliefs by amongst others Van Clève, Le Lorrain, Coustou.

As the usual place for an organ is occupied by the royal gallery it stands instead at the east end in the gallery, a splendid piece of craftsmanship by Clicquot, enhanced by fine carvings based on studies by Robert de Cotte.

The marble altar is attributed to Van Clève. The altar front features a low-relief in gilded bronze representing the *Pietà:* it is the work of Vassé.

The painting in the apse is by La Fosse and depicts the Resurrection.

While the members of the royal family were seated in the gallery, the courtiers stood in the nave.

★★★STATE APARTMENTS

These consist of the various reception rooms – the Hercules Salon and a suite of six salons known as the Grand Apartment – together with the famous Hall of Mirrors and the living quarters where the king and queen would appear in public.

While visiting the palace, it is helpful to remember a few facts concerning the layout of great châteaux of Classical and Baroque inspiration.

Generally speaking, French rulers would spend their day between the ornate reception rooms of the State Apartments – their official, semi-public quarters – and the Private Apartments which afforded a certain amount of privacy. In the 18C, Louis XV and later Louis XVI enjoyed a greater degree of intimacy in the Petits Appartements.

A standard example of State Apartments – The two suites belonging to the king and the queen are placed symmetrically on either side of the central pavilion. Each suite consisted of at least one guard room, several antechambers, the bedroom, the grand cabinet and a number of private salons (it was through these that the two royal suites communicated). At Versailles, this symmetrical disposition was applied only between 1673 and 1682. When Marie-Thérèse died in 1683, there was no question of Mme de Maintenon occupying the apartments of the former queen. Louis XIV moved into new quarters giving onto the Marble Court. His former suite was transformed, at great cost, into a series of reception rooms.

Summer and winter furnishings – In the living quarters of the palace, the hangings were changed twice a year, around the months of May and October. Thus the summer furnishings (silk) would alternate with the winter furnishings (velvet).

The fabric-dressed walls were then hung with paintings inspired by religious themes, by artists of the Italian School: Poussin, Veronese, Titian etc.

★★HERCULES SALON

The salon stands on the site formerly occupied by the fourth and penultimate chapel of the original château. Construction of the salon was started in 1712, the year in which the St Louis Chapel was inaugurated; the decoration was completed by Robert de Cotte in 1736, under the reign of Louis XV.

The salon boasts two splendid compositions by Veronese. **Christ at the House of Simon the Pharisee**★ was a present to Louis XIV from the Venetian Republic. The Hercules Salon was in fact designed to house this huge painting, which has been returned to its precious gilt frame. The second work *Eliezer and Rebecca* hangs above the marble mantelpiece which is richly adorned with gilded bronze.

The ceiling – representing Hercules entering the Kingdom of the Gods – was painted by François Lemoyne, who spent three years on the $315m^2$ - 3 390sq ft fresco. His work met with widespread acclaim, but the following year the artist suffered a nervous breakdown and committed suicide (1737).

★★★GRAND APARTMENT

In former times, the apartment was approached from the Royal Court by means of the Ambassadors' Staircase (destroyed in 1752). It provides a splendid example of early Louis XIV decoration. Note the use of noble materials such as polychrome marble, bronze and copper, chiselled and gilded in the Italian Baroque style. Impressive rock crystal chandeliers hang from the ceiling and candelabra adorn the pedestal tables.

The suite of six salons was sparsely furnished with a few stools, folding chairs, pedestal and console tables. The Grand Apartment – running from the Hercules Salon, dedicated to a man endowed with divine powers, to the Apollo Salon, built in honour of the son of Jupiter and Latona – symbolised the solar myth to which Louis XIV claimed to belong. The six rooms were all built by Le Vau in 1668 and decorated by Le Brun. The salons are named after the subjects painted on the ceiling frescoes.

Three times a week, between 6 and 10pm on Mondays, Wednesdays and Thursdays, the king held court in the Grand Apartment. The ceremony was enhanced by dancing and various other entertainments.

Salon de l'Abondance (Abundance Salon) (b) – At the time of Louis XIV, on the days when the king held court, this salon presented three buffets: one for hot drinks, two for cold drinks such as wine, eaux-de-vie, sorbets and fruit juice, then called "fruit water" *(eaux-de-fruits)*. The walls are hung with the winter furnishings, made of embossed velvet in deep emerald tones. Admire the four portraits of the royal family, painted by Rigaud and Van Loo: the Grand Dauphin, Philippe V, the Duke of Burgundy and Louis XV.

The next two salons were originally vestibules leading to the Ambassadors' Staircase. The magnificent walls lined with marble are in keeping with the ornate decoration of the former main staircase.

Salon de Vénus (Venus Salon) (c) – As in the following salons, the ceiling is painted by Houasse. It features decorated panels framed by heavy gilt stucco.

Salon de Diane (Diana Salon) (d) – This used to be the billiard room under Louis XIV. Observe the **bust of Louis XIV** by Bernini (1665), a remarkable piece of Baroque workmanship. The salon displays several paintings by La Fosse and Blanchard.

Salon de Mars (Mars Salon) (e) – The lavish decoration (wall hangings) is a reminder that this salon once belonged to the royal suite (guard room). Louis XIV subsequently used it for dances, games and concerts. The two galleries which housed the musicians were placed on either side of the fireplace. They were dismantled in 1750. The 18C paintings include *Darius' Tent* by Le Brun and *The Pilgrims of Emmaüs* after Veronese.

The side walls bear Rigaud's portrait of Louis XV and a painting of Marie Leczinska by Van Loo. The martial scenes on the ceiling are attributed to Audran, Jouvenet and Houasse. One of the Sun King's favourite paintings hangs above the fireplace: Domenichino's *King David*, in which he is portrayed playing the harp. It was originally displayed in the king's bedchamber.

Salon de Mercure (Mercury Salon) (f) – This former antechamber was used for gaming on the evenings when the king held court. It was here that Louis XIV lay in state for one week after his death in 1715. Seventy-two ecclesiastics took turns to watch over him, ensuring that four services could be held at the same time between 5am and midday. The ceiling was decorated by J B de Champaigne.

Salon d'Apollon (Apollo Salon) (g) – The former throne room. The throne was placed on a central platform covered by a large canopy. The three hooks to which the canopy was attached still remain. Louis XIV received ambassadors in the Apollo Salon. When he held court, it was used for dances and concerts. The ceiling sports a fresco by La Fosse: *Apollo in a Sun Chariot*.

This room marks the end of the Grand Apartment. Set at a perpendicular angle, the Hall of Mirrors and the adjacent War and Peace Salons occupy the entire length of the main front giving onto the palace gardens.

★WAR SALON

The War Salon is a corner room opening onto the Hall of Mirrors and the Apollo Salon, and features a huge oval low-relief sculpted by Coysevox, representing the king riding in triumph over his enemies.

★★★HALL OF MIRRORS

The Hall of Mirrors was completed by Mansart in 1687. It covered a short-lived terrace (1668-78) that Le Vau had built along the garden front. Together with the War and Peace Salons, it is the most brilliant achievement by Le Brun and his team of artists. The hall is 75m - 246ft long, 10m - 33ft wide and 12m - 40ft high. The 17 large windows are echoed by 17 mirrors on the wall opposite. These are made up of 578 pieces of the largest size possible at the time. This hall was designed to catch the golden rays of sunset.

The ceiling fresco – painted by Le Brun in amber, flame-coloured tones – pays tribute to the early reign of Louis XIV (from 1661 to 1678, up to the Treaty of Nijmegen).

The Hall of Mirrors in the Palace of Versailles

The capitals of the pilasters bear an unusual ornamental feature: made of gilded bronze, they represent the "French order", which combines antique motifs with fleurs-de-lis and stylised cocks (the emblem for French patriotism).

In 1980 the Hall of Mirrors was restored to its former glory. With its crystal chandeliers and new set of candelabra – cast after the six surviving originals – it presents the same dazzling appearance as in 1770 when Marie-Antoinette was married to the Dauphin, the future King Louis XVI.

The Hall of Mirrors was used for court receptions, formal ceremonies and diplomatic encounters. On these occasions, the throne was placed under the arch leading into the Peace Salon. It is easier to picture the hall during court festivities, when it was thronged with elegant visitors in formal attire, brightly lit by the thousands of flickering candles reflected in the mirrors.

The tubs bearing the orange trees, as well as the chandeliers and other furnishings, were made of solid silver under Louis XIV. For a period of ten years, part of the country's monetary reserves was thus shaped into works of art. It was here that the German Empire was proclaimed on 18 January 1871, and that the Treaty of Versailles was signed on 28 June 1919.

The central windows offer a splendid **view★★★** of the Grand Perspective.

★PEACE SALON

Placed at the southern end of the Hall of Mirrors, this salon acts as a counterpart to the War Salon. Originally conceived as an extension of the long hall, it was made into an annexe of the Queen's Suite towards the end of Louis XIV's reign: it communicated with the gallery by means of a movable partition.

Above the mantelpiece hangs *Louis XV bringing Peace to Europe*, a painting by François Lemoyne.

★★QUEEN'S SUITE

This suite was created for Louis XIV's wife Marie-Thérèse, who died in 1683.

Queen's Bedroom (h) – In 1975, after a restoration programme lasting 30 years, this room regained its summer furnishings of 1787. Originally designed for Maria-Theresa, the bedchamber was later occupied by the wife of the Grand Dauphin, Louis XIV's son; by the duchesse de Bourgogne, wife of the Sun King's grandson, who gave birth to Louis XV here; by Marie Leczinska, wife of Louis XV (43 years); and by Louis XVI's wife Marie-Antoinette. Nineteen children belonging to French royalty – among them Louis XV and Philippe V of Spain – were born in this bedroom.

A long-standing tradition ruled that the delivery of royal infants should be made public. Even the proud Marie-Antoinette had to comply with the French custom, surrounded by a crowd of curious onlookers.

The ornamental motifs on the wainscoting and the ceiling were designed and made for Marie Leczinska by Gabriel, while the fireplace, imposing jewel chest, sphinx-shaped andirons, fire screen and bedspread were designed for Marie-Antoinette.

Note the magnificent silk hangings and furnishings decorated with flowers, ribbons and peacock's tails, many of which were rewoven to the original pattern in Lyon.

Salon des Nobles de la Reine (Peers' Salon) (k) – The official presentations to the Queen took place in this former antechamber. It was also here that the queens and *dauphines* of France used to lie in state prior to the burial ceremony. The original fresco on the ceiling, attributed to Michel Corneille, has been preserved. The rest of the decoration was considered staid and old-fashioned by Marie-Antoinette, who had it entirely refurbished by the architect Richard Mique (1785). Furnished with commodes and corner cupboards by Riesener and embellished with magnificent green silk hangings, the salon looks very much as it would have done on the eve of the French Revolution in 1789.

Antechamber (m) – This chamber was used as a guard room under Marie-Thérèse. It was here that Louis XV and Marie Leczinska – and later Louis XVI and Marie-Antoinette – would dine in full view of the public.
A family portrait of Marie-Antoinette and her children by Mme Vigée-Lebrun shows, from left to right, Mme Royale, the Duke of Normandy – who became Louis XVII – and the Dauphin, who died in 1789. He is portrayed pointing to an empty cradle which symbolises the premature death of his sister "Mme Sophie".

Salle des Gardes de la Reine (Queen's Guard Room) (n) – The decoration was the work of Le Brun and N Coypel. It was moved from its original setting – the Jupiter Salon – when the Hall of Mirrors was completed in 1687; the Jupiter Salon was subsequently renamed the War Salon. On 6 October 1789, several of the queen's guards were stabbed to death by a group of dedicated revolutionaries. The Louis XIV decor – featuring sumptuous marble-lined walls – has been beautifully preserved.

CORONATION ROOM

This room was initially used as a chapel between 1676 and 1682. The Parlement de Paris used to hold its sessions in this former guard room. It was altered by Louis-Philippe in order to accommodate several huge paintings depicting the Emperor's coronation. David's second *Coronation of Napoleon* – executed between 1808 and 1822 – lies to the left of the entrance. The original is exhibited in the Louvre Museum (Salle Mollien). On the opposite wall hang David's *Champ de Mars Eagles* and a painting by Gros representing *Murat at the Battle of Aboukir* (1806).

1792 Room (p) – This large, unfurnished room lies at the junction of the south wing and the main central pavilion. The walls are hung with portraits of soldiers, paintings of famous battles and war scenes. Cogniet's work *The Paris National Guard* shows Louis-Philippe proudly sporting his Lieutenant-General's uniform.

★BATTLE GALLERY

Created in 1836 on the site of the princes' suite in the south wing, the Battle Gallery caused quite a stir because of its huge dimensions: 120m - 394ft by 13m - 43ft. It was designed to house the 33 paintings of France's major victories under the *Ancien Régime*, the Empire and the Republic, from Tolbiac *(first on the left when entering)* to Wagram *(first on the right)* by Horace Vernet, Louis-Philippe's favourite painter (who also painted Iéna, Fontenoy, Bouvines and Friedland), and including works by Eugène Delacroix (Taillebourg) and Baron Gérard (Austerlitz).
Take the Princes' Staircase ⑤ down to the Princes' Court.

★★★KING'S SUITE ⓘ

The king's quarters are arranged around the Marble Court. They were designed by Jules Hardouin-Mansart and set up in Louis XIII's château between 1682 and 1701. The style is typical of the Louis XIV period. The ceilings are no longer coffered but painted white, the marble tiling has been replaced by white and gold panelling, and large mirrors adorn the stately fireplaces.

Queen's Staircase ⑥ – Towards the end of the *Ancien Régime*, this was the official entrance to the royal apartments. The decoration of the staircase is extremely ornate: from the top landing, admire the elegant display of multi-coloured marble conceived by Le Brun. The huge *trompe-l'œil* painting is jointly attributed to Meusnier, Poerson and Belin de Fontenay.
The guard room (**1**) and a first antechamber (**2**) lead to the Bull's Eye Salon.

Bull's-Eye Salon (second antechamber) (3) – The salon was originally two rooms: the king's bedchamber between 1684 and 1701 – the part nearest to the two windows giving onto the Marble Court – and a small study. The two were united under the supervision of Mansart and Robert de Cotte. Lightness and elegance are the principal characteristics of this charming salon, which contrasts sharply with the earlier achievements of Louis' reign. Level with the famous bull's-eye – echoed by a mirror on the opposite wall – runs a frieze depicting children at play. Note Coysevox' bust of Louis XIV.
The paintings by Veronese and Bassano have been replaced by a number of royal portraits, including an allegorical rendering of Louis XIV's family by Nocret.
It was in this antechamber that the courtiers assembled before witnessing the rising and retiring ceremonies of the king.

King's Bedroom (4) – This became Louis XIV's state bedroom in 1701. At the centre of the palace, this bedroom, which gave onto the Marble Court, looks out in the direction of the rising sun. Louis XIV, suffering from a gangrenous knee, died here on 1 September 1715. The ritual rising and retiring ceremonies took place in this room from 1701 to 1789. Daytime visitors were requested to make a small bow when passing in front of the bed, which symbolised the Sun King's absolute monarchy.

The King's bedroom is hung with its summer furnishings of 1723 – Louis XV's second year at the palace – and its decor has been scrupulously reconstructed. Beyond the beautifully-restored gilded balustrade lies a raised four-poster bed, complete with canopy and curtains. The gold and silver embroidered brocade used for the bed and wall hangings, upholstery and door coverings has been entirely rewoven.

Six religious works – including Valentin de Boulogne's *Four Evangelists* – lie level with the attica. Above the doors hang *St Madeleine* by Domenichino, *John the Baptist* by Caracciolo and several portraits by Van Dyck.

Council Chamber (5) – Like the Bull's-Eye Salon, it originally consisted of two rooms: the Cabinet des Termes and the Cabinet du Conseil. The decoration of the present room – created under Louis XV – was entrusted to Gabriel. The mirrors dating from Louis XIV's reign were replaced with wainscoting by Rousseau, who produced a splendid Rococo interior.

Over a period of one hundred years, many grave decisions affecting the destiny of France were taken in the Council Chamber, including that of France's involvement in the American War of Independence in 1775.

★★★KING'S PRIVATE SUITE

This suite of rooms, with its superb wainscoting by Gabriel, provides a delightful feast for the eyes. The fine rococo carvings are the work of Verberckt.

King's Bedchamber (6) – The absence of furniture makes it difficult to picture this room in its original state. Owing to the constraints of court etiquette, Louis XV (after 1738) and then Louis XVI (up to the end of the *Ancien Régime*) daily had to leave this room and slip away to the State bedroom, where they "performed" the rising and retiring ceremonies. It was here that Louis XV died of smallpox on 10 May 1774. The original paintings above the doors were taken down and replaced by portraits of the three daughters of Louis XV.

Clock Cabinet (7) – This room was named after the famous astronomical clock by Passemant and Dauthiau, with bronze embellishments by Caffiéri, which was brought to the palace in January 1754: it showed not only the hour, but the day, the month, the year and the phase of the moon. Under Louis XV and until 1769 this cabinet was used as a gaming room when the king held court.

In the centre of the room stands the equestrian statue of Louis XV by Vassé. It is a replica of Bouchardon's sculpture which initially adorned the Place Louis XV – now called Place de la Concorde – in Paris and which was destroyed in 1792.

Dogs' Antechamber (8) – *(Closed)*. A charming passageway off the king's private staircase (known as *degré du Roi*). The decoration features Louis XIV panelling, in sharp contrast with the adjoining rooms.

Hunters' Dining Hall (9) – *(Closed)*. Between 1750 and 1769 hunts were organised every other day in the forests surrounding Versailles. Louis XV and a few privileged fellow hunters would come here to sup after their exertions.

Corner Room (10) – This masterpiece of 18C French ornamental art was commissioned by Louis XV. Gabriel and the accomplished cabinet-maker Verberckt were responsible for the stunning rococo decor.

The celebrated **roll-top desk★** by Oeben and Riesener (1769) was among the few prestigious works of art to be spared in 1792.

The medal cabinet attributed to the cabinet-maker Gaudreaux (1739) is adorned with numerous exhibits in gilded bronze: it bears the 1785 candelabra commemorating the role played by France in the American War of Independence, flanked by two Sèvres vases (bronzes by Thomire). Two corner cupboards made by Joubert in 1755, belonging to Louis XV's collections, were added subsequently, as was a set of chairs attributed to Foliot (1774). The room was originally private but under Louis XVI it took on a semi-official character. In 1785 it was the scene of a formal encounter attended by Marie-Antoinette, at which the King informed Cardinal de Rohan that he would shortly be arrested for his involvement in the Diamond Necklace Affair.

The Corner Room leads through to the Inner Cabinet (11) where Louis XV and Louis XVI kept all confidential documents relating to state affairs, and where they granted private audiences.

Madame Adélaïde's Cabinet (12) – This was one of the first "new rooms" remodelled at the instigation of Louis XV. It overlooks the Royal Court and was designed by Louis XV for his favourite daughter Madame Adélaïde (1752). The ornate decoration features delightful rococo wainscoting and gilded panelling embellished with musical instruments, as well as marine and floral motifs: the cabinet was used as a music room by the king's daughter.

It is believed that the young Mozart performed on the harpsichord before the royal family in this very room, during the winter of 1763-64. Louis XVI later made the room his "jewel cabinet". Note the extraordinary medal cabinet attributed to Bennemann: each drawer is decorated with melted wax, delicately blended with feathers and butterfly wings and carefully poured onto thin glass plates.

Louis XVI's Library (13) – Designed by the ageing Gabriel and executed by the wood carver Antoine Rousseau, this extremely refined ensemble is a perfect example of the Louis XVI style (1774). The austere appearance of the bookcases, in which the door panels are concealed by a set of false decorative backs, is countered by the gay Chinese motifs on the upholstery and the curtains. Next to Riesener's flat-top desk stands the vast mahogany table where the King spent many enjoyable hours in quiet seclusion.

China Salon (14) – This room was used as the Hunters' Dining Hall under Louis XV, and from 1769 to 1789 under Louis XVI. It houses numerous exhibits of Sèvres porcelain, glazed after drawings by Oudry. The whole collection was commissioned by Louis XVI.

Louis XVI's Gaming Room (15) – From the doorway admire the full effect of this perfect vignette of 18C furniture and ornamental art: corner cupboards by Riesener (1774), set of chairs by Boulard, curtains and upholstery in a rich crimson and gold brocade.

Walk down the Louis-Philippe staircase ⑦ and leave by the North Arcade (a public passageway leading through to the park). The room on the ground floor houses a miniature replica of the Ambassadors' Staircase (Escalier des Ambassadeurs). Ask to view the model.

★★ROYAL OPERA

Gabriel started work on the Opera in 1768 and completed it in time for the wedding ceremony of Marie-Antoinette and the future King Louis XVI.

It was the first oval-shaped opera house in France and although it was built during the reign of Louis XV, its decoration was later to be termed Louis XVI: Pajou's work, inspired by the classical models of Antiquity, remains surprisingly modern-looking. The court engineer Arnoult designed the sophisticated machinery required for the new opera house. For banquets and formal receptions, the floor of the stalls and of the circle could be raised level with the stage. This auditorium – its interior decoration made entirely of wood – enjoys excellent acoustics and can seat 700. The seating capacity could virtually be doubled by means of additional galleries set up on the stage.

In the middle of the circle lies the royal box, guarded by a mobile grid and surmounted by an elegant alcove. A number of other boxes, also enclosed by grilles, may be seen up above in the flies.

The low-reliefs adorning the boxes were executed by Pajou. They represent the Gods of Mount Olympus (dress circle), groups of children and the signs of the Zodiac (upper circle).

Although initially reserved for members of the court, the opera house at Versailles was later used for lavish receptions organised on the occasion of official visits. A number of foreign rulers were received at the palace, including the King of Sweden (1784), Marie-Antoinette's brother the Emperor Joseph II (1777 and 1781) and Queen Victoria (1855).

The sessions of the National Assembly were held in the Royal Opera between 1871 and 1875. It was here that the Wallon Amendment was voted on 30 January 1875, laying the foundation stone of the Third Republic. The latest restoration ended in 1957, when the opening ceremony was attended by Queen Elizabeth II and Prince Philip.

★QUEEN'S PRIVATE SUITE ⊙ *plan overleaf below*

These somewhat cramped apartments giving onto two inner courtyards were used as a daytime retreat by the queens of France. Unlike the king, the queen was not allowed to retire away from her State Apartment. The 18C decoration and layout were conceived by Marie-Antoinette, who gave the suite a delicate, feminine touch.

Gold Cabinet (16) – The panelling by the Rousseau brothers marks the revival of Antique motifs: frieze with rosettes, sphinx, trivets, small censers… A lovely chandelier features along the magnificent bronze works. The commode is attributed to Riesener. Naderman's harp reminds visitors that the Queen was an enthusiastic musician in her spare time: she would often play with Grétry, Gluck or even his rival Piccinni. It was in this cabinet that Mme Vigée-Lebrun worked on her portrait of Marie-Antoinette.

Library (17) – Note the drawer handles in the shape of a two-headed eagle, the emblem of the House of Hapsburg.

Boudoir (18) – This little octagonal chamber was used for resting by Marie-Antoinette. It was designed in 1781 by the Queen's architect Mique in honour of the birth of the first Dauphin. The decoration evokes romance and parental love: lilies, hearts pierced with arrows and the famous dolphin.

The boudoir – embellished with blue silk hangings – is furnished with two armchairs by Georges Jacob and the original day couch.

Two of the many prestigious works of art given to the Queen are exhibited here: a clock offered by the City of Paris and a table featuring a tray with fragments of petrified wood (a present from one of Marie-Antoinette's sisters).

The second floor houses Marie-Antoinette's Apartment *(undergoing restoration).*

MADAME DE MAINTENON'S SUITE *plan overleaf below*

This suite *(open only for temporary exhibitions)* was located away from the throngs of courtiers but next to the King's apartments, reflecting a situation enforced by the King during the last 32 years of his reign, with a view to establishing an atmosphere of tact and mutual respect.

The original furniture has been removed and the suite now belongs to the Museum of French History.

The Grand Cabinet (**19**) was a private salon decorated with red hangings where Mme de Maintenon entertained members of the royal family – her favourite was the Duchess of Burgundy – and where Racine recited his famous plays *Esther* and *Athalie*.

★KING'S PRIVATE APARTMENTS

Louis XV did not share the taste for publicity which had been such a dominant trait of the Sun King's personality. Consequently he created a suite of private apartments to which he could retire and receive his mistresses, close friends and relatives.

Some of the rooms overlooked the inner courts, others were located in the attics. They were approached by a series of narrow passages and staircases.

In the privacy of these rooms the King would read, study, carve ivory and wooden pieces or eat on the tiny roof-top terrace, surrounded by tubs of flowers and several delightful aviaries.

The decoration of these apartments was renewed at regular intervals – as were their occupants. Four of the rooms housed Mme de Pompadour's first suite from 1745 to 1750. Louis XVI used the rooms giving onto the Stag Court when he wished to study or indulge in one of his favourite pastimes.

A tour of these apartments is recommended to visitors who are already acquainted with Versailles and who have a particular interest in 18C decorative art.

Madame de Pompadour's Suite – *2nd floor. (Closed).* This was the first suite occupied by Louis XV's mistress between 1745 and 1750. The Grand Cabinet features splendid carved woodwork by Verberckt.

Madame du Barry's Suite – *2nd floor.* The wooden panelling has been restored according to the original decoration. The suite looks out onto the Stag Court and the Marble Court. It consists of a bathroom, a bedroom, a library and a corner salon (**20**) which was one of Louis XV's favourite haunts: he would enjoy sitting here and gazing out at the town of Versailles nestling among wooded slopes.

Dukes' Suite – *2nd floor.* These apartments were occupied by two ministers of Louis XVI, the Duc de Maurepas and the Duc de Villequier. The decoration appears rather austere when compared to that of the royal suites. Most of the furniture was donated by the Duke and Duchess of Windsor.

★★MUSEUM OF FRENCH HISTORY

The museum houses several thousand paintings and sculptures which present French history from the 16C to the 19C.

CRUSADERS' HALLS *(by appointment only)*

They contain a collection of paintings commissioned by Louis-Philippe.

17C GALLERIES

These small rooms – occupying the greater part of the north wing – feature a charming selection of paintings and portraits, also busts and console tables.

Ground Floor – The vestibule by the chapel leads to this suite of eleven galleries. The first six were once occupied by the duc de Maine, the son of Louis XIV and Mme de Montespan, while the last four housed the apartments of the Princes of Bourbon-Conti.

The series of **portraits**★ depicting famous personalities was assembled by Roger de Gaignières, who bequeathed the collection to the Sun King; they include Henri IV, who enjoyed visiting the site of Versailles, and Louis XIII, the founder of the original château. Works by Vouet, Philippe de Champaigne, Deruet and Le Brun tell of the men and the events that marked French history between Louis XIII's reign and the early days of divine monarchy.

The gallery dedicated to Port-Royal features several portraits by Philippe de Champaigne and gouaches attributed to Magdeleine de Boullongne. The rare collection of paintings in the Versailles Gallery illustrates the various stages of construction of the palace.

First Floor – Portraits of the royal family, Mme de Maintenon, Louis XIV's legitimised children and the celebrated figures of the King's reign, painted by Le Brun, Van der Meulen, Coypel, Largillière etc, bring these rooms to life.

Note the set of portraits of famous men (Colbert, Racine, Molière, La Fontaine, Le Nôtre and Couperin) and the vast battle scenes by Van der Meulen, characterised by attention to detail and a true love of nature.

The galleries offer a lovely view of the gardens.

★★★18C GALLERIES

These rooms situated on the ground floor of the central pavilion, once housed the apartments of Louis XV's son the Dauphin, the Dauphine Marie-Josèphe de Saxe and the three daughters of Louis XV, addressed as *Mesdames*. The mid-18C decoration has been entirely restored (furniture, hangings). Many of the works displayed in these galleries were executed by some of the greatest painters and sculptors of the 18C.
Visitors wishing to follow a chronological tour should start at the foot of the Queen's Staircase. From there, walk through the rooms giving onto the South Parterre, the terrace and the North Parterre. The tour ends with the rooms overlooking the Marble Court.

Dauphine's Suite – The Guard Room (**21**) houses a number of pictures representing the rulers who succeeded the Sun King: portrait of the five-year-old Louis XV by Rigaud, another by Belle (1722), Santerre's portrait of the Regent. The fireplace in the Antechamber (**22**), adorned with a bust of the Regent, was taken from the Queen's Bedroom at the time of Marie Leczinska. The Dauphine's Grand Cabinet (**23**) evokes the marriage of Marie Leczinska to Louis XV. It also presents Lemaire's sculpted barometer, offered on the occasion of Marie-Antoinette's marriage to the Dauphin, and several corner cupboards by Bernard II van Risen Burgh (BVRB).
The Dauphine's Bedroom (**24**) contains a Polish-style bed and a magnificent set of six armchairs by Heurtaut. Note Nattier's two portraits of Mme Adélaïde and Mme Henriette, portrayed respectively as Flora and Diana. The Inner Cabinet (**25**) features 1748 woodwork glazed with Vernis Martin. Note Gaudreaux' commode and a writing desk by BVRB.
The Dauphine's Private Cabinets (**26**) *(visited at the same time as the Queen's Private Suite)* were remodelled under Louis XVIII for the Duchesse d'Angoulême, the daughter of Louis XVI: couch formerly belonging to the Comtesse de Provence, antechamber, study-library and servants' quarters.

Dauphin's Suite – The first room (**27**) was used as a library: it boasts magnificent wooden panelling in deep amber tones, enhanced by turquoise relief work. Admire Vernet's delicate seascapes above the doors. The fine furniture includes a flat writing desk by BVRB and one of Criaerd's commodes. The Grand Corner Cabinet (**28**) houses portraits of Mesdames Adélaïde, Louise, Sophie and Victoire by Nattier, as well as some beautiful pieces of furniture by Jacob, taken from Louis XVI's gaming room at St-Cloud.
The Dauphin's Bedchamber (**29**), occupied by Louis XVI's son, has retained its original 1747 decor: wardrobe with lacquered panels (BVRB), commode by Boudin and an 18C embroidered canopied bed. The fireplace is among the finest in the palace.

Lower Gallery – Divided into apartments under Louis XVI and partly restored under Louis-Philippe, the gallery now stands as it did under Louis XIV. From 1782 to 1789 the rooms in this gallery were used by Marie-Antoinette and her children.

Water Gardens and Palace of Versailles

Madame Victoire's Suite – The Sun King's former bathroom and its two marble piscinae underwent several alterations before being used as the antechamber to this suite, occupied by the fourth daughter of Louis XV. The **Grand Cabinet** (**30**) is an exquisite corner room with a delightful carved cornice and panelling by Verberckt. It has retained its original fireplace.

Mme Victoire's former bedroom (**31**) has been furnished with some outstanding pieces, set off by the newly-restored summer hangings.

Madame Adélaïde's Suite – These rooms housed the second suite of Mme de Pompadour, who died here in 1764. Five years later, Mme Adélaïde moved into the suite, which consisted of a private cabinet, a bedroom and a grand cabinet. The **Ambassadors' Salon** (Salle des Hocquetons) (**32**) was an annexe adjoining the former Ambassadors' Staircase, destroyed in 1752. The stately proportions of this room, its *trompe-l'œil* fresco and its splendid marble paving give an idea of how magnificent the flight of stairs once looked.

Note the huge **clock**★ by Claude Siméon Passement with bronze ornamentation by Caffiéri: it dates from 1754 and illustrates the creation of the world.

The last rooms, overlooking the Marble Court, housed the apartments of the Captain of the Guard. They are dedicated to the latter days of Louis XVI's reign and the French Revolution.

The ground-floor suite of Marie-Antoinette, which she occupied during her last days at Versailles, has been partly recreated but of the furniture in the bedroom and the bathroom (**33**) only the console table and the recently re-embroidered bedspread date from her period.

REVOLUTION, CONSULATE AND EMPIRE GALLERIES
South attic (By appointment only)

A detailed exhibition of documents, drawings, engravings, watercolours and paintings, surrounded by wall-hangings of corresponding periods, brings to life the historic encounters, anecdotes, battles, ceremonies and the great figures of the Napoleonic period and the Bonaparte family which changed the course of French history.

19C GALLERIES
2nd Floor – North attic (by appointment only)

Galleries dedicated to the Restoration, the July Monarchy, the Second Empire and the Third Republic – Numerous paintings illustrate the major events which marked this period of French history: the *Entente Cordiale*, cemented with the official visits of Louis-Philippe and Queen Victoria, the conquest of Algeria, the Revolutions of 1830 and 1848, the 1870 War and the Paris Commune, the signing of the Treaty of Versailles. Note the portraits of Louis XVIII, Charles X, Louis-Philippe and his family, Napoleon III and Eugénie.

J. Guillard/SCOPE

PARK ★★★

Facts and figures – The **gardens** cover an approximate area of 100ha - 250 acres and the distance between the palace and their perimeter is estimated at 950m - 3 120ft.

Beyond the actual gardens of Versailles, the enclosed grounds of Versailles used to incorporate the **Little Park** (Petit Parc), which already included the Grand Canal and the Trianon. Under the Second Empire its area gradually shrank from 1 700ha to 600ha - 4 200 to 2 000 acres: a large part of this land was used as a terrain for military training. The royal gates at the exit of the Little Park marked the entrance to the **Great Park** (Grand Parc), a 6 000ha - 15 000 acre hunting reserve surrounded by 43km - 27 miles of walls punctuated by a series of 25 "royal" gates. The Great Park was entirely carved up during the Revolution.

The palace was built on top of a small hillock consolidated by vast loads of earth. The terrace rises above the Latona Basin by a height of 10.5m - 35ft, the Apollo Basin by 30m - 100ft, the Grand Canal by 32m - 105ft and the Orangery by 17m - 56ft.

The flower beds – To ensure that all the beds would be in full bloom during the month of August, the gardeners had to supply 150 000 plants, including 32 000 for the North Parterre, 35 000 for the South Parterre and 35 000 for the Latona beds. Under the reign of Louis XIV, the potted plants would be changed up to fifteen times a year.

★★★GARDENS ⊙
Quick tour: allow 3 hours – Plan overleaf

A typical formal garden – Versailles is a superb example of a genre perfected by André Le Nôtre: the formal garden.

The terrace and parterres provide a perfect balance to the monumental front of the palace which screens the town of Versailles.

Lower down, the Tapis Vert or carpet of grass and the Grand Canal cut across the middle of the grounds, creating a sweeping perspective that extends into the far distance. Numerous groves and straight paths are laid out on either side of this central axis. Their asymmetrical designs, basins and ornamental art add a touch of variety to Le Nôtre's formal layout. The two hundred sculptures which adorn the park here make it one of the biggest open-air museums of classical sculpture. The view towards the south extends to the heights of Satory.

The gardens in former times – Today the branches of the trees lining the paths join so as to form a roof of foliage. In Le Nôtre's time, visitors to Versailles could look up and see the sky. The trees were not planted along the edge of the lanes but set back very slightly: their shadows would not even fall on the statues. The garden paths were flanked with a variety of colourful trellises, and hedgerows averaging 7.5m - 25ft. These were fronted by tubs of orange and pomegranate trees, box trees and clipped yew trees. Louis XV and Louis XVI did not alter the layout of the gardens but under Louis XVI replanting became necessary in 1776. This operation was renewed in 1860 and 1987.

★★★**Grandes Eaux (Fountains)** – *When the fountains are in operation (see Calendar of Events, qv), the gardens may be entered only by the North Parterre, the South Parterre, the Great Staircases of 100 Steps, the two gates at the end of the Grand Canal and the Dragon Gate (at the far end of Rue de la Paroisse).*

This magnificent display of fountains and groves presents a modified version of the splendour of the 18C – known in France as the Great Century. *Brochures of the tour may be obtained at the reception desk.*

Start the tour from the top of the steps overlooking the Latona Basin. Start walking as soon as the fountains begin to play and carry on at a brisk pace, paying special attention to the Ballroom and Apollo's Bath groves, which are open only on these particular days (the latter is not visible from the garden paths). The grand finale *(at 1720 for 10 minutes)* takes place at the Neptune and Dragon Basins. It involves 99 fountains, including the Dragon Basin, reaching a height of 42m - 138ft.

★★★**Illuminations** – *Every year the dates are fixed in advance for the whole season (see Calendar of Events).*

The night illuminations are organised four times a year during summer and end with a fireworks display.

THE GRAND PERSPECTIVE

★★**Parterres d'eau (Water Gardens)** – The two huge basins that front the stately palace constitute a sort of aquatic esplanade where the three main perspectives meet: the central axis, that of the North Parterre and that of the South Parterre. The extremities of the basins bear allegorical statues of French rivers (portrayed as men) and their tributaries (portrayed as women). Lengthways are arranged groups of children at play, alternating with reclining water nymphs. These outstanding bronze sculptures were executed by the Keller brothers.

Degré de Latone (Latona Staircase) – An imposing flight of steps and a double ramp flanked with yew trees and replicas of antique statues lead from the Water Gardens down to the Latona Basin. From the top of the steps admire the wonderful **view★★★** of the gardens and the Grand Perspective.

The two fountains – These stand to the left and the right of the Latona Staircase. They were originally called the "Animal Chambers" on account of the bronze works depicting dogs fighting wild beasts. They were named after the most striking statue of the three that adorn the water basins.

Dawn Fountain (1) – Dawn – whose head is crowned by a star – is the work of Gaspard Marsy. The other two figures are Water and Spring.

★**Diana Fountain (2)** – Le Hongre's statue Air is the one looking in the direction of Dawn. At its side stands the hunting goddess Diana, by Desjardins. The third statue is attributed to Marsy and represents Venus, the goddess of love. These sculptures are among the finest works in the gardens.

All these statues were part of the massive ensemble commissioned by Colbert in 1674: a total of thirty marble sculptures, including 24 statues grouped into sets of six according to selected themes. The four Elements, the four Times of Day, the four Poems, the four Seasons, the four Continents and the four Virtues were to be installed on the terrace fronting the château. The initial plan was however never carried out: the court architects thought it a pity to break the classical lines of the esplanade with a row of great looming figures. Finally it was decided to adopt a more original approach: most of the bronze statues were cast as reclining figures and arranged around the basins of the water gardens.

★**Bassin de Latone (Latona Basin)** – This vast composition by Marsy was the very first marble sculpture to grace the gardens of Versailles (1670). It tells the story of Latona, the mother of Apollo and Diana, who was showered with insults by the peasants of Lycea and prevented from quenching her thirst. She appealed to Jupiter, the father of her children, who promptly avenged the offence by turning the culprits into frogs. The Lizard Basins on the side picture the early stages of the metamorphosis...

Originally the statue of Latona looked towards the palace, a clear indication of how the King viewed the public or private insults concerning his love life.

At the foot of the ramp, to the right, lies the charming **Nymph with a Shell (3)**, a modern replica of Coysevox' statue. The original work – inspired by the Antique model – has been moved to the Louvre Museum.

★★**Tapis Vert** – From the foot of the Latona Staircase, admire the Grand Perspective leading up to the palace and extending beyond the Tapis Vert (Green Carpet), towards the Grand Canal.

This long stretch of lawn is lined with a superb collection of ornamental vases and statues, among them Cyparissus and his pet stag by Flamen and Poulletier's Didon. A stroll along the Allée du Midi leads to the **Richelieu Venus (4)**, executed by Le Gros after an Antique bust that featured among the Cardinal's private collections.

Leave the Tapis Vert and wander down to the south groves.

BOSQUETS DU MIDI (SOUTH GROVES)

★**Ballroom Grove (5)** – This elegant ensemble was part of Le Nôtre's original plans. Shaped as a circular stage, it is surrounded by gentle slopes, grassy banks and tiered rockeries where small cascades tumbled down. This outdoor theatre was used for dances attended by members of the court or a corps de ballet.

Bacchus or Autumn Basin (6) – Attributed to Gaspard Marsy. The basins of the Four Seasons are laid out in the form of a quadrangle flanked by the North and South Groves. These groups of lead figures were recently re-gilded and decorated in "natural tones". *See the Saturn, Flora and Ceres Basins below.*

Queen's Grove (7) – This grove lies on the site of a former maze and was created in 1775, at the time of the great replanting campaign.

In its centre stand a number of bronze statues cast after Antique models: Aphrodite, a Fighting Gladiator etc. The maple groves are a magnificent sight in autumn.

Water Mirror Basin (8) – Of the two basins circling the Royal Isle, the larger began to silt up and was replaced by a landscape garden, known as the Royal Garden. The only one to survive is the Water Mirror Basin (Vertugadin), handsomely adorned with statues.

★**Jardin du Roi (Royal Garden)** – A dazzling sight in summer, when all the flowers are in full bloom, this garden is a welcome change from the formal groves of Versailles. The central lawn is flanked by a charming selection of rare tree species.

Saturn or Winter Basin (9) – The sculpture by François Girardon portrays a winged god surrounded by cherubs amidst ice floes and shells.

★★**Colonnade** – *This grove is usually closed but can be seen quite clearly through the railings.*

Jules Hardouin-Mansart built this circular colonnade in 1685 with the help of fifteen fellow sculptors. One of its most pleasing features is the elegant display of multi-coloured marble: azure, carnation, lilac and white. Observe the carved masks on the keystones and, on the spandrels, the delightful groups of children at play.

★BASSIN D'APOLLON (APOLLO BASIN)

The whole composition was executed by Tuby to designs by Le Brun and is dedicated to the Sun God Apollo.

Apollo is portrayed seated in his chariot, surrounded by marine monsters, rising from the ocean waters to bring Light to the Earth.

ÉTOILE ROYALE

Étoile des
Closeaux

Allée

Tuilerie

Allée

RAMBOUILLET

D 10

Rue

de

la

Div^on

Leclerc

Allée

Allée

de

de

Av.

des

des

des

Choisy

Allée des Closeaux

de

CANAL ★★

de

des

Plat

Menagerie

Petit

Canal

Canal

Aée

du

GRAND

Paons

d'Honneur

Filles

des

Reine

Allée

Allée

Allée

de

la

Reine

Rue

St-Cyr

Porte
des Matelots

Allée des Matelots

Landing Stage

P

de

Allée

d'Apollon

Allée St- Antoine

Apollo
Basin ★

Little Venice

Allée d'Apollon

Trianon

Royal Garden ★

Mail

de

du

Route

Allée

Swiss Pond

Colonnade ★★★

★★★ THE GARDENS

8

9

Vert

★

11

10

12

Quinconce
du Midi

4

13

South Groves

6

Quinconce
du Nord

North Groves

l'Étoile

de

Petit

Avenue

7

5

3

14

Pont

Boulevard

Great Staircases
of 100 Steps

★★ Orangery

South
Parterre ★

Water
Gardens ★★

Latona
Basin ★

1

2

15

16

R. de l'Indépendance
Américaine

North
Parterre

Water Alley ★★

19

17

Neptune
Gate

Porte
de la Reine

R. de l'Orangerie

PALACE ★★★

18

Lower
Parterre ★★

Neptune
Basin ★★

Rue

des

Réservoirs

de

la

Reine

P

PARIS

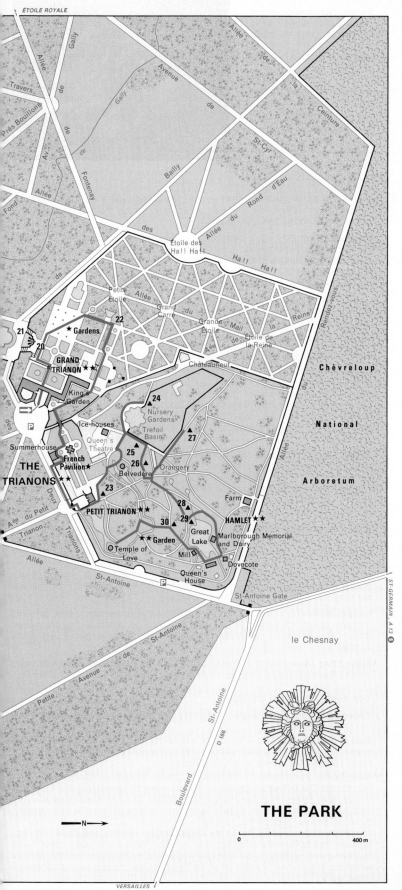

ÉTOILE ROYALE

Chèvreloup

National

Arboretum

GRAND
TRIANON ★★

THE
TRIANONS ★★

PETIT TRIANON ★★★

HAMLET ★★

THE PARK

N →

0   400 m

le Chesnay

VERSAILLES

This basin is continued by an esplanade leading to the Grand Canal. It is bordered by statues, parts of which are genuine antiquities (note the cracks where the different fragments join).

Detail from the Apollo Basin, Versailles

BOSQUETS DU NORD (NORTH GROVES)

Dome Grove (10) – The grove was named after two pavilions crowned by domes which were designed by Mansart. They were dismantled in 1820.
A series of low-reliefs adorns the edge of the basin, representing the weapons used in different countries. It has the unmistakably elegant touch of Girardon. Among the fine statues feature two works by Tuby, Acis and Galatea.

★**Enceladus Basin** (11) – This Baroque composition by Marsy contrasts sharply with the stark realism of the other groups dotted around the gardens. A head and two arms is all that is visible of the Titan Enceladus, slowly being dragged down towards the bowels of the earth by the very rocks of Mount Olympus by which the Titans had hoped to reach the sky (a clear warning to Fouquet).

Obelisk Basin (12) – Conceived by Mansart, this raised basin is surrounded by a flight of stone steps and several lawns. When the fountains are in operation, the central sculpture lets out a gigantic spray of water which resembles a liquid obelisk.

Flora or Spring Basin (13) – Another of the four seasons series by Tuby.

Ceres or Summer Basin (14) – Executed by Regnaudin.

★**Apollo's Bath Grove** (15) – Designed by Hubert Robert in the early days of Louis XVI's reign, this grove heralded the Anglo-Chinese Garden which Marie-Antoinette later adopted for the Trianon park. On the edge of a small lake, a charming artificial grotto houses the **Apollo Group★**. Its lush, verdant setting is a far cry from the austere 17C Versailles. The Sun God, tired by the day's exertions, is portrayed resting, waited upon by a group of nymphs (Girardon and Regnaudin). The horses at his side are being groomed by tritons (Marsy and Guérin).

Philosophers' Crossroads (16) – Flanked by impressive statues. The crossroads offer an interesting sideways **view★★** of the palace (northwest façade). The sweeping perspective on the right is lined with a double row of yew trees and a set of bronze statues, including Girardon's Winter.

NEPTUNE BASIN, DRAGON BASIN, WATER ALLEY

★★**Bassin de Neptune (Neptune Basin)** – *Stand in the central axis, near the statue of Fame*. This is by far the largest basin in Versailles. Its proportions are wildly extravagant by classical standards and it forms a small enclave north of the rectangular gardens. It was designed by Le Nôtre but acquired its present appearance in 1741, under the reign of Louis XV, when it was enriched by a group of lead statues depicting Neptune and Amphitrite surrounded by various gods, dragons and sea monsters (Adam, Lemoyne and Bouchardon).

Dragon Basin (17) – This allegorical sculpture evoking the victory over deep-sea monsters is a direct allusion to the vanquished Fronde, symbolised by a wounded dragon. Though the dragon's body is the original, the remaining pieces were recast in 1889.

★**Allée d'Eau (Water Alley)** – A double row of 22 small white marble basins bears delightful bronze groups of three children, each holding tiny pink marble vessels.

THE PARTERRES AND ORANGERY

Parterre du Nord (North Parterre) – The very first royal suite looked out onto this "terrace of greenery".

Basin of Diana's Nymphs (18) – Arranged around the basin are Girardon's fine **low-reliefs★** which have given their name to the fountain. They were to inspire a great many 18C and 19C painters, including Renoir.

★★**Lower Parterre** (Parterre Bas) – Close to the groves, along its northern and western boundaries, the terrace is flanked by bronze statues representing the four Continents, four Poems, four Seasons and four Virtues. The lead **Pyramid Fountain★** (19), executed by Girardon from a study by Le Brun, combines grace with originality: dolphins, shrimps and tritons.
At the top of the steps leading to the Water Gardens note the **Knifegrinder**, a bronze replica of the Antique statue by Foggini. Coysevox' **Venus on a Tortoise** – called Venus as a Paragon of Modesty under Louis XIV – is a bronze cast, also inspired by Antique sculpture. The original is exhibited at the Louvre Museum and is among the artist's finest works.

★**Parterre du Midi (South Parterre)** – They were laid out in front of the queen's apartments. With their vivid blossoms and their pretty boxwood patterns, these southern flower beds are a hymn to Nature. The terrace running along the Orangery offers a good **view★** of the 700m - 3 000ft long **Swiss Pond** and, in the far distance, the wooded heights of Satory.

★★**Orangerie (Orangery)** – One of Mansart's creations, the Orangery bore the foundations of the South Parterre. It extended south by means of two square corner pavilions which supported the colossal **Great Staircases of 100 Steps**. At the time of Louis XIV, the Orangery housed 3 000 shrubs in tubs: 2 000 of these were orange trees. Today it contains 1 200 bushes, some of which date back to the *Ancien Régime*. The Orangery looks splendid during the summer season, when the orange trees and palm trees (a recent introduction) are brought outside and arranged around the flower beds.

★★GRAND CANAL

The Grand Canal, which was completed in 1670, is shaped like a large cross: the long canal is 1 670m - 5 480ft long by 62m - 204ft wide; the shorter one measures 1 070m - 3 500ft long by 80m - 263ft wide.
The nearby buildings make up Little Venice (Petite Venise) which housed the Venetian gondoliers in charge of the king's fleet (gondolas, models of battleships and merchant ships).

THE TRIANONS ★★ ⊙ *plan above*

Access on foot – *Avenue de Trianon (1km - 1/2 mile) starts at the Neptune Gate and leads directly to the Trianons. The avenue starting from the eastern extremity of the Grand Canal also leads there.*

Access by car – *See map above.*

Fountains – *See Calendar of Events.*

Bicycles for hire – *At the entrance to the park, on Boulevard de la Reine, near the Trianon Palace Hotel.*

★★GRAND TRIANON *2 hours*

A pavilion known as the Porcelain Trianon, decorated with blue and white Delft tiling, used to be a quiet, secluded meeting-place for Louis XIV and his favourite Mme de Montespan. It stood for eighteen years, from 1670 to 1687. When Mme de Montespan fell from favour, the pavilion deteriorated and was eventually taken down. Six months later, Jules Hardouin-Mansart completed the Marble Trianon, a retreat built in honour of Mme de Maintenon.
It was stripped of its furniture during the Revolution. Napoleon I commissioned major renovation work and refurnished the building on the occasion of his marriage to Marie-Louise. The Marble Trianon was restored under Louis-Philippe.
The latest renovation programme took place in 1962 at the instigation of General de Gaulle, who wished to use the Trianon for official receptions.

★★**Château** – Walk past the low railings and enter the semicircular courtyard to discover two buildings with a flat terrace roof, joined by an elegant peristyle. Note the delicate colour scheme with pink overtones. Another wing called Trianon-sous-Bois *(private)* stands at a perpendicular angle to the righthand gallery, but it is not visible from the court.
The peristyle overlooks both the court and the gardens. It was designed by Robert de Cotte and adopted by Louis XIV despite Mansart's scepticism. It was used for banquets and formal receptions.

Apartments – The austere interior decoration has changed very little since the days of Louis XIV's reign. The apartments were occupied by Napoleon and Louis-Philippe and their respective families. The furniture is either Empire or Restoration and the paintings are attributed to 17C French artists.
The Mirror Room (Salon des Glaces) in the left pavilion was used as a council chamber. Admire the splendid Empire furniture and the lavish silk hangings, rewoven according to the original pattern ordered by Marie-Antoinette (the four Continents of the World). The bedroom contains the bed Napoleon commissioned for his apartments at the Tuileries: it was later altered for Louis-Philippe's use. The wall put in by Bonaparte level with the columns has been dismantled and the room has been restored to its original size.
The reception rooms in the right wing were remodelled by Louis-Philippe, who gave them a more personal touch. These salons are enhanced by a collection of paintings by famous 17C French artists, dedicated to mythological subjects.
In Louis XIV's former Music Room (Salon de Musique), the musicians' loggias are enclosed by a series of shutters.
Louis-Philippe created the Family Salon (Salon de Famille), in which the two tables feature numbered drawers reserved for the princesses' embroidery.
The Malachite Salon (Salon des Malachites) was first the Sun King's Grand Cabinet and then the bedroom of the Duchess of Burgundy. It owes its name to the various objects encrusted with malachite offered to Napoleon by Tsar Alexander I following their talks in Tilsit (1807): basins, candelabra, bookcase etc. Malachite is a green semi-precious stone found in Siberia, and is easy to polish.

The Cool Hall (Salon Frais) enjoys a northern aspect. It houses four paintings representing the early days of Versailles, following the plans drawn up by Mansart (display of documents showing the palace and the grounds). The two filing cabinets (1810) and the console table (1806) were executed by Jacob Desmalter from a study by Charles Percier.

The Atlas Cabinet (Salon des Sources) – where Napoleon kept his various maps and plans – leads to the Imperial Suite *(open on request)*.

Placed at a perpendicular angle, the corner **Gallery★** houses an extremely precious collection of 24 paintings by Cotelle. They conjure up a vivid picture of the palace and its stately grounds at the time of Louis XIV. The lovely Empire chandeliers were manufactured in the Montcenis glassworks in the Burgundian town of Le Creusot. At the far end of the Gallery, the luminous Garden Lounge (Salon des Jardins) features a fine set of chairs from Meudon Château.

★Gardens – They derive their simple charm from the impressive displays of flower beds. The terrace of the Lower Gardens (Jardins Bas) (**20**) commands a good view of the Lower Basin (Bassin Bas) (**21**), which is reached via the Horse-shoe Staircase, and of the Grand Canal beyond, seen from the side.

Beyond the parterres lies a charming wood featuring fine avenues, rows of stately trees and several small ponds *(best seen when the Trianon fountains are playing)*. The only sculpture with a mythological theme in the Trianon gardens is Mansart's Buffet d'Eau (**22**), completed in 1703. It pictures the Sea God Neptune and Amphitrite, surrounded by a cluster of smaller statues.

Skirt Trianon-sous-Bois and walk through what was once the king's private garden. It is flanked by two square pavilions which housed the apartments of Mme de Maintenon and Louis XIV towards the end of the Sun King's reign.

To reach the Petit Trianon, cross the bridge erected by Napoleon I, known as Pont de Réunion.

★★PETIT TRIANON *1 1/2 hours*

It was Louis XV's love of gardening and farming that prompted the construction of the Petit Trianon. The King gave orders to build a menagerie (experimental farm) and commissioned his "botanical expert" Claude Richard to design the greenhouses and botanical gardens. A College of Botanical Science was founded and entrusted to the famous botanist Bernard de Jussieu.

Gabriel finished the Petit Trianon in 1768, shortly before Louis XV's reign ended. Mme de Pompadour, the woman behind the initial project, never saw the château. Louis XVI offered the Petit Trianon to his wife Marie-Antoinette. The Queen would often come here with her children and her sister-in-law Mme Elisabeth, relieved to get away from court intrigues and the formal etiquette that was expected from a woman of her rank. She insisted on a number of changes: the grounds were redesigned, a theatre was built and Jussieu's botanical gardens, complete with their experimental hothouses, were destroyed. On 5 October 1789 the Queen was resting in a grotto near the Belvedere when a messenger informed her that the mob was marching on Versailles. She was forced to leave in great haste and was never to return.

Later, Empress Eugénie, who felt great sympathy for the Queen, formed a collection of her personal mementoes and had the château refurnished in 1867.

★French Pavilion – This pavilion was built by Gabriel for Louis XV and Mme de Pompadour in 1750. It is surrounded by an enchanting formal garden. The cornice features a sculpted frieze representing the farm animals that were raised on the estate. Visitors can get a glimpse of the highly-refined interior decoration through the large French windows.

The cool **Summerhouse** at the southern end of the gardens was rebuilt in 1982.

★★Château – The façade facing the entrance courtyard is austere in the extreme, while that giving onto the formal gardens is a perfect example of the Louis XVI period and shows the full extent of Gabriel's talent: the four regularly-spaced columns are crowned by a balustrade and two fine ramps lead from the terrace down to the gardens.

Enter the château and walk up the imposing flight of stone stairs lit by an old-fashioned lantern. The wrought-iron banisters are stamped with a decorative monogram, believed to be that of Marie-Antoinette.

First Floor Apartments – Guibert's craftsmanship is evident in the superb **panelling★★** in the dining room and the salon. The decoration of the dining-room presents fruit, flower and foliage motifs, set off against a jade green background, a welcome change from the "Trianon grey" prevalent throughout the 19C. The salon – partly refurnished by the Empress Eugénie in the 19C (chairs, 1790 pianoforte) – houses one of Riesener's greatest achievements: the famous astronomical writing desk (1771).

The furniture in Marie-Antoinette's bedroom was designed by Jacob and adorned with floral and rustic themes. Jacob also designed several pieces for the comtesse de Balbi: they have been placed in a recently-restored boudoir with unusual movable mirrors.

★★Gardens – This charming Anglo-Chinese garden featuring a brook, several ornamental ponds, some fine tree species and an interesting collection of sculptures was designed by an amateur, the comte de Caraman, and built by the Queen's architect Mique who received advice from Hubert Robert.

Several of the trees are 150 to 200 years old and some were probably planted by Bernard de Jussieu in his botanical gardens. The oldest of all is a damaged pagoda tree (**23**) planted during the reign of Louis XV, which stands near the northeast corner of the château.

Belvedere – This delightful pavilion conceived by Mique was also called the Music Room. It overlooks the Small Lake and the interior decoration offers painted arabesques of the utmost refinement.

Off the winding paths of the landscape garden lies "Charpentier's Garden", planted with remarkable trees; but first enter the grounds of the Grand Trianon to have a look at the superb cedar of Lebanon (**24**) near the Clover Basin, as well as the two entirely-restored 17C ice-houses standing in the background. Return to Charpentier's Garden and note the two huge Wellingtonias (**25**) and single fastigiate oak (**26**). Bear left after the Orangery to an ancient Siberian elm (**27**) with unusually deep striations. Start walking towards the Hamlet. Before the Great Lake may be seen a tulip tree from Virginia (**28**) and two spinneys of stately swamp cypresses (**29**).

★★**Hamlet** – The grounds around the Great Lake are dotted with a dozen pretty cottages featuring cob walls and thatched or slate roofs, inspired by the hamlet at Chantilly (qv). Contrary to popular belief, the Queen was far too steeped in formal protocol to indulge in any farming activities.

The Memorial to Marlborough is a reminder of the popular nursery rhyme, "The chanson de Marlborough", introduced to Louis XVI's court by the Dauphin's nanny. On the way to the Temple of Love, notice a remarkable plane tree (**30**) with thick spread-eagled roots.

Temple of Love – One of Mique's creations (1778), the temple stands on a tiny islet in the midst of the rippling waters. In the centre, Bouchardon's statue shows Cupid making his Bow from the Club of Hercules (original in the Louvre Museum, qv). The sculpture is fronted by a row of Corinthian columns resting on a circular flight of 6 steps.

THE TOWN

Louis XIV decided that plots of land would be granted to those citizens who put in a request, in exchange for a levy of five *sous* for each arpent (3 194m^2 - 3 833sq yds). The new buildings had to conform to the rules laid down by the Service des Bâtiments du Roi, a building commission answerable to the court. The purpose of these measures was to achieve architectural unity. Moreover, in order that the palace might continue to dominate the area, the roofs of the village houses were not to exceed the height of the Marble Court. Today very little remains of these 17C buildings. Most of the old town was completed in the 18C, enlarged and renovated in the 19C.

The Notre-Dame district features the oldest church in Versailles and a few houses built under Louis XIV, situated near the Notre-Dame market-place. The St-Louis district south of Avenue de Sceaux contains the official buildings of the former ministries, the Real Tennis Court or **Jeu de Paume** ⊙ where the National Assembly took their famous oath on 20 June 1789, the "old Versailles" built around the former village square and an 18C estate attached to Stag Park, located close to Satory heights.

★**Musée Lambinet** ⊙ – The museum is installed in the little panelled rooms of the charming hôtel Lambinet, built in 1750 by Joseph-Barnabé Porchon, builder to the King, whose initials can be seen in the wrought-iron work of the façade's balcony. The atmosphere of an 18C residence is recreated with period furniture, paintings (Hubert Robert), sculptures (Pajou, Houdon); numerous objects and documents relating to the history of Versailles are also included.

Room 2 is devoted to ceramics and includes numerous pieces of Paris porcelain from the late 18C known as Old Paris Ware (Vieux Paris), which was noted for its whiteness, rivalling Sèvres ware. Room 4 side-steps to the 19C with the reconstruction of Julia Bartet's "green salon"; the actress, a member of the Comédie Française, was famous for her roles in works by Racine and rivalled Sarah Bernhardt in the role of heroine in Victor Hugo's plays. Earthenwares from Rouen and Strasbourg, together with Chinese porcelain, are exhibited in Room 5. Room 6 contains rare engraved leather blocks from the second half of the 18C, which were used for printing calico known as *Toiles de Jouy* (qv).

The first floor houses material on the Revolutionary period: Charlotte Corday's arrest (Room 9), the events in 1789 at Versailles with the Declaration of the Rights of Man (Room 13), General Hoche – who was born in the town in 1768 (Room 14) – and Marat (Room 16).

On the second floor, Room 23 contains two magnificent abbesses' crosses embellished with rock crystal, which came from Maubuisson and Lys. Rooms 26, 27 and 28 evoke Versailles in the 17C and 18C (note the carved ivory miniatures of the palace and the park). The last room includes items by Boutet, the famous armourer: ceremonial swords and firearms ("armes d'honneur") awarded to the brave under the Revolution and the Empire.

Back on the ground floor, the last rooms display 19C and 20C works of art: Boilly, Isabey, Carrière, Le Sidaner and Dunoyer de Segonzac.

Église Notre-Dame – The church built in the Rue Dauphine – renamed Rue Hoche – by Jules Hardouin-Mansart in 1686 was the parish church attached to the king and his court. The king would attend formal ceremonies such as Corpus Christi here. The requirements of the Service des Bâtiments du Roi (see above) explain why the church presents a flattened front flanked by a series of truncated towers.

A large open-work dome graces the church interior, characterised by Doric embellishments. The nave (explanatory notices) is surrounded by 12 carved medallions representing apostles and figures from the New Testament: these were the works presented by the new entrants to the Académie Royale de Sculpture et de Peinture (Royal Sculpture and Painting Academy) between 1657 and 1689. The axial chapel – the chapel to the Blessed Sacraments – houses the *Assumption*, a 16C painting by Michel Corneille.

Rue de l'Independance Américaine – In the 18C this street housed many buildings occupied by ministries and public services, in particular the Grand Commun – now the Military Hospital – which lodged a total of 1 500 officials. At no 5 stands the former **Ministry of the Navy and Foreign Affairs**, fronted by a magnificent gate crowned by the statues of Peace and War. It was here that an alliance was signed between France and the American "insurrectionaries", acting as a prelude to the 1783 treaties granting the independence of the United States. The mansion has been made into a **public library**.

Cathédrale St-Louis – St Louis' Cathedral was built in 1754 to serve the "old Versailles" and Stag Park, and lies close to the King's Vegetable Garden (Potager du Roi). The west front with its two belltowers, and the dome above the transept crossing are reminiscent of the great classical churches.
Several official celebrations were held at the cathedral: the inauguration ceremony of the States General on 4 May 1789, attended by the deputies who had formed a procession starting from Notre-Dame in Paris; the session of 22 June which authorised the reunion of Clergy and Nobility; the Mass of the Holy Ghost which opened the 1875 sitting of the National Assembly at which the members voted on the constitutional law that founded the Third Republic.
The noble, austere nave still contains its 17C organ and collection of 18C paintings, but the most interesting furnishings are the religious works dating from the 19C.

Carrés St-Louis (St Louis Precinct) – Louis XV gave orders to create a "shopping area" near St Louis Church, along the streets presently named Rue Royale and Rue d'Anjou (1755). The shops – featuring mansard roofs – were arranged around four small squares known as *carrés*: Well Square, Oats Square, Fountain Square and Earth Square. Some of these houses still stand and have been converted into antique shops.

EXCURSION

Arboretum National de Chèvreloup (Chèvreloup National Arboretum) ⊘ – *Leave by D 186 north and turn left before entering Rocquencourt.*
In 1927 a plot of land formerly belonging to the Great Park *(see above)* was offered to the Natural History Museum of Paris so that the Botanical Gardens (Jardin des Plantes) could enrich their collection of tree species. The first steps were to set up a Tree Centre.
Visitors may tour only the southeast part of the park, planted with clusters and rows of conifers. Several types of horticultural species which do not grow locally are cultivated here: a row of Lawson's cypresses, of unusual shapes and sizes; large groups of thujas next to yew trees and weeping conifers. The broad-leaved trees include silver birches and willow trees at the height of their development. The oldest species of all is one of the pagoda trees planted at the time of Louis XV and restored to life thanks to modern arboricultural techniques.

VÉTHEUIL

Population 732
Michelin map 106 fold 3 or 55 fold 18

This former wine-growing district has a lovely riverside setting: it lies on the steep banks of one of the Seine's loops, not far from La Roche-Guyon *(qv)*. The village houses – built with a fine pale yellow stone – are characteristic of the French Vexin region. The small town was made famous by the Impressionists, in particular Claude Monet who lived here for three years and whose wife Camille died in Vétheuil in 1879.

Church ⊘ – Perched right above the village the church makes a picturesque sight, but the Impressionist painters were more interested in the area around Lavacourt, on the south bank of the Seine. From the main village crossroads take Rue de l'Église which leads straight to the entrance steps.
Although the chancel was first started in the late 12C the church was only completed under Henri II, when the last chapels were consecrated in 1850. The building is presently undergoing restoration.

Exterior – The west front dates from the mid 16C: the three levels of Renaissance galleries are flanked by two square turrets. The pier features a 16C statue depicting Charity. The south façade presents a doorway fronted by a Renaissance porch – note the 16C panels. Walk past the 16C nave to the late -12C chancel, which shows the transition from Romanesque to Gothic. A broad view of the elevation of the church reveals small round windows (oculi) on the first floor and a series of stepped buttresses around the east end. The belltower was raised in the 13C: it was the subject of many Impressionist paintings.

Interior – The church houses a number of **statues★** (14C-16C), a few 16C and 17C paintings and several interesting carvings. The first chapel on the left – formerly dedicated to one of the brotherhoods of charity – is enclosed by a Renaissance parclose. In the third chapel stands a lively statue of St James (Burgundian School – 15C) and the north aisle bears a 16C *Ecce Homo*. Note the 14C Virgin and Child in the south transept crossing (Notre-Dame-de-Grâce de Vétheuil) and, in the adjacent chapel, St Veronica, a colourful stone statue dating from the 14C.

VILLARCEAUX ★

Michelin map 106 fold 3 or 55 fold 18
8km - 4 1/2 miles northeast of La Roche Guyon

Villarceaux estate is set in rolling surroundings at the heart of the French Vexin. It is graced by a magnificent setting and two châteaux: a 15C-16C manor house which belonged to the celebrated beauty Ninon de Lenclos, and a Louis XV château.
Approaching the estate from the south, the road from Villers-en-Arthies offers a glimpse of the little 19C Convent Château (Château du Couvent) surrounded by a golf course.

Ninon de Lenclos – When Ninon (1620-1705) died at the age of 85, she had witnessed Louis XIII's reign and the absolute monarchy of Louis XIV. She was acquainted with all the leading personalities of her time and virtually became a legendary figure of the 17C because of her charm and her wisdom: few of her contemporaries could claim to possess such an impressive collection of mementoes. It was at Villarceaux that she received the young Françoise d'Aubigné, the future Mme Scarron and Mme de Maintenon, who 32 years later was to marry Louis XIV. It was also here that she shared a romance with Louis de Mornay, the Marquis de Villarceaux. The youthful Voltaire was officially presented to her shortly before her death.

★**Gardens** ☉ – Follow the itinerary signposted with arrows which leads past St Nicolas' Terrace – note the corner tower – to a series of ponds. The edge of the last pond affords a good **view★** of the south front of the Louis XV château *(private)* built on the terraced slopes. The tour around the ponds leads to the outhouses, which are used for formal receptions, and then to the manor itself and its large stone **tower** ☉.

VILLENEUVE-D'ASCQ

Population 65 320
Michelin map 51 fold 16 or 236 fold 16 – 8km - 5 miles east of Lille

In 1970 the *communes* of Annappes, Flers and Ascq were grouped together to form Villeneuve-d'Ascq, one of nine new towns in France. The three centres of the old *communes* have remained hubs of activity.
From the 1960s universities had established themselves in the Annappes area. The Triolo, Cousinerie, Brigode and Pont de Bois residential and commercial districts developed around the science park (cité scientifique). Industries and research centres followed. Today most of the region's universities are located in Villeneuve-d'Ascq: over 30 000 students are enrolled here.
A stroll through the town reveals new concepts in urban living: overhead pedestrian walkways straddle the main roads; residential areas merge into commercial centres; there are numerous important civic amenities: a 35 000 seater stadium, a cultural centre, museums etc.
The town is linked to the Lille conurbation by a network of motorways and an automatic *métro* system: the Val.
The town's name, Ascq, is a reminder of the tragic massacre of 86 patriots on 2 April 1944, which is commemorated by a monument and a museum (**B**).

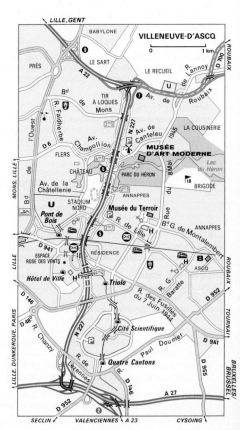

★★Musée d'Art Moderne (Museum of Modern Art) ⊙ – *Leave N 227 at "Château de Flers" exit.* Lying by a lawn above Heron's Lake (lac du Héron), the huge building by architect Rolland Simounet suggests a set of brick and glass cubes. The entrance hall leads to the permanent and temporary exhibitions *(right)*, and to the reception and other services *(left)*: library, cafeteria, lecture rooms.

The collection – Roger Dutilleul's collection, which contains over 230 works from the first half of the 20C, was presented to the museum by Geneviève and Jean Masurel, Dutilleul's nephew. Dutilleul made his first acquisitions in 1907 and from the beginning recognised the talent of artists who were not then understood: one of the first paintings he bought was Braque's *Houses and Tree* which had just been refused at the Autumn Exhibition (Salon d'Automne).

The collection contains many Fauve, Cubist, primitive and abstract works. The Fauve include Rouault, Derain and Van Dongen (*Pouting Woman* – 1909).

Cubism is represented in paintings by Braque *(Houses and Tree, The Factories of Rio Tinto)* and Picasso *(Seated Nude, Bock, Spanish Still-Life)*; this section also contains collages: Picasso's *Head of a Man* and Braque's *The Little Scout.*

Several works by Fernand Léger follow his development from a 1914 landscape to his sketch for a mural (1938), encompassing works such as *The Mechanic* (1918) and *Still-Life with Fruit Dish* and his studies of volume and mass. One room is devoted to Modigliani, seven of whose paintings are included in the collection, together with five drawings. His beguiling portraits reveal subtle plays of line and colour, especially in *Motherhood* (1919), *Seated Nude with a Shirt* (1917) and *The Red-Headed Boy* (1919).

Motherhood by Modigliani,
Museum of Modern Art

Works of abstract art featured are by Kandinsky, Mirò, Klee and Nicolas de Staël. De Staël knew Roger Dutilleul through the painter Lanskoy, who was the collector's protegé, and many examples of the latter's work are also on show.

Outside, a pleasant stroll through the public gardens beside the lake leads to the mills.

Moulins ⊙ – Next to the traditional **flour mill** *(moulin à farine)* stands the **oil mill** (moulin des Olieux) which was used for processing linseed, rapeseed and other plants. In the 19C there were 200 of these oil presses *(tordoirs)* around Lille; this is the last to survive.

Musée du Terroir (Museum of the Land) ⊙ – Delporte Farm in the old centre of Annappes is a typical local *cense (qv)*, built of Lezennes stone and brick; it now houses the museum. In the courtyard and buildings a collection of agricultural tools are displayed, along with traditional workshops: foundry, locksmith's, joinery, saddlery, dairy...

VILLERS-COTTERÊTS

Population 8 867
Michelin map 56 north of fold 13 or 237 fold 8

Villers-Cotterêts is a peaceful little town, almost entirely surrounded by Retz Forest; it was the homeland of the Orléans family until the Revolution and developed owing to the royal passion for hunting. It was the birthplace of Alexandre Dumas senior in 1802.

Birth of the State – In 1535 François I replaced the first 12C royal castle with a Renaissance building and added to the outbuildings which dealt with the management of the royal hunts.

It was here that the King announced the famous Statute of Villers-Cotterêts in 1539 prescribing the substitution of French instead of Latin in public registers and legal documents. Among its 192 articles it stated that parish priests should keep registers of the parishioners' dates of birth and death: here then, are the foundations of the civil State. Previously, except in noble families where records were kept, ordinary people had to rely on the memory of witnesses to prove their civil status. It was another 250 years (1792) before the keeping of State registers was entrusted to the local authorities.

A Child of the Islands – The first of the three generations – grandfather, father and son – of the famous Dumas family was the son of a Dominican settler, Marquess Davy de la Pailleterie, and Marie-Cessette Dumas, a coloured girl. In 1786 Thomas-Alexandre assumed his mother's surname and pursued a career in the army where he later rose to become General, but his Republican opinions led to his being disgraced by Napoleon Bonaparte. He retired to Villers-Cotterêts which was his wife's homeland and lived a quiet life until his death, four years after the birth of his son Alexandre, the future novelist.

Alexandre Dumas' Youth – Many hard years passed for the widow and her son; Alexandre entered the study of one of the town's notaries and copied deeds there until he was 20. One day his mother told him that only 253 francs remained: Dumas took 53 francs as his share, left the rest for his mother and headed for Paris. He played billiards, gambling the cost of his fare to the capital, and won which allowed him to venture forth in the capital with his nest egg intact. His beautiful handwriting landed him a job in the secretary's office of the Duc d'Orléans, future King Louis-Philippe. His prodigious literary career was about to begin.

Château François I ⊙ – In 1806 Napoleon appropriated the château, which was being used as a workhouse; today it is a retirement home. Within the courtyard, the east and west sides are bordered by buildings which retain Renaissance features: high attic windows in brick flanked by pillars crowned with urns. At the far end stands the main front, with a shallow recessed loggia on the first floor.

The **main staircase★** (grand escalier) alone is worth a visit: it is a Renaissance masterpiece, a double flight of stairs dating from the period of François I. The carvings on the coffered ceiling – crowned Fs, salamanders, fleurs-de-lis – are from the school of Jean Goujon. The same motifs are used in greater abundance in the State Room, which was originally the chapel, on the false ceiling which hides the vaulting. The stonework of the Renaissance altarpiece remains. At the end of the gallery *(display on local history)* the **King's staircase** (escalier du Roi), contemporary with the main staircase, has its original decoration of carved scenes from The Dream of Polyphyle.

Park (Parc) – All that remains of Le Nôtre's work are the outlines of the parterre groups and the perspective of the Royal Alley (Allée Royale) ending at a telecommunications tower.

Musée Alexandre-Dumas ⊙ – Three small rooms are dedicated to the famous "Three Dumas" ("Trois Dumas"), Thomas-Alexandre the General, Alexandre senior, author of *The Three Musketeers*, *The Count of Monte Cristo* and *The Black Tulip*, and Alexandre junior, author of *La Dame aux Camélias*.

Alexandre senior was born in the house at no 46 Rue Alexandre Dumas.

EXCURSION

Montgobert – *10km - 6 miles northeast by N 2 and D 2 (left). Turn into a small road towards Montgobert.*

Musée du Bois et de l'Outil (Wood and Tool Museum) ⊙ – The museum is housed in **Montgobert Château**, on the edge of Retz Forest. The 18C building was originally the property of Pauline Bonaparte and her husband, General Leclerc, who is buried in the park.

On the ground floor traditional woodworking tools used by cartwrights, sawyers, coopers, carpenters, joiners etc are displayed.

The first floor is dedicated to the life and management of the forest; exhibition on the role of the Forestry Commission (Office Nationale des Forêts).

The second floor focuses on occupations related to wood within the forest (charcoal burning, woodcutting) together with reconstructions of workshops (joinery, spinning mill, dairy...).

VIMY CANADIAN MEMORIAL

Michelin map 51 fold 15 or 236 fold 15

Vimy Ridge, which overlooks the mining region, was captured in April 1917 by the four divisions of the Canadian Corps, which was part of the British 3rd Army under General Allenby.

The Ridge was the strongest defensive position in northwestern France and of enormous importance: this 61m - 200ft barrier on the plain safeguarded mines and factories which were in production for Germany, and covered the junction of the main Hindenburg Line and the defences stretching north to the coast. Despite the Canadians' great success, however, the German front was not penetrated.

The impressive white stone memorial, which was the result of a design competition won by a Toronto sculptor who said the idea came to him in a dream, is made of "trau" stone from the Dalmatian coast; its construction began in 1925 and lasted 11 years. The two great shafts symbolise the Canadian and French forces; various figures represent Canada, Peace, Justice, Truth, Knowledge... An inscription at the base of the memorial commemorates the Canadian soldiers (over 66 000 of them) who died during the War, and the ramparts bear the names of a further 11 000 men missing, presumed dead.

The foot of the memorial offers views over the old mining basin; the ossuary on Notre-Dame de Lorette Hill *(qv)* can be seen to the west.

To the south, on the slope of the hill, a network of Canadian and German trenches, dug-outs and **tunnels** ⊙ have been preserved, together with shell holes and mine craters. A **visitor centre** provides details of the Memorial, its park and the battle.

Practical
Information

Travelling to France

Passport – Visitors entering France must be in possession of a valid national **passport** (or in the case of the British, a Visitor's Passport). In case of loss or theft report to the embassy or consulate and the local police.

Visa – An **entry visa** is required for Canadian and US citizens (for a stay of more than 3 months) and for Australian citizens in accordance with French security measures. Apply to the French Consulate (visa issued same day; delay if submitted by mail).
US citizens should obtain the booklet *Your Trip Abroad* ($ 1.25) which provides useful information on visa requirements, customs regulations, medical care etc for international travellers. Apply to the Superintendent of Documents, PO BOX 371954 Pittsburgh, PA 15250-7954. ☎ 202-783-3238.

Customs – Apply to the Customs Office (UK) for a leaflet on customs regulations and the full range of duty-free allowances. The US Customs Service (PO Box 7407, Washington, DC 20044. ☎ 202-927-5580) offers a publication *Know before you go* for US citizens. There are no customs formalities for holiday-makers bringing their caravans into France for a stay of less than 6 months. No customs document is necessary for pleasure boats and outboard motors for a stay of less than 6 months but the registration certificate should be kept on board.

By air – The various national and other independent airlines operate services to **Paris** (Charles de Gaulle and Orly) and there are regular flights to **Le Touquet** from Lydd in England. There are also package-tour flights with a rail or coach link-up as well as Fly-Drive schemes. Information, brochures and timetables are available from the airlines and from travel agents.
The domestic network (Air Inter) operates frequent services covering the whole country. There are transfer buses to town terminals and to rail stations. Roissy-Rail, Orly-Rail operate fast rail links to the centre of Paris. The airport at **Lille-Lesquin** – fifteen minutes from the town centre – has good connections with many other towns.

By sea – There are numerous **cross-Channel services** (passenger and car ferries, hovercraft, SeaCat) from the United Kingdom and Eire. For details apply to travel agencies or to:
P&O European Ferries, Channel House, Channel View Road, Dover CT17 9TJ; ☎ 01304 203 388. Ticket collection: Russell St, Dover, Kent CT16 1QB.
The Continental Ferry Port, Mile End, Portsmouth, Hampshire PO2 8QW; ☎ 01705 827 677.
Sealink, Charter House, Park Street, Ashford, Kent TN24 8EX; ☎ 01233 647 047.
Hoverspeed, International Hoverport, Marine Parade, Dover, Kent CT17 9TG; ☎ 01304 240 241.
Maybrook House, Queen's Gardens, Dover CT17 9UQ; ☎ direct line from London 0181 554 7061, Birmingham 0121 236 2190 or Manchester 0161 228 1321.
Brittany Ferries, Millbay Docks, Plymouth, Devon PL1 3EW; ☎ 01752 221 321.
The Brittany Centre, Wharf Road, Portsmouth, Hampshire PO2 8RU; ☎ 01705 827 701.
Sally Line, 81 Piccadilly, London W1V 9HF; ☎ 0171 409 2240.
Argyle Centre, York St, Ramsgate, Kent CT11 9DS; ☎ 01843 595 522.

By rail – British Rail offers a range of services to the Channel ports and French Railways operates an extensive network of lines including many high speed passenger trains and motorail services throughout France. There are rail passes (France Vacances Pass) offering unlimited travel, and group travel tickets offering savings for parties. Eurorail Pass, Flexipass and Saver Pass are options available in the US for travel in Europe and must be purchased in the US – ☎ 212-308-3103 (information) and 1 800 223 636 (reservations).
Tickets bought in France must be validated *(composter)* by using the orange automatic date-stamping machines at the platform entrance.
Information and bookings from French Railways, 179 Piccadilly, London W1V OBA; ☎ 0171 409 3518 and from principal British and American Rail Travel Centres and travel agencies.
Baggage trolleys (10 F coin required – refundable) are available at main line stations.

By coach – Regular coach services are operated from London to Paris and to large provincial towns:
Hoverspeed, Maybrook House, Queens Gardens, Dover CT17 9UQ. ☎ 01304 240 241.
Euroways/Eurolines, 52 Grosvenor Gardens, Victoria, London SW1W OAU. ☎ 0171 730 82 35.

Via the Channel Tunnel – This high-speed undersea rail shuttle link between Folkestone and Calais began operating in May 1994. From 1995 motorists will be able to drive their car onto specially designed double-deck wagons for the 35min trip and drive off at the Calais terminal onto slip-roads feeding directly into the French motorway network. For further information, contact Le Shuttle Passenger enquiries. ☎ 01303 271100.

Motoring in France

Documents – Nationals of EC countries require a valid national **driving licence**; nationals of non-EC countries require an **international driving licence** ($ 10 – obtainable in the US from the American Automobile Club).
For the vehicle it is necessary to have the **registration papers** (log-book) and a **nationality plate** of the approved size.

Insurance – Insurance cover is compulsory and although an International Insurance Certificate (Green Card) is no longer a legal requirement in France it is the most effective proof of insurance cover and is internationally recognised by the police and other authorities.
Certain UK motoring organisations (AA, RAC) run accident insurance and breakdown service schemes for members. Europ-Assistance (252 High St, Croydon CRO 1NF) has special policies for motorists. Members of the American Automobile Club should obtain the brochure *Offices to serve you abroad* (no charge). Affiliated organisation for France: Association Française des Automobile-Clubs, 9 Rue Anatole-de-la-Forge, 75017 Paris. ☎ 42 27 82 00.

Highway Code – The minimum driving age is 18 years old. Traffic drives on the right. It is compulsory for the front-seat passengers to wear **seat belts**; all back seat passengers should wear seat belts where they are fitted. Children under the age of ten should be on the back seat.
Full or dipped headlights must be switched on in poor visibility and at night; use side-lights only when the vehicle is stationary. In the case of a **breakdown** a red warning triangle or hazard warning lights are obligatory.
Drivers should watch out for unfamiliar road signs and take great care on the road. In built-up areas **priority** must be ceded to vehicles joining the road from the right. However, traffic on main roads outside built-up areas and on roundabouts has priority. Vehicles must stop when the lights turn red at road junctions and may filter to the right only where indicated by an amber arrow.
The regulations on **drink-driving** and **speeding** are strictly enforced – usually by an on-the-spot fine and/or confiscation of the vehicle.

Speed limits – Although liable to modification, these are as follows:
– toll motorways 130kph-80mph (110kph-68mph when raining);
– dual carriageways and motorways without tolls 110kph-68mph (100kph-62mph when raining);
– other roads 90kph-56mph (80kph-50mph when raining) and in towns 50kph-31mph;
– outside lane on motorways during daylight, on level ground and with good visibility – minimum speed limit of 80kph (50mph).

Parking Regulations – In town there are restricted and paying **parking zones** (blue and grey zones); tickets must be obtained from the ticket machines (*horodateurs* – small change necessary) and displayed (inside windscreen on driver's side); failure to display may result in a heavy fine.

Route Planning – For 24-hour road traffic information: dial 48 94 33 33 or consult Minitel *(see below)* 3615 Code Route.
See Contents page for the full range of **Michelin maps** covering the regions describe in this guide.
The road network is excellent and includes many motorways, mostly toll-roads *(autoroutes à péage)*. The roads are very busy during the holiday period (particularly weekends in July and August) and to avoid traffic congestion it is advisable to follow the recommended secondary routes *(Bison Futé-itinéraires bis)*.

Car Rental – There are car rental agencies at airports, air terminals, railway stations and in all large towns throughout France. European cars usually have manual transmission but automatic cars are available on demand. An **international driving licence** is required for non-EC nationals.
Fly-drive schemes are operated by major airlines.

Mining has not only marked the landscape with spoil heaps, pit-head gear and miners' dwellings round the pitheads but it has also shaped the rough, proud character of the men. Despite their hard labour and the risks they take (silicosis, unstable galleries, fire-damp explosions such the one in 1906 in Courrières in which nearly 1 100 men were hurt), these black-faced men *(gueules noires)* have a real warmth and deep sense of solidarity. A few museums now recall the conditions of their life and work: the Mining Heritage Centre at Lewarde *(qv)*, the Mining Museum in Bruay-Lobussière (☎ 21 62 25 45), the Mining Museum in Nœux-les-Mines (☎ 21 26 34 64) and the Mining School Museum in the École Diderot in Harnes (☎ 21 20 46 70).

Accommodation

Places to stay – The mention Facilities under the individual headings or after place names in the body of the guide refers to the information given on the Map of Places to Stay which indicates recommended places for overnight stops or longer stays which have been selected for the accommodation and leisure facilities they offer the holiday-maker. The map may be used in conjunction with the **Michelin Red Guide France**.

Loisir Accueil is an officially-backed booking service which has offices in most French départements. For information contact Réservation Loisirs Accueil, 2 Rue Linois, 75015 Paris; ☎ 40 59 44 12.

The '**Accueil de France**' Tourist Offices which are open all year make hotel bookings for a small fee, for personal callers only. The head office is in Paris (127 Avenue des Champs-Élysée; ☎ 49 52 53 54 for information only) and there are offices in many large towns and resorts.

The brochure *Logis et Auberges de France* is available from the French Government Tourist Office.

Rural accommodation – Apply to Maison des Gîtes de France, 35 Rue Godot-de-Mauroy, 75009 Paris, (☎ 47 42 20 20) or 178 Piccadilly, London W1V 0AL, (☎ 0171 493 3480) for a list of relevant addresses.

Bed and Breakfast – Gîtes de France *(see above)* publishes a booklet on bed and breakfast accommodation *(chambre d'hôte)*.

Youth Hostels – There are many youth hostels throughout France. Holders of an International Youth Hostel Federation card should apply for a list from the International Federation or from the French Youth Hostels Association, 38 Boulevard Raspail, 75007 Paris; ☎ 45 48 69 84.

Members of American Youth Hostels should call 202-783-6161 for information on budget accommodation. The publication *International Hotel Guide for Europe* ($ 13.95) is available to members and non-members.

Camping – There are numerous officially graded sites with varying standards of facilities throughout the Picardy, Flanders and Paris regions. The **Michelin Guide Camping Caravaning France** lists a selection of camping sites. An International Camping Carnet for caravans is useful but not compulsory; it may be obtained from the motoring organisations or the Camping and Caravaning Club (Greenfields House, Westwook Way, Coventry CV4 8JH; Tel 01203 694995).

Electricity – The electric current is 220 volts. Circular two pin plugs are the rule – an electrical adaptor may be necessary.

General information

Medical treatment – First aid, medical advice and chemists' night service rota are available from chemists (*pharmacie* – green cross sign).

It is advisable to take out comprehensive insurance cover as the recipient of medical treatment in French hospitals or clinics must pay the bill. Nationals of non-EC countries should check with their insurance companies about policy limitations. Reimbursement can then be negotiated with the insurance company according to the policy held.

All prescription drugs should be clearly labelled; a copy of the prescription is advisable. American Express offers its members a service, "Global Assist", for any medical, legal or personal emergency – call collect from anywhere ☎ 202-554-2639.

British citizens should apply to the Department of Health and Social Security for **Form E 111**, which entitles the holder to urgent treatment for accident or unexpected illness in EC countries. A refund of part of the costs of treatment can be obtained on application in person or by post to the local Social Security Offices (Caisse Primaire d'Assurance Maladie).

Currency – There are no restrictions on the amount of currency visitors can take into France. To facilitate the export from France of currency in foreign banknotes in excess of the given allocation visitors are advised to complete a currency declaration form on arrival.

Banks – Banks are open from 0900 to 1200 and 1400 to 1600 and are closed on Monday or Saturday (except if market day); some branches open for limited transactions on Saturday. Banks close early on the day before a bank holiday. A passport is necessary as identification when cashing cheques in banks. Commission charges vary and hotels usually charge more than banks for cashing cheques for non-residents. Most banks have cash dispensers which accept international credit cards.

Credit Cards – American Express, Carte Bleue (Visa/Barclaycard), Diners Club and Eurocard (Mastercard/Access) are widely accepted in shops, hotels and restaurants and petrol stations.

Post – Post Offices open Monday to Friday 0800 to 1900, Saturday 0800 to 1200. Postage via air mail to: UK letter 2.50 F; postcard 2.30 F; US aerogramme 4.50 F; letter (20g) 4 F; postcard 3.70 F. Stamps are also available from newsagents and tobacconists.

Poste Restante mail should be addressed as follows: Name, *Poste Restante*, *Poste Centrale*, département's postal code followed by town name, *France*. The **Michelin Red Guide France** gives local postal codes.

Telephone – Public phones using pre-paid phone cards *(télécarte)* are in operation in many areas. The cards (50 or 120 units) which are available from post offices, tobacconists and newsagents can be used for inland and international calls. Calls can be received at phone boxes where the blue bell sign is shown.

Internal calls – When calling within either of the two main zones (French provinces or Paris and its region) dial only the 8 digit correspondent's number. From Paris to the provinces dial 16 + 8 digit number. From the provinces to Paris dial 16 + 1 + 8 digit number.

International calls – Dial the code for the international exchange followed by the national code of the country local exchange number and then number. For Paris dial the country 33 + 1 + 8 digit number. For the provinces the country code 33 + 8 digit number. When calling abroad from France dial 19, wait until the continuous tone recurs, then dial the country code and dialling code and number of your correspondent. For international enquiries dial 19 33 12 + country code.

Telephone rates from a public telephone at any time are: Paris-London, about 5.60 F for 1 minute; Paris-New York, 10.30 F for 1 minute. Cheap rates with 50 % extra time are available from private telephones on weekdays between 2230 and 0800, at weekends starting 1400 on Saturdays.

Shopping – The big stores and larger shops are open Monday to Saturday, 0900 to 1830-1930. Smaller, individual shops may close during the lunch hour. Food shops – grocers, wine merchants and bakeries – are open from 0700 to 1830-1930; some open on Sunday mornings. Many food shops close between 1200 and 1400 and on Mondays. Hypermarkets usually open until 2100-2200.

Museum Passes – Combined museum and gallery passes are available in some areas. Enquire locally.

Public holidays – The following are days when museums and other monuments may be closed or may vary their hours of admission:

New Year's Day	France's National Day (**14 July**)
Easter Sunday and Monday	Assumption (**15 August**)
May Day (**1 May**)	All Saint's Day (**1 November**)
V E Day (**8 May**)	Armistice Day (**11 November**)
Ascension Day	Christmas Day
Whit Sunday and Monday	

National museums and art galleries are closed on Tuesdays whereas municipal museums are closed on Mondays. In addition to the usual school holidays at Christmas and in the spring and summer, there are long mid-term breaks (10 days to a fortnight) in February and early November.

Embassies and Consulates

Australia	Embassy	4 Avenue Jean-Rey, 75015 Paris, ☎ 40 59 33 00.
Canada	Embassy	35 Avenue Montaigne, 75008 Paris, ☎ 47 23 01 01.
Eire	Embassy	4 Rue Rude, 75016 Paris, ☎ 45 00 20 87.
UK	Embassy	35 Rue du Faubourg St-Honoré, 75008 Paris, ☎ 42 66 91 42.
	Consulate	16 Rue d'Anjou, 75008 Paris, ☎ 42 66 91 42.
		11 Square Dutilleul, 59800 Lille, ☎ 56 42 34 13.
USA	Embassy	2 Avenue Gabriel, 75008 Paris, ☎ 42 96 12 02.
	Consulate	2 Rue St-Florentin, 75001 Paris ☎ 42 96 14 88.

MICHELIN GUIDES

The Red Guides (hotels and restaurants)
Benelux · Deutschland · España Portugal · Main Cities Europe · France · Great Britain and Ireland · Italia · Suisse

The Green Guides (fine art, historical monuments, scenic routes)
Austria · California · Canada · England: the West Country · France · Germany · Great Britain · Greece · Ireland · Italy · London · Mexico · Netherlands · New England · New York · Paris · Portugal · Quebec · Rome · Scotland · Spain · Switzerland · Washington

*... and the collection of **regional guides** for France.*

Tourist information

French Government Tourist Offices – For information, brochures, maps and assistance in planning a trip to France travellers should apply to the official tourist office in their own country *(addresses below)*.

Regional Tourist Offices – Comité Régional du Tourisme du Nord-Pas-de-Calais, 26 Place Rihour, 59000 Lille, France. ☎ 20 57 40 04.
Comité Régional du Tourisme de Picardie, 11 Mail Albert 1er BP 2616, 80026 Amiens Cedex, France. ☎ 22 91 10 15; Telex 145 320 F.
Comité Régional du Tourisme d'Ile-de-France, 73-75 Rue de Cambronne, 75015 Paris. ☎ 45 67 89 41.
The Regional Tourist Offices (Comités Régionaux de Tourisme) publish information brochures on their own region.

Espace Naturel Régional – For information on the Nord-Pas-de-Calais Regional Park: 17 Rue Jean-Roisin, 59800 Lille ☎ 20 60 60 60.

Departmental Tourist Offices – Fédération Nationale des Comités Départmentaux de Tourisme, 2 Rue Linois, 75015 Paris. ☎ 45 75 62 16.
Office Départemental du Tourisme du Nord, 15-17 Rue du Nouveau-Siècle, BP 135, 59027 Lille Cedex, ☎ 20 57 00 61.
Office Départemental du Tourisme de Pas-de-Calais, 21 Rue Desille, 62204 Boulogne-sur-Mer, ☎ 21 83 32 59.
Office Départemental du Tourisme de L'Aisne, 1 Rue Saint-Martin, 02006 Laon Cedex, France. ☎ 23 20 45 54; Telex 145 896 F.
Office Départemental du Tourisme de L'Oise, 1 Rue Villiers de L'Isle Adam, BP 222, 60008 Beauvais, France. ☎ 44 45 82 12; Telex 530 955 F.
Office Départemental du Tourisme de la Somme, 21 Rue Ernest-Cauvin, 80000 Amiens, France. ☎ 22 92 26 39; Telex 140 754 F.

Tourist Information Centres – The addresses and telephone numbers of the Tourist Information Centres (Syndicats d'Initiative) of most large towns and tourist resorts may be found among the Admission Times and Charges *(qv)* and in the **Michelin Red Guide France**. They can supply large-scale town plans, timetables and information on local entertainment, sports facilities and sightseeing.

Minitel – The French Telecom videotex service offers a wide variety of information *(fee charged)*. Minitel terminals are installed in hotel chains and certain petrol stations throughout the country.
Listed below are some of the telematic services offered:

3614 ED	Electronic service in English
3614 STAR	Nord and Pas-de-Calais information service in English
3615 TCAMP	camping information
3615 MÉTÉO	weather report
3615 or 3616 HORAV	general airline information and flight schedules
3615 BBC	BBC news
3615 LIBE	USA TODAY
3615 MICHELIN	Michelin tourist and route information

Tourism for the Disabled – Some of the sights described in this guide are accessible to handicapped people. They are listed in the publication *Touristes quand même! Promenades en France pour les Voyageurs Handicapés* published by the Comité National Français de Liaison pour la Réadaptation des Handicapés (38 Boulevard Raspail, 75007 Paris). This booklet covers nearly 90 towns in France and provides practical information for people who suffer reduced mobility or visual or aural impairment.
The **Michelin Red Guide France** and the **Michelin Camping Caravaning France** indicate hotels and camping sites with facilities suitable for physically handicapped people.

War Memorials – There are numerous First World War cemeteries and memorials in the north of France, some of which may be found in the chapter on Albert *(qv)*. For comprehensive information contact the Commonwealth War Graves Commission, (France Area), Rue Angéle-Richard, 62217 Beaurains, France; or Commonwealth War Graves Commission, 2 Marlow Road, Maidenhead, Berkshire SL6 7DX, England, ☎ 01628 34221.

Recreation

Information and brochures outlining the sporting and outdoor facilities available may be obtained from the French Government Tourist Office or from the organisations listed below.

Tourist Routes – The Regional and Local Tourist Offices will give information on tourist routes – Routes de l'Histoire, Route des Impressionnistes en Val d'Oise – pinpointing places of interest.

Crafts – Many arts and crafts studios (weaving, wrought iron, pottery) are open to visitors in summer. For courses apply to the Tourist Information Centre.

Cycling – The Fédération française de Cyclotourisme: 8 Rue Jean-Marie-Jégo, 75013 Paris, ☎ 44 16 88 88 supplies itineraries covering most of France, outlining mileage, difficult routes and sights to see.
Bicy-Club de France: 8 Place de la Porte Champerret, 75017 Paris; ☎ 47 66 55 92.
Lists of cycle hire businesses are available from Tourist Information Centres.
The main railway stations also hire out cycles which can be returned at a different station.

Rambling – Short, medium and long distance footpath Topo-Guides are published by the Fédération Française de la Randonnée Pédestre (FFRP) – Comité National des Sentiers de Grande Randonnée (CNSGR). These give detailed maps of the paths and offer valuable information to the rambler, and are on sale at the Information Centre: 64 Rue de Gergovie, 75014 Paris, ☎ 45 45 31 02; or by mail order from McCarta, 15 Highbury Place, London N5 1QP, ☎ 0171 354 1616.
Les Amis de la Forêt de Fontainebleau organise guided tours for the general public.
To receive their programme, send an international reply coupon with a self-addressed envelope to 31 Place Napoléon-Bonaparte, BP 24, 77300 Fontainebleau Cedex.

Fishing – Current brochures: folding map *Fishing in France* (*Pêche en France*) published and distributed by the Conseil Supérieur de la Pêche, 134 Avenue de Malakoff, 75016 Paris, ☎ 45 01 20 20; also available from the Centre du Paraclet, BP 5, 80440 Boves, ☎ 22 09 37 47, and from departmental fishing organisations.
For information about regulations contact Tourist Information Centres or the offices of the Water and Forest Authority (Eaux et Forêts).

Cruising – Two publishers produce collections of guides to cruising on French canals. Both series include numerous maps and useful information and are provided with English translations. The publishers are: Navicarte, Éditions Cartographiques Maritimes, 7 Quai Gabriel-Péri, 94340 Joinville-le-Pont. ☎ 48 85 77 00.
Guides Vagnon, Les Éditions du Plaisancier, 100 Avenue du Général-Leclerc, 69641 Caluire-et-Cuire. ☎ 78 23 31 14.
For further information contact the Association Régionale pour le Développement du Tourisme Fluvial Nord-Pas-de-Calais, 5-7 Avenue Marc-Sangnier, BP 46, 59426 Armentières Cedex, ☎ 20 35 29 07; or the Maison du Tourisme Fluvial, 31 Rue Bélu, 80000 Amiens, ☎ 22 97 88 55.

Motor boating and water-skiing – Enquire at the local Tourist Information Centre or at the resort.

Sailing and windsurfing – Apply direct to the many sailing clubs the length of the coast, from Bray-Dunes to Ault, or to the Fédération Française de Voile, 55 Avenue Kléber, 75784 Paris Cedex 16; ☎ 45 53 68 00.
Windsurfing, which is subject to certain regulations, is permitted on lakes (Val-Joly, Monampteuil etc) and in sports and leisure centres; apply to sailing clubs. Surf boards may be hired on all major beaches.

Hot Air Ballooning – From Maintenon, daily between April and October. Contact Loisirs-Accueil, 19 Place des Épars, BP 67, 28002 Chartres Cedex, ☎ 37 21 37 22.

Landsailing and windskating – The long stretches of beach in the Pas-de-Calais and Picardy regions provide excellent sites for both landsailing (*le char à voile*) and windskating (*le speed-sail*).
The sand yachts used for landsailing consist of three-wheeled go-karts with a sail affixed; they can reach speeds of up to 100km – 62 miles per hour.
Windskating is similar to windsurfing though on land and entails the use of a board with wheels attached.

Riding and Pony Trekking – Apply to the Fédération des Randonneurs Équestres, 16 Rue des Apennins, 75017 Paris, ☎ 42 26 23 23, or to l'Association Régionale de Tourisme Équestre, Le Paddock, 62223 St-Laurent-Blangy, ☎ 21 55 40 81.
The Association Nationale de Tourisme Équestre (ANTE), 15 Rue de Bruxelles, 75009 Paris publishes an annual handbook covering the whole of France.

Hunting – For all enquiries apply to Saint-Hubert Club de France, 10 Rue de Lisbonne, 75008 Paris, ☎ 45 22 38 90.

Golf – The **Michelin Golf Map** of France gives comprehensive details of golf courses. An annual guide is published by Éditions Person, 34 Rue de Penthièvre, 75008 Paris. A map showing golf courses and giving the number of holes, addresses and telephone numbers is available from the Fédération Française de Golf, 69 Avenue Victor-Hugo, 75016 Paris. ☎ 45 02 13 55.

French Government Tourist Offices Addresses

Australia

Sydney – Kindersley House, 33 Bligh St, Sydney, New South Wales 2000. ☎ 612 231 52 44.

Canada

Toronto – 30 St Patrick's Street, Suite 700, Toronto, ONT M5T 3A3 ☎ 416-593-4723.

Montreal – 1981 Ave McGill College, Suite 490, Montréal, PQ H3A 2W9. ☎ 514-288-4264.

Eire

Dublin – c/o 38 Lower Abbey St, Dublin. ☎ 01 300 777.

United Kingdom

London – 178 Piccadilly, London WIV 0AL. ☎ 0171 499 6911 (24-hour answering service with recorded message and information) or 0171 491 7622 (urgent enquiries only).

United States

France On Call Hotline – Dial 900-990-0040 ($.50 per minute) for information on hotels, restaurants and transportation.

Mid West: Chicago – 676 N Michigan Avenue, Suite 3360, Chicago, IL 60611. ☎ 312-337-6301.

East Coast: New York – 610 Fifth Avenue, NY 10020. ☎ 212-757-1125.

West Coast: Los Angeles – 9454 Wilshire Boulevard, Suite 715, Beverly Hills, CA 90212. ☎ 213-272-2661.

CHÂTEAUX OF THE LOIRE - FROM CHAMBORD TO CHINON
THE MICHELIN GREEN GUIDE - NOW ON VIDEO!

Sit back and enjoy a glimpse of the splendours of the Loire Valley from the comfort of your home.
The majestic course of the Loire from Chambord to Chinon evokes the history of the French kings who, charmed by its natural beauty, had magnificent châteaux built in which they installed the colourful pageantry – and intrigue – of their courts, bringing the ideas and easthetics of the Renaissance to France.
To echoes of sumptuous court banquets the Loire takes us past the richly stocked game parks of Chambord and Chinon, which once rang with the sound of the hunt, and the famous vineyards and orchards which have earned the Touraine region its reputation as "the garden of France". Mouthwatering images of local gastronomic delights complete this voyage of discovery, ideally suited both as a tempting preview and as a coulourful reminder of your holliday in the Loire Valley.

Calendar of Events

Events staged several times a year (1)

Saturdays
Chartres .... Chartres Musical Saturdays (classical, jazz, folk music). Tourist Information Centre, Place de la Cathédrale; ☎ 37 21 50 50.

One week in March, one week in September, mainly on Sundays
Chatou 181 fold 13 .... National Flea Market and Ham Fair

May to September, one Sunday a month at 1600 hrs
Marly Park .... Marly fountain displays with hunting horns. Tourist Information Centre ☎ 30 61 61 35

Mid June to mid July and late August to mid September, Fridays and Saturdays
Meaux .... Son et Lumière "Marching towards Europe"

Late June to early September, Saturday evenings
Moret-sur-Loing .... Son et Lumière "Summer Show"

Saturdays (except mid June to mid July) at 1700 and 2200 hrs
Provins .... The King's Challenge Horsemanship Tournament

August to October, Saturdays or Sundays
Royaumont .... Music concerts in the Abbey Information ☎ 34 68 05 50

May to September, 2nd and 4th Sunday of the month, from 1600 to 1700 hrs
St-Cloud .... Fountain display. Information ☎ 46 02 70 01

July to October
Sceaux .... Chamber and classical music concerts in the Orangery Information "Saison Musicale d'été", BP 52, 92333 Sceaux Cedex; ☎ 46 60 07 79

April to October, 2nd and 4th Saturdays of each month, in the afternoon
Vaux-le-Vicomte .... Fountain display in the gardens

Saturdays in May, June and October, Fridays and Saturdays from July to September, from 2030 to 2300 hrs
Vaux-le-Vicomte .... Candlelit tour of the château and gardens

February to July, Saturdays at 1730 hrs
Versailles .... Concerts at the Royal Opera. Information ☎ 39 02 30 00

May to September, every Sunday from 1530 to 1700 hrs
Versailles .... Fountain display with Music in the palace grounds

Some Saturdays
Versailles .... Illuminations of the Neptune Basin, fireworks display and fountain display with music. Tourist Information Centre, 7 Rue du Réservoir, 78000 Versailles; ☎ 39 50 36 22

May to September, 1st Sunday of each month from 1600 to 1700 hrs
Versailles .... Fountain display at the Grand Trianon

Annual Events (1)

Mid February
Le Touquet .... *Enduro des Sables* motorbike race along the beach

Sunday preceding Shrove Tuesday and Shrove Tuesday
Dunkirk .... Carnival
Bailleul 51 fold 5 .... Carnival with the Giant Gargantua

Sunday following Shrove Tuesday
Malo-les-Bains .... Carnival
Chambly 106 folds 6, 7 ... "Bois-Hourdy" Festival

Third Monday in Lent
Hazebrouck 51 fold 4 ...... Pageant in traditional costume and procession of the giants. Carnival the following Sunday

Weekend of Palm Sunday
Coulommiers 106 fold 24   Cheese Fair

Easter Monday
Cassel .... Procession of the Giants Reuze-Papa and Reuze-Maman

Weekends in March
Senlis .... Festival of Baroque Art. Information: ☎ 44 53 06 40

April
**Abbeville and
the Somme Bay** .... Festival of Bird Films

Mid April to early May
Chartres .... Students' Pilgrimage

Last Sunday in April
**Fortified towns in
Nord-Pas-de-Clais** .... Regional festivals

Late April to early May
Barbizon .... Painting Awards

May
Amiens .... Carnival

One Sunday in May
Rambouillet .... Lily-of-the-Valley Festival

Whit Sunday
**Cerny Aerodrome
186 fold 43** .... Vintage Air Show

Whit Sunday and Monday
Arras .... Rat Festival

May and June
Thoiry 106 folds 28, 29 ... Rhododendron and Azalea Festival

Late May or early June
Hazebrouck 51 fold 4 ...... Summer Festival: procession of the giants (Roland, Tisje
                                Tasje, Toria and Babe Tisje)
Bergues .... Beer Festival

May-June
Versailles .... Versailles Festival: concerts, performances. Information
                                ☎ 30 31 20 20

June
Thoiry 106 folds 28, 29 ... Two-week Rose and Peony Festival

Early June
Boeschèpe .... Windmill Festival

Early June (odd years)
Le Bourget Airport .... International Air and Space Fair

1st Sunday in June; 2nd Sunday in June
Chantilly .... Jockey-Club-Lancia Race; Diane-Hermès Race

2nd weekend in June
Marly-le-Roi Park .... Horse Festival; Sale of Secondhand Goods

Mid June
Chantilly .... "Nights of Fire" International Fireworks Competition

3rd Sunday in June
Gerberoy .... Rose Festival
Various windmills .... National Windmill Festival

Last weekend in June
Beauvais .... Jeanne Hachette Festival

Early July to mid August
St-Germain-en-Laye .... "Loges" Festival

July
Opal Coast .... Festival: cinema, music, theatre, dance, animation...
**Fontainebleau
(Grand Parquet Racecourse)** ...... Horse Week: French Show Jumping and Dressage Cham-
                                pionship

July and August
St-Germer-de-Fly .... Music festival: Summer nights at the Abbey. Information:
55 folds 8, 9   ☎ 44 82 55 59

One Sunday in July
Noyon .... Red Fruits Fair

Sunday after 5 July
Douai .... Procession of the Giant Gayant and his family

Second fortnight in July
St-Riquier .... Summer Festival of classical music

Late July
St-Omer .... Procession of floats on the canal

15 August
Dunkirk .... Blessing of the Sea
Cambrai .... Procession with the Giants Martin and Martine

Last weekend of August
Le Touquet .... Flower Festival
Boulogne .... Pilgrimage to the Virgin and grand procession

1st week in September; 1st fortnight in September
Fontainebleau .... Racehorse Breeders' Week; Grand Prix

1st Sunday in September
Arleux 53 fold 14 .... Garlic Fair
Aire-sur-la-Lys 51 fold 14   Sausage Festival

Monday following 1st Sunday in September
Lille .... Grande Braderie Flea Market

Early September
Versailles .... Venetian Nights from the Time of the Kings

Sunday nearest to 8 September
Chartres .... Celebration of Nativity of the Virgin

Friday before the 3rd Sunday in September to the following Monday
Arpajon 106 folds 30, 31 . Bean Fair

3rd weekend in September
Chantilly .... European Polo Trophy

Penultimate weekend in September (odd years)
Senlis .... "September Rendez-vous": open visit of the town (no cars) with musical accompaniment

Last weekend in September
Houdan 106 fold 14 .... Festival of St Matthew (cattle and horse fair)

1st weekend in October
Steenvoorde .... Hop Festival

4th weekend in October
Sains-du-Nord .... Cider Festival

Late October to early November
Berck-sur-Mer 51 fold 11   6 hour landsailing competition

Mid November
St-Jean-de-Beauregard .... Festival of fruits and vegetables
101 fold 33

_____

(1) For places not described in the guide the numbers of the Michelin map and fold are given.

Landsailing, Hardelot-Plage

Admission times and charges

☉ – Every sight for which times and charges are listed is indicated by the symbol ☉ after the title in the text.

Times and charges – _These are liable to alteration without prior notice. Due to fluctuations in the cost of living and the constant change in opening times, the information below is given only as a general indication._ **Dates given are inclusive**.

The information applies to individual adults and, whenever possible, children. For parties, however, special conditions regarding times and charges are common and arrangements should be made in advance. In some cases admission is free on certain days, eg Wednesdays, Sundays or public holidays. Ticket offices often close 30-45 minutes before the actual closing time.

Churches and other places of worship – _These are usually closed from 1200 to 1400, and do not admit visitors during services; tourists should, therefore, refrain from visits when services are being held. Times are indicated if the interior is of special interest and the church, chapel... has unusual opening times. Visitors to chapels are often accompanied by the person who keeps the key. A donation is welcome._

Lecture tours – _Where there are regular, organised lecture tours of towns or their historic districts – usually during the tourist season – this is indicated below._

Guided tours – _When these are indicated, the departure time of the last tour of the morning or afternoon will be up to an hour before the actual closing time. Most tours are conducted by French-speaking guides but in some cases the term "guided tours" may cover group-visiting with recorded commentaries. Some of the larger and more frequented sights may offer guided tours in other languages. Enquire at the ticket office or book stall. Other aids for the foreign tourist are notes, pamphlets and audio-guides._

Ensure no valuables are left in unattended vehicles in car parks or isolated sites.

🖬 – _Enquire at the Tourist Information Centre_ (Syndicat d'Initiative) – _the address of which is shown following the_ **🖬** _below – for local religious holidays, market days etc._

A

ABBEVILLE
🖬 26 Place de la Libération – 80100. ☏ 22 24 27 92

St Wulfram's Church – Guided tours available July and August, 1500-1800.

Boucher de Perthes Museum – Open 2 May to September, daily except Tuesdays, 1400-1800; rest of the year, Wednesdays and weekends, 1400-1800. Closed 1 January, 1 May, 14 July, 1 November, 25 December. ☏ 22 24 08 49.

Bagatelle Château – Guided tours (45min) early July to early September, daily except Tuesdays, 1400-1800; rest of the year, by appointment. 22 F. ☏ 22 24 02 69.

Museum of the History of France in 1940 – Same opening times as the château. 30 F.

AMBLETEUSE

Museum of the Second World War – Open April to 15 October, daily, 0930-1900; rest of the year; Sundays and holidays, 0930-1900. 25 F, children 15 F. ☏ 21 87 33 01.

AMIENS
🖬 Rue du Chapeau de Violettes – 80000. ☏ 22 91 79 28

Guided tours of the town – Apply to the Tourist Information Centre.

Cathedral – Open to tourists daily except Sunday mornings, 1000-1200 and 1400-1800. Closed public holidays. For guided tours ☏ 22 92 77 29.

Son et lumière show – Mid April to mid October, Tuesdays, Thursdays, Fridays and Saturdays with occasional exceptions. Duration 45min. 45 F, child (under 12yrs) 20 F. Booking essential; for information and bookings ☏ 22 91 83 83.

Stalls – Only open to guided tours.

Treasury – Open daily, 1000-1200 (not Sundays) and 1400-1800. 15 F.

Picardy Museum – Open all year, daily except Mondays, 1000-1230 and 1400-1800. Closed public holidays. 20 F. ☏ 22 91 36 44.

Museum of Local Art and Regional History – Open all year, Thursdays to Sundays, 1300-1800. Closed some holidays. 20 F. ☏ 22 91 36 44.

Hortillonnages – Boat tours (1 hour) April to October, daily from 1400. 26 F. Apply to 54 Bvd Beauvillé. ☏ 22 92 12 18.

Stained-Glass Gallery – Guided tours (30min) Mondays to Fridays at 1500. Closed public holidays. Tours of the workshops by request. ☏ 22 91 81 18.

Maison de la Culture – Open daily except Mondays, 1200-2100 (2000 Sundays). Closed during August and on public holidays. ☏ 22 97 79 79.

Zoo – Open April to September, daily except Mondays, 1000-1800; October, daily except Mondays, 1000-1200 and 1400-1700. 18 F. ☏ 22 43 06 95.

ARQUES

Fontinettes Barge Lift – Guided tours (1 hr) mid June to mid September, daily, 1500-1830; rest of the year (closed December to February), weekends and public holidays, 1500-1830. 17 F. ☎ 21 98 43 01.
For boat trips, see St Omer Marshes.

ARRAS
🛈 7 Place du Maréchal Foch – 62000. ☎ 21 51 26 95

Guided tours of the town – Apply to the Tourist Information Centre.

Town Hall – Open all year, daily, 1000-1200 and 1400 (1600 Saturdays, 1500 Sundays and public holidays)-1800. Closed 1 January, 25 December. ☎ 21 51 26 95.

Belfry – Open all year, Mondays to Saturdays, 1000-1200 and 1400-1800; Sundays and public holidays, 1000-1200 and 1500-1830. Closed 1 January, 25 December. 13 F. ☎ 21 51 26 95.

Tours of the Underground Passages – Guided tours (35min) all year; Mondays to Saturdays, 1000-1200 and 1400-1800; Sundays and public holidays, 1000-1200 and 1500-1830. Closed 1 January, 25 December. 13 F. ☎ 21 51 26 95.

Fine Arts Museum – Open all year, daily except Tuesdays, 1000-1200 and 1400 (1500 Sundays)-1800 (1700 15 October to March). Closed public holidays. 13 F. ☎ 21 71 26 43.

N-D-des-Ardents Church – Open, 1400-1600 all year, daily. ☎ 21 23 24 80.

ASTERIX PARK

Park – Open July and August, daily, 1000-1900; May and June, daily except Mondays and Fridays, 1000-1800 (1900 weekends); April, daily, 1000-1800; September to mid October, Wednesdays and weekends, 1000-1800. 150 F. child (3 to 11yrs) 105 F. ☎ 44 62 41 41.

AVON; BY-THOMERY

Rosa Bonheur's Studio – Guided tour (30min) Wednesdays and Saturdays, 1400-1700. Closed public holidays. 15 F. ☎ 60 70 06 19.

AZINCOURT

Musée de Traditions populaires et d'histoire locale – Open April to October, 0900-1800; rest of the year, 1400-1700. 10 F. ☎ 21 04 41 12.

Medieval Centre – Open April to September, daily except Tuesdays, 1000-1900; rest of the year, daily except Tuesdays, 1100-1700. Closed 25 December. ☎ 21 04 42 90.

B

BARBIZON

Father Ganne's Old Inn – Scheduled to reopen in 1995 following restoration. ☎ 60 66 22 38.

Barbizon School Museum – Open all year, Mondays and Wednesdays to Fridays, 1000-1230 and 1400-1800 (1700 October to March), weekends and public holidays, 1000-1800 (1700 October to March). 15 F. ☎ 60 66 22 38.

BARON

Church – To visit, apply to the Town Hall. ☎ 44 54 20 55.

BAVAY

Archeological Museum – Open July and August, Mondays and Wednesdays to Saturdays, 1000-1200 and 1400-1800; Sundays, 0930-1200 and 1400-1900; rest of the year, Wednesdays to Mondays, 0900 (0930 Sundays)-1200 and 1400-1700. Closed public holidays. 12 F. ☎ 27 63 13 95.

BEAUVAIS
🛈 6 Rue Malherbe – 60000. ☎ 44 45 08 18

Guided tours of the town – Apply to the Tourist Information Centre.

Cathedral: Astronomical Clock – Visit all year, daily at 1040 (not Sundays from 15 May to October), 1440, 1540 and 1640. 22 F. ☎ 44 48 11 60.

Local Museum – Open all year, daily except Tuesdays, 1000-1200 and 1400-1800. Closed 1 January, Easter and Whitsun Mondays, 1 May and 25 December. 16 F, free admission Wednesdays. ☎ 44 48 48 88.

National Gallery of Tapestry – Open April to September, daily, 0930-1200 and 1400-1830; rest of the year, daily, 1000-1200 and 1400-1700. Closed public holidays. 20 F. ☎ 44 05 14 28.

BEAUVAIS

National Tapestry Works – Guided tours (45min) all year, Tuesdays, Wednesdays and Thursdays, 1400-1600. Closed public holidays. 18 F. ☎ 44 05 14 28.

Marissel Church – Apply to the Tourist Information Centre or to Beauvais Town Hall ☎ 44 79 40 00 (ask for Service Culture).

BELLIGNIES

Marble Museum – Open March to December, daily, 1400-1800. 10 F. ☎ 27 66 89 90.

BERGUES
🛈 Place de la République – 59380. ☎ 28 68 60 44

Belfry – Open (191 steps up) May to 6 September, daily except Tuesdays, 1000-1200 and 1500-1800. 4 F.

Carillon concerts – Mondays at 1100 and on the eve of festivals at 1700.

Municipal Museum – Open daily except Tuesdays, 1000-1200 and 1400-1700. Closed January. 8 F, child 4 F. ☎ 28 68 13 30.

Den Leew Windmill, Pitgam – Open from April to September, 3rd Sunday of the month, 1500-1900. 5 F. ☎ 28 62 10 90 (Town Hall).

BIÈVRES

French Museum of Photography – Open all year, daily, 1000-1200 and 1400-1800. 20 F. ☎ 69 41 10 60.

BLÉRANCOURT

National Museum of Franco-American Cooperation – Open 15 April to 15 October, daily except Tuesdays, 1000-1200 and 1400-1700; rest of the year, daily except Tuesdays, 1400-1700, and also mornings of weekends and public holidays, 1000-1230. Closed 1 May. 12 F. ☎ 23 39 60 16.

BOESCHEPE

Windmill – Guided tours Easter to September, Sundays and public holidays, 1500-1900. 5 F. ☎ 28 42 50 24 (Town Hall).

BOUGIVAL

Turgenev Museum – Open 20 March to 19 December, Sundays, 1000-1800. 25 F. ☎ 39 18 22 30.

BOULOGNE-SUR-MER
🛈 Quai de la Poste – 62200. ☎ 21 31 68 38.

Guided tours of the town – Apply to Mme Soubité at the Castle-Museum. ☎ 21 92 11 52.

Nausicaa – Open 15 May to 14 September, daily, 1000-1900; rest of the year, weekends and public holidays, 1000-1800. 48 F, child 33 F. ☎ 21 30 98 98.

Belfry – Access via the Town Hall. Open all year, Mondays to Fridays, 0800-1800, Saturdays 0900-1200. Closed Sundays and public holidays. ☎ 21 31 68 38.

Basilica of Our Lady: Crypt and Treasury – Open all year, daily except Mondays, 1400-1700. 10 F. ☎ 21 99 75 98.

Castle-Museum – Open 15 May to 14 September, daily except Tuesdays, 0930-1230 and 1330 (1430 Sundays) -1800; rest of the year, daily except Tuesdays, 1000-1200 and 1400-1700 (Sundays 1000-1230 and 1430-1730). 20 F. ☎ 21 80 00 80.

Natural History Museum – Undergoing redevelopment. Apply to the Tourist Information Centre.

"Libertador San Martin" Museum – Open Fridays to Tuesdays, 1000-1200 and 1400-1800. Closed public holidays. ☎ 21 31 54 65.

"Grande Armée" Column – Open all year, daily except Tuesdays and Wednesdays 0900-1200 and 1400-1800 (1700 October to March). 20 F. ☎ 21 80 43 69.

Le BOURGET AIRPORT

Aeronautics and Space Museum – Open all year, daily except Mondays, 1000-1800 (1700 November to April). Closed 1 January, 25 December. 25 F, child 20 F. ☎ 49 92 71 71.

BOURRON

Château – Not open to the public.

Park – Open 15 April to 15 October, weekends and public holidays, 1400-1800. 10 F. ☎ 64 45 79 03.

BRUAY-SUR-L'ESCAUT

Church – To visit, apply to the presbytery, ☎ 27 47 60 89.

C

CALAIS
🅸 12 Boulevard Clemenceau – 65100. ☎ 21 96 62 40.

Guided tours of the town – Apply to the Tourist Information Centre.

Lace and Fine Arts Museum – Open all year, daily except Tuesdays, 1000-1200 and 1400-1730. Closed public holidays. 10 F, free admission Wednesdays. ☎ 21 46 62 00, poste (ext) 6317.

War Museum – Open 11 February to 19 December, daily, 1000-1700 (1800 June to September). Last admission 45min before closing. 15 F. ☎ 21 34 21 57.

CAMBRAI
🅸 48 Rue de Noyon – 59400 ☎ 27 78 36 15.

Guided tours of the town – Apply to the Tourist Information Centre.

Cathedral of Our Lady – Open all year, daily, 0800-1900. ☎ 27 81 34 71.

St Gery's Church – Closed Sunday afternoons except in July and August. ☎ 27 81 30 47.

Municipal Museum – Open daily except Mondays and Tuesdays, 1000-1200 and 1400-1800. Closed 1 January, 1 May, 15 August, 25 December. 20 F. ☎ 27 82 27 93.

Selles Château – Guided tours (1 hour 15min) by request all year, 0830-1200 and 1330-1800; some Sundays at 1500. Closed 1 May, 14 July and between Christmas and the New Year. 24 F. ☎ 27 78 36 15 (Tourist Information Centre).

CAP BLANC-NEZ

National Museum of Channel Crossing – Open April to September, daily, 1000-1800. 20 F. ☎ 21 85 57 42.

CAP GRIS-NEZ

Museum of the Atlantic Wall – Open May to October, daily, 0900 (1000 Sundays)-1800; rest of the year, Mondays to Saturdays 0900-1200 and 1300-1800, Sundays 1000-1800. 25 F. ☎ 21 32 97 33.

CASSEL
🅸 Grand-Place – 59670. ☎ 28 40 52 55.

Castle Windmill – Open Sundays, 1400-1700; otherwise, apply to the Tourist Information Centre. 12 F. ☎ 28 40 52 55.

Museum – Open June to August, daily except Tuesdays, 1000-1200 and 1400-1800; April, May and September to November, 1400-1830. 12 F. ☎ 28 40 52 55.

Collegiate Church of Our Lady – Open all year, daily, 0900-1800. ☎ 28 42 43 19.

CHAALIS ABBEY

Rose Garden – Open all year, daily except Tuesdays, 0900-1900. 12 F. ☎ 44 45 04 02.

Château-Museum – Guided tours (1 hour 15min) March to 1 November, Mondays and Wednesdays to Fridays, 1400-1830; weekends and public holidays, 1030-1230 and 1400-1830; rest of the year, Sundays and public holidays, 1400-1700. 30 F (includes access to the Rose Garden). ☎ 44 54 04 02.

CHAMPS

Park – Open all year, daily except Tuesdays, 0930 until dusk. Closed 1 January, 1 May, 1 and 11 November, 25 December.

Château – Open all year, daily except Tuesdays, 1000-1200 and 1330-1730 (1630 October to March). Closed 1 January, 1 May, 1 and 11 November, 25 December. 27 F (includes entry to concert, if being held, on presentation of ticket). ☎ 60 05 24 43.

CHANNEL TUNNEL

Information Centre – Open all year, daily, 1000-1900 (1800 October to March). Closed 1 January, 25 December. 32 F. ☎ 21 00 69 13. Information on and bookings for Le Shuttle ☎ 21 00 61 00.

CHANTILLY CHÂTEAU

Museum – Open March to October, daily except Tuesdays, 1000-1800; rest of the year, daily except Tuesdays, 1030-1245 and 1400-1700. 37 F ☎ 44 57 08 00.

Princes' Suite – Same opening times and charges as the museum.

Park – Open March to October, daily, 1000-1800, rest of the year, daily 1030-1245 and 1400-1700. 17 F. ☎ 44 57 08 00.

Horse and Pony Museum – Open April to October, daily (but closed Tuesdays in April, September and October) 1030-1730 (1800 weekends and holidays); rest of the year, daily except Tuesdays 1400-1630, weekends and holidays, 1030-1730. Closed 1 January, 25 December. 45 F, child 35 F. ☎ 44 57 40 40.

Landscape Garden – Same opening times and charges as the park. ☎ 44 57 08 00.

CHARTRES

H Place de la Cathédrale – 28000. ☎ 37 21 50 00.

Guided tours of the town – Apply to the Tourist Information Centre.

Cathedral: Access to New Bell Tower – Open April to September, 0930-1130 and 1400-1730; rest of the year, 1000-1130 and 1400-1600 (1630 October and March). Closed Sunday mornings and 1 January, 1 May, 1 and 11 November, 25 December. 20 F, child 7 F. ☎ 37 36 08 80.

Treasury – Open all year, Tuesdays to Saturdays, 1000-1200 and 1400-1800 (1600 November to mid March), Sundays and public holidays, 1400-1800 (1600 November to mid March). Closed 1 January, 25 December. ☎ 37 21 32 33.

Crypt – Guided tours (30min) April to September, daily at 1100 (not Sundays), 1415, 1530 and 1630 (and 1715 from 21 June to 21 September); rest of the year, daily at 1100 (not Sundays) and 1615. Closed 1 January, 21 June, 25 December. 10 F. Apply to Maison de la Crypte, near the south doorway. ☎ 37 21 56 33.

Tourist Train – Tours (35min) with commentary depart from the cathedral, April to mid October, daily, 0900-1900. 30 F, child 15 F (3rd child free). ☎ 42 62 24 00.

Loëns Loft: International Stained Glass Centre – Open all year, daily, 1000-1300 and 1330-1830 (1800 October to March). Closed 1 January, 25 December. 15 F. ☎ 37 21 65 72.

Museum of Fine Arts – Open April to October, daily except Tuesdays, 1000-1800; rest of the year, daily except Tuesdays, 1000-1200 (not Sundays) and 1400-1700. Closed 1 January, 1 May, 1 and 11 November, 25 December. 10 F. ☎ 37 36 41 39.

COMPA Museum – Open all year, Mondays to Fridays, 0900-1230 and 1330-1800; Sundays and public holidays, 1000-1230 and 1330-1900. Closed 1 January, 1 May, 1 and 11 November, 25 December. 25 F. ☎ 37 36 11 30.

School Museum – Open early September to June, Wednesdays, 1400-1700. Closed during school and public holidays. 10 F, child 5 F. ☎ 37 34 46 97.

Picassiette House – Open April to October, daily except Tuesdays, 1000-1200 and 1400-1800. 10 F. ☎ 37 34 10 78 or 37 36 41 39.

CHEMIN DES DAMES

Caverne du Dragon: Museum – Guided tours (1 hour) daily except Tuesdays, 1030-1200 and 1430-1800 (1900 Sundays). Closed during school winter holidays. 15 F. ☎ 23 22 44 90.

COMPIÈGNE

H Place de l'Hôtel-de-Ville – 60200. ☎ 44 40 01 00.

Guided tours of the town – Apply to the Tourist Information Centre.

Palace – Open all year, daily except Tuesdays, 0915-1730 (1545 October to March). Check in advance for public holidays. ☎ 44 38 47 00. 31 F (20 F Sundays). Lecture tours all year, weekends at 1100 and 1500. ☎ 44 38 47 02.

Historic Apartments – Circuit 1 (King's and Emperor's Apartment, then Empress' Apartment): guided tour (1 hour). Circuit 2 (Prince's Double Apartment and King of Rome's Apartment): guided tour (45min). At weekends, Circuit 2 is available only as part of a lecture-tour group.

Museum of the Second Empire – These rooms are only open on certain days; check in advance. ☎ 44 38 47 00.

Transport Museum – Guided tours (1 hour). May be visited without a palace tour: 21 F (14 F on Sundays).

Museum of Historic Figurines – Open all year, daily except Sunday mornings and Mondays, 0900-1200 and 1400-1800 (1700 November to February). Closed 1 January, 1 May, 14 July, 1 November, 25 December. 12 F. ☎ 44 40 72 55.

Vivenel Museum – Open all year, same days and times as the Museum of Historic Figurines (see above). 12 F. ☎ 44 20 26 04.

COMPIÈGNE FOREST

Marshal Foch's Carriage – Open all year, daily except Sunday mornings and Mondays, 0900-1200 and 1400-1800 (1700 November to February). Closed 1 January, 1 May, 14 July, 1 November, 25 December. 12 F. ☎ 44 20 26 04.

CORBIE

St Peter's Church – Open all year, daily except mornings of Sunday and Monday, 1000-1230 and 1500-1800.

CÔTE D'OPALE

Site of the two Capes – Guided tours in July and August around various natural sites (Cap Blanc-Nez, Cap Gris-Nez, Canche Bay, Slack Dune etc). For information contact Espace Naturel Régional-Littoral Pas-de-Calais, 30, Avenue Foch, 62930 Wimereux. ☎ 21 32 13 74.

COUCY-LE-CHÂTEAU-AUFFRIQUE

Castle – Open April to September, daily, 0900-1200 and 1400-1800; rest of the year, daily except Tuesdays, 1000-1200 and 1330-1600. Closed 1 January, 1 May, 1 and 11 November, 25 December. 20 F. ☎ 23 52 71 28.

Historical Museum – Open April to September, daily, 1015-1200 and 1415-1815 (1430-1830 weekends); rest of the year, daily except Tuesdays, 1415-1815. Closed 1 November and from 25 December to 2 January. ☎ 23 52 44 55.

COURANCES

Château – Guided tours (25min) from 1st weekend in April to 1 November, weekends and public holidays, 1430-1830 (1400-1730 late September to 1 November). 35 F, park only 20 F. ☎ 40 62 07 62.

CRÉPY-EN-VALOIS

St Arnould Abbey – Open Sundays, 1500-1900. ☎ 45 59 17 76.

Museum of Archery and Valois – Open from 3rd Sunday in March to 11 November, daily except Tuesdays, 1000-1200 and 1400-1800 (1500-1900 Sundays and public holidays). 13 F. ☎ 44 59 21 97.

LE CROTOY

Somme Bay Railway – Departure from Le Crotoy and St-Valery at 1530: Easter to September, Sundays and public holidays (daily except Mondays during school summer holidays). Departure from Cayeux at 1530: during school summer holidays, weekends and public holidays. 30-60 F depending on age, and duration of trip. No charge for bicycles. ☎ 22 26 96 96.

D

DAMPIERRE

Château – Guided tours (45min) April to mid October, Mondays to Saturdays, 1400-1800, Sundays and public holidays, 1100-1200 and 1400-1800. 45 F, garden only 28 F. ☎ 30 52 53 24.

DELVILLE WOOD

South African Memorial and Commemorative Museum – Open all year, daily except Mondays, 1000-1745 (1545 16 October to March). Closed public holidays and from 23 December to 31 January. ☎ 22 85 02 17.

DISNEYLAND PARIS

For guided tours apply to City Hall on Town Square, off Main Street, USA. Open all year, from 0900 or 1000: mid June to mid September and mid December to late January, daily to 2300; late March to mid June, daily to 1900 (2200 weekends); January to late March and mid September to mid December, daily to 1800 (2000 Saturdays). ☎ 64 74 30 00. Parking: cars 40 F, motorcycles 25 F.
Disneyland one-day pass: 250 F, child (3-11yrs) 175 F. The ticket allows unlimited access to all the attractions except the "Rustler Roundup Shootin' Gallery". Children under 7yrs must be accompanied by an adult. Two-day pass (consecutive or not) 335 F-475 F, child 240 F-335 F depending on the season. Three-day pass (consecutive or not) 444 F-630 F, child 3155 F-440 F depending on the season.

DOUAI
🛈 70 Place d'Armes – 59500. ☎ 27 88 26 79.

Guided tours of the town – Apply to the Tourist Information Centre.

Belfry and Town Hall – Guided tours (1 hour) July and August, daily at 1000, 1100, 1400, 1500, 1600, and 1700; rest of the year, Sundays and public holidays at the same times. Closed 1 January, 25 December. 8 F. ☎ 27 87 26 79.

Carillon concerts: All year, Saturdays from 1045 to 1145, and at 2100 on Mondays in July and August.

Charterhouse Museum – Open all year, daily except Tuesdays, 1000-1200 and 1400-1700 (1500-1800 Sundays and public holidays). Closed public holidays. 12 F. ☎ 27 87 17 82.

Law Courts – Open to view only as part of a guided tour of the town. Apply to the Tourist Information Centre.

Boat cruises from Quai de la Scarpe – Cruises (30min) available during July and August, Thursday to Sunday, 1400-2000. 20 F, child 10 F.

DUNKERQUE
🛈 Rue de l'Amiral-Ronarc'h – 59240. ☎ 28 66 79 21

Boat tours of the Port – Departure from Place du Minck, Commercial Basin: June, Sundays and public holidays at 1500 and 1630; July to the start of the autumn school term, Mondays to Saturdays at 1030, 1500 and 1630, Sundays and public holidays at 1100, 1500, 1630 and 1730. 38 F, child 30 F. ☎ 28 63 47 14.

DUNKERQUE

Harbour Museum – Open all year, daily except Tuesdays, 1000-1200 and 1300-1800. Closed 1 January, 1 May, 25 December. 20 F. ☎ 28 63 33 39.

Contemporary Arts Museum – Open all year, daily except Tuesdays, 0930-1200 and 1400-1730. Closed 1 January, 1 May, 25 December. 10 F. ☎ 28 59 21 65.

Belfry – Guided tours (20min) April to October, Mondays to Saturdays at 0930, 1030, 1115, 1430, 1530, 1630 and 1730.
Closed public holidays. 12 F. ☎ 28 66 79 21. Access by lift to the 5th floor, then 60 steps up.

St Eligius' Church – Closed Sunday afternoons.

Fine Arts Museum – Open all year, daily except Tuesdays, 1000-1200 and 1400-1800. Closed 1 January, 1 May, 25 December and Carnival Sunday (see Calendar of Events, *qv*). 12 F, free admission on Sundays. ☎ 28 66 21 57.

John the Baptist Church – Closed afternoons during school holidays from 1200.

E

ÉCOUEN

Renaissance Museum – Open all year, daily except Tuesdays, 0945-1230 and 1400-1715. Closed 1 May. 20 F. ☎ 39 90 04 04.

ÉPERLECQUES

Blockhouse – Open July and August, daily, 1000-1900; June and September, Mondays to Saturdays, 1000-1200 and 1400-1900, Sundays, 1000-1900; April, May, October and November, daily, 1415-1800 (1000-1900 Sundays in May); March, Sundays, 1430-1800. Last admission 1 hour before closing. 30 F. ☎ 21 88 44 22.

ERMENONVILLE

Mer de Sable – Open July to August, daily, 1030-1830; June, Mondays to Fridays, 1000-1800, weekends, 1100 (1030 Sundays)-1900; April, May and September, Sundays and public holidays, 1100-1900, some other days, 1100-1830. 94 F, child 74 F. ☎ 44 54 00 96.

F

FELLERIES

Museum of "Bois-Jolis" – Open July and August, daily, 1500-1900; Easter to June and September to 1 November, Sundays, 1500-1900. 15 F. ☎ 27 59 00 64.

FERRIÈRES

Château – Guided tours (45min) all year, daily except Mondays and Tuesdays 1400-1900 (1700 Wednesdays and weekends from October to April). 19 F (includes access to park). ☎ 64 66 31 25.

Museum of Figurative Art – Same opening times as the Château. 12 F. ☎ 64 66 31 25.

Park – Same opening times as the château. 12 F. ☎ 64 30 31 25.

FOLLEVILLE

Church – Guided tours daily except Tuesdays, 1000-1200 and 1400-1800. Apply to Mme Detand, 37 Grande Rue. ☎ 22 41 43 31.

FONTAINEBLEAU   🛈 31 Place Napoléon-Bonaparte – 77300. ☎ 64 22 25 68.

Palace:

Oval Court – To visit apply to the architect's office (Service d'Architecture). ☎ 64 22 34 86.

Main Apartments – Open all year, daily except Tuesdays, 0930-1230 and 1400-1700. Closed 1 January, 25 December and some other public holidays. 31 F (including access to Napoleon I Museum).

Diana's Gallery – Not open to the public.

Imperial Suite – Closed for restoration.

Queen Mothers' and Pope's Suite – Closed for restoration.

Napoleon I Museum – Same opening times and charges as the Main Apartments,

Small Apartments and Deer Gallery – Guided tours (45min) Mondays and Wednesdays to Fridays; enquire in advance. Closed public holidays. 12 F. ☏ 60 71 50 70.

Napoleonic Museum of Military Art and History – Open Tuesdays to Saturdays, 1400-1700. Closed during September. 10 F. ☏ 64 22 49 80, poste (ext) 424.

FOURCHERET

Barn – To visit, apply to M Patria, Ferme Fourcheret, 60300 Fontaine-Chaalis. ☏ 44 54 20 66.

FOURMIES

Textile and Social Life Museum – Open March to November, Mondays to Fridays, 0900-1200 and 1400-1800 (0900-1800 July to September), weekends and public holidays, 1430-1830. 30 F, child (13-18yrs) 15 F. ☏ 27 60 66 11.

FRANCE MINIATURE

Open July and August, daily, 1000-2000 (2300 Saturdays); mid March to June and September to mid November, daily, 1000-1900 (2300 Saturdays in June). 68 F, child 48 F. ☏ 30 51 51 51.

FRIVILLE-ESCARBOTIN

Museum of the Vimeu Region's Industries – Guided tours (1 hour) Easter to 1 November, daily except Mondays, 1400-1700 (1800 weekends and public holidays). 15 F. ☏ 22 26 42 37.

G

GRAVELINES

Prints and Engravings Museum – Open daily except Tuesdays, 1400-1700 (1500-1800 weekends from May to October). Closed public holidays and for 3 weeks around Christmas and the New year. ☏ 28 23 15 89.

GUÎNES

E Villez Municipal Museum – Open all year, Sundays, 1500-1800; July and August, Wednesdays also, 1400-1700. 10 F. ☏ 21 85 53 70 (Town Hall).

GUISE

Castle – Guided tours (1 hour) daily, 0900-1200 and 1400-1800 or 1900 in summer; daily, 1000-1200 and 1400-1700 in winter. 25 F. ☏ 23 61 11 76.

Godin Workers' Co-operative: Museum – Open Tuesdays and Fridays, 1530-1900; Wednesdays and Saturdays, 1000-1200 and 1330-1830; Thursdays 1500-1830. Closed public holidays. 10 F. ☏ 23 60 45 91. Guided tour from June to September, Tuesdays to Saturdays at 1500.

H

HANGEST-SUR-SOMME

Church – Apply to the Town Hall on weekdays (not Wednesdays) between 1600 and 1800, on Saturdays between 0900 and 1200. ☏ 22 51 12 37.

HARDELOT-PLAGE

Château – For information on shows and pageants apply to Huisbois Manor, 62142 Le Wast. ☏ 21 83 38 79.

L'HAŸ-LES-ROSES

Rose Garden – Open mid May to mid September, daily, 1000-2030. 10 F. ☏ 43 99 82 80.

HONDSCHOOTE

Town Hall – Guided tours (30min) all year, Mondays to Fridays, 0900-1130 and 1400-1730. Closed public holidays. ☏ 28 68 31 55.

Noordmeulen Windmill – Guided tours (30min), all year, daily, 0900-1200 and 1400 to 1800. ☏ 28 68 37 97, ring in advance.

HYDREQUENT

Maison du marbre et de la géologie – Open July and August, daily, 0930-1230 and 1430-1830; June and September, daily, 1430-1830; April, May and October, Sundays and public holidays, 1430-1830; during winter and spring school holidays, Mondays to Fridays, 0800-1200 and 1400-1800. 20 F. ☎ 21 83 19 10.

I - J

L'ISLE-ADAM

St Martin's Church – Open all year, 0900 (0930 Sundays)-1200. ☎ 34 69 01 88.

JOUARRE

Tower – Guided tours (30min) all year, daily except Tuesdays, 1000 (1030 Sundays, and public holidays, mid September to March)-1200 and 1400-1800. Audio-visual presentation: 20min. 10 F. ☎ 60 22 06 11.

Crypt – Guided tours (20min): same opening times as the tower. 12 F.

Brie Museum – Guided tours (1 hour) Easter to 1 November, Fridays, 1400-1600, by appointment. 10 F. ☎ 60 22 06 04.

JOUY-EN-JOSAS

Toile de Jouy Museum – Open all year, daily except Mondays, 1000 (1400 weekends and public holidays)-1800 (1700 November to March). 25 F. ☎ 39 56 48 64.

Léon Blum Museum – ☎ 39 46 50 24.

L

LAON
🄵 Place du Parvis-de-la-Cathédrale – 02000. ☎ 23 20 28 62

Guided tours of the town – Apply to the Tourist Information Centre.

Arts and Leisure Centre – Open all year, daily except Mondays, 1200 (1500 Sundays)-1900. Closed between Christmas and New Year . ☎ 23 20 28 48.

Museum – Open all year, daily except Tuesdays, 1000-1200 and 1400-1800 (1700 October to March). Closed 1 January, 1 May, 14 July, 25 December. 10 F. ☎ 23 20 19 87.

Knights Templar's Chapel – Same opening times and charges as the Museum *(above)*.

St Martin's Church – Guided tours May to September, weekends (July and August daily). Apply to the Tourist Information Centre.

LEWARDE

Mining Heritage Centre – Part-guided tours (tour of the mine: 1 hour 30min) all year, daily 1000-1700 (1600 1 November to March). Closed 15 to 31 January, 1 January, 1 May, 1 November, 25 December. High season: 60 F, child (7-17yrs) 30 F; low season: 52 F, child 26 F. ☎ 27 98 03 89.

LEZ-FONTAINE

Church – *When closed apply to M Hannecart opposite the church.*

LIESSIES

Religious Heritage Centre – Open June to September, weekdays, 1400-1800; weekends and public holidays, 1430 to 1830. 12 F, child (13-18yrs) 6 F. ☎ 27 60 66 11.

LILLE
🄵 Palais Rihour – 59000. ☎ 20 30 81 00

Guided tours of the town – Apply to the Tourist Information Centre.

Rihour Palace – Open Mondays to Saturdays, 0900-1900. Sundays and public holidays, 1000-1200 and 1400-1700. Closed 1 January, 1 May and 25 December. ☎ 20 30 81 00.

Countess Hospital – Open all year, daily except Tuesdays, 1000-1230 and 1400-1800. Closed 1 January, 1 May, 14 July, 11 November, 25 December and Mondays of the Grande Braderie and other festivals. 15 F. ☎ 20 49 50 90.

Fine Arts Museum – Due to reopen summer 1995. For information telephone ☎ 20 57 01 84.

Citadel – Guided tours (1 hr) April to October, Sundays at 1500 and 1630. Advance booking compulsory at the Tourist Information Centre. 35 F. ☎ 20 30 81 00.

Town Hall: belfry – Guided tours (30min) April to September, Mondays to Fridays, 0900-1130 and 1400-1600; Sundays and public holidays, 0930-1200. 3 F. ☎ 20 49 50 00.

General de Gaulle's Birthplace – Open all year, daily except Mondays and Tuesdays, 1000-1200 and 1400-1700. Closed public holidays. 7 F. ☎ 20 31 96 03.

Natural History Museum – Open Mondays and Wednesdays to Fridays, 0900-1200 and 1400-1700, Sundays, 1000-1700. Closed some public holidays. 5 F on Sundays, no charge rest of the week. ☎ 20 85 28 60.

Botanical Garden – Open May to September, daily, 0730-2100; rest of the year, daily, 0800 (0730 April) to 1800. Greenhouse: 0730 (0830 October to March)-1130 and 1300-1600. ☎ 20 49 52 49.

LONG

Château – Guided tours (30min) 20 August to 30 September, 0900-1200 and 1400-1700. 30 F. ☎ 22 31 84 99.

LONGPONT

Abbey – Guided tours (30min) mid March to mid November, weekends and public holidays, 1030-1200 and 1430-1830. 29 F. ☎ 23 96 01 53.

M

MAINTENON

Château – Open April to October, Mondays and Wednesdays to Saturdays, 1400-1800, Sundays and public holidays, 1000-1200 and 1400-1800; February, March and November to mid December, weekends and public holidays, 1400-1630. 28 F. ☎ 37 23 00 09.

MAISONS-LAFFITTE

Château – Open all year, daily, 1000-1800 (1700 mid October to March). Closed 1 January, 1 May, 1 and 11 November, 25 December. 26 F. ☎ 39 62 01 49.

MALO-LES-BAINS

Aquarium – Open all year, daily except Tuesdays, 1000-1200 and 1400-1800. Closed 1 January, 1 May, 25 December. 12 F. ☎ 28 59 19 18.

MARLY-LE-ROI

Marly-le-Roi-Louveciennes Promenade Museum – Open all year, daily except Mondays and Tuesdays, 1400-1800. Closed public holidays. 15 F. ☎ 39 69 06 26.

Monte-Cristo Château – Open April to October, daily except Mondays, 1000-1800. 30 F. Guided tours Sunday afternoons. ☎ 30 61 61 35.

Retz Wilderness – Guided tours (1 hr 30min) March to October, 4th Saturday of the month at 1430 and 1600. 30 F. ☎ 39 76 90 37.

MARQUENTERRE

Bird Sanctuary – Open late March to 15 November, 0930-1900. 45 F, child 37 F. ☎ 22 25 03 06.

MEAUX
🛈 2 Rue Notre-Dame – 77100. ☎ 64 33 02 26

Guided tours of the town – Apply to the Tourist Information Centre.

Episcopal Palace (Museum) – Open all year, daily except Tuesdays, 1000-1200 and 1400-1800. Closed 1 January, 1 May, 14 July, 31 December. 15 F. ☎ 64 34 84 45.

MEUDON

Observatory – Guided tours (2 hours) 2nd Saturday of the month at 1430; apply in writing in advance to the Secrétariat des Relations Extérieures de l'Observatoire, 5 Place Jules-Janssen, 92190 Meudon. 30 F, no charge under 18yrs. ☎ 45 07 75 30.

Art and History Museum – Open all year, daily except Mondays and Tuesdays, 1400-1800. Closed during August, 1 January, 14 July, 11 November, 25 December. 15 F. ☎ 46 23 87 13.

Rodin Museum – Villa des Brillants – Open July to September, Fridays and weekends, 1300-1730. 10 F. ☎ 45 34 13 09.

MILLY-LA-FORÊT

St-Blaise-des-Simples Chapel – Open Easter to 1 November, daily except Tuesdays, 1000-1200 and 1430-1800; rest of the year, weekends and public holidays, 1015-1200 and 1430-1700. Closed 2nd fortnight in November and 3 weeks from mid January. 7.50 F. ☎ 64 98 84 94.

MIMOYECQUES

Fort – Open July and August, daily, 1000-1900; April to June and September to 11 November, daily, 1400 (1000 Sundays and holidays)-1800. 25 F. ☎ 21 87 10 34. Wear warm clothing.

MONAMPTEUIL

Lake – April to September: beach, swimming pool, canoeing, sailing, pedaloes, fishing available. ☎ 23 21 60 73.

MONTCEAUX-LES-MEAUX

Château ruins – Open all year, daily, 0900-1900 (1800 in winter). 8 F. ☎ 64 35 92 43.

MONT DES CATS

Parish Church – Open Easter to 1 November, all day.

MONTFORT-L'AMAURY

Maurice Ravel Museum – Guided tour (45min) all year, Mondays, Wednesdays and Thursdays, 1430-1700; weekends and public holidays, 1000-1130 and 1430-1700. Closed 1 January, 1 May, 1 November, 25 December. 22 F. ☎ 34 86 00 89.

Jean Monnet's House – Open all year, Wednesdays to Saturdays, 1400-1800; Sundays and public holidays, 1000-1800. Audio-visual show: 15min. ☎ 45 44 11 77.

MONTGOBERT

Wood and Tool Museum – Open April to October, weekends and public holidays, 1400-1800. 20 F. ☎ 29 96 36 69.

MONTMORENCY

Jean-Jacques Rousseau Museum – Guided tours (1 hour) all year, daily except Mondays, 1400-1800. Closed 1 January, 25 December. 20 F. ☎ 39 64 80 13.

MONTREUIL   🛈 Place Darnéral – 62170. ☎ 21 06 04 27

Citadel – Open daily except Tuesdays, 0900-1200 and 1400-1800. Closed October. 10 F. ☎ 21 06 04 27.

Hospital Chapel – Open some weekends; apply to the hospital ☎ 21 90 01 07.

St Saulve Church – Open daily during school holidays, 0700-1900; rest of the year, Sundays only, 0700-1900.

MORET-SUR-LOING   🛈 Place Samois – 77250. ☎ 60 70 41 66

Riverside Cottage – Guided tours with commentaries (1 hour 30min) Easter to 1 November, Sundays at 1500. 40 F. ☎ 46 33 87 56.

Boat trips – Trips along the Seine, the Yonne, and Loing Canal (departure from St-Mammès – east bank of the Loing) organised May to October, Sundays: Duration 3 hours 30min one way. Information from Vedettes du Val de Seine, 5 Quai de Loing, 77670 St-Mammès. ☎ 60 70 18 18 and 60 70 18 60.

MORIENVAL

Church of Our Lady – Apply to 2, rue de l'Eglise. See notice on door.

N - O

NAOURS

Caves – Guided tours (50min) February to mid November, 0900-1200 and 1400-1800. 42 F, child 33 F. ☎ 22 93 71 78.

NOTRE-DAME DE LORETTE

Remembrance Museum – Open March to November, daily, 0900-2000. 20 F. ☎ 21 45 10 80.

NOYON   🛈 Place de l'Hôtel-de-Ville – 60400. ☎ 44 44 21 88

Guided tours of the town – Apply to the Tourist Information Centre.

Noyon Regional Museum – Open all year, daily except Tuesdays, 1000-1200 and 1400-1800 (1700 November to March). Closed 1 January, 11 November, 25 December. 10 F. ☎ 44 44 03 59.

Calvin Museum – Same opening times and charges as the Regional Museum (*see above*). ☎ 44 44 03 59. Audio-visual presentation: 15min.

OLHAIN

Castle Farm – Open April to November, Sundays and public holidays, 1500-1830 and Saturday afternoons in summer. 20 F. ☎ 21 27 94 76.

P

Louvre Museum – Open all year, daily except Tuesdays, 0900-1800; Mondays (Richelieu wing) and Wednesdays (entire Museum), 0900-2200. Rooms begin to be shut 30min before closing time. 40 F, after 1500 20 F, under 18 years no charge, with identification. ☏ 40 20 53 17 or 40 20 51 51. Guided tours, lecture tours and audioguides are available for an extra charge, enquire in advance.

Invalides, Dome Church and Military Museum – Open all year 1000-1800 (1700 October to March). Closed public holidays. 31 F. ☏ 44 41 44 41 or 44 42 30 11. The ticket is valid for two consecutive days to allow a comprehensive tour of the Military Museum, the Dome Church and the theatre: films on the two World Wars.

Arc de Triomphe – Access to the platform daily, 0930-1830 (1000-1700 October to March). 31 F. Lift. ☏ 43 80 31 31.

Eiffel Tower – Open July and August, daily, 0900-2400; rest of the year, daily, 0900 (0930 mid September to mid March) -2300. Charges for lift: 20 F to 1st floor, 36 F to 2nd floor, 53 F to 3rd floor. ☏ 44 11 23 11.

Conciergerie – Entrance from 1 Quai de l'Horloge: cross the courtyard beyond the archway and descend, right, to the Guard Room (Salle des Gardes). Open April to September, 0930-1800; rest of the year, 1000-1700. Closed 1 January, 1 May, 1 and 11 November, 25 December. 26 F. ☏ 43 54 30 06.

Panthéon – Closed for building works: only the crypt and the upper parts are open. Entrance behind the Pantheon.

Crypt – Open April to September, daily, 0930-1745; rest of the year, 1000-1645. Closed public holidays. 26 F. ☏ 43 54 34 51.

Opéra and Museum-Library – Opera undergoing restoration; Museum open daily, 1000-1700. 30 F. Ring for confirmation. ☏ 40 01 17 89 or 47 42 07 02.

Sainte-Chapelle – Open April to Sept., daily, 0930-1300 and 1400-1800; rest of the year, daily, 1000-1300 and 1400-1700 (1600 Nov. to January). ☏ 42 65 35 80.

Orsay Museum – Open all year, daily except Mondays, 1000 (0900 Sundays)-1800 (2145 Thursdays). Closed 1 January, 1 May, 25 December. 36 F, Sundays 24 F. ☏ 40 49 48 84; recorded information ☏ 45 49 11 11.

Hôtel de Cluny – Museum of the Middle Ages – Open all year, daily except Tuesdays, 0915-1745. 27 F. ☏ 43 25 62 00.

City of Science and Industry, La Villette – Open all year, daily except Mondays, 1000-1800. Closed 1 May, 25 December. 45 F, child (3 to 12yrs) 20 F. ☏ 40 05 70 00, recorded information ☏ 36 68 29 30.

Georges Pompidou Centre – Open all year, daily except Tuesdays, 1200 (1000 weekends and public holidays)-2200. Closed 1 May. 30 F for Museum of Modern Art, 40 F for the Grande Galerie, 57 F for a one-day pass. ☏ 44 78 12 33.

PÉRONNE

Historial de la Grande Guerre – Open May to September, daily, 1000-1800; rest of the year, daily except Mondays, 1000-1700. Closed 19 December to 20 January. 39 F. ☏ 22 83 14 18.

Danicourt Museum – Visit by appointment. ☏ 22 84 01 16, poste (ext) 350.

PICQUIGNY

Castle – Guided tours (30min) July and August, daily except Tuesdays, 1000-1200 and 1400-1800. 25 F. ☏ 22 51 82 83.

PIERREFONDS

Tourist train – *4km – 2 1/2 mile ride (30min) July to 15 September, daily at 1430; 15 March to June and 16 September to October, weekends at 1430. 20 F. 8km – 5 mile ride July to 15 September, Tuesdays and Thursdays at 1430. 35 F. For information* ☏ *44 42 08 77.*

Castle – Guided tours (1 hour) May to August, daily, 1000-1800 (1900 Sundays); rest of the year Mondays to Saturdays, 1000-1230 (1200 Nov. to February). Closed Tuesdays in winter and 1 January, 1 May, 1 and 11 Nov., 25 Dec. 26 F. ☏ 44 42 80 77.

PITGAM

Den Leew Windmill – Open third Sunday in the month April-September 1500-1900. 5 F. ☏ 28 62 10 90 (Town Hall).

POISSY

Toy Museum – Open all year, daily except Mondays and Tuesdays, 0930-1200 and 1400-1730. Closed public holidays. 10 F, child 5 F. ☏ 39 65 06 06.

Art and History Museum – Open all year, Wednesdays and weekends, 0930-1200 and 1400-1730. ☏ 39 65 06 06.

Villa Savoye – Open all year, daily except Tuesdays, 1000-1200 and 1330-1730 (1630 November to March). Closed public holidays. ☏ 39 66 01 06.

PONT-STE-MAXENCE

Moncel Abbey – Guided tours (1 hour) all year, daily except Wednesdays, 0900-1200 and 1400-1900 (1800 October to May). Closed 25 December to 1 January. 30 F. ☏ 44 72 33 98.

PORT-ROYAL-DES-CHAMPS ABBEY

Ruins and Abbey Museum – Guided tour (1 hour) all year, Mondays and Wednesdays to Fridays, 1400-1700 (1730 Saturdays from mid May to September), Sundays and holidays, 1100-1200 and 1400-1700 (1800 from mid May to September). Closed over Christmas period and one week in February. 20 F. ☏ 30 43 74 93.

Port-Royal Granges National Museum – Open all year, daily except Tuesdays, 1000-1200 and 1400-1800 (1730 October to February). Closed 1 January, 25 December. 12 F. ☏ 30 43 73 65.

St Lambert Church – Open Sunday afternoons.

PRÉMONTRÉ

Abbey – *Tour of the exterior only, 0900-1700.*

PRISCES

Church – *Open May to September, daily.*

PROVINS
🚩 Tour de César – 77160. ☏ 64 60 26 26

Guided tours of the town – Apply to the Tourist Information Office.

Pépinières et Roseraies Vizier – *Open all year, daily, 0800-1200 and 1330-1800.* ☏ 64 00 02 42.

Bird-flying show on the ramparts – July and August, daily, afternoons; Easter to 1 November, daily except Mondays, afternoons. 40 F, child (under 12yrs) 20 F, no charge under 6yrs. ☏ 64 60 26 26.

Grange aux Dîmes – Open early July to early September, daily, 1030-1800; rest of the year, weekends and public holidays, 1030 (1400 2 November to March)-1700. Closed 25 December. 17 F. ☏ 64 60 26 26.

Musée du Provinois – Open mid June to 1 November, daily, 1400-1800; April to mid June, weekends and public holidays, 1400-1800. 20 F. ☏ 64 60 26 26.

Tour César – Open all year, daily, 1030-1700 (1800 April to August and weekends from September to November). 17 F. ☏ 64 60 26 26.

Underground Passages – Guided tours (45mins) July and August: weekdays 1400-1730; weekends and public holidays 1100-1800. May, June and September weekdays 1500-1600; weekends and public holidays 1100-1800; from Palm Sunday to 11 November weekends and public holidays 1100-1800. 20F.

Q

QUAEDYPRE

Church – Apply to the town hall, ☏ 28 68 66 03.

Le QUESNOY

Red Bridge Lake – *Mini golf, beach, boats, pedaloes and games.*

Horse-shoe Lake – *Fishing.*

R

RAISMES-ST-AMAND-WALLERS FOREST

Bouvignies Dovecote – Guided tours (45min) April to September, Sundays, 1600-1900. 15 F, children 5 F. ☏ 27 91 20 13.

RAMBOUILLET
🚩 Hôtel de Ville – 78120. ☏ 34 83 21 21

Guided tours of the town – Apply to the Tourist Information Centre.

Château – Guided tour (30 min) all year, daily except Tuesdays and when the president is in residence, 1000-1130 and 1400-1730 (1630 October to March). Closed 1 January, 1 May, 1 and 11 November, 25 December. 26 F. ☏ 34 83 00 25.

Park – Open May to August, daily 0630-1930; February to April and September to October, 0700-1800; rest of the year, 0800-1700. Closed during presidential visits. ☎ 34 83 02 49.

Queen's Dairy and Sea Shell Cottage – Guided tours (1 hour) all year, 1000-1130 and 1400-1730 (1530 October to March). Closed Tuesdays and every other Sunday and Monday. 13 F, child 7 F. ☎ 34 83 02 49.

National Sheep Farm – Guided tours (1 hour) July to September, weekends and public holidays, 1400-1700; rest of the year, Sundays and public holidays, 1400-1700 or by appointment. Closed 24 December to 2 January. 20 F, child (under 12yrs) free. ☎ 34 83 83 09.

Rambouillet Museum – Open all year, daily except Mondays and Tuesdays, 1000-1200 and 1400-1730. Closed 1 January, 25 December. 20 F. ☎ 34 83 15 93.

RAMBOUILLET FOREST

Lakes – For fishing permits apply to the Présidence Syndicale d'Exploitation de la Base de Loisirs des Étangs de Hollande, St-Léger Town Hall. ☎ 34 86 30 61.

Yvelines Wildlife Park – Open May to October, daily, 0900-1800; rest of the year, daily except Mondays, 0900-1800. Birds of prey flying displays March to November. Closed 1 January, 25 December. 40 F, child 30 F. ☎ 34 83 05 00.

RAMBURES

Castle – Guided tours (45min) March to 1 November, daily except Wednesdays, 1000-1200 and 1400-1800; rest of the year, Sundays and public holidays 1400-1700 or weekdays by appointment. 22 F. ☎ 22 25 10 93.

RAMOUSIES

Church – Open on Sundays only. Rest of the week apply to M Francis Navet at the farm opposite the church.
To visit, see the noticeboard by the church door or apply to the presbytery, 50 Rue Huysmans.

RÉTY

Church – Open Sunday mornings or apply to the presbytery, 5 Rue de l'Église.

ROYAUMONT

Abbey – Open all year, daily, 1000-1800 (1730 November to February). Guided tours may be available at weekends. 20 F. ☎ 30 35 88 90.

RUEIL-MALMAISON

Museum – Open all year, daily except Tuesdays, 1000-1200 and 1330-1700 (1630 October to March). At weekends, guided tours (1 hour 30min) only. Closed 25 December to 1 January. 27 F, no charge under 18yrs. ☎ 47 49 20 07.

Bois-Préau Château – Open all year, daily except Tuesdays, 1030-1230 and 1400-1730 (1700 October to March). Closed 25 December to 1 January. 12 F, no charge under 18yrs. ☎ 47 49 20 07.

S

SAINS-DU-NORD

Maison du Bocage – Open March to November, weekdays, 1400-1800, weekends and public holidays, 1500-1900. 20 F, child (13-18yrs) 10 F. ☎ 27 60 66 11.

SAINS-EN-AMIENOIS

Church – Apply to the presbytery opposite the church. ☎ 22 09 51 10.

ST-AMAND-LES-EAUX

Abbey Tower - Museum – Open all year, daily except Tuesdays, 1000-1230 and 1400-1700 (1500-1800 weekends and public holidays from April to September). Closed 1 January, 1 May, 14 July, 1 November, 25 December. 10 F. ☎ 27 22 24 55.

Priory or Magistrates' Building – Guided tours all year, daily except Tuesdays, 1000-1200 and 1500-1800 (not Sundays). Closed public holidays. 1 F. ☎ 27 27 85 00.

ST-CLOUD

Park – Open all year, daily, 0730-2100 (2200 May to August, 2000 November to February). Cars 13 F, no charge for pedestrians. ☎ 46 02 70 01.

History Museum – Open Wednesdays, weekends and public holidays, 1400-1800 (1700 October to February). No charge. ☎ 46 02 70 01.

Fountain Display – See Calendar of Events.

Pasteur Institute – Museum of Applied Research – Open Mondays to Fridays, 1400-1730. Closed during August and public holidays. 20 F. ☎ 47 01 15 97.

ST-DENIS

Cathedral: Tombs and Crypt – Open all year, daily, 1000 (1200 Sundays)-1830 (1630 October to March). Closed 1 January, 1 May, 1 and 11 November, 25 December. 26 F. ☎ 48 09 83 54.

Art and History Museum – Open all year, Mondays and Wednesdays to Saturdays, 1000-1730, Sundays, 1400-1830. Closed public holidays. 20 F. ☎ 42 43 05 10.

Christofle Museum – Open all year, Mondays to Fridays, 0900-1700. Closed public holidays. ☎ 49 22 40 00.

ST-GERMAIN

🏢 38 Rue de Pain – 78100. ☎ 34 51 05 12.

Guided tours of the town – Apply to the Tourist Information Centre.

National Museum of Antiquities – Open all year, daily except Tuesdays, 0900-1715. Closed 1 January, 25 December. 20 F. ☎ 34 51 65 36.

Priory Museum – Open all year, daily except Mondays and Tuesdays, 1000-1730 (1830 weekends). Closed 1 January, 1 May, 25 December. 25 F. ☎ 39 73 77 87.

Maison Debussy – Open all year, daily except Sundays and Mondays, 1400-1800. Closed public holidays. ☎ 34 51 05 12.

ST-OMER

🏢 Boulevard Pierre-Guillain – 62500. ☎ 21 98 70 00

Sandelin Mansion and Museum – Open all year, daily except Mondays and Tuesdays, 1000-1200 and 1400-1800 (1700 Thursdays and Fridays). Closed public holidays. 15 F, or 20 F giving admission to H Dupuis Museum (*see below*). ☎ 21 38 00 94.

Library – Open all year, daily except Sundays and Mondays, 1300-1730; Wednesdays and Saturdays also 1000-1200. Closed public holidays. ☎ 21 38 35 08.

Henri Dupuis Museum – Same opening times and charges as the Sandelin Mansion (*see above*). ☎ 21 38 00 94.

St-Omer Marshes – Boat trips (1 hour 40min) on the *Emeraude* July and August, daily in the afternoon; May, June and September, some Sundays and public holidays. Departure from Neuffossé Canal, beside the D209 to Clairmarais (northeast of St-Omer). Telephone in advance, ☎ 21 98 66 74, or 07 63 49 86.
For a trip on a *bacôve* apply to Mme Lalart, Pont de la Guillotine, Rivage de Tiques, 62500 St-Omer, ☎ 21 95 10 19.

Regional Park – *The Grange-Nature visitor centre is open July and August, daily, 1030-1230 and 1430-1830; April to June and September to October, Saturdays 1430-1830, Sundays and public holidays, 1030-1230 and 1430-1830; rest of the year, weekends, 1430-1730. Rue de Romelaere, 62500 Clairmarais.* ☎ 21 38 52 95.

ST-QUENTIN

🏢 14 Rue de la Sellerie – 02100. ☎ 23 67 05 00

Guided tours of the town – Apply to the Tourist Information Centre.

Antoine Lécuyer Museum – Open all year, daily except Tuesdays, 1000-1200 (not Sundays) and 1400-1700 (1800 weekends). Closed 1 January, 1 May, 14 July, 1 November, 25 December. 8.20 F. ☎ 23 64 06 66.

Town Hall – Guided tours (2 hours) including the Basilica, July and August at 1500. Closed public holidays. 30 F. ☎ 23 67 05 00.

Entomological Museum – Open all year, daily except Tuesdays, 1400-1800. 8 F. ☎ 23 06 30 92.

Isle Marshlands – Guided tour of the nature reserve on the 1st Sunday of each month. Meet at the entrance to the park, Avenue Léo Lagrange. ☎ 23 62 31 27 (Town Hall).

ST-RIQUIER

Church and Treasury – Same opening times as the Regional Museum. Treasury 5 F.

ST-VALERY-SUR-SOMME

Musée Picarvie – Open May to August, daily, 1400-1900; February to April and September to December, daily except Tuesdays, 1400-1900. 20 F. ☎ 22 26 94 90.

Bird House – Open mid February to mid November, daily, 1000-1800 (1900 July and August). 31 F, child 25 F. ☎ 22 26 93 93.

Brighton Lighthouse – Guided tours (30min) June to August, Mondays to Saturdays, 1500-1830, Sundays and public holidays, 1000-1200 and 1500-1830; rest of the year by appointment. ☎ 22 26 60 52.

Somme Bay Railway – See under Le Crotoy.

SAMARA

Site – Open (with guided tour of the museum 1 hour 30min) all year, daily, 0930-2000 (last admission 1800). Closed between Christmas and New Year. Allow 4 hrs. 60 F, child 47 F. ☎ 22 51 82 83.

SARS-POTERIES

Glass Museum – Open all year, daily except Tuesdays, 1500-1800 (1900 Sundays and public holidays). Closed 1 January, 25 December. 12 F. ☎ 27 61 61 44.

Watermill – Open 13 July to August, daily except Tuesdays at 1500; May to 12 July and September to 1 November, Sundays and public holidays at 1500. 12 F. ☎ 27 61 60 01.

SAUVAGE

Wildlife Park – Open all year, daily, 0900-1900 (1800 October to March). 40 F, child 25 F. ☎ 34 94 00 94.

SCEAUX

Park – Open all year, daily, sunrise to sunset. ☎ 46 61 11 21.

Orangery: concerts of chamber music – For a programme, write to "Saison Musicale d'été de Sceaux", BP 52, 92333 Sceaux Cedex. ☎ 46 60 07 79.

Ile de France Museum – Open all year, daily except Tuesdays, 1000-1800 (1700 October to March). Closed 1 January, 1 May, 25 December. 20 F. ☎ 46 61 06 71.

Reference Library – Open all year by appointment. ☎ 46 61 06 71.

Great Cascade – Operates all year, from 1100: to 2000 April and May; to 2100 June and July; to 1900 August and September; to 1700 rest of the year. ☎ 46 61 95 96.

Pavilion of the Rising Sun – Undergoing restoration; for information, ☎ 46 61 06 71.

SEBOURG

Church – Apply to the Café St-Druon, by the church.

SENLIS
🛈 Place du Parvis Notre-Dame – 60300. ☎ 44 53 06 40

Guided tours of the town – Apply to the Tourist Information Centre.

Jardin du Roy – Open February to December 1000-1800.

St Peter's Church – To visit apply to the Tourist Information Centre.

Art and Archeology Museum – Open daily except Tuesdays and Wednesday mornings, 1000-1200 and 1400-1800 (1700 November to 10 January). Closed 1 January, 1 May, 25 December and from 10-30 January. 13 F (includes entry to Hôtel de Vermandois). ☎ 44 53 00 80 poste (ext) 1247.

Musée des Spahis – Open all year, daily except Tuesdays and Wednesday morning, 1000-1200 and 1400-1800 (1700 November to January). Closed late December to mid January. 13 F (includes entry to the Hunting Museum). ☎ 44 53 00 80, poste (ext) 1315.

Royal Castle Park – Open from 3rd week in January to 3rd week in December, daily except Tuesdays and Wednesday mornings, 1000-1200 and 1400-1800. ☎ 44 53 00 80, poste (ext) 1315.

Hunting Museum – Guided tours (1 hour) at 1000, 1100, 1400, 1500, 1600 and 1700. Closed Tuesdays and Wednesday mornings. 13 F (includes entry to Musée des Spahis). ☎ 44 53 00 80 poste (ext) 1315.

St Frambourg Royal Chapel – Open April to October, weekends and public holidays, 1500-1830; rest of the year, Sundays, 1500-1700. 20 F. ☎ 44 53 39 99.

St Vincent's Abbey – Open (exterior only) all year, daily.

Museum (Hôtel de Vermandois) – Same opening times and charges as the Art and Archeology Museum. ☎ 44 53 00 80 poste (ext) 1219.

SÈVRES

National Porcelain Museum – Open all year, daily except Tuesdays, 1000-1700. Closed 1 January, Easter Monday and Whit Monday, 1 November. 17 F. ☎ 41 14 04 20.

Jardies Villa – Guided tours (1 hour 30min) Mondays, Fridays and Saturdays, 1430-1600. 20 F. ☎ 45 34 61 22.

SOISSONS
🛈 1 Avenue du Général-Leclerc – 02200. ☎ 23 53 08 27

Guided tours of the town – Apply to the Tourist Information Office.

Abbey of St John of the Vines – Open all year, 0900-1200 and 1400-1800. Closed 1 January, 25 December. 8 F. ☎ 23 53 17 37.

St Gervase and St Protase Cathedral – Closed 1 January, 14 July.

Museum of St Leger's Abbey – Open all year, daily except Tuesdays, 1000-1200 and 1400-1700 (1800 in May). Closed some public holidays. ☎ 23 59 15 90.

St Medard's Abbey: Crypt – Guided tours (1 hour) all year, 0900-1200 and 1400-1800 by appointment; apply to the municipal tourist office, Cour St-Jean-des-Vignes. ☎ 23 53 17 37. 10 F.

SOLRE-LE-CHÂTEAU
Church – *Apply to the presbytery.* ☏ 27 61 61 76.

STEENVOORDE

Windmills – Steenmeulen: by appointment. ☏ 28 48 16 10. Noordmeulen: Guided tours (30min) by appointment with the Town Hall. ☏ 28 49 77 77. Drievenmeulen: apply at the farm next to the mill.

T

Le TOUQUET

Aqualud – Open mid February to early November, 1000-1800 (1900 6 July-31 August). Late opening Fridays and Saturdays from 8 July to 20 August, 2000-2400. 47 F, whole day 69 F. ☏ 21 05 63 59.

Lighthouse – Guided tours (30min) July and August, 1500-1700. ☏ 21 05 05 41.

TRÉLON

Glass Workshop-Museum – Open April to October, weekdays, 1400-1800, weekends and public holidays, 1430-1830. 26 F, child (13-18yrs) 13 F. ☏ 27 60 66 11.

V

VALENCIENNES
 1 Rue Askièvre – 59300. ☏ 27 46 22 99

Guided tours of the town – Apply to the Tourist Information Centre.

Fine Arts Museum – Reopening following renovation; ring for opening times. ☏ 27 46 21 09.

St Gery's Church – Open all year, daily, 1730-1900 and also Sunday mornings, 0800-1300. ☏ 27 46 22 04.

VALLOIRES

Abbey – Guided tours (45min) April to 11 November, 1000-1200 and 1400-1800. 25 F. ☏ 22 29 62 33.

Gardens – Open April to November, daily, 1000-1800 (2000 June to August). 31 F, child 14 F; combined ticket with the abbey 50 F, child 22 F. ☏ 22 23 53 55.

VAUCLAIR

Abbey – Open all year, 0800-2000. Lecture tours Easter to 11 November by prior appointment with Rev. Père Courtois, Abbaye de Vauclair, 02860 Bouconville-Vauclair.

VAUX-DE-CERNAY

Abbey ruins and grounds – Open April to October, daily, 1000-1800 (1900 Sundays and public holidays); rest of the year and during school holidays, 1400-1800. 25 F. ☏ 34 85 23 00.

VAUX-LE-VICOMTE

Château – Open April to October, Mondays to Fridays, 1000-1300 and 1400-1800, weekends, 1000-1800; rest of the year, during school holidays only. 56 F (includes entry to gardens and Museum of Carriages. ☏ 64 14 41 90.

Candlelit tours: May, Saturday evenings.

Gardens – Same opening times as the Château. ☏ 64 14 41 90

Museum of Carriages – Same opening times and charges as the Château.

Guided tours of the town – Apply to the Tourist Information Centre.

Palace – For all information. ☎ 30 84 74 00.

Exterior – Access to the courts and gardens of Versailles Palace and Trianon, and to the park (13 F for cars) is free every day from sunrise to sunset. Information concerning the Fountain Displays, Illuminations and Aquatic Entertainments may be found in the Calendar of Events *(qv)*.

A **small train** operates between the different sites (35min) within the park: March to November, daily; rest of the year, weekends and public holidays. Departure from the Palace terrace (north arcade). 29 F. ☎ 39 54 22 00.

Bicycle Hire – Available at the entrance to the park, by the Grille de la Reine: July and August, Mondays to Fridays, 1230-1800, weekends and public holidays, 1030-1800; March to June and September to November, Wednesdays, 1300-1700, weekends and public holidays, 1030-1700. Also available within the park by the Grand Canal, March to October, daily, 1030-1700 (1800 July and August). 29 F per hour.

Boat Hire – Boats on the Grand Canal may be hired from March to 1 November.

Château and Trianon	Opening Times	Prices
Open all year, daily except Mondays, 1 May and some public holidays		
Unaccompanied Tours (entrance **A**)		
Chapel	Visible only from entrance doors (lower vestibule and Chapel Room)	
and		
State Apartments	0900-1830 (1730 October to April)	40 F
Grand Trianon	May to September, daily except Mondays, 1000-1830; rest of the year, Tuesdays to Fridays, 1000-1230 and 1400-1730; weekends, 1000-1730	21 F
Petit Trianon	Same opening times as the Grand Trianon	12 F
Guided tours (entrance **D**) *(reservation on site, on the day; duration 1 hour)* – King's Suite – Queen's Private Suite – Mme de Pompadour and Mme du Barry's Suites – Dauphin and Dauphine's Suites – Opera and Chapel – 17C Galleries	0930-1600	23 F supplement

Other rooms in the Palace are open in rotation. For information, ☎ 30 84 74 00.

Fountain displays and Illuminations – See Calendar of Events *(qv)*.

Jeu de Paume – Open only by prior arrangement. ☎ 39 50 36 22.

Lambinet Museum – Open all year, daily except Mondays, 1400-1800. Closed public holidays. 19 F. ☎ 39 50 30 32.

Public Library – Occasional lecture tours of the main rooms. Apply to the Tourist Information Centre.

Chèvreloup Arboretum – Open April to 15 November, Mondays and weekends, 1000-1700. Closed some bank holidays. 12 F. ☎ 39 55 53 80.

VERSIGNY

Château – Tour of the exterior July and September, daily, 1400-1900. ☎ 44 88 04 38.

VERT-BOIS

Château – Closed for renovation. ☎ 20 46 26 37.

Septentrion Foundation – Open all year except August, Wednesdays to Sundays, 1400-1800. 20 F. ☎ 20 46 30 32.

VÉTHEUIL

Church – Open Easter to 1 November, Sundays, 1500-1900; otherwise apply to the Association Notre-Dame de Vétheuil. ☎ 34 78 14 26.

VILLARCEAUX

Gardens – Closed for works.

Manor Tower – Closed for works.

VILLENEUVE-D'ASCQ

Museum of Modern Art – Open all year, daily except Tuesdays, 1000-1800. Closed 1 January, 1 May, 25 December. 20 F. ☎ 20 05 42 46.

Mills: flour mill and oil mill – Open April to October, Sundays, 1400-1800. 10 F. ☎ 20 05 49 34.

Museum of the Land – Open Sundays, 1000-1300. ☎ 20 91 87 57.

VILLERS-COTTERÊTS

Château – Guided tours (1 hour) all year, Mondays and Wednesdays to Saturdays, 0900-1200 and 1400-1700, Sundays and public holidays, 0930-1230 and 1430-1830. 15 F. ☎ 23 96 55 10. Meet at the Tourist Office, 8 Place A-Briand, opposite the Château.

Alexandre Dumas Museum – Open daily except Tuesdays, 1430-1700. 15 F. Closed last Sunday of the month and public holidays. ☎ 23 96 23 30.

VIMY

Vimy Canadian Memorial – Guided tours of the trenches (20mins) and tunnel (30mins) open 1 April to 15 November, 1000-1730. Tunnel closed for the rest of the year. ☎ 21 48 72 29.

W

WALLERS-TRELON

Maison de la Fagne – Open 15 June to 15 September, Mondays to Fridays, 1400-1800, weekends and public holidays, 1430-1830; April to 14 June and 16 September to 1 November, weekends and public holidays, 1430-1830. 12 F, child 6 F. ☎ 27 60 66 11.

Le WAST

Church – To visit apply to Colembert presbytery, ☎ 21 33 30 96 or to Mme Bourdon, ☎ 21 33 32 05.

Huisbois Manor – Guided tours (1 hour) July and August, daily, 1400-1730. 10 F. ☎ 21 33 79 79.

WEST-CAPPEL

St Sylvester's Church – Guided tours all year, Mondays to Fridays, 0900-1800. ☎ 28 68 38 46.

WIGNEHIES

Observation Trails – Open early March to late November, daily. ☎ 27 60 66 11. Trail guides available from the Museum in Fourmies.

WISSANT

Mill Museum – Open 1400-1800. 14 F. ☎ 21 35 91 87.

WORMHOUT

La Briarde Windmill – To visit, apply one week in advance to the Tourist Office, 45 Place du Général-de-Gaulle, 59470 Wormhout, 7 F. ☎ 28 62 81 23.

Jeanne Devos Museum – Open all year, daily except Wednesdays and Sundays, 0930-1200 and 1400-1730; 1st and 2nd Sundays of the month, 1500-1800. Closed public holidays. 12 F. ☎ 28 65 62 57.

Index

A

B

C

Notes

MANUFACTURE FRANÇAISE DES PNEUMATIQUES MICHELIN

Société en commandite par actions au capital de 2 000 000 000 de francs

Place des Carmes-Déchaux – 63 Clermont-Ferrand (France)

R.C.S. Clermont-Fd B 855 200 507

© Michelin et Cie, Propriétaires-Éditeurs 1995

Dépôt légal mai 1995 - ISBN 2-06134402-X - ISSN 0763-1383

Printed in the EC 05.95

Photocomposition : EURONUMÉRIQUE, Montrouge – Impression et brochage: KAPP LAHURE JOMBART Evreux

Illustration de la couverture par Didier WIBROTTE/Pascal VITRY